PACIFIC RISING

PACIFIC RISING

The Emergence of a New World Culture

SIMON WINCHESTER

PRENTICE
HALL
PRESS

New York London Toronto Sydney Tokyo Singapore

PRENTICE HALL PRESS
15 Columbus Circle
New York, NY 10023

Copyright © Simon Winchester 1991

Simultaneously published in Great Britain by Hutchinson.

PRENTICE HALL PRESS and colophons are registered trademarks of
Simon & Schuster, Inc.

Library of Congress Catalog Card Number: 90-71410

ISBN 0-13-807793-2

Manufactured in Great Britain

10 9 8 7 6 5 4 3 2 1

First edition

For Catherine

... it is half
the planet: this dome, this half-globe, this bulging
Eyeball of water, arched over to Asia,
Australia and white Antarctica; those are the eyelids
 that never close; this is the staring unsleeping
Eye of the earth; and what it watches is not our wars.

Robinson Jeffers, 'The Eye', 1941

CONTENTS

LIST OF MAPS

IN GRATITUDE

This book, like many, is the result of an effort that managed at the same time to be both solitary and collaborative. The writing was that part of the task conducted quite alone, and in consequence I bear full responsibility should any errors or infelicities have crept into it. But the preparation and research required the help, advice, support and hospitality of innumerable people, and the debt I owe them is incalculable. Many must perforce pass unnamed, though they will know they are not unremembered. Among those whose help I am delighted to be able to acknowledge in print are:

HM King Taufa'ahau Tupou IV of Tonga; Frances Adamson; Bernard Asher; Merrick and Crystal Baker-Bates; David Bell; Timothy Birch; Peter Boichel; Fergus Bordewich; Cheryl Boynton (Kauai); Graham Boynton (New York); Ian Buruma; Nick Cumming-Bruce; HE Margaret Bryan; Maria Bun; Julian Calder; George Cardona; Sir Jack Cater; Chung Wah-Pui; Captain Peter Clark; Ferhan Cook; Christopher Cormack; Sheila Coronel; John Courtney; Cui Guo-hong; Michael Dobbs-Higginson; John Duncan; Harold Evans; Paul Fabian; James Fenton; Jane and Hamish Fraser; Bill Fullerton; Don George; Mitsuya Goto; Richard Graham; Walter Gray; Adrian Hill; Claire Hollingworth; Jack Howard; Dr Michael Howse; Jane Jamison; Carolyn Johns; Christie Johnson; Frances Lai; David Lange; Sally Loane; William McGurn; Michael Macintyre; Captain Tony Maddern; Yoshinori Maesaka; Mary Ellen Mark; Liza Martineau; R.W. Matheson; Margaret Mara; HE Lawrence Middleton; Stephen Moorbath; Joe S. Moore; Marie-Louise O'Callaghan; Pan Ling; M.G.G. Pillai; Christopher Reed;

George Robinson; Paul Toulmin-Rothe; Itsuko Sakai; Ronald L. Solberg; John Sparrow; Professor Osker Spate; Ben Stein; Richard Stirland; Matthew Strain; Bill Stoops (Seoul); Hal Stoops (Hong Kong); Peter Sutch; John Sulzbach; Yoko Takatsu; Tony and Edith Terry; Nick Thorne; Julia Vickerman; Keith Vitty; Wang Gungwu; Gully Wells (New York); Maggie Wells (Wellington); Philip Wetton; Max Whitby; HE Alan White (Santiago); Tom White (Rangoon); Hans Wiesendanger; Gavin Young.

Gill Coleridge first suggested I might write such a book. Matthew Stevenson, my old friend from New York, encouraged me to continue when I thought the task too great. Lois Wallace and Bill Hamilton were sympathetically interested at all stages. My editors – Richard Cohen at Hutchinson and Paul Aron at Prentice Hall – were equally supportive throughout. But, above all, my wife Catherine deserves my deepest gratitude, and it is only by way of a modest token that the finished book is dedicated to her.

PREFACE

Rarely indeed is one fortunate in being able to live through times in which a major shift in the world's history can be seen to be taking place. The latter half of the twentieth century, however, appears – and probably will appear to historians – to be particularly rich in such moments, and those who live through it peculiarly fortunate to be seated at the feast. The time in which a brand new era starts, a major new nation is born, an idea of global significance is bruited, an invention of profound importance perfected – such things have been there to be witnessed during the lifetime of us all.

One such event, a creaking shift in the plates of world history, took place at some time during the Eighties – or it could have been the Seventies; only long-term historical perspective will be able to fix the precise date – when the world appeared truly to change direction. This came about when the fifty-odd countries now grouped around the Pacific Ocean seemed to take the torch of leadership from those hitherto grouped around the Atlantic, which in turn had taken it four centuries before from a smaller coterie of nations on the shores of the Mediterranean. The implications of such global changes of focus are ultimately profound, yet from so close a vantage point they are not always easy to recognize and define, nor to judge.

Although some historians question whether the primacy of the Atlantic is truly past, and wonder whether the Pacific indeed has the ability to assume the leadership of the world, I have to come clean: I do not. I live on the Pacific's shores and have watched with astonished fascination as, with care and caution, but also with unalloyed ambition, the Pacific has climbed steadily and certainly over the last few decades – since the signing of the Japanese

Peace Treaty in San Francisco in 1951, perhaps – towards its present standing in the world. Now that it seems to be busily achieving a new role, and the great steel mechanisms of leadership are beginning to lock themselves into position for the era just commencing, I thought it appropriate to attempt a portrait of the place and the people from which our planet will soon be taking its directions.

My hope is that the portrait will be thought of as an affectionate one, a reasonably faithful rendering of the human side of this immense new entity. I know very little of economics, and shy away instinctively from statistics which demonstrate the dominance of this nation in this industry, or of that nation in another, or which allow one to ruminate on the changing rates of one state's net average growth, or of one continent's external debt. Readers looking for that information should reach for other volumes, some of which I have listed at the end of the book.

What I have attempted to do is to sketch the faces, to colour in the landscapes, to capture some of the elusive magic of the Pacific and its people. I have been fortunate in being able to spend some years travelling to almost every country and island group (though, try as I might, the four islands of the Pitcairn Group still elude me). Some of what follows tells the story of those travels. Other passages offer thoughts, or the reports of conversations and discoveries made along the way. The whole is a complicated mosaic of many people, tongues and places, religions, philosophies and histories – just as the Pacific itself.

Herman Melville, one of the greatest writers to have grappled with the Ocean and its moods, recognized the complex nature of his subject when he concluded, in *Moby Dick*: "This mysterious divine Pacific zones the whole world's bulk about; makes all coasts one bay to it; seems the tide-beating heart of the earth."

I am certain I have not done – that in a single lifetime I simply could not do – justice to this mightiest of the world's oceans, this "tide-beating heart of the earth". But after all my wanderings about it, I remain fascinated and enthralled by it; and my hope is that perhaps these pages may stimulate a similar sense of fascination and enthralment in the reader.

SBAW
Hong Kong 1990

PROLOGUE

The first dawn on the Pacific Ocean is the first dawn on the world. This happy coincidence – happy, that is, for all those visionaries and seers who speak in sonorous phrases about the "New Pacific Century" and the "Grand Pacific Age", and find such a discovery a perfect symbol of what they're talking about – has been the case ever since 22 October 1884, when a group of scientists and politicians met in a hotel in Washington DC and set down the rules by which the planet was henceforth to organize the keeping of its time.

They adopted the invention of a man named Charles Dowd, who was then employed as principal of the Temple Grove Ladies' Seminary in Saratoga Springs, New York. Professor Dowd, as he liked to be called – and who cut his hair and trimmed his beard to look just like President Lincoln – probably never travelled to the Pacific, nor to very many other places outside America; but he had an abiding interest in his country's enormous and burgeoning railway system, and from that fascination grew a scheme which changed the world – and particularly the Pacific – for ever.

Professor Dowd found it particularly irritating and inconvenient, as did the railway companies and their customers, that in the mid-1860s the continental United States had no fewer than eighty different standards of time. In the state of Pennsylvania, for instance, the Penn Central line ran on Altoona time, which was ten minutes fast on Pittsburgh, while the Pittsburgh, Fort Wayne and Chicago railroad ran on Columbus time, which was thirteen minutes slow. What happened when trains from the two lines converged on Pittsburgh, which of course they did, utterly confused and bewildered the poor steel-workers and their families and all the other benighted souls whose

3

destination this was. It was left to Professor Dowd to come to their aid in 1870 by publishing a 107-page monograph entitled *A System of National Time for Railroads*. This paper, regarded by students of horology as a classic of its kind, suggested that the United States be divided along longitude lines into a number of time zones, each one precisely one hour behind its eastern neighbour.

Crucially he arranged these zones every 15° longitude apart: with 360° around the globe, and 24 hours to deal with, simple arithmetic indicated that each zone should be roughly 15° wide. So America was pared into four – the Eastern time zone, the Central, Mountain and Pacific. When it was noon in New York, Miami and Pittsburgh, so it was 11 in the morning – one hour back – in Chicago, Dallas and New Orleans; at the same moment the clocks in Denver, Butte and Albuquerque would read 10 am, while it would be 9 in Seattle, San Francisco and San Diego. Within ten years his plan, simple and eminently sensible, was agreed by all the railway companies and – shortly afterwards, and to all intents and purposes – by all the states. At noon on Sunday 18 November 1883, all the public clocks in North America were changed to what the *New York Herald* called "the new standard of time agreed upon . . . as an obvious convenience in all social and business matters".

And Professor Dowd's reach swiftly became global: fourteen years after the publication of his monograph and a year after America adopted his system, so the International Meridian Conference in Washington agreed as well: the entire world, not just the American portion of it, should be divided into time zones with Greenwich as the prime meridian. Moreover, it should be divided along the very lines suggested by the modest principal from a small spa town otherwise hitherto and subsequently better known as the site where Ulysses S. Grant died, and where America keeps its Horse-racing Hall of Fame.

There may well be a modest marble tombstone for Mr Dowd somewhere in Saratoga Springs; but each time the television continuity announcer advertises a forthcoming programme as showing at "9 pm Eastern, 8 Central and Mountain" then one might say of the late Professor, *si monumentum requiris, circumspice*.

There might well also be a memorial to Dowd on the tiny island of Tafahi, in the northern part of the Pacific Ocean's only remaining monarchy, the kingdom of Tonga. For Tafahi is the closest populated island in the world to the western side of the International Date Line, which is the obvious corollary to, or the logical antithesis of, the Greenwich prime meridian. Since it is to the west, and the world turns to the east, Tafahi is thus the place which greets the world's new day first; it is the island where the day begins. And where the week, the month, the year, the decade, the century, the next millennium begins. Tafahi is, indeed, "The Island Where Time Starts".

In plain symbolic terms, I thought, no place on earth could be more suitable for opening an account of the newness of the new Pacific Ocean. I had read all manner of learned papers and cover stories in American news magazines talking of the 'Dawn of the Pacific Age' and suchlike: so why not go where that dawn actually happens? Perhaps I might see in the rising of that sun some icon quintessentially Pacific, or think some thought which in a flash would sum up the essential message of the great Ocean. It was a costly venture, of course, since Tonga is a very great distance from almost everywhere; but an admirably far-sighted magazine based in New York thought that a visit to 'The Island Where Time Starts' could make an agreeable tale, therefore handed me a sheaf of air tickets and a small sum in hard currency and told me to be on my way.

And so, on a blustery February evening – in the very middle of the South Pacific summer and, I was warned, of the hurricane season – I flew to within striking distance of Tafahi from an airfield in the Republic of Fiji. I was determined to see the world's first dawn, and to greet the first people on the planet – true Pacific people at that – who were planning to take a stab at their day.

Rupert Murdoch owns a newspaper in Fiji which claims to be "the first with the world's news". In that his is a daily paper, and that Fiji is quite close to the Date Line, probably he is technically correct. But in all other respects Tonga is more rightfully regarded as the closest place* and has an International Date Line Hotel in the main town, Nuku'alofa, to prove it. On the floor of the lobby, a place invariably filled with idle Tongan men of great girth, is a brass bas-relief of the

---

*Pedants will say that the Soviet Union's Big Diomede Island, in the Bering Strait, is actually closer to the Line, since it positively shaves its coast and separates it from America's Little Diomede, only two miles away. But there is no permanent native population on Big Diomede, which can scarcely claim to enjoy the world's first dawn since it is dark there for six months of the year.

Line, set in a marble sea. Charles Dowd's invention gleams dully in the half-gloom, trodden upon by the sandals and the bare feet of a people who, despite the name of their hotel, take little obvious pleasure or pride in knowing their unique status.

But one man knew, and derived considerable pleasure from being where he was. Paul Fabian, the lone British diplomat who gloried in the title of Her Britannic Majesty's High Commissioner in Tonga and Consul for the United States Island Possessions in the South Pacific, had sent me a telex advising me that yes, Tafahi was the first place in the world to receive the day's new time and that, moreover, he had only very recently been there.

I telephoned, down a long and scratchy line. "We're really looking forward to your coming," I could hear him shouting. "Would you like me to fix up an audience with the King here? Perfectly easy if you'd like to see him."

I met Paul Fabian a few days later – a small, bird-like man, quite bald, dressed in a white safari suit and a Panama, and in a perpetual state of fuss about "sending telegrams to London". "First British diplomatic post in the world to open up each day, you know," he said proudly. "That's why you're quite right to come down here to start your travels. Perfect place. Complete Pacific symbol. Admirable choice. Why not pop in for lunch? Not frightfully busy here, must admit. Quite a bit of spare time on the old hands. Better check the wire machine and see if there's anything from London."

But there rarely was. The Foreign and Commonwealth Office had rather greater concerns than Paul Fabian and his tiny High Commission and Residency on the seafront of Nuku'alofa. His was not a mission at the cutting edge of British diplomatic activity. Governments would not be swayed, nor would ministers tremble, on receipt of elegantly crafted and crisply sarcastic Notes written by him on the antique encryption machine which could be seen in a corner of the office, slowly rusting away in the hot, salt air. Precisely why he had been sent to Tonga – what special knowledge or circumstance – was never explained and, sitting as I did for many an evening on the veranda of the magnificent old Residency, watching the fireflies and listening to the surf booming on the reef, I was not too sorely tempted to enquire.

The Fabians had indeed been up to Tafahi, about a month before. His Excellency showed me a film he had taken of the three northern islands of the Tonga group which – being some 300 miles north of

6

the main island – are invariably overlooked by such few visitors as Tonga receives. They were in fact the first of the so-called Friendly Islands to be seen by Europeans: the Dutch navigators Willem Corneliszoon Schouten and Jacob LeMaire spotted them in April 1616.* The Niuas, as the trio are called, are closer to both Samoa and Fiji than to the main Tongan group, and it remains one of the odder quirks of Polynesian history that the islands belong to Tonga at all. (It also renders Tongan maps a most inconvenient shape: to accommodate all the Friendly Islands and all the Tongan seas, a scale map has to be about five times as long as it is wide, though nearly all the population and commerce is bunched in the islands in the far south.)

The most geologically interesting and romantically appealing of the three islands is Niuafo'ou, a sunken volcanic caldera set off to the west. Almost perfectly circular, it contains a virtually circular lake with another almost perfectly circular island in its centre – the whole confection looking like a vast floating doughnut. There is a big bundle of feathers called the incubator bird which lays its eggs six feet down in the hot black sand, and whose offspring emerge huge and fully feathered against the heat. And there is a reputation among world stamp-collectors: since the cliffs of Niuafo'ou are almost wholly steep-to and landings are fatally difficult, mail is – or was until very recently – transferred to and from passing ships by swimmers, who carried the outbound post in oilcloth bags and used bamboo poles to retrieve the inbound letters sealed in tin cans. "Tin Can Island" proclaim the postage stamps, and old ones are said to be almost as sought after as British Guiana Triangulars or Penny Blacks.

The second island is Niuatoputapu, small and triangular, fringed by beaches of the purest white, with palm trees and pandanus pines leaning into the ever-beating trade winds. This island seems overrun with small black pigs (animals so much a part of Tongan life that when Captain Cook presented a pair of hitherto unknown Guernsey cows to the King they were classified as "Cook's pigs", and the name has stuck for cows ever since), and with Australian cruising "yachties" who use the Niuas (as Schouten and LeMaire once did) as the formal port of entry to the kingdom.

---

*They sailed westwards to Tonga after clearing the southern tip of South America and naming it after the Friesland herring port from which they had left, Cape Hoorn.

And then, at latitude 15° 51'S, longitude 173° 43'W,* is the immense, half-mile-high volcanic cone of Tafahi itself – the island where time begins. It loomed in almost every frame of the Fabians' film – a sugar-loaf, bottle-green and black, its cliffs forbidding behind their skirt of angry white water. The guide-books say little: Samuel Wallis visited it and named it Boscawen Island, perhaps after the great admiral of Finisterre; the best vanilla in the Pacific is grown there; and it is rumoured that the finest *kava* – that faintly narcotic drink prepared from the powdered root of a local pepper plant, and an important part of rituals and celebrations in the South Pacific – is Tafahi *kava*, and that it renders all Tafahians perpetually slightly dopey.

So there it lay, 300 miles to the north, utterly cut off from us by the hurricanes which – according to the local weather men – were raging back and forth nearby. It certainly rained a great deal in Nuku'alofa, the gales whipping up the surf into clouds of spume and sending broken branches spinning through the air. The High Commissioner's Residency was flooded, his collection of pandanus mats sodden, his power lines brought down by falling trees. There was a momentary crisis when the telex failed, and he was cut off from London, but two Tongan soldiers arrived on his doorstep in the middle of the storm, saluted smartly, acknowledged they realized his predicament and promised that his links with the outside world would be restored "as a matter of the utmost priority". It turned out to be a matter of enlightened self-interest for Tonga too, since the first thing Mr Fabian did when his line was restored was to pen a telegram to London demanding immediate aid for the islands. And he got it, by return – a promise of a few hundred pounds'-worth of schoolbooks, for which the government of Tonga gave due thanks.

(The *Tonga Chronicle* gave due prominence to the storm the

---

*Theory says it is impossible for a place west of Greenwich also to be west of the Date Line. But politics transcend logic, and the enormous dog-leg that the Line performs around Fiji and Tonga can all be blamed on a colonial governor in Suva, who decided in 1879 that his islands (through which the Greenwich antemeridian passes) should all be on one time, and that should be Antipodean time. Tonga went along with that, but the King of Samoa decided to fall in with American demands and stay a day behind Tonga. His Majesty performed this feat by a combination of calendric sleight-of-hand and flattery: in 1879 on Samoa the Fourth of July was celebrated twice.

following week, though they might have wished for more careful sub-editing. "$10 damage as islands hit by hurricane" read the headline. But readers were also given a piece of gummed paper to stick after the figure ten, written on which was the missing word "million".)

Friendly Islands Airways, the somewhat informally organized internal airline, lost one of its three planes in the storm, spoiling my chances of making an early start for the airstrip on Niuatoputapu. And the inter-island ship, the *Nanasipau'u*, which might have given me a lift up north, chose to ride out the wind in the lee of the island, unwisely put down both anchors, promptly snapped both chains and then drifted helplessly out to sea. When the weather calmed her master spent several days trawling for the missing anchors with grapnels in what the charts said was 30 fathoms of water. He never found anything; when I left he was waiting for a new pair to be brought up from Auckland, and wondering if the insurance company would cough up.

So I waited and waited. And I put in a request to see His Majesty the King.

I had first spied King Taufa'ahau Tupou IV, GCVO, GCMG, KBE, sitting in the royal box in church at Sunday service the week before. Like most Tongan men he was a mighty figure, reputedly weighing nearly a quarter of a ton. The King had his eccentric side. In particular, he was given to unusual enthusiasms. His personal fondness for the sayings of the Reverend Swaggart marked him as a man somewhat out of step with much of the rest of the world; a view reinforced by his apparent keenness on the suggestion of a freebooting American marine that the kingdom become a dumping-ground for spent atomic waste and noxious chemicals. Knowing his passion for cycling (on Mondays, Wednesdays and Fridays) and rowing (on Tuesdays, Thursdays and Saturdays), I had mentioned in my letter that I had stroked my boat, somewhat ingloriously, for two Torpids and two Summer Eights. It seemed as good a way of ingratiating myself as any other: the palace was a protective place, and there was no automatic guarantee that a visiting journalist would be granted an audience. Tales of Tongan royal oarsmanship had recently spread as far afield as Hawaii and Tahiti and I reasoned that it could do no harm to mention my interest, albeit one or two decades old. It worked: next morning there was a note for me in the Date Line:

9

Audience with HM the King, 2 pm in the royal palace. Please wear a tie.

Our meeting was delayed for ten minutes. I had been ushered into the throne room (the throne itself, 8 feet high and needing six men to move it, was carved from a solid slab of oak and had been presented to Queen Salote by the British Government in 1951), and could hear from next door the awful warble of Mr Swaggart's daily broadcast to which the King was apparently listening. The room was crammed with the bric-à-brac of kingship, the usual gifts from brother heads of state around the world: dolls in glass cases, a vivarium, two portraits of George Bush, seals of visiting warships, a porcelain plate from the Republic of China (which keeps a one-man embassy in Nuku'alofa), a map of the moon presented by Mr Reagan, statuettes, umbrellas, a humidor and any number of sets of engraved Waterford glass. There was an elephantine stirring from beyond the arras, the heavy footfall of leather sandals on worn carpets, and the King appeared.

He puffed asthmatically. "Welcome, welcome. You have something to drink? I think the passion-fruit juice is very good this season. You have come from very far. From England, I think. Now tell me, is the *Manchester Guardian* still printed in Manchester? I had heard it may have moved."

Indeed it had, some twenty years before. "Ah well," he chortled. "In Tonga we hear things a little late. But you have come, I am told, because we are the first place on earth to get the dawn. Last with everything else, first with the dawn – a fine irony, isn't it?" and chortling again, he poured more passion-fruit juice into the Waterford glass.

We talked of toxic wastes; the possibility of there ever being true democracy in Tonga ("on paper the place is ripe for revolution, it is true, and our friends in the other islands are experiencing troubled times, so we must be wary"); the complaints about corruption among the Tongan nobility, the curious business arrangements engineered between members of the royal family and the dubious Americans who were forever fetching up at the palace doorstep wishing to bend a royal ear to this scheme or that, with wealth and fame for all; and the most surprising news: his decision to demolish the royal palace.

The King wanted to take me round the garden. He showed me the grass on which Tu'i Mala was wont to graze – Tu'i Mala being a blind Galapagos tortoise which Captain Cook presented to the Tongans in 1777, and which died in 1966 at well over two hundred years old. He showed me the stands of Norfolk pines which shaded the palace, and the view of the seafront, with a new sea-wall being put up by a Japanese firm. A white Range Rover passed, the Union flag snapping from a small mast on the bonnet. The King waved in a desultory way. "Your Mr Fabian, off to collect his letters from home, I daresay. Such a nice fellow, don't you think?"

He walked me slowly out to the garden gate – a kindly old man, more interested in his trees and his plans for the palace, his rowing and his cycling than in the ruder demands of his people for democracy and good government. I wondered as we strolled across the lawn whether he might not in fact turn out to be the last King of Tonga, the final member of a brief and moderately distinguished dynasty. True, there was Crown Prince Tupouto'a waiting in the wings, but he spent little time in Tonga and had a reputation as a playboy – a Farouk-like figure given to white suits and expensive lady friends. He might not be quite the regal material the Tongan people were looking for, and as his wheezing old father – born in 1918, still fit, but neither infallible nor immortal – tottered around the herbaceous borders, I fancied, or perhaps dreaded, that soon we might see the kingdom fall and a republic rise in its place, and the monarchy he represented fall victim to the spirit of the age, as ancient and outworn as Captain Cook's old tortoise.

We reached the low white picket-fence, the only insulation from his subjects that he cared to have. The only protection, too. "Flimsy, eh? Wouldn't stop anyone who really wanted to get me." He grasped my hand and shook it warmly. "So glad you came to see us. Have fun watching the dawn. I shall still be in my bed. But I enjoy knowing that the first sun in the world will warm you here in these islands. It makes me rather proud. That – and you having been an oarsman, too. Really rather proud."

It was another day before the winds died, the seas settled and the Friendly Islands Airways craft was hammered into serviceable shape. And then, at 4 am one pitch-dark morning, I found myself where all along I had planned to be: standing on a steep hillside on a clifftop, waiting for the sun to rise on the world's first dawn of the day. It was a Saturday, the middle of February. The night had been unusually cool, and a slight drizzle was falling. Down below me the surf thrashed and thundered: the Tonga Trench, a precipitous crack in the ocean floor where two of the planet's great tectonic plates crunched together and were folded downwards to melt again, lay a score of miles away. The water was 22,000-ft deep off these islands, though down further south, near Kermadec, it was seven miles to the bottom. But even here I was on the very lip of the world, peering over one of the suture lines of the globe and into the darkness of yesterday.

I had entertained many hopes for this morning. I had imagined, for instance, that I would be able to catch a glimpse of Mount Silisili, a mile-high peak in the centre of Samoa, just a few miles away across the water: I had hoped to do so for no better reason than that Mount Silisili would be enjoying precisely the same clock time as here in Tonga, but exactly one day before. So if I saw the mountain, outlined by the rising sun at dawn, I could say to myself that though it was Saturday morning here what I was witnessing at the same moment was dawn on Friday, the day before. The simultaneous sighting of two periods of time separated by an entire 24 hours seemed a paradox well worth experiencing. Then again, I had this vague vision – a pure fantasy – that schoolchildren would rise from their beds in this tiny village, and would file down to school carrying Japanese-made microcomputers to help them with their sums and their essays. That, it seemed, would be the kind of icon I needed, a truly Pacific emblem – that of South Sea island children beginning the first learning of the world's new day, and doing so by using California-invented high-technology packaged, sold and marketed by the Japanese. Everything about this little scene related to the Ocean with which I had become so enraptured: if ever the peoples of the Pacific were to take over the running of the world, I fancied, it would start with people such as these, using such things in a place like this. And so I waited for the darkness of the Tongan night to lift, my fingers tightly crossed.

In the event, the reality was as different and as perversely non-emblematic as it could be. For a start, it continued to drizzle. The dawn – when finally it came up – did so neither like thunder, nor rosy-fingered. Instead the horizon became vaguely apparent – an uneven charcoal line separating the inky sea below from a deep grey stain of sky above. The stain lightened slowly to reveal lowering clouds moving in from the north; the sea became less ink-like too, and showed itself as a mess of enormous and ever-moving swells picked out here and there by off-white skeins of spray. The fringing reef came into view as well: a ragged line of breakers, huge walls of spume and the ocean hurling itself relentlessly against the coral. If Samoa, Mount Silisili and yesterday were indeed somewhere out there, I would have to take their presence on trust: I doubt if the visibility was more than five miles, and less as the squalls rolled in and drenched me in my eyrie.

As the day began, so the village started to pull itself together. The gloom rolled back until I could see six or seven huts: they were grass-roofed, mean little constructions of board and lath, surrounded by muddy pools by which dozens of small black pigs were wagging their corkscrew tails and chasing each other over the cliffs. Two or three wet and rather forlorn-looking dogs lounged in the mud.

At about 6 o'clock, a light snapped on in one of the huts. I could hear curses and grunts, clothes being pulled on, and the familiar twang as cheap bedsprings were relieved of their customary pressure. I readied my notebook. After all, this was an important moment, a time to savour. Whoever was about to emerge from beneath the dripping straw roof of this tiny hut on this minute hamlet on the eastern edge of this unknown volcanic islet was the first person in the world to rise on this February Saturday morning: *Homo pacificus*, the symbol of all I had travelled half a world to see. He would, I knew, be an immense and magnificent man, his shirt half open, his *ta'ovala* mat secured with its waistband of coconut fibre. He would spy me and bellow "*malo e lelei!*" I could wish for nothing more (unless, of course, his daughter followed, bearing a Toshiba lap-top computer, and skipped down the hill to school).

The door creaked open. The figure framed in the light was shorter than I had expected, thin and stooped; he looked up at the sky and cursed a guttural curse, then started buttoning his fly. He wore no *ta'ovala*, no coconut-fibre belt. I coughed, and he looked up; a grey little man with spectacles, standing there in the mud surrounded by the squabbling pigs, he looked the very antithesis of magnificent immensity. Rubbing his glasses clean, he peered intently over at me through the thin rain.

"*Gröss Gott!*" he exclaimed. He came a little closer and his face broke into a lopsided grin, half amazed, half delighted. "*Guten Morgen, mein Herren!*" he said. "*Wilkommen in Tonga.*"

It turned out that my *Homo pacificus* came from Dusseldorf. There was, I realized, an easy explanation. Tonga had signed a treaty with Germany in 1876, and there had been a German coaling station on Vava'u. Then at the end of the century Britain, fearing for her own security in the trans-Pacific sea-lanes, swapped rights to Tongan waters with those she had in Samoa, giving Samoan trading rights to

Germany and the United States, and keeping Tonga's for the Empire. The corollary is that British influence in Tonga is still immense; but Germany still has relict links from before 1899, and this dampish little Dusseldorfer was a case in point. His sister, he explained, had married a Tongan, and the couple now lived in Mainz: not perhaps the most attractive of men, he had been invited out to stay among the substantial ladies of the islands to see if he, too, could forge any links. Thus far, he had not enjoyed any success.

A moment later and the girls of the house tumbled out – Sophia, Anna and Salome. All large, cheerful girls in their late teens, to my great relief they wore long skirts and mats around their waists, tied as tradition dictates with a braided *kiekei* band. They asked me in for tea, and we all listened to the morning news on Radio Tonga, crackling over the miles from the aerials down in Tongatapu. The King, the announcer said, was leaving that night to attend the funeral of the Emperor of Japan.

Salome, the most talkative and pretty of the trio, took me aside. Training to be a teacher and with a wisdom that belied her years, she explained that it was her half-brother who was now living in Mainz and had suggested that Erich (the Dusseldorfer) travel down to Tonga to look for a wife. "But he is rather lacking in grace," Salome said. "It is unlikely he will go back successful. There is very little connection now between our people and you Europeans. We prefer to take our husbands from among each other. Not like the old days when we looked up to you. Now we have our own pride, and people like him have no place here."

I was enormously glad she had made that little speech for the mere sight of Erich – the knowledge that a man who worked as a painter in a Ford Taunus factory and was, in his own way, a type-specimen of Atlantic man, with no known connections with the new Ocean, had somehow fetched up on a remote Pacific island – was disturbing the entire thesis I wished to construct. There was no use pretending it hadn't happened: I had wished for a pure Pacific experience, a truly new world experience at the dawning of this day, yet it had become hopelessly muddied with a relic of the old world and the Ocean whose time, we are now supposed to believe, has passed.

But Salome had placed it all perfectly in context, and by doing so had made Erich an unwitting ally to the theme. For *of course* the Pacific is still influenced by the Atlantic that once dominated the world: the ties that bound the world together yesterday – personified by the men and women who came out from the West to trade or to peddle religion, to colonize, annex, smuggle or fight – these ties still exist today, though more weakly, with less influence and fewer and fewer people enrolled in the process. The crucial difference now is as Salome had declared, and is as true on a small and insubstantial island group like Tonga as in the capitals of Japan, Chile, Queensland or Korea: the difference is that the peoples of the Pacific no longer have a reason to look up to those adventurers from the old Atlantic. They have their pride, their new confidence and assertiveness. "We are a Pacific people," I heard said on many occasions, "and we are proud."

I said my farewells to Salome and her sisters and shook hands with Erich, who gave me a sheaf of letters to airmail when I got back to Hong Kong. A boat returned me to the little coral landing-strip; Friendly Islands Airways took me down to Tongatapu; and within half a day I was settled in a small hotel in Auckland, waiting for the weekly Cathay Pacific jet home. I had seen the island where time begins, and had come to the sorry realization that the Pacific, the vastest of all oceans, is a far more complicated entity – if indeed it could ever be regarded as such – than it was possible to imagine.

For if nothing else, by the time I had flown another twelve hours north from Auckland, and my jet had settled me on to the runway at Kai Tak airport in Hong Kong, I was still on the periphery of the Pacific Ocean. I was still in a place washed by the waters which had thundered off Tonga, where there was a king with a nation of Brobdingnagian subjects, a million pigs and a tradition of wearing clothes made of pandanus leaves and coconut string. I was still on the shores of the same great sea and yet had been transported into quite another world, a place on the edge of a China which seemed to have nothing in common with those islanders so forgotten and so far away. Except, of course, the Ocean itself.

Trite though it may sound, the Pacific, unlike its sister seas, is an ocean of many worlds indeed – and at the same time by being so has become *the world ocean*, as dominant and all-encompassing as its immensity suggests it has to be. To fathom its many mysteries, to grasp its vastness and try to understand its wholeness, I then realized would be a very considerable task.

The event that set the modern Pacific on its unrelenting climb towards world dominion happened, by an entirely appropriate coincidence, to be the first ever shown clear across America, on coast–to–coast television.

The inauguration of the 3,000-mile link of co-axial cables and microwaves took place on an unusually hot Saturday morning, 8 September 1951, for the reporting of the momentous happenings then reaching their climax in the gaudy and Italianate opera house in San Francisco. The ceremonial that unrolled before the cameras was displayed, just as it happened,* on television sets (black and white only) in living rooms, offices and bedrooms from Presque Isle in Maine to Key West in Florida, and in all salient points between such as New York, Pittsburgh and Washington DC.

The event that prompted this sudden electronic integration of the nation – with all the then unrecognized implications, good and bad, for those who lived there – was the formal signing of the Japanese Peace Treaty. This treaty, written on a mammoth parchment document that was said to hold more signatures than any other treaty in world history, was signed by 49 of the participants in the Second World War. It formally returned to Japan the sovereignty she had lost in her atomic-bombed defeat, and enabled her to recommence her ambitious ascent towards economic supremacy – a climb which, though frustrated and corrupted before, was this time and at last to culminate in her present astonishing success. And with Japan's success came the beginnings of the Ocean's success: a new economic axis had been created.

However the era of the Pacific probably had its true beginnings nearly a century before, and at the behest of that most unremembered of all American presidents, Millard Fillmore. No other act of his dismal presidency deserves mention;† but in an irony perhaps lost on his many detractors, his single decision in March 1852 to despatch a naval expedition to Japan, under the command of Commodore Matthew Perry, has had an ineradicable effect on world history.

Perry's foray to the Orient marked the true beginning of America's

---

*The word "live" was coined in Britain in the 1930s to describe such coverage by radio: only after the San Francisco conference did the combination of television's popularity and American informality remove the quotation marks.
†When he had finished his undistinguished term, he ran again as candidate for the infamous "Know-Nothing Party" in the poll of 1856. He didn't win.

global role; it marked the emergence on the world stage of Japan, after two centuries of a xenophobia that almost bordered on paranoia; and it allowed the creation – nervous at first, but gradually becoming more and more pronounced – of a trans-Pacific axis between, put at its most basic, California and Honshu – an axis around which the fortunes of today's Ocean, and much of today's world, revolves.

America's interest in the Pacific, dating from the end of the eighteenth century, was almost certainly fired by the telling in dockside bars and merchants' cafés of gaudily embroidered tales of the explorations of Captain Cook: why, the mariners of Boston and New York wondered out loud, should the Ocean that washed their continent's western shores be traversed and charted by a navigator all the way from North Yorkshire, and by Frenchmen and Portuguese too? And so, in the early years of the nineteenth century American sailors set out in contest, the seaward extension of those landlubbers who, to use John L. O'Sullivan's famous phrase of 1845, sought their "manifest destiny" on land by expanding ever westward, to the very edge of the continental United States.*

Those mariners set about whaling, settling, plundering; they established a presence in Hawaii; they shared with Britain the spoils of the Chinese treaty ports; they took Samoa; they befriended Korea; they seized and settled Midway, Wake, Guam and (a spoil of an Imperial war) the Philippines – thus creating a series of stepping-stones, a lifeline of tropical islands that led all the way to that greatest and most elusive prize, the Middle Kingdom, China. But the most notable act of all this trans-Pacific ambition – when seen from today's vantage point, if not necessarily so at the time – was President Fillmore's decision to send out Commodore Perry and his "black ships", to bring sense to the isolationist shoguns who in almost Carthusian seclusion, ran the state of Nihon.

Matthew Calbraith Perry, with his minuscule armada of two frigates and two sailing vessels, arrived at the heavily fortified port of Uraga – at the very mouth of Tokyo Bay – on 8 July 1853. Japanese warships, puny in the extreme, surrounded him. The Commodore†

---

*O'Sullivan's prophecy, written in the *United States Magazine and Democratic Review*, was for "the fulfilment of our manifest destiny to overspread the continent allotted by Providence . . ." The occupation of the Texas Republic, the occupation of Oregon Territory and the war with Mexico were all stirred into life by liberal use of the phrase.

†Though he called himself Admiral to impress the locals.

refused pointblank to leave. He would, he insisted, complete his mission to deliver a pouch of documents from President Fillmore – by force, if no one was deputed to receive the papers personally.

Despite their stubborn pride and the risk of loss of face, the Japanese soon realized that Perry's ships were far superior to their own. They withdrew their blockade, and sent their Prince Toda to collect the package. In what was regarded then as some perverse flourish of American protocol, "Admiral" Perry then gave the papers to two of his black mariners – "the best-looking fellows of their colour that the squadron could furnish" – and instructed them to hand them over. They were to deliver, with the greatest of courtesy, the inaugural diplomatic traffic between the newly-emerging America and the soon-to-emerge Japan.

The initial shock felt by the Japanese wore off quickly enough, once they had read the letters and considered their implications. The Commodore was back in Tokyo Bay seven months later, in the depths of the following winter. This time he came with nine ships, and a determination to win agreement from the Japanese – and he did precisely that, concluding a treaty of peace and friendship that – unknown to all its signatories – was to have consequences of shattering proportions. The collapse of the shogunate and the restoration of the Meiji throne was but one effect, from which a myriad of others flowed: the revival of Japanese nationalism and her imperial designs, the invasion of China, the florid plans for a Greater East Asia Co-Prosperity Sphere, the bombast and cruelty of the Pacific War, the creation in America of the atomic bomb, its eventual use over the two great cities of Kyushu, and Japan's consequent defeat, post-war disgrace, ruin and decay.

All of this, it can surely be argued, flowed seamlessly from that fateful meeting between two black American sailors and a princely envoy from the Kyoto court in the harbour at Uraga, and by the handover of a letter written by a president who, less than a year later, would be languishing in Buffalo in the beginnings of what should be – by this reckoning alone – quite undeserved historical obscurity.

It took the San Francisco Peace Treaty of 1951 to place the official seal of international forgiveness on Japan's decade of distemper; after which, and ever since, Japan has raced ahead without once looking back, achieving all she had sought by war and conquest without the firing of a single shot or shell.

Few commentators at the time saw in the conference the beginnings of the Pacific age. Most were far too taken with the spectacle of Andrei Gromyko, then the Soviet Union's deputy Foreign Minister, trying – and failing – to break the conference apart. The newspaper-reading public – and the television audience of some 40 million who had never before been treated to live pictures from the Californian coast – revelled in the pictures of Gromyko and his Polish and Czech "wrecking crew" (as John Foster Dulles put it) who complained, harangued, sulked and finally walked out as amendment after amendment was defeated by the other conferees. All praise was given to Dean Acheson, the conference chairman, for his handling of the "Reds"; and there were lurid tales told by a reporter who smuggled himself into the Soviets' rented mansion disguised as a plumber ("socks and panties dangled . . . orange peels littered the floors . . . five to seven beds had been squeezed into every bedroom . . ."). There was even supposed to be a plot to assassinate Gromyko by ramming a beer truck into his motorcade (and a meat truck did overturn on the road shortly before the cars were due). America was fascinated by the Russians' presence in their prettiest city, and duly ignored the real significance of what was going on.

It took well over an hour for the first 48 delegates – who included no Soviet bloc nation, nor India, nor Burma, nor either of the Chinas, nor a scattering of other countries who could not bring themselves to accept Japan's word – to file up to the podium to sign.* And then, with a solemnity and dignity appropriate to the moment, the Japanese Prime Minister Shigeru Yoshida stepped up to sign. He had flown in via Honolulu, but reportedly had not deigned to glance over at the still-visible wreckage of Pearl Harbor, just off the runway. He and his five brother delegates (though there were 74 in the full Japanese team, and 70 correspondents) were dressed in morning coats and striped trousers, "to show Japan's modesty and sincerity", as Yoshida said. They signed – and the war was officially over, the peace had begun.

Very few of the seers got it right. Freda Kirchwey, writing in *The Nation*, came close:

*And to be given a brand-new fountain pen to memorialize the event.

. . . already the British are worrying about cheap Japanese goods flooding markets absolutely essential to the export trade . . . Norway is worried about fishing rights. . . . Many nations are apprehensive because the treaty establishes no controls to prevent the ruthless industrial and trading practices that built Japan's pre-war commercial empire. And all the powers. . . . fear the rapid rise of Japan's war-making capacity, industrial and political as well as military. They know that a new balance of power in Asia has been created by the Treaty. . . .

By "new balance of power" Freda Kirchwey (and most other writers who made this same point) meant a balance between Japan, Korea, Formosa, China and the Soviet Union. There was little thought that the "balance" would ultimately rest between the two old enemies, Japan and the United States; nor that the entire Pacific Ocean and all the countries around it were to become, to a greater or lesser extent, dependent upon and in thrall to these two protagonists in the conference. As everyone left, clutching the fountain pens and the sugar-pastry city crests handed out by an exuberant San Francisco mayor, so the world's thoughts were principally, and thankfully, concentrated on the reality that one war was now definitely over while another – that raging across the Ocean in Korea – was beginning to look as though it might end soon. (It did not.) The idea of the emergent Pacific was not in anyone's mind, and in any case the reality of it was not to appear for many years.

But it did steal up on us, in the way eras have a habit of doing, some time in the late Sixties and early Seventies. The West, the Atlantic world, may have been firing rockets to the moon and fighting a war in Indochina, but the benefit of hindsight indicates now that in other ways it was gripped by a blinkered and introspective mood, absorbed by its own internal problems. Understandably so, for these problems were grave indeed: the Kennedys had been killed, likewise Dr King; the streets of Paris and London were furious with the sounds of protest; the cities and university towns of America were in turmoil: race relations, the draft, mind–expanding drugs, the Weather Underground, Dylan, Daley, psychedelia, the National Guard; a cause for a riot, bomb or occupation was to be found everywhere, every day. It was not a time for students of the world to ponder the great matters of global history, to care about the great beyond, to notice the unleashing of distant energies. Yet being unleashed they most certainly were.

The turning point, the moment when the era rightly began, came during those years between America's Sixties triumph – Neil Armstrong's first footsteps on the Sea of Tranquillity in 1969 – and that most doleful moment of the Seventies, when the last US Marines were evacuated from the roof of the embassy in Saigon in 1975. And the indicator of the moment, regrettably, has to be a statistic: the simple fact that from the late Sixties and the early Seventies onward, more than half the world's goods and services, more than half the world's trade, had its origins within the domain of the Pacific Ocean. If in no other sense than economic, the world's focus had switched from East to West, from Greenwich to the Date Line, from Atlantic to Pacific. This part of the planet meant business.

Statistics – unpalatable, indigestible and ephemeral though they may be – tell much of the story of the world's sudden recognition of the Pacific. Some – such as those asserting that most of the world's people now live around the Ocean – are questionable (as will be explored shortly). Others, which display the higher growth rates of the Pacific countries, the greater *per capita* incomes of their peoples, and the steadily increasing volumes of iron ore, oil and containerized trade crossing the Pacific, are powerful indicators of an undeniable trend. But, though statistics are objective icons for the disinterested observer – or powerfully distorting tools for the polemicist – once in a while a particular set of figures will leap from the page of some dust-dry tome to offer up an image more illuminating than all of a dozen reports like those in the bibliography relating to this chapter.

Others interested in this Ocean may have already found their choicest figures: the one that brought the Pacific's surge so very much alive for me – when hitherto it had been no more than the muffled beatings of a warm, blue and very distant sea – related to an event seven miles above the surface of the earth, some time during a night in 1984. Probably, though this can never be wholly proven, the night of Friday, 4 May 1984.

Like any wide expanse of sea, the Pacific Ocean is criss-crossed with commercial air-routes. These are flying lanes, arranged more or less like the lanes of a superhighway, each given a name and a number, all clearly designated on maps, and designed by the

International Civil Aviation Organization's Air Navigation Commission to allow civil aircraft to fly in relative safety when far from land. To say the Pacific is *criss-crossed* is, perhaps, too strong – the Atlantic has a number of routes that cross each other, and its Jepperson high-altitude charts are so filled with intersecting lines that to an untutored eye, they resemble the early stages of weaving. In contrast the Pacific, being so huge, and travelled across by aircraft that tend (at least for now) to fly principally between East and West and back again, manages to contain its major routes within a few distinct bands.

The five "main roads" that run between Anchorage and Tokyo are the main tracks across the Pacific for aircraft running between any of the American or Canadian west coast airports on the one hand, and any of the Asian traffic centres, Tokyo, Seoul, Taipei or Hong Kong on the other. These routes, known as ATSs, or Air Traffic Separation routes, are designated Red 220, Red 580, Amber 590, Red 591 and Green 344, and they carry the bulk of traffic across the Ocean. Pilots using them plot their journeys across the uninterrupted emptiness of the Pacific by plotting a course between a series of way-points, random but fixed points above the Ocean that are each given five-letter nonsense names – Neeva, Nytim, Nokka, Nabie, among a host of others – from above which the planes report their positions to the Pacific's oceanic control centres at Tokyo, Anchorage and Oakland, California.

These heavily-travelled, perpetually busy airways are supplemented by others currently less hectic but growing fast both in use and consequence. There is, for instance, a route between Tokyo and Honolulu – known, because it is not fixed in cement, as it were, as the TYO-HNL Flexible Track System – which carries millions upon millions of Japanese to and from honeymoons and shopping expeditions; there are routes now between Honolulu and San Francisco, between Honolulu and Nadi (in Fiji, and pronounced Nandi), Nadi and Tokyo, and Nadi and Sydney, between Los Angeles and points south-west. (Fiji, despite its relative economic unimportance, has become a major centre for air traffic controlling, refuelling, stopovers and crew changes.)

Oceanic controllers there, as well as in Honolulu and Auckland, watch the blips on their radars, or plot positions of unseen aircraft on immense plastic charts, as do French-speaking specialists hunched over their radar screens outside Papeete, in Tahiti. To the north and west of these last the skies are cluttered; only to the east of Tahiti is the Ocean left to its own devices.*

This, then, was the situation on what I shall call that Friday, early in the northern summer of 1984. It was late on Friday evening in London; in the cities of the western Pacific – Tokyo, Hong Kong, Seoul, Vladivostok, Sydney – it was early Saturday morning. In those of the eastern Pacific – San Francisco, Hawaii, Easter Island, Anchorage, Pitcairn – it was mid-afternoon, on Friday. Professor Dowd's line dividing Friday from Saturday rendered it late Saturday morning in Tonga, and slightly later on Friday morning in Samoa, just a couple of hundred miles away. So the exact time – and day – of this statistically important happening depends very much on where it was recorded. Since planes tend to fly by Greenwich Mean Time, it is convenient to say it took place on the evening of the Friday.

What happened is recorded as a statistic. There are about 700 Boeing 747s in operation around the world, and rather fewer Douglas DC10s and Lockheed L1011 Tri-Stars: the so-called jumbo jets, the wide-bodies, those given the suffix "heavy" – as in "Cathay Pacific 200-Heavy" – by the air traffic controllers. Until that Friday night slightly more than half the planes actually up in the sky, flying between the cities with runways that can handle wide-bodied jets, were doing so – across the Atlantic Ocean. They were flying between London and New York, Philadelphia and Frankfurt, New Orleans and Madrid, Montréal and Paris, Chicago and Lagos, Rio and Cape Town, Buenos Aires and the Canary Islands and a score of other places besides.

But from late that Friday night the scene suddenly shifted. Most of the world's big planes known to be in the air at that time were recorded by the traffic controllers as being not above the Atlantic Ocean at all, but above the Pacific. It was a development that had been long foreseen, and it was inevitable. But somehow, of all the facts and figures that had and have been adduced to bolster the arguments in favour of the dawning of a new Pacific age, this one seemed the most appropriate.

The jumbo jet is after all one of the most potent symbols of this century. The simple statistical confirmation that the majority of them

---

*There is but one recognized air route in the region, passing between Tahiti and the Chilean capital of Santiago, via Easter Island. Otherwise the lonely, cloudless skies of the South-Eastern Pacific see no scheduled civil aircraft at all.

were from 1984 onwards – and probably from that particular Friday, though one cannot be certain – in the skies above the Pacific Ocean was (for me and I suspect for most who came to know) the first and final affirmation that from now on this part of the world was the centre of things.

Official recognition of the change came thick and fast during the presidency of Ronald Reagan. In June 1984, a scant four weeks after the jumbo-jet statistic became known in the world's aviation lobbies, the President made a particularly memorable speech. He was in Dublin – an improbable place for a display of Pacific oratory – when he declared:

> This century has brought the Pacific nations many hardships, and many difficulties and differences remain. But what I found everywhere [on a recent tour] was energy, optimism and excitement. More and more there is a sense of common destiny and possibility for all the peoples of this great region. The vast Pacific has become smaller, but the future of those who live around it is larger than ever before.

Then again, in a later speech, the President warmed to his theme: "You cannot help but feel that the great Pacific basin – with all its nations and all its potential for growth and development – *that* is the future."

Or: "The Pacific is leading mankind into a new age of enterprise and progress. The Pacific Basin is being transformed into one of the most dynamic and productive regions in the world. The pattern of growth, stability and co-operation found in this region offers a unique and promising vision for the future."

And finally, in the same year, all trace of the tentative vanished: "The Pacific is where the future of the world lies."

After such endorsements from a man who, despite being a migrant from the Mid-West has been transformed instinctively into a prime example of *Homo pacificus*, it would have been a foolish and almost unpatriotic American who professed otherwise. And so, come the mid- and late 1980s, the rhetoric flooded forth. At Georgetown soirées and Bel Air fund-raisers, in the think-tanks and the magazine offices, in the halls of academe and (dare one say it) in the offices of publishers, the Pacific suddenly became *fashionable*. A phenomenon – *Pacific chic* – began to arrest the attentions of those on the dinner-party circuit, and it became desirable, nay essential, for the United States to think Pacific, be Pacific (though with a capital "P") and, above all, to develop a Pacific policy.

"There is a shift in the centre of gravity of US foreign policy," said a State Department seer, Mr Lawrence Eagleburger, "from the trans-Atlantic relationship toward the Pacific basin and particularly Japan."

"There is now a new reality in the world," said George Shultz, the Secretary of State, "though the world may not comprehend it. In economic development, in the growth of free institutions, and in growing global influence, the Pacific region has rapidly emerged as a leading force on the world stage . . . a sense of Pacific community is emerging."

Sometimes the rhetoric became positively and absurdly hyperbolic. Senator Gary Hart, who in 1985 was busily courting public attention for his attempt* on the American presidency, declared that "we are all members of the community of nations surrounding the Pacific. The Pacific has become the twentieth century's fountain of youth."

And further: "Economically," a governor of California declared, "the sun is now rising in the West."

The Russians were not backward in coming forward, either. In July 1986 Mikhail Gorbachev, speaking in the great Pacific port of Vladivostok – the name means "Rule the East" – made what turned out to be a seminal address displaying the Soviets' keen interest in the region. He spoke of the "renaissance in world history" that was taking place along the rim of the Pacific, and declared that his country – the greater part of which, he told his audience, lay "East of the Urals" – was about to develop a coherent attitude towards it and its people. "The situation in the Far East, in Asia and the Ocean expanses adjoining it, where we are permanent inhabitants and seafarers of long standing, is to us of national, state interest."

Mr Gorbachev's words – and the wave of shrewd and generally conciliatory diplomatic actions that followed – sent a tremor through the American diplomatic establishment. The Pacific, it had long been supposed, was America's private playground – no super-power had bothered about the Ocean before, and the assumption of American naval supremacy in its blue waters was unchallenged. There were

---

*Later brought to an abrupt halt, after revelations about his over-exuberant behaviour on board a boat – in the Atlantic.

the inevitable demands that the new Soviet "threat" be repulsed: the United States, some thought, should forget about the Europeans and concentrate its diplomatic and military skills entirely on the Pacific.

Wiser counsel suggested a more cautious approach. Mr Paul Wolfowitz, President Reagan's State Department specialist on the subject, did indeed talk of the United States "reasserting our appropriate role in the Pacific region – a very strong and involved role – and even many foreign observers give President Reagan a large share of the credit for that." But the whole process of reassertion and realignment must be performed with care. "We must pay great attention to the Pacific, as it is one of the most important regions of the world. But if we do that at the expense of other vital interests . . . we will have made a mistake."

But the underlying theme was that expressed by a Japanese, Zenko Suzuki, in 1982 – a theme that has since proved an undeniable stimulus to politicians and rhetoricians in need of a new and very positive cause. "We are today standing at a historic crossroads," Mr Suzuki told a conference in (most appositely) Hawaii, "a crossroads where the many civilizations encounter each other in this Pacific region. We are witnessing the birth of a civilization which nurtures ideas and creativity precisely because it is so rich in diversity. This is the beginning of the Pacific Age, an age which will open the doors into the 21st century."

Mr Suzuki's flourishes merely echoed and embellished words that had been uttered with signal prescience almost exactly eighty years before, by John Hay. "Western history," Theodore Roosevelt's Secretary of State declared in 1902, "began with a Mediterranean era, passed through an Atlantic era, and is now moving into a Pacific era." And Hay himself was an echo of an even earlier huzza for the region. William Seward, President Lincoln's Secretary of State, the man who had committed the legendary "folly" of buying Alaska for rather more than $7 million, made an even more provocative forecast in the mid-nineteenth century: "The Pacific Ocean, its shores, its islands," he said, "will become the great theatre of events in the world's hereafter . . . henceforth European commerce, European thought and European connections, although becoming more intimate, will nevertheless sink in importance."

Setting such contentions assertions aside, it is evident that in terms of all the human and material resources it contains, the Pacific is indeed a remarkable prize. But it is what the more energetic and motivated of these human resources – her people – have managed to do with the material resources that – to quote from just three current claims, which some might think exaggerated – has triggered an economic revolution, caught the rest of the world unprepared and given birth to a whole new era and a brand-new geography.

Many metaphors are used. On one rather bloodless level, the phenomenon of the New Pacific is the consequence of what happens when all the curves by which we define a region's resources suddenly reach their peaks simultaneously, and produce a wave of dramatic geometric harmony – the whole wave being far greater and more impressive than the sum of its component curves. In a more romantic mode, it is as though a thousand lone voices have suddenly and unexpectedly found common cause in one majestic chorus, which is now drowning out the discordant notes heard from beyond the main stage. Or again, it is as though the disorganized and random bursts of photons present in a beam of white light were suddenly all being accelerated and agitated to precisely the same frequency and directed at the same spot – to produce the awesome source of energy that we have come to know as the laser.

But whether a wave, a chorus or a laser is used as a metaphor, the common feature to be found in all comparisons is, quite simply, *power*. The Pacific, once merely big, is now endowed with very considerable power which seems likely to grow and grow, to a pitch that mathematicians will say is amenable to extrapolation, but which is actually, in terms of its effects, quite unimaginable. It will presumably then decline, and some presently unconsidered part of the world – perhaps Africa, or Arabia – will rise to prominence; but for the moment there is little doubt that the Pacific era is beginning, it will reach its full flower in perhaps two or three decades, and will then enjoy or suffer the supremacy known to other oceans and regions in the decades and centuries past. How long it endures – how long the Pacific wave will stand before it breaks, how full the chorus sings until it wavers, how long before the brilliance of the light begins to dim – cannot even be guessed.

A Library of Congress report on the region, commissioned in 1986, began thus:

27

The Asian Pacific Rim has been transformed in the past 25 years into a major world centre of commerce, industry and economic activity. The region today rivals North America and Europe in many of the key indicators of economic power. The unprecedented economic achievements of the region have forced governments and firms in North America and Europe to re-examine their policies and practices to remain internationally competitive, and have led to predictions that the countries of the Asian Pacific Rim will eclipse North America and Europe as the centre of world economic power and dynamism in the 21st century. They are growing . . . at breathtaking rates. . . .

The figures are breathtaking, too, as a random sampling will illustrate:

In 1965 the Pacific countries – leaving out the US and Canada – produced goods and services worth $183,000,000,000, sixty per cent less than that of Western Europe; by 1985 this figure had increased eight-fold, to $1,700,000,000,000 – a mere thirty per cent less than Europe.

The Pacific countries are now America's largest trading partner – they first outstripped the Europeans in 1985, when they sold goods worth $121 billions to the United States, compared to the $116 billions'-worth that came from Southampton, Marseilles, Rotterdam and Hamburg.

Thirteen of the Pacific nations – the US, Canada, Japan, Australia, New Zealand, Hong Kong, Malaysia, Singapore, Indonesia, Thailand, Brunei and the Philippines – now account for half of the world's growth.

The four "little tigers" – Hong Kong, Singapore, Taiwan and Korea – have growth rates which, at between eight and eleven per cent, are more than double those for most of the rest of the world. (Germany grew at 2 per cent during the period 1973–84; Hong Kong grew nearly five times as rapidly.)

The western American states are in on the act, too – Oregon, California and Alaska are growing at seven per cent – twice the rate of the remainder of the country. In 1950 the gross personal incomes of those living in the five Pacific states amounted to just over a quarter of those living in the 18 Atlantic states; by 1982 it had risen to very nearly half. The population had gone up too – from 30 per cent of the Atlantic states' population in 1960 to 37 per cent in 1982.

The sum of the gross national products of Japan and China

and the "little tigers" will, by the year 2000, equal that of the United States.

In 1995 Japan will own a tenth of all American assets, a figure brought about in part because of the weakness of the dollar against the yen, but also because the Japanese manage to save three times as much as do the Americans, and have that much more spare money to invest.

Los Angeles is set to take over from New York as the busiest port in the world. Hong Kong shot past Rotterdam in 1987 to become the world's busiest container port. Forty per cent of American trade with the Pacific is carried on ships that arrive in the port of San Francisco.

The figures are almost endless. And what they all display, rather too baldly though highly effectively, is the simple economic importance of the Ocean.

What they do not tell, however, is the human dimension of the Pacific story – the human reasons behind the staggering growth of the region, the ways in which this virtuoso performance actually affects the lives of the men, women and children of the Pacific, and the ways in which the Pacific people are different in outlook, aspirations, fears and needs from those who live beyond the Ocean. The figures report on what and where and when; the pages that follow will, I hope, give some answers to the how and, most important, to the why. Why, if the Pacific era is upon us, has it all happened here?

Ever since the Portuguese annexed Goa in 1510, the Europeans have had their eyes on or have in some ways dominated Asia and the Pacific; Western ideas have triumphed here as everywhere else in the world. But now, at long last, it seems as though this might be ending: the much vaunted triumph of the West may be faltering in this, its first confrontation with a region and a group of peoples who are as confident and as proud – and as rich and powerful – as the Westerners have long been.

Yet is this really so – could European dominion, and the subsequent dominion of America, really be at the beginning of a decline? And further, is it really possible – given the varieties of people, the gigantic distances and the vastly differing ideological systems to be found in the Pacific – that this part of the world could assume the mantle of leadership? Could it triumph, with its Galileos, Einsteins, Picassos, Beethovens and Aristotles – thinkers and seers of Pacific origin, who will one day come to imprint their views and creations as firmly as did their Mediterranean and Atlantic forebears?

Or is it all an illusion, a phantasm derived from mere figures, a figment of journalistic imagination, an evanescent creature of dream and the wishful thinking of those for whom history is proceeding too slowly, and who would prefer to see an era change during their lifetimes rather than to live within the dulling envelope of merely one? I hope that the succeeding chapters will go at least some way towards building flesh and sinew, face and character – even if it happens to be, as on Tafahi island, a North German face and character – on to the dry, lifeless bones of economists' figures.

THE GREAT OCEAN

On the face of the planet there lies, assembled into one immense and complicated but always inter-connected body, a quantity of some 329 million cubic miles of water – the sea. This body, because it contains fifty thousand million million tons of sodium chloride and similarly massive quantities of other dissolved salts, is undrinkable by most living creatures, but in scores of other ways is central – vital, indeed – to the existence of all life.

What might at first seem an enormous volume of fluid accounts in fact for a mere one million million millionth of the total volume of the planet. (A trifling proportion, perhaps – though students of the trivial are usually intrigued to learn that all the dissolved salts in the sea, were they to be dried out, would be enough to cover the entire land surface of the planet to a depth of 150 feet.) To better appreciate the size of the sea, one can perhaps imagine it heaped up into a cube. Each side would be 690 miles long – about the distance from London to Inverness, or Washington to Atlanta.

But of course the water is not heaped up into a cube and so it is perhaps more appropriate, though less convenient, to think of this mass of salt water in its actual context – as a veneer-thin skin which lurks in those troughs and valleys which fall below the mean circumference of the earth's planetary spheroid. If the earth is thought of as a billiard ball, then the water upon its face is like hammered gold leaf, adhering to some imperfections in the ball more tightly than to others, and in yet others not adhering at all. It is held there and is permitted (or forced) to move only very slightly to and fro – though in very complicated ways – by the influences, sometimes combined, sometimes separate, of that variety of proximate gravities exerted by the sun, the moon and the nearer planets.

Thanks to the condition of the atmosphere above it this body of water may appear, at closer quarters, either tranquil or chaotic, storm-swept or calm. Depending on its latitude and the season, it may be a deep warm blue or an ugly, tepid green – or its surface may be frozen hard and white into ice, on which creatures may walk. Depending on the geology, the tectonics and thus the topography of the earth's surface beneath it, it may be many miles deep or some few fathoms shallow. It invariably supports an unimaginably vast quantity of living creatures, from submicroscopic unicellular beings via countless varieties of fish and plants and crustaceans to the mightiest whales – and thus the mightiest living creatures – that are known to exist.

The sea is statistically a very much more impressive body than the land it surrounds. For a start it is far larger – 71 per cent of the earth's surface is sea, only 29 per cent dry land. Only in a very few latitudinal bands is there more land than sea: thanks to Europe and Asia, that stretching from 45°N to 70°N is dominated by land, as is that (because of Antarctica) between 70°S and the South Pole. Elsewhere, and particularly south of the equator, the sea rules: north of 84° there is no land at all, and between 45°S and the Antarctic Circle there is to all intents and purposes none either (just The Bluffs in New Zealand, a sliver of Patagonia and a few islands, unshakable relics of the British empire). The average depth of the sea is 12,430 feet – much deeper than the average height of the land, a mere 2,760 feet. And the sea's greatest known depth of 36,200 feet exceeds by more than a mile the height of Mount Everest.

From mankind's point of view the varying configurations of these 329 million cubic miles present a variety of conveniences and opportunities. It is a body that simultaneously defines the continents and divides them from each other; at the same time it knits together some of their distant and improbably linked civilizations, as well as their anthropologies and histories. The water can be both a barrier to our travel and a pathway for our commerce.

It displays an endless variety of moods: lonely, majestic, dangerous, fickle and serene. It is always powerful. Perhaps not always as immediately dramatic as an exploding volcano, devastating earthquake nor a hurricane-force wind – but in terms of a sustained exertion of strength, it is probably the most powerful earth-borne entity known.

34

The sea is the primal source of all living things on earth. It is an immense graveyard, thought of by some as a sacred and unspoiled resource. It is used by others – by far too many – as a dumping-ground for the unwanted, the unsung, the unspeakable. For many it is the way home; for others the way *from* home, a medium that encourages escape, change, exchange and exile. Accordingly, and because of its vast size, the sea inspires the greatest emotional responses of loving and loathing among those who occupy their business upon its surface. It can be the focus of inconsolable grief; it inspires poetry and literature, symphonies and songs.

To any visitors from another planet, it would be the most obvious and most dominant feature of this one. But only lately have we come to think of it as one body, however large and interconnected it may be. Not long ago geographers were wont to divide it into its most impressive component bodies, and to call them the Seven Seas. (These were the Arctic and Antarctic, the North and South Atlantic, the North and South Pacific, and the Indian Oceans. Other impressive bodies of water – the Mediterranean, the Caspian, the Black, the Baltic – were not included in the list.) Slowly, as geography became a more refined and philosophical diversion, so this way of subdividing the sea evolved into the simpler concept of just Five Oceans: the northerly and southerly subdivisions of the Atlantic and Pacific dropped, we were left with the uncomplicated vastnesses of the Oceans Arctic, Antarctic, Atlantic, Pacific and Indian.

Then again, at the turn of this century, a geographer named Otto Krümmell decided that both Seven and Five were too many, and that there should be only the Three. The Arctic and Antarctic Oceans, Krümmell decreed, were simply polar integrands of those oceans which had equatorial legitimacy: only these latter – the Atlantic, the Pacific and the Indian – were, in his scheme of things, true oceans.

The progressive simplification continues. Today even more reduction has taken place: now the more pedantically-minded geographers dispense with talk of any subdivisions, perhaps hesitating to diminish so mighty a feature of the globe by paring it apart and apportioning its sections hither and yon. They now call it what an extraplanetary visitor – a being unmoved by tales of historical discovery, disinterested in the results of political argument and unaffected by the predicted consequences of commercial trends – would probably call it himself. They remind themselves that it is all linked, one body of water, one mass of 329 million cubic

35

miles of brine, and with unaffected simplicity they call it the World Ocean.

For the purposes of this book, however, I plan to use Herr Krümmell's definition of 1897 from his *Handbuch der Ozeanographie*. It is worth bearing in mind, though, that his three oceans are in fact all part of one, and that their individual behaviours are all part of the overall behaviour of the planet's hydrosphere, where all winds and currents, ambient temperatures and barometric pressures – and, just possibly, all human behaviour too – are part of one hugely complicated, ever-mobile, mathematically-insufferable and only marginally predictable global machine. The workings of the Atlantic Ocean are affected by what happens in the Indian Ocean. The Indian Ocean pays close heed to what occurs in the Pacific Ocean. The Pacific is affected by everything and in turn it, too, affects everything else.

Taken alone the Pacific Ocean can be, like any other, defined in a variety of ways, depending on whether the observer is a geographer, geologist, cartographer, military strategist or fashionably up-to-date economist. Sometimes the definitions can border on the eccentric: the American admiral who commands all his country's ships, airmen, soldiers and marines in what the Pentagon regards as "the Pacific" – as in the admiral's official title CINCPAC, Commander-in-Chief, Pacific – holds sway over an ocean which has its westerly shores off Mombasa, and is arbitrarily cut off along a line running due south from the border between Mexico and Guatemala. Thus "the Pacific", as seen from the Pentagon's decidedly Atlantic eyrie in Arlington, Virginia, includes all the Indian Ocean, yet excludes that 10 per cent of the true Pacific which abuts the coast of South America (and, even more surreal, is actually administered from the office of the Commander-in-Chief, Atlantic, in Norfolk, Virginia).

The genesis of this particular definition, which we might call "the military Pacific", has more to do with American imperial history than with logic. But in recent years a more rigorously scientific approach has unwittingly given some credibility to it – at least to the Pentagon's arbitrary gift of an eastern frontier for the Ocean. It is all to do with satellites.

The geostationary communications satellites placed high above the Pacific to link the banking and trading centres of South-East Asia, Japan and Australasia with those of North America preside over a "window" of the planetary territory of geometrically fixed size – rather as if a cone, a dunce's cap, the height of which is equivalent to the altitude necessary for a satellite's geostationary orbit, had been set down over the ocean. The maximum diameter of this window, at the equator, is about 150° of longitude – so for the satellite to be able, say, to "see" Singapore on the very western periphery of what one might call "the economists' Pacific" – a definition we will consider in a moment – its window must end in the east somewhere near the longitude of Mexico City. As indeed do the windows of most Pacific communications satellites.

This is simple enough to test by observation. Any international satellite dish one might see in Vancouver or Los Angeles will point toward its "bird", low on the western horizon – the Pacific satellite. A dish in any Pacific city east of the longitude of Mexico City – Lima, say, or Quito, or Santiago – will be cranked down in the direction of an equally low point on the *eastern* horizon – for just as American naval vessels involved in exercises off the Pacific coasts of Peru, Ecuador or Chile are regarded as being part of the US *Atlantic* Fleet, so communicators, for reasons of pure geometry, think of these countries' capital cities as part of the *Atlantic* communications network.

Balboa and Magellan might have found the classification very droll, but the fact remains that for purposes of cartographic, organizational and now administrative convenience, the Pacific Ocean is simply far too big.

There are, however, more conventional definitions of the Ocean's limits.

To a geologist, for instance, the Pacific Ocean is a very sharply defined depression of the earth's surface which has been formed as a result of the complicated processes of plate tectonics. Put another way, the area which can properly be called the "tectonic Pacific" is one of relatively low altitude that is bounded by a ring of islands and mountains which have been – and are still being – formed by the geological processes that occur when one tectonic plate bumps into and grinds against another. The main and more or less stable plate that dominates the area is known, hardly surprisingly, as the Pacific Plate; surrounding it are a number of equally large, or smaller plates such as the Australian, the Nazca, the North American and the Cocos Plate.

Were one to define the Pacific in terms of its tectonics alone, then it would be a sea considerably shrunk from that to which we are accustomed. Its boundary – the boundary of the Pacific Plate – would follow the west coast of North America, but it would then turn sharply south and pass to the seaward, as it were, of both the Galapagos archipelago and Easter Island, before curving to the south of New Zealand, along the spine of South Island and emerging back into the sea near the hot mud springs of Rotorua. The Pacific boundary-line would then pass to the seaward of Tonga and Fiji, curve back westwards to New Guinea, head north and east through Guam and Iwo Jima, pass off the eastern shores of the Japanese chain, head up to Kamchatka and rejoin the North American continent off the Aleutians.

This supposed boundary of the Pacific Plate almost exactly parallels what was once called the Andesite Line: a zone surrounding the Pacific, on the outer edge of which are found rocks of an andesitic – acid – variety, and within which nearly all the rocks are of a more basic kind, using the word in its chemical sense. In excessively crude shorthand: there are light-coloured rocks that form themselves into sharp peaks and very explosive volcanoes (Mount St Helens, Krakatoa) on the outside of the Line; while there are dark-coloured rocks that give rise to rounded hills from which flow copious amounts of benign lavas (Mauna Loa) within it. When the Line was adduced, the science of plate tectonics was unknown; the mechanics are better understood today, and I shall return to them later. For now the geologists' definition is sufficient: the tectonic Pacific is a body that is only about 70 per cent of the area of the conventionally accepted Ocean, and omits the coasts of all the South American and most of the South-East-Asian countries. This is a definition which, while perhaps satisfying the intellectual appetites of a few myopic geophysicists, and considerably more satisfying than that of the Pentagon, still bears little relation to reality.

Yet neither does what we might call "the economists' Pacific". This, though, is probably the most popular modern vision of the Pacific – a vision of a place of unbridled growth, vigour and wealth, one that has helped to spawn modish concepts like the Pacific Rim, the Pacific Basin and the Pacific Community (each of which will be considered in detail later). But the "Pacific" which has led to such thinking is a very different place from that dreamed up by soldiers or geologists, and once again is some way removed from the real, warts-and-all Pacific to which later chapters will be devoted.

It is a collection of those countries which generally have two things in common: they abut on to the ocean, and they are in some positive – always positive – way economically or politically vibrant. Japan is a good example, invariably on every list, as is the other side of that particular economic equation, the United States; South Korea is always there too; Taiwan invariably; Hong Kong and Singapore usually; the Philippines on occasion. Some countries – Australia, Fiji, New Guinea, Mexico – are included in some definitions, omitted from others. And a whole host of other countries – North Korea, Chile, the Solomon Islands, Colombia – hardly ever get counted by the practitioners of the dismal science, despite their admirably Pacific qualities. So a Pacific as defined by such minds might fall within the appropriate longitudes and latitudes, but it would be riddled with holes, a discontinuous mess, a collection of unconnected pieces of sea and land established principally to prove an argument about an entity of which they make up only a fraction.

The geographers and the oceanographers, politically disinterested a *corps d'elite* as they are, offer us two uncomplicated versions of the Pacific. The first is what we might call the "technical Pacific" – that immense body of water lying to the seaward of all the island arcs and groups within the Ocean's obvious continental margins. It is in places almost congruent with the tectonic Pacific; its outline follows the Andesite Line along the western margin of the Pacific Plate, from Kamchatka to Christchurch. But on the eastern margin it keeps its own counsel: instead of heading out to sea to follow the line of the Easter Island Ridge, this Pacific Ocean boundary stretches (with only three minor hiccups) directly down the American coasts, from Attu Island in the Aleutians to Diego Ramirez Island off Cape Horn. This is thus the most nearly recognizable of all the Pacifics we have considered so far.

However, it is the next and last version which can most reasonably be regarded as the true Pacific. This uses the technically-defined Ocean as above, except that all the hiccups that interrupt the passage of its boundary have been removed by the relatively simple process of granting to it all of the so-called "marginal seas" to which logic (and political reality) suggest it can lay claim. The three hiccups on the American coast are the Gulf of Alaska, the vast and confusing mess of nameless bays and inlets and fiords between Skagway and Vancouver, and the Gulf of California. Excluded from the technical Pacific, these are now part of the real Pacific.

Would that the other coasts were so simple! To perform the same task on the other side of the world, the following eleven major seas – all on the continental side of the Andesite Line, all secure on their own tectonic Plates – need to be included (we are proceeding northwards and clockwise, from a point somewhere south of New Zealand): the Tasman, Solomon, Coral, Bismarck, Philippine, South China, East China and Yellow Seas, the Seas of Japan and of Okhotsk and the Bering Sea.

There are lesser seas which must also be included, in particular the fifteen around the islands of the East Indian archipelago: the Sulu, Celebes and Molucca Seas, the Gulf of Tomini, the Halmahera, Ceram, Banda, Arafura (which may or may not contain the Gulf of Carpentaria, depending on which atlas is used), Timor and Flores Seas, the Gulf of Boni, the Bali Sea, the Makassar Strait, the Java and Savu Seas; and there is the Gulf of Thailand, the Strait of Malacca, the Singapore Strait and the Inland Sea of Japan.

Add to this the Great Australian Bight and the Bass Strait – for if we did not, it would be difficult to regard Australia as a Pacific nation, which would indeed be a foolish error – and we have arrived at what seems the most appropriate and comprehensive definition of our goal: one oceanic bloc, twenty-four marginal Seas (of which one is designated Inland), five Gulfs, four Straits, one Canadian Confusion and one Australian Bight.

All told that is some 69,370,000 square miles (and 173,700,000 cubic miles) of sea (though the Scottish mapmakers Bartholomew omit all the waters south of Australia, as well as the Timor and the Savu Seas, and come up with a total of 67 million square miles). Whatever the precise total, it is through these waters – found north and south of the 13,235 uninterrupted miles separating Malaysia from Colombia, and east and west of the 9,600 miles lying between Big Diomede Island in the Bering Strait and the Cape Adare in Antarctica – that the axis of the world, some would have us believe, is now turning.

The Ocean thus defined is almost immeasurably vast, its size only imaginable in terms of other immensities. Its area takes up fully one third of the entire earth's surface; it makes up half of the World Ocean. Twice as large as the Atlantic and getting on for three times the size of the Indian Ocean, it is bigger than all the land surface of the earth, including Antarctica, and with Africa counted twice. It has the deepest sea known – 36,200 feet, nearly seven miles. Not unexpectedly, perhaps, it contains that spot on the world's surface that is most distant from land – where the longitude 118° 30'W intersects 47° 30'S is an equal 1,560 miles from the nearest coasts of Chile, Peter Island in Antarctica and an uninhabited British colonial possession, a member of the Pitcairn group called Ducie Island.

Moreover it is, as so vastly important a body of water perhaps should be, the original ocean of the world, the so-called Panthalassa. If one accepts (and not everyone does: there are some vocal Soviet opponents of the idea) the theory of continental drift propounded by Alfred Wegener,* then the present configuration of the planet derives from the break-up of a single super-continent which he called Pangea, which comprised two lesser continents called Gondwanaland and Laurasia, and a shallow marginal sea named the Tethys. Some then inexplicable process forced the supercontinents to break into immense component parts which became (in the case of Gondwanaland) Africa, South America, India, Antarctica and Australia and (in the case of Laurasia), North America, Europe and continental Asia.

The slow fission of Gondwanaland produced two oceans – the Indian, where Africa, India and Antarctica were hauled away from each other; and the southern portion of the Atlantic, where South America and its clearly closely-fitting neighbour Africa (which possessed an uncanny coastal match first noted by Francis Bacon) sprang apart. Laurasia's similar explosion gave rise to the North Atlantic, and the Tethys was widened to produce the Mediterranean and all the other shallow seas that decorate the central parts of Asia and southern Russia.

*Although Wegener's famous theory was published in 1915, drift was in fact alluded to rather earlier by a catastrophist with the magnificent name of Antonio Snider-Pellegrini.

But Panthalassa, as Wegener called it, had already been born. The events that he suggested (his theory fell out of favour in the Twenties, and has only been revived since the study of palaeomagnetism indicated the strong likelihood that the continents *had* drifted, and in continuous directions at regular velocities) were supposed to have started to take place 600 million years ago. The Panthalassic sea that supposedly surrounded the proto-continents is thus at least that old. Australia drifted up and into it (and is still drifting northwards, at an infinitesimal rate); but very little else. The immense, landless mass of Pacific water is more or less as it always has been.

Its size and its stability have come about largely because, unlike the other oceans, the Pacific is made essentially of one tectonic plate – one of the eight* plates that cover the surface of the earth. Plate tectonics appears to be the device, unexplained in Wegener's day, that permits the continents to drift: it is a process whereby the rigid, relatively cool plates that cover the earth's hot and partially plastic asthenosphere, forty miles down, shift slowly about, colliding and separating from the other plates by turn. The processes that occur when these plates meet is now thought to form the basis of all the planet's tectonic processes – from the formation of continents and mountain chains to the making of ocean deeps, island arcs, volcanoes and earthquakes. The structure of the Pacific – its enormous, landless centre, its contorted and congested peripheries – is due entirely to the plates of which it is constructed and the manner in which they have moved in relation to each other.

I have mentioned that the Ocean's enormity and stability derives from the dominant presence of one plate – the Pacific Plate. Probably the largest on the earth's surface, to me it bears a passing resemblance to a somewhat distorted version of a face that was popular in Eighties amusement arcades – that belonging to a creature called Pac-Man. If it is possible to conjure up such an image, then imagine the "head" facing to the left, the west.

The top of the "head" – the northern boundary of the plate – runs from the Alaskan coast near Seward, along the line of the Aleutian Islands to the Komandorskiye Islands off Kamchatka. The top of the "face" then runs along the Kuril Islands to Japan, staying always on the ocean side of these chains – down through the Marianas

---

*Or twelve, or six, or twenty-six, depending on which plate theorist has the floor.

– Saipan, Guam, Palau – to a point just east of the Spice Islands, which played so large a part in the saga of Magellan and his attempted circumnavigation.

Then Pac-Man's "mouth" begins – a jaw that turns inward, eastward, along the northern coast of New Guinea, through New Britain, the Solomons, the Torres Islands, the New Hebrides and New Caledonia. Next the upper jaw ends, the lower begins, the outline turning back south-westwards through Samoa, Tonga and the Kermadec Islands to the Bay of Plenty in New Zealand (where, in a typical display of tectonic activity, there was a major earthquake with considerable damage and injury in 1987). The lower jawbone continues through both the North and South Islands of New Zealand until it reaches the "chin", then begins a slow doubling back along an unseen series of mid-oceanic ridges that curve through the roaring forties, become the back of Pac-Man's skull and turn back up towards warmer water, surfacing briefly as Easter Island and the pinnacles of Sala y Gomez, and joining the scalp and the hairline at the Mexican coast, Baja California and the west coasts of America, Canada and, finally, Alaska once more.

This great plate – adorned with a few "hot spots", where plumes of magma have spurted to the surface randomly to form such agglomerations of islands as the Hawaiian chain, the Marquesas, the Tuamotos, the Tubuais and that tiny British possession the Pitcairn group – is almost universally deep, has a floor covered with siliceous oozes and red clays* and is dotted with millions of volcanic abyssal hills discovered by the trailing of arrays of echo-sounders. Most important, though, is the fact that the Pacific Plate is moving. It is floating, propelled by convection currents deep in the mantle, at between six and sixteen centimetres a year, towards the north-west.

This movement, which though tiny in real time is immense in the aeons of geological time, is wholly responsible for the other dramatic features of the Pacific. For there are other plates surrounding the Pacific Plate and they jostle and crash against each other, like ice floes at break-up time; and as they jostle so they ride up against each other, pushing each other deeper, cracking and bending as they do so – only on a global scale, and with extraordinary consequences.

---

*But few river deposits, since virtually none of the world's rivers force themselves through the coastal mountains to drain into the Pacific.

There are essentially two processes at work, one to be seen at the western edge of the Pacific and the other towards the east.

In the west, the Pacific Plate meets two other major plates, the Eurasian and the Indo-Australian. The collision is slow, mighty and spectacular. What is believed to happen (and plate tectonics is still only a matter of intelligent conjecture, not amenable to the kind of proof most sciences demand) is that the Pacific Plate, being composed of heavier, oceanic rocks hits the Continental Plate and is forced down beneath it – "subducted", and propelled hundreds of kilometres downwards, towards the region of the mantle where it melts and becomes the stuff of volcanoes once again. It takes a little of the Continental Plate with it, producing a rare and exotic melt of rock; and as it goes down and melts, and as its volume changes and its physical chemistry alters, so this deep-diving mess of ocean rock contorts and winces, and deep-seated earthquakes and violent eruptions occur.

The subduction takes place at an angle – the Pacific Plate is being forced down, but forced onwards too, so the line of its descent is a gentle plane inclined at perhaps 30°. The eruptions, however, occur directly above the point of strain in the asthenosphere where they happen – meaning that a line of volcanoes and volcanic islands occurs to the landward side of the colliding plates. Between the islands and the edge of the two plates is one further feature – a series of ultra-deep trenches in the sea-bed, where the Pacific Plate is being forced down to meet its original maker.

The order, then, is always the same: Pacific Plate, trench, volcanic island, earthquake zone, Continental Plate. And it is repeated time and again around the Ocean's western margin. Take, for instance, the North Pacific. As one progresses outward from the sea, there is the classic order: the Japan trench; the Japanese Islands; Fuji-san; the great Kansei earthquake zone; the Sea of Japan; the Asian continent; Siberia. Or again, further south, in the true West Pacific, the order once more: the New Guinea trench; New Guinea; the volcanoes of Manam, Kaul and Long Islands; deep-seated earthquakes; the stable continental mountain ranges of Central New Guinea; the continent of Australia.*

*Further to the south-east the subduction goes the other way, with the Indo-Australian Plate passing *beneath* the Pacific Plate: here the trenches, from the Pacific perspective, are on the outer side of the island arcs.

The line of trenches indicates precisely where the Pacific subduction zone begins, exactly where the Pacific Plate collides with its neighbours. The Aleutian trench is thus where it hits the North American Plate; the trenches of Kurlin, Japan, Bonin, Mariana (the deepest in the world, with a hole of 36,201 feet), Yap, Palau and Manus indicate its collision with the Eurasian Plate; the Mussau, Solomon, Vitiaz, Torres and New Hebrides trenches show where the Pacific Plate overrides the subducted Indo-Australian Plate; and the Tonga, Kermadec, Hikurangi, Hjort, Iselin and Balleny trenches demonstrate the effect of bumping into the same Indo-Australian Plate and passing beneath it. And on the landward side of all the trenches (except those between the Solomons and the New Hebrides, where they are on the seaward side) are the island chains – Japan to New Zealand – whose birth is in whole or in part a consequence of all that colliding and jostling beneath the blue horizons.

The reverse is happening in the eastern part of the Ocean. Here the Pacific Plate, bowed, stretched and strained by its westward movement, is moving away from its neighbour – in this case a relatively small fragment of lithosphere known as the Nazca Plate. And the very opposite processes obtain: instead of cold rock being forced down, hot rock springs up to fill the void between the two separating plates. A line of oozing volcanic vents – a sharp, steep ridge below the sea surface – runs from San Diego, via Easter Island south-westwards. Along this line new ocean floor is being generated: the material lost by being subducted into the mantle is being replaced by black coils of basalt easing their way out of cracks and fissures on the sea-bottom.

This sea-floor spreading, as the phenomenon is known, is happening at an impressive rate: near the Galapagos Islands the sea-floor is expanding at eight inches a year; down by Easter Island, by nine inches. It is a process of oceanic generation and destruction – generation in the middle, destruction at the outer edges – that is peculiar to the Pacific Ocean. (The Atlantic, though dominated by an enormous mid-ocean ridge where new sea-floor is being created at a modest rate of about an inch a year, is home to only two very small subduction zones, with volcanoes and trenches, in the Caribbean and the South Sandwich Islands, and therefore is not being destroyed at its edges as rapidly as it is being created in the middle; the Indian Ocean is similarly undramatic – a mid-ocean ridge once again, but a single subduction zone where its eastern plate collides with the

45

Eurasian Plate and produces the volcanoes that – like Krakatoa – line the southern side of the islands of Java, Sumatra and Timor.)

There is, finally, one other possible relationship that mobile plates can enjoy: those which neither collide nor diverge may simply slip past each other, rotating in relation to one another around some imagined pole. This is happening right now in the eastern Pacific – the Pacific Plate is sliding north-westwards, while the North American Plate is sliding south-eastwards, and the two strain and rub as they do so. Enormous tension can build up along the margin of the two plates and occasionally explodes into immense earthquakes which can, if they strike inhabited portions of the land surface, wreak terrible damage. One such place where the two plates are edging past each other is at the San Andreas Fault in Northern California: the consequences of a major release of tension along that line are too well-known, and too horrific, to bear repeating here. The earthquake of October 1989 reminded San Franciscans of the awesome power of the thing.

In summary, the Pacific is not simply the biggest and the deepest quarter of the world ocean. It is the most active and most geologically interesting – a test-bed, an ever-mobile demonstration of all the major forces and processes that shape the great structures of the planet. Vulcanologists and headline-writers talk about the "Ring of Fire", the "Halo of Energy" that surrounds and encloses the Pacific; there are 336 active volcanoes surrounding the Pacific, as against a mere 94 in all the Atlantic and Indian Oceans. The phrases have become metaphors, some writers suggest, for all the zest and excitement that drives the Pacific's inhabitants ever onward. And they are indeed appropriate metaphors – for this, geophysically-speaking, is where the planet's action really is, the axis of the earth's creativity, the centre of its growth.

The eponymous notion of Ferdinand Magellan's men that the Mar del Sur was a pacific sea, blessed by fine weather and pleasant breezes, was more or less correct – at least, for that region of the Ocean through which they first sailed and where their optimism was at its height. But elsewhere – particularly to the west of the Date Line, and north of the 40th parallel – the Pacific can be anything but pacific, and may be as savagely destructive as any stretch of water known.

The general weather system of the Pacific is determined by the

46

emptiness and uninterrupted smoothness of the Ocean – of the area above which, as all over the planet, air pressures build and wind patterns develop. No vast islands with walls of rock or ice stand to disrupt the progress of the wind. There are no sand deserts or snowfields or rain forests to lift or deflect the breezes, or raise or lower the temperature. So the climate conforms almost totally – to the east of the Date Line – to what is called the planetary weather system, the theoretical system of winds and pressures that would exist if the earth was a near-perfect spheroid unencumbered with continents, mountain chains and other complicating nuisances. Winds blow as they should, in the directions that physics tells us they should, at the right speed and in the proper season. The steadiness of the breezes is quite remarkable: nowhere else on earth is the weather so stable.

Nor so perfect. In the region of the trades – the south-easterlies (between the equator and Capricorn) and the north-easterlies (to the north of the equator, up to the Tropic of Cancer) – one can count on endless days and weeks of steady, 13-knot winds, a delightful lack of high humidity and temperature, and skies that are either cloudless or decorated with small white patches of flat-bottomed cumulus cloud, always poised a third of a mile above the sea. It is perfect sailing weather: a yacht can cast off from San Diego in January, coast southwards before a good southerly blow and then catch the trades which will take her almost clear across to the Philippine Islands without the need for a single sail change. There will never be more than a stray shower; the waves will never be more than three feet high, with a scattering of white horses when the breeze runs into double figures. No sailor who has ever crossed the tropical Pacific at the right season will forget the idyll of the passage.

However, the weather is very different to the west of a sinuous line that curves down from a point off the east coast of Japan and then very roughly parallels, a thousand miles out, the outline of Asia – curving in towards Borneo, out over New Guinea, down around the Solomons. The simplicity and pleasing symmetry of the trades is suddenly quite destroyed by the influence of the Asian land mass and its monsoonal – seasonal – climate. The immense summer heat of the Asian deserts, the low pressures they generate above them, the consequently varying winds – all these features dominate the weather of the western Pacific (and much more so in the northern hemisphere, where the ocean is overshadowed by two immense land

47

masses, compared with the relatively landless margins south of the equator).

So in winter the trade winds are strengthened and diverted, and are almost reversed in summer. Good south-westerly blows are dominant during the Asian summer; cold north-easterlies during the winter. The change from one monsoon to another can be sudden, and dramatic. One February evening I was in a ship, northbound through the South China Sea. It was bitterly cold, the chill wind roaring down from Siberia raising immense grey seas, through which the ship plunged head-to in clouds of spume. The crew all looked liverish and unhappy. But by next morning the gales had dropped – though it was still very cold – and the sea was glassy, doldrum-like. Then by lunchtime a line of waxy, yellow-white clouds was spotted abaft by the starboard lookout, and before long a breath of hot and humid air was wafting over a ship which, in a matter of moments – since its metal was still so cold – was dripping with condensation. By nightfall the air was tropical, the humidity was unbearable and every fan was on, every *punkah* louvre open and every air conditioner roaring away. In no more than twenty hours and with 400 sea-miles beneath our keel, the miserable Asian winter had given way to the equally miserable Asian summer, and all newcomers on the ship knew full well what the monsoon was all about.

But however unpleasant monsoonal conditions can on occasion be, they are as nothing compared with the fearsome storms that hurl themselves on the Pacific with terrible regularity. The Atlantic and the Indian Ocean receive their due share of tropical cyclonic storms too, but in the Pacific, because of its vastness, they are visitations of destruction and tragedy like nowhere else in the world.

The storms have different names, depending on where they are generated and where they hit. In the north-east Pacific, they are known as *hurricanes*; in the south-west, as *cyclones*. In a long stretch of vulnerable Asian land between Vietnam and Japan they are *typhoons* – the Chinese words for "big wind"; in the Philippines, which suffer each summer from the most dreadful storms, they are *baguios*; on the west coasts of Mexico and Central America, *cordonazos*; and in north-western Australia, *willy-willies*. Officially, in the neutral world of the meteorologists, they are known as tropical revolving storms –

the most energetic and destructive of all the planet's natural surface phenomena.*

The storms seem to be formed in the strangely disturbed band of atmosphere that lies athwart the equator between the two trade wind regions, and is known as the intertropical convergence zone. How and why they form is still not known; all that can be said with certainty is that winds begin to twirl anti-clockwise around a fixed point of steadily diminishing atmospheric pressure, and this circulating system then begins to move, invariably in a westerly direction, its internal pressure steadily falling and the gales inside it picking up speed as it does so.

By the time the storm is fully formed it may be as much as 400 miles wide, moving at perhaps 20 miles an hour, and with winds near its core raging at well over 100 miles an hour. If this beast then hits land, there can be destruction on a titanic scale – floods, ruined houses, uprooted trees, broken bridges, the ruin of crops and the death of livestock, and loss of human life. In the less well-developed countries, where warnings of impending storms are poor and precautions minimal, whole tracts of countryside can be inundated, entire villages swept away, vast communities decimated. India suffers terribly; the Philippines too; and the low-lying parts of eastern China.

In Hong Kong, where there is a well-oiled storm warning machine piloted by the staff of the ancient Royal Observatory, the entire community becomes rather gaily caught up in the summertime ritual of typhoon watch.

Idle – or perhaps not so idle – mention may be made on the radio news of a distant tropical depression known to be forming somewhere close to an exotic and encouragingly far away island – Yap, maybe, or Truk, or the northern Marianas. The colony pricks up its ears.

The circulating system wanders a little closer, deepens, is classified under a new title – a moderate tropical storm – and is given a name, Agnes perhaps, or Bob, an innocent, unassuming, rather cosy, old-fashioned sort of name that makes no connection in anybody's mind with a swirling mass of warm air and piled clouds that is bearing down on the coast, thunder and lightning flickering from its belly,

---

*Earthquakes can be much more terrible, but are regarded as sub-surface phenomena, despite their principal effects being very much on the surface.

49

the waves beneath it being whipped up into a fury. Across in Hong Kong the marine department raises a single beacon on a flagpole on Green Island, the No. 1 signal: all Hong Kong is now formally aware that a typhoon may be forming within 500 miles.

Next day Agnes (if that is what the storm is called) keeps to a westerly track, hurrying a little more, deepening a little more. Now it has been upgraded still further to a severe tropical storm: winds at the centre, measured by radar and by American air force planes despatched from the big bases in Japan and the Philippines, are gusting to eighty miles an hour. Shipping is advised to keep well clear, and masters begin to make the complicated storm-avoidance manoeuvres well known to those familiar with these waters in this summer season. In Hong Kong the No. 3 warning is hoisted: a little coloured blip appears at the bottom left of the colony's television screens, a constant reminder that a typhoon alert may soon be declared and the emergency drills so well practised in the territory brought into force.

And already the thin strands of cloud, the outer rings of the immense, whirling storm, begin to drift over the southern islands – Po Toi, Sung Kong, Waglan Island, the Ninepins – and the wind and the waves begin to bustle about in the harbours. The junks start to roll heavily in the swell. Fishermen on the distant banks beat for home. The old sampan-ladies begin to tie up their wares, wrapping everything in layers of black plastic and hessian sacking. The typhoon shelters at Aberdeen and Mong Kok start to fill with craft, their prudent masters and owners looking uneasily at the eastern sky as it blackens and darkens, and as the wind begins to sing in the telephone wires, the unsecured edges of roofs begin to flap and creak, and the streets are busy with flying litter, and dust.

And then, shortly before noon next day the Observatory announces that Typhoon Agnes will strike Hong Kong, head on, imminently. The No. 8 signal is raised and the colony goes into its well-known emergency rituals. Schools empty. Shops shut down. All businesses, factories, financial markets, the airports – everything – are declared closed. The entire colony scurries home. The Star Ferry keeps on going, its little green ships bucking across the harbour in the growing swell until the last stragglers from Kowloon have made it to Hong Kong, and those bound north from the island have reached their goal. And then, for ten, twenty, forty hours or so the millions sit back to watch the show as the huge tropical storm lashes and bursts and howls its way around the islands, shaking, shuddering and drenching the place as if it held all the concentrated fury of nature and had decided to unleash it upon this one unfortunate spot.

To go out in a Hong Kong typhoon is to experience an almost pleasurable madness. The banshee-like wail of the wind is majestic. It is almost impossible to stand up, and you haul yourself from building to building, from stanchion to stanchion as if on board a ship rounding the Horn in a nor'wester. The air is dangerously alive with the objects – pieces of tin, small stones, branches, tiles – being hurled along by the wind. The horizontal rain stings like grazing bullets. You only venture outside once.

Most people who have been seasoned by these violent irruptions stay indoors, where they hold typhoon parties, or watch the progress of the storm on the television. On every channel earnest-looking men with maps and pointers, looking like war-gamers in some fiendish Pentagon basement, demonstrate – predict, even – the inch-by-inch path that the storm is taking, noting that it usually passes off to the north, but may perhaps curve back upon itself and go in for a second strike.

But then, with a final burst of rain and a final howl of the gale, it is all over – the only cyclonic visitation of the year, perhaps. The storm signals are reduced in urgency, from No. 8 to 3, to 1, and then the last is taken away. The dead and injured – and often there are casualties, particularly in the poorer areas, or the more remote parts of the New Territories countryside – are taken away; the power lines and landslips are repaired; the beached ships are tugged off the reefs; the cost is counted; and the colonials take to watching, with a curious mixture of pride and nostalgia, as the storm – "our Agnes" they'll call it – wanders away, does some more smashing and battering in Taiwan or the Yangtze valley before petering out, quite spent, and becomes just another statistic for the record books.

The truly mighty storms are remembered for years, though the frequency of destructive typhoons is depressingly high in some corners of the Pacific – the Philippines, for instance, and Japan. In 1979 alone, for instance, devastating storms named Cecil, Irving, Mac, Sarah and Vera struck the Philippines: three in Luzon, one in Leyte, one off Samar. In one storm, 46 inches of rain fell in 24 hours. And unlike Hong Kong, the Philippines is ill prepared* for

*Or if prepared, at least ill-able to cope.

floods, high winds and landslips, and there is invariably much loss of life, generally ignored by the rest of the uninterested world.

There is one final and decidedly non-pacific phenomenon that occurs only in this ocean – the tsunami. This tidal wave is a product of the combined efforts of the jostling of the crustal plates and the behaviour of the deep Ocean through which the resulting shock waves are transmitted: a small nudge in southern Chile can set up a wave that streaks across the entire Pacific in a matter of hours, with unimaginably enormous force. In deep water the travelling wave may be only a few feet high: but on those rare occasions when such waves reach shallow water, or coastlines, they can rear up and explode with fearful consequences. The infamous Chilean case, in May 1960, began with an earthquake deep in the subduction zone between the Nazca and the South American Plates: scores of people died near the town of Puerto Montt. But it was the resulting tsunami that did the greater damage: it lumbered away to the north-west, speeding up and gathering energy as it did so. It hit Hawaii fifteen hours later, wrecking boats and beaches, ruining the Waikiki tourist trade; and twenty-four hours after being triggered in southern Chile, it hit Japan, 10,000 miles north. When it hit it was travelling at more than 400 miles an hour: no one expected it, and hundreds of Japanese living along the coasts of Hokkaido and Honshu were drowned. Warning stations were then established all over the Ocean, and a big "tsunami early warning system" was set up in Hawaii, an island chain through which all major long-haul waves, it is reckoned, were bound to pass.

The almost ceaseless trade winds of the central Pacific propel the Ocean's surface waters westward on both sides of the equator, forming the basis of the two enormous – but essentially very simple – circulatory systems of currents that dominate the Ocean. The two equatorial currents, interleaved by the equatorial counter-current, take waters from the American coast across to New Guinea and Mindanao: then one heads north, taking warm water to the Japanese coast as the Kuro Shio. This warm water collides, at around 36°N, with the southbound cold Oya Shio – part of the small, anti-clockwise current system in the Bering Sea – causing huge and navigationally hazardous fog banks to form, four days out of ten.

The main north Pacific current system continues in a clockwise direction – the mixed, cooling waters of the Bering Sea and the Kuro current turning east and then, when they reach the coast in the region of Seattle, turning south to form the cold California current, source of all the San Francisco fogs and a challenge for the more courageous of Oregon sea-swimmers.

Much the same takes place, though in mirror-image, in the south Pacific. The southern equatorial current is diverted south, past the Solomon Islands, and goes on to bathe the Great Barrier Reef – and, indeed, much of the Australian coastline down past Sydney – in the tropical water of the east Australian current. It then turns east, joining the endless eastern drift of the southern Ocean current, before heading back up north once again along the coast of Chile and Peru, as the Peru current.

Although there is no South Pacific equivalent of the foggy collision of the Kuro Shio and the Oya Shio, there is one crucially important peculiarity about the currents off the South American coast which has a bearing on the economic livelihood of tens of thousands of people.

It is associated with a phenomenon known, somewhat inelegantly, as *upwelling*. Upwelling occurs when offshore winds – like, in this case, the south-easterly trades – persistently drive water away from the land, and the sea replaces that water by allowing cold bottom water to *well up* from below. The effect off the coast of Ecuador is twofold: first, the waters off the Ecuadorian coast (a few degrees north and south of the equator) are unusually cold – indeed, so powerful is the upwelling that a belt of this oddly cold water extends west from Ecuador for nearly 3,000 miles.

The second, and economically important, consequence is that the "new" water from the ocean bottom is dense with phosphate, nitrates and many other nutrients liked by planktonic life – with the result that this belt of water is stiff with plankton. The food chain being what it is, these same waters are alive with fish, and the skies and islands are dense with birds. Fishermen scurry all over the seas catching anchovies; quarrymen have long made a living scraping guano from the bird-rich islands. All told, the upwelling of the cold waters of the south-eastern Pacific has long been a source of considerable economic importance.

But occasionally, and for reasons not quite understood, the upwelling suddenly stops. The trade winds weaken, the waters off the Ecuadorian coast are not pushed relentlessly out to sea, there is no consequent need for any replenishment. In addition the lack of upwelling allows a tongue of the equatorial counter-current (which normally passes into and flails pointlessly about in the Gulf of Panama) to head further south, into the region of the northbound Peru current. In the years when this inexplicable phenomenon occurs – and it usually happens around Christmas, and so is known by the local fishermen as El Niño – the plankton suddenly vanish, the fish die and the birds fly away or are left to starve and rot.

The fishermen come back with their holds empty; the islands have neither birds nor guano; it is said that the strength of the smell of the gases from the millions of tons of decaying fish is such that it can blacken the hull of a passing ship – a phenomenon known as the Callao Painter. The gallows humour disguises the very real misery that El Niño causes; not only are there no fish to harvest, but the arrival of the rogue current, reaching down all those unfamiliar and unwelcome degrees of latitude, invariably causes heavy rains, soil erosion, landslips and added misery to the towns along the Peruvian and Ecuadorian coast.

During the last ninety years El Niño, one of the Pacific Ocean's more enigmatic problems, has occurred nine times – in 1891, 1925, 1941, 1953, 1958, 1965, 1973, 1976 and 1983. The mechanisms of the upper atmosphere and the deep sea that cause it to spoil so many Latin Christmas times are still unknown; but there is beguiling evidence that whenever El Niño appears in the Pacific, so the monsoon rains in India are perilously sparse, the winters in the continental USA are unusually harsh, and there is a further episode of drought in that wretched quarter of Africa known as the Sahel.

Further study is necessarily being completed; but the evidence of linkage between the simultaneous appearance of climatic phenomena in Kansas, Chad, Bihar and in the south-eastern Pacific Ocean suggests what all geographers have known for many years – that the globe works as one complete system, one vast interactive machine, and that the divisions man has forced upon it are no more than crudely artificial devices for our own intellectual convenience.

The resources presently known to exist on or beneath the land surface of the Pacific are stupendous in their extent and importance. There are few diamonds to be found, nor is there much cocoa; and considering the amount of space the Pacific commands it might seem a little odd (unless one remembers the geology) that only a fifth of the world's proven oil reserves are there. (Most of those lie off the minute sheikdom of Brunei and are the personal property of the Sultan, who is in consequence the world's richest man. Brunei is also the world's wealthiest country, with a GNP per inhabitant of $21,000, half as much again as that of the United States.) But just about everything else exists, and in spades.

There is more than half the world's coal – much of it in Manchuria; half the world's uranium – much of it in Australia; half the world's natural gas; nine-tenths of the silk, 67 per cent of the cotton, 63 per cent of the wool; huge iron mines, great deposits of silver and, it has lately been found, a girdle of epithermal gold lodged in the volcanic rocks from the Solomon Islands to northern Japan. Lihir Island, off the west coast of New Ireland (itself sitting off the north coast of Papua New Guinea) is said to have the world's largest gold deposit – though as it sits inside a volcano the deeper the miners dig, the hotter they get.

In terms of similarly world-beating deposits, there is nickel in New Caledonia (the mining establishment once ruled the island in the name of France); aluminium at Weipa on the Cape York peninsula of Queensland; iron in the Hamersley Range of Western Australia; lead, zinc and silver at Broken Hill; uranium near Darwin and in the tiny Queensland town called Mary Kathleen; copper and lead at Mount Isa, whose smokestack is the tallest structure in northern Australia. Malaysia has the world's biggest tin deposits, while the South Jianxi and Guangdong provinces of China are rumoured to have the most tungsten. The Ok Tedi mine in Papua New Guinea seeks to reduce to ground zero a massive mountain of copper capped with a summit of gold. There is yet more tungsten in the Yukon, vast deposits of copper and molybdenum in Arizona, still more copper and molybdenum in both northern and central Chile. And dotted in mines and quarries from New Zealand clockwise around to Easter Island, the ocean is littered with cobalt, zirconium, titanium, antimony and almost everything else under the sun.

And with almost every mineral, so also every kind of food and crop. There is rice in abundance, of course: China, Japan, Indonesia, Thailand, Burma, Vietnam and Korea produce (and then consume) most of the world's annual crop of 400 million tons of the grain of *Oryza sativa*. (Of the centres of the world's rice culture, only India and Bangladesh lie outside the region we have defined as the Pacific.) Most of the world's beef, mutton, pork, fish, eggs, wheat, wool, cotton, sugar, groundnuts, palm oil, soyabeans, bananas, tea, oranges and pineapples come from Pacific countries: only wine, potatoes, apples, cocoa and milk come predominantly from countries beyond the Pacific pale.

However, the distribution of all this food is patchy. There is still real malnutrition to be found in islands of the Philippine archipelago. I have seen children with the classic symptoms of kwashiorkor – distended bellies and rheumy eyes – sitting aimlessly in dingy hospitals outside silent sugar mills on Negros Island, and wondered how such tropic abundance could possibly spawn such misfortune. Nutritionists and cartographers still draw the so-called "hunger line" through Asia and the Americas; the poorer people who live in those countries that are sandwiched between Mexico and Chile, and between North Korea and New Guinea, exist on diets of fewer than 2,250 calories a day, and thus go to bed each night hungry.

And herein, of course, lies one of the ruder ironies of the Pacific: that among all this economic vibrancy and dynamism there are still the familiar evils we currently associate only with Africa, or with countries that are at war: illiteracy, hunger, a vertiginous growth of population, disease, overcrowding, slums. Beside the glitter of all the Pacific wealth there are still pockets – becoming ever smaller, the governments and their statisticians insist – where the unhappiness and squalor of the inhabitants remain an insult, a disfiguring blot on the Ocean's otherwise gleaming escutcheon.

As their national borders are currently defined, and as this book has decided to define the Pacific, thirty-three countries lie around the margins of the Ocean. Twenty-three more lie within it. They can be grouped, more or less efficiently, according to the usual geographical rules. The peripheral Pacific, for instance, can be divided into six.

Australia and New Zealand, originally settled by white Europeans and still following a generally Protestant tradition, are usually regarded together – though it is worth noting that if their native aborigines and Maoris still dominated their populations, both countries would be regarded as South-East Asian, joined ethnically and culturally across the Arafura Sea. But in fact the Sea does divide this new Antipodean culture from the ancient traditions of South-East Asia, and so renders the countries separate and distinct from their neighbours.

The South-East Asian Pacific nations comprise, among others, the world's largest Islamic country, Indonesia; the only Asian Christian country, the Philippines; the world's richest country, Brunei; what is probably the world's poorest country, Kampuchea; the busiest port-city, Singapore; as well as Thailand, Malaysia, Laos, Vietnam and Papua New Guinea.

The Gulf of Tonkin and the Vietnamese frontier is the arbitrary point at which South-East gives way to North-East Asia – the industrial powerhouse of the Pacific, the region that most economists and businessmen mean when they idly refer these days to "Asia". In terms of its population, China dominates, of course; but there is also the old Portuguese colony of Macau; the thoroughly modern British colony – though soon to be "retroceded" – of Hong Kong; the Republic of China on Formosa, now known as Taiwan; Japan; the two implacably hostile Koreas, North and South; and the Soviet Union. The range of ideologies, climates, ethnic varieties, economic standing and futures apparent in this spread, between the islands of Hainan and Sakhalin, invariably defies imagination.

And then the Date Line is passed, and we are into a segment of the Pacific best known for its unrivalled prosperity and good fortune: here is the United States, sharing with Japan the suzerain's role; and, sandwiched between its two continental divisions, the Dominion of Canada.

Next, pushing further south, we enter what seems to be a perpetually troubled and impoverished region, between Tijuana and the Darién Gap – Mexico, distinguished in global terms these days solely by being the site of the planet's largest city* – and a succession of Isthmian countries. We tend to think of most Central American countries as somehow linked by the Caribbean Sea to the Caribbean islands and cultures; but all the republics have Pacific coastlines – and so Guatemala, El Salvador, Honduras (with a scant 45 miles of Pacific shoreline along the Gulf of Fonseca), Nicaragua, Costa Rica and of course Panama can rightly (if pedantically) be thought of as Pacific nations.

Finally, the sixth Pacific segment contains those countries that, until lately, have been utterly excluded from consideration – those of South America. Colombia, it is true, still seems to regard herself as an Atlantic nation – her trade goes principally through the Caribbean port of Cartagena rather than through the dire and crime-ridden

---

*Unless there is some drastic and improbable happenstance there will be 35 million people living – and living very poorly – in Ciudad Mexico, DF, by the end of the century.

wharves of the Pacific port of Buenaventura; but Ecuador (which has island possessions in the Ocean) and Peru seem to be becoming further and further entwined in Pacific matters; and Chile – ah, Chile! She, the "bootlace" of Latin America, has the longest coastline of any country on the Pacific – 3,317 miles, longer by far than the entire Pacific coastline of Australia, which is a mere 2,450 miles from Cape York to Tasmania. Although she is very much a latecomer, Chile is now furiously building her Pacific interests and ambitions. The links she is forming – trade with China and Korea, New Zealand and Australia – are deliberately aimed at ensuring that Chile in particular, and South America in general, is becoming very much a legitimate partner in the Pacific of the future, no matter that the local cultures and traditions, combined with the sheer distance from the Pacific's economic heartland, have always hitherto militated against the continent's inclusion.

Within this great encircling babel of tongues and cultures, aspirations and rivalries, lie the Pacific islands, regarded from afar as idyllic and palm-fringed and all more or less the same. But they are not at all the same, being invariably grouped into three – Polynesia, Melanesia and Micronesia – on the basis of complicated formulae relating to the race of the islanders, their languages and their geography. But in contrast to the sturdy independence of the encircling nations, many of the island-groups within have still to shake off the mastery of foreign powers, and remain in subjugation.

European colonizers have left their marks all over the central Pacific – in the name of protecting sea-lanes, submarine cable routes, or the native peoples themselves. These marks have proved almost indelible. For although the tide of imperialism has ebbed considerably in most of the remainder of the world, some of the Pacific islands are still too small and their governments too feeble to stand alone as independent states. The consequence – and most would regard it as regrettable – is that old empires, or their sub-imperial nominees, look after them even now. Not one of the three island groups escapes.

In Polynesia, the largest of the groups – an immense, tilted isosceles triangle of islands with its apex in New Zealand and its other angles in Hawaii and Easter Island respectively – only Western Samoa, Tuvalu and Tonga are now nominally independent. France has huge possessions – the Tahiti group, the Marquesas, the Tubuais and the Tuamotus, as well as those of Wallis and Futuna well to the west. The New Zealand goverment looks after the Cook Islands, Niue and Tokelau; the Americans have Samoa, and the British look after the four islands of the Pitcairn group, selling stamps for the islanders to help them keep up their revenues.

The Melanesian group, stretching in a broken line to the east of the immense and mountainous island of Papua New Guinea, includes the Solomons, Vanuatu and Fiji, each an independent, free-standing state; but the Australians look after Norfolk Island, and there are French possessions too, in New Caledonia and the Loyalty Islands, with gendarmes, soldiers from Lyons and Marseilles, and offices of that wondrously-named bureaucracy, the DOM-TOM, which concerns itself with the *Départements Outres-Mer et Territoires Outres-Mer*.

And finally the Micronesians, up in the north-west of the ocean – here Kiribati* and Nauru are independent, Guam is a self-governing American territory, and the others – Yap, Ponape, Truk, Kosrae, the Marshall Islands and Palau – are part of the old post-war US Trust Territory, now doing their best to keep afloat. It would be idle to pretend that any of the Pacific islands have the kind of economic importance possessed by, say, Korea, or Malaysia, but in addition to potentially immense political importance and no small amount of charm, they have a symbolic significance – for they are what the world still thinks of when confronted with the single word, *Pacific*.

The countries of the Pacific are now inhabited by half the world's people – 2,400 million of them. The figure is slightly spurious, though. Some countries – New Zealand, say, and Japan – are obviously wholly Pacific; but Australia, the United States and Canada are shared by the two oceans that lap their eastern and western shores; and Russia, at least in the years prior to the Gorbachev speech at Vladivostok, was a country whose traditions and ethnic roots were quite obviously Atlantic and Baltic. To count the Soviet Union's

---

*Pronounced Kiribas, that being the closest thing the islanders could manage to their old colonial name, the Gilbert Islands, after Captain Gilbert of HMS *Charlotte*, who landed there in 1788. His colleague on HMS *Scarborough*, Captain Marshall, went on to land on islands now administered by the USA.

275 millions as "Pacific" people is stretching the point a little, and it might be more appropriate to count only those living east of the Urals. Similarly it might be proper to consider as "Pacific" only those Americans who live west of De Soto, Missouri (the median point of the population, moving slowly ever-westward as the people do the same), or, in Australia, those east of Alice Springs. But the complication of such an operation would be considerable; and it is reasonable to say that the entire population of the Pacific nations, even if they inhabit the Atlantic seaboard, can make use of the goods that are carried across the Pacific Ocean. So, while noting that single caveat, the figure of 2,400 million can be allowed to stand. Half the world's people, like one third of her surface area, is by this reckoning Pacific.

These Pacific peoples speak 1,200 of the world's languages. Most of them, in number if not necessarily in influence, speak Mandarin Chinese. A sizeable proportion – the Americans, Canadians, Australians, New Zealanders – have as their first language the most supranational of all tongues, English. (And an even more sizeable fraction – nearly all Filipinos, for instance – have English as a back-up.) Those living between Tijuana and Puerto Williams speak Spanish. Some languages are peculiar to one region, yet intimately related to others beyond – like the 500 or so Austronesian tongues which not only link speakers in Vietnam and Cambodia with those in Fiji, Malaysia, the Philippines, Sulawesi and Borneo, but also reach out to the inland mountains of Taiwan, the North Island of New Zealand, and to the speakers of Dobu in the d'Entrecasteaux islands and of Trukese on Truk. There are important languages only spoken in their countries of origin – Japanese, for instance, and Korean; some Pacific languages unrelated to each other or to any other linguistic group on earth: Ainu, for example, which is not spoken outside Hokkaido Island in Japan and has no relationship at all to Japanese; and Gilyak, which is used only by a very few people on Sakhalin Island – a place known only as being the birthplace of the actor Yul Brynner,* and near where the Korean airliner KE 007 was shot down in 1983.

Superimposed upon this immense bewilderment is an equally confused gallimaufry of religions. The Marind of New Guinea believe

---

*The son of a mining engineer from Mongolia and a gypsy from Romania, for many years he kept his Sakhalin name, Taidje Khan.

that fire has its origins in sex, and so indulge in a rite whereby a girl has to be raped in order to keep that fire alight. Some Melanesians worship the memory of President Lyndon Johnson.* Trobriand islanders use the tug-of-war, cricket, the collection of yams and great and freely expressed sexual enthusiasm as the planks of their complicated beliefs. Anyone in Hong Kong with a problem – be it so trivial as to know which horse to place a bet on, or so crucial as to know whom to marry – can ask the god Won Tai Sin, whose temple is to be found in the middle of a vast housing estate in north Kowloon, and who came to fame by turning boulders into sheep. Queensland aborigines believe they can sing a man to death, and indeed recently managed to sing the state's premier – a white man, a New Zealand migrant who cared little for "black fellows" – out of office. Every Easter, a number of brave Filipino men allow themselves to be crucified – with real nails driven through their palms – in an attestation of their faith.

Basically, though, the line of 150°W longitude divides the Pacific into the religious groups that really matter, in terms of the Ocean's success. To the east of that line the dominant religions belong to the Christian-Hebraic schools; to its west the societies have their roots in Confucian-Buddhist beliefs. To the east are Roman Catholicism and Protestantism, Mormonism and Judaism, Jimmy Swaggart,† Billy Graham and Oral Roberts. To the west are Mahayana Buddhism, Shinto, Taoism and, in a strangely aberrant appearance, the Islam of Indonesia (and even more odd, Hinduism on the island of Bali). Above all – though only formally practised by large numbers of zealots in South Korea – is Confucianism, a philosophical system now 2,500 years old, but which underpins the entire belief system of almost everyone who (whether under communist rule or not) lives between the Yalu River and Cape York.

And, as the Canadian writer Eric Downton put it in 1986, "societies with Confucian-Buddhist roots are proving more effective in coping with the industrial and technological challenges on the eve of the twenty-first century than [are those countries with a] predominantly Christian-Hebraic heritage."

---

* The President made an unscheduled stop while on the way to South-East Asia. Local people, awed by the sight of Air Force One and the posses of Secret Service guards, assumed the plane's passenger to be a god.

†Who, as mentioned in the Prologue, is nonetheless very popular on the island of Tonga, the King being an unabashed fan.

Confucianism, in other words, is central to the coming triumph of the region: we shall examine it in more detail later, and perhaps will come to recognize its new strength, its new status on the world's political and economic stage. For the teachings of the Sage, suddenly, have established themselves as an almost indestructible Oriental adhesive, helping to bind so many of the region's member-societies together.

The Pacific, as is surely now evident, is an Ocean which, while long trying to assume some kind of unity, is plagued by a grossly inconvenient diversity. It is after all, an entity which gives house room to people as different as Chilean gaucho and Japanese silk farmer, Californian software writer and Australian brewer, Tongan noble and Panamanian politician; it encompasses men and ideas more disparate and discordant than any to be found within the borders of any other physical entity on the planet.

But now – listeners insist – some distant harmonies are being heard. Some trans-Pacific resonances are being detected, some symmetries noticed; there is some recognition of a sense of common purpose and design. A few Atlanticists, as one might term the doubters, decline to recognize or admit that such things exist. But to those for whom such patterns are becoming real, and for whom some rational explanation of the shift is required, then it can fairly be argued that the spreading ethic of Confucianism – exported in the last hundred years or so to every nation on and within the Pacific coastline by the tens of millions of overseas Chinese who have acted as its accidental evangelists – is crucial. It can be argued that it has played a significant – one might even say the most significant – role in producing all those patterns and distant harmonies that are being recognized as signalling the onset of the Pacific Age.

APPROACHES

I

From a Peak in Darién

Towards the eastern end of the Republic of Panama, a few hundred
yards away from a tiny Darién settlement known as Santa Fé, is
a small somewhat dilapidated hut, roofed against the rains with
sheets of rusting corrugated iron. It is currently home to a family
of Choco Indians, their head a middle-aged farmer known by the
local people as William. Not Guillermo, as might be expected in a
Spanish-speaking community, but William, *pur et simple*.

William's life – like that of nearly everyone else in Santa Fé
– appears to be both blameless and obscure, and is occupied
principally with the farming of bananas and taro plants on the
shallow hillsides that slope down to a sluggish tributary of the
Rio Sabanas. He has lived in his rickety hut for most of his fifty
years. His parents lived there once – and generations before them
– on this patch of land, if not in this particular accommodation.
But now the earlier generations have all passed on, and today
William's home is crowded with his wife, several small children,
an assortment of chickens and a gaggle of small, excitable black
pigs. In short, it is very much the kind of hut in very much the
kind of village with which Darién is amply overstocked. Neither
the village, nor the house, nor William is at all remarkable in any
obvious way.

Except that in one rather less than obvious way, William is very
special indeed. There was one aspect of his life which had made
him so – of which I had heard talk long before on some obscure
wanderers' grapevine. Via the half-reliable morsels of intelligence
that pass from continent to continent along this jungle-drummed,
smoke-signalled messageway, it appeared that William the Choco

of Santa Fé in Darién was possessed of an unusual link with a great historical moment.

He had insisted, so the story went, that he knew – and his knowledge was said to be based on information handed down from Choco ancestors long dead but unforgotten – what no one else in Panama knew (or apparently wanted to), and no one in the world of historical scholarship knew either. This small shard of antiquarian knowledge which he claimed was the precise location of the hill, the peak in Darién, from which Vasco Núñez de Balboa was reputed to have first glimpsed the Pacific Ocean on the morning of Tuesday, 27 September 1513. William, it was rumoured, could lead a man to the very spot where the Pacific Ocean was first seen by the first European explorer – a place in space and time that changed the historical progress of the world.

The story might or might not have been apocryphal. William may or may not have been a rogue and charlatan; there are said to be many such in Panama, which as a crossroads for the modern world radiates a special magnetism for crews of ne'er-do-wells. But I had been sufficiently intrigued by the stories I had heard of William to want to find out. Accordingly, one winter's day when I was at a suitable jumping-off place in America, I decided to see if I could find him. I had the somewhat faint hope that he might lead me to the place and permit me to stand where Balboa had stood – on the very peak which John Keats, with the kind of monumental mistakenness permitted under the principle of poetic licence – declared was occupied by:

> . . . stout Cortez, when with eagle eyes
> He stared at the Pacific – and all his men
> Looked at each other with wild surmise –
> Silent, upon a peak in Darién.

I went to Miami and booked myself aboard a late-night Pan American jumbo jet to Panama City, arriving shortly before dawn in the pullulating and insufferably hot shanty-capital sprawling beside that most famous of all entrances to the world's greatest of seas. When Panama City awakened, and after I had taken a small breakfast of pineapple, *café con leche* and a hard roll or two, I rented a small white Japanese car, acquired a map from the official cartographers who conduct their business under the curious name of the Instituto

Geografico Nacional Tommy Guardia, and set out to look for Santa
Fé, for William – and for the Pacific.

I was thus occupied by precisely the same ambition which had
driven Vasco Núñez four and a half centuries before. Like him, I
knew that this great and peaceful ocean was out there somewhere.
I just wanted to lay my eyes upon it. I too wanted to stand, silent
or otherwise, upon that peak in Darién.

It was in December 1511 that the King of Spain had given Balboa
the job of Captain-General of the fledgling colony of Darién. The
post was offered as somewhat grudging recognition* that he had
been a signal success as leader of the first European colony in South
America, a village called Santa Maria de la Antigua, on the Atlantic
coast of the Isthmus. His success led to some intimacy with the
Indians, who told him that a vast sea lay off to the west – a sea,
and a land, infinitely rich in gold.

Peter Martyr d'Anghiera, the Italian court historian (though to
the Spanish court) who was the inventor of the phrase "the New
World", the man who first announced the existence of a substance
called India-rubber, and the principal contemporary chronicler of
Columbus and all those others who explored and travelled to the
"Orbe Novo" in the fifteenth century, wrote an extraordinary account
of how Balboa first heard the definite news. It seems that during
a period of good relations between the Spaniards and the native
Indians, the cacique of one local tribe had become blood-brother
to Balboa, and had actually persuaded the Spaniard to help him
prosecute a local war. (Quite conceivably the *conquistadores*, like most
colonial conquerors, believed in policies of divide-and-rule, of which
this small conflict was but one example.) Whatever, once the battles
were over and the cacique's tribe had won, the man made Balboa a
gift – a quantity of gold ornaments so gaudy and so valuable that
squabbling broke out among the Spaniards as to who should have
which piece, how much the minor colonial leaders should get, how
much Balboa himself should receive.

Suddenly the cacique's son, who had watched the scene in dismayed silence, lost his temper. Richard Eden, who translated Peter

---

*Grudging because some courtiers had laid charges against Balboa, and King
Ferdinand was half-disposed to believe them.

Martyr's works, quotes the young Indian as shouting to the Spaniards:

"What is the matter, you Christian men, that you so greatly esteeme so little portion of golde more than your own quietnesse . . . If your hunger of gold bee so insatiable that onely for the desire you have thereto, you disquiet so many nations, . . . I will shew you a region flowing with golde, where you may satisfy your ravening appetites. When you are passing over these mountains (poynting with his finger towarde the south mountaines) . . . you shall see another sea, where they sayle with ships as bigge as yours, using both sayles and ores as you doe, although they men be naked as wee are . . ."

Balboa – as avaricious, arrogant and adventurous as any of his brother *conquistadores* – decided in an instant that he must go and see for himself. He sent news home to Spain, demanding reinforcements of 1,000 men – the number the cacique had warned him would be required to defeat such forces of hostile Indians along the way. Official Spain was immediately excited. A force was raised, an expedition was organized – but Balboa, it was ordered, should not be its commander; that task should go to a bitter rival, Pedro Arias Dávila. The Pedrarias expedition, as it is generally called today, left Spain with 2,000 men in April 1514.

But Balboa had beaten them to it; he had decided not to wait. Seven months before, while Castile was – in his intemperate view – still dithering, he had set sail from Santa Maria for the coastal town of Acla, at what Indians told him was the narrowest and least topographically inconvenient part of the Panamanian isthmus. With Leoncico snapping genially at his heels, with a force of 190 Spaniards and with several hundred more local guides and porters embarked on a fleet of nine canoes and a small ship named the *Chapinera*, Balboa set out for Acla on the morning of Thursday, 1 September 1513. He was bound, as his biographer puts it, "for Careta, the Pacific, and immortality".

Only 92 men at arms and 2 priests began the route-march, for Balboa was a prudent organizer, keenly interested in security, and he insisted that the others from Santa Maria remained at the base camp, denying them their expected encounter with immortality. Enlarged by an escort of servants and porters and the sixteenth-century versions of groupies and hookers, the marchers made an impressive column half a mile long. Day by day, under the hot September sun, it wound its way steadily south-westwards, stopping for a few hours here, for half a week there, while Balboa attempted – in most cases, successfully – to make and consolidate friendships with the leaders of the tribes on whose lands he trod.

The men crossed the low hills of the Serrania del Darién, then proceeded to cut their way through the jungles in the valley of that great central Panamanian river variously called (depending on whose map you buy) the Chucanaque and the Abanumaque. On the far side they came to the Sierra de Quareca, hills which, though not particularly high, did give the party – many of them clad in heavy metal cuirasses and leg-armour – some relief from the steamy, insect-ridden heat of the lowlands. But here Balboa's persuasive charm did him no good: a Chief Torecha, leader of a tribe of mountain Caribs, set about defending his lands, and there was a brief and bloody battle which the Spaniards (hardly surprisingly) won.

Yet they were anything but magnanimous in their triumph – at least not once they discovered, to their corporate Castilian horror, that some of the patricians of the region were "soiled by the infamous vice", the "abominable sin", of homosexuality. Nothing so riled a sixteenth-century *conquistadore* as the knowledge that some men indulged in sodomy, and Balboa felt no compunction in setting the dreadful war-dogs on the culprits and having them torn to pieces in full public view.

It was a grisly episode indeed, one which inevitably detracted from history's judgement of the epochal events that were to follow. One can perhaps understand why John Keats, writing his first mature work of poetry, managed to confuse Balboa with Cortez; a young and sensitive man, Keats may well have balked at including a figure capable of such wanton cruelty in a sonnet devoted to such tender sentiments.

Balboa left Quareca the next day, 25 September. There now follows – among yesterday's narrators and today's historians – one of those minor disputes of chronology from which whole doctoral theses are constructed and careers built, or destroyed. We need not bother with the details, save to say that it is quite certain that all the contemporary accounts of Balboa's triumph – which mention that he first saw the Pacific at 10 am on Tuesday, 25 September – are wrong. 25 September 1513 was a Sunday.

It is also a near-certainty that the discovery was not made on a

Sunday. To these ardent Catholics, *domingo* was a day with peculiar significance. One can be perfectly sure that had such a momentous event happened on the Lord's Day, that fact alone would have been reported over and over again, the comfortable synchronicity of it all being a matter for boundless pleasure. That the particular day of the sighting was never regarded as special, and is almost brushed aside, suggests that it *was* a Tuesday – and the nearest Tuesday to the reported date is the 27th. Choosing this date also allows Balboa and his company a little breathing space: they can spend two full days marching from the unpleasantness in Quareca to the summits of the coastal range – rather more reasonable a period than the few hours that elapse if we believe the earlier date.

This, then, is the historical moment: 10 am, Tuesday, 27 September 1513. As for the historical place – technically, says Balboa's biographer, the peak was not in Darién, nor was it actually a peak. Cartographic logic suggests it was in fact an isolated hill that stands above the headwaters of the Rio Congo – an unspectacular 1,800-ft-high hillock, somewhat denuded of trees, a short distance away from a rudimentary track (made by wild pigs, or cattle, or perhaps by people long ago) which can still be discerned in the jungle.

Antonio de Herrera's *History*, published in Madrid eighty-eight years later, records the moment thus. Balboa:

> . . . commanded his armie to halt, and himselfe went alone to the toppe where, having sighted the Mar del Sur, he knelt down and raising his hands to Heaven, pouring forth mighty praises to God for His great grace in having made him the first man to discover and sight it. Having made this pious demonstration, he signalled to all his people to come up, and they in their turn fell on their knees, rendering thanks to God for this great favour, while the Indians stood amazed at the rejoicing and the ecstasy of the Castilians . . .

Two days later, on 29 September, the Feast of St Michael and All Angels, Balboa and his men arrived on the shores of the great sea, to take possession of it for God and for Castile.* The ceremony was supposed to start at 2 pm on the 29th: the Gulf on whose beach the men found themselves had been named San Miguel because of

*It took only a single day for one Alonso Martin who, cheekily, found his way to the oceanside and paddled out in a dugout, demanding that his colleagues witness that he, and not the Captain-General, was the first in the new ocean.

the happy coincidence of the feast day. But it very nearly had to be postponed. No oceanographer, when Balboa first strolled down to the gently lapping waters on the morning of that day, he had no reason to suppose that the ceremony – which would involve him standing ankle-deep in the water, the better to annex it – could not begin on schedule.

But he knew nothing of the Pacific's tides. The tidal range in the Caribbean sea off the north coast of Panama is very modest – no more than a couple of feet. The tidal variation of the Pacific on the south side, however, is most impressive – a good 18 feet under normal circumstances, more than 20 feet at springs. And when the Captain-General and his men turned up in the afternoon – all in polished armour, and bearing a gaudy new flag adorned with the arms of Castile and Leon and a Madonna and Child – they were dismayed? embarrassed? horrified? amused? (history does not record) to find no sea in sight; just hundreds of yards of black and rank-smelling mud. No claim to the new ocean could be made by standing in a nearby bog – Balboa knew his law. And so the group waited, and waited, until not long before dusk the sea raged in "with great impetus", and the process of annexation could begin.

To judge from the surviving accounts of the *escribano* detailed for the occasion, it was a ceremony that today would have been ideal grist for the television networks.

There stood Balboa, his shield on his arm, his cuirass gleaming on his chest, the brilliant new banner in one hand and his naked sword in the other, his plumed helmet giving him a stature far more considerable than offered by his height alone. He waded into the sea until the waters lapped against his knees while Leoncico splashed happily along behind him – perhaps reflecting how far he and his master had come since both were smuggled in a flour barrel on a boat to Darién.

The great man paced back and forth, uttering as he did so a formula of annexation appropriate to the moment:

"Long live the High and Mighty Sovereigns, Don Fernando and Doña Juana, Kings of Castile and of Leon and of Aragon, et cetera, in whose names and for the royal crown of Castile I take and assume royal possession corporal and present of these austral seas and lands and coasts and islands with everything annexed to them or which might pertain to them in whatever manner or by whatever reason or title might or could exist, ancient or modern, in times past, present or to come, without gainsay whatsoever.

"And should any other prince or captain, Christian or infidel, of whatever law or sect or condition he may be, pretend to any right to these lands and seas, I am ready and prepared to deny him and to defend them in the names of the Kings of Castile present and future, whose is this empire and the dominion of these Indies, islands and mainland, northern and southern, with their seas, in the arctic pole as in the antarctic, on both sides of the equinoctial line, within and without the Tropics of Cancer and Capricorn – so that each thing and part of it belong and appertain most completely to Their Highnesses and to their successors, as I declare more at length by writ setting forth all that may be said or can be said and alleged in behalf of their royal patrimony, now and for all time so long as the world shall last until the final universal judgement of all mortals."

Few annexations come more comprehensive than that. It is largely thanks to this one moment of history that there currently exists an unbroken line of Spanish-speaking nations through 90° of latitude from Tijuana in northern Mexico to Punta Arenas in southern Chile. One can reasonably say that Balboa's triumph ultimately gave us San Diego and Los Angeles, Santa Barbara and Yerba Buena, San Ysidro and San Onofre, San Clemente and San Francisco. At this distance, we may find Balboa's antics in the surf laughably pretentious; but at the time the sighting of the *Mar del Sur*, as he felt compelled to christen the new sea, was a formidable discovery indeed: the implications of its swift and secure passage into the hands of Spain were profound in the extreme. The fact that Balboa caused the Ocean to become a Spanish lake, in effect, would come to be recognized as one of the most important stratagems in the development of the modern world.

There is a tragic postscript to the tale of Vasco Núñez – a man judged by today's historians to have been "as kindly, loyal and competent a *conquistadore* as ever brought the cross and the banner of Castile overseas. . . ." By the time the news of his triumph had been transmitted home to the Court, the Pedrarias expedition was on its way. It was a considerable party: 2,000 men in twenty ships, and headed by an intemperate ruffian whose only qualification for replacing Balboa as Governor of Darién was that his wife was the daughter of one of Isabella's ladies-in-waiting.

The contrast between the two men was as profound as their

rivalry was to become. Balboa was constructive in his approach to the Isthmus, generally compassionate to the Indians, inventive in his plans for exploration and the furthering of Imperial aims. (He achieved a great feat of maritime engineering by building ships on the Atlantic shore, transporting them bodily over the hills he had explored and sailing them off into the Pacific.)

Dávila, however, was a bully, a cruel and insecure man whose constant attacks on the Indians succeeded in turning them from "sheep", as Balboa called them, into "fierce lyons". Eventually the contest between the new Governor and the man he had replaced became violent: Balboa and four of his colleagues, summoned from their Pacific base to discuss "matters of common concern" with Pedrarias, were instead arrested. They were accused of rebellion, murder, treason and – ironically, in view of the circumstances – the mistreatment of the Indians. There was a show trial, the five were beheaded in public and their heads placed on poles. "And in a building that stood ten or twelve paces from the place where they were beheaded, one after the other like sheep", wrote a Spanish historian, "was Pedrarias, watching them between the canes which formed the walls of his house. . . ."

A statue to Balboa stands near the Pacific exit of the Panama Canal, in the town named in his honour. He is standing as he must have stood that afternoon on the shore of the Gulf of San Miguel, four-square and haughty, bucklered, helmeted, spurred, and looking out over the greatest ocean in the world.

I took a rather simpler route than Balboa – the Pan-American highway out of Panama City. This is a road of great promise, as one might expect of a highway that is paved almost all the way from Barrow in Alaska to Ushuaia in Argentina, and is – at 16,000 miles – the longest continuous route in the world. A formal concept since 1923, millions of American dollars have been spent on it and it has been virtually complete for years.

Complete, that is, except for one irritating – and one might have thought, locally embarrassing – gap, in Panama. The Darién Gap. No road has ever been built clear across Darién; nor, one imagines, will one ever be built. Balboa might find it amusing: nearly five centuries later, the land he crossed in the sixteenth century on foot has still not been completely bridged for those crossing it by car.

I found this less amusing when, on the outskirts of a grimy little town called Chepo, the highway quite simply fell apart under my wheels. One second I had been speeding at fifty miles an hour along a ribbon of uninterrupted concrete; the next, to the wide-eyed amusement of a group of policemen standing beside a checkpoint, there was a loud crunch, every shock absorber on the Nissan thudded home to its end-stops and I found myself dead in the water by a pothole large enough to accommodate half Balboa's army. The dust began to clear after half a minute. A donkey grazed morosely beside me. The policemen guffawed. The air was full of mosquitoes. It was very hot and sticky and, as the dust cleared still further, so the hills ahead shimmered in a pale blue haze.

It took an hour to free the Nissan from what I assumed to be its grave, and persuade its bent and battered metal to press on southwards. The road worsened as I edged gingerly down along the country's sunken spine, vanishing at times in coils of thick black mud. Elsewhere tractors had scoured deep gullies separated by huge ridges that threatened to strand the little car with its wheels thrashing uselessly in space. The bridges were awesome in their fragility and ill-repair: loose plates of iron rattled and slipped away to reveal brief visions of dark and menacing deeps, filled no doubt with crocodiles, man-eating fish and swimming snakes. In several places the road simply ceased to exist at all – there were cliffs, a hole 50 feet wide and 10 feet deep. A muddy cut through the jungle showed where the last car had passed around it. A rusting hulk at the bottom of the pit showed where the last car hadn't.

Five hours later, after I had passed beneath a crudely-lettered blue notice board that welcomed travellers to the unpeopled jungle vastness of Darién, I came to a wooden sign that said simply "Sante Fé". I turned off to the right. The car protested as it settled into muddy pools, heaved itself out, scraped through fields of boulders and crossed innumerable rickety bamboo bridges. Finally I passed rows of sombre-looking huts, blackened by cooking smoke and infested by scores of small children and large dogs. There was a small shop, stocked with boxes of soap powder, dried and blackish-red carcasses of goats, tins of condensed milk and posters of Madonna. Outside a low, white cement building with a radio aerial stood a tall negro with distinctly West African features, wearing the neatly pressed uniform of an inspector in the *Carabiñeros Nacional*. He waved me to a halt, and then proceeded to ask why on earth I, a *gringo*, had driven all this way, to what was evidently one of the least visited and least remarkable villages in all Panama.

My Spanish, at least when I attempted to speak it, was execrable. So I wrote my request on a sheet of paper. The brief dialogue I later found preserved along with the car rental papers:

"*Es posible, con los miniculares, a vuer el Mar Pacifico sur los montañas?*" I gestured to the low hills rising to the west of his police station.

"*Si,*" the policeman wrote. I was encouraged.

"*Donde Señor Balboa – el primero conquistadore – quando el vuer el Mar Pacifico?*"

The policeman smiled broadly, then wrote quickly: "*El Hindio William conose el te puede llebar. Pero le reconose algo al cabo y ami. . . .*"

So . . . the Indian named William did exist and, moreover, he lived close by. The policeman, who was even now shutting up his office, was evidently going to guide me there. Fifteen minutes later, having banged and bumped our way up another track heading directly for the low hills, the two of us came to the small tin-roofed hut which I had imagined and there, standing before it, was the single link required to bring Balboa's journey and mine into their final conjunction. William, busily digging some unrecognizable vegetable out of the mud, was wearing gumboots and the jaunty remnants of a straw hat. (Not, however, a *Panama* hat, since those are only worn in Ecuador.) When the policeman told him what was wanted he removed his hat, wiped his brow and looked at the sky – it was mid-afternoon, and there would be only three hours of light remaining. Then he gestured towards the rise ahead, and to a path snaking into the undergrowth. "*Dos horas,*" he said, and without a backward glance, began walking up the hill.

Panama City, like most Central and South American capitals, is littered with statues of, temples to and mausoleums occupied by the famous, the not-so-famous and the forgotten. In nearly all the Spanish-speaking world it is almost axiomatic that any half-significant event, any battle, revolution or skirmish is memorialized in an extravagant confection of marble and gilt, with crosses, acanthus leaves, Castilian doggerel and an invocation of the deity. One might reasonably have expected, therefore, that the one historical *event* for which Panama is known (and there is a clear distinction to be drawn here between an event

75

and an *accomplishment*, for obviously the Canal is Panama's best-known triumph and has become its own memorial) should be remembered in an impressive construction, no matter how far from anywhere or how difficult of access the site may be.

But Balboa's hill – if that really is the hill to which William takes his occasional visitors – is quite unmarked. It is exactly as the explorer's biographer predicted it would be: 1,800 feet high, half-covered with jungle, a little way off the trans-Isthmian Indian tracks and somewhat detached from the rest of the Sierra – an outlier, distinct and somewhat aloof. It is in Darién, however – at least so far as Panama's administrators are concerned. And from its summit it is entirely possible to see a stretch of water which – whether to a sixteenth-century viewer innocent of the details of geography, or to a well-versed wanderer five centuries later – could only be an ocean.

It seemed remarkably near: a flat blue sheet, crawling as in Hong Kong with the skeins of hidden currents, stippled and rippled by breezes, and turning brassy gold where it met the horizon on to which the sun was now setting fast. One or two small boats inched ahead of tiny trails of white water. To the left – the south – were the indentations of a swampy, evil-looking coast, where the shores of Panama curved and recurved to form the immense and nearly landlocked Gulf of San Miguel. But to the right the level sea stretched far away – an ocean on which a westbound mariner sticking to this latitude need not (once he had cleared the complicated coastline of Panama itself) strike any land whatsoever until he met the Philippine Islands of Mindanao, Palawan and the skerries of the Sulu Sea, 13,000 miles away.

No other ocean is as wide. The distance from Panama to Palawan is more than half the way around the world. And this was the ocean that Vasco Núñez de Balboa had found – an immensity quite unimaginable but a void which, he must have known, was now no longer unbridgeable.

It would be agreeable to report that on at last sighting the ocean I, like Vasco Núñez, promptly prayed a lot, rejoiced even more, cut down a fine tree and erected a cross, then had the expedition secretary carefully write down the names of all my companions for posterity. But in fact it was rapidly beginning to get dark. The negro policeman was quite keen that I should stay the night in Santa Fé.

William was more eager that he should show me some papers he had recently received by post from America. And I was keen to return to Panama City to catch my plane. So we hurried back down the hill, and to William's little house.

The papers to which he had referred, and which he kept in a tin box underneath his bed, contained an unexpected coda to this small adventure – an unfortunate little postscript which reminded me how Captain Scott must have felt when he reached the South Pole only to find that Amundsen had beaten him to it.

For I was not the first to have stood in Balboa's footprints.* The papers that William held related how, just two months before me, a man named William Dobelle (describing himself as being "on the artificial organs faculty at the University of Utah" and the director of a "medical device company in New York and Zurich") claimed to have visited Balboa's hill. He reported that he had come in by helicopter, and had claimed the hill as Balboa's on the advice of William, and in a formal note to the Explorers' Club of New York, of which he was a member.

Dr Dobelle had found the whole experience so extraordinary that he had issued a press release (no less) recounting the adventure, and had sent copies to William from his office in Farmington, New York. Such were the papers which the Choco kept under his bed: written on a Macintosh, sent from Manhattan, claiming a triumph with which William seemed notably unimpressed.

The modern world from which I had briefly stepped aside seemed to come crowding in again. Once I had said my thanks and farewells to William and to the immense policeman who had silently accompanied us throughout the afternoon, I headed away down the rutted tracks, rather glad to be back on the road and off back to Panama City. Like Captain Scott, I was in a hurry to get home.

It was not an easy journey. I had two punctures and was forced to abandon the Nissan. I had a long and wary walk through the pitch-dark jungles – my wariness stemming from having sighted a large tarantula strolling down the road for its evening constitutional. After what seemed an interminable period of tiptoeing down the road

---

*I knew I was not the first to *try*: King Leopold of the Belgians had organized an expedition in 1954, but he found nothing of note.

I managed to hitch-hike a lift on the roof of a logging truck. I then waited until midnight in a tiny village where the local people plied me with beer and chickens until I could barely move. Finally, ten hours after I had started I arrived at Tocumen airfield, back in one of the least pleasant cities in the Western hemisphere.

But a mile or so away from Panama City, linked to it by a discreet network of roads and side-streets that become suddenly cleaner, neater, less tropic, less obviously corrupted, is a city that bears the great *conquistadore*'s family name. The city of Balboa looks for all the world like a suburban Texas town – it has green lawns of tough-leaved grass, cyclone fences, large split-level houses, young housewives in sunglasses and hair-curlers driving Camaros on their way to the Safeway, American flags – and American troops. For Balboa stands at the Pacific terminus of the Panama Canal – one of the most remarkable examples of man's enduring engineering skills, one of the legacies of Balboa's discovery and march. Before I left for San Francisco I spent a few days wandering the considerable length and the decidedly inconsiderable breadth* of the Canal, newest of the major approaches to Balboa's ocean.

A ship's master passing through the Panama Canal need have no concerns about having to navigate his way successfully into the Pacific. He doesn't have to steer at all; he doesn't look at his compass; he need not even run his engines: his vessel is quite literally pulled out of one ocean and into the other by a sextet of electrically-powered (and Japanese-made) trains called "mules" which run on American cast-iron rails beside the lock-gates of the Canal: all the captain has to do is stand on the bridge and watch, listen to the genial Yankee twang of his assigned American pilot and experience a transport of delight.

*The narrowest parts of the Canal are the locks – Gatun, Pedro Miguel and Miraflores – where the concrete walls are only 110 feet apart. The length, too, is limited to 1,000 feet. Such restrictions, which presented no inconvenience to the dainty little ships of 1914, mean that only specially small vessels can now make the 51-mile transit. Enormous container vessels, such as the round-the-world monsters operated by Evergreen Shipping, unload their cargoes at Balboa and transport them by rail to the Atlantic port of Colon, where an identical vessel loads them for the remainder of the voyage. Since 1986 a joint US, Japanese and Panamanian consortium has been examining how to improve the present Canal, or how best to augment it, since the isthmus of Panama is the sole barrier to economic freedom of trade between the Atlantic and the Western Pacific Oceans.

For a passage through Panama is very much a delight. While it must be admitted that the republic in which it is set down has its less attractive aspects,* the Canal itself is a thing of unexpected spectacle and beauty. Its sheer size is impressive, of course, and a first-time transit from Atlantic to Pacific will be something of a revelation – the ship does not head due westward to get to Balboa's ocean, but south-east. Further: a quirk of the Coriolis Force means that the journey is slightly uphill, with the Pacific Ocean about six inches higher than the Atlantic.

But the beauty of George Washington Goethals' eighty-year-old construction becomes apparent within moments of arrival. Lake Gatun, into which the ships pass on a due southerly track after leaving the Caribbean and easing through the first set of locks, is an immense inland lake – though an artificial one created by the damming of the Chagres River. The Tiger Islands, the Brujas Islands and the Trinidad Islands are the summits of drowned hills, covered with tropical jungle and noisy with a hundred kinds of colourful birds. (There are spiders too: an engineer, inspecting the Lake as it was filling, reported seeing a half-drowned tree covered with what appeared to be black foliage: he paddled alongside, then shot away as fast as his blades could carry him. The "leaves" were tens of thousands of tarantulas, clinging to the branches to delay their inevitable death.)

The route turns south-easterly after Gatun, through the deep chasm of the Gaillard Cut – eight miles of near-straight canal where the labours and tribulations of all Goethals' thousands of men become dramatically evident. Here, truly, one can see writ large the truth of the Canal Commission's simple motto – "the Land divided, the World united" – or applaud the brief laureateship of the poet Stafford who wrote, to celebrate the Canal's opening day in 1914:

> In freedom let the great ships go
> On freedom's errand, sea to sea –
> The oceans rise, the hills bend low,
> Servants of Liberty.

The Cut – 500 feet wide from shore to shore, 45 feet deep,

---

* With President Manuel Noriega, shortly afterwards removed by an American invasion force, one of the most egregious examples.

illuminated at night by a blaze of red and white lights – is of a size to dwarf the vessels passing through it. From down on deck, the cliffs rise up to the sky, quite blotting out the sun; from 400 feet up at the viewing platform on Contractors Hill the passing tramps, container vessels and car carriers look like toys. Far below, on the winter's day when I stood and watched, the *Aleksandr Ulyanov* – a 30,000-ton general freighter – was grinding slowly northbound, back to the Atlantic, back to Mother Russia; a comfortable-looking, rust-stained Greek liner called the *Corfu Reefer* had passed heading south.

The *Mar Mediterraneo* was waiting in the Pedro Miguel locks. The *Hyundai No. 205*, carrying cars from Pusan to Savannah, was coming through the Miraflores. And there seemed an almost endless queue of freighters, tankers and oreships waiting in the roads at each end, some at anchor, some jostling politely for the lock entrances. Thirty ships make the nine-hour transit through Panama each day: 11,000 a year, carrying more than 130 million tons of cargo to and from every country on earth. Warships, pleasure boats, container ships – Britain's royal yacht *Britannia* was due some days later – all saving themselves 8,000 miles and three weeks of sailing round the Horn. None seemed to begrudge handing over the thousands of dollars in tolls payable in cash by each ship to the Canal Commission, which brought in more than £150 million in 1988. And few aboard, whether captain or crew, seemed anything less than awestruck during the entire nine hours that a transit usually takes.

I watched the crew of a grubby Polish reefer vessel: they were taking pictures of each other against the background of the Gatun Locks; three hours later, they were gazing with rapt attention at the passing majesty of Culebra; their cameras were out again for the Pedro Miguel, for the distant flags of the American bases, for the Miraflores Locks, and for the immense red-white-and-blue *bandera* of the Panama Republic that waved lazily from the summit of Mount Ancon, over the old wooden houses of Panama City. And as the ship freed herself from the mule-lines and her screw began to churn up a wake of umber, sludgy water, and she picked up speed towards the marker buoys and the farewell beacon on Flamenco Island, I was sure I could see the seamen still, pointing their cameras back – now with long lenses all – towards the statue of Balboa which stands on the Panama City seafront, with the great man gazing out at the Ocean into which the Poles were now, at long last, sailing.

2

The Strait That Shall Forever Bear His Name

Once Balboa had found the Ocean, so in their droves the explorers emerged to circle, probe and colonize it, but first – in that most daring of all endeavours – to cross it.

No one could be sure how wide it was. No one could be sure where lay the *Terra Australis Incognita* which Ptolemy had postulated, and which Mercator had argued was a necessary balance for a spherical world, without which the whole planet might simply topple over to be lost among the stars. No one knew the weather, the currents or the winds. There was only one certainty, one small piece of reasoned and deduced fact which spurred the would-be circumnavigators onwards. This certainty was that the Spice Islands, the Moluccas, lay at the farthest side of the *Mar del Sur*, or of whatever might lie beyond the waters that Balboa saw.

The position of the Spice Islands was more or less well known. Traders buying nutmegs and cloves from Arabian merchants had been aware of their existence for centuries; Marco Polo knew roughly where they were, for he saw junk traffic in the ports of Cathay* loaded down with spices and manned by suntanned crews who had clearly come there from the south.

Then, in 1511, a Portuguese expedition led by Antonio d'Abreu discovered them. His party of three ships had travelled from Lisbon

---

*Cathay, although now taken to be coterminous with modern China, in fact referred only to North China: the Russian word for China is still Kitai, from which the Mongol word for Cathay is itself derived. South China was always known as Mangi – so the airline Cathay Pacific, which is based in the south Chinese territory of Hong Kong, should by rights be called Mangi Pacific. Marketing strategists apparently rejected linguistic accuracy in favour of popular acceptance.

out to Malacca with Albuquerque, thence down the Strait and past the immense island of Borneo to the confused archipelago where all spices known to man grew in wild profusion. To reach their goal d'Abreu's men had gone halfway round the world from Europe to the Orient, and always in directions with an easterly component.

This single geographical fact, though dictated by circumstance, was of great political and imperial importance. For since the Treaty of Tordesillas, signed in 1494, all the unknown world to the east of an imaginary line drawn 370 leagues west of the Cape Verde Islands would belong to Portugal; everything to the west of that line would belong to Spain. So far as the Atlantic and the Indian Oceans were concerned, there was no problem; but what about the other side of the world? Where, the scholars and the diplomats debated, was the antimeridian of the Tordesillas line? No decision had been taken in those first decades of the sixteenth century. Conquest, squatters' rights, annexation, *force majeure* – these cruder tools of geopolitics might well dictate its eventual position. Thus the Moluccas discovered by going eastabout would, by the logic of some explorers, belong to Portugal. The Moluccas claimed by a party going westwards might belong to Spain. So while d'Abreu and his colleagues went off eastwards, even braver or more foolhardy men – following the banner of Castile – were determined to discover – heroically and, as it turned out for many of them, fatally – the way to reach this same Orient by travelling outwards to the West, across the vast unknown. It meant the acquisition of knowledge, to be sure; but it also meant the envelopment and direction of the Orient by Spanish *adelantados*, for the greater glory and expansion of the vast empire of Spain.

There is thus a nice irony in the fact that the man who undertook the seminal voyage, and did so in the name of Spain, was in fact Portuguese. He was born Fernão de Magalhães, and the Portuguese – "he is ours", they insist – rarely care to acknowledge that he renounced his citizenship after a row, pledged his allegiance to King Charles I – later to become the Emperor Charles V – and was given a new name: Hernando de Magallanes. The English-speaking world, which reveres him quite as much as does Iberia, knows him as Ferdinand Magellan.

There is a statue to Ferdinand Magellan in the main square of Punta Arenas, at the southernmost tip of Chile. He sits by a globe with his back to the police station, looking south towards the Cabo de Hornos Hotel, towards the low hills of Tierra del Fuego and the unseen coast of the distant Antarctic. Another monument to him is in the main square of the city of Cebu in the central Philippines, a canopy with the kind of gaudy murals one expects in this flamboyant tropic city. The paintings illustrate the notable moments of his forty years of life, including that most singular to the Filipinos, the bringing of Christianity to their islands. Nearby, on a small, marshy, mosquito-ridden island called Mactan – the site of Cebu airport, and some of the region's hundreds of guitar factories – there is a simple memorial (looked after by a caretaker with the improbably contradictory name of Jesus Baring) of which more later. Doubtless there are other statues to Magellan – near Sabrosa in Portugal's Trás-os-Montes, where he was born; in Sanlucar de Barrameda, from where he set sail. But the life that will be always remembered stems from a journey which will never be forgotten – that commemorated by the space of sea between the statues in Chile and Cebu, a distance of some 12,000 miles. Edward Gaylord Bourne, in his masterly series *Spain in America*, written at the beginning of this century, offers a view with which few would take issue:

> The first navigation of the Straits of Magellan was a far more difficult problem of seamanship than crossing the Atlantic . . . . Columbus's voyage was over in thirty-five days; but Magellan's had been gone a year and weathered a subAntarctic winter before the real task began – the voyage over a trackless waste of waters exactly three times as long as the first crossing of the Atlantic . . . *Magellan is to be ranked as the first navigator of ancient or modern times, and his voyage is the greatest single human achievement on the sea.*

Yet when he set off on 20 September 1519, with a royal mandate to search for a passage through to the *Mar del Sur*, and thus to determine for certain that the Spice Islands were within the Spanish domains, he had not the foggiest notion how far he might have to travel. Not only was there great perplexity about the existence of a Strait – for all the men in their five little ships knew, Balboa's Panama and the Columbia that Columbus had sighted in 1499 might be the equatorial portions of a continent that extended without a break to the Antarctic pole, and the Southern Sea would be quite unreachable from the west. And even if a break were to be found, the five *naos* and the 277 men would have to sail – how far? Schoener's globe of the world then known shows Japan a few hundred miles off Mexico; the historian López de Gómara says that in his negotiations with the

Emperor Magellan always insisted that the Moluccas were "no great distance from Panama, and the Gulf of San Miguel which Vasco Núñez de Balboa discovered". He would rapidly discover precisely what "no great distance" meant.

The five vessels that would soon make history – the *Vittoria* (now generally known as the *Victoria*), the *Trinidada* (the *Trinidad*), the *San Antonio*, the *Concepción* and the *Santiago* – were small* and, until Magellan set to work on them, hopelessly unseaworthy. ("I would not care to sail to the Canaries in such crates," wrote the Portuguese consul in Seville, with obvious pleasure. "Their ribs are soft as butter.") They set sail from the Guadalquivir River under the proud corporate title of the *Armada de Molucca*, amply armed but hopelessly provisioned, with crews composed of men of nine different nationalities† and of innumerable and in many cases mutually antagonistic temperaments. There was one Moluccan slave, Enrique, who would act as an interpreter if the crossing was accomplished. There was a journalist, too – or maybe Antonio Francesca Pigafetta was a Venetian spy, since he came from Venice, was an acquaintance of the Doge and could well have been told to keep a wary eye on Spanish imperial ambitions in the East. Be that as it may, Pigafetta's diaries of the journey remain the classic source for all future accounts of the voyage: he had joined the ships, he said, because he was "desirous of sailing with the expedition so that he might see the wonders of the world".

The sorry tales of sodomy and mutiny, of yard-arm justice and abrupt changes of command, and all the other trials that attended the Armada on its path south and west across the Atlantic, do not belong here. The truly important phase of the journey was to begin on Candlemas Day, 2 February 1520, when the vessels left their anchorage in the River Plate, near today's Montevideo, and headed south. No charts or sailing directions then existed for the coast beyond Cabo Santa Maria: no one had ventured this way before. From this moment on the sailors were passing through virgin territory, with unknown coasts, increasingly terrifying seas and temperatures that went steadily downwards day by day.

They began to see penguins – "ducks without wings", they called

---

*The *San Antonio* was the largest, at 120 tons; the *Victoria* was 85 tons, and the little *Santiago* a caravel of only 73 tons.
†Including a lone Englishman, one Master Andrew, from Bristol.

them, *patos sin alas* – and "sea-wolves", or seals. They explored every indentation in the coast off which they sailed – and with depressing regularity each indentation, even though some of them were very large and tempted the navigators to believe that they might be the longed-for straits, proved to be a *cul-de-sac*.

They spent much of the winter, from Palm Sunday until late August, in the centre of a chilly and miserable bay at what is now Puerto San Julián – a winter made doubly wretched by an appalling mutiny and the consequent executions and maroonings that Magellan ordered; by the stranding and wrecking of the *Santiago*, which the Captain-General had sent on a sounding expedition; and by the realization of the dreadful damage done to the remaining ships by the constant chomping and feasting of those plank-gourmets of the seas, the teredo worms. But one important discovery was made at Puerto San Julián: these southern plains were inhabited by enormous nomadic shepherds (though they herded not sheep but the little wild llamas known as guanacos, and they dressed in their skins). Magellan captured a number of these immense people – one pair by the cruel trick of showing them leg-irons and insisting that the proper way to carry them was to allow them to be locked around their ankles. Women were brought aboard the ships, too – but the crews, despite so many months away from female company, did not find much sexually attractive about them. They were immensely hairy, had breasts that hung down at least a yard and were used by the males as beasts of burden. But the men liked the giants' tricks: one used to swallow and then regurgitate long arrows, as in a circus; and another, who allowed himself to be called Juan and learned some biblical phrases, caught and ate all the rats and mice on board, to the entertainment of the men and the pleasure of the cook.

Magellan, who like everybody else was awed by their size, called these men "*patagones*" – "big feet"; the land in which he found them became – and has been, ever since – Patagonia.

Despite the amusement such indigenes provided, the months at anchor in so depressing a place wore on Magellan, and by late August he was off south again with the four ships that remained. Two men had been left behind, marooned on his orders for mutiny: they had a supply of wine and hardtack, and guns and shot; but when other, later expeditions entered the Bay they found no trace of them. They may have been killed by the giants; they may have starved to death; all the men of the Armada remembered were the pitiful wails of the pair echoing over the still waters as the ships sailed back into the open sea, and south.

By the time the flotilla had reached a latitude of 50°S, and had stopped again for rest and replenishment, the men were becoming restive once more: their plea now was – if the expedition wanted to reach the Spice Islands, why not turn east towards them and pass below the Cape of Good Hope, as usual? Magellan refused, of course – except that he was evidently frustrated enough at the lack of success in finding a way through to promise that if no strait was found by the time they had eaten up another 25° of latitude, he would turn east as they wished. The murmurs stilled. The weather became colder, the seas outside rougher and stormier. One wonders if the Captain-General had any idea of the utter impossibility of navigating at 75°S, for on this longitudinal track his ships would be stuck fast in the thick ice of the Weddell Sea, hemmed in by the unimagined continent and unendurable cold of the Antarctic.

The four ships got going once again on 17 October. Four days later on 21 October 1520, a day celebrated throughout the Catholic world as the Feast of St Ursula and the Eleven Thousand Virgins*, Magellan sighted a headland. Cabo Vírgenes, which is today surmounted by a lighthouse that flashes a powerful beam every five seconds, as well as with a foghorn and a radio direction beacon, is perhaps the most navigationally important point on the Atlantic coast of South America. For this modest Cape, as Magellan and his men were soon to discover, marks the eastern end of "the Strait that shall forever bear his name" – the entrance, at long last, to the *Mar del Sur*.

At first they had no idea that the stretch of pale, shallow water beyond the Cape would present them with anything more than another disappointment. Ranges of immense, snow-covered mountains crowded into view: there could, Magellan thought, be no possible exit. Nonetheless he ordered the *San Antonio* and the *Concepción* into the headwaters of the bay – only to be horrified when he saw them being swept by unsuspected currents and winds into a huge maelstrom of surf and spindrift, and on to a wicked-looking spur of black rock. He had already lost the *Santiago* – now it was

*Ursula was a fourth-century Cornish girl murdered in Cologne by the Roman Emperor Maximian, along with either eleven or eleven thousand young girls under her protection: Columbus named the Virgin Islands after her.

beginning to look as though two other ships were doomed. The whole expedition was turning, it seemed, into a fatal shambles.

But he had no time to dwell on these particular miseries, for an immense storm broke and his own ship, the *Trinidad*, and the *Victoria* alongside, were themselves imperilled. Men were hurled overboard, one vessel was dismasted, the other nearly turned turtle several times. And the storm went on and on and on; when finally relief came to the exhausted crews, it seemed the only recourse was to turn tail and head for home. The expedition was over, an abject failure.

Yet just at that moment – one occasionally suspects that the myth-makers have been at work on the story – the lookout sighted sails on the western horizon. They were indeed what they could only have been – the two scouting vessels which had returned, safe and sound. Yet the joy Magellan must have felt at realizing his men were still alive was as nothing when he saw, as the tiny *naos* drew closer, that their yardarms were hung with bunting, that music was playing and the crews were dancing, singing and shouting. It became clear in an instant that they had found the *paso*.

> Suddenly, [as an account of their voyage puts it] they saw a narrow passage, like the mouth of a river, ahead of them in the surf, and they managed to steer into it. Driven on by wind and tide they raced through this passage and into a wide lake. Still driven by the storm they were carried west for some hours into another narrow passage, though now the current had reversed, so what appeared to be a great ebb-tide came rushing towards them. They debouched from this second strait into a broad body of water which stretched as far as the eye could see toward the setting sun . . . .

By the application of good marine logic – tasting the water and finding it salty, then making sure the ebb- and flood-tides were of equal strength (both tests which argued against this body of water being a river) they realized that they had, indeed, discovered the way through. Magellan, overjoyed and believing that his ultimate goal was within his grasp, brushed aside the doubters' view that he should, despite the discovery, turn back *eastwards* for the Moluccas. "Though we have nothing to eat but the leather wrapping from our masts," he declared, "we shall go on!"

The Estrecho de Magallanes, as Admiralty Chart No. 554 is content to call it, is as darkly beautiful as it is useful. Before I first visited I supposed wrongly that, since the latitudes are more or less the same, the coastline would be vaguely similar to that of Maine or New Brunswick. But it is in fact much starker, more hostile, more grand. From the east, the direction taken by Magellan, the land begins flat and windswept, mean grassland with tumbleweed rolling endlessly before the gales. The wind reduces such trees as there are to stunted survivors. There are virtually no deciduous trees, aside from a few beeches seen halfway along the Strait near the modern coaling-station of Punta Arenas. In consequence there are no autumn colours to be viewed in surroundings that look as though there should be – no golds and flaming reds to set off the whites, blues and blacks of snow, water and rock.

In summer the box-leafed barberry, or *calafate*, blooms – bright yellow flowers, small blue berries. There are sphagnum bogs and spiny bushes and, also in summer, thousands of tiny polar flowers of apparent delicacy but great toughness. The wildlife is very different, too – penguins, guanacos, seals, Patagonian foxes, sea-lions. There are birds both magnificent – *Diomedea exulans*, the wandering albatross, and five almost equally remarkable family members – and flightless, like the ostrich-like rhea and the ludicrous steamer duck.* Some birds are sinister: the *Carnero*, a mean-spirited grey monster, is said to delight in picking out the eyeballs of shipwrecked sailors.

The Strait is not an easy place for sailing vessels: ". . . both difficult and dangerous, because of incomplete surveys, the lack of aids to navigation, the great distance between anchorages, the strong current, and the narrow limits for the manoeuvring of vessels', says the pilot manual. (Had Magellan and his men read today's pilot they would, no doubt, have been reluctant to try to pass through.)

The coastline is now Chilean territory on both banks, save for a minute touch of Argentina at the very western entrance. (Cabo Vírgenes is part of the Argentine Republic, and there are two lighthouses at Cabo Espíritu Santo on Tierra del Fuego, one belonging to Argentina, the other to Chile, the frontier in between; their duplication causes much confusion to seamen.) The shores are littered with the relics of stranded vessels: just on the seaward side of the first narrows – the Primera Angostura – are two magnificent old ships. One is reduced to her ribs; the other still has her steel plating and her funnel. Both are home to seabirds and seals and all manner of grasses and flowers. They have

*Which can paddle at 20 knots, and overtake many ships.

88

washed up on a shingle strand beside a lonely and barely habitable estancia. Bored gauchos sit out of the wind, sucking *yerba maté* from gourds; their horses munch at the thin grass in a desultory fashion. The place is apparently being slowly abraded by a fine, stinging dust blown across Patagonia by the unceasing gales. The wrecks are less exposed to the weather than they might be, lying in the lee of a hill called, improbably, Mount Sutlej. (Though perhaps not quite so improbable: a hulk I once saw stranded in Port Stanley in the nearby Falkland Islands was called the *Jhelum* – and both Sutlej and Jhelum are names of rivers in the Punjab. Where, I have often wondered since, are South Atlantic ships or hills or plains named after the other three Punjab rivers – the Indus, the Chenab and the Ravi?)

The two narrows are narrow indeed – the first no more than half a mile wide and, before the opening of the Panama Canal in 1914, crowded with a mass of shipping. Today only the occasional vessel passes by; when I was there, a couple of Polish trawlers bound for repairs in Punta Arenas, an oiler from the American Navy bound for an Antarctic research ship. A shabby little ferry chuckles across every couple of hours, taking lorries and a few cars on the quickest route between Patagonia and Tierra del Fuego.*

Once through the narrows, and having explored and discounted tempting-looking passages that turned out to go nowhere – *Bahia Inútil*: one can almost sense Magellan growling with irritation as he named this immense body of water *useless* – the Captain-General entered the narrow waterway that would eventually take him into the neighbour-ocean. He had turned a corner. Until now his ships had been on a southerly course, the weather becoming even colder, the unexpected winds known now as *williwaws* threatening to dash his vessels against the steep cliffs. But now, having passed Cape Froward at nearly 54°S, he was heading north, and would not be so far south again ever in his life.

By now he had lost another ship. Though he did not know it the

---

*The island was named Tierra de los Fuegos, the Land of Fire, by Magellan, because of the awesome night-time sight of hundreds of camp-fires set by the local Indians. Today there are no Indians left, but the place still burns with great spouts of flame from the dozens of oil-rigs dotted across both the Strait and the lower stretches of the eastern shores.

San Antonio had turned tail and was even now on her way back to Spain, "bearing a cargo of falsehood against Magellan". (She also took away supplies that were vital for all the fleet – a third of the Armada's biscuit supply, a third of its meat, and sixty per cent of its currants, chickpeas and figs.) Her captain quite probably sighted the Falkland Islands on his way back – something about which Magellan was never to know nor care. He had but three vessels left and despite urgent pleas from his men – now demoralized again, fretful once they realized another ship was gone – to abandon the voyage and sail back to the Guadalquivir, he pressed on north-westwards, passing through scenery of a wild grandeur and beauty he had never known before. The trio of vessels (with a combined weight less than one of today's jumbo jets) passed the tip of a small island where it was clear the two oceans' waters met – the point is now named Crosstides – and through the Paso Tortuosa. Then, deciding boldly not to enter another beguiling-looking passage which, had he done so, would have wasted very many miles and many days (it is now called Canal Jeronimo, and leads into an immense maze of lakes and passageways), he sailed directly north-west, up the Paso Largo and finally into the Paso del Mar.

Here huge surges of Pacific water – sensed as mere vibrations once they had rounded Cape Froward – now rocked their boats from stem to stern. Stiff westerly winds made forward passage difficult, and the little boats had to tack this way and that within the narrow confines of the Strait's exit, before the funnel began to widen and the open sea to present itself. Magellan, now perfectly confident of his discovery, named the waters Estrecho do Todos los Santos – All Saints' Strait. It was a name that would swiftly give way to his, once his heroism and navigational skill were recognized back home.

There is some dispute about the date upon which *Trinidad, Victoria* and *Concepción* passed into the Mar del Sur. Antonio Pigafetta, the journalist (or Doge's spy) says 28 November; one distinguished eighteenth-century historian says the 27th; another of equal distinction puts it a day earlier. Whichever is correct, we know that Magellan named the final cape Deseado, "for we had long been desiring it". We also know that "the iron-willed Admiral" broke down and cried on hearing that Balboa's ocean had at last been sighted. (Unhappily his chosen name Deseado barely survives today; the dramatic and unlit cliff on Isla Desolación that marks the western exit of the Strait is now called Cabo Pilar. Deseado is a smaller cape to its south, generally ignored except by sentimental mariners of whom there are, these days and in these waters, rather few.)

The day when the ships passed the tip of Desolation Island was rough and stormy – the typical robust westerly weather for which Cape Horn is notorious. The mariners spent the night in such shelter as they could find from the 30-knot winds, drenching squalls and menacing waves. At daybreak, though, they passed out into the ocean proper, still heading to the north-west to get out of the miserable cold. They passed the Strait's tiny guardian islands, the Evangelistas – where there is now both a lighthouse and a Chilean signal station – and sailed into an evening that suddenly became magically serene.

Ferdinand Magellan assembled his men on deck. Father Pedro de Valderrama, the *Trinidad*'s padre, stood on the poop deck and called down on the crew of all three remaining vessels the blessing of Our Lady of Victory. The men sang hymns. The gunners fired broadsides. And Magellan – just as Balboa had done seven years before – proudly unfurled the flag of Castile.

But he had none of the grandiloquence of Vasco Núñez; he uttered none of the proud formulae Balboa had uttered in the Gulf of San Miguel. What he said – if contemporary accounts are to be believed – includes the first use of the word that, as a geographical descriptive and identifier, is central to this book and, if one accepts the dominant economic theses of today, central to the future development of the planet.

"We are about to stand into an ocean where no ship has ever sailed before," Magellan is said to have cried (though it has to be reiterated that there is no *hard* evidence that he did so). "May the ocean be always as calm and benevolent as it is today. In this hope I name it the *Mar Pacifico*."

And just in case it was not Magellan who first uttered the word, then perhaps it was Pigafetta: "We debouched from that Strait," he later wrote, "engulfing ourselves in the Pacific Sea."

Unknown to Magellan and his crew – for they lived fully three centuries before Alfred Wegener advanced his theory of continental drift – the spot where they chanced upon the new ocean is one of the great tectonic landmarks of the world. A few miles from where the tiny ships first "debouched from the Strait" is a spot which marks one of the suture-lines of the planet, one of those rare sites where can be seen the brushstrokes of creation. I went there once, to see a place that was thus twice blessed, by histories both recent and more ancient.

I had travelled down to Punta Arenas, which the biblical authority of the *South American Handbook* said was the best jumping-off point. Within two days of leaving the warm winter of Hong Kong, I was standing shivering in the endless summer gales of the roaring forties on the shores of the Magellan Strait – if not obviously at the edge of any tectonic plates, then certainly at the very edge of the world.

It was New Year's Eve and the midnight sky was still bright: Punta Arenas is at 53°S, and although on a similar longitude to Halifax has been shunted, by Professor Dowd's descendants, into the same time zone as New York – all of which means that it stays light for a great deal longer than in most cities, and we celebrated the coming of the New Year in almost broad daylight. The few ships out in the harbour sent up fireworks and flares, and the low hills around town echoed with the wail of sirens and foghorns – at least until the dark did set in at about three in the morning. By that time I had made drinking friends in the Hotel Cabo de Hornos with a couple of young American teachers down from Ecuador who had long wanted to visit the Towers of Paine, the very spot where – geologists had written – the two tectonic plates in which I was interested had come together. They spoke good Spanish: if they promised to interpret for me, I said, I'd rent a car and give them a ride.

The next morning the wind still blew from the west. Beyond town, beyond the extraordinary cemetery for the pioneers who had created the place and the Indians who had tried to frustrate them, and once the shanties had petered out, the Patagonian landscape was flat and treeless and the gale howled across it without ceasing. For a few miles, as we hugged the shore of the Strait, the northbound road was paved; but once we had passed a junction and the track leading eastwards across to Argentina, it reverted to rutted gravel and the wind blew little spirals of dust across it, like ectoplasmic tumbleweed.

We saw a great many sheep, of course, grazing on the peat-grass and the bog-myrtle; and every once in a while, some miles back from the road, an *estancia* – a collection of farm buildings like white dolls' houses, tiny on the immense plain. Some owners had tried to plant pines as windbreaks, but they were stunted little trees now, huddling themselves for protection in the shadow of the buildings.

I stopped to take a photograph of one *estancia* that I knew belonged to a Scottish family who had lived there for five generations: even from two miles away I could hear the rhythmic clattering of the tin roof as it was lifted and dropped by the gales. The womenfolk would no doubt be beside the wood stove, talking over the din of the roof as they did their needlework; the men would be in the wool-shed, cleansing and grading the fleeces in time for the next lorry down to port. Scotland must have seemed a fair way away, and no chance this year of a real Hogmanay.

At a place called Morro Chico there was a tiny inn where we sat around the stove ourselves. We were given mugs of coffee and slices of black bun, a dark Christmas-time cake that had come from Scotland too. The innkeepers – I had enough Spanish to recognize their curious Patagonian accent, all rolling rs and glottal stops – took me outside to show off a baby rhea they kept in a pen. It had been hit by a passing lorry, and they joked that it would never fly again. It was a joke because rheas, which look like small ostriches (only with an extra toe on each foot) cannot fly anyway. This one hobbled about gamely, seemingly eager to get back to the open plains.

Soon after Morro Chico the plains began to undulate and then, in the distance, we spied the mountains, the southern Andes. The road was now backing west towards the sea, and towards the place where I fancied we might see evidence of major geophysics at work. We first met Pacific waters at the windswept village of Puerto Natales, and suddenly there were mountains all around us: mountains and glaciers, and curious seabirds and dolphins and spume-whipped sea, the water a vivid blue under a cloudless sky. It was breathtaking in its beauty. The exiles from Ecuador – more accustomed to jungle and soggy heat – had gasped unashamedly as we rounded the bend above the cliffs, and they remained quite mute, awestruck, as we circled down into town and parked outside the Hotel Eberhardt for a dish of the king crab, *centolla*, and a mug of beer.

The ocean which appeared to stretch across all our visible horizon was in fact a loch, Ultima Esperanza, a sea-loch that reached 200 miles inland and from where Pacific shipping could, in theory (if the master was good and the compass correct) navigate its way deep inside the Andean chain. There was a small cutter parked at the jetty, and a sign taped to the Eberhardt window said that for

$15 each she would take us right up to the foot of the Balmaceda and Serrano glaciers which spilled from the southern tip of that immense high-altitude sheet of white that was the Patagonian ice-cap.

But we were driving to the ice-cap anyway and needed to reach the peaks by nightfall. So we contented ourselves instead by watching a troupe of steamer ducks – quite flightless, like the rhea – whizzing maniacally through the waves, chasing a fishing-boat. They may not be able to fly and one doesn't like to enquire too deeply into how elegant they look below the waterline, but steamer ducks – their wings gyrating through the water like paddle-wheels – can make 12 knots, and more in a following wind.

There were another 100 miles of flatland, of dust, sheep, rheas and distant mountains before we were stopped at a police post. A trio of grumpy officers, all Pinochet look-alikes, demanded our passports, eyeing us curiously lest we be Argentine spies. We then passed beneath a ranch fence: Parque Nacional Torres del Paine, it announced, and in the distance over a range of low brown grasslands were the sharp spires of a dozen oddly-shaped mountains, twisted and contorted and coloured like no other mountains we had ever seen before. This, at last, was the place where the engine work of the world was on view, just beyond the brow of the hills ahead.

It is worthwhile, perhaps, placing these Towers in the context of their geology. As I mentioned previously, there are six major plates covering the surface of this planet, and ten or so that are classified as minor (though even minor plates can be as big as entire continents). These plates float, relatively coldly and stiffly, on the warmer and more mobile outer surface of the earth's mantle. They slip and slide against each other – somewhat ponderously, since they proceed at no more than a foot a year and sometimes a great deal less. But they are for ever *moving* and, where they meet in head-on collision, in what is known as a *subduction zone*, they produce one of the great geological dramas of the planet.

Generally speaking, a subduction zone is the place where the major business of the earth's surface is done. One of the colliding plates crumples upwards and then grinds down, sliding beneath the onrush of the other. As it descends towards the mantle it melts; thousands of deep-focus earthquakes are triggered as gobbets of molten rock screech and burst against each other; the edge of the upper plate, meanwhile, contorts and rises tortured into the air, producing a range of soaring peaks.

There are volcanoes and fault lines and a ceaseless tremor of activity. The ocean floor is scored and fissured, and a suture line miles deep plunges through it in sudden counterpoint to the nearby mountain-building. From the deepest point of a new trench to the highest point of a newly created mountain range can be ten miles, maybe more – the greatest difference in the shape of the planetary spheroid anywhere. The whole area, a band 50 miles wide and hundreds or maybe thousands of miles long, is alive – rearing and plunging, writhing and creaking – as the future shape of a portion of the world is determined for the next aeon of geologic time.

Geophysicists are perhaps not best known for their romantic souls, and when they invented the dire appellation subduction zone, they probably overlooked the fact that precisely because of all this sub-terranean frenzy, each one is an area of quite extraordinary beauty. The contorted peaks of the Torres del Paine rise at the very site of collision of two of the world's largest plates – the South American and the Antarctican Plates. Where they smash into each other, at fully one resounding inch a year, in one of the primal dramas of the earth's creation, they form the summits and the valleys that even now were beginning to fill our windscreen as we headed deep into the park.

A shepherd, a *gaucho*, rode past us, ahead of a sea of sheep. There must have been 5,000 head corralled into convoy formation by a quartet of big black dogs. The *gaucho* was a swarthy old man in a red woollen cap and a leather jacket; his saddle was a grubby sheepskin, and the horse's nose was bridled with a yellow wool *cabeza*. He waved at us as we passed and then, noticing something, gesticulated wildly into the air. "*Condor!*" he cried. "*Condor!*"

And sure enough, gliding effortlessly through the eddies and the down-draughts from the peaks ahead, were six mighty Andean con-dors, the biggest birds in the world. *Vultur gryphus*, I had been told, was not in as grave danger of extinction as its California cousin. It was a magnificent vision: the mighty, black-winged birds, their wings fully 10 feet from tasselled tip to tasselled tip, rose and fell in the cold wind against a background of the brown earth below them, the deep blue sky above them and, behind them and nearly circling us all, the great grey fortresses of the Andes, sheer walls of ice, snow and rock nearly two miles high.

As the plains became higher and colder, so another memorable Andean beast appeared – the guanaco, country cousin to the llama, brother to the vicuña and the alpaca, and properly regarded as a small and humpless camel. Herds – if that is the proper collective for guanacos – grazed peacefully on the alpine plants. They stood their ground as we passed; few people travel this way, and none would ever think of harming one of these gentle creatures. Moreover, as the guide-books say of the guanaco, "when annoyed, they spit."

Now we were at 2,000 feet, the grasslands and such trees as there had been were below us. The lakes huddled in the valleys – Lakes Grey, Nordensköld and Pehoé – were speckled with small icebergs, and at the end of Lake Grey we spied the white winding-sheet of a glacier edging its way down from the ice-cap. The wind was biting. The peaks – the Towers – had closed in above us, presenting a glowering, vaguely terrifying immensity. They cast a shadow a mile wide, within which there was just the howl of the gale, clouds of dust and the occasional flurry of hail. A primal place indeed. As we glanced at each other, we shuddered with apprehension.

But we had another few hundred feet to manage before we saw our goal. We scrambled up the hillside on the left bank of an enormous river which thundered down a precipitous cascade of rapids into a foaming cauldron, raging with wind-whipped mist. We could barely hear ourselves think. A few blades of grass clung to the otherwise barren slope, the gale tugging all the while at their roots. Swirls of clouds billowed down from the Towers and the glaciers hung vertically, suspended like gigantic icicles, while flocks of birds scattered and spun before them, helpless in the wild turbulence.

Finally we breasted the saddle in the lower ridge, what in the Welsh mountains, and latterly in the Himalayas, we would call the *cwm*. Darkness was falling. Behind us we could just make out the glimmer of lamplight from the tiny hotel on Lake Pehoé, where we should be dining on river trout, *bife chorizo* and good Chilean *pinot noir* before the night was out. If, that is, we survived the cold and managed to avoid being hurled by the wind into that bottomless pit at the base of the waterfall. Already the night air was laying hoar-frost on the rocks, and a gleam of thin ice was sparkling on the surfaces of the flatter stones.

It was dark behind . . . but there was sunset ahead. Sunset, and the

Pacific Ocean. Now we were huddled against the wall of sheer, pale grey rock that soared seamlessly into the sky, up into the ice-white clouds above. Ahead of us the land fell away, became green, then brown, then evolved into a crazed fretwork of islands and sea-lochs, lakes and strange peaks. Could that be, perhaps, the Isla Esperanza and, beyond, the much larger Hanover Island, Isla Jorge Montt and the chunk of rock the Royal Navy (who found it) once called Cambridge Island, but which was now the Isla Diego de Almagro?

To the left, I fancied – though the light might be playing tricks – I could see the horns of Cape Pilar, the western end of the Magellan Strait, and to the right the prouder outlines of Imperial Fortune, Mornington Island and the pleasantly ambiguous Isla del Duque de York. But ahead, beyond all this minor geology, stood the Pacific Ocean, painted blinding gold by the sun, but endless and vast, and terribly, terribly deep.

So here at last, this point at which I stood, was the very place, the geophysical start-line at which two of the world's great geologic plates met. Ahead of me, in the glorious sunset, was the level and quite stable monolith of the Antarctican Plate. Behind me, in the dark, was the similarly undisturbed sheet of crust known as the South American Plate. They met, collided and contorted somewhere deep below, some miles ahead of me, beneath all that sea and ice and beyond that jumbled mess of islands. Beneath my feet and beside me to my right, were the sheer pale grey rocks that were the andesitic relics of all the ancient turbulence and torture which had been and was still being caused by the plates' gentle, turgid but quite inevitable meeting.

This, then, was one of the great suture lines of the world, a place which marked a turning point in the history of the planet.

It was too cold to stand and stare, and the wind kept buffeting us dangerously each time we tried to gaze across at the Ocean. So we turned back eastwards instead, and hurried down the hill. Above, in the dark, there was a rumbling from the Towers of Paine, the crackling sound of old rock being broken by new ice and the skitter of smaller stones plunging down a crevasse. We looked back and up, and for a moment the Towers' summits were flecked with gold, before the sun slid down behind the unseen horizon and all Chile was plunged into blackness.

3

"Primus Circumdedisti Me"

The concept of the Pacific Ocean, the greatest physical unit on earth, had been born. Balboa had seen it; Abreu had ventured on to its western edges; Magellan had discovered how to reach its eastern periphery. Now it was up to the explorers to try to comprehend the enormity of their discovery, to probe it, to determine its lateral extent, to search for the enigmatic *Terra Australis Incognita* and to define both its frontiers and those of the immense body of water that contained it. Yet before they could do any of this they – or, more specifically, Magellan, since this was his determined aim and that of those who sponsored his venture – had to sail across it.

So the Captain-General ordered the sails and the rudders of his three little vessels set to carry the shrunken – but now at long last triumphant – Armada northwards. He thought it might take three or four days to reach the Spice Islands. This was a savage underestimate – a tragically optimistic forecast based, quite probably, both on the terrible inability of long-distance navigators to work out how to calculate longitude (an inability which ensured that not a single estimate then available to Magellan was even 80 per cent of the true size of the ocean), and on the scale that he assumed from a little globe (boxed in a costly wooden holder) that he is said to have taken with him.*[1]

---

*This globe was said to have been a copy of the famous model constructed by Martin Behaim, cartographer-royal to the Portuguese court – and if Magellan did in fact use its scale to suppose the half-week crossing of his new ocean, then the irony is more than apparent: for the globe, or the information on it, would have been smuggled out of Portugal to a Captain-General who was sailing on an adopted pennant. How droll, the Portuguese mandarins might have remarked, that Magellan's expedition was well-nigh decimated by disease and starvation

Not that anyone suspected tragedy as they breezed to the north of Cape Deseado. Far from it. Once the Armada had reached the lower southern latitudes, the winds began to blow balmily and unceasingly from the south-east. They were trade winds, just like those well-known in the southern Atlantic and Indian Oceans, and they were pleasantly warm, their effect being to produce nothing but splendid sailing. No undue swells. No angry squalls. No cyclonic outbursts. Just endless days and nights of leisured spooming before the powerful breezes. "Well was it named Pacific," wrote Pigafetta much later, confirming his master's choice of name, "for during this period we met with no storms."

For weeks and weeks he managed, by dint simply of wafting before the winds with sails unchanged, to miss every single one of the islands with which the Pacific Ocean is littered. He was not even nearly shipwrecked and his course, recorded sedulously by his pilot, Francisco Albo, shows him – almost uncannily – leading his vessels decorously *past* the Juan Fernandez Islands, *past* Sala-y-Gomez and Easter Island, *past* Pitcairn, Ducie, Oeno and Henderson* and, indeed, past everything else. His astrolabe, his crude speed-recorder, his half-hour glass (which any watchkeeper would be flogged for holding against his chest, since to warm it so would make the sand flow faster, the half-hour pass more quickly and the watch be more rapidly over with) served him admirably: he plotted the likely course to the Spice Islands and, more or less, his ships took him there.

Any deviation could have caused disaster (or serendipitous benefit, depending whether he made contact at day or night). Had he strayed 3° north of Albo's recorded track, he would have hit the Marquesas; 3° south, he would have come to Tahiti. He was 100 miles off Bikini. He passed within half a day's sailing of razor-sharp coral reefs, thundering surfs, huge spikes and lances that would have ruined his ships for ever. It seems, at this distance, that some guardian angel had

---

which came as a direct consequence of his basing his navigational calculations on stolen Portuguese intelligence material.

* The latter recently the subject of a failed purchase offer by a retired coal mining millionaire from Frog Level, Virginia, who wished to use it as a centre for Pacific eugenics, producing a master race much in his own image. The British Foreign and Commonwealth Office, which administers the uninhabited speck of coral, refused to sell it, arguing that a fruit-eating pigeon and a flightless bird called the Henderson rail might be unnecessarily affected by the Virginian's eugenic exertions.

Magellan's tiny fleet under her benevolent watch, assuring him of deep waters and fair breezes – the plea of every mariner, even today – for days and nights too numerous to count.

Yet in fact this providence proved on closer inspection to have a less than kindly face. For six weeks out of the Strait, Magellan's men began to die. The monotony of a landless passage, the unchanging direction of the wind from the stern, the blazing sun – all this was bearable, perhaps. But what was not bearable nor, it turned out, survivable, was the lack of food (and of proper food) aboard the sea-locked ships.

Magellan cut the rations soon after turning west, so alarmed was he at the lack of landfall. Much of the biscuit and meat, the chickpeas, currants and figs had already gone, carried back to Europe on the treacherous *San Antonio*. But now such food as the three ships carried began to rot under the soggy tropic airs. The penguins and seals they had caught and killed in Patagonia started to fester and turn putrid; maggots raged through the ships, eating the clothes and supplies and rigging; the water supplies turned scummy and rank. The men began to develop the classic symptoms of scurvy – their teeth loosened in their gums, their breath began to smell horribly sour, huge boils erupted from their shrunken frames and they sank into inconsolable melancholia.

By the turn of the year the men had started to die like flies. One of the Patagonian behemoths whom Magellan had persuaded aboard was, despite his immense physique and power, the first to go: he begged to be made a Christian, was baptized Paul and then died. By mid-January a third of the matelots were too sick to stagger along the decks: their food was limited to scoops of flour stained yellow by the urine of rats, and biscuits riddled with worms and weevils.

Depression and deep anxiety afflicted Magellan, too. At one point he flung his charts overboard in a fit of rage. "With the pardon of the cartographers, the Moluccas are not to be found in their appointed place!" he is said to have cried. The travellers did in fact strike land in late January – a tiny island they called St Paul's, which seems to be the minute atoll now called Poka Puka, the northernmost of the French *circonscription* of the Tuamotu Group.* They stayed a week, replenishing their water-butts, and feasting on turtle eggs and *bêches*

*And, four centuries later, the first island to be spotted by Thor Heyerdahl aboard the balsa raft *Kon-Tiki*, after his long drift westward from Callao in Peru.

de mer. They left in optimistic mood – surely, they surmised, this island must be the first of a vast skein of atolls and lagoons that stretched to the now-close Moluccas. But it was not to be: the ships had barely traversed a third of their ocean when soon the hunger pains, the racking thirst and the sense of unshakable misery began to try the men again, and once more the dying began.

More and more terrible the voyage steadily became. By 4 March the flagship had run out of food completely. Men were eating the ox-hides and guanaco-skins used to prevent the riggings from chafing (and not in fact too bad a diet, so long as the scurvy-ridden teeth hung in). The smell of death, the knowledge that it was both inevitable and impending gripped the crew. And then dawned the 6 March and a seaman called Navarro – the only man fit enough to clamber up the ratlines – spied what everyone was waiting for: land, steep-sided, tree-covered and with native huts adorning the lower shores.

A great cheer went up. Cannon were fired from ship to ship. Men fell to their knees in prayer. A squadron of tiny native dug-outs, lateen-rigged, were seen to speed out to meet the Spaniards. Magellan had reached the islands he first called *Las Islas de las Velas Latinas* and then, once enough of his cargo had been filched, the *Islas de Ladrones*, the Islands of Thieves. He had reached the Mariana island that we now call Guam. The Pacific had been crossed. The voyage that the Captain-General had supposed might take three days had in fact occupied three and a half months. He had left Cabo Deseado on 28 November 1520, and dropped anchor in Guam on 6 March 1521 – a passage of ninety-nine days which even today's atomic submarines might find irksome.

He stayed in Guam for only three days, to rest, to make minor repairs, to take on food (such as the "figs, more than a palm long", which must have been bananas) and fresh water. (He had not careened his ships since Patagonia and their barnacle-heavy hulls must have made progress sluggish indeed.) Then he set off, still towards the Moluccas, standing down for the south-west and to the Philippines – islands of which all travellers to these parts had often heard, but to which no European had ever been. The Spice Islands, it has to be recalled, were the Armada's prescribed goal: the official mandate and ambition of Magellan was to discover, name and seize in the name of Spain the immense archipelago that lay to their immediate north.

The only Briton on the expedition, Master Andrew of Bristol, died on the short passage: he was never to see the islands which, a novelist was later to write, were "as fair as Eden, with gold beaches, graceful palms, exotic fruits and soil so rich that if one snapped off a twig and stuck it into the ground it would start straightaway to grow".

Magellan made his landfall on 16 March at the island now called Homonhon, a small skerry at the southern end of the large Philippine island of Samar. Two days later, the first contact was made with Filipinos – though the name Philippines was not to be given until 1542, when Villalobos named them after the Infante, later to become Philip II. (Magellan's name for them was less inspired, although politically more innocuous: he called them after Lazarus, the saint on whose dedicated day he first sighted them.)

The significant moment came two days later still, when the ships sailed down through the Gulf of Leyte and the Surigao Strait.* Once through the Strait, Magellan landed at the island that guarded its entrance, Limasawa. Eight natives sailed out to the *Trinidad* in a small boat and on the Captain-General's orders, his Moluccan slave Enrique hailed them.

In a moment that must, for an instant, have seemed frozen in time, it became clear that the men understood perfectly. Their language was being spoken to them by a man on a ship which had come to them from the east. The linguistic globe had been circumnavigated. A man who had originated in these parts had travelled to Europe across Asia and around Africa, and had now returned home by the Americas and the Pacific: Enrique de Molucca may well have been, strictly speaking, the first of humankind to circumnavigate the world, but he was never to be honoured for so doing.

Nor, by the unhappy coincidence of ill-temper and wretched misfortune, was Ferdinand Magellan ever able to savour his own triumph either. Just six weeks later he was dead, cut down on a Philippine island in a skirmish that is as unremembered as the place in which it happened is unsung – a flat, muddy little island called Mactan, where they have built an airport to serve the city of Cebu.

The circumstances of his end are riven into every Iberian school-child's learning, even today. The ships' crews wanted to press on for

---

*This was where, more than four centuries later, one of the last truly great naval battles of the world was fought, when Admiral Halsey reduced the Japanese Imperial Navy to vestigial strength, and prepared the way for the ending of the Second World War.

the Moluccas – one Spanish officer knew his brother was waiting for him at Ternate, and all the others were keen to reach their official goal. Magellan was happy to continue with his exploration of the Philippines, however; he seemed well-disposed to the people, and enjoyed the relative ease with which – whether pagan or Muslim, for Islam had a considerable foothold in the southern islands – they took to Christianity. (It is perhaps worth remembering that the Catholic faith which Magellan and his priests brought to Samar and Cebu and northern Mindanao flourishes still today, that the Philippines is the only dominantly Christian country in Asia, and that the power and influence of the Church has not been insignificant in such recent political developments as the overthrow of President Ferdinand Marcos. Magellan's legacy survives, and in remarkably good shape.)

But the sewing of the seeds of that legacy were to be Magellan's undoing. His horribly inglorious end came in late April, five months after he left his Strait, victorious. The hubris generated in the wake of that triumph was to come violently into confrontation with Nemesis.

The precise circumstances are these. Magellan had demonstrated what he felt was his superior status to the local Rajah of Cebu, and had made Christians of him and his followers. He had declined to pay the customary tribute, saying that no representative of the greatest emperor on earth could or should do so. His arrogance was meekly accepted; but not all the local rajahs, nor all their country cousins, felt bound by such complicity. Least fettered of all was the minor Rajah of Mactan, a man named Cilapulapu, now known to all Filipinos simply as Lapu Lapu. (In any case *ci* means simply "the".) He was not going to pay fealty to this Christian interloper, come what may. He cared little enough for the Rajah of Cebu, let alone for his new-found foreign friends.

The Spaniards soon had wind of this rebellious mood, and on 27 April Magellan and sixty of his men paddled across the narrow strait to Mactan, in an attempt to bring Lapu Lapu to heel. "You will feel the iron of our lances," he had been told by a Siamese trader used as interpreter. "We have fire-hardened spears and stakes of bamboo," replied a defiant chieftain – "come across whenever you like." Following Magellan to watch the battle being prosecuted on his behalf, the Rajah of Cebu was forced to observe what proved to be a rout.

The waters at the northern end of Mactan island are very shallow and degenerate into warm swamps. A selected forty-eight Spaniards, dressed in full armour, had to wade the last few hundred yards to do battle with the Mactan warriors. They were at a dire disadvantage. The enemy attacked with great vigour, and Magellan's pitiable invading force was thrown into disarray. They fought for an hour, thigh-deep in the water, then Magellan plunged his lance into the body of an attacker but was unable to withdraw it quickly enough. It was a fatal delay. Another native slashed Magellan's leg with a scimitar and he staggered. Scores of others crowded around him as he fell and, as Pigafetta was to write, "thus they killed our mirror, our light, our comfort and our true guide".*

There is a monument near the spot where he fell. It is a tall white obelisk, guarded solicitously for the last fifteen years by the man with the splendid name of Jesus Baring. There are two accounts of the event, one engraved in English on each side of the cross, and Señor Baring derives much amusement from showing his occasional visitors – and there are very few, considering how globally important this spot should be – how markedly they differ.

The one on the monument's eastern side – the side which pedant geographers will recognize as marginally nearer to the Spanish Main – records it as a European tragedy. "Here on 27th April 1521 the great Portuguese navigator Hernando de Magallanes, in the service of the King of Spain, was slain by native Filipinos . . ." On the other side, by contrast, the event is seen as an Oriental triumph – an heroic blow struck for Philippine nationalism: "Here on this spot the great chieftain Lapu Lapu repelled an attack by Ferdinand Magellan, killing him and sending his forces away . . ." Mr Baring points at the latter and roars with laughter. "This is the real story. This is the one we Filipinos like to hear!"

Lapu Lapu is thus the first – and to many people here the greatest – of Filipino heroes.† These days his memory is being revived, his exploits retold, and his adventures are being made the stuff of comic strips and films and popular Visayan songs.   Each April there is a full-scale re-enactment of the battle of Mactan on the beach, with an improbably handsome Cebuano film star playing the part of the

*It is worth remembering at this point that Fernão de Magalhães was a native Portuguese – of whom it used to be said, because they were such energetic explorers, "they have a small country to live in, but all the world to die in".
†His heroic stature is diluted somewhat by his having to share his name with that of a very popular fish.

semi-naked hero and, when I was last there, "the Philippine Air Force officer Mercurion Fernandez playing the role of the armour-clad Magellan". The two sides struggle gamely in the rising surf until that epic moment when officer Fernandez contrives to collapse into the shallow sea, and grunts his last. The assembled thousands then cheer their hero, and Mr Jesus Baring basks contentedly in his briefly reflected glory. Such is the pride in the Rajah of Mactan that there are firebrands – in Manila as well as in Cebu – who believe their country should shed its present name – reminder, as it is, of colonial conquest – and be reborn as Lapu Lapu Land.

Little more needs to be said of the tiny Armada now, save to note what most popular historians choose to forget: one of the ships, the doughty little *Victoria* – at 85 tons the second smallest of the original five – did get back to Spain. The *Concepción* was scuttled; the flagship *Trinidad*, which tried to make for home via the Pacific once more, and was blown up north as far as Hakodate in Japan, was captured by a Portuguese battle group and became a total loss in the Spice Islands which had been its original goal.

But *Victoria* scudded home under the charge of Juan Sebastian d'Elcano, previously the executive officer of the *Concepción*. She made Timor, discovering that the local natives attached bells to their foreskins and liked to attract women by urinating fiercely at them and thus making a jingling sound which the women found impossible either to ignore or resist. She reached Mossel Bay (or Port Elizabeth) in South Africa, passing without harm (other than a broken foretopmast and a badly strained main yard) through the most dangerous sailing waters on earth, where freak waves which can cause modern oil tankers to founder are experienced. She doubled the Capes Agulhas and Good Hope, then made the Cape Verde Islands where they discovered that – despite meticulous log-keeping – they had lost a whole day from their calendar. (Professor Dowd's International Date Line, which they had crossed without knowing it, was of course the culprit: the concept of the need for such a line was, however, profoundly unimaginable.)

They picked up Cape St Vincent in early September, and on 6 September made the harbour of Sanlucar de Barrameda whence they had set off almost exactly three years before. Two day later they were tied up beside the quay at Seville, home.

Juan Sebastian d'Elcano had brought just 17 men back with him: 266 had set out. Circumnavigation was a costly business.

But it was to be well rewarded. Juan Sebastian was given an annual pension and a coat of arms as handsome as it was aromatic: a castle, three nutmegs, twelve cloves, two crossed cinammon sticks, a pair of Malay kings bearing spice sticks, and above all a globe, circled by a ribbon emblazoned with the motto: *Primus circumdedisti me* – thou first circumnavigated me. For d'Elcano *was* the first true circumnavigator, even though he had sailed at Magellan's behest and had performed (with only one proto-mutinous slip, for which he had been forgiven) just as his Captain-General had directed.*

These days he is largely – but not absolutely – forgotten. When Australia held her 200th birthday party in January 1988, a procession of the greatest of the world's Tall Ships swept through the Sydney Heads, past Circular Quay and underneath the coathanger bridge to the anchorage at Darling Harbour. I had just been to Mactan and to the Magellan monument, and my mind was still filled with the brilliance and tragedy of the expedition. So it was with pleasure indeed that I was able to note – with considerable surprise – that the lead vessel of the huge Armada was a brilliant Spanish four-masted barque hung with the ancient arms of Castile: she was the *Juan Sebastian d'Elcano*. Crowds of happy Australians cheered her onward: but none, so far as I could gather by asking, knew after whom she had been named, nor why.

*He was to die four years later in mid-Pacific, while working as captain of another vessel dispatched to try to seize the Spice Islands for Spain.

4

Down the Malacca

I had made my approaches to the Pacific twice thus far – once down the Isthmus of Panama, from where the first European glimpsed and then claimed the Ocean; and next along the Strait of Magellan, whence the first round-the-world sailors embarked on the most challenging part of their journey. To render this beating of the Ocean's bounds properly symmetrical – to come at it now from its western and Asian side, not merely via the Americas – it seems appropriate to relate a third approach run towards its edge – the run that underlines the strategic and commercial importance of today's Pacific Ocean: the passage through the Strait of Malacca.

It is said that if you take an aeroplane and fly eastwards from the Arabian Gulf to Tokyo Bay along the main sea-lane, there will never be a point at which you cannot see at least three oil tankers. On each of your horizons there will be a couple of giants bound for Japan, their gunwales nearly awash from their load of a quarter of a million tons of crude. Below you, and slightly to the north of the line of the eastbound ships, will be another tanker, empty and in ballast, so high out of the water that her red-lead skirting is above the waterline. She will be heading away from Japan, back to collect another load, and to turn around once more.

Fifty miles behind her, and fifty miles ahead, will be more empty tankers. And as the plane flies on so yet more ships – some full and heading east, others empty and heading west – will appear inexorably, relentlessly, so sometimes it seems as if an immense floating pipeline has been created on the sea, taking Arabian oil outwards to feed the insatiable appetites of the Japanese economic machine.

This procession of ships, set in unintended formation, line astern, begins its progress at Kharg Island, Kuwait, Bandar Abbas and a dozen other pumping stations, where the ships are fed before they start their stately journeys east.

First, the cortège lumbers through the hot waters of the outer Gulf, past Dubai and through Hormuz – the American Navy perhaps observing the convoys her vessels seek to protect. Then the line heads into the open ocean, past Oman and Muscat, out into the Arabian Sea, heading for a passage through that delicate filigree of islands known as the Laccadives and the Maldives, where the Indian Ocean proper begins. It ducks south of Sri Lanka (with perhaps the old British lighthouse at Dondra Head just visible, winking on the port beam), passes through the Ten Degree Channel between the Andamans and the Nicobars, then trims its course a little east by south for the run down to Singapore, through the Strait of Malacca.

Everything gets squeezed together in Malacca, as though in some enormous sub-marine sandwich. General cargo ships making passage between Le Havre and Shanghai, reefer vessels working from Hamburg to Vladivostok, passenger liners from Bangkok to Trieste, aircraft carriers from Manila to Mombasa, coasters bustling between the ports of Sumatra or along the Malay States from Penang to Singapore. And fishing boats, too – scores upon scores of drift netters and purse-seiners, trawlers and small factory ships, and what seems like a thousand tiny skiffs each crewed by a man with a bamboo pole, hoping for a bite of yellowfish to take home to the village in a creek up beyond the mangrove swamps.

The Peninsular & Oriental container ship *Cardigan Bay* makes the journey, Pacific-bound, once every four months. The day I passed through, Captain Peter Clark was in command of his 70,000 ton vessel, with its 3,000 containers and a crew of 31. He had collected some extra cargo – a couple of hundred boxes – at Port Swettenham (or as the Malays like to call it now, Port Klang). It was late evening when the cranes completed their loading. The Captain whistled tunelessly as the three Klang tugs edged us away from the quayside, down the silent and black Klang River, and into the most congested and most difficult of all the ocean gateways.

We reached the Strait some time after midnight, and prepared to edge out into the navigation fairway. Everyone on the bridge peered nervously right and left, doing the maritime equivalent of the highway crossing code. Ships in traffic separation schemes like that in force in Malacca keep to the right, so to get out the *Cardigan Bay* had to ease herself across the path of northbound ships, then out into the southbound – Pacific-bound – lane. The running lights of a score of vessels streamed slowly past up ahead, majestically cruising their cargoes up and down the Strait, quite oblivious to our determination to get in among them. It didn't look at all easy.

"Here comes a widger now!" exclaimed Captain Clark, suddenly exasperated. We had found the ship on our ARPA radar, a now-compulsory device that automatically warns navigators if any vessels nearby happen to be on a collision course. And this "widger" most certainly was. The radar burbled, then beeped angrily. A green light began to wink, and unseen electronic devices drew lines and patterns of dots that ended up right across our own course: in eight minutes, if neither the oncoming ship nor the *Cardigan Bay* took action, there would be a crash.

Captain Clark pulled out a computer print-out headed "DDVs", fresh in from Singapore Radio, and set it beside the chart. It was a list of all the truly big ships – the deep draught vessels – that were known to be coming our way as we turned the bend. He examined it closely in a pool of dim light. There was the *Tokitsu Maru*, 259,000 tons, proceeding at ten knots, drawing sixty feet of water and clearly full of oil. The *Japan Daisy*, the *Esso Languedoc*, the *Meishomaru*, the *Tottorimaru* – "nearly all Japanese tankers, see?" – all heading south. The newcomer, now six minutes away, was ploughing north.

"There she is!" the Captain cried, and jabbed his finger at Index No. 744 on his list – a supertanker named *Yukon Leader*, 257,000 tons of steel and ballast, heading north. "That's probably her. She rounded the Raffles Lighthouse six hours ago. Should be around here by now, somewhere fine on the port bow." And as one, four pairs of binoculars turned towards the bow, and a little to its left, as the captain, the officer-of-the-watch, the lookout and the radio operator all scanned the horizon. Until – "Got her, sir!" one of them yelled, and then we could all see her – a distant dazzle, the light on her foremast a little lower than that on her mainmast, the green of her bridge wing lantern showing she was starboard side on, heading north.

Normally the rules of the road require that the ship which has the other on her starboard side gives way – so in this case the *Yukon Leader* should have come around. But as we were coming out into the roads the Captain felt it would be prudent for us to do the giving way. He telegraphed down for "half speed both", ordered the helmsman to steer us to port, and we made a course to "nip around her stern", as he put it. ("Nipping" not being quite the expression for a 20-knot container ship easing herself around the back of a 15-knot supertanker.) We managed to perform all this, whereupon the ARPA radar ceased its burbling and fell quiet, telling us the collision was not about to happen after all. *

And by dint of more weaving ourselves for almost an hour through the warp and woof of a dozen more moving ship-tracks, we eventually found ourselves in the southbound fairway, steering south-east. All we had to do now was drive, and worry.

Worry about whether northbound ships would stray into our paths; worry about whether ships ahead of us would go too slowly and risk being poked up the stern; worry about whether big boys behind us would try to race past and shove us into the shallows of the Sumatran mangrove swamps; or whether "little widgers" would play chicken beneath our bows; or if all the navigation lights were working; and if our engines were firing nicely (they weren't: a piston had just burned out in a pyrotechnic spectacular, and the chief and his men had to labour for half a day lifting a new one – taller than a man – up and into the singed cylinder).

But all that apart, things went smoothly enough. The Malaysian towns of Port Dickson and Melaka – or Malacca as it once was, where the rattan canes come from – slipped by to port. The Sumatran villages of Labuhanbilik and Bengkalis gleamed weakly to starboard. The great diesels thundered behind us; the lights of passing ships slid past. The night thinned, the water began to glisten steely grey and a hazy dawn came up over Singapore.

Then, all of a sudden, after six hours' steaming, we were at the Strait's end. We had reached that spot on the Ocean where all Japan-bound ships must turn hard left, where the waters of the Indian Ocean are put behind and the Pacific Ocean, as defined in the terms of this book, finally begins.

It is a place mighty in its inconsequence. There is just a tiny buoy with a radar beacon on top – a buoy known as the South Cardinal

---

* Not long after our journey a very real collision took place at almost the same spot. The 8,350-ton American destroyer the USS *Kinkaid* was hit amidships by a small freighter, the *Kota Petani*. One American was killed, five were injured and the warship, with a jagged gash in her flanks, limped into Singapore for repairs. The US Navy promptly announced a 48-hour suspension of all operations, worldwide, to give its sailors safety lessons.

Beacon, a wretched little thing that bobs about in the waves looking as though it has been long forgotten by its mother. In the old days the imposing stone monster of the Raffles Light would be the left-turn signal: but now the Japan-bound ships keep far away and turn instead at the South Cardinal, which has a light that makes six quick flashes every fifteen seconds, the better to distinguish itself from all the other illuminations of this oriental Coney Island.

Precisely as we reached this point, with the buoy under our bows, so Captain Clark called, "Port Thirty!" to the helmsman, and the *Cardigan Bay* began to shift left, and shift and shift, and shift some more until her head was pointing directly up to the north-east and Tokyo was in the windscreen, more or less.

The Pacific lay ahead. Now that the sun was fully up, the Ocean was burning hot and had a strange steely gleam about it. Tiny islands topped with jungle and then crowned with a gantry and a warning light littered the Roads. The fairway was crowded with ships on their way out, the bridge radar screen a drift of confetti of passing ferryboats and fishermen and of vessels riding glumly at anchor, awaiting new orders. Bumboats crewed by cheerful rogues with importunate grins scurried up to the sides of newly arrived vessels – like ourselves – hoping to make a few dollars bringing the crews ashore for a night in town, or from selling cigarettes, newspapers, or the other delights of civilization.

On this horizon the Pacific is very much the Orient – all Somerset Maugham and Joseph Conrad, all heat and mystery, oleander, silk, cheroots and Tiger Balm, and a whiff of that unmistakable, unforgettable and always strange Pacific perfume compounded of lushness, incense and decay. Lying at anchor in the Singapore Roads, all manner of Pacific fantasy and legend is conjured up.

Oh! what a town it was back then!

Every Oriental costume from the Levant to China floats through the streets of Singapore – robes of silk, satin, brocade and white muslin, emphasized by the glitter of barbaric gold. Parsees in spotless white, Jews and Arabs in dark rich silks, Klings in Turkey red . . . Bombay merchants in turbans and full trousers with crimson silk girdles; Malays in red *sarongs*; Sikhs in pure white Madras muslin, their great height rendered nearly colossal by the classic arrangement of their draperies; and Chinamen of all classes, from the coolie in his blue or brown cotton, to the wealthy merchant in his frothy silk crêpe and rich brocade, make up an irresistibly fascinating medley . . .

Isabella Bird – seemingly one of the great fashion-writers of her age, were this a characteristic passage – got it right. Singapore a century ago was truly irresistible – a faraway colonial possession that was in all ways (not merely the sartorial) extraordinary. It was seductive, alluring, faintly wicked, slightly dangerous and quintessentially Oriental. In its 225 square miles of jungle, village, harbourside and slum, you could rub shoulders with every imaginable manifestation of the Eastern life – Bengalis and Manchus, Javans and Pathans, Hakka, Malacca, Thais and Cantonese. All this vast Babel functioned under the benign supervision of more or less enlightened Englishmen, who by turn administered and exploited their subjects, and in between times played host to visiting armadas and fortune-hunters, occasional desperadoes and innumerable wandering potentates.

Singapore then was joss-stick and opium pipe, bridge and tennis and mah-jongg, a gin sling of an evening and a tiger shot dead under the billiard table in the Raffles Hotel.

That was all a century ago. It was much the same fifty years later too, when the British surrendered the place to the Japanese and General Yamashita renamed the island Syonan, the Light of the South, and sent tens of thousands of his enemies to suffer and die in Changi prison. Then again, when Lord Louis Mountbatten retook the place, opened the prison gates, tore down the rising suns and returned the territory to its rightful name (which appropriately for the Empire, had come from the Sanskrit phrase for Lion City) most of the old magic returned once again, if a little sobered by the War. Wanderers fetching up in the Singapore of the Fifties found it outwardly unchanged – exotic and erotic, hot and steamy, perfumed and malodorous; all jungles, lizards, mangoes and gaudy snakes, and a thousand little boats bobbing on the pale blue mirror of an equatorial sea.

But back in those Fifties and Sixties, the old place *was* changing, and fast. As the complicated politics of the Malayan peninsula cranked out the new post-Imperial order, so new leaders with fresh visions for the place took office. They – and in particular a young Cambridge-educated Hakka named Lee Kuan Yew – began to hammer the exotic into the efficient, and to turn this wayward corner of the world into something of which they, and all the East, could be proud. So roads, skyscrapers, railways and bridges started to replace kampongs, swamps and tracts of tropical grassland, and with frightening speed Singapore began to embrace, experiment with and finally become "modern".

Thus nowadays, while much of the Orient that I could see from the *Cardigan Bay*'s bridge-wings had not greatly changed – Sumatra, just on the southern skyline, is very much as it was, and Johore, a veil of hills to the north, is precious little altered either – Singapore herself has become a very different place. If Mrs Bishop – as Isabella Bird was formally styled – were to alight today from one of the bumboats bobbing below she would be confronted instantly by one of the many sobering realities of modern Singapore: forget the brocades, the frothy crêpes and the colossus-making draperies – most Singaporean men nowadays wear what look like pale imitations of Brooks Brothers suits, while the women dress from the local equivalent of bargain basements at J.C. Penney. Neat, tidy and prosperous they may all look. But Oriental they most certainly do not. And as with the clothes, so with the city: neat and tidy, peaceful and crime-free, prosperous and ordered it may be – but Oriental, sadly, it is no longer.

Hence what is perceived (by Singaporeans) to be Singapore's most pressing current problem. In the headlong – and it must be said, spectacularly successful – rush to modernity and efficiency, Singapore, the world's busiest container port, home of what travellers year after year vote the best airline, the cleanest and most law-abiding of Oriental cities – even more so than Tokyo – has also become, to put it frankly, deadly boring.

This has been suspected, rather uneasily, by most strangers who have flown here during the last five or six years. Something of the exotic vitality, the magic spark, seemed to be going out of the old place. No one really managed – or dared – to say how or why that might be until a few months ago. Then suddenly it became more or less official: in the late Eighties the *Economist*, no less, published the results of a survey suggesting that Singapore was the "World's Most Boring Place" (or, as a captious friend pointed out, "Second Most Boring", since the "Most Boring" would be intrinsically interesting by virtue of being so honoured).

Anyway, "Most" or "Second Most" or whatever, what stung the locals – as at least a dozen told me in highly indignant tones – was that Singapore was said to be *even more boring than Libya*.

But, one had to say that this was very nearly so. It was all so dreadfully *regulated*, so marvellously ordered. No litter. No spitting.

No music. No hawker stalls. No smoke. No incense. Huge notices in the parks displayed long lists of the dozens of prohibitions in force. Taxi drivers were forbidden to play their radios in their cars. The slums were all torn down. Cameras were installed in public-housing elevators to make sure no passengers misbehaved, and urine-detectors were put in some of them as well, to stop the lifts between floors and trap the incontinent miscreants until the police arrived. The bumboats, with their wicked lascar skippers and their immense gypsy-like families, were moved on from their moorings on the Singapore River since they polluted the stream so badly. The people who had once lived so colourfully on the water were asked to live in hutches high up in cliff-like tower blocks, like the cave-dwellers of the North-West frontier. A word last referred to with admiration in pre-War Bavaria – *eugenics* – began to be heard again in Singapore, as it was suggested by social planners that bright parents might be encouraged to bear children, those with few "O" levels positively discouraged, and that meetings and possible marriages of young graduates be organized through a programme of government-subsidized sea cruises; for a few dollars you could go on a cruise for a week and encounter and consolidate a relationship with a suitable breeding partner.

The *Love Boat*, as it was christened, set sail each week, and if you were bright, and single, you could apply to cruise up the Malay coast for a few days for even fewer dollars. The Singapore government would hope that you would then meet someone of the opposite sex aboard and – given the erotic effect of the sea-swells and the soothing zephyrs – would start on the road towards procreation and the ultimate demographic betterment of Singapore. To the eugenicists' chagrin, there were disappointingly few takers, however.

All this may or may not have been laudable for Singaporeans, but it was rapidly inducing terminal narcolepsy among those who came to visit. Back in the Seventies, airline passengers bound between Europe and Australia did so quite contentedly. They came and stayed, on average, for four days. They shopped for cheap cameras and scent; grazed through the remarkable variety of restaurants and had their first (and probably only) tastes of sea-slug and lemon-grass; flirted safely with the mild dangers of Eastern vice. In particular they went to the infamously iniquitous Bugis Street, where they ordered a Tiger beer or two, sat out in the warmth of the equatorial evening and ogled the nightly procession of women – some of whom, of course, were not women at all – who glittered and teetered past in *cheongsam* and six-inch heels, touting for custom from the sailors.

But then the government, in another fit of modernizing frenzy, tore down Bugis Street – and suddenly there was no longer a single thing which seemed worth doing in Singapore.

Word soon got around and passengers stopped disembarking from the long-haul jets. The cruise ships started to talk of calling less frequently; those travellers who stayed did so for two days and not four; the hotels began to empty and discounts were on offer everywhere. (A couple of years ago I complained that my room in the Hilton was noisy: I was offered a 50 per cent discount, then 90 per cent, and ended up paying $8 a night, so terrified was the management of losing such revenue as a single guest provided.)

The local exchequer – which reckoned to get a sixth of its foreign exchange from tourists – started to panic and in 1984 set up a task force to investigate. The report, which came out in record time three years later, made sobering reading: there was a "deep malaise" which required "urgent action". The government had torn down everything worth seeing, the prices in the shops were too high, there were no taxis. All was now concrete and glass, shopping centres and leisure complexes. The new Singapore was no more exotic than Tulsa or a Harlow New Town, but with rather worse humidity. Small wonder that no one wanted to go there.

The government came up with a plan whereby it agreed to spend a billion Singapore dollars – $450 million – to preserve, to revivify, to refurbish and recreate. The plan was said to be "chockful of leisure ideas" and there were schemes to create plenty of new "attractions". Local beaches were to be made "more alluring" and something called a "coralarium" was to be built near one of them. Raffles Hotel was being transformed into "the Crown Jewel of the visitor industry" or – somewhat more mysteriously – "the anchor in the heritage link". Bumboat cruises on the Singapore River were to be resumed. Preservation programmes in Chinatown, Little India and Arab Street were started to ensure that the "original ambience" was maintained.

Critics remarked that it seemed very much as though the city-state of Singapore was being turned, panic-stricken, into a vast Oriental theme park, another Eastern Disneyland (Tokyo has a real Disneyland, in Chiba, on the east side of the Bay). It can be costly to criticize Singapore (many newspapers and magazines – the *Asian Wall Street Journal* and the *Far Eastern Economic Review* in particular – have had recent cause to reflect on having dared cock a snook at Lee Kuan Yew: both were banned; the latter sued) and it would be churlish not to admire the Singapore government's efforts during the last two decades; it has built for its people a new city, helped to create for them a stunning success, yet in so doing ruined that part of itself which seemed to its planners (mistakenly) less relevant to its future fortunes. An error was made then, and a major effort is now being made to correct it.

Gazing up from the ship, wondering at the gleaming skyscrapers which were even now twinkling in the morning sun, it was difficult to imagine that Singapore ever really had a past. From where I stood on the *Cardigan Bay*'s bridge, this gleaming vista just might be that of a city newly risen from the shore, a town utterly without history, an instant vision of the success and dynamism of tomorrow's brave new Pacific world.

5

Across Siberia

Liverpool Street station, an old and smelly warehouse of a terminus in a grey corner of East London, has no Edwardian bas-reliefs on its grimy walls, displaying Elysian visions of departing passengers' destinations. Euston once had an arch (now demolished) that listed all the faraway halts on the Midland Railway; and there are splendid old stations across Europe and America which soothe or tempt their clients with paintings of distant corniches, prairies, canyons and steppes, the implication being that a ticket bought *here* might – with a little invention and a lot of time – ultimately take you *there*, with all the attendant magic and romance.

But at Liverpool Street there is nothing, except for dog-eared gravure prints of the Backs at Cambridge and views of The Wash. Certainly there are no portraits of Polynesian girls with orchids behind their left ears, thick black hair tumbling across their mahogany breasts, smiling down on the morning rush-hour crowds from above the posters for Alka-Seltzer and Pears Soap, and Awayday excursions to Cromer and Clacton. There are no gouache illustrations of palm trees leaning into the trade winds, no mosaic representations of white sand beaches and skies of rain-washed blue. Neither hint nor suggestion, in short, that it might be possible to reach the shores of the Pacific Ocean aboard a train that begins its journey here.

Yet it can be done, and with comparative ease. You start by proceeding to Platform 9 in the main line engine-shed and board the 9.40 am boat-train to Harwich and the Hook of Holland; or, more precisely, by buying a ticket for one of the longest rail journeys on earth, and one that links – in a more symbolic and spectacular manner than the great trans-American and Canadian lines – the Atlantic and the Pacific Oceans.

I had already begun to work on getting the necessary tickets and visas (for East Germany, Poland, the Soviet Union, the Mongolian People's Republic* and China) when a colleague suggested I might like to try to buy a through ticket from the window at the station itself. It seemed both fatuous and facetious; but I allowed myself to be persuaded, and one rainy afternoon stood in a queue behind figures buying weekly seasons to Southend and Diss. We all shuffled forward, inch by wearying inch, until I reached the window and peered down. I assumed as haughty an accent as I could muster: "One single, first class, to Hong Kong, please," I requested brightly.

The man barely looked up. "Oh yes, guv," he said, in a tone which might have been tiredness, or scorn, or both, "and was you wishing to proceed via Khabarovsk, or go the long way via Ulan Bator?"

He had me. I was forced to retreat, to mumble something about not being quite sure, and that I would have to find out, when he barked, "Next!" and the man behind me stepped up and demanded two cheap-day returns to King's Lynn.

Next day, though, armed with a sheaf of tickets from an agency in London that specialized in such things, I was aboard the 9.40 am boat-train, sitting down to a British Rail breakfast and idly watching the marshy outskirts of north-east London speed by in the rain.

Three days later and a stone obelisk on the right-hand side of a low Ural hill marked the end of Europe, the beginning of Asia, the start of Siberia, the beginnings of places which had been and would now be influenced by the Pacific. And, as if on cue, the weather turned more extreme. The larch forests were thick with powder snow, while those legions of admirable ladies who sweep it from the switches and grease the signal levers wore trousers under their skirts, acknowledging the chill.

The train was always on time, at every station – though, since the system runs to *Vremya Moskovskaya* or Moscow time, steady progress across the time zones occasionally became more confusing. We arrived at Novosibirsk, for instance, at what the clocks on both train and station said was 10 am, except that the setting sun suggested it was much later – and indeed enquiry indicated all Novosibirsk was sitting down to tea, it being locally 3 pm. To add to the mix of chronological mayhem, the train's dining car runs to local time

*Which in the vernacular is Bügd Nayramdakh Mongol Ard Uls, and was written thus on the clip-in visas that the Mongolian Embassy eventually issued.

and opens for dinner each evening at 6 pm. No matter that watches, clocks, stomachs all believed it to be lunchtime – the buxom lady was serving dinnertime caviar and borscht and then closing for the night, with no further food till breakfast, which began at about 1 am.

I stopped at Irkutsk for three days – getting acclimatized, I kidded myself. Irkutsk folk are not unlike those people from Dallas, ever boastful, and with reason. Everything there is bigger, colder or wider than anywhere else in the Union. I liked it, thought it a happy sort of place, and spent many hours strolling through the deep Siberian snow, which by day sparkled in the sunlight and at night gleamed silver under a giant moon. A Dutch friend I had made on the interminable passage across Poland and Western Russia left here, for he was continuing on Train 20 to Peking: I waved him farewell as the massive express slipped slowly away through a blizzard, and saw him shake the hands of new-found chums, a Buryat couple with the eyes and noses of the Far East, now not so distant.

Next was a slow and local mail train bound for Mongolia – no "soft" class here, but the conductor gave me all four berths of a hard-class compartment, plenty of room for the baggage and plenty for me. The train was full of Red Army soldiers bound for the eastern border – for there was still some tension in Moscow's relations with China, no matter that the situation in Europe had altered so radically. They were an amiable bunch who shared food with me (for on this local train there was no such luxury as a restaurant car) and were entranced with Polaroid pictures and the silver-covered almonds I had bought from Fortnums in London. They sang soft melodies at night, and were delighted when I persuaded the technicians who controlled the train's PA system to put a Beatles cassette on it and we all listened as "Hey, Jude" wafted out across the Trans-Baikal mountains.

Dawn came up in Ulan Bator, the coldest capital city on earth. I stayed a few days, bracing myself for temperatures at which steel snaps like china, skin goes hard and leatherlike and speech becomes impossible after only moments in the wind.

The United States did not until very recently recognize Outer Mongolia, regarding it merely as a province of China. There is an American ambassador now, but when I visited Ulan Bator there was, as since the war, but one resident Western envoy – a Briton – and I called on him in his splendid white-painted Embassy. He was a magnificent figure, the very image of Charles Laughton, and he gave me lunch, with no suggestion of an appointment. "Don't see many strangers here, old man," he explained. "Let's hear the gossip from home." I rather fancied his eyes glistened a little as we left, for he wouldn't see another stranger – especially in winter – for many weeks and months to come. "Think of us," were his last words as he closed the Embassy door. "Think of us."

Of all the railway trains running anywhere, my next conveyance, the once-weekly express that plies between Moscow and Peking via the Mongolian capital – unnamed, and known only as Train Number 4 – must be one of the finest. Its compartments are panelled with wood, its adornments are all solid brass, its restaurant cars serve caviar and champagne (once beyond the Soviet border, that is), its elderly Chinese staff (for it is the proudest express of the Peking Railway administration) are impeccable in manner and quietly attentive to their duty. Everything was spotless – even the coal-fired samovars seemed fed with scrubbed nuggets of fuel – and the two days were an episode of seamless luxury.

From Train Number 4, I watched the camel trains wandering purposefully across the Gobi skyline; I was duly fascinated once again by the bogie-changing operation at the Chinese frontier (for China runs on Euro-rails, her railway administration having learned its lessons from Western imperialists); and from within this express I was amused to hear loudspeakers at the border welcoming me into the world's biggest People's Republic to the most incongruous tune of that great London pub song "Roll out the Barrel". Next morning I was able to take my breakfast – such is the magic of this train – in the very shadow of the Great Wall itself, talking pidgin to the gentle Mongol attendants in the restaurant car.

However the next train, a domestic Chinese monster that took me from Peking down, away from the cold of North China to the palm trees of the south, was very different, best forgotten. There were the same German-built carriages, massive and secure; yet these were not pleasantly seedy but uncared-for and dirty, the corridors jammed with smokers, the dining cars awash with animal bones and puddles of rice. It seemed a longer journey than it was, a rude introduction to the reality of China, one I was glad to end.

Finally, after some shunting and doubling-back in the marshalling yards of Canton, the train chugged up to the last frontier. High on a hill above a grey and grubby river, I could see at last a solitary Union Jack and a tiny fort from which came the occasional glint as a British soldier swept the view with his binoculars – not, it should be said, to warn of war, but to keep out those immigrants who otherwise would stream in illegally from China, bound for the fleshpots of Hong Kong. The Iron Curtain here – along with Korea's, one of the two remaining in the world – was built by the non-Communist side, and is aimed at keeping people Out, not In.

For a few moments I was on foot – shunting and shuffling my bags across the Friendship Bridge and then having men of the Hong Kong government stamp my passport, and policemen with royal crowns adorning their cap-badges wave me through and on to the final train of the Kowloon and Canton Railway Company – the first on the entire run not owned and operated by the state.

Air-conditioned, quiet as silk, painted a glistening red and gaudy with advertisements for Coca-Cola, McDonald's, Tissot and Gucci, the border train took just thirty minutes to complete the final run.

As, softly, it shushed against the terminal buffers, I calculated I was 8,565 railway miles out from Platform 9, Liverpool Street – a station opened by Queen Victoria – and here I was on Platform 2, Kowloon, opened six years before by that great lady's great-great-grand-daughter. But, as one might expect in this most bustling of cities, there was no time to admire the foundation stone, for a red limousine had already drawn up at the kerb and an elderly, uniformed Chinese driver was enquiring if I was the gentleman from London, and if so welcome, and would I care to be driven through the tunnel across to Hong Kong island, and to see what I had come all this way to see – the Pacific Ocean, in all its South Chinese manifestation?

Victoria Peak may not be the highest point of the British Crown Colony of Hong Kong – Tai Mo Shan, under whose shadow I had passed on the last leg of the rail journey, is fully twice as high at 3,140 feet – but it is and long has been *The Peak*, the only hill that matters. "It rises 1,200 feet above the level of the sea* and stretches its solid bulk across the whole line of the city, effectually shutting out the south-west breeze – and all the cool air to be had during the six months of a most oppressive summer when everyone gasps for want of that needful aliment." In the heyday of the Empire the Chinese were banned from living above the 788-ft contour line, and the Europeans built immense mansions there with names like "Skyhigh",

*Actually 1,181 feet, though Sir Rutherford Alcock's *The Capital of the Tycoon* was written in 1863, before the surveys had achieved today's accuracy.

"Cloudlands" and "The Eyrie". They were – and to a declining degree, still are – members of a community given to ostentation, profligacy and occasional madness. In the 1860s a Mr Belilios, a Jew who had amassed a considerable fortune and by his riches managed to soothe the anti-semitic attitudes of the older colonials, kept a camel which hauled his goods and chattels up and down the steep slopes, and which spat as enthusiastically as the Chinese sedan-chair porters in whose path it stoically trod.

The High Level Tramway – now better-known as the Peak Tram – was built to help the Europeans dispense with camels and sedan chairs. Opened in 1888, it provided then as now a tram which departed every fifteen minutes for a terminus built in a *cwm* just shy of the summit. The journey takes eight minutes and at times the rails slide upwards to a near-impossible gradient of one in two, at which point the steel hawser that hauls up the tramcar and its fifty passengers sings out with the strain and rises so high in the air that rollers have to be fixed to the archways of some of the bridges to stop the cable wearing away the stonework.

It was to the Tram that the driver took me, and advised me to sit behind the Governor's bench (promptly cleared for His Excellency should he ever wish to ride). We rose with a whoosh: the air, which at sea level was pleasingly balmy like a spring day in Manhattan, became quickly less warm, and as we rose at alarming angles through the high-rise jungles of Upper Victoria and Mid-Levels so it became immediately clear why the *taipans* had long favoured The Peak for their houses – the same reason they chose Murree, Simla, Ootacamund and Kandy: because it was so much cooler than below.

But "cool" in the tropics means mist: the warm and wet south-westerly breezes, pushed upwards 1,800 feet or so to where the temperature is two or three degrees centigrade lower, precipitate their moisture as a fine grey blanket of mist which hangs on The Peak like a thick growth of moss from April to September. Residents whose houses are so grand must shut away their decent clothes to keep down the mildew: strange amphibian creatures are discovered in bookshelves and in storage bins; walls bulge and peel every few months as the insidious, creeping fog strips away the paint. The case of Jarndyce versus Jarndyce might as well have been contested up on The Peak in the summertime as in the foetid courts of Limehouse, so dank and dismal does the place become, so invisible the surrounds, so foreshortened the view.

But this midwinter's day was quite different. The air was clear and bright, almost frothing with freshness and zest. The northward view from the ascending tram was brilliant, never-ending – an immense panorama of skyscrapers and winding roadways, the deep blue harbour crisscrossed by the white trails of speedboats, hoverfoils and Star Ferries, the low buildings of Kowloon, the jets rising and falling above the ends of the arrow-straight runway of Kai Tak, and then beyond, like an old Chinnery watercolour, the brown, green and blue hills of the New Territories and China fading into the far distance, limitless and enigmatic, like China herself.

The Reverend James Legge, who lived in Queen Victoria's Hong Kong for more than thirty years – he left shortly before her Golden Jubilee – once wrote: "I sometimes imagine Britannia standing on The Peak and looking down with an emotion of pride upon the great Babylon which her sons have built." Even more so today: the sight of Hong Kong from the summit of her peak is one of the most heart-stopping views on the planet, so immense and so concentrated an amalgam of man's best and worst, richest and poorest crammed on to the narrow plain halfway up the steep hill below. And the unending sound: a huge urban roar that resounds upwards like a prolonged shout, yet stuttered and punctuated with the chattering of 10,000 pneumatic drills as they tear, rend and smash up more of the old city to make way for another layer of the new.

But it was not towards the north that I was here to look. I had to climb another 600 feet from the tram terminus at Victoria Gap (truly the very last terminus out from Liverpool Street, thus making my total journey out from London a triumphal 8,600 miles) up to Victoria Peak itself. Here the granite had been grassed over and arranged with trees that were still an approximation of the ancient pleasaunce the British had created, a walking ground for meditation and escape where profit and restlessness do not quite intrude, where one may simply stand and stare. There is wild indigo and daphne, frothy bushes of jasmine and banks of rhododendron, and at the very peak a small stall selling cold drinks and bars of chocolate, a shelter with a pair of telescopes, and a gravel walkway shaped like a dumb-bell, with the huge gantries of the Cable and Wireless signal station on the north side and on the south side – the Pacific Ocean.

Here it was at last, sparkling and shimmering in the late afternoon light, so very blue, so splendidly and subtly alive and energetic, and yet above all so very *Pacific*. So different – and in so profound a slew of ways – from the last great sea I had crossed, between Harwich and the Hook: back there all seemed greyness and salt, swell and gale and seagulls, with rusty old ships battering their way past wicked sandbars and shoals along the antique trade routes linking crumbling unromantic ports, places like Rotterdam and Felixstowe and Blyth and Esbjerg, and the dour old dockyards of Rostock, Immingham and Kiel. Here the sea was a thing of colour and beauty, its surface tinged by the gold of the late sun: a third of a mile below me, the water's surface was coiled with the sinews of unseen currents, its hammered-steel surface serrated by the tracks of immense long-haul ships bound to and from the great ports of the world – Yokohama, San Francisco, Calcutta and Panama, places as romantic and perfumed with intrigue as any in the world. But lest one imagine the Pacific here was only a roadway for great commerce, there were also scores of tiny fishing craft converging on Aberdeen harbour, all scurrying home with their catches in time for tea.

Dark islands formed crouching silhouettes as the sun inched down towards the south-west. I was looking due south: slightly off to the west was Lamma, with its two-chimneyed coal-fired power station, wild heathy hills, fishing villages and score of restaurants (on the shores of Picnic Bay) serving the best sea-food Hong Kong's ever-hungry masses can buy. To the east there is the shoulder of Chung Hom Kok with its radar aerials and the dishes with which British Intelligence eavesdrops on the world; further over still lies the hump of Stanley where the British Army has its finest barracks and whence Cable and Wireless sends and receives all the telephone, telex and facsimile traffic from and for Hong Kong's six million. A little further still, past Beaufort Island and the Hakka-run island of Po Toi is the strange little doubled-up skerry of Waglan, where the Imperial Lighthouse Service once built their most easterly bastion of granite and concrete and silvered glass. The Waglan Island Light survives still,* and

*Though no longer manned: the last keeper went back to Kowloon in 1989; computers run Waglan now, and sound its foghorn when the winter mists hang low across the approaches to the Roads.

even as I watched it began its evening flashing, marking the boundary of Empire, defining the edge of the sea where the Queen's Writ ran.

But due south the sea opened up to a wide expanse of ever-darkening blue, a few faraway islands staining its surface with small black shadows. This, indeed, was the outer rim of the Pacific Ocean, though but a very tiny part of it. The coast I could glimpse from this eyrie – perhaps thirty miles from west to east – was the merest fraction of the coastline, the sea ahead a pitiful fraction of the volume and might of an ocean that is almost unimaginably huge.

Such unthinkable immensity, and I was at the edge of it, perched high above a tiny corner called the South China Sea, an entity bordered by the islands of Taiwan, Luzon, Palawan, Borneo and Sumatra, and by the Malay peninsula, Cambodia, Vietnam and South China. What I was seeing, though it was growing fainter by the minute, was but a minuscule portion of the Pacific – yet a portion that was nonetheless four times as large as the North Sea from which this journey had commenced.*

Now the lights were coming on in the houses and tenement blocks of Aberdeen and Repulse Bay. The fishing boats were all in and a large junk – so-called, really just a junk hull with a tall poop-deck and a big motor, and minus the distinctive sails – was dipping in towards the quay at the Marina Club, having given some newly arrived businessmen the obligatory tour of the harbour. Out in the deep fairway of the Lamma Channel the big ships were still crawling inbound and outbound, monster container vessels, tankers, bulk carriers and tramps linking Hong Kong with the great outside, icons of the trade that gave this colony – the world's classic entrepôt state – its first breath of life.

Watching the ships rumble their way silently down the Channel reminded me that in the car which had brought me from the station I had glanced through the ten-page supplement, *Trade & Transport*, which readers of the *South China Morning Post* receive twice each

---

*The South China Sea, at 895,000 square miles, is the largest of the component seas of the Pacific: only the Bering Sea, at 876,000 square miles, comes close. By comparison, the Mediterranean is 967,000 square miles, the Red Sea 169,000 and the Baltic 163,000 – a fifth the size of the South China.

week and which most of them throw away. But some do not, and for them it is a supplement offering far greater rewards than the blandness of the rest of the paper, which is one of the most profitable in the Murdoch empire (Murdoch being a quintessentially Pacific operator, and a man much taken with providing news and information for the thousand-million-odd citizens of China). For the supplement lists, in a series of a hundred or so advertisements, the forthcoming voyages of each and every ship – including those that crawled below – which plans to arrive at and depart from Hong Kong.

It is a wonderful ten pages of utter escape, a dissertation on faraway and carefree romance that must provide vicarious bliss (or savage frustration) for a rock-bound Peak resident, shut in by mist and lack of money and condemned to near-eternity in the congestion and unending din of Hong Kong. Whose heart would not race a little on reading of the *Trident Dolphin* now loading for Aqaba, or the impending arrival of the MV *Atacama*, flagship of the Great Andean Service, bound for Valparaiso?

The advertisement showing the sailing times of the *Atacama* caught my eye. It was such a fine name. The very idea of a shipping line offering something called a Great Andean Service seemed pioneering and bold, and grandly titled too, like the Bombay, Baroda and Central India Railway, or the Irrawaddy Steam Navigation Company. It had a ring to it – a peculiarly Pacific ring, a bit of dash and style. And it offered, as it happened, a revelation.

For when I looked more carefully at the front page of the supplement, one fact became abundantly clear. Almost all the major journeys to and from Hong Kong were now Pacific journeys: ships that plied to the old country, to England, Africa and India, were fewer now than once they had been. There seemed a maritime rebirth going on, a change of emphasis, an abandonment of one set of ties and the construction of another.

The *Oriental Knight*, for instance, was bound for Sydney, Melbourne and Brisbane; *Mulpha Kuang* for Manila; *Al Mirqab* for Singapore; *Kyowa Hibiscus* for Honiara, Pago Pago and Apia; the *Oceania Express* was off to Yap, Koror, Truk, Pohnpei, Kosrae and Majuro; the *Makalu* would leave in a day or so for Los Angeles and San Diego; the *Tendai Maru* was bound for Suva, Wellington and Dunedin; *Asian Jade* for Adelaide; *Ming Chun* for Yokohama; *Glory Ace* to Kobe;

Yi Chun to Pusan; *Promoter* and *Chungking* for Port Moresby and Rabaul.*

Page after page of ships criss-crossing the Pacific Ocean then followed. To be sure, there were big vessels still plying back and forth to Southampton, Hamburg and Bremerhaven – no suggestion that the links with Europe or Atlantic America were diminishing. But what did seem clear was the increase of business, of trade, of shipping connections within and across the Pacific Ocean itself. The ley-lines had long been there – my old *Times* school atlas displays the main routes, Los Angeles to Sydney, Honolulu to Panama, Tokyo to Vancouver. But today there are many more such twinned cities, a dense network of skeins of shipping routes and trading networks, the warp and weft of a new fabric of global commerce. These days there are formal and regular maritime links between such ports as Shanghai and Iquique, Kagoshima and Port Hedland (of which more later), Bundaberg and Astoria, Nauru and Oakland, Ulsan and Auckland and – in a revival of the most venerable of all trans-Pacific shipping services, the Manila Galleons – Manila to Acapulco.

There is also a route plotted on today's navigational charts between the towns of Port Hedland in Western Australia and Kashima in Central Japan. It is this route, between two ports that were unknown and unsung as little as two decades ago, which provides for us the framework of a characteristic and illustrative course of today's Pacific. The story of what lies between these two small and ill-remembered ports, and on the course that ships' masters make to pass from one to the other, tells much of the story of the Ocean and its fortunes as it comes of age, and of the course that the Pacific and its member-nations seem destined now to take.

*There were also six ships in Hong Kong waters that day – the *Ever Govern*, *Ever Lyric*, *Ever Guide*, *Ever Gleeful*, *Ever Vigour* and the delightful-sounding *Ever Gleamy* – that belonged to the most successful (and mysteriously-owned) shipping company in the world, the Taiwan-based Evergreen Line. It is the only company that runs express round-the-world services, east-bound and west-bound: its ships are always on time, charge far less than anybody else, and are kept as gleaming as a new pin.

CONNECTIONS

ONE: Bands of Steel

I

The Cutting Edge

It is still possible to find prospectors in the outback of the Northern Territories and Western Australia – real, unadorned, curmudgeonly prospectors of the old school. They come into town once in a while, perhaps to stake a claim or to order up an assay – furtive old fellows, grizzled of beard and leathery of skin, each one with a burro (or, these days, a plane), an adze and an army surplus trenching tool, a patched tent and a burned-out billycan, with water bottles and claim pegs dangling from the saddle stock, and a hessian bag of samples clutched tight in gnarled, red-rimmed old hands.

Most prospectors, in Australia as everywhere else, wither and die on the land they once scoured for their living. But some – the men who struck it rich, who found the gold, or the uranium, or the iron – have become legendary figures, folk heroes of great wealth and power, exemplars of the Great Australian Dream. One such is Lang Hancock, the man who discovered iron in the blazing remoteness of a tract of western Australian range country they call the Pilbara.

Mr Hancock is a big man, in more ways than one (his biography is titled *Rogue Bull*). He is known throughout the country for his extreme views, his impatience, his frustration, his friendship with the hydrogen-bomb king Edward Teller, his professed immunity to radioactivity and his oft-expressed scorn for the "eco-nuts" who would hinder the wholesale excavation of Australia. He is, as one might imagine, an inexhaustible source of colourful quotations – and by happy chance the author of a thought that will serve as a convenient epitaph for modern Australia and the country's principal role in the Pacific.

"My message remains the same . . ." he told an English author who visited his mansion at Wittenoon – a mansion so astonishingly appointed that, were iron as glamorous a commodity as oil, it might be Australia's Southfork – "Dig or Die. The fundamental basis on which all modern civilization rests is *mining*. Without minerals we could not harvest our food, till our soil, build our machines, supply our energy, transport our goods.

"Our horn of plenty starts with a hole in the ground."

Like it or not, Australia has long been a country better known for her mining towns than for the grace and charm of her principal cities. Schoolchildren know all the names: Ballarat and Bendigo, Broken Hill and Kalgoorlie, Mount Isa and Mary Kathleen.*

The dominant image of Australia with which I and most of my generation grew up was of an agreeably rough place, stiff with quarries and spoil heaps, littered with winding gear, blasting caps, ore trains and the brutish romance of rough-and-ready company towns which had been set down miles from anywhere, in huge ochre plains that they referred to as being at "the back of Bourke" or "beyond the black stump". If Sydney Opera House ("that bunch of nuns in a rugger scrum", as someone called it) had been built, then it hadn't managed to struggle into my schoolboy consciousness. True, the Harbour Bridge (the famous coathanger) had always been there, though in my imagination it served to frame a steady stream of ore carriers constantly lumbering away down through the Heads with thousands of tons of the continent aboard, and orders to dump them down on the far sides of the world.

Even today, much though Australians would like to think of themselves as sophisticated participants in the mainstream of world affairs, the mind's eye is fixed rather less on the country's modern achievements than on the benefits and challenges of her geology. Ayers Rock. The Nullarbor Plain. The Barrier Reef. The Big Red Centre. The Kimberleys. Coober Pedy. These are what many an outsider still thinks of when asked to contemplate "Australia".

And as with the image, so with the reality. So far as the Pacific is concerned Australia is a place to excavate and to mine, a place that will serve the region best if it is allowed to become what its people so desperately *won't* want it to become – a great big hole

---

*The town, now shrunk to a population of a mere 800, was one of Australia's main uranium centres until 1962: it was named in 1954 after the wife of the prospector who found the ore body, Norman McConachy.

in the ground. "A bloody great quarry is what we are now," said a dyspeptic Queenslander who was showing me around. "And a bloody big spoil-tip is what they'll leave behind." Or as Gough Whitlam, perhaps the country's most interesting prime minister, once said, "Australia spent the first half of the century as a farm for the British. Now it looks as though we may spend the second half as a quarry for the Japanese."

The biggest iron-ore mine in the world is in Australia, at a place called Newman. A prospector named Stan Hilditch happened on the outcrop of ore in 1957 – ore that was so rich his hammer almost rang when it struck it – on the flanks of a 10-mile hill called Mount Whaleback. The mountain is memorably distant from civilization: a bus from Perth, speeding along the empty roads at 60 miles an hour, takes 15 hours to get there. (And Perth is a long way from anywhere too: closer to Singapore than to any other big Australian city, it is said to be the most isolated regional capital in the world, and was once asked to turn all its lights on for American astronauts so that it could be seen from space, a brilliant pinprick in a sea of otherwise total blackness.)

Hilditch's discovery was on a truly enormous scale: Mount Whaleback and all the other ridges of the Ophthalmia Range were smeared with the rich black bands of some of the highest grades of ore known. There were incalculable quantities of the stuff: more than enough for this empty immensity they call "the Gaba"* to offer an endless supply of cheap iron to every imaginable customer between Shanghai and Santiago. But when news of the find became known it caused precious little excitement – no more and no less than that which triggered when, twenty years before, Lang Hancock had made his celebrated find over at Mount Tom Price, 100 miles to the west. For the simple fact was that no matter how much ore might be buried beneath "Australia Fair", the world wasn't about to get any of it. A total ban on iron-ore exports had been official Australian policy since 1938.

The reasoning behind the Australian ban is complicated, and was based on a policy of specific economic hostility – by the United States – towards the then rising star of Japan. It is still thought by some historians to have had a not insignificant influence on the events leading to the start of the Pacific War. According to today's

*Standing for the Great Australian Bugger-All.

explanations – not available to the frustrated prospectors at the time
– Japanese diplomats heard in 1930 all about the possibility that huge
reserves of iron might be found in the deserts of Western Australia.
Approaches were made by Japanese steelmakers and mining companies – principally to Broken Hill Proprietary Ltd, the biggest of
their Australian opposite numbers – suggesting that a joint venture
be formed, thus guaranteeing Japan a regular supply of a mineral that
her burgeoning industries badly needed and which, for the Japanese,
was expensive and scarce.

But Washington, half a world away, would not countenance such
a deal. Half a century had elapsed since Commodore Perry's "black
ships" had forced Japan to emerge into the real world, and it was
now becoming all too clear to America that the newly-emergent
Japan was rapidly blossoming into a very powerful force indeed.
Too powerful, Washington decreed: ways must be found to inhibit
her exuberant growth, to curb her ambitions. One such way was
to demand of Australia that she resist such Japanese blandishments.
For, as the Americans saw it, a Japan with guaranteed iron supplies
would be an even more dangerous nation than was then imagined.
Australia fell into line, but in a curiously dog-in-manger manner:
Canberra banned all iron-ore exports, but to the rest of the world
as well as to Japan, pleading rather weakly, on the strength of a
report by a government geologist named Mr Woolnough, that her
own resources were far too low for her own needs.

It is now acknowledged that the consequence was quite the reverse
of what Washington had intended. The notion that a Japan guaranteed iron would be dangerous evolved into a reality that a Japan
denied iron would be even more so – for, denied something she
so badly needed, she simply armed herself and prepared to go out
and get it. Hence (without too much hyperbole) the beginnings
of the Greater East Asia Co-Prosperity Sphere, hence Nipponese
Pacific ambitions and militancy, hence Pearl Harbor, hence the
Pacific War, the atomic bomb . . . the direct and indirect consequences of the discoveries of those old prospectors were great
indeed.

But with the Pacific War over and with *realpolitik* making itself felt
in Canberra, so the apparent need for the iron embargo diminished.
The ban was reluctantly relaxed in 1960 (although some in the
Australian government still believed firmly in Mr Woolnough's
twenty-year-old warning that there might not be enough iron for

Australia's needs alone). Immediately – indeed with almost indecent haste – Stan Hilditch promptly staked his claim to Mount Whaleback, and was granted a reserve a year later: it was a claim that was to make him an immense personal fortune, and to create in Western Australia the true foundation stone of the Pacific economic boom. The haematite ore he had discovered – originally assumed to be so far from civilization as not even to be worth the attentions of a single pick and shovel – was found by the assayers to contain no less than 64 per cent iron: small wonder it clanged against the prospectors' hammers. Within weeks, platoons of astonished geologists quickly identified no fewer than 44 ore bodies on and around Mount Whaleback: 3,450,000,000 tons of ore that would yield perhaps 1,500,000,000 tons of iron. The potential for building 700,000,000 Toyota Corollas lay beneath a single mountain range. What once had appeared a find of no economic significance at all turned out to be the single most important source of iron in the hemisphere.

If the mine itself – as the Pacific's, and the world's, largest – is reckoned to lie at the very base of the Ocean's economic success, then the small corps of men who work on the actual faces, hewing the ore away from its cliffs, can be considered the true cornerstones of the edifice – or, to change to a more comfortable metaphor, the men who are literally at the cutting edge. In the same way as curiosity impels the discovery of the sources of rivers, the highest peaks or the most remote promontories, so I felt impelled, when I first visited the Ophthalmia Range, to discover the man who on that particular day stood at the cutting edge of the Pacific boom.

He was called Alan Thompson, and a few years before he was hired for this particular job – a job that was endowed with a symbolism of which, he confessed, he was blissfully unaware – he had been that most lowly of Australian stereotypes, a kangaroo-shooter.

"Lower even than the dunny man, I was – a real larrikin, a wild bushman, even worse than an abbo." He worked for a petfood firm, conducting his slaughter for the culinary pleasures of unseen poodle dogs.

It was the simplest kind of work. He would spend his days in beer-fuddled idleness, then take his battered pickup out at night to hunt for 'roos. He would dazzle the creatures with a spotlight, pick them off with his rifle; when his "eye was in" he could kill sixty a night. Then he would sleep, take the carcasses off to the depot in the morning and buy more beer for the day ahead. "I was low, very low. You believe me, I was low."

Today, however, Alan Thompson plays an altogether different role – one which, though he is unaware of it, is earning him a small but not insignificant place in the economic history of the world. He is one of a *corps d'elite* among the great contingent of Australian mine workers; it is he who, with perhaps a dozen others on each of the four daily shifts, claws from the red Australian earth the very metal to make the products which so aptly symbolize the new Pacific boom. From his shovel – though shovel is hardly the word for the immense electric-powered Harnishfeger crane that costs $2,000,000 and can scoop up sixty tons of ore at a time – pour the raw beginnings of scores of millions of Sony Walkmans, Nissan Sentras, Daewoo computers and Hyundai supertankers that are apparently in demand everywhere from Aberdeen to Acapulco.

He had taken a job with the Newman iron-ore mine, far out in the remotest outback, ten years earlier. His decision was made very much on a whim: it seemed just possible that a long-term living might be made in iron ore, something more respectable than the hunting of *Macropus cangaru*.* He was more right than he knew. Newman has since become the biggest iron mine in the world, the greatest opencast pit in a country that, whether it likes it or not, is coming to be regarded as a continent-sized opencast pit – a pit designed for no other purpose than to supply the Pacific economies with raw commodities. Alan Thompson is thus the very first link in a complicated chain of manufacturing and trading that stretches all round the world, and which, in economic terms, utterly dominates its current economic condition.

His air-conditioned cab (two long ladder climbs are needed to reach it) towers thirty feet above the Proterozoic dust. Before him, his only view all day, is a huge red cliff, laced with a tracery of silver-black ore bodies so rich in iron that one shovel-full will provide sufficient steel to make twenty-five Honda Civics, or the works for enough Pioneer CD players to supply the demand in West Germany for nearly six weeks.

In between issuing commands for his shovel to munch its way into the cliff he reads a Wilbur Smith novel; his greaser, a trainee

---

*There is a certain irony in his chosen career, in that "kangaroos" is the common word for mining shares on the Australian stock exchanges.

shovel driver named Lionel Sanders, plays with the Toshiba stereo, trying to tune in a rock station. But Newman is way out in the bush, "far beyond the black stump", and radio stations are distant luxuries; all Sanders can get is a howl of empty air.

He only turns on the motor in his shovel when the first of the fleet of Warbco "Haulpaks" arrives – gargantuan trucks designed to carry 200-ton loads of ore off to the crushing mills a mile away. The Haulpaks are dangerous beasts: never overtake one on the right, the miners caution – the driver has no visibility on that side, and if he turns he'll flatten you and your car with his twelve-foot tyres, and never even feel a bump. "You've got to have a hell of a lot of respect for these things," says Thompson, as he drops twenty Hondas-worth of ore on to the truck, making it bounce heavily on its man-high springs. "They have a life of their own. You sometimes feel they're taking over."

For eight hours a day – except for short breaks for "smoko" (the same word, oddly, that is used by shepherds in the Falkland Islands, and by Patagonian gauchos) – Thompson and Sanders chew their way deep into their assigned cliff. They remove 1,500 tons of ore every hour, 20,000 tons a day – a hundred Haulpaks'-full. Eventually, after a nearby row of immense and noisy plants (one charmingly known as a "beneficiation" plant) crush, grade and concentrate the rich blackish ore, it is all dumped into wagons for a 300-mile rail journey to the sea, and the beginning of its Pacific voyage.

The railway is owned by the mining company, which claims that the trains which run along it and down to the loading quays at Port Hedland are the longest in the world. The train drivers, despite Western Australia being half a world distant from New Zealand, are nearly all Maoris. It seems they have the same kind of inexplicable affinity with railroading as do the Anglo-Indians (with decidedly British names, like Mr Aloysius Jones, who can still be found shunting in Madras) across on the Indian subcontinent.

I arrived one day to take the 7.15 am ore train – 240 trucks, five engines, the whole structure two miles long and weighing 30,000 tons. It was being driven by Messrs Wick Maniapoto and Dick Thorby, Maori drivers known locally as "the koalas" because their life is of such legendary comfort. "We are a protected species – the union looks after us real good," says Mr Maniapoto and he opens the throttle, the five engines throb and the huge snake of ore cars begin to rumble north. "Some of the miners back in the pit complain about how good the drivers" conditions are. We're often the cause of squabbles – and believe me, there are a lot of squabbles at Newman. All the mines, in fact. That is one of the reasons Australian ore is pretty expensive. But then there's such a lot of it, and it's so rich, and so near the customers, they buy it anyway."

The journey from mine to port takes six hours, most of which is downhill except when it traverses a small range of hills called the Chichesters where two extra engines – to make a total of seven – are brought on to help heave the two miles of ore-wagons up and over. The countryside is brick-red, fiercely hot, and dotted with black spinifex bushes and stunted gum trees, all desiccated by the pitiless Australian sun. There's not a lot to do except drive and eat (the drivers have prodigious appetites, and are given snap-boxes the size of small trunks filled with gallon bottles of milk, whole hams, trays of hardboiled eggs and enough bread to feed a fair-sized village). They count the kangaroos – of which it turns out there are more than 140 identifiable variants – and tell 'roo-related stories of great antiquity (like that of the Briton who knocked down his first kangaroo on the road, felt sorry for it and put his jacket round its shoulders. When he wasn't looking it got up and bounded away, taking his jacket with passport and American Express gold card off into the bush, never to be seen again).

By mid-afternoon we are at the coast, and the dusty, lonely outpost of Port Hedland. Alan Thompson's ore, and that of all the other faraway diggers, was unloaded from the train by machines that wrestled each wagon up and over on its back, and allowed the ore to cascade down almighty chutes, each time with a deafening roar and an explosion of bright red dust. Endless chains of house-sized iron buckets then hoisted the ore on to mile-long conveyor belts which rose steadily skywards before tipping it, in an unending dark stream, on to the summits of Matterhorn-sized stockpiles on the quayside. High up in the control rooms, brawny men in shorts punched computer buttons to move the belts from summit to summit, so that all were equally immense, and pushed other buttons and pulled levers that triggered enormous spray cannons which shot water on to the piles, to stop the fresh sea breezes from blowing the ore away. More men in hard hats watched over a battalion of rotary cutters that scythed into the mountains, quarrying for one last time to move the ore out onto other, horizontal conveyers that led from the store-mountains to the quaysides, and to the ships themselves.

And what a small armada invariably awaits! Out in the roads, beyond the sandbanks and the tide rips, is a silhouetted line of long, black supercarriers. The ships are hove to, imperturbable, unmoving in the slow swells, thin spirals of blue smoke rising from their funnels. There is the *Pohang* from Korea, the *Slurry Express* from India, the *Pacific Pride*, the *Iron Pacific*, the *Japan Linden* and the *Esperanza Marina* – tens of thousands of tons of empty hulls waiting to carry away immense chunks of old Australia to be remade into the new products of Korea and Japan.

There is a slight problem in the loading dock. A crane operator, distracted by a tense moment in the cricket match to which he was listening, had kept his loading button pressed for a few seconds too long, and a little Shanghai ore carrier had mistakenly received twice as much ore, unceremoniously and suddenly dumped into her hold, as she was designed to be able to carry. She lists heavily to port; the Chinese crew, told to try to shift the stuff out again, are demanding extra pay; the master is furious; the crane driver is about to be sacked; the master of the *Africa Maru*, patiently waiting his turn to load, is charging demurrage rates of £10,000 a day . . .

It takes a full day before someone manages to solve things, after which the grubby little Chinese ship is under way, grossly overloaded and wallowing on the tide, on her twenty-day voyage to the Yangtze. The huge bulk of the Japanese-registered *Africa Maru* slides into her place on Berth A, the conveyors begin to whine and the floods of red ore start to cascade into the dark emptiness of her main holds. It will take twenty hours for her to be filled to the brim; by the flood tide she will lumber her way north out to sea again, and another ship will take her place.

Back at Newman, Alan Thompson is still crunching his way into the mountainside – one that the mine's explosives experts have softened up with fifty tubes of ANFO (a powerfully percussive mixture of ammonium nitrate and fuel oil) inserted in holes. To him the Pacific boom he is told he is helping to create is an unimaginable thing, ephemeral and all but meaningless. "I"m more bothered by what happens to Australia," he says. "I see the other countries round about us getting on better than we are, and it troubles me.* Sometimes I feel like pulling out, going off to Tahiti or somewhere, taking up gardening, breeding birds." (Mr Thompson has an abiding interest in tropical finches, and keeps 200 in a cage in his garden.) "The Aussie dollar's weak, the economy's in trouble, Canberra doesn't know what the heck it's doing. You tell me I'm part of the Pacific boom. What boom? It may be okay up in Korea and Japan, but sure as eggs it's not down here. I sometimes get the feeling we're being used; we're a sort of Third World to them, just a place to dig up and turn into something better. I'm not sure Australians are exactly impressed about that."

And with that he kicked his huge electric shovel into angry life again. The greaser resumed his fruitless search for more good stereo rock music – music with which he might drown out the jarring sound of his native Australia being chewn up and dumped into the back of the waiting trucks, to be sent off on its long voyage across the sea.

*In the mine office one supervisor had been reading a gloomy paperback called *Poor Nation of the Pacific*, and had shown me a remark made by Lee Kwan Yew to the effect that the Australians had to choose whether they were going to be the loafers of the region, or its most energetic. "Toss another prawn on the barbie and crack us a tube of Foster's," the supervisor said. "That's the most energetic thing the average Aussie does these days."

2

Hauling Australia Away

It had been a slightly inauspicious beginning for the 4,000 sea miles home when the *Africa Maru*, waiting to get in to collect her load of ore, ran aground six cables out from Port Hedland Roads. There is a treacherous and unpredictably mobile sandbar just beyond the outer marker buoy, and on this blazing summer's day it must have shifted right across the fairway, directly into the path of the 54 feet of draught that the ballast-laden ship was sporting. (It would be churlish, of course, to suppose any error on the part of the Japanese deck officers.)

She was easing in from the open sea, running at perhaps five knots on a slight swell, her navigator checking on the leading lights and the entrance to the dredged channel; then all of a sudden she stopped, with neither a shudder nor a groan, without a single saké bottle being knocked to the ground in the wardroom. Some of the young officers standing on the bridge tilted very slightly to for'ard, and then recovered, rather as if the ship had hit an unanticipated patch of rough water. Otherwise it was an accident of supreme gentleness, a stranding most singularly lacking in drama. The master, an impeccably polite young man named Shigetaka Takenaka, had the grace to look embarrassed, told everyone we would have to wait for a bit more tide, and whistled up the tug that was in any case preparing to help us swing into the berth, to head out to sea and give us a little help. Captain Takenaka, quite unflustered and not bothered by any of the problems of "face" with which Western Pacific peoples are supposedly beset,* was on the radio to Port Hedland pilots; lazy

---

*When John Gunther asked "eight representative Chinese" in the late 1930s what China needed most one said, "Honesty – the abolition of Squeeze and Face." Little has changed: the existence of the very concept of Face, and the (cont. over)

Australian voices could be heard in the background muttering about the bloody Nips hitting the bricks and couldn't someone take driving lessons and how we'd better go out and help the buggers off . . . .

Meanwhile an Indian ore-ship, the *Slurry Express*, which had been lurking out to sea listening to the distress which had befallen her sister, was now eagerly waiting to jump the queue, to take the *Africa Maru*'s place at the quayside. "Port Hedland Radio, Port Hedland Radio, am I having your good permission to come in alongside Berth Alpha?" the radio officer called in impeccable Chowringhee English. "Negative, *Slurry Express*, negative," replied the port captain. "Wait your turn. Fall in line after *Africa Maru*. Wait your turn." The silence that followed had a true Bengali eloquence. The delay, one could hear the master telling his agent over another VHF frequency, might well be interminable. Who would be knowing when the blessed Japanese ship might be refloated? The tide was now almost at its highest, and tugs might not be able to pull her off. Demurrage costs were high. The sun was insufferably hot. Waiting in the slow swell to take on 50,000 tons of dusty ore must then have seemed, even to the most seasoned of lascars, the punishment of purgatory.

A jaunty little pilot boat appeared down on the starboard side and two young men, their faces tanned like old Morocco by the endless West Australian sun, skipped up the companionway and were on the bridge within seconds. "G"day, Captain," said the senior pilot, who introduced himself as John Lindsay, "and me mate, Vince Nolan – like the artist, you know. Got yourself into a bit of bother, eh?" Captain Takenaka shrugged, and looked worried. "The tide will peak in fifteen minutes. We must be off then or we will have a problem," he said, with steely control.

The bridge began to fill with earnest-looking young men, all ready to carry out the master's orders with unquestioning precision. A small white helicopter whirled down from the sky and landed on a for'ard hatch, collecting Mr Nolan who would, the master was told, coordinate the two tugs which had just arrived from port. One tug attached itself to the bow, the other leaned its hessian-snouted

---

monumental risk of ever losing it, still inhibits the taking of risks so necessary for invention and originality. But Captain Takenaka's apparent repudiation of the demands of Face was one early indication for me that, at least among the younger professionals, the concept is losing ground. John Gunther would be proud, though Squeeze – institutionalized bribery – remains.

prow against the stern-plates of the *Africa Maru* and began to gun its engines, producing a cloud of black oily smoke above and a roar of sandy foam behind.

The engine-room alarm warbled softly. Captain Takenaka picked up the phone and listened intently to a Japanese voice on the other end, his brow furrowing as he did so. He replaced the receiver and sucked air in through his teeth – the unmistakable signal of an Oriental in trouble. John Lindsay recognized the eloquence of the gesture, and cocked an interrogative eyebrow.

"Number 2 engine is apparently short of power," said the Captain. "Engine room says maybe give us ten minutes more. There is nothing I can do." He looked at his watch. John Lindsay looked at his. The young men glanced at the bridge clock on the bulkhead, with its red segments before the hours and the quarters. The clock read 3.27 pm; high tide in the Port Hedland Roads was at 3.43. A deep silence fell on the assembled company. The faint sound of helicopter rotors ahead, and the grumble of the stern tug from behind. Someone cleared his throat. The clock ticked. A notice in Japanese mentioned that the ship's air-conditioning plant would be shut down that day for overhaul, and the bridge was very hot – though an officer had opened the bridge-wing door, and a faint breath of hot air wafted in off the mirror-smooth sea.

The clock clicked to 3.30, then 3.35. At 3.38 the telephone warbled. Captain Takenaka picked it up silently at the first sound. "Hai?" he intoned softly. He put down the instrument gently, and with a series of gliding movements and near-silent commands that blended into an instant of fluid control, started a series of procedures that, he hoped, would get the 135,000-ton vessel moving and swinging out of danger. "Port ten. Half ahead Number 1 engine. Full ahead Number 2 engine. Stern tug full ahead all. Bow tug full ahead all." And to each command came the response: the midshipman called back the rudder angle as the repeater clicked down the course. The engine-room telegraphs rang and swung over to confirm their selected speeds. The Sony radios that two young officers out on the bridge wings held to their ears crackled into life and both men acknowledged that the orders had been sent and received, and that the tug captains had switched to full power and were pushing and pulling as demanded.

At first there was nothing, other than the belching roar of the tug engines and the low and distant thunder of the *Africa Maru*'s 26,000-horsepower Sulzer diesels – made, like the ship herself, by the sister company for whom her load of iron ore was destined, Sumitomo Heavy Industries, of Yokusaka, near Tokyo. Everyone, Captain Takenaka included, peered anxiously at the sea, trying to detect some sign of movement, like commuters stuck in a train outside Paddington station who, transfixed by the appointments they'll miss, positively will the engine to start and the passing scene to begin to pass once again. And at first, just as outside Paddington, there was no movement at all . . . nothing.

Then a tiny bamboo-and-glass wind-chime, which some fanciful sailor had suspended above the starboard doorway by a piece of sisal,* began to clink. Everyone looked at it. At first it uttered only the most imperceptible and seemingly random noise. But after ten seconds more or so it was rocking to and fro regularly, its tiny splinters of glass tinging one against the other, impelled by a force that, though unseen, was recognized by everyone on the bridge as what it could only be – the sea. Someone cheered, though stifled his enthusiasm as the Captain muttered more orders into the annunciator. "Port five. Full ahead both engines. Bow tug ease away. Stern tug half ahead port engine."

We were free. The outer channel buoy, which for the past six hours had been stuck tantalizingly in the port windscreen, was moving now, in and to the left as we began to circle towards it. The bow tug began to fall in beside us as our speed took us past her. The helicopter whirled over our bows and Mr Nolan said he'd have a cold Swan's Lager waiting in the bar for John Lindsay once the ship had docked. "Daft buggers," said Lindsay. "Couldn't drive a bloody dodgem car."

Twenty-four hours later Captain Takenaka's vessel was fully laden with 135,000 tons of Western Australia, had eased her way back out of the roads and sneaked safely past the fickle sandbank, and was heading north for Japan. In twelve days' time the contents of her five mighty holds would be ashore, destined for the hands of the alchemists of Nihon, to be turned from dull Antipodean earth into glittering Japanese motor cars – a quintessential process of the new Pacific.

She started on a course of 020°, weaving her way past the reefs and shoals of the north Australian coast, where the Indian Ocean

*This had a classical four-character prayer pasted beside it. "To appease the Gods of the sea," a crewman whispered.

blends into the Timor Sea. The low coast was a thin green blur to starboard: after dark the watchkeeper pointed out the gleam of lights from Broome, a town once famous for its mother-of-pearl industry. In Victorian times half the world's pearl buttons came from Broome, the young man said; but he omitted to mention that Japanese Zeroes had attacked the town in March 1942 and destroyed all the planes at Broome airfield – five American, twelve Dutch and two British – in an incident that has since passed into local lore as "Australia's Pearl Harbor". *

Soon the coastline had vanished altogether and the *Africa Maru* was out in the open ocean, wallowing with a ponderous rhythm as she heaved her bulk at 14 painful, creaking knots through the long swells. The reefs slipped by: Imperieuse, Clerke and Mermaid, Ashmore, Hibernia and Seringapatam, marine testaments all to a legion of long-forgotten hydrographers and explorers. Then it was dawn again, and the ship was through the Timor Sea and into the Savu Sea, Indonesian islands were all around, and the master doubled up the watch for the tight and twisted passage through the Alor Strait, with Lomblen Island and its mile-high volcano looming high and green on the port side.

Then still more seas came and went as fast as the island chains that laced the Indonesian archipelago. The Savu Sea gave way to the Flores Sea, and that soon became the Banda Sea which later still, and once the ore-carrier was safely through the wide passage between Buru Island and Pular Sanana, evolved into the Seram and then the Molucca Sea. And this latter, the young Japanese steersman was quick to note for all on the bridge who were interested (he said he had taken a history degree at his university in Fukuoka), was the sea which washed the Spice Islands themselves, to which the great explorers from Portugal journeyed and where they first glimpsed the western boundary of the Pacific, 500 years ago. (The Spice Islands, it will be recalled, were the intended goal of Magellan's trans-Pacific expedition, part of a vain attempt to render them part of the Portuguese empire. A Spice Islander travelling with Magellan,

*One of the destroyed planes was carrying a sealed brown paper package holding thousands of pounds' worth of diamonds, being spirited out of Java for safe keeping in Australia during the Japanese occupation of the Dutch East Indies. The packet was later found in the wreckage on the beach, but many of the stones were gone: a local Chinese tailor and three other men were arrested, but many of the diamonds are still unaccounted for half a century later.

Enrique the Moluccan, was able to interpret for the party when the ships made landfall in the Philippines, and claimed them for Spain instead.)

Nutmeg and cloves had drawn men here, if for no other reason than that they perked up the taste of the otherwise dull fare that Europeans slapped down on their earthenware dinner plates. Wars had been fought and thousands had died to keep the essential trade in them alive. It might seem a little difficult to believe today, except that nutmeg – the seed of an evergreen tree known as *Myristica fragrans* – was a most remarkable spice: it had been a rare and precious incense in the days of the Holy Roman Empire, had later been used to flavour the disagreeably tasteless puddings, sausages and drinks of the fifteenth and subsequent centuries, and had been found by early quacks to relieve skin irritation and mask the symptoms of rheumatism. But fashions change. Nutmeg and cloves are still exported from the Moluccas, true; but the sea lanes to their west are no longer alive with the carracks that brought them back to Lisbon and Venice via Cochin and Calicut. Today they are more likely to be clogged with great tankers and ore-carriers, heading north with thousands of tons of rich red earth – a commodity that the Sultans of Ternate and Tidore and all the other nutmeg czars of old, having no interest in metallurgy, would quite probably have refused to dignify with their contemplation.

We were leaving the Molucca Sea and heading out over the six-mile deep known as the Philippine trench when Captain Takenaka pulled a new chart from the drawer. It was called *The Whole Nippon* – a title that seemed somewhat ambitious, since it displayed an area of land and sea stretching way beyond what we customarily think of as the Japanese island group. The main islands of Honshu and Hokkaido, Kyushu and Shikoku were there of course, centre-stage; and the Ryukyus, which included the infamous island of Okinawa,*

---

*Okinawa, which the Japanese fought bitterly to retain during the closing stages of the Second World War, remained under American control until 1972. One side effect of US rule was that cars drove on the right side of the road. But early one summer Sunday morning, soon after the Japanese had re-established their rule, such islanders as had cars were ordered to resume driving on the left side – probably the only case of a left-side "victory" in modern times. The Swedes were the last to order such a change – but went the other way, falling in line with their Continental and American colleagues. Japan, with Britain and most of her old Empire, remains staunchly sinistrally-ordered.

were there too, extending almost to the coast of Taiwan. One can forgive the Japanese for including Sakhalin Island and part of the Kuril chain stretching down from Kamchatka (four islands of which are still vehemently claimed by Japan, but which the Russians decline to relinquish). But when a map entitled *The Whole Nippon* goes on to include islands far away from Japan, tiny assemblages of coral and limestone like the Marianas and Carolines, as Captain Takenaka's appeared to, one wonders how extensive Japanese ambitions truly are – or were. It is as though the Ordnance Survey had published a map entitled "Great Britain" which showed France and Spain as well; Gallic and Iberian chauvinists might fairly grumble at how imperial pretensions died hard – as they had, apparently, with the publishers of the chart used by the *Africa Maru*.

For the truth was, though few outside the closed world of Japanese scholarship now care to remember it, that from 1914 onwards almost all the islands now looking up on our starboard side were, indeed, part of the Japanese Empire. The Caroline and the Marshall Islands and those tiny sun-bleached morsels of land that now make up the Federated States of Micronesia were all part of the colony known as the Nan'yo Gunto – the South Sea Islands. It was the taking of the Nan'yo that triggered among millions of Japanese an intense desire for world dominion – and which led, in ways emotional and practical, to the beginnings of Japanese intervention in the Second World War.

Japan's interest in expanding her boundaries was a phenomenon that coincided almost precisely with the ending of the shogunate and the restoration of the Emperor system. Many reasons have been put forward to account for it – the chauvinism that was so often associated with or was a by-product of Meiji liberalism, the romanticism of Japanese democratic thinking of the time, or the simple fact that an enormous samurai class, now no longer needed to prop up the shoguns, wanted employment.

Whatever impelled the imperial interest in the South Seas (a minor misnomer, since Japanese colonialism in the region was all to the north of the equator), the idea of languor, beauty and tropical mystery certainly became a vital part of Japanese mythology within a decade of the restoration of the Meiji house: books with titles like *Great Exploits in the Southern Seas* and *The Great King of the Islands*, written by men who probably had never travelled to a coral atoll in their lives, won huge popular approval. Suddenly, as an echo of America's "manifest destiny" to expand west, it became the destiny of Nippon to expand south. "It is our great task as a people to turn the Pacific into a Japanese lake," cried the Diet member and journalist Yosaburo Takekoshi. "Who controls the tropics controls the world."

There is no evidence to suggest that military strategy played a significant part in Japan's early attempts to colonize the islands – although as it later turned out they became of crucial strategic value. True, early naval training voyages carrying civilian passengers provided the reading public and the Imperial Palace with accounts of the Pacific islands; but it seems today as though Japan's interest in the region was as much dictated by the realization that no one else had spoken for it, as for the thought that one day it might be used as a springboard for even more grandiose plans of world dominion. Germany had annexed the Marshall Islands for no sound reason – and Japanese political thinking, so far as we can gather, merely reflected that, with Germany moving in, the Pacific was beginning to fill up. So we'd better have a slice of it, thought Tokyo, before it is too late.

In a reversal of the British maxim, trade was followed by the flag. Tiny trading companies were established in the eastern Caroline Islands, on Truk, Ponape and Kusaie, where copra, coconuts and fish were exchanged for whatever manufactured goods – tin trays, knives and buckets – the islanders seemed to want. The traders wrote home with eloquent descriptions of their Elysian new homes, where there was ample space for settlement, boundless opportunities for trade and money-making, and endlessly perfect weather, peopled with guileless and pliant natives. Back home, especially if the letters arrived in winter-time when chill rains fell on Tokyo and the farmers in Hokkaido huddled under ten feet of snow, the South Pacific must have seemed tempting indeed. "Japan's destiny," wrote a journalist who had cruised the Marshalls in 1888, "lies in the vast reaches of the hazy ocean."

Thanks to the Great War and the diplomatic adroitness of a Japan which had reached full political wakefulness in little more than half a century, the Pacific islands fell swiftly into the hands of Nippon. In the late summer of 1914 it took only a few moments of cynical calculation for Japan to realize that it would be prudent, wise and profitable to join the European Allies in their fight against Germany.

Tokyo presented Berlin with an ultimatum, urging German forces to withdraw from her possessions in China and from the Marshall Islands. The Germans stayed put: the Japanese Imperial Navy removed them. By October 1914 there were Japanese naval units occupying Ponape, Truk, Kusaie, Palau (even now faintly visible on the long-range radar of the *Africa Maru*, 30 miles off the starboard bow) and Angaur – though oddly Tokyo only ever admitted to the capture of a tiny atoll known as Jaluit, and refused to allow Allied naval vessels to enter the Marshall or Caroline waters, where they might discover otherwise.

When the war ended Japan laid proper claim to the islands; Viscount Ishii suggested to the American Secretary of State that it could keep them as "souvenirs" and for "sentimental reasons". The generals and admirals in Washington had long seen through such arguments, and soon persuaded the politicians to take a similarly alarmed view of Japan's growing imperial attitude. But what argument could fairly be made? Other countries were picking over the bones of Germany's Pacific carcasses – Britain, Australia and New Zealand, for instance, had their eyes on New Guinea and the islands of the South Pacific, and therefore could hardly look Japan straight in the eye and dispute the logic and legitimacy of her claim. They could only worry about the likely consequences.

The League of Nations eventually permitted Japan the luxury of a formal mandate over the islands, thus bringing to fruition the colony of Nan'yo. The Americans retained their links with Guam and Wake Island but elsewhere – in the Carolines to the south, the Marianas to the north and the Marshalls to the east – the rising sun of Japan fluttered defiantly in the trade winds. It would continue to do so for the next three and a half decades, until the war of the Pacific, and the bloody conquest of each one of the island groups by the forces of the United States.

Yap was somewhere on the starboard horizon now, invisible and far away; it had been a vital cable crossing-point once, and the Americans had been loth to let Tokyo control it, and eager indeed to win it back; other islands, all evidence of the dramatic tectonic behaviour of this part of the western Pacific rose and fell away on the long-range radar. We were on a heading of 010°, speeding above the deeps to Iwo Jima and the Bonin Islands, an unchallenged part of Japan for 120 years and once classified, somewhat eccentrically, as part of Tokyo Metropolis. The British had annexed them once, in 1825, and had named one rock Lot's Wife, and the best anchorage in Chichi-jima in the splendidly non-Pacific style of Port Lloyd Harbour.* The fight for Iwo Jima was one of the fiercest of the war – more than 4,000 Americans and 22,000 Japanese died in the struggle for Meatgrinder Hill and Mount Suribachi, and the famous photograph by Joe Rosenthal of the Associated Press of the US Marines raising the flag on the top of Suribachi has proved one of the more enduring images of American triumph ever published.† The United States returned them to Japan in 1968, four years before the return of Okinawa and the remainder of the Ryukyus.

But the Marianas, the Carolines and the Marshalls were never to be returned to Japan. Their strategic position was deemed too vital to the security of the ocean for the Japanese to be let loose – and there was little doubt about their strategic value. The submarines sent off to help (not that they did: most ran aground) the carrier force that attacked Pearl Harbor had been dispatched from Kwajalein in the Marshalls. Three of the Japanese forces assembled for the invasion of the Philippines were assembled in the Palaus. Bombers from Saipan struck the American base at Guam; and the attack on Wake Island was masterminded by the Japanese Fourth Fleet headquarters on Truk. The same strategic value proved vital once the tide of war had turned: the atom bombs which destroyed Hiroshima and Nagasaki were lifted by B-29 bombers that took off from the US Air Force base on Tinian, a hitherto insignificant Mariana island just south of Saipan.

It is Saipan – way off to starboard, invisible to all our radars – where the most mournful memorial to those days can be found and, in a neatly coincident irony, where the extraordinary contrast of the Japanese past and the Japanese future can best be witnessed.

On Saipan the undoubted melancholy fuses with what Westerners would consider the utterly bizarre. It was on Saipan, after all,

---

*Other rather endearing morsels of British imperial history can be found nearby: Port Hamilton was constructed on the Korean skerry of Komun-do, and the most southerly point of China, on Hainan Island, was called Cape Bastion until the humourless hydrographers of Peking retitled it Chinmu Chiao.

†Some find it droll that the statue modelled on the image, which now stands near the Pentagon, has become a near-legendary meeting place for homosexual Washington men.

that hundreds of Japanese civilians – mostly women and children – hurled themselves off the two precipices (now named Suicide Cliff and Banzai Cliff) at the north of the island; and it was here that the garrison of 30,000 men, supposedly secure in their caves and pill-boxes, were whittled down to a mere 600 after the furious American bombardments. They had counted on Admiral Ozawa's ships from Manila coming to their aid, but the battle of the Philippine Sea, otherwise known as the "Great Marianas Turkey Shoot", put paid to that, and the fall of Saipan became the most costly of all outpost defences that Japan was to mount.

Now, two kinds of Japanese visit Saipan, and by doing so illustrate the two very different attitudes the Japanese now have towards the South Seas, the Nan'yo, they once so coveted.

The first kind visit once a year, in small and well-organized expeditions sent out by the Bereaved Families Association of Japan. Their task is simple, if morbid – they are there to comb the tangantangan jungles of northern Saipan, or the caves on Banzai and Suicide Cliffs, for the bones of those who fell in battle. And each year they find them: huge troves of skulls, femurs, scapulae, tibia and vertebrae; and they bundle them in burlap sacks and – under the constant invigilation of a group of Buddhist priests – carry them to a pyre where, with all due ritual and keening, they are cremated and their souls, their *kami*, permitted at last to escape the bonds of earth.

The second kind of visitor is that more usually seen all around the world – and indeed two of the watchkeepers on board the *Africa Maru* as we passed nearby admitted to having been themselves. They, of course, are the modern Japanese tourists and (as with the crewmen here) youngsters on honeymoon. Planes fly in daily from the airports outside Tokyo and Osaka, each bringing hundreds of well-off, polite, earnest Japanese who will stay at the Saipan Hyatt and the Saipan Inter-continental hotels, laze in the sun, eat their sashimi, buy their souvenirs and have their pictures taken as they will in every other peaceful and unchallenging resort town within ten thousand miles of Japan.

And while these visitors may wish – and are probably able – to buy their Louis Vuittons, their Guccis and their Giorgio Armanis in the duty-free shops there, the residents of Saipan itself will be buying goods by Sony, Seiko, Panasonic and Nissan; in both ways the Japanese have created a beachhead on Saipan, one far more seductive and appealing and, so far as one can see, more lasting too.

And not just on Saipan. The Carolinians drive Nissan cars and there are Sony Walkmans sold on Rongelap and Jaluit; the Nationalist Chinese have them also in Taiwan; when the ancient Rovers and Buicks that have long served as taxis in Rangoon finally fall apart, they are replaced by Sentras and Corollas; the Japanese economic empire has spread its beguiling tentacles among the Filipinos across Luzon; and perhaps even up in the cold and foggy latitudes of the Kuril Islands and Sakhalin Russian soldiers of the Red Army are tuning in their National radio sets and playing tapes on their JVC cassette decks.

Captain Takenaka's map was thus perhaps not as ambitiously titled as I had supposed. One way or another, the Whole Nippon is what this part of the world seems destined to be.

As if to underline our steady approach to the empire of the sun, there were now increasing numbers of flocks of small Japanese fishing boats on the horizon of these hot, hammered-pewter waters. Many, the lookout explained, were drift-netters, their crews employing a technique recently much condemned by the environmental lobbyists, since the nets – nearly invisible to a human eye, let alone to that of an average myopic fish – can often stretch thirty miles down-current, snaring species both wanted and unwanted, yet resulting in the killing of all. There is indeed something macabre about watching the shaking machines worrying the dead fish from the nets as they are brought in, mile by mile: the platoons of men who stand beside them separate the fish into two – those likely to find favour with customers at the Tsukiji market in Tokyo are tossed into the ice-holds while the rest, dead or dying, are thrown back into the sea. There they float, belly-up, in the drift-netters' oily wake. It all looks too greedy to be good, and it was with some relief that American tuna canners said in 1990 that they would henceforward use other methods of snaring their prey, and stamp "Dolphin Friendly" on cans that held fish caught in more humane fashion.

The Japanese long-line tuna-boats were out in force too. It was not until the 1920s that the Japanese began to fish beyond the protection of their own home waters. Then they began long-lining* for tuna off Taiwan in the Thirties, off southern Indonesia and the Eastern Pacific in the days before the Second World War, and they now take their search for sea-creatures as far away as the Falkland Islands and the South Shetlands, where the cold waters produce a peculiarly robust kind of squid that Japan's millions (and Korea's even more so) like to eat between meals. These days the scale of Japanese fishing is so vast as almost to defy belief: the country's fleets, working from some 1,500 fishing ports both great (like Kushiro, at the northern tip of Hokkaido, which lands nearly a million tonnes annually) and small, take in more than 13 million tonnes of fish a year.† The Food and Agriculture Organization in Rome divides the World Ocean into fifteen areas: Japanese boats are active in them all, taking one per cent of the catch even in faraway ocean areas like the Western Indian Ocean and the South-western Atlantic. In the North East Pacific, the richest fishing grounds on the planet, the Japanese take nearly half of the 20 million tonnes fished out each year – the little boats we could see from the bridge-wings, and which winked at us with their Aldis lamps at night, were thus the outward and visible sign of an immense economic phenomenon.

At night that phenomenon is visible from beyond the stratosphere, too. As soon as dusk falls over the Sea of Japan scores of squid-catchers set to work: by shining brilliantly powerful arc-lights down into the sea shoals of cephalopods can be duped into thinking that nightfall has been postponed, and can be lured back to the surface and bagged by the watching crewmen. To appear sun-like to the sinking squid, the lights are of remarkable brightness and the purest white; so bright the lights, and so numerous the fishing craft that

---

*The technique, which is applied on a similarly massive scale, involves lines up to 120 miles long with hundreds of dangling hooks, each baited with a chunk of frozen *Scombresox saurus*, a sort of garfish of which tuna are inordinately fond. As many as 3,000 hooks lurk in the water awaiting the schools of yellowfin, albacore, bigeye and bluefin, and all for the insatiable appetite for tuna-based sushi and sashimi which the Japanese display. American passion for raw Japanese fish has declined somewhat as American passions are wont to do: it seems not to have dented the volume of tuna scooped up by Japanese long-liners, who are busy as ever.

†This figure suggests, since most of the catch is eaten domestically, that each Japanese consumes 100 kilogrammes of fish a year, or an amount equivalent to twice his own body weight.

carry them that a passing astronaut noticed them as he peered down into the blackness of the Oriental night. Where his maps told him to expect empty ocean he saw instead a sprinkling of tiny dots of diamond brightness, like a dusting of snow on a background of velvet: the Japanese squid-fishermen, labouring through the small hours to help satisfy the needs of the trenchermen of Tokyo.

We were still too far away to see any land, either by eye or by radar. Somewhere off our port beam – we were at 25°N now, having reached about as latitudinally far to this side of the equator as Port Hedland had been on the other south side of it – were the Ryukyu Islands, and Okinawa. I had been to Okinawa a few months before, and though struck by many aspects of its singularity – the people, for instance, are far shorter, darker and more Chinese-looking than most mainland Japanese – I remembered best of all that alone in the west Pacific, it was a place where the locals staged, of all things, bull-fights. *

On Okinawa the bulls do not tussle with man, but with each other. Two enormous, beer-fed beasts are led by their devoted trainers into an earth-banked circus: a gong is sounded and the bulls, muscles rippling, legs straining, nostrils flaring as they snort with effort, push against each other like a pair of sumo quadrupeds, all mass and grunt. The audience, mainly farmers from the surrounding valleys, urge on the bull on which they have placed a wager of the odd yen or two. After a while one animal clearly becomes the dominant; he pushes his friend to the edge of the circle, or perhaps even causes him to stagger or fall. But neither beast ever gets hurt – only the wallets of the losing farmers and the face of the losing trainer suffer, and both are eminently mendable.

Okinawa is a historically curious place, the largest island in the chain of the Ryukyus that extends between Japan and China, like stepping stones (or "the tail to the rocket of Japan" as a fanciful

*As a convenient example of trans-Pacific connections it is perhaps worth remembering that Mexico, where bull-fighting is very much a way of life, is a Pacific nation too. Anthropologists know of no link between Okinawa and Mexico, which in any case use very different styles of combat; but there are Spanish riding customs still practised in Hawaii, where the influence of Castile lingers still. The Mexican silver dollar, though, was standard currency in the Orient until recently, and the first regular trans-Pacific shipping service – the Manila Galleons – linked Manila and Acapulco.

writer, presumably a Sinophobe, noted in the mid-Sixties). Chinese influence was once paramount: from the fourteenth century China laid claim to the islands, and the Kings of the Ryukyus were obliged to pay tribute to the Emperor in Peking. But in 1609 the Shimazu family – one of the greatest of Japanese warrior clans, based at Kagoshima in southern Kyushu – conquered the islands and forced the Ryukyu kings to give fealty and pay tribute to their Satsuma fief, thus making them doubly damned and doubly taxed. The Meiji restoration changed everything: in 1879 the new government in Tokyo formally annexed the islands and organized them into a new prefecture, and China accepted the new masters as *de facto* rulers. There was a final dispute a few years later when a group of Okinawan fishermen drifted off course on to the beaches of what was then called Formosa (now called Taiwan), and were promptly executed by the Chinese. China apologized after the inevitable barrage of complaints, and in penitent mood announced it had formally agreed that Japan owned the Ryukyus, and for good.

The last war brought devastation to Okinawa as to almost all major Japanese island possessions: the defeat brought American occupation troops, sailors and airmen storming into what a US marine handbook later called "the keystone of the Pacific in the free world's fight against the spread of Communism": at the time of writing there are 88 American military installations on the Okinawa Islands, and Kadena air base is one of the most important in America's purported defence of the Pacific. Big bombers, equipped with all manner of ordnance, thunder down the runways endlessly; the island swarms with off-duty GIs, rendering much of the architecturally tasteless capital city of Naha even less attractive than it might otherwise be.

But outside Naha the island itself has a tropical languor to it, with farmers – their houses hiding behind walls of coral, protecting them from the violent typhoons which bear down from the central ocean – raising sweet potatoes and rice, pineapples and sugar cane. The remoter islands are becoming tourist resorts for those few Japanese who think Hawaii is too far to fly for white sand beaches and leaning palm trees. But the environmentalists object: plans to build a runway on the coral reef on Ishigaki-jima are the subject of violent opposition, and have turned into a national issue, debated in the Tokyo Diet. Rarely otherwise do the affairs of the Ryukyus enter the wider curriculum of mainstream Japan.*

I had taken a small ferry down to Ishigaki-jima once; it seemed the prudent choice, given the row over the aerodrome, and proved to be a transport of utter delight. The little white ferry-boat left Naha port at teatime, as an enormous harvest moon was rising from a mirror-calm sea. There was a silky breeze which, as I stood on deck, seemed to have a comfortable and caressing quality. There was good cold Kirin beer in the small café, the rumble of the engines was soothing, my cabin was small, neat and cosy and I slept perfectly – to wake at dawn with the ocean stretching boundlessly on all sides, not an island in sight.

I took breakfast and then climbed to the bridge to see where we were. A few score miles north of Miyako, it turned out – Miyako, one of the few Ryukyu islands untouched during the Second World War, and best known for its unspoiled villages of old cottages built of coralline limestone, and the high typhoon walls of a great age. Outside Hirara Town there is a stone, five feet high, known as the *Bubakarisu* – said to have been erected there by the Chinese when they first placed the Ryukyu kings under their suzerainty. Any islander taller than the stone would, the Chinese masters decreed, have to pay tax and tribute, either in money or more commonly, in the pretty blue kimono cloth called *jofu*, swathes of which I remember seeing hanging over the limestone walls, drying and fading in the intense near-tropical sun.†

*Most schoolchildren know the unusual role the Ryukyus play in the record books. There is a species of wildcat found in the jungles on Iriomote Island; the world's largest moth, the *yonagunisan*, lives on Yonaguni Island; the *habu*, a deadly snake, can be trodden on just a few miles from Naha; and the perfectly lethal *fugu* fish is caught in the seas off the archipelago. The *fugu* can be and is made into expensive sushi and sashimi, but only if the lethally poisonous gut section is removed by a highly skilled and government licensed *fugu* chef. Men have been known to murder and, indeed, to commit suicide by bribing the *fugu* chef to leave traces of the gut in the sushi. Death, of a peculiarly uncomfortable kind, follows within minutes.

†There is a curious German monument at Hirara Port, harbinger of later friendships and enmities. Emperor Wilhelm I had it erected in 1873 as thanks for the Miyako islanders having given a ship and safe passage to the crew of a German trader that foundered on the rocks. Forty years later Japan set herself against German expansion in the Pacific, and scooped up all her tropical islands; thirty years after that Tokyo and Berlin were firm colleagues in the Axis.

It was just before bouillon-time when the reef-fringes of Ishigaki-jima began to etch the for'ard horizon – though the 1,500-ft-high Mount Omoto had been in sight from the time the low silhouette of Miyako was beginning to slip away on the port quarter. Ishigaki Town was no more than a large village, dominated by an old samurai's residence built in 1819, when the Shimazus and the Chinese were running the place in uncongenial tandem. There was an eighteenth century *shinto* shrine, and a temple to the female Buddha figure known as *Kannon*,* where the fishermen still pray before setting sail. There was hibiscus and bougainvillea, banyan trees and lily forests, and the more sheltered coasts were lined with mangrove swamps – all extremely un-Japanese, a very long way from Fuji-san. I rented a bicycle during the afternoon and pedalled slowly around – becoming ever more forgetful that this island was part of a land which had given the world the Walkman, the Landcruiser and high-definition television, the *geisha*, the *samurai* and the ethos of *bushido*. I was reminded of Kauai, the island at the far end of the Hawaiian chain, all flowers, beaches, spirit homes and old houses – though this was considerably less developed than Hawaii, with very few cars and a great deal more charm.

From here Japan was a far country, without a doubt. An islander I met told me that from the summit of Mount Omoto it was possible to see Hsueh Shan, the 10,000-ft summit peak of Taiwan. On this occasion, my first visit to Ishigaki, it was a late autumn evening – I left Haneda airport in a thin chill drizzle – and probably while these blue seas were booming against the reefs in this part of Japan a blizzard was lashing down on Hokkaido, the maple trees were red in the Tokyo parks, there was a big autumn storm off Matsue and the view of the temples in Kyoto was subtly altered by woodsmoke and the outlining of an early frost. Japan, it struck me then, is much more than just a far country – she is far larger than mere cartographic

---

*In both Japan and China, the sex of *Kannon* is open to doubt – in the rest of the Buddhist world, where he is known variously as Avalokitesvara, Natha-deva or Kuan-yin, he is indubitably male (and in Tibet is regarded as the *bodhisattva* who introduced the famous mantra *om mane padmehum*). The Japanese *Kannon* is seen in a variety of forms; *Senju* has 1,000 arms, *Jun-tei* has only 18, *Ju-ichi-men* has four hands and eleven heads. He or she is noted as the creator of the fourth world – the universe in which we live – and protects against fire, wild beasts, assassins, robbers and shipwreck, which is why the Ishigaki-jima fishermen venerate her (or his) shrine.

representation might suggest, a country with geographical heft and consequent pride, a nation that, like the similarly-scaled Great Britain of 10,000 miles away, was such stuff as empires are built on.

"The tail to the rocket of Japan" turns out to be a more appropriate metaphor than that mid-Sixties writer had imagined. For not too many miles north of Okinawa, at the point where tail joins rump, is the site where modern Japan currently looks up and outwards to the next empire to conquer – the empire of space. Japan maintains her small corps of space scientists on her southern periphery, on an island called Tanegashima, working quietly away at Nihon's next frontier.

From 100 feet up inside the vehicle assembly building, the scene appears pure Cape Canaveral. Here and all around is a forest of white-painted gantries, a spaghetti-like mess of hydraulic tubing, acres of protective gold foil and an army of men in helmets and white cotton shoe-covers. Half a mile away and slightly distorted by the shimmering of the afternoon heat, is the launch pad, its base pitted and flame-scarred by innumerable tests and rocket firings. Below and beyond this apparently familiar scene are the blockhouses and the telemetry aerials, the tanks for liquid hydrogen, oxygen and helium, the fire trucks and the escape slides. And beyond all that is the coastline, the coral reefs and the seamless blue of a tropical sea.

But closer examination suggests that Canaveral is a very long way away. Tucked in between two small segments of the aluminium wall of this tower, at the very point in the assembly building where the snout of the rocket protrudes into the sun, is a small confection of paper and wood no more than six inches by two.

The wood is a sliver of bamboo, split at the top; inserted into it is a small piece of hand-made mulberry paper, folded into convoluted arabesques by (it was explained) an amateur origami-master. Four small *kanji* ideographs are written on the paper in black brush-strokes, four more in red. A technician in a white plastic helmet provides a translation.

The black characters, he says, present a formal prayer to the Shinto god of Thunder, a plea to ensure that storms keep well away from the tower. The sentence in red makes polite obeisance to an even more exalted member of the pantheon, asking that the rocket shall be allowed to make its journey successfully into and through his domains.

"Very Japanese," said the technician half apologetically. Then he grinned. "And so far very effective. Every single one of our space rockets has worked perfectly. The Gods seem to have smiled on our space programme."

Indeed. The Japanese Space Centre on Tanegashima – Lotus-Seed Island, so-called because of its shape – has quietly and formidably been projecting Japan and Japanese technology beyond the earth's atmosphere since the beginning of the Eighties. With little by way of drum-rolls or fanfares, rocket after rocket has soared up, tilted elegantly south-eastwards above the tracking stations on Okinawa and Christmas Island, and eased itself into orbit after orbit of seemingly easily attained perfection. Communications satellites, navigation satellites, weather satellites, television broadcasting satellites . . . one after another they have been tossed up into the skies and parked neatly somewhere above Japan, as if emerging from some infernal Honda assembly-line. And like Hondas – so reliable they are more like hairdryers, someone remarked with envy* – the satellites have been unwrapped and switched on, and then have proceeded to work faultlessly until such time as someone gets bored with them and tosses them away on to the intergalactic rubbish heap.

However, during all its recent history and despite its consummate success, one aspect of Japan's space effort has irritated its directors, has offended their collective sense of pride. Substantial portions of the rockets assembled on and launched from Tanegashima have been *designed and made abroad* – in America, mainly. Japanese rocket technology was not sufficiently advanced, nor the budget of the Japanese Space Agency sufficiently generous, to permit otherwise. But by the middle of 1989, all of that changed.

A new rocket, known simply as the H-2, was in the final stages of design when I arrived on the island; its engine was to be brought down to Tanegashima for its first static test firing a few days later. The significant thing about this rocket – far larger than anything else ever known in Japan, and as powerful as the major-payload monsters being used elsewhere in the world – is that all of it is being designed and made in the factories of Japan. The Japanese space programme is thus about to become fully home-grown. And largely because of the new and very apparent sense of national pride sparked by the building of the H-2, Japan's space programme appears set to

---

* "You take it out of the box, it works perfectly for ten years, and then you throw it away and buy a new one."

take off – the pun is perhaps forgivable – in a most spectacular fashion:

> We have many plans [says Yoshinori Maesaka, the mild-mannered and rather bookish director of the Tanegashima space centre who showed me round one hot, steamy afternoon]. We believe we have at long last developed a first-rate launch vehicle that can place good-sized payloads into useful orbits. We have a proven record of efficiency – one hundred per cent efficiency, in fact. We have a good launch site, and we are building a new complex of pads for the new rocket. And we are very cost-effective, too. So all told we think the world will look to Japan for its satellite launches in the next century. We have gone about this slowly and steadily. Now we are ready.

It is more than twenty years since Japan set up her National Space Development Agency. Its goals – rigidly confined by the twin principles of "harmony with social necessity and national resources" and "for peaceful purposes alone" – have been as modest as its budget: today the annual expenditure on space is only 124 billion yen, a reasonably handy sum when translated into dollars ($1 billion), but somewhat trifling when expressed as a fraction of the total government spending of 54,000 billion yen. (A mere one tenth of one per cent: the US spends proportionately ten times as much.)

The frugality of the effort is readily apparent. At Tanegashima there are only 90 government employees, and in between launches most of them return to laboratories on the mainland where they can be more usefully employed. Kunio Hirata, the head of the Propulsion Test Division, offers another example: a system developed at the Centre for saving some of the liquid hydrogen used in static engine tests. "The Americans and the Russians just let their excess hydrogen burn off during a test. We found it was so expensive that we decided to recapture it and recompress it into a liquid. It looks rather mean-minded to outsiders, but we are keen on economizing. And of course, it works out less expensive for the consumers, too."

And consumers are what the Japanese are now eagerly seeking. The H-2 rocket – designed by Fuji Heavy Industries, the casings made by the Kobe Steel Company, the solid rocket boosters by Nissan Motors, everything bolted together and lifted up with motors made by Mitsubishi Heavy Industries and launched from a complex made by Kawasaki Heavy Industries – has only a fairly limited set of duties for Japan herself. A big weather satellite is due to be launched in 1993, an advanced earth-observing satellite six months later – and thereafter whatever large chunks of hardware are deemed consonant and "harmonious" with Japan's needs and funds. The major real purpose of the H-2 is to launch other customers' hardware and turn the whole effort into a characteristically profitable display of Japanese business acumen.

Satellite launching is a cut-throat business these days, as Japan knows well. Director Maesaka had no illusions:

> We're up against the European Ariane, China's Long March [the Mark 3 of which was used to launch AsiaSat, a Pakistan to Sakhalin communications satellite owned by a Hong Kong consortium, in the spring of 1990], the Space Shuttle, the Russian Proton, even the Indians and the Israelis. But we believe we can score with our reliability – we reckon we have a 60 per cent confidence level and the rocket hasn't even been fully tested yet. We believe our cost will be the same or lower than the others. We have built a rocket that makes a very minor disturbance to the environment – it is a very "clean" rocket. And we can offer to put two tonnes of payload into geostationary orbit – four tonnes with modifications – or ten tonnes into low earth orbit. Taking all aspects together the Japanese rocket will be the most competitive.

There are two obvious snags, however, the first a fact of simple geography: the Tanegashima launch site sits at 31°N latitude, meaning that the increasingly popular parking place for satellites (up above the equator) is a long way off, and requires extra launch time and power for every pound of satellite. (An Australian consortium is trying to win approval and backing for a private commercial satellite launch sit at Cape York, in far northern Queensland – its advantages being near-perfect weather for 300 days a year, and a location less than 10° longitude south of the equator.)

The second snag is more recognizably Japanese: the hundreds of tuna fishermen who ply the waters down-range from the island have objected to having rockets fired over their heads, and to the huge bits of discarded hardware that would fall all around them. Meeting to consider the threat, they formally demanded severe limits on the number of launches each year.

"And the fishermen are very powerful," says director Maesaka. "They managed to convince the government that we should only launch during four months of each year. So that's what we do – we launch our rockets only in January and February, August and

September. The rest of the year" – he gestured sadly at the empty gantries – "we don't do anything."

In the harshly competitive world of satellite business, it must be admitted that a country which can only put up its customers' payloads during one third of each year is running at a pretty serious disadvantage.

That aside, however, one suspects that the unstoppable enterprise of Nippon – the word chosen to be painted on the side of each H-2 rocket – will somehow prevail.

Next morning, quite suddenly, the *Africa Maru* was well out of the tropics and in the cool grey waters of the continental shelf. We had altered course slightly to starboard, and Japan was but a few miles off on our port beam. The entrances to Osaka Bay and Tokyo Bay loomed up and fell away, vague patches of settled grey cloud suggesting their approximate position. The sea was now filled with enormous ships. On every side, steaming into ports like Chiba, Kawasaki and Yokohama were fully-laden oil tankers wallowing heavily up from the Gulf via the Strait of Malacca; gaily coloured grain ships from New Orleans, Tampa and Hampton Roads; reefer ships and container carriers crammed with frozen beef and pork from the downs of New South Wales; coalers from Newcastle* and bauxite carriers from the Queensland ports of Weipa, Hay Point and Gladstone. And doubtless there were ships here from a little town with the unlovely name of Gove, way up in the Australian aboriginal territories of Arnhem Land, on the Arafura Sea. I had sailed in a yacht from Gove many years before, and one day as we bucked in the swell from a bauxite boat sliding out from the buoys the skipper (a tough young woman from Sydney) had wondered out loud where the cargo might be going. "All for the bloody Nips, I s'pose," she had said. "Tearing up our country and turning it into bloody cars, that's all they do. We're just a bloody quarry now."

They had said more or less the same thing in Newman and here, a few miles out from the smoggy sprawl of Tokyo Bay, was

---

*The Australian Newcastle, that is; it may export coal and have neighbour towns called Wallsend and Stockton, but only a few miles out all memory of Geordie country fades, and names like Kurri Kurri, Dongog and Bulahdelah replace those that, to a Briton, sound so comfortably familiar.

the vision they had all feared: that of Australia, compressed into long steel boxes, arriving in chunks off the shores of Japan, to be melted down and hammered out for the greater good of the heirs of those men who had bombed Darwin and Broome, had threatened to invade Queensland, and who had killed – in so many vicious ways – thousands of Australians doing no more than defend their own corner of the Pacific. For an Australian patriot, the vision was a bizarre and cruel nightmare.

We were bound for the more modest port of Kashima, on the low coast of Ibaraki prefecture. This Kashima – not to be confused with a less commercially important town of the same name over on Kyushu, where there is a particularly lovely Inari shrine with a number of beautifully-sculpted images of foxes – is about as far east of Narita airport as Tokyo is to the west of it. It is rarely visited by foreigners not involved in maritime trade, though a large blue sign points to it, just beyond the entrance at Narita airport.

The pilot boat arrived alongside as we reached the outer marker, and we then swept majestically in along the fairway – no sandbars to interrupt our progress here, no swaggering Australians to grumble at our presence. Here was all efficiency, clipped commands, precision and a singular lack of emotion; by lunchtime, eleven days out from Port Hedland, the *Africa Maru* was tied up alongside and Captain Takenaka and his 29 crewmen were scurrying down the ship's companion-way to a weekend off at their homes in the Tokyo suburbs. It was left to the Kashima port handlers and the conveyor belts of Sumitomo Metal Industries – alongside whose smelters we were parked – to whisk the five holds clean of all those thousands of tons of red Australian earth, and begin to turn them into steel.

3

William the Conqueror's Car

There was a pleasing symmetry in the arrival of the *Africa Maru* at a Sumitomo plant. She had, after all, been built at the Oppama shipyard of Sumitomo Heavy Industries – Sumitomo Jukikai Kogyo KK – and her engines (based on the classic Sulzer design for marine diesels) had been constructed at their Tamashima plant. Now she was berthed here in Kashima alongside the main steel mill of Sumitomo Metal Industries (Sumitomo Kinzoku Kogyo KK), home from the sea.

Like so many other giants of modern Japanese industry, the Sumitomo group is the child of one of the great merchant houses of the sixteenth century, one of the shopkeepers to the shogun who flourished under the protection and favour of the Tokugawas. The first celebrated member of the clan was Sumitomo Masatomo,* who began a copper mining, smelting and refining company and,

---

*There is a confusing convention about the format of Japanese names, which surfaces for the first time here. Mr Sumitomo's family name is here placed first, before his given name, Masamoto; while with other Japanese mentioned thus far in the book, like the *Africa Maru*'s captain, Shigetaka Takenaka, the Western approach is adopted – placing the family name last. The rough-and-ready rule has it that Japanese living or known before the Meiji restoration in the mid-nineteenth century are given their names in the Oriental style, family name first; while those known during the rule of the post-Meiji emperors are accorded Western nomenclature. Not all writers do this – some rather strict-minded authors say that since Japan is an Eastern country then, like China, the family name should come first in all cases – hence the recent prime minister of Japan is, to them, Nakasone Yoshihiro. Rather than burden readers with an additional complication I will adopt the imperfect and illogical rule: a modern Japanese gets his name last, a figure of obvious antiquity remains as he knew himself.

despite the ban on exports – indeed, on trade and any significant foreign contact – was permitted to ferry his copper to customers overseas. The range of the clan's interests began to expand under the Meiji emperor, at the time when the other vast conglomerates, known generically as the *zaibatsu*, began to form – companies like Mitsui and Mitsubishi, dynastic cartels of vast power and influence throughout Japan. They, Sumitomo included, reached their apogee shortly before the war; indeed, many would say it was the *zaibatsu*'s influence which encouraged Japan's aggressive attitudes in 1941. A dozen family-run empires controlled 80 per cent of Japan's industrial, commercial and financial enterprises in the days immediately before the Pearl Harbor attack – the *zaibatsu*, the moneyed cliques, enjoyed untold and unchallenged power. By the end of the war Sumitomo, one of the mightiest of them all, controlled no fewer than 135 enterprises through its parent holding company, Sumitomo Goshi Kaisha.

General Douglas MacArthur, in his reforming role as Allied commander of the occupation forces in post-war Japan, broke up the *zaibatsu* empires – or supposed that he did. But it didn't take long for the old hierarchies to reassert themselves; while MacArthur may have successfully dismantled the archaic system of Japanese aristocracy by abolishing the House of Peers and thus atomizing the influence of the old dukes, marquesses and viscounts, he could not entirely wreck the system by which the Japanese managed to amass their fortunes. So by the mid-1960s the old family names were back in evidence again, though this time under the guise of what became known as the *keiretsu*, conglomerates that were (as was once said of Mitsubishi) more republican, less monarchical, more dominated by complicated systems of interlocking shareholdings than by the power and influence of single families. The *keiretsu* system is every bit as conservative an economic force as that of the *zaibatsu* days, but it has a healthier and more democratic bent to it now – even though a survey showed that, in each of Japan's twenty major industries, companies associated with the three greatest old *zaibatsu* – Mitsubishi, Mitsui and Sumitomo – accounted for anywhere between a third and a full 100 per cent of total production.

Sumitomo today is an empire of several dozen companies, based in Tokyo and Osaka, but with offices and factories spread the length and breadth of Japan and, indeed, throughout the world.

The Hong Kong telephone directory, for instance, lists 45 numbers for Sumitomo entities, from Sumitomo Bank via Sumitomo Forestry to Sumitomo Property & Casualty Insurance Company. Sumitomo Metal Industries, which can trace its ancestry directly back to Masatomo four centuries ago, is a particularly vast and powerful star in the constellation; known as Fuso Metal Industries during MacArthur's days, it resumed its family name once he had departed and the legacy of American reform was waning. It was beside its wharves and conveyor belts, and against its skyline of converters and electric furnaces that the *Africa Maru* berthed that autumn morning: the extendable scoops were lowered deep into the holds, the chains began to clank and whirr, and the first of tens of thousands of tons of Newman ore began to pour on to the dockside storage mounds, to be smelted into Sumitomo steel, to be rolled, tempered, quenched and burnished, then transported to another factory where they would be transformed into thousands of editions of that product which, perhaps more than any other, has come to symbolize the modern Japanese economic dominance of the world: the motor car. In this particular case, cars from a company that is one of the relative newcomers on the Japanese industrial scene (having held its name since only 1934), the Nissan Motor Company Ltd.

Nissan was not one of the *zaibatsu*. Its name was not that of a family,* but was derived from the words *Nippon Sangyo*, meaning Japanese industry. Nonetheless the company, formed by a brash Thirties arriviste named Yoshisuke Ayukawa, played an enormous role in the war – perhaps even greater than that played by the Sumitomos and Mitsuis, who were regarded by men like Ayukawa as grey and conservative oldsters, lacking the kind of world vision that the generals and the admirals seemed then to hold with such passion and conviction.

Though Ayukawa-san was Nissan's godfather, it was actually a remarkable *American* inventor, William Gorham, who can most accurately be given credit for fathering the first Nissan-built car, the Datsun. William Gorham, who took the Japanese name Katsundo Goahamu (which can be taken as meaning William the Conquerer),

---

*Nor even an approximation of one – like Toyota, which was the marketing department's suggestion for stiffening up the name of that company's controlling family, Toyoda.

was the son of a China-based travelling rubber salesman. He was a great tinkerer, inventing, among other things, the Gorham motorized rickshaw and a diesel engine for Japan's armada of small fishing boats.

Gorham and Ayukawa met in the early Twenties, the transplanted American demonstrating the so-called Gorham-shiki car, a very crude beast that was essentially fashioned from two bicycles and a motorcycle engine. When Ayukawa set up Nissan, he hired Gorham to design the first car, and Gorham in turn hired other Americans from Detroit to come over the Pacific to help. The first Datsun came off the production line in 1933, Japanese-financed but entirely American-designed. Those Americans who quake at the nation of today's trade deficit might do well to remember the role one of their own played in its beginnings.*

Ayukawa's intimacy with the militants in the armed forces meant that the Nissan company, as it grew in the late Thirties and early Forties, became a constant ally of the country's ultra-nationalists – the hotheads who formed the care of the Japanese military in those heady pre-war days. The company went so far as to become a prime mover in the whole sad affair of the Japanese annexation of Manchuria, and the establishment of the Japanese territory of Manchukuo, with the former emperor of China, Henry Pu Yi, installed as its puppet head of state. Nissan's holding company – now merged with Hitachi – moved its headquarters (for tax reasons, the firm lamely explained) to Manchukuo's administrative capital, Changchun. Huge Nissan-Hitachi factories were built in and around Harbin (designed by the Japanese rulers of Manchukuo as the industrial capital).

It remains one of the finer ironies of the modern world that China's present struggle to become a properly industrialized nation owes much to men like Ayukawa, who left behind so great an industrial legacy in Manchuria. The hope of Ayukawa and his uniformed friends was, of course, that Manchuria would become Japan's major manufacturing out-station, from which the tanks, planes and guns would be fanned out to assist in the speedy conquest of the rest of Greater East Asia. The Russian parachutists who landed in Harbin

*William R. Gorham remained in Japan throughout the war, unscathed, but under a kind of benign house arrest. When he died in 1949 he was still tinkering, this time helping Canon to design 35mm cameras.

in 1945 soon put paid to such folly – but the fighting was desultory, the Japanese quickly capitulated and the factories remained, less ruined than those in mainland Japan which had been pounded into near-extinction by the waves of American bombers. Before long the Chinese, then the Communist Chinese, subsumed them into their otherwise war-wrecked economic structure.

After the war Ayukawa, like so many of his colleague industrialists, was purged. MacArthur's team decided, perhaps not unreasonably, that a man who had played so intimate, if perhaps not technically so culpable, a part in the Japanese war-machine should not be allowed to resume his work and position as if nothing had ever happened. So despite his brilliance and his connections – his mother, for instance, was niece to a man who had been a powerful adviser to the Mitsui family – and despite his likely ability to prise Nissan from the mire of the ruined Japan, he was banned as a Class A war criminal. (He did, however, manage to become a member of the Japanese Diet, so his disgrace was not comprehensive.)

The effect of his dismissal, coupled with the purging of other senior Nissan executives and the near-total wreckage of Nissan's production lines in and around Tokyo, meant that the company was effectively impotent: however much it might have wanted to get back into the manufacture of motor cars, it couldn't man-age. Moreover the work force was extraordinarily militant – the same proletariat which had rebelled in Britain's post-war elections, replacing Winston Churchill and the Tories with the modest Clement Attlee and a reforming Labour Party, was now on the rise in Japan, only even more so. In Japan, after all, the old order had failed and been seen to have failed: the militarists, the gerontocrats and the sycophantic drones of the *zaibatsu* had lost the war they had pledged to win. And so, in the view of the labour unions, they were to be punished. The greatest weapon of the working class is, of course, the threat to withdraw its labour – and this weapon the Japanese workers began to wield with a vengeance, bringing an already crippled and groggy nation to its knees.

Nissan was savaged by the strikes. Both sides employed the ugliest of methods: there were immensely cruel kangaroo courts staged by workers attempting to break the will of Nissan supervisors (and often succeeding). The company hired tattooed and often drugged gang members to break up union meetings and protests. Production plummeted: in 1950 the two working factories of the Nissan Motor

Company produced 11,072 old-model lorries and just 865 motor cars. All the books recorded losses. Other than pride and face, there was precious little keeping the firm alive. A miracle was needed.

On 25 June 1950, Kim Il Sung, *wunderkind* of the then unrecognized state of North Korea, duly provided one by marching his troops across the 38th parallel of latitude and into the Republic of South Korea. The bitter, bloody and (in terms of territory gained and lost) quite pointless war that lasted for the following three years was the perfect tonic for Japan's manufacturing industry. The Americans, whose forces led the immense United Nations effort to thwart the combined armies of North Korea and of her ally, the newborn People's Republic of China, needed lorries, jeeps and repair facilities close to the action. "A gift from the Gods," was how the Japanese Prime Minister described the war: and though the plants and assembly lines inevitably slowed once the armistice had been signed at Panmunjom in 1953, to all intents and purposes the blue touch-paper had been lit. Japan – and Nissan – were on their way.

The company's first real triumph came in 1958, when a rising young advertising manager at Nissan, Yutaka Katayama – a man obsessed with cars, engines and speed* – decided to enter two of the company's sturdiest products in a 19-day, 10,000-mile rally around Australia along some of the roughest roads in the outback. Everyone, Japanese and Australian, thought Katayama (his image as a well-born but delightfully dotty inventor enhanced by his having once designed an ultra-light peasants' car called "The Flying Feather") was certifiable. But, *mirabile dictu*, a Datsun car called Mount Fuji, designed like and apparently as comfortable as a tank, won. (The driver had driven tanks during the war.) Katayama returned to Tokyo's Haneda airport in triumph: thousands of cheering Japanese, their morale and honour buoyed up by news of the event, lined the roads into the city centre. Japan had not only astonished the motoring world, but she realized she had done so. It was this small but powerfully symbolic triumph in Australia that prompted Nissan, and all her sister companies too – for the infection of the victory spread widely, far beyond those

---

*When he became manager of Nissan's operations on the American West Coast, and took a house in Palos Verdes, he claimed that he collected more speeding tickets than any man in town. In the end, and to avoid losing his licence, he hired a chauffeur.

directly involved – to begin, with furious energy, to gear up for what they have all done so successfully ever since: to export their products around the world.

A modest consignment was duly dispatched eastwards across the Pacific: one small Datsun car, one small Datsun pick-up truck and four small Nissan engineers, led by a shy and extremely proper Nissan bondsman named Teiichi Hara, arrived on the quayside in Los Angeles later that summer. Their mission was heretical; they came as iconoclasts. To a nation whose best-informed engineers and salesmen responded to their every presentation with "I didn't know the Japanese made cars," they had to sell the extraordinary notion that not only did they make cars, but they could make very good cars – and, moreover, cars eminently suited to American roads, to American traffic, to the fantastical (by Japanese standards) style of life of the average American, and to the American wallet.

But Hara-san's team came also to do what no other visitors seemed to have attempted before: they came to *learn*; to see what American driving conditions were really like, to assess the potential competition (in essence the Volkswagen), to see what modifications, if any, were necessary before their little Datsun could think of making it on the American market. They came to gather intelligence – first as single spies, then in battalions. It was an approach that would reap rich rewards.

The car they had brought along would have been quite familiar to students of the American automobile in any case. Fundamentally the same vehicle as that designed by the now legendary inventor and honorary Japanese, William Gorham, it was not a true passenger car at all, but more like a taxi. It had all the subtle charm of a small tank, the acceleration of a lawn-mower, the brakes of a rowing-boat and the appearance and sound of a sewing machine. It was built to be a survivor; its body was made of thick steel plate which had been rolled out like pastry by such mills as the punch-drunk Japanese steel industry could bend to the task. The car was in consequence heavy and ponderous; turning the steering-wheel made you think the road was covered with treacle.

Mr Hara's team had little money to spend (they had to move into a flea-pit of an hotel in Los Angeles since they could not afford to pay more than $6 a day) and they spoke precious little English. They felt poor, quite inadequate, when they measured their standard of living against the amazing picture that presented itself: this America of chromium, vinyl and rock 'n' roll, of great cuts of beef and gallons of orange juice, of freeways and vast mansions and the endless fields of grapes, asparagus and cattle-crammed grassland. But they persevered, testing their little Datsun by running it back and forth along the freeways (they had no test-tracks of any value back home, nor the use of any in America), tinkering with it each evening, refining the gears, the dampers, the springs, the shock absorbers and the timers until it began to approach the kind of performance they imagined would be acceptable.

There is a celebrated moment in Nissan's history when the little car was humming happily along the San Diego freeway near Bakersfield, and a Volkswagen driven by an extremely unfriendly-looking man with an even more unfriendly-looking passenger pulled alongside. The two cars met a mile or two from the long uphill run that marks the edge of the San Joaquin Valley and decided – drivers glaring at each other – to race. They began neck-and-neck on the flat; but as the road began to rise so, incredibly, the German car began to fall back. By the time they had reached the summit the competition was nowhere in sight: the Datsun, it was now a proven certainty, was at least as good a performer as the best-selling import. The Japanese company could compete, and with its head held high.

The visit, the vanguard of a Japanese attack which one might argue has had a far greater global effect than that started at Pearl Harbor seventeen years earlier, did not end at all auspiciously. Mr Hara was driving the now modified Datsun along the freeway; his colleague engineer Shin Maki was in the passenger seat. Suddenly the American car ahead braked. Whether Hara-san was guilty of the familiar sin of tail-gating will never be known; but the Datsun ploughed into the back of the American car and the borrowed car with the two other engineers aboard ploughed into the back of the Datsun. Mr Maki went through the windscreen, scratched his face and had two front teeth knocked out. He found them, and stuck them back in their sockets with another great American discovery the team had made, Wrigley's chewing gum.

When the party arrived back in Tokyo next day the entire Nissan board was at the airport, eager beyond belief to know if the Gorham-designed Datsun could be adapted to suit the American market. It was destined to be an unforgettable moment in Nissan's corporate history – and also in the history of what has come to be known as Japan, Inc, too. But the moment was ever so slightly marred, for as

Shin Maki stood to make his formal address to the president and board of directors, he suddenly clapped his hand to his mouth: the chewing-gum had inexplicably lost its adhesive powers, and his two front teeth had fallen out.

Toothless though Mr Maki may have been, the board was impressed by his report. Ships leaving Yokohama port for Long Beach began to fill with Datsun cars, made specially with the steering-wheel on the left (for the Japanese still drive on the left, and need their steering-wheels on the right), destined for America. America didn't like them at first – motoring writers called the Datsun the "mobile coffin" because of unbearable, engine-generated heat inside the car. But slowly, as visiting engineering groups known as "U-teams" (for United States) modified, modified and re-modified the cars, and as the competitive prices of the Japanese imports started to make an impression on consumers, sales began to take off.

A few score a month at first, then a few hundred a month, then the first thousand – and then Yutaka Katayama, the young advertising manager who had entered a pair of Datsuns in the trans-Australia rally in 1958, was appointed head of Nissan's US West Coast operations. Katayama was a man possessed of ideas, a commodity all too seldom found among those from the Confucian tradition. They were, moreover, radical ideas, at least for their time. Above all, he wanted to bridge the Pacific Ocean that, he reasoned, so deeply divided Japan from America, East from West. He wanted to shrink the Ocean, to bring about understanding, to make the obvious connection of Kyushu to California, of Tokyo to Tucson, of Oregon to Okinawa.*

And he listened to the drumbeat of America. He learned what the dealers wanted, and what the public wanted. He revelled in the frequently-announced news that yet another Nissan dealer had become a millionaire and years later, back in Tokyo, had a map in his office emblazoned with dots showing their location. He was proud of them, as though he had fathered their fortunes. And as their fortunes

---

*David Halberstam, who tells the Katayama story well in his remarkable account of the Japanese car industry, *The Reckoning*, recounts how Katayama introduced kite-flying competitions between American and Japanese colleagues on a disused lot beside the San Diego freeway. He was fascinated by the difference – the Americans charging into the wind like frontiersmen of old, the Japanese almost secretly sidling into the breeze, backing up and releasing their kites gently into the currents. The empty lot eventually became the headquarters of Nissan America.

increased, so did those of Nissan. Sales of the company's cars in America increased steadily throughout the Sixties.

In 1964 Nissan entered the list of the top ten importers for the first time. In 1965 sales were 1,000 cars a month. By 1966 Nissan was sixth, selling 22,000 cars annually (a still negligible total when ranged against Volkswagen, which in 1966 sold 420,000 of its Beetles). In 1969 the figure was up to 58,000 sales in America.

But of even more symbolic significance was the fact that the year before, 1968, Japan had at last surpassed Germany in total car production. The Germans were still selling more cars to America, but Japan – so close to ruin so very few years before – was now second in the world to the United States in total car production, and closing the gap fast. It was closed in the mid-1970s, and the positions are now wholly reversed: today Japan makes more than 13 million cars a year, and has outstripped production in the United States (where Henry Ford had invented the very concept of the automobile assembly-line) by nearly two to one. Something like 3 million Japanese cars are now sold in America each year, and such is the rapacious expansion of the Japanese industry that their plants built inside the United States now make 800,000 cars annually for distribution on the American market, and in 1985 one Japanese car-maker, Honda, became the fourth largest car-maker in the country after General Motors, Ford and Chrysler. The Americans had lost the battle to make the world's colour televisions; now they were losing the battle to make the world's cars. The world's cars, televisions, radios, stereos, ships, girders, steel pipes, tractors, cranes, personal computers, cash registers, wristwatches – all were now being made, mostly, on the shores of the Pacific Ocean.

Not much more than a day after the *Africa Maru*'s arrival at Kashima port, the finished product which has been melted, refined, forged, pressed and rolled from her cargo of dark red earth leaves the Sumitomo factory. Scores upon scores of shiny rolls, ten tons each, of the -millimetre-thick steel sheet ordered by the Nissan Motor Company leave on their one-way journey out of Ibaraki prefecture. Some of the steel goes straight back to sea, and is loaded on to small coasting ships for transfer to the Nissan factory down in distant Kyushu, the most westerly of the main Japanese islands.

The rest leaves the factory's main gates on low-loader trucks,

173

bound for the four main Nissan car-producing plants sited on Honshu – all of them, like most of the best of today's Japanese industry, sited in the unimaginably vast metroplex fast conjoining the two cities of Tokyo and Osaka. You cannot escape seeing this apotheosis of industrial development if you travel on one of the Shinkansen "bullet trains" between the two: what (if an innocent visitor to Japan) you might have fancied would be 300 idyllic miles of classically Oriental scenery – all Fuji-san and willow-shaded lakes rendered as if on an ancient woodcut – turns out instead to be 300 endless miles of factories, large and small, with chimneys, neon signs, looping superhighways, dormitories, parking lots, bowling alleys, test-tracks and offices, and yet more factories and chimneys and the occasional vision of the distant sea, this too being adorned with container yards, shipbuilding cranes, port terminals and still more chimneys and office blocks. For an hour or so you take it, expecting that it will thin out and here at last will be the country of your dreams. And so it does thin out, for as brief a moment as it takes you to glance down at the *Japan Times*, before it resumes – it being the outskirts of Mishima or Shizuoka and Hamamatsu or Nagoya or Yokkaichi, or the city of Osaka itself.

The four Nissan plants are at Tochigi, very close to Kashima and thus to the north of Tokyo; Murayama, in the north-west of the city, where the company makes both cars and forklift trucks; Oppama, down near the American naval base at Yokusuka, south of Tokyo; and Zama, in a small town an hour to the south-west of the capital. Zama* makes its cars primarily for export, and thus is the next link in the complicated chain which takes iron-rich earth from Australia and delivers motor cars to their principal destination on the far side of the Pacific.

Zama is a small town in the shallow valley of the Sagami river, a few miles upstream from the better-known town of Atsugi which is attractive enough to see the occasional tourist. The Sagami is known for its sweetfish, an olive-coloured kind of sea-trout that migrates upriver to spawn, and which Japanese fishermen catch with the help

---

*An entirely un-Japanese name – and though the executives at the Nissan Zama plant say they regard themselves with pride as foot-soldiers in the front line of a sales war, they are generally unaware of the repute of their more famous namesake, now a small and sleepy town in deepest Tunisia. The battle of Zama was the last encounter of the Second Punic War, a long and brave piece of fighting which ended when Hannibal's forces were routed by the Romans.

of trained cormorants: watching these birds dive, often by lamplight, to spear the delicate little fish and deliver them back to their keepers presents a charming counterpoint to the factory scene that dominates so much of the Sagami Valley. Particularly a factory scene like that presented by Nissan Zama, a place as typically impressive – and, to a Western competitor, as frightening – as any of the modern Japanese monsters of manufacturing.

The factory, which was built as a lorry plant in 1965 (it reverted to car-making five years later) stretches over 212 acres, with 133 acres of buildings – three full-blown assembly lines, paint shops, stamping shops, warehouses, tool-sheds and immense multi-storey storage buildings that hold the new cars until they are ready to be whisked off to the dockside. Though there are more than 5,000 men and women employed at Zama – many of them sleeping in company dormitories beside the No. 2 body assembly shop – most of the actual building of the cars is performed by robots. The scene on the lines has the terrifyingly dehumanized aspect you would expect: bright orange machines with tubular and telescopic arms weave and dance and kneel and whirl before the objects of their brief worship – objects which, as they progress beneath the lines of orange engines, gradually evolve from mere shapes of cast metal linked to unfamiliar assemblages of girders and rods, into larger and more obviously car-like entities until, shiny with chrome, glass and paint, and with a final curtsey to and caress from their robotic makers, they bump down from the assembly rails on to their rubber tyres and are driven off by humans to the warehouse.

It was one year after the Zama plant opened in 1965 that the car that would turn out to be the most popular of the Nissan range was sent to be built there. This was the Datsun 210, soon to be rechristened (as the Datsun name was gently stifled) the Nissan Sunny or, to confuse matters more, the Nissan Sentra (as it is known in the United States). The Sentra has been – still is, with half a million of the model selling around the world each year – so important a car in Nissan's history that there is a small museum devoted to it inside Zama's main gate. Production has been continuing at Zama for more than two and a half decades, and most of the 35,000 cars made there every month are Sunnys and Sentras still: of the ten Nissan ships leaving Japan for America each month, four are filled with cars from the Zama plant, and most of the vehicles in the holds are Sentras, destined for the same roads on which the old boneshaking rattletrap of a

Gorham-designed Datsun had been tested back in the summer of 1958.*

There are, of course, different models, depending on the outlook, needs and self-image of the person who is the target customer. There are estate cars for the suburban family, saloon cars for salesmen, racier-looking models for the younger customer – "two doors or four doors? Sedan, sports coupé or wagon? Standard, E, XE or SE? Each delivering Nissan quality at an affordable price," as the brochures put it rather more seductively. (And available in twelve colours, from Vail White to Thunder Black.)

To make one Sentra car uses 1,700 pounds of Sumitomo's steel. This statistic would be more than usually tedious were it not for the fact that faraway Alan Thompson, it may be remembered, scoops up 60 tons of iron ore from the cliffs at Newman with every bite of his electric shovel. Provided the ore is rich enough, 40 tons of steel will be smelted by Sumitomo from 60 tons of Australian ore: so simple arithmetic will show that Mr Thompson's brief action of chewing into the cliff, collecting the ore and dumping it into his accompanying Haulpak will net him the makings of no fewer than 77 Sentras. Mr Thompson was not a man who was fully aware of his unique position at the cutting edge of the Pacific boom. He might appreciate things a little more now, were he ever to learn that he plays so handsome a part with each swing of his shovel.

The road connecting Zama with the port of Yokohama is neither long nor straight. It winds through Yamato and Imajuku and near the old town of Kanagawa† before reaching the port on Tokyo Bay. It is along this road that, each day, dozens of car transporter

---

*In 1988 a total of 247,000 Nissan Sentras were sold in the United States. But 112,000 of these were assembled at Nissan's own factory in Smyrna, Tennessee, meaning that 135,000 were shipped across the Pacific – 11,500 every month, or nearly four ships-full.

†Where, on 31 March 1854, the first treaty was signed between Japan and a Western nation, the United States – a treaty that formally ended more than two centuries of Japan's self-imposed *purdah*. One of the results of the Treaty of Kanagawa was the appointment of a minor New York politician, Townsend Harris, to be the first US consul to Japan, based at Shimoda nearby. It was two years before Harris travelled to Edo (now Tokyo) to meet the *shogun*. His encounter led to the 1858 Harris Treaty, opening five ports to American trade – one of them the precursor of today's Yokohama, whence a vast tide of Nissan cars travel to the United States, grotesquely imbalanced by the small trickle of American exports passing the other way.

lorries thunder eastwards, each one carrying twenty new Nissans away from Zama and down to the waiting ships. Every convoy of four trucks represents one load of Australian ore: thirty trucks make the 20-mile journey every day, to place another 600 cars gently down on the dockside. They will then be loaded, driven by dockworkers up the ramp and in through huge steel doors let into the hull or the stern, on to one of the gigantic car-carrying ships which wait to transport them and their constituent iron across the Pacific to the American west coast, 5,000 sea miles away.

4

Driving the Deficit Home

The MV *Rainbow Ace*, one of three vessels which the Nissan Motor Company has on a long-term charter, is a typical model of what is known as a ro-ro car-carrier, an utterly bizarre-looking ship, all hull and bulk with neither grace nor dignity. The moment I spotted her bright green hull, tied along the Yokohama dock, I knew I had seen her once before, a long, long way from here: not on the edge of the Pacific but in the very middle of the Indian Ocean, while I was sailing on a small yacht thousands of miles from anywhere.

She had crept up to have a close look at us during the night, and we spotted her at dawn. The entire ship's company, it seems, was standing on her bridge-wing looking down at the unexpected sight of a tiny yacht in so vast a sea. A thin voice came from above, heavily accented. "Are you OK? Do you have any problem?"

I gave the thumbs-up – *no problems down here*, I signalled, *all fine*. "Is good. We go," the voice returned. The ship sounded its siren, three times, for "God Speed and Bon Voyage", and began to inch away. There was an obvious explanation: her deck officers must have spotted what had appeared to them to be a crewless yacht, a veritable *Marie Celeste*, bobbing about in an untramped corner of the Ocean. They had sidled over to us, perhaps planning to set down a boarding party – only to see us appear on deck. They could resume their journey, and immediately did so – thundering alongside, the water churning white from the ship's bow, the rumble of her diesels becoming briefly deafening as her engine room came alongside, and then the huge maelstrom at her stern.

Rainbow Ace, it had said on her stern plates. *Kobe*. And streaming from the jackstaff was a white flag with a central red disc. "Japanese car carrier," said the skipper laconically. "Bloody ugly bugger, don't you think?"

But now the MV *Rainbow Ace* was leaving Yokohama, fully laden with 3,000 brand-new Nissan cars, for a non-stop passage to Seattle. If the master accepted the recommendations of that most august of British Admiralty publications, *Ocean Passages for the World*, she would be following the so-called Great Circle route to the North American coast. It is easy enough to imagine what the Great Circle route is by thinking thus: if a line were drawn from Yokohama to the very centre of the earth, and another from Seattle to the same central point, and if those two lines were thought of as the edges of a plane, then where that plane emerges from the surface of the earth is the Great Circle that connects Yokohama and Seattle. On a flat sheet of paper it does not look like the shortest route; but in the world of spherical geometry it is, and ships would be well advised to follow it.

In theory. However, in the basement of a sprawling office block in Sunnyvale, California, near where the US Navy built its first base for dirigibles, is a group of men and machines who are paid large sums of money to think otherwise. The firm is called Oceanroutes, Inc; it is owned by one of the mightiest of the so-called "hongs" of Hong Kong, John Swire and Sons, and its business (put bluntly) is setting the Admiralty straight. For a not inconsiderable fee, it tells ships around the world just how they should get from this port to that, taking into account all the many variables and imponderables with which the seas are filled, which the ancients involved in writing *Ocean Passages* could never have imagined.

Perhaps the most important and often most difficult of his many tasks is the decision that a ship's master takes on how best to get his vessel, his cargo and his crew quickly, economically and safely across the deep. *Ocean Passages* offers the accumulated wisdom of five centuries of ocean-going seamen over every known route in the world. Wanting to pass from Southampton to Panama? Halifax to Lagos? Yokohama to Seattle, as does the *Rainbow Ace*? The Lords of High Admiralty will always have a recommended passage:

> For ships bound between the East Coast of Japan and the west coast of North America in the months of the Northern winter, from September to May, masters are recommended to proceed . . . by

the more southerly route to Seattle. On this route bad weather is unusual, and the strength of the adverse current should not be felt after leaving Japan.

Using such magisterial advice, and then taking into account the innumerable peculiarities that make *his* ship, on *this* route, in *that* season, different from any other – the type of cargo, the amount of freeboard, the date of the last service given to No. 2 engine, the current cost of oil, the fact that the chief engineer's daughter is about to get married, whatever – the master will devise a route. He will check the likely weather – the pilot charts for the ocean will tell him the probable winds, currents, wave heights and likelihood of storms – and make further adjustments before starting his main engines, weighing anchor, easing hawsers, slipping springs and casting off. What happens then depends on his experience, his skill, his luck – and the weather.

In all probability, were the master of the *Rainbow Ace* to take the Admiralty advice and proceed via a route slightly to the south of the Great Circle (south, also, of the rhumb-line route, which is the apparent "straight line" between the two ports, if seen on a standard Mercator map projection) he will arrive in Washington State on time, having used the minimum fuel and with his vessel, cargo and crew in good shape. But there is a good chance he may not. He may well encounter a massive and unpredictable mid-ocean storm; he will have to divert round it, his men will suffer days of sickness and lowered morale; his precious cargo of Nissan cars may be battered, or soaked, or may have broken their securing chains and shifted about under the endless pounding of the sea. He may then limp into Seattle six days late, his tanks near-empty, his crew dog-tired, his Sentras damaged. How much better if he had had due warning of the storm, and had taken evasive action long before he even left port.

Hence the recent establishment of a number of so-called weather routing firms, of which Oceanroutes is one – and a convenient one to include, since it is based on the Pacific and owned by a Pacific-based corporation. Its ultimate directors are Englishmen and Scotsmen based in the centre of Victoria, Hong Kong; but the staff who really matter are principally technical men – meteorologists and marine engineers, aided crucially by banks of enormous computers that digest just about all known weather data recorded for the world's seas.

On the eve of the departure of one of its vessels, a shipping company tells Sunnyvale where it is bound, what it is carrying and the ship's size and shape. The Oceanroutes control centre – deep below a suburban street on the outskirts of Sunnyvale, with rooms alive with clattering printers, fax machines, radios and plotters, and hung with charts and perspex screens scrawled with a rainbow of chinagraph renderings of hurricanes, williwaws and typhoons – works out a sensible way to get from the one port to the other; and will then radio and telex its suggested route back to the master on the vessel's bridge. Then it will keep in touch with the ship for the duration of its voyage; if the duty weathermen spot a storm bearing down on the planned route of *Rainbow Ace* (whose position will be plotted with Chinagraph, hour by hour, on one of the perspex wall charts) they will be on the radio to the bridge within minutes, with their computer-aided recommendations for a quick and cheap way to get around it – the plan being to make faraway ships make money for their owners, and bring them home safely with their cargoes and their crew.

The Admiralty routes, it has now been found, are rarely the best for today's fleets of high-speed ships. Vessels on the winter crossing between Yokohama and Seattle, for instance, should pass on a much more northerly track than their Lordships recommended since, according to an Oceanroutes analysis, "the more common scenario to be found between latitudes 30°N and 50°N during the winter months is one of prolonged gale to storm head conditions . . . extended periods of high speed reductions are caused by weather along routes that pass through this area . . ."

Oceanroutes takes over where the Admiralty leaves off. The firm has taken the complicated business of designing ocean passages from the courteously elegant admonitions of the nineteenth-century Admiralty to the bloodless but infinitely more reliable and efficient prognoses of met-man, satellite, and computer. And by all accounts, though the seafaring romantic may sigh with nostalgic regret, the machine-made passage is the better bet.

Had Magellan entered the Pacific Ocean through the Bering Straits, rather than via "the Strait that shall forever bear his name" – or, to put it another way, had his first encounter with the ocean been close to latitude 50°N rather than precisely opposite, latitude 50°S, where his little fleet actually made its first entrance – he almost certainly would not have called it the Pacific. He selected that name for the simple reason that the sea off the coast of what is now southern Chile was exceptionally placid: after the heaving greyness of the seas of the South Atlantic, and the wind-whipped and dangerously tide-ripped waters of the Magellan Strait, the ocean itself was blue and calm and benign and well – Pacific.*

But had he encountered it where the *Rainbow Ace* was due to go, the name would have been very different indeed. For the North Pacific Ocean is a region of grotesquely appalling weather. Deep depressions come spiralling in from the poles; there are high winds and enormous waves, the waters are peppered with icebergs driven out of the straits; bitterly cold currents – the Kamchatka and the Oya Shio – meet warmer streams from the south to create immense fog banks of density unknown elsewhere in the world. And as if to add to the misery of this awful place, the countries that abut on to it seem to glare at each other over disputed islands and territory, and cover the islands they own with fortifications, air bases and naval dockyards where no one ever cares to be sent, where morale is low and tempers run high. The Pacific north of the 50th parallel, at least on the western side, is one of the least congenial places on the planet.

As the *Rainbow Ace* moved away from her berth in Yokohama, so Japan dismissed her with an appropriate augury. A powerful submarine explosion ripped open the sea off the small town of Ito, on the Izu Peninsula – just off the ship's starboard beam. It was the first time a volcanic explosion had been recorded here for 3,000 years – though it had been well known for a long time that Izu (as a place exactly on the western edge of the Pacific tectonic plate and thus showing all the violent potential of any subduction zone) would suffer an eruption at least once in a while. The day the ship left Yokohama was an ominous day for a Japan that waits expectantly for the great Kanto earthquake to come and level Tokyo again: the Izu volcano seemed a dire warning, and not even the most committed of Japanese chauvinists seemed pleased to see that the explosion created another small portion of Japanese territory by heaving out of the seabed and up into fresh air.

But the ship soon left the volcanic smoke and steam behind,

---

*Others have wondered at Magellan's impetuous naïvete. "That great sea, miscalled the Pacific," mused Charles Darwin, who knew the sea off the Galapagos Islands, as well as in more southerly latitudes. "The Pacific is an even nastier ocean than I had imagined – very much nastier than the Atlantic," wrote the wife of the Governor-General of Canada, the Marquis of Dufferin and Ava.

turned around Cape Nojima and rumbled northwards into the colder Pacific, leaving Japan to port. The waters off this part of Japan are a deeper blue than those further offshore: sixteenth-century hydrographers noticed this and named the northbound current that causes the phenomenon the Kuro Shio, the Black Current. It helped our speed by a good couple of knots: we passed Kashima, where the Australian steel had been delivered in only half a day, and (though we soon entered the colder region of the southbound Oya Shio current) we were shortly abreast of the island of Hokkaido, the northernmost of the country's four main islands. Hokkaido is best known, perhaps, for either the beer that comes from Sapporo, the splendid hot spring at Noboribetsu (one of the few places in Japan where men and women still bathe together, though the prurient behaviour of con temporary Japanese men is about to put paid to the practice even here) and the presence on the island of about 12,000 of the hairiest people on earth, the Ainu.* Thanks to the cold currents and the merciless winds from the north, the winter weather on Hokkaido is harsh: it is an island that sometimes seems more Siberian than Japanese.

The parallel is apposite: recent history and modern politics has in fact made Siberia a closer neighbour of Hokkaido than strict geography should permit. It has also left a legacy of argument and bitterness, and few are the Hokkaidoans who can ignore the lowering presence of the Soviet Union, just a few miles from their shores.

At one point the distance is just two and a half miles – possibly the narrowest of maritime frontiers. Standing below the lighthouse at Nosappu, on the very eastern tip of Hokkaido, you can see quite clearly the outlines of the Habomai Islands rising low out of the grey waters. If you look through the lighthouse-keeper's telescope, you can see soldiers on the nearer of the Habomai skerries; the men are clearly in a small monitoring post, keeping watch over the 4,000-yard-wide Goyomai Channel – and on Japan. For though the telescope is probably not powerful enough for the identification

---

*These Caucasoid interlopers in a land of Mongoloids are an anthropological oddity, celebrated for the brown hair that grows liberally over much of their bodies. The Japanese, who are not without racialist tendencies, treat them poorly – to the obvious resentment of the Ainu. An Ainu woman is said to have approached a Japanese man and demanded to know what it was that was peculiar about the Ainu – why did the Japanese regard them as if they were freaks? She asked in all innocence, though she had a vivid blue moustache tattooed around her lips, and a heavy blue beard.

of cap badges or uniform, the soldiers are members of the Red Army. Russians. The islands are not known as the Habomai Islands in the Soviet official gazeteers, nor in the British Admiralty charts: they are known by the name they were given in the late 1940s, when the Soviet Union claimed them: Ostrov Zelnyy.

The claims to the Kuril Islands – that long chain of 56 islands and rocks stretching from Kamchatka to Hokkaido* and forming the outer barrier between the Sea of Okhotsk and the Pacific itself – are complex in the extreme. The Russians have a fair historical claim to the islands: in the seventeenth and eighteenth centuries Russian explorers founded a settlement, and Siberians left the questionable comfort of their continental homes for the rude shock of life in the Kurils. But in 1855 the Japanese, uneasy about having Russians so dangerously close to Hokkaido, captured a group of the more southerly Kurils, renaming them the Chishima-retto; twenty years later, under the terms of the Treaty of St Petersburg, the Japanese took them all, and Sakhalin Island to the west was partitioned – the southern half stated to be Japanese, the rest declared undeniably Russian.

The Second World War put paid to the treaty. The Russians, who cynically entered the war for only the few days between the dropping of the atom bomb and Japan's inevitable, neutron-activated, suit for peace, stormed down from Kamchatka and Siberia and secured all of Sakhalin, and all of the Kurils, for herself. (The Yalta Agreement had, in any case, ceded the islands to Moscow's control – one of Marshal Stalin's many pleasures from having hosted, and thus attended, the Allies' meeting.) The Japanese protested at the seizure of the four most southerly islands – Shikotan, Kunashiri, Etorofu and Habomai – and at the high-handed manner in which members of the Japanese population living there were rounded up, told they had no business trespassing on sovereign Soviet territory and brusquely transported to Hokkaido.

The Russians paid no heed: the islands' names were changed to Shpanberga, Kunashir, Polanskogo and (as we have seen) Zelnyy, and the international community was asked to validate the claim. Japan, of course, has never agreed – and to the extent that the international community cares much about the happenings on the

---

*The margin of the Pacific tectonic plate, once again, with all the volcanic activity – the "ring of fire", the "halo of energy" – for which such margins are known. 100 volcanoes have been logged in the Kurils, 30 of them active.

edge of the Sea of Okhtosk, it has tended over the years to throw in its lot with the Japanese. But all to no avail: the Russians, keen to protect the Kurils as the gateway for their atomic submarines passing between the huge naval base at Vladivostok and the North Pacific, have shown no sign of ever relinquishing their gain. In the early 1980s Moscow decided to order Far Eastern Command to deploy about one division of soldiers on the four islands, to base squadrons of MiG-21 and MiG-43 jets there, to arm the islands with 133mm cannon and secure them further with *Hind* ground-attack helicopter gunships. Any Japanese fishing vessel having the temerity to stray into what the Russians consider their territorial waters is harshly dealt with.

Russia may be currently eager to foster good relations with Japan – for so very long her traditional Far Eastern enemy – but on this particular issue there is as yet no public sign that Moscow is likely to relax its stand. Diplomats say they expect a change before long, however: with the Gorbachev economy in such a shambles, and the yen so magnificently abundant, a simple equation can, they say, be worked out – a few billion yen for a few hectares of long-lost real estate. But publicly, at any rate, the Russian attitude today is like that of the British in their Imperial heyday: *what we have, we hold*. All rumours of any deals are stoutly denied. For now, despite the evident ending of the Cold War, the security of the Vladivostock-based Pacific submarine fleet is, it appears, still paramount.

The *Rainbow Ace* rumbled on into the foggy gloom. The waters grew colder and the sea had a sullen, oily look to it, as though it was coated with some kind of fishy scum. From time to time, this being one of the funnels that collect Japan's sea-borne trade from America's West Coast ports, she would encounter another vessel. On the second evening out, when she was somewhere off the profoundly inhospitable coast of the Kamchatka peninsula* the captain spoke over the VHF radio to one of his sister ships, the *Aurora Ace*, back from carrying Nissans to New Westminster

---

*Kamchatka is a dreary place, known for its tundra, volcanoes and hot springs – the site of the Soviet Union's only geothermal power station, and the Pacific's only herds of reindeer. But linguists are fascinated by it: the Palaeo-Siberian group of languages includes the fabulous Luorawetlan family, one of whose members is Kamchadal, which is spoken by a mere 500 people in the very south of Kamchatka. The interest stems from the linguists' constant search for a link between Eskimo and Korean, the latter being a tongue which, like Basque and Finnish, is of unfathomable affinity.

(just south of Vancouver) and Los Angeles. I had always wondered what car-carrying ships transported on their homeward legs, and we relayed a message to the master. "Containers-full of hay," he replied. "And lumber. And tobacco. Some new cars – Cadillacs and Lincolns are quite popular in Japan, you know. And a few second-hand cars, too – I've got a Lagonda on board, I think, for a collector. But we're mainly loaded with hay. We're very light. Not so easy to handle in big seas. And there are some plenty big seas up ahead for you."

The *Aurora Ace* passed a couple of miles off to starboard, her navigation lights obscured by mist or spray, rocking slowly back and forth under the influence of the swells. We were in deep water once again: the Kuril-Kamchatka trench lay beneath us, the Zenkevich rise – showing where the Pacific Plate was buckling up like a too-hastily rearranged carpet before plunging down to its volcanic and seismic roots – off a little to the right of our track. The names on the submarine charts had the kind of properly dignified ring to them of which old maritime explorers would have approved: there was the Emperor Seamount Chain a few hundred miles to the east, the Mapmakers Seamounts behind us and, many more thousands of miles away, the Chinook Trough and the Mendocino Fracture Zone.* However, we plunged on north-eastwards, eventually – and in the foulest of North Pacific storms – crossed the Aleutian rise and the Aleutian trench and entered the waters of that most inhospitable group of islands which, like giant stepping stones, link Kamchatka with Siberia – the only American territory to be invaded and briefly conquered by the Japanese during the Second World War.

There are about seventy Aleutian Islands, stretching in an arc more than 1,200 miles from end to end – from Fort Randall, on the western tip of the Alaska Peninsula, to the Commander Islands, in Soviet territory and on the far side of the westwardly-kinked Date Line. Follow the longitude line down from Attu Island, which is the farthest from the American mainland (and one of the two islands captured by the Japanese), and you will come across islands that are more obviously Pacific – places like Mili, in the Marshalls; Tarawa,

*But the Hess Rise, which led a trail of small subsea hills down to Midway and the Hawaiian Islands, was oddly familiar to me. Harry H. Hess, the former professor of Geology at Princeton and author of a great tectonic theory of Sea Floor Spreading, had been my guest once at a dinner in Oxford. We dined rather too well, got lost in the fog, and arrived an hour late for the speech Professor Hess was due to give. Oxford took many years to forgive me.

the capital of Kiribati; Tuvalu, once the Ellice Islands; the outer reefs of the Fiji group; and the Three Kings Islands, off the northern tip of New Zealand. Coral and palm, blue sea and lagoon – how much more typical are these islands of 175°E and its passage down the length of the Pacific. Attu, by contrast, is an utterly wretched place – permanently cold, eternally foggy, treeless, windswept, without beauty, calm or even the serenity of Arctic solitude. It is, perhaps, one of the worst places in the world.

Vitus Bering, a Dane in the service of Peter the Great, discovered and mapped the Aleutians in 1730, in an expedition noted for its setbacks and discomfort;* he returned for more punishment in 1741, lost one of his ships to their vile rocks, lost many of his sailors on their shores (and named numerous islands after his Russian crewmen), then died of scurvy on one of the Komandorskiye group, now in Russian hands but named Bering Ostrov in his well-deserved honour. Bering saw no pressing need for any Imperial conquest of the islands – they guarded nothing, except the Strait to which he had given his name and which led to and from nowhere (since Gamaland, the landmass that eighteenth-century Russians suspected linked Asia and America, did not, he discovered, exist). But the sea-otter and the fur seal had impressive skins, and the islands teemed with them: such conquest of the area as the Russians ordered (which extended, in the name of the Russian-American Company, to Alaska itself) was for commercial reasons alone – and the only commerce was in fur. The Americans bought Alaska in 1867, found gold on the mainland and promptly lost interest in the outlying islands: they left the native Aleuts to hunt and trap the fur-covered beasts themselves; surely the islands' only reason for existence.

Japan had no abiding interest in fur either when, two centuries later, her Imperial ambitions turned briefly to the Aleutians. The capture of Attu and Kiska was essentially a sideshow to the main Pacific war, but it was a sideshow of unusual symbolic significance for both sides.

The decision to strike against the Western Aleutians was part of the so-called "Second Operational Phase" of Japan's war plan. The first – the strike against Pearl Harbor, Hong Kong, the Philippines and

---

*He was given his marching orders in Finland, yet had to set sail from Kamchatka. His crossing of the unexplored and trackless Siberia, a heroic exploit in itself, took him three years before he even put a boat in the water.

Singapore (where, in perhaps the only droll moment of this dreadful period, Raffles Hotel had to undergo a ceremony renaming it the Shonan Ryokan) – was formally concluded on the 42nd birthday of the then Emperor Hirohito* with the capture of the city of Rangoon.

There was much argument in Tokyo about the thrust and direction of the Second Phase. Some admirals wanted to invade Australia – but the army, not having a spare one hundred divisions, balked at such Napoleonic folly. Others wanted the immediate seizure of Hawaii, and one group wanted to destroy Allied forces on Ceylon as a prelude to the invasion of India. Calmer voices – notably Hirohito's – were soon heard. "The fruits of victory are tumbling into our mouths too quickly," the Emperor told Marquis Kido, his Lord Privy Seal, on 9 March 1942. There was vague talk – later amplified by historians into a dull roar of "victory disease" which afflicted Tokyo's military leaders – a disease whose symptoms were a combination of hubris, haste, strategic myopia and a fatal overextension of resources. With perfect hindsight it is possible to see that the attack on Pearl Harbor itself was the worst of all possible Japanese strategies, since it would rouse a rich and powerful America into a coldly uncontrollable fury that would not abate until the war was won. There are those who would argue otherwise, but even agree today that the debate in the Tokyo spring of 1942 between the host admirals and the generals and Imperial palace functionaries, over precisely which stratagem would be the key to the Second Operational Phase of the war (which path would be taken to ensure the eternity of the Greater East Asia Co-Prosperity Sphere, as Japan's fanciful new empire was to be called) was a debate that led inevitably and inexorably to Tokyo's defeat. The winning candidate was that proposed by the architect of the Pearl Harbor attack, Admiral Isoroku Yamamoto himself; it called for the engagement and utter destruction of the American Pacific Fleet, and the simultaneous expansion of the Japanese sphere of influence to the longitude of 170°W, at the very doors of Hawaii and, significantly, inside Alaskan territory.

Wake Island at 170°E had already been taken; so had Tarawa and

*Since his death in early 1989 Hirohito has been known in Japan only by his era-name, Showa. For reasons similar to those offered earlier in this chapter – and principally to avoid confusion – most Western use keeps to the name by which the Emperor was known from the moment of his elevation to the Chrysanthemum Throne on Christmas Day, 1926.

Abemama in the Gilberts; now Yamamoto wanted to cross the Greenwich antimeridian and the Date Line and have the American Fleet lured into battle at Midway Island, 117°W of Greenwich and only seven degrees away from the target line. (Midway was a cable station on the Hawaii-Luzon route, and provided a refuelling stop for planes flying between San Francisco and Manila. It had little other importance.) At the same time, Yamamoto ordered, troops should make landings on American Arctic territory – the latter an easily-inflicted punishment with, he imagined, disastrous consequences for American morale. Kiska Island, the most ambitious of his intended conquests, also lay at 177°W – and as it happened Midway and Kiska were as close to the American mainland as the Japanese forces were ever to reach: from the moment of their having stretched out to these otherwise insignificant skerries – the infantrymen up north, the aircraft carriers in the warmer seas around Midway – they were progressively beaten back and back until, three years later, came Hiroshima and Nagasaki and the end of the Pacific War.

The Battle of Midway, one of the most decisive naval battles in history – "the greatest sea battle since Jutland" wrote the Commander-in-Chief, Pacific – was in fact an encounter almost entirely conducted by aircraft. All the ships which fell victim to the three days of fighting did so after being bombed or torpedoed by planes, not by the gunfire of each. It was this unusual aspect of the battle which proved to be the undoing of the Japanese; for though they had sent the cream of their Imperial Navy to the scene, they did not have – could not have, since they were so far away from any of their territories – the land-based air cover that might protect their ships from the Midway-based and carrier-based planes sent against them by Admiral Nimitz. So Admiral Yamamoto had to watch and listen with deepening dismay from his flagship *Yamato* as three of his carriers and one of his heavy cruisers were destroyed in a celebrated six-minute air attack on the now (to Americans) glorious Fourth of June, 1942.* The tide of war was promptly and decisively turned. Until Midway the Japanese had never lost a battle; after it they never won another.

But in public relations terms the loss at Midway was quite con-siderably offset by the triumph on the Aleutians. On the same day

*The day now holds more gruesome memories – 4 June 1989 saw the Chinese army move suddenly and violently against the students on Tiananmen Square in Peking, and it is a date that may be commemorated in North-East Asia, and perhaps around the world, for many years to come.

that the huge carrier force had launched its initial attack in the south, a smaller naval and air force under Admiral Kurita 2,000 miles to the north crept through heavy fog and rain – fog so thick the cruisers had to turn on searchlights to see where they were going – to within 200 miles of Unalaska Island, and launched a raid against the American naval base at Dutch Harbor. The raid had twin purposes; to soften the Aleutians' resistance, and to try to divert the Americans' attentions away from the principal theatre of which the Aleutians was, as we have noted, a mere sideshow. And in the first of its objectives, the Dutch Harbor raid was a success. (The second was never likely to have been won: the Americans had already cracked the Japanese naval code, knew that Midway was Yamamoto's cherished objective, and were waiting for him.) Many of the Catalinas that the US Navy used to patrol America's most miserable outposts were wrecked – enough, the Admiral concluded, for the outer bastions of the Aleutians to be attacked, and then invaded.

The invasions were scarcely on the scale of Normandy. Attu Island had a population of no more than a few dozen Aleut Eskimos, and the ten staff of a weather station. Kiska was uninhabited. And though Japanese press reports giving details of the unfurling of the Rising Sun on sovereign American territory offered the impression that the conquest had been achieved after great heroism and with much spilling of noble Japanese blood, the fact soon emerged that there had been no American opposition at all. The Japanese flotilla, realizing there was no need to hang around in the cold and stormy waters, promptly turned southwards to see if it could help with the débâcle around Midway. But to Admiral Yamamoto's further chagrin (which brought on another bout of his legendary stomach cramps) two of the heavy cruisers involved in the Aleutian triumph collided with each other and had to limp home under heavy escort, ruined for many weeks. They were effectively out of a fight that was in any case clearly on the way to being lost.

Having seized the western Aleutians without taking Midway rendered the Japanese position even more isolated, and only precariously defensible. This was made abundantly clear six months later, when the US Pacific Fleet decided that its first mission of 1943 was to replant the Stars and Stripes on Kiska and Attu. The way to do this, the C-in-C, Northern Pacific Command decided, was to isolate the islands still further by intercepting all the approaching Japanese convoys, and thus denying the garrisons all supplies. (The US Army, somewhat reluctantly, occupied Amchitka Island nearby and flew sorties in light bombers the 60 miles across the strait – the Oglala Pass, as it is now called – to help soften Japanese resistance.)

The February weather was even more appalling than usual. The first decisive American victory came on 18 February, in the very waters on which the *Rainbow Ace* was now steaming. Admiral Charlie McMorris intercepted two enemy transports that were trying to sneak supplies onto Attu, then went in and bombarded the Attu garrison, giving them a good hiding into the bargain. Attu began to get nervous.

The Japanese admiral commanding the Fifth Fleet ordered all his available resources – four cruisers and four destroyers – to bring in the next two-transport supply convoy. American naval intelligence failed to decode the signals ordering the escort group to set off, and when McMorris stumbled across this powerful group of shipping a month later off the Komandorskiye Islands, he was aghast. He had only a small cruiser group – far too small a force to withstand the Japanese. But he stood his ground nonetheless: for four hours, beginning at sunrise on 26 March, he pounded the Imperial naval vessels with shellfire so intense that they withdrew. The transports never did reach Attu, neither then nor a fortnight later when two destroyers tried unsuccessfully to breach McMorris's tough little blockade. All was thus set for invasion: the troops began to embark on American landing ships in San Francisco at the end of the month, and arrived in mid-April at Fort Randall, a bleak port at the upper end of similarly unpleasant-sounding Cold Bay, on the westernmost tip of Alaska.

By the time the force had fully assembled there were 11,000 men of the 7th Infantry Division – an immense gathering of men and material for such a flyspeck of a town as Fort Randall, but in the proper perspective just a small, faraway portion of the huge Operation Cartwheel, a series of no fewer than thirteen immense amphibious landings by which the United States intended to begin recapturing the lost ground of the Pacific.

Aleutian fog not surprisingly delayed matters. But on 11 May, eleven months and one week after the Japanese first waded ashore on Attu, American forces moved quietly towards the icy surf, guided by the submarine *Nautilus* (which had also taken part in the Midway operations, and whose successor, the first atomic-powered submarine in the world, went on to sail in even colder waters, traversing the entire Arctic Ocean under the North Pole).

Resistance was, at first, pleasingly limited. The "several thousands" of Colonel Yamakazi's men who were expected to defend the beaches never materialized, and the 7th Infantry swept on to the shores anticipating an easy time of it. They might have known better – the resistance eventually put up by Yamakazi's men was both in the best spirit of *bushido* and an ominous warning to those American soldiers and marines who would later try to dislodge the Japanese from Saipan, Okinawa and Iwo-jima. For the men on Attu fought brilliantly, careless of the fact that they were outnumbered five to one and that they had been all but abandoned by their colleagues in the big Japanese supply bases on the Kuril Islands. A fleet had been despatched north from Truk, and big cruisers were coming up from the Kurils – but Imperial General Headquarters decided, quite simply, that the game was not worth the candle. There were other, more significant targets to defend. Yamakazi would have to fight on as best he could.

The Americans dropped leaflets urging him to surrender, but he ignored both the pleas and his plight. Like a wounded wolf, he retreated into a defensible lair at the end of Chichago Harbor, from where he fought on stubbornly, his men progressively running out of food, water and ammunition. On 29 May, his position quite hopeless, the colonel led his men down the steep hillside to make one last-ditch *banzai* attack on the Americans. It was the biggest *banzai* assault of the entire war – a thousand men tearing down the icy hill, screeching out "Japanese drink blood like wine!", throwing themselves uselessly against the bayonets and machine guns of the stupefied American soldiers.

It was a pitiless business. Only 28 men were taken prisoner, out of 2,500 who had held the island. One thousand Americans died in the assault. It was a lesson in both American organization and power, and Japanese courage and determination. Repeatedly pitting such attributes against each other was to cost the blood of both nations dearly before the war was finally won.

Kiska Island, by contrast, was quite deserted when 35,000 astonished infantrymen stormed ashore two months later. The Japanese knew the island was indefensible and, in a daring and brilliantly executed operation involving two cruisers and six destroyers, carried out under the cover of thick July fog, evacuated all 5,000 of their troops within an hour and sped with them back to the Kurils. For once the weather that so dogs all intra-Aleutian voyages, whether by

Bering on the *St Peter* or Nissan Sentras aboard the *Rainbow Ace*, had proved a kindly soul.

Today the Aleutian Islands bristle with American military bases, not so much for fear of a new upsurge of Japanese nationalism but because of the proximity of Soviet Siberia. Amchitka, for instance, was used as a site for underground atomic bomb testing – the Arctic twin of Bikini. The Coast Guard is on Unalaska. The US Navy has a large station on Adak – reckoned by many to be punishment quarters. I once knew a man in the naval public information office at Subic Bay in the Philippines who had thought he was going to be posted to the naval liaison office in London. I saw him the day he received his orders and he appeared to have aged five years in as many minutes. His Luzon tan had faded and he looked like the Pilsbury doughman. He stared down at the buff telegram form. "Adak fucking Alaska," he kept murmuring to himself, in utter disbelief. "Adak fucking Alaska. What in fuck's name did I do wrong?"

Of precisely what solecism my friend had been judged guilty was never to be explained. But no doubt the US Navy would have tried to bolster his morale, to reassure him of Adak's key role in protecting the United States. From Adak are managed the two parallel arrays of submerged sonar detectors which, one running parallel to and north of the Aleutians, the other parallel to and to the south, supposedly check on the movements of Russian submarines in and out of the vast hiding-ground that is the Pacific. Ballistic missile submarines wander from their pens at the Siberian ports of Petropavlovsk, Magadan, the new port of Sovetskaya Gavan, Vladivostok and the North Russian port of Murmansk, and they gather in large numbers under the polar ice. Whether they then move out into the Atlantic through the North Sea or the Greenland-Denmark gap, or to the Pacific through the Bering Straits and around the Aleutians, is something only the submarine SOSUS chains can detect: Adak, like Keflavik in Iceland, is a miserably-located but apparently vital installation on the main North Pacific SOSUS chain – and someone, after all, has got to do the job of manning it. That, or something like it, is what my Subic friend would have been told within hours of stepping off his transport plane into the gales and fog of his new home.

But perhaps the most important Aleutian base is that on Shemya, whose lights we could see off to port as we sliced on a barely east-by-north course through the forty-mile passage between the Attu and the Kiska Groups (more properly called the Near Islands and the Rat

Islands). Not that Shemya is any more popular than Adak. It is an air force base, and the men call it The Rock, just as inmates of Alcatraz were wont to do. It is so forlorn and isolated a place that one tale has passed into Shemyan folklore: in the late 1960s a North-west Orient Airlines jet made a forced landing on the all-weather strip on Shemya and the crew – including one stewardess – were briefly entertained at the officers' club. A Mr Elwin Williamson of Natick, Massachusetts, who was serving on the island at the time, said the stewardess was the only woman he had seen in a year, and the chair on which she had been sitting was later auctioned among the enlisted men.

Shemya is home to a small detachment of converted Boeing 707s, known as RC-135s, which are assigned to the highly-classified Cobra Ball programme by which the air force and its intelligence organization, the Electronic Security Command, seeks to find out about Soviet missile testing in and around Siberia. The grey-and-white, black-nosed planes – which can stay in the air for more than ten hours at a stretch – fly out from Shemya towards the Kamchatkan coast on virtually daily missions. They are packed with monitoring equipment – special high-speed cameras with powerful lenses and high-resolution film that can capture pictures of missile warheads in flight and banks of receivers for intercepting and decoding the missiles' telemetry signals.

Since Kamchatka is one of the Soviet Union's principal rocket test firing sites – the missiles are supposed to fall harmlessly into the vastness of the world's vastest ocean – and since Petropavlovsk on the eastern Kamchatkan coast remains one of the most important of Russian naval bases, the presence of such intelligence-gathering men and machines in the Aleutians is reckoned by the Pentagon (and more particularly, by the National Security Agency in Fort Meade, Maryland) to be vital. The men who have the ill-fortune to work there apparently feel otherwise; and as the loom of the Shemya Base lights slipped out of sight behind our wake, and became lost in the gloom and icy spray of another bitter sub-Arctic evening, one had to sympathize with them. Like Adak, Attu and Amchitka, Shemya must be a dismal place to have to live, even for a day.

The man who directs the lives of those inhabiting the bases lives in somewhat more salubrious surroundings, 2000 miles and a whole climatic world away. He is an Admiral, and at the best of times a difficult man to find.

The first report, when once I went to seek him, said he was in

Madagascar. Then, that he was on an official visit to Fiji. Someone said he had been seen in Karachi, and a naval attaché at the British consulate had met him at a cocktail party on Bahrein Island. Then his advisers let slip that he had been appearing before a committee of Congress in Washington for a week or so, and had come back on station for a three-day trip to Korea, Japan and Northern Luzon; it was not very often, the aides said, that he was back at home base in Camp H. M. Smith, on the island of Oahu in Hawaii. Perhaps this was not altogether surprising for a man whose responsibilities included the defence of Western interests over fully one-half of the earth's surface – 100 million square miles of land and sea (mostly sea) – the supreme operational head of the most devastating military force assembled anywhere on the face of the earth.

And more. The Admiral is commander of naval, air, marine, coast-guard and army power whose influence stretches from the sands of the East African coast to the icebergs of the Ross Tableland, from the fog here in the Bering Straits to the gentle swells of the Sulu Sea, from the land of Mongols to the bars of San Francisco. A man, moreover, who so infrequently settles in one place for more than one moment that he rarely has time to see anybody other than men and women in uniform, or their rulers and directors.

When first I saw him the sun was glaring down over the glittery stacks of Waikiki, the surf was up and Diamond Head glowed gold. Camp H. M. Smith was, as the taxi-meter showed, quite far away – and, as it turned out, in style as well as distance.

It had nothing in common with the hula-skirt, Coppertone, beach-bum image of Hawaii. Instead it was a rather uninspiring collection of breeze-block huts halfway up a hill, all strictly business, no fun at all. From the entrance gate – guarded by a truck-sized Marine, for this is a Marine camp (and H. M. "Howlin" Mad" Smith was a Marine hero) – you could see the grey slabs of warships down below in Pearl Harbor. In the middle of the Roads lies the strange, inverted white concrete arch that is the memorial to the USS *Arizona* and the "day of infamy" in December 1941. The sunken battleship is Hawaii's second biggest tourist attraction, though mostly for American visitors; the Japanese tend to stick to the beaches and the shops, or to their habit of buying houses and tracts of Hawaiian land.

But the view was of no immediate consequence: passes had to be verified, salutes exchanged, corridors tramped through, doors unlocked, and military men in a glorious crescendo of rank had to signal approvals and mutter passwords. Until finally the linoleum gave way to carpet, the breeze-block outlines became smothered in soothing pastel paints, and oil portraits of the men of "Old Navy" – Nimitz, Halsey, John Paul Jones – replaced the charts, maps and safety warnings which had covered the walls below. "Welcome aboard!" cried an ensign, and a thick oak door opened to reveal the anteroom – the outer cabin, they call it, a heartbeat away from the Commander.

Despite the calming of the world elsewhere, the Admiral who presides from the inner cabin has still to deal with what America perceives as a superabundance of local crises – both actual and dangerous, as well as potential and alarming – in the vast sphere of his oceanic domain. On any day the questions keep rattling in. Will the North Korean army smash down the fences on the DMZ and once again invade the South? Will the Philippines' battling Communist rebels – still Communists, though far behind the fashion – triumph in Negros, or the Islamic separatists in Mindanao, and bring down Cory Aquino's fragile government? Or if not Marxists, what about the right-wingers and disgruntled bandits in the Philippine army? Or the threat of simple assassins, gangsters who loathe Americans and wish them out of their former colony, and who threaten to murder those who go to the girlie bars of Olongapo and Ermita?

Then again, have the Russians moved a new aircraft carrier into the Vietnamese port of Cam Ranh Bay? Which foreign power is trying to enter into a new tuna-fishing treaty with Kiribati, and why are the Cubans opening an embassy in the capital of Vanuatu? What dangerously pacifist legacies has the old New Zealand Prime Minister instilled in the heart and mind of the new? Does the continuing outflow of Indian nationals from Fiji spell coming economic instability in Suva? Will the new (and, oddly, *ethnic Japanese*) president of Peru put paid to the excesses of the Maoists of the fearsome movement called the Shining Path? What of China since Tiananmen? And what of Hong Kong in the last few years of British rule?

There are marginally lesser problems too, one of which in fact had caught the office's attention on the day I arrived. What to do about American sailors who become infected with the AIDS-triggering HIV while on shore-leave in Mombasa? Do we keep our carriers away from East Africa and let that fall to troublemakers too?

And so on and so forth. One can be more rapidly persuaded here than anywhere else that the modern world centres on the Pacific

Ocean. The Atlantic and its congruent seas bristle only with the alarums of yesterday – the Middle East, South Africa, Northern Ireland – and resonate to the new rhythms of collapsed Communism, a reunited Germany, an amiable Warsaw Pact, a half-pointless NATO, and a cold war ended without armistice but by the general consensus that it had run its course. In its own way, history had come to a temporary end in Europe.

But according to the geopoliticians and Pentagon advisers of Camp H. M. Smith, the Pacific bristles with the problems of tomorrow's world: problems of the new geopolitics, problems without established answers, problems which all the superpowers (for all three border the Pacific, which is another reason for the Ocean's unique importance) have an interest in solving, or exploiting, or making worse.

Politicians and diplomatists are there to endeavour to settle these problems, and to try to seize any opportunities for advantage that their solutions present. But to give additional weight to their arguments – or, of course, to deal with the mess they will leave if they fail – are the armouries. These – the stocks of weapons, men and machinery that are held in the bases, encampments and fortresses in and around today's Pacific – constitute the most fearsome assemblage of apparatus for making war to be found anywhere on the planet. And the Western, Allied stocks of all these weapons, men and machinery are under the practical day-to-day command of the Admiral whose office is in the panelled cabin at the quiet centre at the Camp.

In the days before our meeting, staff in a variety of offices sprinkled around Pearl Harbor did their level best to provide a list of all the military units which the Admiral actually *does* command. This proved a formidable task: 362,000 people work directly under the Admiral's flag. Via a bewildering array of acronymic titles, his word percolates through fleets, aerial combat units, army battalions and marine forces – all the way down to platoon dental teams on Truk, paymasters in Alaska and Forces Post Office clerks in Japan and on Diego Garcia.

Thus there is, under USCINCPAC (the Admiral), another (slightly lesser) Admiral who commands the two Pacific Fleets and is called USCINCPACFLT; an Air Force General who is known as USCINCPACAF; an Army General who is CINCWESTCOM, the Commander-in-Chief, Western Command; and another man called COMFMFPAC who controls the Marine Fleet Force, Pacific. A long way down the line come such magnificent creatures as USCINCPACREPSWPAC, who is the Admiral's official representative in the South-Western Pacific. He is based in Fiji, and the brass plaque on his door is said to be longer than many of the ships that sail into his harbour.

Given the size and complexity of this immense force, there are some pockets of near-total lexicographical insanity. Take one of the most important commands that is directly answerable to the Admiral – the 45,000-strong, ever-alert and battle-ready group of men and women who make up the United States Forces, Korea. Their own particular commander is an army man and he has the following problem, as explained by one of the officers beavering away for me in Honolulu:

USCINCPAC (the Admiral) exercises operational command of the Eighth United States Army (EUSA) through the subordinate unified commander (the General). The commander, who has his headquarters in Seoul, Korea, is also Commander-in-Chief, United Nations Command (CINCUNC); Commander-in-Chief of the Republic of Korea/United States Combined Forces Command (CINCCFC); and Commander, United States Forces, Korea (COMUSKOREA). As CGEUSA he reports to the Department of the Army; as CINCCFC he reports to the ROKUS Military Committee; and as COMUSKOREA he reports to USCINCPAC (the Admiral).

I met the General, the centre of this bureaucratic whirlwind, on the golf course outside his headquarters in Seoul one day. He was accompanied by an Englishman named Captain Richard Margison, who turned out to be commander of a Coldstream Guards platoon that was guarding him – because the General was a United Nations commander as well as an American commander, and because during the Korean War the British Army was part of the UN force. Oddly, Captain Margison also turned out not to be English at all, but an American with a huge farm in upstate New York. An American, working as a platoon commander in the British Army? It was just what I was coming to expect in the kind of fantastic, Alice-in-Wonderland world with which I was dealing in what the Pentagon, with unintended irony, calls "the Pacific theater".

Captain Margison explained another of the complexities of his General's life: he apparently has one staff assistant whose specific task is to intercept and reply to any letters and memoranda that the General writes *to himself* – which he does a great deal, it seems, because he wears so many hats and they all need to know what each of the others is doing. "You sometimes feel you're going mad," said Margison, whose three-month tour was nearly up, and who looked forward eagerly to rejoining his Coldstream messmates back in Hong Kong.

Away from the lexicographical and organizational nightmares, the Admiral's armoury remains fairly straightforward. It is also truly massive. The most mobile of his battle platforms are, of course, the ships: around 220 of them, with the giant nuclear-powered aircraft carriers like the *Coral Sea* and the *Carl Vinson*, and the old battleships – 60,000 tons of doorstep-thick steel such as the *New Jersey*, the *Iowa* and the *Missouri* – leading the pack. There are an undisclosed number of Ohio-class Trident strategic submarines, prowling for months on end, sneaking into the Sea of Okhotsk or trawling at periscope-depth through the outer harbours of Vladivostok, or wandering on limitless patrol scores of feet below the region's Seas – the Tasman, the Bering, the Arabian, the Japan, the East China, the South China and the Coral.

Then there are the smaller warships, those with a more strictly limited purpose: guided-missile cruisers and destroyers, assault ships and frigates, oilers and submarine support bases, electronic warfare command and control ships, one salvage tug made in England, and the TAK-6 Fleet Ballistic Missile Resupply Ship which looks as though it should be filled with bananas but which in fact holds enough atomic warheads to blow the world apart. All told 32 attack submarines, 6 aircraft carriers, 76 surface combatants, 33 amphibious ships and 54 auxiliaries.

There are 238,000 navy men and women out there, organized into two Fleets – the Third, which deals with the Pacific from California out as far as the Philippines, and the Seventh, which takes in all the Western Pacific and the Indian Ocean too; and there are 1,900 navy planes and 700 Marine aircraft and helicopters. There are the mighty bases at Subic Bay and San Diego, the stations at Guam and

Okinawa, those on the Japanese mainland and up near Seattle, and the strategically vital leasehold base on the British colony of Diego Garcia, which sports 1,170 navy men and a good deal else besides.

In blue-water terms alone, the Admiral commands a fearsome machine for the prosecution of a war.

But there is much more. There is the Pacific Air Force, with bases at Hickham Field and Wheeler on Hawaii itself; three gigantic installations in Japan – Yokota, Kadena and Misawa; four – Kunsan, Osan, Suwon and Taegu – in Korea (where some are soon to be run down, thanks to the recent easing of tensions); and Clark Air Base in the Philippines, with its scores of fighters, transport aircraft and spy-planes. In Guam, too, there is a detachment of strategic bombers – not under the Admiral's direct control but answerable to the commander of Strategic Air Command across in Omaha, Nebraska, and filled to the gills with atomic bombs. The Admiral has more than 330 Air Force planes at work for him and presumably does not begrudge CINCSAC – the initials are inevitable – the odd collection of hardware on Guam.

The Pacific army is no mean force either. The Eighth Army is specifically dedicated to Korea; IX Corps and all its many brother units are in Japan: and Western Command is based in Hawaii, down the road from Camp Smith. WESTCOM, with the elite 25th Infantry Division at its core, supposedly has the ability and the equipment to go anywhere and fight any war, whether brushfire or the stuff of history, between the shores of Lake Victoria, the oilfields north of Anchorage and the suburbs of Auckland.

And finally the Marines, toughest of the lot. The Admiral has twenty-one battalions ranged from quonset huts on Diego Garcia to air-conditioned barracks in Yuma, Arizona. There are Heavy Helicopter Squadrons, Tank Battalions, Assault Amphibian Battalions and Marine All-Weather Attack Squadrons. Strangest-sounding of all is a unit called the Near Term Prepositioned Ships Program Brigade, which is based in Arizona but does most of its work out in the Indian Ocean, ready to save the Gulf oil-fields, the ports of Southern Pakistan, VOA's transmitting station being built outside Colombo (from Tamil guerillas), or to carry out any other task which the Admiral – on orders from the Oval Office – has in mind.

Assuming that a cold war of sorts is still being fought across the Pacific, the Admiral's Soviet opposite number is the holder of an office that in Pentagon-speak would be called CINCFETREC, the Commander-in-Chief, Far Eastern Theater, Regional Command. Navy men whom I met in Honolulu noted with some disdain that the Soviets traditionally select an army man for the post; on the day I met the Admiral it was a coarsely ungenial bear of a man named General Ivan Moiseyevich Tret'yak. He was 63, stood six feet tall and weighed twelve and a half stone. The US Navy knew where he had been to school and what his interests were, and an aide produced a rather fuzzy photograph showing a thickset man with a slight squint. Where was he based? "Classified information," the aide chipped in, before an answer could be offered. But a week later I had a letter saying it wasn't classified at all and in fact General Tret'yak had his headquarters at Chita, 700 miles east of Irkutsk. "Not much fun for him in winter," said one of the officers. "Not a patch on Hawaii."

But back up in the gloom of the far Pacific north, we ploughed ever onwards, doubling back down through the Aleutians once more as our Oceanroutes navigation plan had us weave through the Unimak Pass and out beyond the fog banks, into open water. Alaska was some hundreds of miles off our port flank now, and from time to time we spied an oil tanker heading south, fully laden, from the port of Valdez, where since 1977 the Alaska Pipeline has brought North Slope Crude down from the mighty field at Prudhoe Bay * There were American cruise ships, too, bringing blue-rinsed ladies from Milwaukee up to see the glaciers, the seals and perhaps even the salmon-eating bears of Kodiak Island.

I suddenly sensed that the waters on this side of the Date Line seemed in some inexplicable way more homely, more comfortable, less obviously polyglot, despite our lumbering presence. They had a certain *feel* of America about them, though for no obvious reason save the shipping: the water itself was grey and cold still, while the seabirds were no different and uttered squawks in equally unintelligible tongues. Perhaps, I fancied, it was all to do with the names on the charts – Cape Fairweather, Salisbury Sound, Mount Edgecumbe, Chatham and Dixon Entrance had a kind of domestic ring to them, a sort of familiarity I had not known since leaving Port Hedland many weeks before. The radio, too, burbled with

---

*When, after years of wrangling over the possible environmental consequences of the Trans-Alaska Pipeline, it was decreed that it should be built, no American steel mill was able to produce pipe of the right size and quality. Only the Japanese could oblige – a trans-Pacific connection of the Seventies that in its own way is as beguiling as the Nissan car-carrier's connection of today.

American accents, and from time to time the master spoke to Coast Guard watch stations and passing boats, and there was a refreshing breeziness in the exchanges; the voices rang with the confidence and self-assuredness that is so characteristically American. In short, it felt good to be back again, after a long, long time away.

It was six years, in fact, since I had last been around these waters – aside from innumerable visits to Anchorage airport, when I had been spilled, complaining, from flights proceeding from European cities like Brussels and Amsterdam to such Asian capitals as Seoul and Tokyo, flights somewhat misleadingly advertised as proceeding "over the Pole". (The development of the new Boeing 747-400 series of jumbo jets in the late 1980s would change all that, however, and would spell the eventual end of such nightmares as enforced fuel-stops at Anchorage for long-haul flights – a development of immense importance to the life of the Pacific, as will be explained in a later chapter.)

My last visit had been to a town called Ketchikan, which was even now 100 miles or so off to the left, the east of the *Rainbow Ace*. It had been a strange odyssey, occupying a fortnight of a February in the early 1980s when I was living in New York and working for one of the livelier British newspapers. A small Associated Press paragraph datelined Ketchikan had chattered in over the wire machine, and to those of us living a pleasantly flabby life in Manhattan it was a tale that smacked of heroism of the old school. I called London, packed an overnight bag (that would have to serve me for ten times as long as I expected), flew cross-country to Seattle, met a photographer who was similarly impressed by the tale's potential and then took a smaller jet up to Ketchikan itself.

"Spread wings of a prostrate eagle," the town's name supposedly meant, according to a brochure which obligingly published a translation of Tlingit Indian vernacular: but it looked too dreary a place to have much association with eagles, what with the endless drizzling from a slate-grey sky and the all-pervading smell of sour lumber, steam, glue and fish. There were perhaps a dozen streets, all of which either ended in the sea or petered out into the pine forests with which Revillagigedo Island* was wholly covered. There was a pulp mill at one end of town, belching steam; there was a sawmill at the other,

*Not to be confused with the world's only other Revillagigedo, an island some few hundred miles off the coast of Mexico.

with its pepperpot-shaped sawdust furnace oozing smoke; a clutch of orange-painted fishing boats hugged the small dockside, clustered beside a rusty old coaster settled deep in the water from which fresh supplies – boxes of oranges and bananas, cheese and chocolate – were being unloaded. It looked like a frontier town, connected only by air and by sea to a country of which, for most of the time, it can hardly have seemed an integral part.

The story was very much a frontier tale. It seemed that there was a West Virginian named Wortman who lived in town with his three teenage children, two girls and a boy. By all accounts he was a quiet sort of fellow and not particularly well off – he had been a miner in the Appalachians until he was laid off back in the Seventies, and had come up north to work as a jobbing carpenter and handyman. He kept his own counsel, the neighbours said; the family lived in a very ordinary frame house, with a rusty and beaten-up old Chevrolet pick-up. There was no wife.

His only luxury – his pride and joy, one might say – was a 30-foot sloop, the *Betsy*, which he had built himself in his back garden. She was a tough little wooden craft, seasoned, wizened and tempered by the cold and the waves – a boat that was, in more ways than one, something like Wortman himself. He boasted that she could go anywhere, and in coastal Alaskan waters such a claim was not one to be made idly. These were, the locals said, the toughest waters in the world. (Locals always say such things, of course. By the absolute standards of world-ranging mariners, *the* most difficult are usually said to be found off the Wild Coast of the Transkei, in South Africa.)

It seems that one of the two Wortman daughters had front teeth that were shaped with a little less than the perfection demanded by today's American teenagers. The girl demanded that she visit the local orthodontist – a visit that Wortman reckoned would set him back many hundreds of dollars, and which prompted him to come up with an alternative plan.

Orthodontists, he said, were every bit as good – but a great deal less costly – down in Canada. Why not go down to the nearest Canadian town which was likely to have such a surgeon – Prince Rupert, British Columbia – and moreover, why not go aboard *Betsy*? It would prove a useful exercise in sailing, it would be fun and would enable the young Miss Wortman to have her teeth made presentable at minimal cost. All three children readily agreed. *Betsy* was duly loaded with food and supplies, and the four set off one Saturday morning in a half-gale, southward along the Clarence Strait, bound for the frontier and Prince Rupert, 100 miles away.

It proved an easier voyage than they had imagined. The little boat chuckled along for a day and a half, and by nightfall on the Sunday they were at the mouth of the Skeena River and at the terminus of the Canadian National Railway, in the 16,000-strong town named after the first Governor of the Hudson's Bay Company, back in 1906. (Prince Rupert had been one of the main assembly points for American forces due to take back Attu and Kiska Islands in the Aleutians from the Japanese, as recounted earlier.) They checked through passport and customs control and spent the next day, Monday, shopping and sightseeing and having the youngster's teeth fixed. By mid-morning on Tuesday they were ready to set sail again: the weather was calm, the sea was slight, the air temperature a little above freezing. They should be home by Wednesday morning.

It was shortly after midnight that *Betsy* ran aground. One moment they were peacefully asleep, curled around each other to ward off the gnawing cold of the far North-Eastern Pacific in February. The next there was a terrible splintering crash, and they were flung into a maelstrom of icy water. It was pitch-dark and spitting with sleet, and as they struggled to the shore – a thin line of white surf could just be made out pounding against the island they had seemingly hit – they tried their best to salvage something from the wreck. They found each other first; their accumulated possessions included a few spars of wood and a bag of onions. The "panic bag" which most prudent yachtsmen stash away, ready for just such a moment, had vanished.

The four huddled together on the rocky beach through the night, soaked, freezing and frightened. But by morning something of the spirit which persuades or compels men to go to such places as Ketchikan, Alaska – and being an American, Wortman could have lived in warmth and comparative comfort anywhere from San Francisco to St Augustine – had apparently come alive. The father and his thirteen-year-old son, aware there was no time to lose, built a crude shelter for the girls, lashed together some spars of driftwood and, realizing that the tiny islet on which they had stranded was of no possible use for survival, took off for the long, low island they could see off to the west. They both wore jeans and sweaters, but neither had any shoes; those had gone down with the *Betsy*.

It took the pair a little less than a week to stumble and hobble their way along the island, through snowfields and across frozen rivers. They trapped Arctic hares; they ate the seeds of wild sedge, and lichens. They were in terrible shape, their feet blackened with frostbite, when finally, just as they were about to give up and turn back to where the girls had been told to wait, they found a small fisherman's hut down by the water's edge. They broke in. There was food – chocolate, oats, dried milk, raisins – and there was fuel for the cooker. And most important, there was a working VHF radio. Wortman cranked it into life and broadcast a "Mayday" message before collapsing on the bunk, exhausted.

The orange-and-white Coast Guard rescue helicopter from Sitka was with them in an hour and the sisters, astonished at their good fortune, were picked up thirty minutes later. The girls were in surprisingly good condition – ample testimony to the benefits of female puppy-fat, though to augment that the pair had found some molluscs on the beach and had eaten them, cold; and they, also, had savoured the delights of Alaskan lichen. The girls were taken straight home; Wortman and his son were whisked off to the Ketchikan hospital, and had to have a number of their toes amputated. Within a couple of days, though limping a little, they were back in business.

Such was the story we had to tell. The family was reluctant to talk at first – reticence and stoicism being the handmaids of Arctic living. No other reporters had come up to Ketchikan, though, and within a day we were being regarded as the most curious of animals, fêted and shunned by turns. We stayed ten days in town, and came to know almost every inhabitant and most of the very few civilized square miles of Revillagigedo Island. It took all our reserves of persistence, charm, petty bribery and rat-like cunning to breach the walls of silence that surrounded the Wortman family – and it took all the stoicism and financial underpinnings which are the normal complement of a faraway editor's desk to keep us in town while we did so. Eventually it all paid off: the piece, handsomely illustrated, duly made it into the paper in London, and was sent by syndication around the world – and, indeed, back to America and Alaska itself – thus helping to create the small legend of "The Man from Ketchikan". There was a long article in the *Reader's Digest* some months later, under the rubric "Drama in Real Life"; and there was a book, privately printed, called *Almost Too Late*.

But in all other respects the Wortman family and Ketchikan slowly faded both from the public mind and from mine too – until I noticed the name of the dreary little town in the *Rainbow Ace* chartroom, and wondered idly about the current appearance of Miss Wortman's teeth, and the state of her brother's and her father's ruined feet. I wondered too whether we might see the reincarnation of *Betsy* bobbing along beside us, but that, not surprisingly, was not to be.

Gazing over the taffrail towards the distant, snow-capped peaks that afternoon, I found myself musing on just why adventures such as that of the Wortman family have a tendency to befall Westerners – why one so rarely reads of such a thing happening to a Japanese family, to someone from Korea or China. Did they never put to sea in boats – did they never go exploring, wandering for the sheer sake of wandering? Were they somehow reluctant to take the risks of exploration and pioneering, the breaching of conventions so often entailed in travels of both body and mind?

There must surely, I said to myself, have been *some* risk-takers, some men from this corner of Confucian Asia who would have made the leap in the dark that is sometimes necessary to accomplish the extraordinary, to go to places never before known, to attempt to move knowledge and society on another notch or two. Of course, the Chinese are now spread around the world – an immense hegira has taken place that will be related in a later chapter – and not a few went to their present homes by sea. But racking my brains that afternoon I could come up with only one famous name: Admiral Cheng Ho from Kunming, the Chinese explorer who found his way to Africa in the fifteenth century. And he was not a product of the Confucian tradition at all: he was a Muslim, the son of a hajji.*

His voyages were unusual, in any case. The European travellers who followed him – Vasco da Gama, Marco Polo, Magellan, Balboa – did so for reasons that were, if not always creditable, at least practical. They travelled to conquer, to trade, or simply to discover. In other words, there was a rational purpose to their journeying. But

---

*Further, the Admiral's "proper" Chinese name was not Cheng, but Ma – and this was said to have been derived from Mohammed, since one of his antecedents was Mohammed, King of Bokhara, a typically restless Central Asian who could well have engaged in the kind of exploration that the more ethnically and ethically mainstream Chinese, both of the fourteenth century and today, would scarcely contemplate. To scotch the notion, held dear by believers in machismo, that courage is directly proportional to body-levels of testosterone, it is also worth recalling that Cheng Ho was a eunuch.

when the Ming court permitted Cheng Ho to begin his series of huge naval expeditions – and huge they were, with more than 70,000 men travelling on some of the voyages in immense, specially built ships* – the sole purpose was no more and no less than display. The Ming emperor, Yung Lo, was content merely to show to such of the rest of the world as was interested that he was master of the most powerful empire on the face of the planet. He had no interest in interfering, nor in plundering. If the countries his navy visited concurred with his self-image of power and grandeur, then those countries were helped, insofar as China was able to do so, with any little local difficulties they might have; if, on the other hand, some were so foolish or shortsighted as to dispute China's claims to be global suzerain then, with a contemptuous shrug of their shoulders, the emissaries of Ming would sail away in search of more pliant states.

The motive for Cheng Ho's expeditions may have been questionable, by today's Western standards; but his achievements are undeniable. His first voyage, which began in 1405, shortly after he had been ennobled as "Commander in Chief of Missions to the Western Oceans" by the Emperor, involved 62 ships and 27,800 men. It took two years, during which Cheng went to Champa (now the southern part of Vietnam), Siam, Malacca and Java, then to Calicut and Cochin on the south-west tip of India, and the island of Ceylon. Two years later he was back in Ceylon where, despite the Ming intention to roil no waters, he became involved in a dispute that prompted him to take the king back home with him as captive. The third voyage took him to Hormuz, where today's tanker-choked Straits are (choked principally with tankers bound for Japan). In 1413 – the energy of the man seems to have been prodigious – he went past Hormuz to Aden and Dofar, with a Chinese mission visiting Mecca, and the fleet itself visiting Brava and Malindi and almost reaching today's Mozambique Channel.

It was on this journey that Cheng Ho discovered a giraffe, and became so enchanted by its strangeness that he had it captured and hobbled, and brought it back as a gift for the Emperor in Nanking. Yung Lo thought it an amazing beast; his courtiers even more so, one of the more sycophantic of them suggesting that it was a specimen of a fabulous animal known as Chi Lin that, according

---

*Some were as much as 2,500 tons burthen, and Marco Polo was said to be deeply impressed to find the officers aboard had private bathrooms.

to Chinese mythology, appeared only during the reign of a perfect sage. Yung Lo, who was no fool, brusquely told the official to stop being so silly.

The Cheng Ho travelling circus continued its wanderings until 1433. They reached the island of Timor, close to the Australian mainland, leaving one small legacy of their visitation in today's Chinese tongue. The ideographs still in use for the island give the sound "Tee-mor' only when said in the dialect of Foochow, which is where Cheng Ho's fleet originated. All the other islands nearby have as their Chinese names sounds which are similar to their native names only when pronounced in the dialect of Amoy, whence most of the current settlers came.

But once Yung Lo had died, the curious impetus behind the Admiral's journeys began to evaporate. The Imperial Navy had suffered a number of small, but irritating defeats, and naval prestige was low; the Grand Canal had just been completed, and the huge convoys that travelled its thousand-mile route from Hangchow to the new capital at Peking consumed an inordinate amount of capacity in the southern shipyards; the court eunuchs who directed the expeditions were, as usual, involved in bitter disputes with the Confucian scholars who infested the bureaucracy. So the Ming Navy, which had the staggering total of 3,800 ships in 1420, was allowed to fall to pieces; Cheng Ho made his final trip to Africa in 1431, and brought back an ostrich. He died in 1435.

But aside from this remarkable character, the explorers, navigators and adventurers of the world were almost wholly of Western origin. Why, one may wonder, did it happen that Westerners sailed out to China, while no Chinese ever sailed out to see the West? Why were there Western trading stations in such places as Canton and Nagasaki – and yet no Chinese trading to Liverpool, nor Japanese to Rotterdam? Why was it that Westerners ran an annual trans-Pacific galleon service from Manila to Acapulco and back, yet no Chinese ever tried to turn a profit from a steam-packet shuttle between Recife and Lisbon? What force kept Easterners at home, and what converse energies impelled Westerners – like Mr Wortman of Ketchikan, or Sir Edmund Hillary, or Scott and Amundsen, or Lewis and Clarke – to wander, to root out, to look beyond the farthest hill and around the next corner?

It was a pleasing way to pass an Alaskan afternoon, standing gazing out at the sea, pondering idly the nature of the Eastern mind, thinking that it might be this all-pervading, all-powerful, omnipresent entity called "Face" that somehow lay behind the difference. For Face is a commodity only measured by its loss, only honoured in the breach. To possess it is the norm, and thus quite unremarkable. To lose it is the universal horror. All Eastern situations are thus carefully calculated to afford to all participants the maximum opportunity for retaining Face. No risk is to be placed before anyone that might result in public failure, no matter how trivial it might seem to others – for no matter how trivial, failure would involve some inevitable and thus utterly humiliating loss of Face.

To carry this argument to its logical conclusion, one can say that any situation involving a possibility of failure, a risk, tends to be shunned by many adherents to the Confucian way (not that Confucianism speaks of Face, nor would approve of such aversion and fear; and Face is not peculiar to adherents of Confucius alone – from the Brahmaputra to the most northerly tip of Hokkaido, from Buddhism to Shintoism and via everything within, Face is all).

To get into a small boat and sail through heavy seas for a hundred miles presents a very considerable risk of failure – possibly failure with fatal consequences. A Westerner might think it irresponsible, the act of a lunatic, but he would have no intellectual opposition to it. Someone whose cultural background was steeped in the concept of Face would perhaps have more inbuilt hostility, more spiritual opposition, more of an instinct for self-preservation than would allow him to countenance the taking of such a gamble. His opposition would stem from his knowledge that the risk, by its very definition, courted possible failure, and thus awoke all his most appalling fears of how such failure would inevitably appear to those around him. And those around him would judge him on his failure, just as he would judge others upon theirs. Without meaning to reinforce any stereotypes, it seemed to me a most convenient if not necessarily rigorously true explanation for there having been so few Chinese sailing expeditions in the past, so few Korean Mount Everests – so few indications, in short, that Eastern pleasure can be a consequence of taking risk. Except, of course, gambling – and as the tables at Las Vegas so heavily populated by Hong Kong Chinese amply display, there are few more avid players of baccarat and roulette on the face of the earth. So was there any truth in this at all? Were Face, Risk, Invention and Exploration really to be linked, and grand theories of the differences between East and West really to be posited here? It really was too cold now, and the wind turned like a blade beneath my anorak, so I banished such thoughts for the moment and scuttled off below.

Next morning, brisk and sunny, we were passing the Swiftsure Bank Lightship at the mouth of the Strait of Juan de Fuca, pinioned between Canada and the Continental United States – the "Lower Forty-Eight" as some Alaskans still call them, with mock contempt – heading for our destination port, the city of Seattle. The *Rainbow Ace*, sniffing the air like a horse on the final moments of its gallop, seemed to accelerate, to ride more friskily, the closer she came to home.

"A few more moons," the old Indian declared, "a few more winters – and not one of our descendants . . . will remain to mourn over the graves of a people who were once more powerful and hopeful than yours." The old Indian was Chief Sealth, the venerable and titular leader of the Suquamish and Duwamish tribes* who had made their home in the hills and valleys around Puget Sound. His speech – probably made more florid than its delivery by some unknown master of Victorian prosody – was delivered in 1855, after he had formally ceded his land and that of all his people to the white newcomers, and after he had agreed to leave and let the whites get on with building the new city they would name after him. Old Sealth had been born at the end of the eighteenth century, scion of a proud and untroubled tradition; he died in 1866, and the location of his passing – Port Madison Reservation, Washington – says much of the price he paid for dealing with the white man.

The town was not called Seattle from the beginning. It was on a drizzly November afternoon in 1851 that the schooner *Exact*, on her way from Portland, Oregon to the Queen Charlotte Islands in Canada, turned off into the shelter of Puget Sound and stopped at a headland that seemed to lead to a likely-looking settlement-ground. The party who agreed to disembark, ten adults with their twelve children, staked claims and – perhaps because of the rain, the mud and the misery of the place – promptly called their new home town Duwamps.

It was not a name to last much longer than it deserved. A doctor,

*These casual names actually refer to the places in which the Indians later lived; their technically proper tribal names, Makah, Quileute, Chimakum and Kwalhioqua are lost to all but specialists in the aboriginal peoples of North America.

David Maynard, arrived at the settlement in the spring, made friends with Chief Sealth and decided it would be both flattering to the Chief and euphonious to the ears of potential settlers to rename it Seattle – an approximation of the way the Indians pronounced their leader's name. Sealth himself was not so sure: once he had died, he said, his spirit would be disturbed on every occasion that the name – his name – was mentioned. Dr Maynard, who did not entirely understand this argument, nonetheless was so eager to have the name of Duwamps changed that he agreed, on behalf of the new community, to levy a small tax on all new settlers to help ease the Chief's posthumous discomfort.

Sealth himself seems to have been a towering figure on the landscape of the Pacific Coast Indians – a people racially and culturally closer than most American Indians to their Mongoloid forebears who had come over the Bering "land bridge" from Asia some 20,000 years before. He, for instance, was converted by French missionaries from his shamanist beliefs and became a Catholic, a minister who led his people in morning and evening services. (The shamanism of the Coast Indians* had much in common with that still found in Japan and Korea, though no Asians (so far as I have seen) fashion the enormous totem poles that are such a hallmark of Pacific Indian communities.)

Sealth's friendship with the white settlers has made him a controversial figure among his own descendants. Many of today's more militant Indians – like those with whom I spent many a cold day on the Pine Ridge Reservation in South Dakota in 1973, during the small rebellion that came to be called "the Second Battle of Wounded Knee", denounced him as a traitor, a man who sold out his people. And there is no doubt that Sealth did agree to the terms of the Treaty of Port Elliott, ceding Indian land to the whites, and agreeing with unbearable docility to put himself and his brothers and sisters into reservations, and not trouble the settlers any further. Yet his speech, an inexpressibly sad testimonial to the plight of a powerless people

---

*Coast Indians worship, among other beasts, the salmon, which exists in these waters in such abundance largely because the Kuro Shio, the warm current we last encountered off Japan, extends its tendrils to the coasts of Washington and British Columbia. The anthropological and religious links between Asia and this corner of North America are thus amply matched by a marine connection quite unknown elsewhere: the waters off California suffer from another current, are very cold, and support no salmon. The local Indian culture is in consequence very different.

who tried in vain to stem the advance of white – and thus American – progress, suggests he was acutely sensitive to what was happening. He was a man perfectly attuned to the historical context of what befell his people.

A few more moons [he had said]. A few more winters – and not one of the descendants of the mighty hosts that once moved over this broad land or lived in happy homes, protected by the Great Spirit, will remain to mourn over the graves of a people once more powerful and hopeful than yours. But why should I mourn at the untimely fate of my people? Tribe follows tribe and nation follows nation, like the waves of the sea. It is the order of nature, and regret is useless. Your time of decay may be distant, but it will surely come, for even the White Man whose God walked and talked with him as a friend cannot be exempt from the common destiny. We may be brothers after all. We will see.

We will ponder your proposition, and when we decide we will let you know. But should we accept it I here and now make this condition: that we will not be denied the privilege without molestation of visiting at any time the tombs of our ancestors, friends and children. Every part of the soil is sacred in the estimation of my people. Every hillside, every valley, every plain and grove, has been hallowed by some sad or happy event in days long vanished. Even the rocks, which seem to be dumb or dead as they swelter in the sun along the silent shore, thrill with memories of stirring events connected with the lives of my people, and the very dust on which you now stand responds more lovingly to their footsteps than to yours, because it is rich with the blood of our ancestors and our bare feet are conscious of the sympathetic touch. Our departed braves, fond mothers, glad and happy-hearted maidens, and even the little children who lived here and rejoiced for a brief season, will love these sombre solitudes and at eventide they greet shadowy returning spirits.

And when the last Red Man shall have perished, and the memory of my tribe becomes a myth among the White Men, these shores will swarm with the invisible dead of my tribe. And when your children's children think themselves alone in the field, the store, the stop upon the highway, or in the silence of the pathless woods, they will not be alone. In all the earth there is no place dedicated to solitude. At night when the streets of your cities and villages are silent and you think them deserted, they will throng with the returning hosts that once filled them and still love this beautiful land. The White Man will never be alone. Let him be just and deal kindly with my people, for the dead are not powerless. Dead, did I say? There is no death, only a change of worlds.

The old Chief's eloquence, polished and honed though it may well have been, stands today as one of the sadder memorials to the fate of millions of American Indians. His final plea did him no good: he and his followers were sent off to a reservation at Suquamish, on the Kitsap Peninsula on the far side of the Sound. We passed it in the *Rainbow Ace* as we turned in towards the docks in Elliott Bay: on the map it is now marked as the Port Madison Indian Reservation, between Appletree Cove and Miller Bay, sandwiched between the little suburbs of Kingston and Indianola, and not far from where the huge atomic submarines growl in and out of the ocean at the great naval base at Bremerton.

There were woods, small frame houses, winding streets and then, behind them all, looming off to the west and sheltering them from the Pacific storms, the mighty and snow-covered Mount Olympus, 8,000 feet of ancient volcano, glaciers inching down from beside its summit – an appropriately memorable place for the old Indian chief to rest.

These days the Indian population of Washington State remains one of the largest in the country. There are eight large reservations – Port Madison counts as one of the smaller, and is not included in the lists that cover such major tribal homelands as those of the Puyallup, the Tulalip, the Lummi and the Spokane.* Indians who have watched helplessly as their native skills have vanished in the face of technical progress – their unparalleled knowledge of the ways of the salmon, for instance, supplanted by the needs of the canning industry and by the mechanization of the purse-seine fishers – now cling pathetically to the gunwales of civilization. A huge percentage of Washington's Indians – or native Americans, as they rightly prefer to be known – are indigent.

Much has been written on the fate of the American Indian, and maybe the present standing of the Suquamish, the Tulalip and others of the Pacific North-West is little worse than that of the Oglala Sioux in the Dakotas, the Navajos in Arizona or the Mohawks of

---

*Near Spokane is a small university and prison town named Walla Walla, unknown in most of America yet familiar to much of the citizenry of Hong Kong, 6,000 miles away. The small motorboats that cross Victoria Harbour after the Star Ferry has shut down for the night are known as *walla-wallas* because, it is said, the man who first owned one came from the town. It sounds like a tall story, but short of the name being an approximation of the engine's burbling note, there is no other explanation.

New York State. But to a visitor newly arrived from Asia, where ethnically similar men and women seem to be enjoying such vast success and reaping such enormous benefits from their labours, the trans–Pacific contrast is prodigious. The Japanese crewmen on our ship were quick to notice it – to see the few Indians who were lounging around on the waterfront and to spot them because, unlike most of the other stevedores, these were men who shared with the crew a certain similarity of appearance, something more than a hint of common origin.

The crewmen, hard-working, smartly dressed, eager young Japanese, looked down from the high decks at these idle, unkempt, half-drunken men – and I fancied that they shuddered with the recognition that something peculiarly awful had befallen men who were, in a sense, their blood-brothers. There was little that they could or wished to do. One of the crew remarked that Westerners spoke admiringly of the "work ethic" that is such a dominant feature of the Confucian tradition, the Asian mind – and then went on to point out that a contrast such as that between the evident attitudes of the Japanese crewmen like himself and the Indian dockworkers down below gave the lie to any suggestion that this ethic has a basis in heredity. The Japanese, it has long been recognized, are far from shy when it comes to pointing out, as now, the existence of a stereotype in others who, like all the world, appear inferior to themselves.

It was cold and drizzling when we docked, and it remained that way – classical North-West weather, the captain said, and "just like Britain" – for most of the ship's brief stay. Our 3,000 Nissans – the product of just forty scoops-full of Australian iron ore and all the technical expertise of the Zama plant – emerged from the doorway in the ship's side and into the rain, at the rate of about two each minute. White-coated Japanese drivers raced them out and down the ramp and into the parking bays so that, before the ship's engines were properly cool the acres of dockside below us presented a checker-board of gleaming colours and sheens, a vivid demonstration of the immensity of Japan's export trade with the Western world. The thought that it was a mere thirty years earlier that Teiichi Hara had arrived on the quayside in Los Angeles with just one small and primitive Datsun car and one equally unimpressive Datsun lorry seemed barely believable. Nor was it easy to believe that in the first seven hours of our stay in Seattle, the *Rainbow Ace* disgorged more new Nissans on to American soil than the total number of cars built by the entire Nissan empire throughout Japan in 1950.

Put another way: the 3,000 cars that roared sportily out of our ship's hold represented four years" production at the rate of 1950: at the rate of 1989 it represented just three days' worth, and at the Zama plant alone. Rarely can there have been a more dramatic illustration than this of the post-war recovery of Japanese industry. The illustration was starkly underlined by the Seattle harbourmaster's insistence that the *Rainbow Ace* leave her berth as rapidly as possible. Another vessel was in the roads, waiting to use the same parking space.

According to the harbourmaster's files, the new arrival was MV *Bell Flower*: Japanese flagged; registered in Tokyo; on long-term charter to the Nissan Motor Co. Ltd. She had left Yokohama eleven days before. A facsimile of her manifest was on hand with US Customs: she was loaded with 3,000 passenger vehicles from the Zama factory – a further 3,000 Japanese imports, bound for the docks in Seattle and the countryside beyond.

Nissan's American distributors, based in Los Angeles, decide which car goes where – which of the hundreds of dealers from Bangor in Maine to Anchorage in Alaska receives what number of Sentras in which colour and in what style. In Seattle there is one main dealer, Pacific Nissan, Inc. on East Pike Street – I used to run past the showrooms each dawn, and would see the new cars gleaming under the lights in the front parking lot. The firm received six of the cars from the *Rainbow Ace* and they were all sold – all on credit, with specially low interest rates – three days later. It would be pleasant to say that I had seen one being driven down Interstate Five a day or so later, but in fact when I looked the highway was far too crowded with all kinds of Japanese cars – and from a distance most of them, I have to confess, look exactly alike.

CONNECTIONS

TWO: Threads of Silk

I

The Men

At the corner of Jirón Paruro and Calle Ucayali, near the centre of the grey old Peruvian capital city of Lima, is Chinatown. To Westerners it has the reputation of being a less than friendly place. "Watch out," suggests the *South American Handbook* in an uncharacteristically tactless aside, "for pickpockets and thieves." If it is, for what the Cantonese call *gweilos* – white ghosts, foreigners, outsiders – a less than congenial quarter, then there is an explanation.

There are said to be 30 million Chinese scattered in Chinatowns around the world, the consequences of an intermittent hegira which has been going on, by choice or compulsion, for the last five centuries. Most have emerged from the comfortless exactions of the Middle Kingdom within the last century; they are spread, statisticians tell us, through 109 of the world's countries. And while it is undoubtedly true that the Chinese have clustered in cities far from the compass of their native land – in New York and London, Cape Town and Mombasa – it is around the Pacific that they are most obvious, eager participants in the new social and economic order of the times. "Ah! The Chinese in Manila!" exclaimed a specialist in the field, on observing the vast department store in Makati where Imelda Marcos was wont to buy her shoes, and which was owned by a wealthy but unknown Fukienese. "His home in Chinatown. His heart in Amoy. His money in San Francisco!"

Once, when I was searching for the common threads that bound the new Pacific together – the sutures which might render this unimaginably vast ocean as much of an entity as the Mediterranean once was – I read about the Chinese community in the port of Valparaiso, in Chile. It was not an especially large community, nor was it overly prosperous. Most of its members had come from Shanghai; they ran restaurants and small shops, a few businesses that by and large catered to the community itself. Like so many Chinatowns it was a more or less self-sufficient place – introspective, self-satisfied and secretive.

But in the waters off Chile there are quantities of the enormous shellfish called abalone, so prized by the Chinese for the apparent (though unproven) stamina-enhancing qualities of its meat. The Chilean Chinese fish for it, and send it back home packed in containers to the abalone-dealers in Shanghai. There is thus a small skein of trade which has been woven, unexpectedly, between two places as far removed from each other across the Ocean as it is possible to be – a fine line of commerce that reaches out from a big port-city at the far south-eastern corner of the Pacific Ocean, across to another big port-city at the far north-western corner.

Perhaps, I then thought to myself, it is possible to imagine a spider's-web of such silky bonds linking every city on every Pacific shore, with a Chinese at each end of every link as its common feature. From the Chinatowns of Manila to those of Vancouver; from the Chinese in Callao to those in Dalien; from those in Xiamen to Chinese in Sydney. They, I concluded, were what really connected the Pacific together: the members of the greatest diaspora in the world, the overseas Chinese.

As I looked more closely at the subject, so more specific and more easily comprehensible trans-Pacific bonds emerged: the inward-looking nature of today's Pacific is not a phenomenon confined to its populations of expatriate Chinese. But there can be no doubt that these Chinese, people from so many regions, with so many customs and ambitions and such an extraordinary history, are playing a tremendously significant role in the development of the new Ocean: the matter of Chinatown's coming to Lima, and of the coming of other Chinatowns and Chinese to towns and countries elsewhere on the Pacific's shores, can go some way towards explaining why, and how.

The Chinatown of Lima is one of the oldest in the world*: the

*New York's is older, having been in place officially since 1844. Bangkok has had a Chinatown ever since the city was founded at the end of the eighteenth century. London, though, did not possess the genuine article until five Cantonese restaurants opened on Gerrard Street in 1965.

graveyards there date back to the middle of the nineteenth century, and there are records of Chinese immigration having taken place as early as 1849. But the 1870s were the zenith; and what happened during those years when scores of thousands of young Chinese men were landed at the Peruvian ports – and which was to be echoed during the creation of Chinatowns all around the Pacific at about the same time – remains one of the great untold modern horror stories – a reason, perhaps, for the absence of wholehearted congeniality at the corner of Jirón Paruro and Calle Ucayali.

The Peruvians, who had enjoyed the services of the negro slaves brought by their former colonial masters, the Spaniards, had taken only thirty years to decide on the morality of slavery: emancipation was the announced policy of the *mestizo* president, Ramón Castilla, when he began his second term in 1855. The negroes were freed; liberal opinion was mollified. But the Peruvian landowners, with their immense haciendas, were restive: they needed labour, armies of cheap and willing workers who would permit them to reap the profits to which they had become accustomed. And so Castilla, who needed the support of the landowners as well as of the liberals and the workers, permitted them to import thousands – and later scores of thousands – of Chinese coolies. The story of the transport of these wretched and unfortunate men across vast stretches of Ocean remains one of the least known and most undistinguished chapters in Pacific history.

Like the black African slaves of a century before, the Chinese of Victorian times – despite not being, technically, slaves at all – were preyed upon by profiteers at home, subjected to the most terrifying indignities, transported to faraway lands in conditions of appalling privation and then, quite literally, worked to death. Coolie-brokers established offices in the newly opened Chinese treaty-ports: Canton, Amoy, Foochow, Ningpo and Shanghai. Men called "crimps" would round them up and herd them into the dockside slave-pens, the barracoons.

Since demand for these inexpensive and energetic workers far outstripped supply, almost any technique imaginable was used to gather them up. "The buying and selling of piglets" – *mai chu-chai* – was the Chinese phrase used in reference to the coolie trade – an apt summation of the squalor of the business. There was another phrase too, still used in English: "a Chinaman's chance". It means, quite simply, no chance at all – no chance to get away from the ceaseless exactions of the coolie-mongers.

Peasants and slum-dwellers from the villages and cities were simply kidnapped and press-ganged*; beaten by thugs until they were senseless, they would sign their contracts either because they could not understand or because they were terrified of further punishment; they were trussed into sacks and sold like meat; they were tricked into gambling for their future – with loaded dice, drugs or rice wine on hand to ensure they lost their bets. And if they resisted – they were tied up by their thumbs, kept bound in ice-cold water, or more callously tortured, until they agreed to sign. Any who tried to escape from the barracoons were beaten to death: "to prevent their cries being overheard gongs were beaten, fireworks were discharged," a "piglet" from the Macau depôt was later to recall.

The brokers would size them up and dispatch them to the ships that would take them off to their uncertain fates – and to journeys on the high seas as appalling as anything the Africans had to endure on the notorious "Middle Passage".†

There are descriptions of a barracoon in Amoy where hundreds of contracted workers – not slaves in the strict sense, but men who had been driven to accept five-year contracts at a pitiful monthly wage which would only begin to be paid "upon arrival" – were gathered to wait for the receiving ships. "They were stripped naked, and stamped or painted with the letters C (California), P (Peru) or S (Sandwich Islands – Hawaii) on their breasts, according to the destinations for which they were intended . . ."

If the "Middle Passage" was a nightmare for the Africans, so the far longer journey crossing the Pacific was a seemingly endless progress of horror for the Chinese. The official amount of space allotted per "piglet" was 8 square feet – a portion of decking a scant 6 feet long and 16 inches wide. When as many as 1,000 coolies were loaded on to a single vessel, they had to lie on top of one another like animals. They took their own rice and water – the ship's master

---

*Though not, oddly, "Shanghaied": the term applies specifically to men lured into service in the crew of a foreign-going ship.
†The crossing of the Atlantic – the "middle passage" of an African slave's journey into bondage – was appalling indeed. The ships in which up to 600 slaves were confined, horizontally, in spaces 6 feet long and 16 inches wide had fatality rates of an average 13 per cent: so many dead black men were slung overboard that sharks would pursue the vessels all the way from the Guinea Coast to Virginia.

had no responsibility for feeding them, and if calms or storms forced a delay it was quite commonplace for some of the passengers to die from simple starvation, or dehydration. The number of deaths was ferocious: the annual mortality rate on the voyage between Canton and Callao in 1862 rose to 41 per cent, and that from an average of 26 per cent. Suicides were frequent: one release from the endless orgies of beating and flogging. "From China to Peru", a phrase much in use at the time, signified with grim accuracy a journey from which there was no return.

To ensure the arrival of sufficient coolies to satisfy the customers, vessels invariably made the passage grossly overloaded: the rationale among the coolie-dealers held that, while all of a 300-strong cargo might arrive alive, 350 of a 600-strong consignment would too – an extra 50 men, an additional profit, for the mere inconvenience of having 250 Chinese die. "Passengers – what passengers?" growled the steamer captain in Conrad's *Typhoon*. "The Chinamen! Why don"t you speak plainly? Couldn't tell what you meant . . ." The coolies were no more than livestock, and only marginally profitable livestock at that. The traders seemed to cleave to the proposition which Sydney Smith was once quoted as advancing – that to kill the Chinese was as useless as killing flies in July.

When the coolie-ship *Don Juan* caught fire in mid-passage in 1871, the escaping crew reportedly battened down the hatches and let the Chinese burn to death. The coolies aboard the *Napoleon Canevaro* murdered the captain and crew, set fire to the ship and perished with her. The *Cayalti* was reported on arrival in Hakodate as having neither master nor crew, but forty Chinese and the decks stained with blood. The American captain of the *Robert Browne* ordered the coolies' queues cut off, whereupon the Chinese rose up and murdered him. The trade – in which Britons* played an unseemly role – was as deadly as, for the merchants, it was profitable.

Between 80,000 and 100,000 coolies were landed in Peru between 1849 and 1874 – figures which suggest that, given the rate of attrition, 6,000 men were leaving China's shore each year, just for work on the

---

*A Mr Tait, "a British subject who has the advantage and influence which his being Spanish, Dutch and Portuguese consul gives him", was the principal trader of Chinese workers in Amoy in 1850. Other trading companies have evolved into today's familiar and more respectable firms: Jardine Matheson, for one; Boustead, Guthrie for another.

Peruvian haciendas. Ships by the dozen lay at anchor in Hong Kong and Macau, waiting to carry the greatest floodtide of humanity ever known into the waiting arms – and fetters – of employers all around the globe.

On arrival at Callao (Lima's main port) or at the more northerly coolie-decks at Paita, the men were either whisked off to the sugar-cane fields by employers who had contracted for them a shipload at a time; or else they were lined up on the wharves to be inspected by prospective employers – purchasers – and to have their muscle-tone assessed, their bodies poked and prodded. They then filtered out into every aspect of Peruvian menial life – such that, as the Shanghai writer Pan Ling discovered, their ubiquity became the subject of Spanish poetry:

> There is no place where you do not find the Chinese
> From the sacking of guano,
> To the cultivation of the valleys,
> From waiting on the tables
> To cleaning the streets.
> He is even the servant of the commoner,
> And there is no activity – you understand? –
> On which he does not diligently embark.
> And the people of the country?
> They are thinking of becoming gentry!

But their putative gentrification did not prevent them from marrying the newcomers. Peru today has a bewildering and tightly formalized hierarchy of racial mixtures which reflects this, for included among such familiar categories as the *mulatto* and the *mestizo* are such oddities as the *injerto* – the consequence of a marriage between Chinese and Spanish (i.e. white) Peruvian – and the deliciously named *chinocholo*, a breed resulting from the congress of Chinese and African blacks.*

---

*Blacks in Peru held the Chinese in particularly low esteem. After all, they had been imported as slaves themselves by the Spaniards, and once they had been emancipated by Castillo, and placed in positions of authority over the new peons, they went about their new task with great relish. "Negroes . . . are said to have regarded the Chinese as their successors, and to have enjoyed cracking the whip over the yellow labourer as it had once been cracked over them." Given the natural racial antipathy of Chinese towards black, this reversal of social positions had a dangerous irony about it.

Though the exertions required in the cane fields were dreadful enough, nothing could have prepared the newcomers for the labours of the guano deposits with which Peru is uniquely blessed (as it is, similarly uniquely, with reserves of bismuth, *alpaca* wool and the world's most nutrient-rich vegetable, a goosefoot with the spinach-like leaf known as *quinoa*). Guano – cormorant, pelican, gannet and (particularly on the Lobos Islands) Pacific seal guano – is one of the principal sources of fertilizer in Peru, and Peru is one of the world's greatest sources of it. In the latter half of the last century, indeed, guano (the word is the Spanish for dung: in Peruvian it is *huano*) was the country's greatest export, enriching both the national coffers and the landowners whose cliffs birds and seals happened to select for their evacuations. But extracting it was a decidedly unpleasant task: the blacks did it first and then, inevitably, the Chinese.

Pan Ling quotes an American consul in Lima who reported in 1870 that the Chinese contracted to work on the guano islands had to clear 100 wheelbarrow-loads of the foul-smelling phosphatic dust every shift, and that those who collapsed from their exertions had to work on their knees to pick out the small stones with which the excrement was liberally littered. An English observer commented that "no hell has ever been conceived by the Hebrew, the Irish, the Italian . . ." that was as terrible as the guano fields in which the new Chinese were forced to labour.

The combination of the dire conditions and the tyrannical employers drove as many Chinese to suicide as had ended their lives on the coolie-ships: guards had to be posted on the shores of the guano islands to ensure that no Chinese rushed into the sea to drown; and it is said that the limbs of the stunted trees which grew out of the guano beds were often found weighed down with the bodies of Chinese workers who had hanged themselves as a means of escape. Some of those who did not choose to end their own lives conspired in bloody rebellions which ended the lives of many others: the first of the Chinese risings in Peru took place in 1870, when a planter and his three dinner guests were surprised at dinner by a mob of Chinese who fell upon them and slaughtered them all at table. This particular outbreak of violence – "a bloody and impotent protest against horrible wrongs", as a prescient Lima newspaper was to write – spread far afield. In one town the white citizens took refuge in a church, but according to a survivor, the women there "suffered a terrible fate, their persons were violated and their bodies cut in pieces, their heads cut off and placed on poles, and shown to those inside the church . . ."

However, the situation gradually changed for the better, thanks to an important evolution in the situation back in China.

The Chinese government's attitude towards the emigration of its citizenry was ambiguous, to say the least. Technically it was illegal, the Emperor specifically forbidding the spiritual pollution that would inevitably result from any forays into the outer darkness, the land beyond the Middle Kingdom. Yet by the beginning of the nineteenth century, there had been an unusual and prolonged period of calm within China – a calm that allowed a massive and dangerous increase in the country's population. There were about 150 million people in China in 1800; by 1850 there were 410 million – yet there had been no obvious change in the country's wealth, or in its abilities to house the new bodies, feed the new mouths and teach the new minds: the result was poverty, lassitude, corruption and a growing breakdown in public order and discipline. Allowing the people to leave – and thus permit an easing of the head of steam – was the obvious choice for the Chinese mandarins.

So permit it they did, in a corrupt fashion characteristic of the times. Beginning in 1845, shortly after the British formally ended the African slave trade, Chinese customs and immigration officials at the newly-recognized coolie ports extracted taxes – protection money might be a better phrase – from the emigration firms, and promised to look the other way when the ships left port. But they rarely allowed the emigrants to return, for to admit them back would be to accept that they had left in the first place – and leaving was contrary to the Imperial edict.

The abuses of such a system were legion. The secret underworld societies – dominated by members of the "Heaven and Earth League", better known by its English name, the Triads – essentially ran the brokerage business. Local government teetered on the brink of collapse before the extortionate demands of the gangsters. Immense fortunes were being made. Scores of thousands of coolies were dying. The semi-legitimate, semi-voluntary emigration scheme – the so-called "credit-ticket" plan by which the emigrant bought his ticket from the ship's master with a promise to reimburse him from his wages overseas – was merging imperceptibly with the indentured-labour schemes. By the beginning of the second half of the century the business (and its political implications) were looking overwhelming and ugly: Britain and France resolved to do something about it.

First they legalized emigration, at least in Canton, where they had influence over the Chinese administrators. Then they regulated it: brokers were licensed, crimps outlawed, officials could not put the "squeeze" on migrants, ships' masters were ordered to make their vessels habitable. All manner of lofty language was invoked to justify the properly regulated flow of Chinese to the West: a British document spoke of how "the Chinese choosing to take service in British colonies or other parts beyond the sea are at perfect liberty to enter into engagements . . ."; an American paper, even more grandiloquent, was positively Lincolnesque in dealing with so grubby a topic: the United States and the Manchu Emperor had recognized "the inherent and inalienable right of man to change his home and allegiance, and also the mutual advantage of free migration and emigration . . ."

The Chinese hardened their demands. Pushing their still "official" ban on emigration into the shadows, they demanded that any coolie shipped overseas should be given a free return passage by his employers, and that the period of indentures be limited to five years. The British and French signed such an agreement – the Emigration Convention of 1866 – though, under pressure from their planter-colonists, they both failed to ratify it. Nevertheless they looked with haughty disapproval on those who flouted its principles; most notably they excoriated Portugal, which permitted the most wanton abuses to flourish in Macau, where 40 barracoons had sprung up within a single year.

Despite its sometime hypocrisy, over the years their pressure worked – such that by the mid-1860s, when scheduled steamer services in and out of the South China ports were replacing the old clipper ships, a good proportion of Chinese emigration had become more or less free. The odours of the crimp and the chain gang – as well as the buying and selling of "piglets" – were fast starting to evaporate. Large numbers of the Chinese going overseas in the latter years of the nineteenth century were doing so under their own steam – to try to make their own fortunes rather than merely enhance those of the people for whom they worked.

An advertisement for clipper passage to the New World proclaimed:

All Chinamen make much money in New Orleans!
Chinamen have become richer than Mandarins there.
Pay, first year, $300, but after
Three years there will make poor workman very rich
And he can come home at any time.
On the ships that go there passengers will find nice rooms
And very fine food. They can play all sorts of games
And have no work. Everything nice to make man happy.
It is a nice country. Better than this.
No sickness there and no danger of death.
Come! Go at once. You cannot afford to wait.
Don't heed the wife's counsel, or threats of enemies.
Be Chinamen, but go!

But it was gold rather than the goalless lures of the shipping companies that took the first Chinese credit-ticket travellers – and all those who had not been sucked up into the coolie trade – to the West Coast of North America.

The prospect that the California soil might hide an abundance of mineral riches had been published as far back as Elizabethan times: Richard Hakluyt, in his *Principall Navigations, Discoverys and Voyages of the English Nation*, 1589, wrote of Sir Francis Drake's New Albion as a place where "there is no part of the earth here to bee taken up, wherein there is not some speciall likelihood of gold or silver . . ." James Marshall, a New Jersey carpenter, amply confirmed Drake's suspicion when, one warm winter's afternoon in January 1848, he discovered flakes of pure gold in the mill-race of the sawmill he was building on John Sutter's land near Coloma, not far from the present-day Californian capital of Sacramento.

The discovery at Sutter's Mill turned America on its head: where once the focus of the young country's progress and expansion had been the East, now all of a sudden there was an excellent reason to hitch up the wagon, to brave the depredations of the Indians and the painful miseries of cholera, and to go West. Indisputably, there was gold in the hills. Sutter and Marshall tried to keep their discovery a secret, but as the word leaked out so the first of thousands descended on to the property, building makeshift camps from which to search for the apparently ubiquitous placer deposits. The trickle of prospectors turned into a great stream, which over the years became formalized into a near-highway running between Philadelphia and San Francisco Bay: "As we neared the California trail," wrote Horace

Greeley in 1859, a decade after the rush had begun, "the white coverings of the many emigrant and transport wagons dotted the landscape, giving the trail the appearance of a river running between great meadows, with many ships sailing on its bosom."

They took the overland route; they took the boat around the Horn; they took clippers to Panama and hiked across the malarial swamps of the Isthmus – 80,000 men and a few women poured into the fledgling state to try their luck and make their fortune. They built new towns around the goldfields – Rough and Ready was one, You Bet another; Rich Bar and Mormon Bar, Jenny Lind and Bear Valley, Carson City, Virginia City and Sacramento City – some still vibrant settlements and cities, others preserved as museums of a fabulous age, some now wrecked and dead, ghost towns of dust and tumbleweed. But in their heyday it was to places like this that the thousands of new Americans came – and they were joined in short order by men from overseas, particularly by the most egregious gold-lovers on the face of the earth: the Chinese.

There was already a small colony of Chinese living in San Francisco, families from the Cantonese districts of Namhoi, Punyu and Shuntak who had emigrated to work as merchants and traders. But now came the fortune-hunters, men from Sze Yap or the so-called "Four Districts" of Toishan, Sanwui, Hoiping and Yanping – clambering in their thousands on to every available boat plying between Canton and the Pacific Mail Steamship docks in San Francisco, to labour in the placer fields, under whatever hardship, for as long as it might take to ensure they came home rich. They called San Francisco Gum San: the gold hills.

The San Francisco Customs House records 20,000 Cantonese miners passing through its books in 1852. Some were bold entrepreneurs working for themselves, some bound to Chinese gold contractors, some indentured to American mining firms. They were duly registered by the semi-secret and thus ill-regarded (by Westerners) Chinese Consolidated Benevolent Association – the Six Companies. This fearsome organization, regarded (not altogether unfairly) as the beginnings of the Chinese mafia, had enormous power over the lives of its members: its leadership, composed mostly of men rather closer to racketeering than to altruism, possessed the ultimate power of being able to grant the immigrants permission to leave America for home – a power more honoured in the breach, particularly to those whose obligations in the credit-ticket business remained unfulfilled.

The very existence of the Six Companies, the burgeoning of other secret societies known to Americans as "tongs" and the closed and introspective nature of Chinese society . . . all this, coupled with their prodigious appetite for work and stoic acceptance of any burdens did much to arouse the antipathy of the white Americans, the immigrants from the Old World. "The Chinaman is dreaded," wrote Lafcadio Hearn, "because of *his power to underlive the white*." To be sure the American whites savoured the pleasures of having small, tough yellow-skinned men to do the work that they found hard or distasteful: but there was something about their lack of complaint that many Americans interpreted as dumb insolence, which made them infuriated and provoked them to loathe and fear their newly arrived colleagues. Xenophobia was in any case fashionable; the Know-Nothing Party,* dedicated to halting non-white (and German) immigration, was enjoying some popularity, and one of its successors, the American Party, made some political headway in California demanding a total ban on the employment of Chinese and other Orientals in the state's industries.

Robert Louis Stevenson, whose association with the Pacific Ocean is more journalistically intimate than is generally recalled, lived for a while in San Francisco and was appalled by the way the Chinese were treated. He loved the city's Chinatown:

> . . . by a thousand eccentricities [it] drew and held me . . . I could never have enough of its ambiguous, interracial atmosphere . . . never wonder enough at its outlandish, necromantic-looking vegetables, set forth to sell in commonplace American shop-windows, its temple doors open and the scent of the joss-stick streaming forth on the American air, its kites of Oriental fashion hanging fouled in American telegraph-wires . . .

But it was precisely this ambiguous interraciality which appalled the lumpenproletariat of the city. The Chinese, Stevenson noted, were called "hideous vermin", and the Americans "affected a kind of choking in the throat when they beheld them". American Party rallies

---

*As President, Millard Fillmore allowed his name to be put forward as the party's candidate in the 1856 election – a curious move for a man who, three years before, had been sufficiently worldly to dispatch Commodore Perry to open up trade with Japan. His candidacy was in any case a political disaster: he failed dismally, and retired, to be forgotten, in Buffalo.

resounded to cries of "Kill him! Lynch the greasy slave!" They were often referred to as Mongolians, even in polite society. There was a widespread belief that they could do any labour and bear any hardship and pain because their nerve endings – uniquely in the human race – grew further from the skin: they could not feel discomfort, but they had a special power to inflict it: they were prodigious torturers, a demonically cruel people. It is perhaps no surprise that laws were enacted to ensure they paid higher taxes than others; that they could not testify against a white American in court (though the reverse, naturally, was encouraged); and that they could not stand eligible for full American nationality.

In 1877, by which time the hostility of the American worker to these implacably mysterious immigrants – who seemed to be taking much of his work – had reached flashpoint, riots broke out: a wave of killings and lynchings as grave as those seen in later years in the Deep South, and directed against another imperturbable and unfathomable people. Chinese laundries, shops and restaurants – any business foolhardy enough to display ideographs on its shingle – were routinely and savagely attacked; Chinese men – Chinamen being the preferred term of the day – were mauled and beaten in the street; police who dared try to stop the whites attacking the Chinese were themselves insulted, taunted and attacked. The docks of the Pacific Mail Steamship Line – symbolic of the tide of immigration, since its ships had brought most of the Chinese into town from Canton – were attacked, a lumber yard next door was set on fire and firemen who came to douse the flames were set upon.

As in San Francisco, so in Seattle to the north – where Chinese were forcibly evicted from their homes by white mobs and marched to a ship, the *Queen of the Pacific*, in the vain hope that the master would sail them all back home – and in every one of the western states: 55 outbreaks were counted in one year. American politicians found that by inserting anti-Chinese rhetoric into their speeches, votes could be easily won, and a whole slew of increasingly discriminatory legislation found its way on to the statute books – laws, for example, that barred Chinese children from state-funded schools, and denied the Chinese employment in any public body "except in punishment for crime".

But they did have one champion, a man who allowed them to play the leading part in building what has become America's greatest Chinese memorial: the trans-continental railway. Charles Crocker, one of the "big four"* who organized the construction of the Central Pacific road from Sacramento across the rugged massif of the Sierra Nevada Mountains, hired thousands of Chinese workers – first from the Chinatowns of the west coast cities, later from the farms of Guangdong province itself – to undertake tasks that (it is now tempting to think) could not have been performed by members of any other race on earth.

Crocker's specific task was to build a railway from Sacramento across into the state of Utah, where his line would meet those of the Union Pacific road then being built (under much less arduous circumstances) west from Omaha, Nebraska. Initially he was reluctant to hire the Chinese at all. In 1863, when the building began, there was plenty of work but not enough labour: men and boys applied and were put to work with no questions being asked. Children – youngsters twelve years old – were paid 75 cents hourly to help get the railway going. There were plans to import 5,000 rebel prisoners from the civil war camps in the east, but the war ended and the plan had to be abandoned. Then there were schemes to use peons from across the border in Mexico, but everyone agreed that the *mañana* attitude would hardly help a project with such urgent deadlines, so that plan also died stillborn.

In early 1865, the line had advanced 56 miles east from Sacramento to Illinoistown (soon to be renamed Colfax, after Grant's vice-president paid a visit), and had come close to the legally-accepted beginnings of the Sierra Nevada. Here the work began to get very difficult, and the decision was taken by Crocker at least to give a trial to the hitherto unhirable Chinese. J.H. Strobridge, the Central Pacific's tyrannical superintendent, was implacably opposed to the idea: in his view the diminutive, rice-fed men were weaklings, physiologically incapable of accomplishing the kind of work needed. They were, he harrumphed, worthy only of washing shirts and raising vegetables: the idea of them building a railway was preposterous.

Except, ventured Crocker, hadn't the Chinese built . . . the Great Wall? And wasn't that structure – in those days charmingly, if wrongly, believed to be visible from the moon – an even greater

*The others – Collis Huntington, Mark Hopkins and Leland Stanford – all left their mark too; the latter, a former Governor of California, founded his eponymous university, which is perhaps the greatest of today's Pacific education and research institutions.

achievement than the Central Pacific seemed destined to be? It was an unanswerable argument, and Strobridge was about to cave in when there came an unexpected ally: a sudden wildcat strike involving 1,000 of his white workers. With a grunt of resignation, but no loss of face, Strobridge agreed to give fifty Chinese workers a try. They had been hired from the worked-out placer deposits, from laundries, kitchens and the market gardens in the Central Valley. Oscar Lewis, in his masterly account of the building of the railway, recounts how the men

. . . were herded on freightcars in the Sacramento yards and hauled to the end of the track. They disembarked, glanced without curiosity at the surrounding forest, then tranquilly established camp, cooked a meal of rice and dried cuttlefish, and went to sleep. By sunrise they were at work with picks, shovels and wheelbarrows. At the end of their first day of prodding industry Crocker and his engineers viewed the result with gratified astonishment. Those who through the day had been momentarily expecting the weaklings to fall in their tracks from exhaustion permanently revised their opinion of the Chinaman's endurance.

Henceforth they were officially regarded, as the Central Pacific's president read into the record, as "quiet, peaceable, patient, industrious and economical".

The company offered $40 a month to every able-bodied Chinese who cared to come and work: 2,000 blue-denim-clad Cantonese were employed in the first six months and the line – hitherto progressing through the brush of the foothills at a few hundred feet a day – now began to streak through the cuttings and over the embankments that were a necessary part of the ever-steepening ranges. The partners began to react with disbelief to the weekly distance reports, which wildly exceeded their expectations. So far as the railroad bosses were concerned, the Chinese were a godsend.

"Cholly Clocker", as they came to call their sudden benefactor (who in return called them "Crocker's pets"), played fair with them too: each month he would arrive at the construction sites, riding on his old sorrel mare laden with two leather saddle-bags filled with coins – 50 lbs of gold in one, a hundred of silver in the other – and press the cash directly into the workers' uplifted palms. The gesture was important for the company's public relations: contractors whose angry white employees had argued that the railroad's Chinese were held in virtual serfdom were told smugly by Stanford that "no system similar to slavery . . . prevails. . . . Their wages . . . paid in coin at the end of each month, are divided among them by their agents . . . in proportion to the labour done by each . . . . These agents are generally American or Chinese merchants, who furnish them with supplies of food, the value of which they deduct monthly . . ."

Anger within the contracting firms abated and – despite the threats of reprisals in San Francisco as the docks filled ever more regularly with boat-loads of Chinese from the farms around Canton (for by 1866 Crocker had decreed that 15,000 Oriental men should be working on his line) – so did the threatened resentment in the camps themselves. The white workers up in the hills found they were suddenly relieved of the need to wield picks and shovels, and instead were promoted to become overmen and team leaders. This new regime reinforced their idea of their own racial superiority, since the Chinese were invariably subservient to them even if they did have the gall to rise earlier and go to bed later, and to work all the hours in between.

But the ability of the Chinese to work long and hard was not the only factor. They were adventurous and inventive, too – ingenious in a way which led to the phrase "damn" clever, these Chinese". For example: to deal with the pressing problem of drilling dynamite holes far up on sheer and inaccessible rock-faces, they lowered themselves from the summit edge in small wicker baskets, using a system of pulleys. And when, at the notorious pass known as Cape Horn, they somehow had to fix the railway to a smooth vertical face, dozens of them – dangling in baskets a thousand feet up in space – chipped laboriously away at the granite until they had carved a thin ledge in the wall and then, standing upon this tiny ledge, widened it until it could accommodate the railway itself. Many transcontinental travellers who, three years later, passed over the Cape and looked out of their carriage windows into open space, grumbled that they were afflicted by vertigo – forgetful of those whose vertigo might have been far worse for having built the rails in the first place.*

*Vertigo was the least of it: hundreds of the Chinese died in construction accidents, or froze to death in the terrible Sierra Nevada snowstorms. One newspaper reported in 1870 that fully 10 tons of Chinese bones – the remains of 1,200 workers – had been shipped back to the Middle Kingdom for burial.

There was racial as well as commercial rivalry between the two onrushing lines. The Union Pacific's bosses wagered that any one of their "Hibernians" could outwork three of Crocker's "Chinamen" – a bet that often led to ludicrous situations. Perhaps the silliest was realized when it emerged that the two sets of surveyors – one moving west ahead of the Union Pacific road, the other pushing eastwards in advance of Crocker's Central Pacific – had at one stage in late 1868 actually passed each other in the eastern Nevada flatlands, running parallel just a few hundred yards apart and not meeting at all. As it happened, the Oriental work crews and their grade-line invariably seemed to be positioned a few hundred feet up a hill above the survey line of the Irishmen: boulders were often rolled down the slope, forcing the Hibernians to scatter in terror. To get their own back the Irishmen, adept in the use of black powder, once in a while liked to lay their charges much too far to the north of their own line – occasionally blowing up a platoon of Chinese for good measure. As always, the Chinese were phlegmatic about their losses – though they took the opportunity to use their equanimity as a bluff one day when they destroyed an immense section of Irish line, a blast that took half a village with it.

It was the Chinese, of course, who won the race. Thanks to a rockfall which delayed the Union Pacific crews for 24 hours, Crocker's teams were the first to reach Promontory Point, Utah – the otherwise undistinguished hamlet formally designated by Congress as the point where the American continent should be joined by the new iron roadway. And it was there, on 10 May 1869, that a colour party of these new American Orientals played a suitably rewarding part in one of the great little ceremonies of the coming Pacific dawn.

The Central Pacific train, with its Chinese tracklayers to the fore, was at the Point on time: the Union Pacific special, filled with dignitaries and soldiers of the 21st Infantry bound for the Presidio at San Francisco – a hint of one way in which the new line would soon be used – was unaccountably late. The 500 spectators who had gathered – workers from Canton and Kilkenny; grandees in the Mormon hierarchy and painted young whores from across the line in Nevada; writers, artists and photographers – were at first irritated and then soothed by the shabby magnificence of it all.

On this memorable day the Chinese looked most splendid. Their denim pantaloons had been freshly scrubbed, their long queues* newly greased and braided. A hand-picked group of the most muscular among them – and during these past years some had developed amazing sets of biceps and triceps – carried the final rail into position and lowered it on to a specially polished laurel sleeper. (The thesis that skeins of overseas Chinese trading links are what truly connect today's Pacific may be tricky to prove; to allege that it was the Chinese (the Cantonese) who actually knitted transcontinental America together is – given the events of that rainy May afternoon in Utah – a fair assessment of a technically unassailable truth.)

There were prayers – lots and lots of prayers, most particularly from a Massachusetts divine who, it was later judged, rose far too enthusiastically to the moment. (The telegraph operator, exasperated, tapped out in morse once he had finished that "We have got done praying: the spike is about to be presented.")

Would that it were only a single spike. The Chinese lowered their final rail on to the sleeper, and watched patiently as an entire hedgehogful of pointed objects was hammered in, retrieved and hammered in again. There was a silver spike from the Comstock lode in Nevada; an alloy spike of Arizona gold, silver and iron; gold and silver spikes from Montana and Idaho; then two more spikes of pure gold from California, with a silver sledgehammer for driving them in. It seemed the invited guests were pathologically incapable of driving any of them into the holes provided – none of the contemporary accounts suggests that over-indulgence played any part in their incompetence.

The final spike was due to be pummelled into place by Leland Stanford, president of the company and former Governor of California. Since he was no better than the rest, the final memorable seconds of the ceremony had to be fudged by the telegraph operator. The plan was for the telegraph signal caused by the actual electrical contact between Stanford's silver hammer and California's golden

---

*Worn proudly by the Chinese in nineteenth-century America (though often with Western-style felt hats) in spite of the fashion having been imposed on them by their hated Manchu Imperial house. Patriotic Chinese inside China loathed them, rightly regarding them as a symbol of their subjugation. But in foreign lands they wore them with a defiant pride – a symbol which the more primitive Americans came to scorn. "Chink, Chink, Chinaman, sitting on a rail/Along comes a white man and cuts off his tail" was a refrain popular among more than the juveniles of the latter part of the century.

spike to resound across the nation, and cause a ball to drop from a pole on the Capitol Dome; for fire bells to ring in San Francisco; for cannon, factory whistles and hooters to sound from Seattle to Miami, from Boston to San Diego. But Leland Stanford – for what reason? Myopia? Drink? Undue excitement? – missed, his silver hammer clanging uselessly against the Chinese-laid final rail. Thanks only to the quick thinking of the telegrapher, who simulated the hammer-blow with his morse key, did the historic signal flash out from Promontory Point to all America, and beyond. The vice-president of Union Pacific then hammered the spike home into the laurel sleeper. The line was finally laid, the continent finally spanned. And China, unwittingly, had a new memorial: the beginnings, if historians care so to judge it, of a new kind of Pacific-centred, Oriental Imperialism.

Much of this account has been concerned with the Chinese as migrant labourers: the armies of tough, wiry, nimble, uncomplaining men who happened to lie at the very bottom of China's immense and Byzantine society. But it would be wrong to suppose that only common working men emerged from the Middle Kingdom to populate the outer reaches of the world. Since the long Oriental hegira began in the fifteenth century, after Admiral Cheng Ho's remarkable naval expeditions had demonstrated the size (and the potential for profit) of the lands beyond China, so a stream of ambitious and energetic voyagers have sought their fortunes abroad. The modern Chinatowns and the nature of the Chinese who populate them reflect the complicated admixture of types, ethnic backgrounds, traditions, attitudes and abilities which were brought by the settlers of the past – a far more complicated mix than if all the Chinatowns had been inaugurated by men captured by crimps and shipped off to work on the railways and in the sugar fields and the guano islands – and leavened by the more openly ambitious and more obviously free-willed settlers of today.

In South-East Asia, the Chinese seem to be omnipresent, inescapable, part of the warp and woof of every country between Vietnam and India, Luzon and Timor. "I have written a great deal about the Chinese and very little about the Malays," Isabella Bird felt obliged to explain in a travel narrative she published about the peninsula in 1879, because "the Chinese may be said to be everywhere, and the Malays nowhere." As went Malaya a century ago, so goes all Asia today:

the store from which Imelda Marcos bought her shoes in Manila
was owned by a Chinese;* likewise the drug overlords of Kuala
Lumpur and the shrewdest Port Moresby entrepreneurs are Chinese;
it is difficult to conduct business in Jakarta or Bangkok without their
involvement. To quote an old Chinese adage about Hong Kong and
Canton, they are as close to the economy of what they termed the
Nanyang "as the lips are to the teeth".

The *Nanyang* – the word is similar to the Japanese *Nanyo*,
encountered aboard the *Africa Maru* – means literally Southern
Ocean, but has come colloquially to signify South-East Asia.
It is through this area that the Chinese have long spread their
intellectual, cultural and commercial influence – as long ago,
indeed, as the third century AD, when official missions were
dispatched to report on the countries bordering the Nanyang. Half
a millennium later Chinese Buddhist pilgrims voyaged to India,
stopping at many Nanyang ports en route. The Sung Emperors
of the twelfth century encouraged trade with the region, and
the Mongols too – once they had conquered China – happily
did business with the inhabitants of Nanyang itself, and with
the Arab traders who reached the area from the west. All this
was long before the eunuch Admiral and his giraffe-capturing
expeditions to Mogadishu: the intimacy between China and her
southern neighbours has been profound for the better part of two
thousand years.

This explains why, of the clearly definable groups of overseas
Chinese, it was the merchants, the moneylenders and entrepreneurs
who arrived first – which explains in its turn why the attitudes and
sympathies of these mercantile classes underlie all overseas Chinese
life today, and generally colour Western attitudes to the Chinese as a
people known for cunning and monetary shrewdness. It is probably
fair to say that the Chinese communities overseas are no longer
regarded as particularly adept at building railways or panning for

*Corazon Aquino, who replaced Ferdinand Marcos as President in 1986, is of
Chinese origin. The Filipino family name is Cojuangco, a portmanteau made up
of the original Chinese name Co, the second of the two original given names Kuan,
and a Hokkienese suffix, Ko, which means "elder brother". The ancestral village,
Hung-chien-t'sun, is 90 minutes' drive from the city of Amoy; nearly everyone
there has the family name Co, and Mrs Aquino's paternal uncle, Co Guan Hing,
lives in a house decorated with photocopies of a *Time* cover showing the heroine
of Malacañang.

gold: it is their financial skills – the underlying reason for the first Chinese migrations – that are best-known today.

Direct descendants of these commercial travellers – traders, artisans, skilled workers – are to be found scattered all across the Nanyang. There are Hokkienese in Jakarta and Manila; Chuichows (or Teochius) in Thailand; Hakkas – the gypsy-like "guest people" – in Sabah and Sarawak (and oddly, though irrelevantly here, in Jamaica). The families have lived in their new homes for generations; yet, like so many Chinese abroad, they have rejected the need to become totally or even marginally assimilated into their newly adoptive population. They live apart – in Chinatown; they huddle together in their laager; they retain their peculiar traditions; and, to a greater or lesser extent, they direct many of the crucially important aspects of the economy of the land in which they live. Yet, by and large, they immerse themselves in anonymity and humble circumstance. I once saw a shuffling old man in Davao, the wretched capital city* of the southern Philippine island of Mindanao. He wore grubby white shorts and a torn vest, and was barefoot, but a Filipino friend told me he was the wealthiest man in Davao: a landowner, restaurateur and property developer whose only ambition was to pass on a fortune to his six children. Like all the Filipino Chinese businessmen he paid off both the government protection racketeers and those working for the Marxist New People's Army: however costly, business insurance was more crucial to the Chinese than ideology, at least in the short term.

"Jews of the East" is a widely used sobriquet telling much of the complicated cocktail of envy, disdain, fear, dislike and admiration with which such men are regarded. Their sheer ability to work all the daylight hours and more, to drive themselves unceasingly, to wage unremitting war on torpor and sloth, to seek ever new fields for profit and self-advancement, to urge upon their children the absolute need for learning, hard work, filial piety, respect, duty and the constant acceleration of the family fortunes – the ability and dedication of the Chinese to pursue such lives has left the rest of the world gasping in their wake. They were never liked; but they were always respected and invariably essential. "One finds [the Chinese middleman] everywhere," the historian Victor Purcell wrote. "One

*Said to be the biggest city in the world, thanks to a typically grotesque Filipino attempt on the record books made by redrawing the city's boundaries. Most of the land is covered by barely penetrable jungle.

needs him everywhere. One must accept him, while limiting as far as possible the bad effects of his role."

In simple chronological terms the second group of Chinese to venture abroad in large numbers was the contract workers – the coolies – who have been discussed above. Unlike the volunteer entrepreneurs of the decades before, most of them were sent very long distances, travelling clear across the Pacific rather than simply across the home waters of the Chinese empire. Just a few went to Sumatra and the Malayan peninsula; but hardly any to the Philippines or Thailand. Some of the railway builders, cane-field workers and gold-miners came home from the Americas and the Antipodes when their contracts were over, true; but many stayed; and there can be little doubt that the difference between on the one hand the discreet Chinese dominance of many of the Nanyang economies, and on the other the relative economic isolation of the North American and Australian Chinese communities, stems from the very different kinds of Chinese who first populated the regions. Astute and enthusiastic members of the mercantilia took off for the cities of the Nanyang; armies of the Chinese proletariat – not all of them entirely willing – ended up in the goldfields of the Yukon or slaving through the snowfields of the Donner Pass for the likes of Mr Crocker.

Today, things have changed yet again. Chinese are still leaving for the West . . . but not from China. They are re-migrants – men and women who, for one reason or another, have decided to leave the country to which they or their ancestors first migrated, and go elsewhere. They are to be found dotted all around the Pacific – Chinese from Malaysia now in Perth, from Taiwan now in Los Angeles; Chinese from Vietnam in Vancouver and now, and above all else, Chinese from Hong Kong – in Toronto, Los Angeles, Melbourne, Calgary, Sydney, San Diego, Auckland, Wellington, Newcastle, Townsville . . . .

The extraordinary situation of the British dependent territory of Hong Kong, made all the more so after the infamous "incident" of 4 June 1989 in Peking when scores – perhaps hundreds – of students were killed by soldiers under orders to enforce martial law regulations, is generally beyond the scope of this chapter. But in one respect – the emigration of large segments of its now anxious and mistrustful population – it splices with uncanny neatness into the same story as that of the coolies, the crimps and the Nanyang Chinese.

The end of British Hong Kong is due at midnight on 30 June 1997, after which Xianggang (since Peking will be in charge, the Mandarin transliteration will obtain officially, rather than the Cantonese *Heung Gong* of today) will become a Special Administrative Region of the People's Republic. The six millions who lived in the territory at the time the agreement between Britain and China was signed in 1984 accepted it, *faute de mieux*, without demur. But since then, and in steadily increasing numbers, they have demonstrated their disdain for the pact and their loathing for the barbarisms of Deng Xiaoping's China by leaving Hong Kong for good – for Canada, Australia, the United States and any other climatically and monetarily congenial nation that would take them in. Sixty thousand a year – one per cent of the population – were reported to be leaving in 1989 and 1990, a figure considerably higher than that annually leaving China during the height of the coolie trade.

Unlike the coolie days, when an overcrowded China would shed few tears at the prospect of losing a tiny proportion of her less commendable citizenry, Hong Kong could ill afford to lose anyone. Moreover, the people being leached from her population in the late Eighties were, generally speaking, her most shrewd and skilled white-collar workers – men and women with knowledge of computers, banks, aircraft engines, textiles and the fine art of selling and marketing. They who were the very essence of the colony, the greater part of the reason for its staggering success.

At the time of writing neither government – either of Britain or Hong Kong – had come up with any kind of plan to save the situation; while China had not begun to behave in a manner that might render her exculpated, in the eyes of the anxious Hong Kong Chinese, from the horrors of the "Peking Spring". So the exodus, the blood-letting went on. It was to the advantage of the other Pacific democracies, of course, that such highly talented, well-organized, energetic and enthusiastic immigrants were on offer as potential new blood; and the more prescient and less prejudiced of these countries eagerly established migration offices in Hong Kong to seek out the best and the brightest Chinese who might wish to make their new – and safe – home in this new land or that new city. Hong Kong was being bled to death by uncertainty, a pervasive lack of trust and what many fairly recognized as the incompetence, the wishful thinking, the naïveté and the extraordinary lack of interest displayed by the departing British. Some have noted that Britain's exit from one of its most grand colonial possessions has been tawdry and ill-considered;

still others will argue the contrary and insist that Britain had no alternative but to act – or to fail to act – as she did. However, the effects of all this action or inaction were undeniable: the great Pacific diaspora of overseas Chinese, the so-called *hua-i*, was growing in the late Eighties by 60,000 bright and ambitious new souls every year, to the undeniable benefit of the Pacific and the consequent loss of poor old Hong Kong. Death by 60,000 cuts each year seemed the most undignified end for a territory which had served Britain in general – and a few great British families in particular – so ably and profitably for the century and a half of its Imperial existence.

The existence of the Chinese communities in big cities around the Pacific has not, however, been wholly beneficial. Since the arrival of the very first Chinese in the very first Chinatowns 150 years ago – in Lima for the sugar, or San Francisco for the gold – a new word has been coined to indicate a whole new chapter in criminal behaviour: the Triads. The silent, beguilingly cabalistic, hauntingly mysterious, heavily romanticized and little understood Mafia of the Chinese underground.

Triad societies have existed for more than two centuries, the first being formed in China for the relatively benign purpose of ridding the country of the loathed Manchu emperors. The idea was born of symbolism: a union of Heaven, Earth and Man – the triple union, *San Ho Hui*, hence the word *Triad* – could (the early organizers supposed) become powerful enough to drive out the Tartar despots. It failed in its early ambition – the Manchus were not overthrown until 1912 – but the society itself flourished and spawned clones, all deeply secret, with complex rituals and initiation ceremonials, its members given to bizarre and often violent behaviour. Like so many societies in which secrecy plays a central role, so the activities of the Triads became ever more dubious and nefarious – leading to today's situation in which, by and large, the Triads have evolved into a globe-encircling network of Chinese-directed villains, as wealthy and influential an organization as the Sicilian Mafia and (being Oriental and supposedly unfathomable) a great deal harder for the world's police forces to detect, penetrate and neutralize. Triads are in short a public enemy, a menace to society.

The epicentre of the Triads' world is, and probably will continue to be until the middle of the Nineties, Hong Kong. Its relatively free-and-easy, undisciplined, unpoliced inner world was infinitely more attractive to those who sought profiteering on the grand scale than was China, with its omnipresent ears of the State, gargantuan machinery for detection and repression and very limited potential for those in search of a fortune. So out from Hong Kong, to every city on earth sporting a Chinatown or a Chinese community, fan the acolytes of the Triad world – acolytes from no fewer than fifty societies which the Royal Hong Kong Police currently believe to exist.*

The internal structure of a Triad society varies little. To those lonely and unfulfilled young men who apply to join a group, it is satisfyingly cabalistic in its nomenclature. Much revolves around numerology – this number being auspicious, that being invariably fatal, and so on. The *Capo di tutti capi* equivalent is the so-called Dragon Head, who sports the number 489: very few of this highly regarded rank are known to exist and, in consequence, are regarded with awe by the Chinese public.

However, the only confessed Dragon Head brought before public scrutiny in recent years was considerably less than an awe-inspiring figure. In person, he was the very opposite of the type imagined by the press and its readers for the leadership of so dreaded an organization. Far from being a character by Reginald Kray out of Oddjob, Mr W.Y. Heung, the 489 of a sizeable Chiuchow Triad known as the Sun Yee On (which means New Righteousness and Peace, public sentiments at considerable variance from the practices – loan-sharking, protection, drugs and prostitution rackets – that its leaders favour), turned out on his appearance in court to be a bookish sort, mild-mannered, eminently forgettable. With his dark suit and white shirt, neatly trimmed and parted hair and well-shone shoes, he might well have been a Chinese under-manager at IBM. His "cover", his respectable job, was as a solicitor's clerk in a law firm in central Hong Kong; it was in his office there, amidst all the trappings of legality, that he interviewed would-be office-bearers of the Sun Yee On, coming practitioners in lawbreaking of the most grotesque kind.

(Mr Heung's father was a Dragon Head before him. He won a Commendation from the British Forces' commander in the colony

---

*Many of the overseas Triad bosses have old affiliations with the Hong Kong Police – an organization that was, until the establishment of the extraordinarily powerful ICAC (the Independent Commission Against Corruption), about as venal as a police force can possibly be. Pan Ling quotes a Toronto specialist in North American Triads as saying that in his territory "a common denominator among high level Chinese organized crime figures is a former affiliation with the Hong Kong Police."

just after the war, since via the syndicate he controlled he was able to organize neighbourhood patrols that were of great help to the Allied troops. But the Commendation did him little good; he was deported to Taiwan in the 1950s.)

The rank immediately below Dragon Head is the Second Marshal, or number 438; below him is the Red Pole, or 426, whose duties include fight-fixing and, as the title suggests, arrangements for the punishment of miscreants; below him the White Paper Fan, 415, is a counsellor and administrator of the gang; and then the Straw Sandal, 432, who collects debts and organizes the protection rackets. The lowest members of Triad society – but nonetheless members, wielding considerable power and influence at street level – are the 49 Boys.

The membership drive begins at school: young boys who appear more friendless or rootless than most, or the kind of work-shy youngsters who populate the amusement arcades and roller-rinks on the Kowloon peninsula, are easy prey for the Elder Brothers, the recruiting-sergeants of the Triads. The merest suggestion of friendship and camaraderie, of involvement in an organization with tradition and pride, the macho temptations of tattooing, uniform-wearing, secret handshakes and passwords, proves powerful medicine. Peer pressure, the awesome prospect of gaining face and acquiring some standing in gutter society – all these factors ensure a constant flow of young men who agree to the Triads' probation period, the *lam dang long*, the hanging of the blue lantern, that invariably precedes formal initiation.

Once inside the society, a new recruit maintains the rules of Triad secrecy with total rigidity: his parents may never know of his affiliation – indeed, they may regard with pleasure his newly disciplined behaviour, apparent politeness and more polished appearance. But out on the street, away from the scrutiny of the uninitiated, he is a delinquent villain: running small rackets, collecting protection money, distributing drugs. If he does well he may be promoted to one of the more responsible divisions of the society – the prostitution wing, the drug-smuggling arm, the gambling and loan-sharking business. He may become involved in one or another of the uncountable front organizations that give the Triads a veneer of respectability.

If he has a fair degree of nous, street-smartness, contacts and shrewdness, over the years he may grow rich, wield much influence and come to rub shoulders with the more obviously established and, crucially, criminally unblemished members of colonial society. He will distribute money to charity; his photograph will appear in the *Hong Kong Tatler* or *The Peak*; he will take tea in the Clipper Lounge of the Mandarin Hotel and play tennis at the Hong Kong Country Club. In other words, he will come to exist in that blurred nether-world of middle-class Hong Kong where the legal and the monstrously non-legal mingle unashamed and contented – a situation which goes a long way to make Hong Kong the elegantly gold-edged sink of iniquity that the outside world has long supposed it to be.

The Sun Yee On is perhaps the best-organized and most powerful of the Triad syndicates – though not the best known: that honour belongs undoubtedly to the 14K,* spread as it is through every Chinatown from Amsterdam to Valparaiso. The last time there was a census, in 1978, the membership of Sun Yee On ran to 33,750, of which 1,267 were full office-bearers. Twenty-one such office-bearers were based overseas – a dozen in Macau, one in New Zealand, three in Britain, four in the United States. Drugs are the syndicate's main business: they dominate the heroin market in Holland, for instance, and are fast displacing the Sicilian gangs as the chief suppliers of Asian narcotics in New York City.

There are many others: the Wo Sing Wo (which in the 1970s had a beautiful, Roedean-schooled Chinese model named May Wong working as a Straw Sandal, peddling heroin in London; Scotland Yard ran an extensive secret operation to uncover her); the Wo On Lok, which recently displaced the 14K as the dominant force on the Amsterdam drug market; the Big Circle Boys, responsible for all manner of jewellery robberies in Hong Kong; the Bamboo Union, whose political links with the ruling Kuomintang in Taipei became all too well known when they murdered an American-Chinese writer in San Francisco, for having written critically about Taiwan's then president, Chiang Ching-kuo; the Four Seas, who along with the Bamboo Union control Taipei's flourishing prostitution industry; the Frogmen – Vietnamese-Chinese who, during the war, were employed by the South Vietnamese army as underwater demolition

---

*So named because its first meeting, convened by a group of secret police chiefs of the Kuomintang, was held in April 1949 at No. 14 Pao Wa Street, Canton. Its first object, like that of the original Heaven and Earth League two centuries before, was openly political – in this case to consolidate popular support against the Maoists. It was only when the syndicate failed in its political ambition – after Mao won and declared the People's Republic that same October – that the men of 14K turned to crime.

experts – now operating in New York's venerable Chinatown; the Young Turks, Singaporean Chinese working in the seedier quarters of Sydney; and the Saigon Cowboys, who despite disclaiming all links with the China all Vietnamese profess to despise, use methods precisely similar to those of the Triad societies to reap profits from the Western underworld.

Jade dealing, heroin smuggling, nightclubs, casinos, bars, discotheques, funeral parlours, dragon dances, lion dances, Cantonese pop concerts, kung-fu extravaganzas, Oriental herbalists – in all of these and a hundred more fields with appeal both for the Chinese overseas subculture and for some of the more romantically-inclined Westerners, the Triads exert a powerful hold. The police try to control and crush them: their hydra-headed siblings rear up again, in other guises, in other places, eternally, infuriatingly – like weeds, ants, cockroaches.

In Hong Kong, in the early summer of 1990, there was an impressive display of Triad muscle and police helplessness. A number of brand-new apartments suddenly came on to the market in a suburb of Kowloon. The Triad leaders decided that, given the highly speculative nature of the housing market in the colony, they could well make a killing by buying up the flats en masse and selling them a few weeks later. Since many gangs had the same idea at the same time, this pitted several Triad gangs against each other. One took the initiative, and ordered no fewer than 1,000 of its members to stand in line outside the apartment sales office – each sporting a white glove on his right hand, and with money for the deposit in his jacket pocket. The men came down in air-conditioned buses, as well organized as football supporters or members of a church outing. The police did nothing that day, nor the next, when the Second Marshal of the Triad gang held a press conference in a local seafood restaurant.

The Triads, the police who pursue them around the world insist, are only as powerful as society allows them to be – a trite enough excuse, one might suppose, except that Chinese society – at least to many frightened and wary Westerners – does seem to be unusually tolerant of wrongdoing on the kind of massive scale in which their secret societies appear to indulge. Probably the ordinary overseas Chinese is as ignorant of and untainted by the doings of the Triads as the ordinary Italian is distant from the perverse activities of the Mafia. As yet, there have been few demands by any overseas Chinese for an end to the use of the word Triad (while Italian immigrants are much more sensitive about the use of the word Mafia); and despite the outcry over the showing of the colourful epic *The Year of the Dragon*, a film devoted to the menace of the Chinese gangs in Lower Manhattan, the overall Chinese concern about white Westerners' reaction to them appears to be relatively limited.

By Jirón Paruro and Calle Ucayali in Lima or Yamashita Park in Yokohama, behind Gerrard Street in West London or Mott Street in Manhattan, along Ongpin Street in Manila, by the Rue des Gravilliers in the 3rd *arrondissement* of Paris or to the south-west of the Singapore River, the world's old established Chinatowns are sharply delineated and – for both the Chinese and their sometime disquieted Western neighbours – comfortingly static. (New Chinatowns, like that in Monterey Park in Los Angeles, have sprung up in the outer reaches of some cities and are of quite a different genre – suburban, modest, quiet and about as prosaic and dull as any American suburb from Westchester County to Marin.) In the traditional Chinese quarters, the symbols are invariably the same. There is usually a great gate, decked out with dragons and painted in scarlet and gold; there are innumerable restaurants, splendidly exotic food markets, store-fronts advertising jewellers and quacks, old ladies in samfoos and men in straw hats, Cantonese cinemas showing kung-fu films, gambling halls – in basements, and invariably illegal – where mah-jongg or fan-tan is played unceasingly. The telephone company has obligingly (though usually rather tastelessly) designed its booths to look like small pagodas; the city has given its street signs ideographic transliterations; and the roadways are often crowded with tour buses from within which wide-eyed and blue-rinsed ladies from the Mid-West gaze, uncomprehending, at their only brush with the strangeness of the Orient.

And there will be fortune tellers, herbalists and grocers' shops (selling ground deer antlers, bundles of leaves of every species imaginable, dried ox penises and copious amounts of a substance called Bezoar, an accretion culled from the stomachs of cloven-footed beasts and said to be antidote to all known poisons). Doubtless these grocers will sell, or wish to sell, ready-roasted ducks which they will hang, or wish to hang, in racks at the front of the store, the better to attract custom. But in the United States – the country which made substances like clingfilm and Listerine and professions like hygienist and allergist the icons of a new national religion – the idea of hanging cooked ducks out in the air and on the street was anathema. In San Francisco in the early 1980s the practice was banned; burly policemen were wont to wander into the depths of Chinatown there and issue tickets to bewildered Hokkienese shopkeepers, ordering them to answer in an American courtroom for having the temerity to indulge in a method of displaying food that they had known for centuries before.

Mr Art Agnos, a redoubtably liberal politician who is now the Mayor of San Francisco, had long been thought of as a friend of the city's Chinese. After all, in 1961 he had condemned a bill in the California state senate that made the eating of dogs illegal; while not overly keen to munch up Rover himself, he thought such legislation was unnecessary and, moreover, an insult to the state's ever-growing population of Chinese (who largely cleave to the principle that anything with four legs that is neither table nor chair is edible). He won many friends then; he won a great many more in 1982 when, as a state assemblyman, he co-sponsored a bill making it perfectly legal to hang up ducks in the windows of Chinatown store-fronts: and when the bill passed and the hygiene-maniac lobby lost, he became a hero fêted by every duck-monger in the city.

Since then Mr Agnos has become Mayor (an influential lady named Rose Pak set up "Chinese-Americans for Art Agnos" in 1981; it was an improbable-sounding election machine, but one that evidently functioned well). His Chinese friends have since prospered as in no other non-Chinese city in the world. There are Chinese in highly responsible positions in the city government: the Deputy Mayor is a Mr Ho, the Port Commissioner a Mr Wong, the Planning Commissioner a Mr Hu, the Public Utilities Commissioner a Mr Chin and, perhaps most extraordinary, the Police Commissioner is a Mr Lee.*

There are Cantonese investors everywhere; and while it is true, as in most Pacific coast American cities, that the Japanese investors are the most heavily involved – something to be discussed in the chapter on Los Angeles – the Hong Kong Chinese are coming up fast, thanks in no small measure to the eagerness of Mr Agnos. The value of Californian property held by Japanese investors is said to be in the region of $6,000 million; that of Cantonese investors, $2,000 million. And in San Francisco itself the Chinese – who, moreover, were nearly

*Pius Lee, in full. The Cantonese stint nothing when they choose English first names for themselves: Byron Cheung, Greenstreet Kan, Pluto Mak, Mimsy Wong, Cézanne Leung, Slump Cheng and Hello Ng are well-known figures in today's Hong Kong.

all educated either at Diocesan Boys' or St Stephen's school in Hong Kong – are said to own fully one tenth of the buildings in the city centre: the city's second largest hotel, three of the biggest banks, chains of clothing stores, innumerable restaurants and dry-cleaning businesses.

One is bound now to suspect that this is how the Chinese influence across the Pacific is set to expand and consolidate itself. The thin strands which first brought Chinese trade across what is called in Cantonese "the Great and Peaceful Ocean" – the abalone, the gold, the jade, the Bezoar, the jars of Tiger Balm – are still there, of course; the crime is there, likewise the Triad-dominated ruination which is increasing ominously; emigration is still there as a factor in the Chinese equation, and will continue to increase for at least the coming half-decade as a direct consequence of the growing instability of Hong Kong.

However, the signal difference we are seeing now is that the Chinese have entered the big league. They are no longer the ubiquitous, shadowy, wealthy bit players in the vast commercial theatre that is the new Pacific. They are no longer mere traders and dealers, compradors and fixers, men who live by *cumshaw* and *squeeze*, men who accost strangers in hushed voices and say they can always get it – heroin or hashish, a stereo amplifier or a nice small boy, a diamond or a shoe factory – and can get it cheap, or wholesale, and who then always know someone's brother or uncle who can acquire this and repair that and fix that and sell, sell, sell. . . .

Today's Pacific Chinese are increasingly rich; increasingly influential and becoming, to the crusted establishments of the pioneering families, almost respectable. As yet, they may not get into the favoured housing estates at Pacific Heights or Pebble Beach; they may not be on the boards of the Chambers of Commerce, or the San Francisco Symphony or the flashier country clubs. But they are getting on: their children do prodigiously well at school, and are going on to do even better at university. A new generation is in the ascendant, which is breaking free both from the traditional Confucian constraints of its own society and from the smudged reputations gained in the gold rush towns, the railway camps and the crowded alleys of Chinatowns themselves. And while the Triads continue to sour the public image of the new Chinese, the impact of the law-abiding, the industrious, the studious and the properly ambitious is undeniable. More than a century after setting out from the Middle Kingdom, the Pacific Chinese appear to have come of age.

2

The Master

On the eastern outskirts of the unlovely city of Taipei, in a modern office building of the rather severe ordinariness characteristic of today's Taiwan, is the headquarters of an organization known as the Examination Yuan. From here are administered all of the multiplicity of school and civil service tests that are offered for the citizens of the Republic of China, to help them clamber up the ladder of academic and professional success.

The president of this esteemed organization is a Mr Kung or, were his name to be rendered into the kind of Chinese used on the mainland, Mr Kong. His first names are Teh-cheng (in Taiwan) or Decheng (on the other side of the Strait). For the purposes of this introduction, and for reasons that will shortly become clear, I shall refer to him as Mr Kong Decheng.

Seventy-seven generations and more than 2,500 years separate this Mr Kong from the man called Kong Fuzi, who was born near and lived in the small town of Qufu in what is now Shandong province, in Eastern China. The present Mr Kong is hugely proud of his familiar connections, and the Taiwanese are proud of being able to count him among their number. For Kong Decheng is the seventy-seventh direct lineal descendant of the man whose Latinized name – so devised by Jesuits in the sixteenth century – renders him perhaps the most familiar of all the millions who have ever lived in the Orient. Kong Fuzi, or Master Kong, who was born in 551 BC and died seventy-two years later, is known in the West today simply as Confucius.

The five systems of belief which have come to dominate mankind's history – Buddhism, Christianity, Hinduism, Islam and Confucianism – differ markedly one from another: that much is obvious, if only from the vast amounts of treasure spent on armaments to defend each from the predatory or malevolent intents of the other. But Confucianism enjoys a difference of a greater order, in that it is manifestly not a religion. No worshippers bow down before bronze statues of Confucius, nor sprinkle his image with rose-water and waft scented smoke before him. No acolytes prostrate themselves five times daily, their heads towards where they believe Qufu to be sited. No member of the Confucian school is abjured to make a sign of the cross upon forehead, breast and shoulders, to indicate fealty to a long-dead prophet crucified upon such a shape. And none of the followers is bound to bathe in sanctified streams or endure vastly complicated and sometimes fatal penances, in the hope of placating members of some immense and bizarre Confucian pantheon.

Confucianism is spared the normal excesses of the organized church. It is a system that manages to exist and flourish without the benefits of patriarchs or metropolitans, deacons and rural deans, pardoners, caloyers, Moderators, imams, Knights Templar, suffragans, Popes, sufis, archflamens or archimandrites. There are no cantors or altar-boys, beadles or vergers, nuns or thurifers. There is in the Confucian way no matins or communion, no compline or benediction. Confucians do not inhabit presbyteries or ashrams. They do not have the strange habits of the Premonstratensians or the corns of the discalced friars, nor the bloodied shoulders of the Shi'ite followers of the Imam Reza. They distance themselves from such practices as the tonsure and the Yarmulka, the veil and the cowl, the cloister and the vats of holy water. And there is no such thing as a Confucian missionary.

Yet hundreds of millions of Pacific people – including all the Chinese, both within and without the Middle Kingdom – are the undeniable heirs to one of the most pervasive philosophical systems devised. There may be many overlays to this philosophy: the people in question may claim themselves to be Buddhists (of one kind or another), or Christians (of similarly bewildering variety and shades), or Muslims (of the two major schools, and of *their* multiplicity of sets and subsets), or agnostics or atheists or dogmatic Communists, their dogma shaped by one or another pantheon from Lenin to Trotsky and Mao to Lin Piao. But beneath the fripperies of such outward belief, the inner mechanisms, their guiding spirituality is – to a greater extent than is either admitted or recognized – shaped by the precepts of the long-dead scholar from Qufu, the Master Kong.

He was born a quarter of a century before the Buddha, of a family of threadbare aristocrats. His seventy-two years were lived out against a background of extreme dislocation – not an unusual phenomenon in a China which throughout its history has enjoyed little in the way of protracted periods of stability (this century alone having seen some of the varieties of tyranny, anarchy and organized shambles which have characterized Chinese life for the better part of 3,000 years). His parents died when he was a small child, and he eked out the kind of living offered to the cadet branch of a fairly good family, the recipient of some small benefits of patrimony. He took care of a state park; he supervised some Shandong provincial granaries. And he studied: he studied, so legend has it, for all the spare hours that were gifted to him, believing that knowledge lay at the very foundation of benevolent government. Indeed, as one of his many (and in this case, more popular) biographers was to note from the Confucian scripture, the famous *Lun yu*, or *Analects*:

> In order to propagate virtue to the world, one must first rule one's country;
>
> In order to rule the country, one must first rule one's family;
>
> In order to rule the family, one must first regulate one's body by moral training;
>
> In order to regulate the body, one must first regulate one's mind;
>
> In order to regulate the mind, one must first be sincere in one's intentions;
>
> In order to be sincere in one's intentions, one must first increase one's knowledge.

And benevolent government was much needed in the China of the day. The warring between the feudal barons, the constantly usurped authority of the Emperor, the fickle and corrupt local officials, left the peasant classes prey to all manner of misery. Poverty was everywhere; starvation was all too common. Confucius, who witnessed this distress and was greatly affected by it, realized that he – so learned and so relatively well connected a figure – just might have some chance of bringing it to an end. He might be able, he thought, to encourage kindly governance and stability to flourish in its place – and to achieve this goal he began to compose a structure, a philosophical approach to government and good social order which he believed would bring China's travails to a close. Once his views were properly formulated and codified he tried to persuade his local neighbourhood warlords to place him in a commanding position so that he could put his ideas into practice: the rulers either ignored him or, supposing him to be a dangerous radical, deliberately decided to have no truck with him at all.

Through his middle years Confucius thus became a teacher – a small-time public philosopher who would hold small seminars in his house in Qufu, to which he would invite intelligent young men from the towns nearby and school them in the cultural and historical, musical, poetical and human attributes of his country. He placed a premium on sincerity and intellectual attainment; he disapproved mightily of the Chinese aristocracy and of "connections", of the power of influence, wealth and social standing. Those who came to be taught by Master Kong had only to be clever, keen and sincere: once accepted and tutored, then they could – and indeed did – enter the government service (still denied to Confucius himself), and set about administering the land in as benevolent and wise a fashion as each graduate could manage.

When he was in his fifties the local rulers realized that they had a celebrity on their hands, and offered him what appeared to be a senior post in the government. But it had no real power and Confucius, aware that he was wasting his time and energy, quickly resigned from it. He spent much of his later life wandering from state to state – many of them at war with each other, thus rendering his odyssey an extremely dangerous one – looking for a ruler who might allow him into a position of real power where he might put his ideas to work. But as in Shandong, none in the vast lands of North China would entrust state administration to him – fine, authoritative and learned a figure though each ruler apparently recognized him to be. And so he came back to his home province, taught for five further years and then died. He had achieved little enough in his lifetime, and was consigned to his grave as a prophet singularly without the honour of his own country. Ten years later, on the other side of the world, Socrates was born; yet the basic forms of Socratic scholarship, and the aristocracy of the intellect, were already in the making far away and long before in China.

His immediate legacy was seemingly less than legend supposes it to have been. His books, of which there are said to be so very many, may well not have been written by him, or even edited or approved by him. His aphorisms and precepts, the collected fragments of his literary output that make up the *Analects*, were probably recorded, rewritten and retrospectively given his authorship by the many disciples who followed him. Meng-tze – whom the Jesuits called Mencius, and who lived a century later – did much to interpret and extol the works of the sage. By 221 BC, two and a half centuries after the death of Confucius, his ideas had been sufficiently widely proclaimed and had seized a sufficiently large proportion of the popular imagination to prompt an upsurge of fear and loathing of them among the ruling classes.

When the first of the Ch'in emperors took the throne – the first of the dynasty that gave China its name – there was a vicious campaign to wipe out the Confucian philosophy and exterminate its liberal and (for the nobility) inconveniently meritocratic protocols. The Emperor Shih Huang Ti ordered the burning of all Confucian books and the burial, alive, of practitioners of Confucian scholarship – those who, had the new ethic been a proper religion, would have been its priests. This same Emperor was the builder of the Great Wall, and is best remembered for that achievement: his attacks on thought, and the attempted destruction of literature, set in train a tradition which has remained a feature of Chinese life and society every bit as permanent as his granite wall.

His empire was violent, but brief; by the time the Han dynasty was properly established in 206 BC, the pendulum had begun to swing back. By the time of the great Han Emperor Wu, the Confucian scholars had been formally rehabilitated and the foundations were being laid that would render Confucianism the official state religion – or, since it was not an actual religion, the philosophy by which China was to be officially organized until the revolution of 1911 and, many would say, until the present day. During Wu's reign, from 141 until 87 BC, the country began to enjoy a period of fragile stability; under these conditions Confucianism started to achieve an authority and a central place in Chinese life that it was never, despite innumerable attacks from all kinds of quarters, to lose.

More than 1,200 years later, there was one further period of reinterpretation of the precepts of Confucian teachings, under the scholar Chu Hsi. He breathed new life into a dogma that was in danger of becoming sterile and stagnant: he codified the varieties of Confucian thought which had become evident since the reinterpretations of Mencius; he stole some of the better aspects of Buddhism and Taoism from the scholars of those creeds; and he laid the foundations for modern Confucianism – Neo-Confucianism – said by many to underpin the new economic success of the Pacific. Indeed, a good reason for including Confucius in this short list of Pacific icons might have been wanting, had not Chu Hsi reinvigorated the philosophy in the twelfth and thirteenth centuries, during the closing years of the Sung dynasty. The economic success of Singapore, Japan, Korea and their neighbours – which outsiders, rightly or wrongly, ascribe to the application of the tenets of Confucius – might more properly be laid at the door of Chu Hsi. "Virtue is the root," declared one of the Neo-Confucianists. "Wealth is the result."

What, then, did Confucius teach, what did Mencius codify and to what did Chu Hsi give more sparkle and fizz, and a relevance that was to last until today? This religion–that-is-not-a-religion, this philosophy-with-temples, this missionary-less movement that has spread halfway around the world – what makes it what it is?

The central theme can be summed up in a single word: order. The codes by which Confucius wished the world and its people to live their corporate lives are all designed to bring order and harmony to society and to each and every one of its members. The discipline and order that he felt was central to society gaining its rightful happiness was to be achieved, he declared, by its members doing nothing to each other that they would not wish done to themselves. (A good five centuries before Christ said much the same in the Sermon on the Mount.)

But of course there was much more to Confucius than that. His *Analects* amount to 20 sections and 496 chapters – 300 rules of major ritual and 3,000 minor observances that would, if perfectly learned, give to the scholar the competence to govern his country and his people well. For another central theme of Confucian teachings – the theme that undoubtedly alarmed the Chinese warlords who later tried to purge the nation of his memory – was that the tradition of rule by nobility had to be replaced by a new tradition of rule by the intellectuals. An immense structure of examinations and tests of varying degrees of difficulty was established to create a new ruling class – a class selected purely upon merit, and under a set of rules that had utter disdain for the hereditary privileges which obtained in feudal China, and which exist today in some relatively primitive societies (and in many of the more obviously class-ridden aspects of contemporary Britain).

Those who believe in the success of modern Confucian societies need look no further for the reason than the legacy of Confucian education, and the ruthlessness of the examination systems. In Japan, Korea, Hong Kong and Singapore there is much the same competitive ferocity among the schoolchildren today as there has traditionally been in Confucian China – though few ordeals are as awesome as that personally invented by the sage and known as *kai ke chu shih* – "the enlisting of talent through the civil examination system".*

Although personally invented by the Master Kong, it was not until the Sui dynasty in the sixth century that such examinations began to be regularly staged – although there are records showing that as early as 165 BC, during the enlightened years of the Han dynasty, a system of recommendation and testing was used to select government officials, and that written and oral tests, administered by the Emperor himself, divided the winning candidates into the *virtuous* and the *irreproachable*, with all the concomitant benefits such commendations would bring. Confucius himself ran a small school, as mentioned earlier, entry into which was dictated solely by a young man's intellectual merit. The idea of a thinking elite was firmly established by the time Confucius died, even though it took 1,000 years for a Chinese emperor formally to take on board his ideas for competition.

And what competition the examinations then turned out to be! There were four levels of test – those for the officials of the district government, those for the provinces, those for running the nation's capital (which moved many times, thanks to the vicissitudes of Chinese history) and those administered within the Imperial Palace itself. Since the invigilators imposed no limits on the age of candidates, men as old as 99 (in one case) and boys as young as 11 presented themselves for testing.

The provincial capital examinations were in many ways the most important. They were held every three years, staged in the Examination Yuans of the various cities – Xi'an, Canton, Shanghai, Harbin, Urumqi among them – under conditions of great security and order.

*Taking the tests was also known as "going through the Dragon Gate", since students passing into the closely guarded compounds where the examinations were held had to pass through a doorway known as *Lung Men*, or Gate of the Dragon.

The specially constructed buildings were immense; as many as 8,000 candidates had to be housed for the three days of written tests, so as well as watch-towers and guardhouses there were stores, kitchens and dormitories, and row upon row of cubicles in which the candidates sat their papers.

The cubicles had no furniture, save for two planks. One was placed higher than the other during the day, and was used as a writing desk while the student sat on the lower. At night time both were set at the same level, and the two used as a bed. The student would bring his own papers and calligraphy brushes, as well as food. He would be subjected to a full body search as he entered through the Dragon Gate, and only then did he receive his papers. Any cheating – often tried and often (since the invigilators worked from towers with a full view into the open-doored cubicles) detected – was punished mercilessly. The most minor infraction of the rules resulted in thirty strokes, the most major in several hundred, and even slow execution (the court stranglers were particularly adept – with their steel wires – at gradually throttling the life from a body. One strangler proudly noted that he could take a full thirty minutes to suffocate a man, "during which process every bodily opening poured forth its contents.").

For three days and two nights the students laboured, writing lengthy papers on the inner meanings of the doctrines of the Buddha and of Lao Tse and of the Master Kong himself. There would be tests on history, and current affairs, and from time to time aspirants to the higher official positions would be asked to write poems, or compositions in rhythmic prose. Sometimes the strain of it all was too great and a candidate died of prostration: a hole would be cut in the Yuan's wall and the body removed, since under Imperial edict none could open the Dragon Gate until the examinations were declared to be over.

These provincial examinations represented but the first of the hurdles – though the only hurdle for most candidates – that lay between a man and the highest offices of state. Those who did best in the first papers were called to the capital for a stiffer series of examinations, and the few who passed these were ordered to attend upon the Emperor himself, who presided over a one-day academic festival known as the *tien shih*. This was by all accounts a colourful and impressive affair – gongs and fireworks, formal court dress and Imperial finery, the papers composed by the Lord of Ten Thousand Years himself, and to be answered within the confines of

seven sheets of exquisite and handmade parchment. A great feast
was staged for all who were summoned to attend, and the names
of those who succeeded, and who might reasonably expect to be
appointed Ministers of the Chinese Empire, were carved on great
stone tablets, to be remembered by all in the years to come. It was
no coincidence that the official Chinese name for the philosophical
system of Confucius was and still is (as it resurfaces, if the excesses
of the Cultural Revolution really are over and allow it to) *ju chiao*, or
the Doctrine of the Literati.

Sadly, for so boldly inventive a system for assuring a fair and
equitable approach to governance, the Confucian education system
– though not Confucianism *in toto* – inside China slowly ebbed into
extinction. The Peking Examination Yuan, tucked beneath the city
walls, was demolished in 1900, the bricks used to repair damage to
the foreign legations occasioned by the rebellious Boxers. But though
the system fell into disrepair in China where it was born, the strictness
and rigorously competitive nature of the schools in neighbouring
nations and states bears witness to its legacy: in Japan, South Korea,
Hong Kong and Singapore – and of course in Taiwan, where an
Examination Yuan still exists to promulgate Neo-Confucian testing
for the civil service – the numbers of children who can read and
calculate, and who are by all other measures to be regarded as well
educated, are well up into the high 90%s in all cases. In Japan, where
the Confucian educational practices are most clearly echoed, 99 per
cent of the population is literate: in the United States, according to
the scholar Jonathan Kozol, 16 per cent of white adults are functional
or marginal illiterates – a figure that rises to 44 per cent among the
black and 56 per cent among the Hispanic quarters of the community.

(Confucianism has rested in the core of Japanese society for at least
thirteen hundred years. Prince Shotoku's famous "Constitution of 17
Articles" – though it may have been for him, rather than by him –
contains the prescient remark that "the management of State affairs
cannot be achieved unless it is based on knowledge, and the sources of
knowledge are Confucianism, Buddhism and Shinto." The awe with
which the infant Japan regarded the magnificence of China's T'ang
dynasty, which held sway from the seventh to the tenth centuries,
further consolidated the influence of Confucian teachings. And the
very concept of *Bushido* – the infamously spartan ideal of soldiery,
which led to the *kamikaze* and so many of the other honour-bound
insanities of modern war – have Confucian teaching as their basal

principle: the Tokugawa shoguns lent their entire authority to the tenets of Neo-Confucianism, regarding Buddhism as a philosophy that was suitable for the lower classes, but Shinto and Confucianism as better suited for the Lords of Learning and the Warriors of State.)

Order, meritocracy and – the third leg of the Confucian tripod – a concept denoted by the Chinese character *jen* and meaning, broadly, brotherly kindheartedness and magnanimity. Man, the scholars reasoned, was inherently good: he had all the love and magnanimity stitched into his genes. But once in a while it became confused or diverted, so that he needed a hugely detailed code of political maxims and rules of social conduct to function properly, and to harness his *jen* to its best effect. This code, summed up in the *Analects* – or in the various now semi-official books of Confucian aphorisms and known in shorthand as the Five, the Six, the Nine, the Twelve or the Thirteen Classics* – suggested conduct in every field of human endeavour from love of art, music and good food to fellow-feeling for one's peers, and to that single best-known aspect of Confucian life, filial piety. Children were meant to obey, respect and ultimately care for their parents: this was the true foundation, Confucius decreed, of a properly ordered society. It was the absolute primary virtue, and in cases of conflict piety preceded all others.

There were strict rules governing the conduct of relations between others as well; filial piety was but one (though the dominant one) of the so-called "five cardinal relations" – that between sovereign and subject, brother and brother, husband and wife, and between friends. Confucius laid down laws whereby these relationships might be most harmonious and profitable to all concerned – the establishment of a common ethical way of life that covered business dealings and social intercourse with everyone, by everyone else.

If from all of this fog some ideal of the Confucian man appears, he will be shaped approximately thus: he will be clever, finely educated, discerning and imbued with an unerring sense of taste and style, and

---

*The Thirteen Classics include the most famous Confucian work, the *I Ching* (the Classic of Changes); *Shu Ching* (Classic of History); *Shih Ching* (Classic of Poetry); *Chou li* (Rites of Chou); *I li* (Ceremonies and Rituals); *Li chi* (Record of Rites); *Tso Chuan* (Tso's Commentary); *Kung-yang chuan* (Kung-yang's Commentary); *Ku-liang chuan* (Ku-liang's commentary); *Lun yu* (The Analects); *Hsiao Ching* (Classic of Filial Piety); *Erh ya* (a dictionary); and *Meng-tzu* (Mencius). The lesser numbers refer to collections of fewer than these, though *I Ching*, *Shu Ching* and *Shih Ching* are common to all.

with an unyielding love for the better things of life – good music and painting, fine food and wine, a liking for an evening of good tobacco in a long churchwarden. He will, however, be no snob: his position has been gained by hard work and ferocious competition, with no social or economic advantage to give him a head start. He will be a man who enjoys the common touch – easy in the company of kings, yet comfortable with men who are his intellectual and social inferiors. He will have a fierce respect for his country and the system under which it is ruled; though he may once as a student (like today's young and fiery students at the Korean universities) have felt an obligation to correct injustice if he ever spied it, and to have raged against those whom he felt had perpetrated it. He will display unending respect for his elderly parents, and will tithe them much of his income, and they will live with him no matter how inconvenient or cramped this might be. He will likewise honour the memory of his ancestors, taking good care to visit their graves, to keep them tidy and blessed. He will expect obedience and respect from his children too, and will brook no argument or dissent. He will expect them to labour hard at their studies, as he did before them, and as did his parents and grandparents in years past. He will treat his friends well and with respect. He will be courteous. He will be kindly. He will work hard, in honour of his parents, his superiors, his nation, his leader. He will, in the eyes of Westerners, be an impossibly endowed pillar of rectitude who seems to have stepped from the lines of Kipling's *If* by way of Norman Vincent Peale, and he will present a formidable foe to anyone who, from a foreign and less morally organized nation, might seek to oppose his views or the fortune he amasses from his philosophically-buttressed labours.

From such assumptions are born the assertions that fuel the belief that the world is entering the Pacific Century. A most eloquently expressed example appears in a Canadian publication from 1986. "If the East Asian centers of industry and technology have surpassed the Western capitalist nations' performance, that means they have by far outrun the Communist countries. So we come to an immensely important point. *Societies with Confucian-Buddhist roots are proving more effective in coping with the industrial and technological challenges on the eve of the twenty-first century than is . . . society with its predominantly Christian-Hebraic heritage . . .*"

*

260

And yet in academia a century ago – and more recently still, in popular journalism – the very opposite was being stated. Something called the Protestant ethic was adduced, to account for the enduring success and the sum of achievement of Western societies. No Catholic society – Ireland, Italy, Argentina – could perform as well. No Islamic society could cope. No Eastern state had the wherewithal. The triumphal leaders of global progress, men like Max Weber were wont to argue, would always be England, Germany, America and Russia, because the ethic by which they organized their societies was naturally attuned to profit and the magic of capital. Professor J.M. Roberts, an English historian of great repute, argued much the same in a lengthy BBC television series of the early 1980s, *The Triumph of the West*. The West (though not exclusively in his view the Protestant West) had discovered gravity, split the atom, painted *Sunflowers*, built great empires, made the motor-car and the aeroplane and written an immense corpus of world-spanning music; by sombre contrast, the East had invented fireworks, painted over and over again scenes of birds sitting disconsolately on twigs before a panorama of grey mountains, had tried to give the world impossibly difficult and quite pointless languages and had discovered almost nothing and invented even less. The East, in short, was in terms of human achievement a waste of a hemisphere.

Yet now the argument is being turned upon its head. The nations which have long suffered the yoke of the Protestant ethic are now (it is remarked by seers of varying degrees of credibility) stumbling, aimless and decadent, weary from all their years of global leadership, exhausted by their inventive efforts. In their place, spurred by such common goals as educative effort, filial piety and duty to nation, are rising the new Pacific stars of the cosmos – and all of them are peopled by men and women who are, if they know it or not, Confucian in their upbringing and outlook.

Not that all of Asia is being swept along by this spring tide of success. The Philippines, sad and forlorn, still lag behind. There is not much by way of economic miracle evident on the huge islands of Java or Sulawesi. The Papua New Guinea archipelago remains poor, save for those spots in the jungle where prospectors have discovered copper, gold or oil. Burma is a total mess. Unremitting civil conflict in Nicaragua and El Salvador has crippled such hopes as the smaller nations of the central eastern Pacific might once have had.

Such argument serves only to bolster the assertion of coming

Confucian supremacy. The Philippines is Catholic. Indonesia is Muslim. Papua New Guinea is many things, but not Confucian to any significant degree. Burma is as close to a wholly Buddhist state as the leaders of the Burmese Socialist Programme Party will ever permit. And the tiny countries grouped around the Isthmus have all sworn eternal devotion to Rome. Such Pacific nations as remain, the apologists continue, are both successful and Confucian. The situation speaks for itself.

Or it would, were there not one major flaw in the argument – the presence of China. This epicentre of Confucianism, this land which had given birth to and had nurtured and languished under the teachings of the Master Kong is manifestly not the success story that by rights, and by this argument, it ought to be. The discipline and filial piety and *jen* are all there – although to anyone who spent much time in the urban bleakness of modern China, *jen* seems in pretty short supply. Confucius is still a brooding presence, his teachings are still more profoundly effective than anything Mao or his successors have attempted to instil in the collective unconscious of the reborn nation. And yet the country is an unmitigated economic disaster. (As is Vietnam next door, also deeply Confucian in beliefs and practices. Her troubles, though, can largely be ascribed to war-weariness, and there are many who cling to a fervent belief that Saigon is about to arise anew, to be transformed into a hybrid of Bangkok and Marseille, an unrivalled success story for the next century.)

The true economic success stories of the moment are confined to just a few, albeit highly impressive performers – Japan, South Korea, Taiwan, Hong Kong and Singapore. These are peopled with undeniably Confucian stock,* and the same basic formulae apply in each case: a high premium is placed on education, on duty, on parents, on ancestors, as well as on such less laudable concepts as "face" and "squeeze". Each state in consequence enjoys a remarkable degree of social cohesion – "an unbelievable display of social solidarity and community responsibility", as Herman Kahn once put it. (Kahn was referring specifically to consensus on family planning that had lately been adopted in each society, and which demonstrated to him – since family planning was inimical to standard Confucian practice, where

---

*Though Korea is presently enjoying an enormous interest in Christianity, with noisy evangelists holding huge open-air services in the city centres, and the rooftops jammed solid with red neon crosses.

as many sons as *could* be born were born – that powerful forces of social discipline were at work. Probably he would have reached much the same conclusion had he been shown almost anything else.)

The citizenry in these states tend to prefer muscular governments peopled by authoritative, paternal figures – Lee Kwan Yew of Singapore being a perfect example – rather than submitting themselves to the undisciplined rigours of true democracy. The concept of rule by a scholarly gentry – such as the swells, British and Chinese, who still run Hong Kong without benefit of any say from the people themselves – still goes down well with the common people. They want no politics of the kind they all too often read about outside. The verbal fisticuffs on the floor of the Lok Sabha in New Delhi, or the sophomoric abuses bellowed even in the House of Commons in London would represent, to most thinking voters in a Confucian nation-state, an unseemly by-product of popular sovereignty. Political maturity brings in its train excessive behaviour even in Confucian societies, of course; the Japanese Diet can on occasion prove extraordinarily juvenile, and in the 1989 Taiwan elections a young woman candidate mimicked Italy's *La Cicciolina* by taking off her blouse in public and displaying her breasts to the voters – a performance somewhat out of line with the austere standards of Master Kong, and unlikely to win wholehearted approval by any interpreter of the *Analects*. But these exceptions do not dilute the principal reality, that by and large Confucian peoples favour tough government, good discipline and order. True democracy, rough edges included, is a luxury in which they are not, whatever aspiring politicians might wish, particularly interested.

Hong Kong, peopled largely by Chinese whose affection for Confucius has not been contaminated by state socialism – which must surely be blamed for inhibiting the natural tendency of modern Confucianism to bring forth rewards up on the mainland – offers as good an example as any of the modern disciple. We will call him James Chan and he works for a British *hong*, or trading company, named Inchape Pacific. He is 44, married with two children, and he oversees a group of young Chinese in the business of selling office machines.

Mr Chan comes into the office each morning at a quarter to nine, assembling his staff for a meeting at ten minutes to the hour. He is never late, and will accept no excuse from anyone who is: those who struggle in after the deadline are fined – $50 for the first occasion, $100 for the next, $200 for a third and so on. Mercifully his system recycles itself to zero each month: he was savvy enough to realize that staff who might well be late a dozen times in a year would have to pay a fine considerably more than their annual income.

He runs his office along strictly hierarchical lines. Everyone on his floor has a rank and there are at least seven ranks, from tea-boy and clerk to section supervisor (which is what Mr Chan is) in the single open-plan, cockroach-infested and smoky office over which he holds sway. Everyone in his office must display deference to those of senior rank and studied indifference to those below. When he is in the presence of men above his own station, he declines to sit down, and will laugh each time that they do even though (his English being poor, and most of his seniors being English) he has no idea what they are saying. Only those employees of a certain rank may write internal memos. Books must be kept on the lower shelves of desks belonging to those of a certain grade, though employees of a certain seniority may keep books on a higher shelf too. Everyone must wear identity badges at all times, the rank thus being visible one to the other.

He insists on seeing all inbound correspondence, on signing and countersigning all outgoing papers, on approving all decisions, affirming all minutes, initialling all orders. His secretaries must call him "sir".

He works unceasingly, though in truth his "work" often involves playing an elaborate and endless game on an office computer. Each Monday he gathers his senior colleagues about him for a meeting that lasts until ten at night. They play a lot of endless games at the meeting. He says that to leave the office late gives him considerable status among his superiors, even though he is not actually working while he is there. After his meeting he goes out for Chinese dinner with his colleagues and drinks with them until eight or nine on most other evenings, particularly enjoying Napoleon brandies. He has taken only one seven-day holiday in the last three years – a bus trip to Europe, where he passed through seven countries in five days of non-stop driving. He believes holidays should not be taken, that they are "morally wrong". He insists he has a duty to work as hard as possible, to make as much money as possible to spend on the education of his two children. Both these children go to private school, and he expects to find them working at their books when he returns home at ten or eleven each night. Of his wife he says little, and no guests are ever invited to his home. It gives him more "face" to entertain them at a restaurant, preferably one of great showiness and cost.

He instructs his salesmen on the ethics of their craft – ethics that would have turned even Willie Loman's hair white. The end justifies any means, he tells them. They may lie, cheat and harass to any degree in order to make the sale. They may have no loyalty to the product they sell: if he detects such dangerous tendencies in his salesmen, he may well pluck them from selling one product (to which they appear to be becoming attached) and set them to selling another. "He may like computers – so I put him on copying machines. To teach him that selling is all. Making money is the only reason for our being here." The high-pressure activities often result in mistakes, and furious customers, but nonetheless Mr Chan insists his staff never apologize. They may make excuses, blame the customer for failing to understand, blame others in the organization, blame paperwork or translation problems – but never take the blame themselves. "It is important for the team that they always feel they are on top, that they never lose face."

It seems a bleak and cheerless life that Mr Chan has chosen to live. He smokes incessantly, and is preternaturally lined and worried-looking. He looks 54, not the decade younger that his identity card proclaims him to be. His home is small, populated by his wife and two children, his own mother and his wife's mother – the two older women cordially disliking each other, the one believing the other socially and intellectually inferior. The ladies retire to their box-like bedrooms, leaving the rest of the family in the small living room. There is a table, two nylon-covered sofas and some straight-backed chairs, and in the corner is a large cage of noisy, ever-squawking birds. The television, a big new Sony Trinitron, is always on, and loud. The dominant colours of the decorations are red and gold, and the flat has a brassy and angry feel to it. It is not a peaceful place, not a place for contemplation or quiet. There are no books, other than children's textbooks. A couple of dog-eared copies of the Hong Kong fashion magazine *Joyce* and an Inchape company journal lie on top of the television. The neighbours are loud, though it is said there is no crime to speak of in the neighbourhood, and the Chan family may come and go at will, and at any hour, without the kind of fear they might experience in a less well-disciplined society.

Mr Chan thinks of himself and his surroundings as Confucian. He sees his devotion to his aged mother and mother-in-law, his strict regard for punctuality, order and rank, his pride in his own achievements "based on my efforts alone, you know" as firm evidence that he has learned much from the writings of the sage. He does not question the precepts – he does not actually recall what any of them say, never having actually read them – nor does he ever seek any outside religious assurance save from the gods at the Wong Tai Sin temple, where he will go once a year or so to have the geomancers offer answers to questions that might then trouble him – whether to hire this person or back that horse, invest his money in that stock or share. He is a long way divorced from the idea of the Confucian "cultivated man".

Yet James Chan, and millions like him with similar attitudes, aspirations and ambitions, represent the driving forces behind the economic success of Hong Kong and its neighbours today. Is it worth it? Is this what the Master Kong might have wished when first he began to utter the precepts, the rules and the Rites? Looking at Mr Chan it seems, from time to time, that it could not possibly be so. Rather it appears that what drives so many of the successful businessmen of Asia is actually a perversion of all that Confucius stood for, yet something that masquerades as the consequence of his teachings.

The "reciprocity" that the Master claimed lay at the foundation of his social ethics – the "I shall do unto you as you shall do unto me" – how does that square with James Chan's undoubted avarice, his ruthlessness, his admitted lack of scruples, his decision to place money above all other considerations? Then again – constancy in friendship is highly praised, Confucius believed: how, then, can today's Confucians claim to believe such precepts when friends are so often victims of the ruthlessness that drives the businesses of modern Asia? Has the Confucian ethic perhaps vanished clear away in the face of today's economic realities – and do we merely parrot the idea that Confucian-structured societies are more successful than those following other systems of belief? It is hard to believe otherwise.

In the strict sense, Confucianism remains fitfully alive in some corners of the Western Pacific. In Hong Kong, for instance, there is a flourishing Confucian Hall, a Confucian Young Men's Association and a number of Confucian schools; in 1984 an attempt was made to publish an English magazine, a *Journal of Confucius*, to spread the word of the Master. It did not last. In Korea the best preserved of all Confucian rituals takes place each May in the Chongmyo shrine, where the remains of the Yi dynasty monarchs are preserved. The Yi Dynasty Association stages the ceremonial, accurate in every detail, and many tourists come to watch the extraordinary sacramentals with the blazing robes, strange headgear, arcane musical instruments, the movement and low chanting, the clash of cymbals and the offered feasts. But one senses that the memorial is designed more to honour a regal dynasty than a majestic philosophy, and that all the dressing-up has a political edge to it – an expression of a wish to resurrect better times and better rulers, rather than a longing for a return to the strict rules written down in the *Analects*, or the *I Ching*.

Possibly only in Qufu, in Eastern China, where it all began 2,500 years ago, can one really capture something of the flavour of it all. The town itself – 100,000 of the country's half-million residents owning the surname Kong – is less ugly than many in modern China. The 76th Yancheng Duke, as the descendants of Confucius were known, argued in 1904 that the Peking to Shanghai railway would, were it to pass through Qufu, interfere with the energy waves radiating from the Master's tomb. Fearful of the wrath of the sage, the railway authorities agreed, and Qufu has been spared the dirt that Chinese railways bring in train, as it were.

The temple of Confucius itself, and the 460-room Kong family mansion where the various Yancheng dukes have lived since the Master himself died in 479 BC, remains more or less intact, spared from the vagaries of Chinese history for two millennia. It was inhabited until 1950 by Kong clan chiefs who pursued habits of near-Imperial luxury and apparent (but always denied) decadence: children played with toys made of kingfisher feathers and gold; there were banquets of 130 courses; when the dukes ventured beyond the mansion walls the citizens of Qufu had to press their faces into the muddy earth once they spotted the vanguard runners, who warned of the ducal approach with banners proclaiming "Make Way for the Wearer of the Two-Eyed Peacock Feather" or "Possessor of the Yellow Ribbon of the First Grade".

Hall after hall, passageway after passageway leads ever deeper into a mansion still crammed with the collection of a score of centuries. One entire suite, gawped at from behind glass screens by huge numbers of spitting Chinese peasant-tourists, is filled with the wedding gifts for a celebration held in 1935: silver, glass, bolts of unopened silk, swords of jade and sandalwood. Those who lived there were warned, despite the opulence, to live in accordance with the sage's wishes – to drink deep at the well of learning and to live comfortably as part of the intellectual nobility. But no more: to live badly was to commit a heinous sin.

The temple itself, entered as are all Chinese temples through the South Gate, is exquisite. One passes, in order, through a rose-madder wall, along a marble causeway, through a forest of cypress trees, over a marble bridge seemingly fashioned from clouds, past a forest of vertical stone tablets supported on tortoises, and up to the central temple chamber itself – marble, upswept eaves of ancient tiles, a thing of utter loveliness. But as with so much in China, romantic fantasy is only permitted to go so deep: inside the temple is a garish plaster statue of the Master, and the heaving masses of the Chinese proletariat who have come to see it jostle and spit and chew melon seeds most unattractively. Politics intrude, too. Faded Red Guard slogans can still be seen on the Master's walls. And, though none of the museum staff will admit it, the Guards also desecrated the Kong graves, threw out the skeletons still clad in their ornamental burial robes, hitched trucks to the bronze images of Confucius and his followers and dragged them through the streets. "Down with the Confucian curiosity shop!" they cried. Nowadays, though there has been some slight relaxation in the attitude to Confucius, the Chinese police still try to prevent pilgrims burning paper bundles in the burial ground – the burning being a sign of respect for the departed spirits. Anyone entering the grounds is searched for concealed paper – "spirit money" it is called – and so an elaborate charade has to be acted out whereby the visitors enter without paper . . . only, once inside, to catch bundles of it thrown in by friends. Then they vanish among the trees and, out of sight of the guards, indulge in their fiery prayers.

Why did you come, someone asked a miner who was fingering the marble in the inner sanctum. "Because we don't have to condemn Master Kong any more. Because he is permitted." Such sentiments betray, of course, one legacy of the Master's teaching – an almost unquestioning respect for authority. "We don't *have* to condemn him," the miner said – a reminder of the sense of obligation to the intellectual nobility that Confucius himself had helped to create.

28 September is celebrated throughout the Confucian world as the birthday of the sage. In Taipei, where the teachings are still regarded as state ideology, the ceremonial is particularly grand. The rituals are supervised each year by the president of the Examination Yuan, Kong Decheng, whose position as 77th direct lineal descendant of

Kong Fuzi gives him a special place in the Republic of China's official society. Mr Kong is also the official spokesman in Taiwan for modern Confucianism, and as such the foremost public authority for the interpretation of the sage's teachings. And he has no doubts, however debased the philosophy may seem to have become in some levels of commercial society, that Confucianism holds a key to future success.

> Confucius can be applied to almost any area of life [he will say to visitors]. You can apply it to international relations by remembering that Confucius taught that we should always behave fairly to one another. That means that strong countries must not take advantage of weak and struggling ones. Why did Hong Kong, Singapore, South Korea and Taiwan make such great economic progress in recent years? Because Confucius taught us to think of other people first. In a Confucian society, bosses and workers don't see themselves as antagonists, but as brothers who have a duty to cooperate with one another.

In theory, that is what they have done in the country lying just a few miles off Taiwan's western shore. Communism and Confucianism share many precepts. China is where Confucianism was born, and where Communism may finally come to die. Yet neither system appears to have worked for China herself. Perhaps China and her millions are beyond the abilities even of Confucius to direct. And yet again, for a China that weaves her influence so very subtly around the Pacific and the world, perhaps not.

3

The Money

I have suggested that the silken web that holds together the edges of the new Pacific has been spun in large part by the Chinese who, during the last century, have fanned out from the Middle Kingdom to all the shores of the Ocean. The web so constructed has been anchored in large part also by the tenets of Confucius – denatured and distorted though his teachings may now have become, given the mercenary realities of the times. But what the web itself constitutes – what common interest and shared purpose actually connect the devoutly Confucian trader in Seoul with his counterpart in Fiji, the Cantonese broker in Vancouver with his opposite number in Brisbane, or head office in Shinjuku with the sales team in San Mateo – is commerce: the simple and ancient mechanisms of business and trade. And central to the conduct of trade is, of course, the commodity called money.

While first the British pound and then the American dollar took over from the Swiss gold franc and the Mexican silver coin to dominate world trade throughout the present century – just as the franc and the "Mex" had taken over in their day from the doubloon and the moidore – so another currency is now becoming increasingly central to the conduct of trade across the new Pacific Ocean. The global dominance of a national currency has much to do with the notion, if not the practice, of Empire: sterling's salad days coincided neatly with those of England's rule of half the world; the dollar is a still-present indicator of the pre-eminent importance of the United States in the conduct of the planet's commercial affairs. But now the torch appears to be passing and a new currency, a new indicator of leadership – of the idea of a new Imperialism – is fast rising to become the world's new fiduciary standard. The newcomer of the world market is the form of money constructed principally for use within the island group of Japan: the yen.

There are precious few constants in the story of the yen. For a start, it is a stripling among the monies of the world, being not much more than a century old. Then, as one might expect with so adolescent a financial instrument, it is given to moments of wildness and abandon: the rates at which it is exchanged for the other major currencies of the world vary terrifyingly, often such as to make bankers and investors tremble.

The power with which the yen is gifted – or has been, in recent years – is utterly unpredictable: at the moment of writing Japan has just bought (essentially out of petty cash) such supposedly enduring symbols of American greatness as Columbia Pictures and the Rockefeller Center and the Seven-Eleven group of convenience stores. While there is much fear-inducing hyperbole – it is still the British, and not the Japanese, who are by far the biggest holders of American property – Japan is said now to own a fifth of the city centre of Los Angeles. What Japan and her mighty yen will have done by the time this chapter is completed, or printed, or read, is impossible to divine or imagine. One can predict with certainty only this: that whatever gesture, purchase or decision is made – underpinned by all the immense amounts of available specie washing around in the Tokyo banks – will be impressive and profound, and will have an impact on Western pride that may range from dismaying to devastating.

All this comprises something of an apologia for the observation of some aspects that may well be transient. In common with the exchange rates that determine its value, nothing relating to the yen can ever be fixed. So some elements of its current status may only remain valid a decade, a year, a month or a day from now; other remarks and conclusions may have the shortest of lives, like the Ephemera; some things which seem true today may be their very antithesis tomorrow. Yet the yen's status as a part of the connective tissue of the Pacific community will surely remain a verity, whether Japan continues to enjoy her present good fortune or even if she suffers a reverse: simple confidence in the assertion allows this account to proceed.

There is, though, one other constant. On the obverse of the modern 5,000-yen note – there are notes of three denominations in circulation today, the others having values of 10,000 and 1,000 yen – is a head-and-shoulders portrait of a man of apparently great dignity and bearing. To judge from the comfortable upholstery of his cheeks, he has a slight tendency to corpulence; he wears small round spectacles framed in steel and sports a fine moustache; he has a wing collar and grey silk tie, and a jacket which one has to assume is morning dress: the formal attire of a Japanese statesman of half a century ago.

And indeed a statesman is exactly what he is, or was. His name was Inazo Nitobe* and the fact that to the left of his portrait on the currency note there is a Lambert projection map of the Pacific Ocean, from Singapore to Ecuador, from the Bering Strait to Stewart Island in New Zealand, indicates the field over which – a century ago – he ruled intellectually supreme. Nitobe-san was Japan's "Father of the Pacific", colonialist and academic whose writings and arguments helped convince the post-restoration Japanese that, after all those centuries of internal conflict and external hostility, foreign expansion – the building of an Empire – was the probable key to future international success. The Greater East Asia Co-Prosperity Sphere, the vastly ambitious idea of global dominion that lay at the root of Japan's Pacific War, had its own origins in (among other factors) the writings of Inazo Nitobe and those who followed his nationalistic – if liberally expressed – beliefs.

For he was a liberal, a humanist and a devout Christian – but a nationalist without doubt, though American-educated (Johns Hopkins), and with an American wife. His early career was spent entirely in the fields of teaching and academic administration, an ascent culminating in his appointment to the first chair in Colonial Studies at Tokyo University, from which pedestal he mouthed sentiments of what would now be regarded as breathtaking audacity, but which in their time would have found their echo in those of a Curzon or a Palmerston. "Colonial rulers should take care to maintain pride in themselves," he declared. "Merely being kind to colonial subjects is insufficient. Primitive peoples are motivated by awe." He wrote a classic book about *Bushido* and was clearly a firm believer in this code by which the Japanese nobility had conducted their affairs in all the centuries leading up to the war. It would, he thought, take subject peoples a good eight centuries to make the necessary evolutionary steps towards the higher civilization that Japan represented. But he counselled kindness and understanding towards these lesser mortals, who at the time were simply the

*The note titles him properly Nitobe Inazo; but as mentioned in an earlier footnote, I stick to the Western convention that the names of Japanese prominent since the Meiji restoration are written Western-style.

Koreans, Formosans, Manchus and the islanders of the Nanyo who were discussed in an earlier chapter. Doubtless his sentiments would have later applied to the Han Chinese, the Singaporeans and Malays, the Filipinos, Indonesians and Burmese who fell under the ultimate control of the Showa Emperor.

> Do we govern an unwilling people [Nitobe asked] for their sake or for our own? As to the general unwillingness of any colony . . . to be governed by a power alien to it, there is little doubt. A colonial government has received no consent of the governed. Nor is there much reason to believe that a colonial power, white or brown, bears the sacrifice simply to better the lot of the people placed in its charge. The history of colonization is the history of national egotism. But even egotism can attain its end by following the simple law of human intercourse – "give and take". Mutual advantage must be the rule.

I find something nicely droll about the placing of the portrait of this thoughtful but arrogantly confident imperialist on the treasury bill. After all, here is a man who spent the better part – or at least the better-known part – of his career providing, perhaps unwittingly, part of the intellectual stimulus behind Japan's ambitions for military hegemony over Greater East Asia, not to say the world. He was not the father of the war, not by a long chalk; indeed, when the Bank of Japan announced in 1981 that it planned to distinguish the note with his picture, it was at pains to portray him as a peacemaker, and to record his six-year tenure as a permanent vice-minister of the League of Nations. But the soldiers whose hunger for world domination took them on that long and tragic path from the beginnings of the Japanese empire in south Manchuria in 1895 to its end in the waters off the coast of Midway Island in 1942 knew of his thinking and his writings, and must have taken no small comfort and sustenance from his words.

Although their military plans came to naught, the story of Imperial expansion (of a kind) did not end with the atom bombs, the surrender or the Peace Treaty. By dint of her energy and acumen in business and manufacturing Japan eventually came to exercise a kind of economic hegemony over the world instead – and the device by which she exercises such dominion today is of course the currency unit, the yen: from which Nitobe-san, his ambitions finally and ironically realized, stares unblinking and benign. Was that at least partly the reason for the Nippon Ginko – the Bank of Japan – so honouring him?

Is there some kind of elaborate and sardonic joke being played on all us *gaijin* by the treasurers of Nihon – reminding us of Japan's imperial triumph, however differently it was gained? Whatever the reason, the presence of that imperturbable, pleasing and rather kind old face seems to give the yen – or at least the 5,000-yen note – an even greater symbolism than is offered by its simple existence as a Pacific icon.*

The yen was born officially in 1869, two years after the Emperor Meiji took back the reins of power from the last of the Tokugawa shoguns. Before that Japan's internal financial organization, like Japan herself, had been a desperate shambles. The various clans issued their own paper money, and there were charming oblong gold coins, the so-called *oban* and *koban*, decorated with Paulownia flowers and issued by the shogunate. A survey conducted by the Finance Ministry in 1868 showed that during the Tokugawa period 244 clans had issued paper notes in an astonishing 1,694 denominations, and 14 magistrates' offices and 9 retainers of the shogunate had issued currency as well. Clearly something had to be done to straighten matters out – for purposes of international trade, if nothing else. How could Japan trade with the outside world if the currency complications meant that a man from Sapporo could not easily buy from a merchant in Tokyo, who could not in turn pay for goods from his supplier in Osaka?

The answer was to unite the currency into one: the yen, symbolized for the international audience by an amalgam of its initial Roman letter and two horizontal lines, thus ¥. The word derives from the Chinese *yuan*, which means round thing, or dollar, or coi, and the Chinese character for *yuan* is very occasionally used to denote it:

---

*Japan is unusual in many senses, but the question of placing Inazo Nitobe's portrait on the note raises a subsidiary issue that points up another aspect of the nation's uniqueness. For it is a country singularly lacking in acceptable heroes. Whose portraits, after all, could the country place on its banknotes? Not the present, nor a recent emperor, since to reproduce his picture is the basest lese-majesty. Not a *shogun* of old, nor a *daimyo*, for fear of offending a competing family, nor any of the ancient emperors, for fear of incurring the wrath of Amaterasu, the first of all rulers of Nihon. The Bank officers had to choose men who were "safe" – poets and Nobel laureates like Yukichi Fukuzawa and Soseki Natsume who appear on the two other currency bills. In that context the choice of Nitobe-san was almost certainly not to be regarded as a joke: he was a good, solid and as noncontentious a figure as a country of such ancient sensibilities could come up with.

more usually, though, a character that looks like a small standing cupboard denotes the yen.* This is a *kanji* character – unlike the Japanese phonetic scripts, *hiragana* and *katakana*,† and the *romanji* used for Western consumption – and is a derivative of the Chinese. It should by rights be instantly recognizable in China: but it is not, until it is explained that it is a *simplified* Chinese character for *yuan*, a kind of stripped-down and slightly rearranged version of the original.

The yen, which was originally minted in Osaka,‡ was divided into two smaller generations: the sen, of which there were (and still are) a hundred to the yen; and the rin, of which there are a thousand (and thus ten to the sen). The sen, made of copper or bronze, was often called (as were so many eastern coins of small denomination) cash – a word that shares a common origin with the one English speakers use to denote money in a more general sense.

Early examples of the usage of the currency show its starting value. In 1875, four years after the yen – which had been struck in gold as a standard and in silver for use in foreign trade and in the Treaty Ports – became the official currency, William Jevons in his classic text, *Money and the Mechanism of Exchange*, noted that "even Japan has imitated European nations, and introduced a gold coinage of twenty, ten, five, two and one-yen pieces, the yen being only three per mille

---

*To dispose of another linguistic matter, the noun yen, a craving, has a probable Chinese origin too. But it comes from the Mandarin yin, meaning a craving for opium, and is first quoted in English in 1876, around the time the Japanese currency was being introduced into the Western prints.

†The fact that the Japanese and the Koreans have invented phonetic scripts is taken by some to indicate their intellectual and cultural superiority over the Chinese, who have not. Boswell's *Life of Johnson* records a dialogue that illustrates the view, Johnson having triggered an argument by calling the East Indians barbarians. Boswell: "You will except the Chinese?" Johnson: "No, Sir." Boswell: "Have they not arts?" Johnson: "They have pottery." Boswell: "What do you say to the written character of their language?" Johnson: "Sir, they have not an alphabet. They have not been able to form what other nations have formed." Boswell: "They have more learning in their language than in any other, from the immense number of their characters." Johnson: "It is only more difficult from its rudeness; as there is more labour in hewing down a tree with a stone than with an axe."

‡The Osaka mint was established under one Major William Kinder, the former Master of the Hong Kong Mint, who came from the colony with six assistants. The machinery was all British – indeed, the British had played a significant part in helping to reorganize the post-Restoration currency in Japan: the Hongkong & Shanghai Bank was quick to support the new currency, which munificence prompted the Japanese to decorate the manager of the Yokohama branch.

less in value than the American gold dollar." Twenty years later the *Daily News* remarked that "the sen is nominally equal to a halfpenny, though in fact only worth half that coin." By the turn of the century the yen's value was tumbling: Japan, wrote *The Times* in its issue of 16 January 1904, "has . . . specie to the unprecedented amount of 113 million yen, or £11,300,000". Then again, on the eve of the Second World War, John Gunther records one yen as being worth 27 American cents. From near-parity with the dollar in 1871, to an exchange rate of sixteen to the pound three-quarters of a century later – the currency seemed anything but powerful in its stripling years. Would that the situation today were in any way similar, is the current cry of the Western bankers.

During the first half of the twentieth century the yen was no more than another foreign currency, playing a lowly and largely unnoticed role in the financial undergrowth while sterling, and later the dollar, enjoyed or suffered unchallenged supremacy in the world markets. Not that the Japanese economy was anything but a model of propriety and success: a prescient onlooker could see in the Japan of the early Meiji days some clues as to her likely performance in the longer term. For instance, she was eager to husband her capital, encourage personal savings, export her goods aggressively and remain independent of foreign bankers (rarely, if ever, borrowing money abroad and, like China, running the risk of ending up in thrall to Wall Street or Mincing Lane).

She had been a debtor nation before the Great War (in which she sided with the Allies against Germany, winning all Germany's possessions in the South Pacific and laying the foundations for her later Imperialist adventures), but afterwards emerged as a creditor nation, taking sound commercial advantage of the European countries' propensity for destroying each other on the battlefields. From 1913 until 1919 her foreign trade tripled, and her standing as a creditor nation remained until the outbreak of the Pacific War, her currency generally healthy and strong, though largely ignored by the world financial community.

In the wake of the war, after the defeat and surrender aboard the battleship USS *Missouri* on 2 September 1945, everything changed. The Japanese economy had been ruined, her cities had been flattened, the social and physical structures of the country had been damaged and distorted beyond recognition, the leaders were gone, the administration was a gibbering wreck. There were foreign masters in control in Tokyo now, General MacArthur's men, who in the name of the victorious West were to punish those who had prosecuted this most terrible of wars, to rewrite the nation's constitution, to purge the country of its (in the Western view) archaic and interlinked systems of nobility and divinity, and to try to bring some semblance of order to an economy whose total collapse had left Japan prey to all the forces of anarchy.

As part of the package the yen was devalued massively. It took four years of argument before the MacArthur occupation government fixed a new rate for the currency of 360 to the dollar in April 1949. The yen that went for an American quarter before Pearl Harbor had a value of a little more than a quarter *of a cent* afterwards. In symbolic terms, it was a swingeing reverse for a currency a mere seven decades old which, in its brief lifetime, had performed so very well (barring a sizeable devaluation in the Thirties, calculated to spur the economy during the latter days of the Depression). But a cheap yen was necessary, the Americans decreed, to help promote the exports with which the Japanese could – if they worked as hard in defeat as in the days when they briefly scented victory – drag themselves back into the civilized and perhaps even the prosperous world.* "We wanted the Japanese to be able to export," remarked one of the Americans involved in managing the Japanese economy on behalf of the occupation government. "We wanted them on our side politically. We figured that 90 per cent of Japanese exports could sell at 300 exchange rate, even though some were profitable at 200. But we didn't want to be wrong on such matters."

The rate – established because "we wanted them on our side politically" – had an enormous impact on Japan's economy, which in any case was in tatters. Imports – such as were permitted in those dire days after the fighting was over – became immensely costly. Yet the exports that Japan might start to ship to the outside

---

*The Japanese capacity for dragging themselves up and out from under their problems is a consequence of many factors, ranging from the Confucian ethic, via face, to avarice. Many theses remain to be written on this most absorbing of modern topics. One of their undoubted mentors, however, was the Haddington shopkeeper's son, Samuel Smiles, author of *Self-Help*. The book was published in 1859, four years before Admiral Perry's visit and nine years before the fall of the shoguns and the restoration of the Emperor. Within a decade the book had been translated and had sold a million copies – in a country that had a population then of only thirty million.

world could not be built without money to prime the pumps of the devastated factories. There was, however, American aid. And there were American loans, won with humiliating perseverance by Japanese businessmen who felt they had nothing to lose by going on their knees to their conquerors' banks. These two sources of funds were all that lay between a fearful vision of Third World destitution and the emergence of Japan into the community of modern nations.

It is by looking at this grim period in Japan's modern history that we discover the most dramatic examples of her financial recovery. To take one illustration, in 1947 Japan decided to repair her wrecked textile industry and approached the bankers of Wall Street. Every single one considered the request for $60 million, and each one balked at the impertinent notion: it eventually took a Pacific coast institution, the Bank of America (incidentally, then the world's largest bank) to come up with the money.

Precisely forty years later, when the Bank of America itself was in deep financial trouble – having, among other problems, seriously over-extended itself by lending vast sums to impossibly spendthrift Third World debtor nations – it turned to the one banking system sufficiently rich and generous to arrange a rescue operation: the Japanese. A consortium of thirteen Japanese banks put together a package of $130 million to see the San Francisco bank through its crisis – an Androclean reversal that says much about the astonishing change in Japan's fortunes in the four decades since the ruin and degradation in which she found herself at the War's end.

This reversal of Japan's world role – from defeated bankrupt to (as she is now) the world's greatest creditor nation – has been accomplished with remarkable, almost miraculous speed. As recently as 1957, when the first primitive Nissan cars were being shown to bemused dealers in California, Japan was importing twice as much as she exported, despite the prohibitive cost of virtually everything from outside, for which the Bank of Japan had to pay in foreign currency. The situation had not changed much by 1965: just after the triumph of the Tokyo Olympics, sceptics were making wisecracks about Japan's chronic over-production and her inability to sell the exports she so desperately needed to sell. "The Japanese economy," *Look* wrote in 1965, "is like a confectioner desperately eating his own chocolates on a raft, hoping that a passing ship will stop to purchase his surplus."

But then *Look*'s ship did indeed stop, and it started to buy the chocolates – the cars, television sets, cameras and small and exquisitely designed pieces of electronic wizardry which the Japanese factories began to turn out with such efficiency and zeal – with glorious and prosperous abandon. Suddenly, the nation which had had as its *leitmotif* the phrase "export or die" ever since the War was at last managing to export its goods, and in increasing and eventually gargantuan amounts. The consequences were beyond the bounds of their economists' wildest expectations.

The yen started to become a desirable currency, and its value began to inch up. Washington, increasingly alarmed at the toehold Japanese products were gaining on the American shores, started to urge, cajole and even force the exchange rate upwards, so that the yen became increasingly expensive and Japanese exports grew ever more costly and difficult to sell. But at the same time as the steady and largely involuntary rise in the yen's value began to affect the country's exporters, so it started to prove a blessing in other areas of Japanese life: Japan began to amass reserves in its coffers, and reserves that were starting to be worth a great deal in the international marketplace.

The legendary, almost Calvinistic propensity of the Japanese for saving money, for buying with cash, for scorning the *gaijin* barbarisms of credit, for endurance, fortitude, stoicism and asceticism – all these started to pay off. And so long as the export boom continued the effects began to tell. Japan finally started to enjoy real prosperity, yet at the same time came to an unspoken collective agreement that it would not succumb to the temptation of throwing all its hard-won gains away in the feckless and reckless manner so familiar in the West. A student travelling abroad in 1964, for instance, was permitted to take only $30 with him; and a scientist recalls arriving in the United States in 1957 with several cameras – not for photographing the Grand Canyon and Niagara Falls, but specifically so that he could sell them in order to live. Japan's wealth in 1970 stood at a mere $5 billion: every effort was made, collectively and with Confucian-inspired enthusiasm, to conserve this money and help it grow.

External forces had conspired to change the value of the currency on many occasions. President Nixon forced a revaluation in 1971. The Six-Day War of 1973 (and the consequent Arab oil embargo) and the 1979 revolution in Iran are still recalled with horror in Tokyo: these were the events that placed Japan's essential flow of oil between the Gulf and Tokyo Bay at risk, forcing the yen downwards on both occasions. Yet during both the "oil shocks" –

the *shokkus* – of the Seventies the Tokyo car-makers enjoyed sudden and unexpected good fortune: they were in any case making cars that consumed far less petrol than most American-made vehicles, and thanks to the battering their currency was taking these cars were being priced lower and lower, making them all the more tempting for the American consumer. Back at home the companies sought ways and means of making their production ever more efficient; their financing became increasingly creative so that each minute fraction of every possible advantage was recognized, targeted and won. The export figures began to inch their way upwards.

The Japanese industrial and export machine of the 1970s – advised, co-ordinated and given "administrative guidance" by the twin jugger-nauts of the nation's miracle-building, the Ministry of International Trade and Industry and the Ministry of Finance – was now fighting across the new world economic battlegrounds with the same skill, determination and intelligence being displayed by the Vietcong's General Giap in the war that was coming to its inevitable conclusion 2,000 miles to the south-west of Tokyo. Giap's inventive, barely believable military stratagems, which outwitted and outfoxed his cumbersome enemies – France at Dien Bien Phu, and the United States through the length and breadth of his country later – were being echoed in economic terms by this newcomer nation, so recently vanquished, so utterly humiliated and, one might have thought, so rigorously disbarred from participation in the new economic order. But now, as the economist George Soros wrote in the *New York Review of Books* in 1987, Japan was fast becoming the leading economic power in the world, via a process unlike anything ever witnessed before. "There has been," Soros wrote, "no transfer of economic power as rapid as the one now taking place."

During the oil crisis years, Japanese trading firms coming to America had to arrange "standby credit" before they could obtain loans from American banks; these same banks charged a so-called "Japanese pre-mium" to Tokyo businesses trying to raise capital on the New York and London markets, which in the mid-1970s utterly dominated the world and could do more or less as they pleased. But now the shoe is on the other foot. American banks – like the Bank of America, as noted above – routinely approach the big Japanese institutions for help: Japan's current foreign assets stand at more than $130 billion; by 1990 they will be at $400 billion; by 1995, $558 billion. The country is the dominant financial power, and before long will be the biggest creditor nation in the history of the world. The Rising Sun has risen indeed, and with extraordinary dispatch.

The patterns have changed as profoundly as the figures. In the 1960s a third of Japan's exports were of textiles. By 1980 this was only 5 per cent. Such change was a consequence of the external influence which did so much to concentrate the Japanese planners' minds – the oil shocks of the 1970s. For although it is true that the most immediate and visible impact of these shocks was to trigger foreign demand for Japanese cars, they also reacted to teach the men of MITI and the Ministry of Finance the need to increase production in the newer, more technologically intensive industries, and thus to minimize the risk of being held hostage to fortune by the oil producers.

Therefore, spurred on by exhortations from these ministries to pull together, to perform the national duty and make the patriotic gesture of redefining their goals, Japanese companies went on a hi-tech binge: by the late 1970s they were filing three times as many patent applications as their counterparts in West Germany, and half as many again as the United States. By 1986 the country was far and away the greatest producer of semiconductors, making four times as many as all the European countries put together. To those watching on the outside the revolution in the Japanese economy which had taken place as a direct consequence of the oil embargo was a thing of awesome power and speed.

It was also remarkable to note that such an apparent bastion of the free market was so ready to take direct advice – verging on instruction – from its government. What was happening in Japan was an example of the kind of amalgam of economic and political principles which, while unfamiliar to the West, appeared to work for the common good and in a most impressive way. A centrally-planned free-market economy? – a contradiction in terms, one might think; except that in the world of the Confucian mind-set it appears no contradiction at all.

There are indications – too complex and evanescent to explore here – that the years during which Japanese exports dominated the world are slowly coming to an end. The price of the yen shot up between the winter of 1985 and the spring of 1986, due principally to the manipulation by the Saudi Arabian government of their oil production, and the resulting dramatic fall in the price of oil around the world. The Japanese economy, still mightily dependent upon oil,* was viewed as garnering huge benefits from such a fall in its price. The yen was in any case beginning to edge up on the foreign exchange markets, because the Western industrial nations had reached a formal decision among themselves to weaken their own currencies in an attempt to limit Japanese exports to each one of them, by making such export prices higher. So at the time of the Saudi decision the yen had strengthened from about 230 to the dollar to around 200. With the sudden free-fall of oil prices the yen strengthened enormously: within weeks the dollar was trading at 160 yen.

I recall suffering a direct consequence of the sudden rise: I had arranged to meet a friend of mine in Tokyo early one morning out in the city suburbs, and foolishly – because I was late, and not sure I could work out the journey on the underground railway system – hailed a taxi. The fare was 48,000 yen. As I handed over nine crisp notes adorned with the face of Nitobe-san, and a small fistful of change besides, I knew that I was going to be faced with a problem. Only when I returned to the hotel did I calculate the cost of the ride: there and back had cost me $635, and the two whiskies I bought at the clubhouse set me back a further $45.

All of a sudden Japan became, for outsiders, a frighteningly expensive place. But if it was expensive for foreigners going into Japan, Japanese products sent out of the country were also becoming costly in the extreme. No longer was a Honda Civic a cheap small car; no longer was a Nikon F-301 an inexpensive camera, nor a Sony Walkman an item from the bargain basement. Japanese products were universally of excellent quality, no doubt; but those made in Japan were of a fearsome cost. The Japanese manufacturers began to build their factories abroad: everywhere from Cebu in the Philippines to Smyrna in Tennessee. And the Japanese government, watching the yen becoming increasingly expensive a currency, started to come to terms with the probable reality that the supremacy of Japanese products abroad was now likely to tail off.

However, there was no particular concern over this likelihood. For during the golden years – perhaps no more than fifteen of them from

---

*How very differently things might have turned out had Pacific geology not placed Japan on a chain of islands made of volcanic rocks, but instead settled the Japanese close to a selection of sedimentary anticlines that might have yielded them oil of their very own.

the mid-1970s until the 1990s – of their export-led triumph, the Japanese had amassed one other commodity that they would now be able to export in vast amounts, in place of (or perhaps for a while in addition to) their cars, their stereo sets and their steel pipe (as used to construct the Alaska pipeline, the American steel mills no longer being competent to make it*). And this commodity was of far greater significance to the long-term well-being of the world than either the consumer products or the heavy industrial goods that had brought Japan to this happy state. The new commodity, of which Japan had apparently cornered the market by the late 1980s, was quite simply: money.

They had gathered it unto themselves in such vast quantities by dint of one remarkable aspect of their personal, Confucian-inspired self-discipline. The Japanese, like citizens of no other consumer society in the world, have been officially enjoined to save their earnings, and they stash it away in vast amounts in banks.

Japanese savings habits, and their recent effects, need to be put into context. What I have said above, about the extraordinary rebirth of the Japanese economy in the forty years since the end of the Pacific War, might suggest that the phenomenon of their success is something new. Far from it. Japan took a conscious decision to become a major industrial power soon after the Meiji restoration: by the 1930s she was near the top of the league, and had been a net creditor nation from the time of the Great War until the attack on Pearl Harbor spelled her undoing – if only in the short term. The organization of her industrial might was based on the silky ruthlessness and unassailability of the giant cartels, the egregious *zaibatsu* of Mitsui, Mitsubishi, Sumitomo, Yasuda and Okura, who in the 1930s controlled more than 60 per cent of the total wealth of the nation. "Mitsui," wrote a wide-eyed John Gunther in 1938, "is a colossus beside which organizations like Du Pont, Standard Oil, Imperial Chemicals seem like children."

After Nagasaki and the USS *Missouri*, and under the not-always-benign invigilation of General MacArthur and his staff, the *zaibatsu* were supposedly purged, their aristocratic leaders blamed personally for the part they played in the war machine. New conglomerate

---

*It was outside Pittsburgh that, as a direct consequence of competition from Japanese steel-makers, a small town became so economically depressed in 1989 as to be the only place in the world where a McDonald's closed for lack of business.

empires arose, establishments with shareholders in which the direct influence of the old noble families was markedly diminished. The new organizations were known as *keiretsus*, and it was clear almost from their inception that, however idealistic the Americans had been in advocating the fission of the cartels, this was not going to happen.

Freed from any obligation to direct their production to any military forces (which post-war occupied Japan was forbidden from having) the *keiretsus* could engage wholly in producing commercial goods for export; and when they became rich, as they inevitably did, it was discovered that only a very few of the old *zaibatsu* leaders had been purged, that the old families were leading many of the new conglomerates and had almost as great an influence on the post-war economy of Japan as in the years before. One may not often hear the phrase "the house of Mitsui" these days, but there is little disputing that the power of those various organs controlled by Mitsui – Mitsui Bank, Mitsui OSK Shipping Lines, Mitsui Electronics – is immense.* The same is true for almost all the others.

What this meant for the reconstruction of Japan's economy under MacArthur was that the men who actually directed the national recovery *knew what they were doing.* They were experienced figures, privileged, trained for leadership, men familiar with the business practices and personal habits of a nation that, in reality, had spent the better part of the century – interrupted only by a brief but savage war – as a powerful and prosperous industrial nation. They realized in double-quick time that they had a number of choices to make, and three identifiable possibilities sprang to their minds. They could invite foreign – meaning American – investment to help reconstruct themselves. They could borrow huge sums of money from overseas. Or they could nationalize the shattered remains of their industries and, at least for the first decade or so, pursue a rigorously centrally planned and controlled economy.

However, the greybeards of 1946 decided that none of these plans offered what was really needed. Having concluded that a rigid centrally planned economy was politically unacceptable, they chose

---

*When one of Van Gogh's famous *Sunflowers* series was sold by Christies for $40 million, the Japanese buyers were Yasuda Fire & Marine Insurance. Yasuda, led by the baron of the same name, started as a money-lending business and became Japan's biggest banker in the Thirties, bigger even than Mitsui.

neither to invite foreign capital nor to borrow it. To raise capital, they decreed, a domestically-generated surplus had to be created; that surplus would come through personal savings. Battered by war and now trapped in penury, the Japanese people would be asked to suffer more and accept less, by withholding part of anything they earned in the coming years and putting it into the bank. If they did that, they were assured, then generations of Japanese yet unborn would come eventually to enjoy the fruits of their labours.

Thus the first task of the post-war reconstruction was the creation of the machine that was to generate all this capital – a national savings machine of greater scope and efficiency than anywhere else on earth. Seen with the advantage of today's hindsight, the invention of this machine was the key to Japan's modern success – an engineering triumph like no other.

The consequent invention was part mechanical, part conceptual. The mechanical side involved the creation of what became the world's largest financial institution – the so-called *maruyu*, or Japanese postal savings bank, which took money in at the 22,000 post offices, paid savers a negligible amount of annual interest (on which, however, no tax was charged), and enjoyed total assets of about $1,000,000,000,000. The conceptual side involved the furnishing of a policy that would encourage and indeed demand savings from the people. It exhorted them to make gestures for reasons of patriotism, to undergo a further period of austerity and to endure the national sacrifice.

The bonus system was introduced and expanded, giving workers large payouts at the end of each year – a "thirteenth-month" payment, it was often called – which (the employers invariably suggested) would be better placed in a *maruyu* account than spent. Tax benefits were introduced: up to certain levels no tax at all was levied on saved earnings, and the wily Japanese managed to get around the ceiling regulations, as the authorities knew they would, by opening many accounts in many family names. So until January 1988 when, because of the abuses, measures to tax *maruyu* savings were in fact introduced, the Japanese family was able to salt away almost limitless amounts of money with reasonable freedom from pain, to earn a small increment on the growing sum each year, and avoid paying the government anything for the privilege. Compared with the exactions imposed by the revenue bosses in Western nations, the policy seems generous to a fault.

By offering only paltry interest rates, the savings institutions were able* to lend money out – to corporations wishing to expand, or government agencies wanting to enhance the nation's infrastructure – at low rates too. There is an inherent private Japanese attitude – Confucian, it has to be said – towards financial prudence and conservatism. It is an attitude that favours savings, in a precise mirror-image of the way that the modern American attitude favours and fosters consumption, expenditure and instant gratification and, as a necessary corollary, a constant desire for credit. The difference is crucial: the one is the formula, as Japan has demonstrated, for unrivalled commercial success; the other is calculated, even for a country with such massive natural resources as the United States possesses, for debt and slow and inevitable decline. Some optimists believe that a country so rich in people and resources as the United States can never suffer a terminal demise; but in order to begin the return to its deserved standing, it must reverse its present profligacy and adopt the habits of its more successful – and these days success generally denotes Pacific, and specifically Japanese – peers.

I remember travelling on a TWA jet one night, sitting beside a voluble but interestingly philosophical Asian. The attendant offered drinks: I ordered Coca-Cola, my new friend water. He turned to me with a strange gleam in his eye. "Why you drinking sugared water?" he suddenly asked. "It rots your teeth. It makes you fat. It is no more thirst-quenching than this water – you are sensible enough to know that as a fact. So why do you drink it?" I mumbled a reply, slightly stung by his attack. It tastes good, I ventured; I drink it because I like it, because it makes me feel good. His finger shot out and waggled infuriatingly before my face. "Aha!" he said, triumphant. "Instant gratification! The pursuit of happiness through the pursuit of pleasure! It is

---

*And still are: in 1988 the average yield on a household savings account in Tokyo was a mere 1.76 per cent. But depositors were still attracted: in the same year 16.5 per cent of income was still being saved in Japan, compared with 4 per cent in the US. As a result of the first figure, the bank prime interest rate to borrowers was far lower in Japan than in the US: a first-class borrower in Chicago might expect to pay 8.75 per cent in 1987, while his opposite number in Sapporo would shell out only 3.38 per cent, less than half as much.

simply not a sensible way to run your life. Think about it. Pursue happiness through achievement. Pleasure is a mere temporary phenomenon. I am happy. I am thin. I have good teeth." (He grimaced at this point, showing me a mouthful of titanium-oxide tombstones.) "And I am now quite rich and my children will be richer. All because of seeking to achieve, not seeking to consume! Change your ways! Think Asian!" I went to sleep exhausted soon after this exchange; but I have come to recall it many times, particularly now.

The savings ethic spreads through all classes, all generations. I have two friends, sisters living in a tiny flat in Fukuoka, a town at the western end of the *Shinkansen* bullet-train line from Tokyo. Both women have two jobs. Yoko works during the day as a receptionist at a local hotel, and in the evenings in a small and expensive whisky bar, the Lexington, a few blocks from the office. Yorie spends her daylight hours working as a secretary and receptionist for a computer software company (with which Fukuoka, the centre of Japan's rather uninspiring version of Silicon Valley, abounds); three nights a week she changes into a short black skirt, a sheer white satin blouse and black fishnet stockings, and works as a hostess in a men's club – but "quite respectable, I just talk and give them whisky, no touchy-feely, no Pink Salon-type of behaviour" she insists.

Each month Yoko makes ¥110,000 as a receptionist, ¥45,000 in the bar; her sister takes in ¥105,000 as a secretary, ¥60,000 as a hostess. Their rent for the rabbit-hutch of a flat in which they live – a total of 350 square feet for the two of them – is ¥40,000; their other expenses, transport, clothes and food come to around ¥200,000. And the rest they save: between them, they save ¥80,000 a month – a quarter of their combined earnings. Yoko is 25 years old: she now has ¥2,800,000 in her *maruyu* account – at the current average exchange rate, that amounts to a little more than $20,000. Her sister has a similar sum – money that the pair will use, perhaps, to help buy a house "when we are a little older, and if we don't get married".*

The two girls present a type example; their house-buying plans indicate the general aspirations of the current Japanese middle class,

*Both girls, being over 25 years old and single, are known in the cruel vernacular of the Japanese marriage market as *kirisimasu keeki* – Christmas cake; of no use after the 25th.

aspirations which have an enormous effect on the more general health of the national economy. Very few Japanese, for instance, buy houses when they are young. They are content – bowing to the eternally expressed demands, the "mass self-hypnosis", as critics of Japan have called it, for patriotism, austerity and labour for the national good – to rent tiny flats, to have a standard of living which modern young Americans would find intolerable. But when (in their forties) they do manage to buy a house, they do so with cash. Assuming they remain single, Yoko and Yorie may have amassed a quarter of a million dollars in twenty years' time. They can buy a small house for half this sum, with cash, and they can invest the rest – perhaps in shares rather than in the bank – and earn a higher interest rate than they have been accustomed to at the post office. They can earn decent money from their investment, improve their house, sell it and move to a larger property, becoming increasingly prosperous, yet without once having owed anybody anything. In other words, they can reap the rewards of twenty years of frugality and self-sacrifice.

Neither woman has a credit card. Neither carries a cheque book. If they want something, they pay cash. They have a number of prepaid magnetic cards – for the telephone, a fast-food restaurant, the subway train, the local cinema. But they write cheques only for the rent and the power bills. The rest involves settlement with crisp notes adorned with the pictures of Nitobe-san or his two colleagues, and perhaps a few coins as well.

The overall picture is more enlightening still. Japan and America are both nations producing immense wealth. America, however, over-consumes that wealth – on average, in the late 1980s, it has been consuming fully 3 per cent more than it makes. But in Japan quite the reverse is true: the Japanese under-consume, and by no less than 20 per cent. Immense sums of money are thus left over, to accumulate interest and thus generate more wealth, or to help lift the country to more dizzying heights of sophistication and efficiency, ownership and power. The concomitant happiness and self-confidence generated for the Japanese is evident on all sides; as is the reverse, stated so aptly by Mr Micawber more than a century ago, and from which the United States is suffering today.

The statistical reality of the newly found Japanese financial power is truly staggering. Daniel Burstein, an American writer who has chronicled the growing power of the yen in recent years, notes in stark detail the way in which the tables have been turned:

●All ten of the world's top ten banks – in terms of their deposits – are Japanese. The biggest of all, Dai-Ichi Kangyo, has assets of ¥41.2 trillion – $290,000,000,000.

●The big four Japanese stockbroking and securities trading houses – Nomura, Daiwa, Nikko and Yamaichi – are four of the largest in the world; judged by the market value of its stocks, the biggest, Nomura Securities, is twenty times larger than America's best-known brokerage house, Merrill Lynch. Nomura has 131 branches in Japan, offices in 21 countries. With assets of a quarter of a trillion dollars, its profits before tax – $4.1 billion in 1987 – matched the profits before tax of *the entire American stockbroking industry*. After tax its profits in 1987 were $2 billion. Yoshihisa Tabuchi, the current Nomura president, is quoted as saying (while sitting beneath an original Chagall in his office), that:

> We want all customers. We aspire to serve all nationalities, all borrowers, all issuers, all investors. We wish to be like Japanese manufacturing companies which sell the same products to people in every part of the world. The growth of our company is a function of the Japanese capital market being opened and liberalized. History shows money *must* circulate out of a capital-surplus nation into the world economy. The London merchant bankers played this role when capital accumulated in London. For most of the twentieth century the United States played this role. Now the time comes when the Japanese must fulfil their responsibilities. It is in this area that Nomura finds its reason for being.

Had Tabuchi lived in an earlier era, one Nomura colleague remarked of him, "he would have been a shogun."

●In terms of the value of its stocks the single Japanese company, Nippon Telegraph & Telephone, is worth more than the *combined* total value of A T & T, IBM, General Motors, General Electric and Exxon.*

●The Osaka Stock Exchange is the fourth largest in the world, and is bigger on market value than the American Stock Exchange. Although 100 per cent of a class of Japanese schoolchildren could

*NTT does not win a single mention in the 1987 edition of the *Encyclopaedia Britannica*. A T & T has three.

289

locate the United States on a globe, and nearly as many could locate New York on a map, only half that number of Americans could accurately place Japan. One can assume that few – schoolchildren or stockbrokers – would place Osaka correctly, even if they were familiar with its name.

●Japanese banks control 10 per cent of the American retail banking system. The assets of Japanese banks operating within the United States are greater than the combined assets of Citicorp and J.P. Morgan.

●Several areas of domestic American finance – the business of issuing letters of credit that guarantees the underwriting of municipal bonds – are now actually *monopolized* by Japanese finance houses.

●The Japanese acquisition of Columbia Pictures, which Sony bought from the Coca-Cola Company, and the sales of such symbolically American institutions as the Rockefeller Center and the Seven-Eleven chain are the latest in a parade of effrontery. In mid-1989 the Japanese owned (among others) CBS Records, Firestone Tires, most of the Citicorp "ski-slope" skyscraper in Manhattan, as well as the Mobil, Exxon and ABC buildings; the *US News & World Report* building in Washington; the Dunes Hotel in Las Vegas; a real estate portfolio in Hawaii worth $6.5 billion, which includes three-quarters of the equity in twenty hotels on the Waikiki waterfront;* 18 per cent of the Paine Webber securities group, 16.7 per cent of NeXt Inc, the computer firm spawned by the Apple Macintosh creator, Steve Jobs, the Mark Hopkins Hotel in San Francisco (plus all the Inter-Continental Hotel Group of which it is a flagship), and 13 per cent of Tiffany & Co, the jewellers.

●Until very recently, the world's richest man was an American named Sam Walton of Walmart Stores. Now it is Mr Yoshiaki

---

*Hawaii is so popular a destination for Japanese holidaymakers – particularly for young couples on their honeymoon – and so attractive for Japanese investors, that it has the appearance of being an almost wholly Japanese state. "Although the US flag still flies there," said one American news magazine, "Hawaii looks well on the way to becoming an economic colony of Japan." And as with Hawaii, so with California. One leading Japanese financier suggested, apparently not facetiously, that once the yen had risen to a value of 100 to the dollar, a common US-Yen world currency could be created, from which would stem the idea of the State of California becoming jointly owned by the two countries, in which Japan could expand and build without let or hindrance.

Tsutsumi, the head of the Seibu Railway (many Japanese railway lines still being privately-owned).

●There were – despite the caution and prudence of most Japanese – a number of unashamedly decadent crazes in the Tokyo streets during 1988. One involved drinking tea into which tiny specks of pure gold leaf had been stirred, another the eating of sushi similarly decorated with filigrees of .999 gold; yet another for breathing in, at 200 yen a time, sixty-seconds' worth of mint-flavoured-but-otherwise-pure oxygen; and another for dropping ice from Antarctic bergs into the finest and oldest of available single malt whisky (a sacrilege that would confirm most Scotsmen in their prejudice against the Japanese). And ever since the late 1980s the Louis Vuitton luggage shop in Hong Kong has attracted a queue outside almost every day – all the shoppers being young Japanese women, often Tokyo secretaries, for whom a Vuitton handbag was a mere incidental, easily affordable in a local currency that (since it was pegged to the US dollar) was ludicrously inexpensive.

A friend named Itsuko, a part-time translator in Tokyo, would fly down to Hong Kong for a weekend twice a year, together with two colleagues who worked behind the counter in a Japanese airline office: the trio would visit Louis Vuitton, Gucci, Cartier and Dunhill, return with their purchases to the Mandarin Hotel and take tea each afternoon, and speculate on what other bargains they could snap up before the plane left to take them home. "So cheap! So cheap!" they would cry. "Any country that bases its money on the American dollar is, just for now, so cheap for us. It is just wonderful, don't you think?"

The goods would be a great deal cheaper than when Itsuko started on her regular pilgrimages to the colony, back in 1984. The present standing of the yen as the world's most impressive currency owes everything to decisions taken in that same year in Washington and Tokyo by representatives of President Reagan, which resulted in the establishment of a landmark pact known as the Yen/Dollar Agreement, widely regarded as – for America – the most disastrous legacy of the Reagan presidency.

The agreement had its origins in the assumption that Japanese export success – very considerable at the time Reagan came to power

– was largely based on the cheapness of the yen. It needed, the president and his council of economic advisers decreed, to be raised in value against the dollar. Donald Regan, the American Treasury Secretary, arrived in Tokyo in March 1984, determined to "play hardball" with the Japanese (who, not unnaturally, wanted to keep the yen low and their exports cheap and thus competitive). "We think the yen is probably weaker in relation to the dollar because of the fact that it's not an international currency," he told the Japanese, in terms unexpectedly blunt and embellished with all manner of threats of punitive responses if they did not do as they were told. "If there were more demand for the yen, the yen would be stronger . . ." The Tokyo markets, he blustered, just had to be opened up to American investors and traders and speculators. Regan was the Commodore Perry of the 1980s: he would open up Japan for his financial friends and allies as Perry had done for those of President Fillmore a century and a half before. In the view of most sensitive watchers of the Japanese scene, the hubris of the man was barely credible.

And the Japanese backed down – or seemed to. The Yen/Dollar Agreement was signed. The barriers to American financial institutions operating inside Japan were to be dismantled, or at least lowered; the yen itself was to be made into a truly international currency to be traded just like the dollar. It was not only a manifest triumph for American good sense but also a reminder of her power. The consequences, Regan assured his president, would be a dramatic diminution of the trade surplus that Japan enjoyed over America; Washington and New York would resume their contented roles as supervisors of the destiny of the free world, while Japan would recede into the outer darkness reserved for the lesser races.

In fact – despite a meeting of the major industrial countries a year later at the Plaza Hotel in New York, at which all agreed to mount a concerted campaign to inflate the value of the yen – precisely the reverse of what Regan had promised occurred. The yen did indeed increase in value, and the dollar did indeed decline. The dollar fell from 260 to 180 yen to the extraordinary (in psychological terms) figure of 123 yen. The phrase *endaka* – "high yen" – entered the Japanese financial and popular lexicon. Yet the trade deficit did nothing but worsen. In 1984 the average monthly deficit with Japan was $3 billion. In 1987, after the Yen/Dollar Agreement and the Plaza Hotel arm-twisting pact, the deficit was running at $6 billion – and America's total deficit, with all its trading partners, was an all-time record of $17.6 billion. The accumulated Japanese surplus between 1981 and 1987 rose to $300 billion.

The power of the now truly internationalized yen started to become enormous, incredible and soon unassailable. The overall effect of Mr Reagan's attack on his own dollar was to take every one of the yen that the Japanese had collected in their four post-war decades of saving and trading, and double their value at a stroke. "Reagonomics", so laced with the kind of machismo only Hollywood could contrive, was being shown to have been dangerously wrong, the product of provincialism, arrogance and sheer economic stupidity, all of it emanating from the White House of the day.

For how did the Japanese react in the wake of the two agreements, which in theory spelled such economic disaster for their country and for their industries? In characteristic Japanese fashion, they prepared for more self-sacrifice and hunkered down for yet another long session of belt-tightening. They started to lecture their managers and their workers about the paramount interests of the nation, of moral duty, of the revered precepts and hallowed *Analects* of the Confucius who had guided them so wisely down the centuries . . . .

Deciding on a collective policy towards the prices of their exports, they developed an *endaka* philosophy. If the yen rose in value by 10 per cent, they would grin and bear it and not raise their prices at all. If it rose by another 10 per cent, they would raise their prices to the American consumer by 3 per cent. Another 10 per cent rise, another 2 per cent price increase, and so on. And to offset the results of such a policy, which could indeed be calamitous, they would seek to make money, or minimize the losses elsewhere – either by cutting their own costs and expenses or, more importantly, by indulging in the electronic high-technology, high-speed, computer-aided financial wheeling and dealing which has come to be known by its invented name, so often followed by an exclamation mark: *zaitek!*

The Nissan Motor Company, which provides such a symbol of today's trans-Pacific connections, will once again serve here to illustrate the overall Japanese reaction to Mr Reagan's battle plan of 1985. Stung by the free-falling dollar, the company actually made a small operating loss in 1986, before a new programme of cost-cutting efficiencies began to take effect. But thanks to creative *zaitek!* investing in the same year, Nissan actually made an overall profit – 75 per cent of it due directly to returns on its investments rather than on the sales of cars. With such a profit up its sleeves the company could well afford, provided it was not greedy (and it had been urged to do so as part of the patriotic self-hypnosis mentioned earlier) to keep its prices down, however well the yen was forced to perform. Which is just what the company did: a Nissan car that sold in the United States in 1984 for $9,000 and which, given the drop in the dollar value from 260 to 130 in 1987 should by rights have cost the buyer $18,000 in that year, was actually pegged for sale at $11,000.

At the same time as the Japanese car-makers kept their prices artificially low – though the use of the word artificial in this case means that they accomplished the feat by cutting costs and profit margins and made money elsewhere and by other means – the American domestic manufacturers (assuming the Japanese would actually be forced to raise prices substantially) increased their own prices to make greater profits. In other words, they tried to cash in on the expected effects of the Yen/Dollar and Plaza agreements; the Japanese battened down the hatches and devised clever means of minimizing their losses; and the American consumer, making the final judgement that Japanese products were in any case better designed, better made and better value for money than their American counterparts, went on buying Japanese goods anyway. The consequence was economically painful and, for the Washington policymakers, professionally humiliating: Japan continued making money hand over fist, the American trade deficit became steadily larger and larger, and the value of Japan's assets increased to levels unimaginable by even the most doom-laden seers of a few years before.

This brings us to the extraordinary situation of today – a situation that must, however, be viewed in the context of the opening caveat. There are few constants in this story, and the situation I have attempted to describe may be very different now at the end of this brief tour from that which obtained at the beginning. Volatility, in the confused and confusing world of modern financial markets, is all.

But at the end of the Eighties and the beginning of the final decade of this century, the singular most important underlying feature of this saga – a trinity of features, though essentially united as one – is this: Japan is now the world's largest creditor nation, the United States the world's largest debtor nation and, most crucially of all, Japan now finances fully one third of the total American national debt. She performs this unenviable task by virtue of having become, in recent years, by far the biggest purchaser of American Treasury bonds. At each auction, as the United States re-finances the staggering burden of the world's greatest debt, the Japanese securities firms are there buying, buying, buying. They bought 80 per cent of one issue in 1986; they routinely buy a third to a half of all new long-term bonds the US government issues.

The corollary to such massive purchasing, such creative use of the vast sums of surplus money sloshing about in Japan's huge banking system, is this: the global hegemony which the United States still enjoys – particularly in the wake of the evident collapse of totalitarian socialist regimes in the Eastern bloc, which places an ever greater premium on the alluring model of the "American way", to be copied by these newly emerging free markets and societies – is now being financed in large measure by the Japanese. It has an irony far distanced from the simple fact of the ironies of the Pacific War in that its victor is being eventually conquered by the vanquished. The more interesting irony has much to do with the profound changes fast taking place in today's world – and in particular the undeniable fact that the bastion of the Judaeo-Christian ethic in the West is now being propped up by the bastion in the East of the Buddhist-Confucian ethic, an ethic which, as we have already seen, is regarded by many as poised to dominate the globe in the coming years.

What, in the longer term, will result from this dependence and, more ominously, from the possibility that it will founder on some as yet unseen hazard, is anybody's guess. Many are the doomsayers. "The possibilities of a stable international order may vanish," mutters one. There could be "direct confrontation" once again.* "Wake up, America!" says one business magazine. "We have spent too much, borrowed too much, and imported too much. We have lived beyond our means, relying on foreigners to finance our massive budget and trade deficits. The bill is now coming due."

And a bill to be paid in a currency which, little more than a century old, is rapidly and unstoppably evolving into the Pacific currency of today, and in all probability the global currency of tomorrow.

---

*In such a spirit a Congressman from Texas, one Jack Brooks, has gone on record recently as opining that the praise President Truman merits for having dropped two atom bombs on Japan should be muted for the simple reason that "he should have dropped four".

ICONS

Victorian engineering, Edwardian physics and the infinite complexities of today's technology have all played a significant role in knitting together the distant shores of the Pacific Ocean. Trade, navigation and cultural connections produce their own special forms of intimacy between alien peoples. But, whether stated in the milled brass of a century ago or the germanium wafers of today, the achievements of science provide the mechanics for those connections to take place at all – connections which present no small challenge when they are to be conducted across a sea which (at its widest) is half the circumference of the planet. The devices that enabled the peoples of today's Pacific to talk and even to see one another across thousands of miles of Ocean; to travel fast and directly between one another's countries, cities and islands; and (no matter what their linguistic background or ability) to explore and utilize the awesome power of computing science, seem worthy of iconic status: three highly visible symbols of technology's triumph over the majesty of what was once recognized only as an unbridgeable distance.

I

The Messengers

Fanning Island, which is actually four islands so far away as to be thought of as one, is said to constitute the most beautiful and unspoiled tropical atoll in the world. It lies nearly 4°N of the equator and 159°W of Greenwich, and is thus almost exactly in the middle of the South Pacific. Nowadays it is called Tabuaeran. Its neighbours are known as Teraina and Kiritimati: before they gained their independence from Britain and were part of the Gilbert and Ellice Islands Colony, they were known as Washington and Christmas* Islands.

Discovered by an American naval captain of the same name aboard the brig *Betsy* in 1798, Fanning enjoyed nearly a century of relative tranquillity: but on 5 January 1897 its elysian peace was suddenly disturbed. A body with the magnificent title of the Imperial Pacific Cable Committee decided (after a lengthy conference in London, where men of great distinction pored for hours over maps and charts of the seas between British Columbia and New South Wales) that it would invite tenders for the construction of a communications cable clear across the Pacific Ocean to link by telegraph these two hitherto unconnected outposts of the Empire. The proposed monster cable, part of the vanguard of a telegraphic revolution that since 1851 (when the English Channel Submarine Telegraph Company offered its first

---

*The vague but apparent similarity between the islanders' word "Kiritimati" and our word "Christmas" (the atoll was found by Captain Cook on Christmas Eve 1777) displays a charming attempt to render a colonial name into a language utterly devoid of the sound and letter "s". The newly independent nation of which Kiritimati is a part is, of course, Kiribati, which is pronounced *Kiribass*, and is the best the locals can do to match the name given to the island group by the colonial masters, The Gilberts.

gutta-percha-covered wire for service between Dover and Calais) had been linking the nations and the continents to each other, would do so, the IPCC decided, in a series of mighty leaps: it would make its first trans-maritime excursion from Queensland to New Zealand overland; would pass from Doubtless Bay on the tip of the North Island of New Zealand to Norfolk Island, 500 miles to the north-west; would plough on from Norfolk Island to Suva in Fiji – another 1,980 miles; would snake from Suva a further 2,040 miles up to Fanning Island, just north of the equator; and from Fanning Island would jump the 3,485 miles to Bamfield, just outside Vancouver. Fanning Island, therefore, was to be hoisted from tropic obscurity to become a pivot point for the longest link in a vital chain of global communication over which, as Alfred Lord Tennyson had put it:

> Britain's myriad voices call
> Sons, be welded each and all
> Into one Imperial whole –
> One with Britain, heart and soul!

Once the decision had been made to buy the idea and build the project, the unlovely and decidedly non-Pacific city of Newcastle upon Tyne slips briefly into the story. Back in 1902, when the various colonial governments had given their assent to the building of the Pacific Cable, it was realized that there was no cable ship then built capable of carrying the kinds of loads needed to span such immense distances. After all, to lay a cable across the Atlantic's narrowest point – Shannon to Newfoundland, say – required only 2,000 miles of the elephantine coils of copper and gutta-percha. But to bridge the distances involved in the Pacific Ocean required two or three times that amount; a technological leap in the dark that required a bold new set of thinking and some powerful new equipment.

Newcastle came to the rescue: a vessel named the *Colonia* was built at the yard of Wiggin Richardson (now, like most of the old Tyne shipbuilders, closed down), and steamed to London to load 8,000 tons of cable into her mighty hold. She then crossed the Atlantic and doubled the Horn, and arrived off the Canadian west coast. On 18 September 1902 she set out from the cable terminal at Bamfield, near Vancouver, paying out the first miles of the Imperial Pacific cable from the cast-iron slipways on her bow. The Geordies had designed her well: she steamed south-westwards at a steady 8 knots, eventually arriving in perfect calm, blue seas, in light trade winds, off

English Harbour on the west coast of Fanning Island on 6 October, having laid the world's then longest stretch of telegraphic wire in just eighteen problem-free days. Fourteen more days were to elapse before the cable-ship *Anglia* completed the final link between Suva and Fanning; on 31 October Sir Sandford Fleming, former Chief Engineer of the Canadian National Railway, universal time-keeping pioneer (like Professor Dowd, the champion of the International Date Line) and father to a Pacific Cable which had been three decades in the making, telegraphed a message. He sent it on the shortest possible journey – from his office in Ottawa to that of the Governor-General of Canada in his office across the street. But he sent it via the new cable, so when the message was received back in Canada it bore a notation to the effect that it had already been to New Zealand and back. The time clocks showed that it had travelled the 15,672 miles in less than two minutes.

Cable transmissions along the line then began in earnest. In the early days they proved less than wholly accurate. One celebrated message was sent from Australia to London to report on the deeply dull fact that an Antipodean dignitary had inaugurated the building of a new railway line. It read: "GOVERNOR-GENERAL TURNS FIRST SOD". By the time it arrived in London it had been transmogrified to: "GOVERNOR-GENERAL TWINS FIRST SON", a message duly picked up by an eager newspaper which promptly published a story to the effect that, "Lady Kennedy, wife of the Governor-General of Queensland, gave birth at Government House yesterday to twins, the firstborn being a son." The story might have had great veracity had not the Governor-General at the time been 80 years old and a bachelor.

Fanning Island enjoyed her pivotal status as the Pacific's most remote and most vital cable station for more than sixty years, and those who lived in the tiny station near Bicknell Point enjoyed their time there too. It was by all accounts an easy life: the station was a long, two-storey affair shaded by palm trees, a few yards above the beach on the western side of the atoll: on the lagoon side was a small pier where the company canoes were kept, and one could spend off-duty hours strolling about in the ever-calm waters beneath the unblinking eye of the tropical sun. There was a good library; there was a small schooner kept down at English Harbour which one could take out to sea; you paid for your goods at the store in Australian currency, though when you posted a letter you used New Zealand stamps. The 200 islanders, mainly Gilbertese, were a friendly crowd and lived on the south side of the atoll in a shanty town called Baerau: they worked copra for the great Australian trading firm of Burns, Philp and Company, and a few of them kept bees which produced honey for an apparently enthusiastic little market in San Francisco. Everyone posted to Fanning by the Cable Company seemed to like the place, and even if it became on occasions a trifle, well, *boring*, you had only to think of where you might next be posted – the rain and traffic back in London, the harsh heat of Dubai or the grim crowding of Lagos – to sit back in your easy chair, light up another cheroot and (before checking once more the imperturbable meters recording the passing messages between Calgary and Canberra) reflect on how deucedly *fortunate* you had been to draw this particular straw.

However, there was a brief moment when the stalwarts of Fanning Island were interrupted from their reverie. It was September 1914: war had broken out in Europe, and one of the first actions taken by the British in August was to order their various cable ships to raise and cut all the submarine cables linking Germany to the outside world. It was a matter of weeks before the Germans struck back; London had assumed they would, and in fact had predicted with some accuracy that they would attempt to cut Britain from her colonial allies by slicing both the Indian and Pacific Ocean cables at their very weakest points – Cocos-Keeling Island in the case of the former, and the remote and ill-defended Fanning Island in the Pacific. And "ill-defended" was the phrase: despite anticipating some kind of attack on the cables, the War Cabinet had done almost nothing to prepare the operating staff to repel their probable aggressors: the 26 men and 4 women (all white, notes the Official Report) who worked for the Pacific Cable Board on Fanning were left to preserve the integrity of the Vancouver to Brisbane cable with just a handful of elderly rifles and revolvers, which they buried in the coral sand at various places marked on a map locked in the cable office safe. It was to be an uneven contest.

The Royal Navy in London, and from their great Pacific base at Esquimault on Vancouver Island, sent occasional word down the line. Early in September came a message suggesting that the heavy cruisers *Nürnberg* and *Leipzig* were sniffing around the Gilbert and Ellice Islands and might happen upon Fanning Island any day. The Fanning wireless operator stuck a note on his desk. The four women, a little unnerved by the proximity of rapacious Huns, insisted that watches be kept at night; a few days later a lookout spotted two vessels, a French merchantman and a collier, heading straight for Fanning. Much relief was expressed, and the cable station superintendent organized a greeting party to set off in a whaler to welcome the matelots, and perhaps persuade them to stay and help the islanders ward off attack by the onrushing Germans.

But of course it was all a trick, not cricket at all. The "French" boat lowered two whalers of its own, which were duly rowed ashore and on grounding disgorged parties of distinctly unfriendly and decidedly non-Gallic toughs armed with rifles and fixed bayonets. The Tricolour was lowered from the merchantman's jackstaff and replaced by the Imperial Eagle: tarpaulins were whipped away from a bundle on the foredeck, and a Maxim gun was trained on the cable station. Fanning Island was about to suffer its inevitable fate: the scalpel was being wielded, as expected, by members of the cruiser *Nürnberg* which now sat at anchor half a mile offshore, her crew having removed all suggestion of her having ever been French.

The raiding party broke into the control rooms, forcing the operators to raise their hands, take them off the Morse tappers and cease all communication with the Empire. Then the Germans systematically smashed all the equipment with pickaxes. They took dynamite and gun cotton and blew up the boiler-rooms, dynamos, refrigerating plants and diesel engines; they sawed down the flagpole and took it away in sections as souvenirs; they read through the confidential papers and learned of the hidden stashes; they set to digging, and took away the guns and ammunition and $3,000 in emergency funds. But to their credit they left the private bungalows alone, did not injure a soul, behaved with the utmost courtesy during their twelve hours on Fanning (the *Nürnberg*'s captain apologizing profusely to the cable superintendent) and, most notably, they failed completely to find the ends of either the Vancouver- or Fiji-bound cables.

So although the operators in Canada realized within seconds that the cable had been cut at Fanning somehow, it proved child's play to repair it and restore the link between British Columbia and Queensland in a matter of days: once the engineers had arrived at the atoll, a jury-rigged connection was established in two days, and the whole cable properly repaired at a cost of a mere £5,000 after a total interruption of just a month. The *Nürnberg*, meanwhile, was tracked to the Falkland Islands and sunk.

It is probably worth telling briefly the story of what happened at Cocos-Keeling Island, over on the far side – the Indian Ocean side – of Australia. The basic circumstances were similar to those on Fanning: a crucially important Imperial cable link, lying quite unguarded, with a staff of untrained and innocent youngsters out from the Home Counties. The attacking cruiser in this case was the *Emden*, which behaved just as badly as the *Nürnberg* by erecting a dummy funnel made of canvas to make the cable operators believe her to be a British naval vessel.

However, the lookout on Cocos had his wits about him. When the ship was spotted he cabled to London first that "a strange vessel" was approaching and then, putting two and two together, that she was in fact the *Emden*. He continued passing messages about the attack as the Maxim gun was trained on his office and the marines poured ashore from their whalers, and he managed to do so until his dynamos were dynamited and he was ordered to take his hands off the Morse tappers and stand up against the wall. The Germans then – with the same utmost courtesy as on Fanning – wrecked everything in sight, but they wasted many hours hacking up a piece of cable which led down the beach but was in fact quite unconnected to anything. They then left – only to discover to their horror that the *Emden* herself, far from waiting on their return, was in fact sailing out of the tiny harbour without them: a Royal Australian Navy cruiser, alerted by the cable messages to London, had made all speed to Cocos and stumbled upon the *Emden in flagrante delicto*.

The Australians attacked: the German captain decided to leave the boarding party to fend for itself on Cocos and turned tail – eventually sustaining terminal damage on North Keeling Island, a few miles away.

The German marines turned back to Cocos, made immediate prisoners of the somewhat perplexed cable office staff and ran the Imperial Eagle up the flagpole. But being good North Germans, they soon realized that island life was not likely to be for them, and looked for, found and promptly commandeered a means of escape: a three-masted topsail schooner, the *Ayesha*, which belonged to the Scots eccentric, Sidney Clunies-Ross, who owned the island. They took half of the cable station's supplies on board, together with 150 gallons of fresh water and some clothes, and set sail – freeing the even more perplexed cable staff once again.

Then, while life on Cocos returned rapidly to normal, the Germans aboard *Ayesha* sailed on to Bombay, captured a small British steamer and went on to land somewhere near Aden. They then trekked overland to Hodeidah in the Yemen and a further 400 miles north through the desert to El'Lith, where they conceived a splendidly ambitious plan to attack the Hedjaz railway – only to be attacked in turn by Arab mercenaries and driven to Damascus and, eventually, Constantinople. They arrived back in the Fatherland in June 1915, seven months after their whalers had settled into the waters at the harbour entrance to Cocos Island and triggered a series of events that was to change all their lives in the most dramatically interesting manner imaginable. (The commander, Herr von Mugge, went on to write a book about his exploits: in the Thirties it was something of a best-seller.)

Telegraphy, to return to the subject in hand, was an invention that required only relatively simple technology and gave forth in consequence only relatively simple results. The telegraph cables (like that passing through Fanning Island) transmitted electrical charges to signify the passage of the letters and words making up the various messages. A letter was translated into Morse code; the relevant Morse key was depressed: a current flowed down the line; a signal was received at the other end; the Morse was decoded into the original letter.

But telephony, which as the natural successor to telegraphy transmitted the actual sound of a human voice, needed infinitely more complicated resources. No longer was the mere passage of an electrical current sufficient – the human voice needed electromagnetic waves to be dispatched, and over a wide spectrum of radio frequencies. Cables could not at first handle such transmissions, and all early transoceanic telephony was performed by short-wave radio transmitters with immense aerials and hugely powerful, power-guzzling devices to hurl the signals into the ether. It took until 1956 for science to come up with the right answers for cable transmission: then a consortium organized by the British Post Office, A T & T and the Canadian government built TAT-1, the first trans-Atlantic telephone line: it passed between Oban in western Scotland and Clarenville in Newfoundland, and allowed 36 simultaneous telephone calls to go on between subscribers on the American mainland and Europe.

It was not long before the Pacific was similarly bridged. COMPAC, the Commonwealth Pacific Cable, was opened in 1963 ("Are you there, Mr Prime Minister?" said Queen Elizabeth to what she hoped was John Diefenbaker, in Ottawa) at a ceremony in the Grand Pacific

Hotel in Suva.* The new giant, capable of carrying 82 simultaneous two-way telephone calls, crossed the ocean from Sydney to Vancouver via New Zealand, Fiji and – crucially – Hawaii. Fanning Island was thus bypassed, and a year after COMPAC formally opened for business the venerable sexagenarian telegraph wire was closed down and pensioned off. The staff on the island were relieved in 1964 and the old office – timbers still sturdy, tin roof still preserving the instruments from the summer rains – was closed.

COMPAC's inauguration was untimely, to say the least. Eighteen months before the party at the Grand Pacific a small rocket had been fired from Cape Canaveral in Florida, carrying in its nose a small cylinder of steel, titanium, selenium and glass that was expected by its inventors to sound the death knell for the submarine telephone cable. This cylinder, the world's first orbiting telecommunications satellite, was called Telstar. Weighing just 170 lbs, it had been designed by Bell Telephone and launched at dawn on 10 July 1962, into an inconveniently elliptical orbit that rose to 3,000 miles above the earth from a low point of 600. The receiver installed to "talk" to it as it shot up from one horizon and sank quietly below the other could handle more telephone calls than all the telephone cable and radio channels then connecting the United States with the rest of the world. A new means of long-distance communication had been born, and the world's cable-makers and cable-layers scratched their heads and wondered if they had just been put out of business, and for ever.†

The sky soon began to fill with these canisters – some spinning, some static, some orbiting high, others orbiting low, some fast,

---

*A rather forlorn if architecturally spectacular dump, wrongly regarded by romantics as the Raffles of Fiji. But it has a history: Somerset Maugham went there two years after it had opened in 1914: "It is cool and empty . . . . The servants are Hindus, silent and vaguely hostile . . . . The food is very bad, but the rooms are pleasant, fresh and cool . . ."

†As if to underline this assertion I found myself attending a rather dispirited meeting on a rainy day in spring 1988, in a small hotel in suburban Vancouver. The meeting, which was attended by Fijians, Papuans and Hong Kong Chinese as well as Australians, New Zealanders, Canadians and Britons, had been called to bring to a formal end the life of the COMPAC, after a quarter of a century of sterling service. The end came when someone banged a gavel on the table, a dozen white folders were snapped shut and a few of the participants lit up cigarettes. "Are you there, Mr Prime Minister?" seemed a remark made all too long ago and besides, John Diefenbaker had died nine years before.

some slow and, as soon as the penny dropped and rockets came to be designed that could shoot that high, some orbiting at the same speed as a point on the earth's equator and thus appearing to stand still: to be *geostationary*, though they were in fact moving very fast and at 22,300 miles above the earth's surface, were very high up. Geostationary satellites thus became the key to uninterrupted global communication – there was no longer to be any "waiting for the bird", no thumb-twiddling while waiting on that "window of opportunity" as the orbiting satellite came into view. Other than a handful of specialist satellites designed for military reconnaissance or scientific measurement, nearly all the satellites fired up from Canaveral or Vandenberg, Kourou or Tanegashima, or else hoisted from the cargo bay of the space shuttles, were placed almost precisely above the equator. Once in orbit, they remained apparently more or less where they were.

Although one of the more spectacular long-distance telephone calls – that between President Kennedy and the Prime Minister of Nigeria, in 1963 – went via an early Atlantic satellite, it was across the Pacific that television made its most spectacular transoceanic appearance: Syncom 3, positioned just above Professor Dowd's International Date Line, was used in the northern autumn of 1984 to transmit the Tokyo Olympic Games to the rest of the world. Since the televising of the event did inestimable good to the international reputation of the Japanese capital, one may fairly say that the super-Pacific satellite of the day – though by modern standards a puny beast, 28 inches wide and weighing a mere 78 lbs – helped create today's image of Tokyo, playing the part of a Pacific icon in a way that helped make the city an icon of the region too.

Today there are dozens of commercial satellites hovering silently along the equator above the Pacific: a regularly-published global satellite chart maps their positions, lest anyone should try to park another in a site already taken. Taking the western half of the Pacific as extending from approximately 95° East of Greenwich – above Rangoon, and the western tip of Sumatra – to the Greenwich anti-meridian, the satellites currently overhead or shortly to be placed there are, according to the chart, as follows:

Statsionar-14 and *Gorizont-05*, operated by the Soviet Post Office; *Chinasat-3* and *PRC-18*, operated by the Chinese; *Statsionar-21*; *Chinasat-2*; *Palapa B-2P* and *B-3*, owned by Indonesia; *PRC-15*; *Statsionar-15*, *Statsionar-D06* (for diplomatic wireless transmissions) and the similar Soviet *Raduga-15*; *Avsat-5*, operated by Aeronautical Radio Inc; *Sakura-2 A* and *-2B*, run by the Japanese Space Agency in co-operation with Nippon T & T (which incidentally is by far the world's largest company according to the value of its stocks); *More-140*, *Gorizont-14*, *Gorizont-06* and *Statsionar-16*, all Russian; *Pacstar-1*, owned by Papua New Guinea; *PSI-1*, run by Pacific Satellites Inc; *Avsat-4*, from Aeronautical Radio Inc; *Intelsat-V-F1*, *Intelsat PO-PR1*, *Marisat-Pacific-103*, *Intelsat-VA PAC2*, *Intelsat IVA-F3*, *Marecs B2*, *Intelsat PO-Spare*, *Intelsat V-F8* and *Intelsat MCS PAC A* – all of the last belonging to the international organizations established to allow the world to keep constantly and reliably in touch with itself.

And in April 1990 a Long March rocket launched from western China hoisted into orbit *AsiaSat*, a huge drum made five years before by Hughes in Los Angeles. Bought *second-hand* by a consortium of businesses based in Hong Kong, it had been put on sale at a knockdown price because it had gone wrong while out in space on its first venture, had been retrieved by the Space Shuttle and brought back to earth and to Los Angeles for refurbishment and sale. Three years and a great deal of paperwork later, the gleaming new-looking device was pushed back up into space by courtesy of a Chinese rocket, and now provides telephony and television for a vast slew of western Pacific nations below, stretching from Sakhalin across to Burma, and beyond.

It would be agreeable to be able to report that satellites are romantic beasts, sturdy masses of cast iron adorned with rococo scrollwork and gold leaf, proud in their dominion over the fragile earth below. Kipling had written of the Undersea Cables as

Joining hands in the gloom, a league from the last of the sun
Hush! Men talk today o'er the waste of the ultimate slime
And a new Word runs between: whispering, "Let us be one!"

But would he, could he write of these new-fangled objects, sitting silently up in space, inhaling and then passing on all the idle chatter of humanity below? On the face of it the subject seems ripe for a poet's interest – and if not a Kipling, then at least a McGonagall. Until, that is, you see the satellites themselves. I spent a while in the Hughes Aircraft Company's great warehouse of a factory beside Los Angeles airport, being shown down a long row of glassy black drums which before long would be hurled into outer space to commence

308

their lonely vigil. But try as I might to extract some noble sentiment from the sight, I managed only to feel rather depressed. Perhaps it was the coldly antiseptic appearance of the place: everyone padded around in slippers and whispered, as if afraid to wake some unseen patients, and the visit was treated with a kind of reverence as if we were all in the presence of a mighty Force.

A typical Hughes satellite constructed for Intelsat stands about 40 feet tall, a massive greenish-black drum with, at its upper end, an array of hinged arms and legs all covered with gold foil. (Beside the site where each satellite is being built hangs a roll of pure gold foil, looking no more special and costly than a roll of kitchen paper: from time to time one of the white-coated workers tears a sheet from it – a wedding-ring's worth, by the looks of it – and wraps it around a protruding arm or leg to ward off dangerous radiation and reflect sudden spurts of damaging heat.)

The arrays are the aerials themselves – a couple of large diameter dishes, about 6 feet across, for the lower frequency radio signals, and a pair of smaller ones for the higher frequencies. Once the satellite has been placed in orbit, a radio command sent from earth (picked up by another hinged antenna that snaps open the moment the satellite is deployed) will cause all these aerials and antennae to unfold, like flowers on a warm spring day. Then the upper part of the satellite will begin to spin, so that it becomes gyroscopically stabilized and keeps what the engineers charmingly call "the right attitude". The lower part of the drum – covered with thousands of the glistening greenish-black squares which are actually panels of solar cells – will absorb the heat and light energy from the sun,* and convert it to electricity to keep the entire satellite and its radio transponders – the crucially important but unseen innards of the device – doing what they are designed to do: receiving signals from earth, amplifying them and directing them out again to somewhere else down on the planet below. One satellite can deal with 12,000 two-way telephone conversations at once, and transmit two channels of television – ten times as many phone calls as the most powerful cable ever laid.

The "birds", as the great monsters are still called, are all controlled

---

*Except during solar eclipses, when the satellite passes through the earth's shadow: nickel-hydrogen batteries then keep the power up for the vitally important few moments of cold and dark. Down below no one has the slightest idea that communications have been in any danger of collapse.

from the Intelsat headquarters near Washington. I was on a remote tropical island once when one of the satellites hurtling along above us "went down", and we all had to reposition our aerials to the spare "bird" flying along nearby. The engineers had been working all night, cranking the satellite dish a few thousands of seconds of arc this way and then the other, so that it pointed at the precise spot in the sky where the spare satellite was due to be moved. Back in Washington the engineers were preparing the coded instructions to their "bird", telling the tiny rocket motors in the orbit and altitude control propulsion system to fire with this much force for that number of seconds. A few moments before six in the morning, when a new Pacific day was just beginning its glorious uprush from the East, Washington came on the line. Loudspeakers in our tiny control room began to crackle with the calmly urgent voice from the American capital, giving instructions that had to be obeyed to the letter, failing which our island would lose its connection to the satellite and, with it, our few thousand people would lose their links with the world.

"Repositioning routines for Intelsat Five-eight" the voice intoned, referring to the eighth satellite launched, back in 1984, of a particular type, V-A, manufactured by Ford Aerospace. "All locations should now be locked on to coordinates one seven nine decimal nine three six east, zero zero decimal five north." The technicians checked their instruments and nodded at each other – just as other technicians were no doubt doing, up in Guam and Saipan and down in Tonga and Brisbane and across in Anchorage and Tahiti, in summer and winter, today or tomorrow: it made no difference to the unblinking neutrality of the satellite on which side of the equator or which side of the Date Line sat its customers – it merely needed to be able to talk to them, and to do this it required to be placed where the engineers in Washington promised they would place it, and to have the aerials down below trained precisely on to its antennae.

"Repositioning motors firing in five seconds. Lock-on one minute sixteen seconds after tone," came the voice. Oscilloscope traces, bright yellow against green, formed lazy lines on a dozen screens. Hands fell on "Aerial Lock" buttons. There was a sudden sound from Washington. "Motors fired. The bird is moving. Repeat, the bird is moving." The seconds ticked past in total silence. A small river of sweat trickled down the temple of the chief technician, but his hand hovered certainly over the red aerial lock button.

Then, as the aerials started to "see" the satellite which was now moving into the field of view, the oscilloscopes suddenly began to froth with confused lines as they started to detect signals which our aerials were receiving from the transponders. At first there were patternless lines and dots, the visual equivalent of static and snow; then, almost imperceptibly at first, a number of signals began to distinguish themselves and the harsh sound over the speaker began to assume the shape of a musical tone – high and faint, fairly rough-edged, but becoming smoother, louder and more distinct as the seconds passed.

"Ten seconds from the bell," said Washington, automaton-like. A gong sounded and the unseen American began a countdown, second by second. The tone became ever louder and clearer. The oscilloscope pattern revealed itself as a bell-shaped line, its summit becoming increasingly pointed and clear in the centre of the screen until suddenly with a ". . . three . . . two . . . one . . . lock" the announcer called for 100 satellite dishes across the Ocean to lock on to this new arrival. Our engineer pressed his button exactly on cue and a dozen dials flashed to maximum readings, the oscilloscope filled with a bright green solid line. We appeared to have trained our aerial precisely: it remained only to test the quality of the line. I dialled a number in Los Angeles; it was picked up in seconds, and the friend to whom I spoke remarked that it sounded as though I was speaking from the house next door.

One might have imagined that the story would stop there: the progression from Aldis lamp to telegraph wire, from telephone cable to geostationary satellite, seems in retrospect to have been a perfectly natural evolutionary process, and one might suppose that any further advance in trans-Pacific – meaning ultra-long distance – communication would lie in some realm presently unimagined. After all, that is how progress tends to operate. But something outwardly curious has befallen the communications business – something which started to become apparent every few months during the late 1980s with the appearance in Hong Kong harbour of a large white ship with the distinctive curved arrow of Cable & Wireless on her funnel.

She was the cable ship *Cable Venture* and, in spite of the proliferation of satellites in the skies above her (to which she was intimately connected via the white domed aerial marking her as a subscriber to Marisat, the International Marine Communication Satellite service), she was reportedly in the business of laying cable again. Satellites, the word went round, were – in certain circumstances and for certain purposes – out of date. It had suddenly become more sensible and economical to lay cables born of a wholly new technology on the Ocean floor once more: suddenly it seemed as though the communications revolution of which the satellite-launchers had spoken so keenly a quarter of a century before had turned back upon itself, and come round full circle.

Today's cable ships the *Venture* and the *Enterprise* for Cable & Wireless, the *Long Lines* and the *Charles L. Brown* for American Telephone & Telegraph are not laying the kind of elephantine-scale cables that used to end up on Fanning Island; nor are they putting down the plastic-sheathed copper wires that carried telephone calls beneath the seas during the Sixties and Seventies. The new cables snaking up from their huge holds are slender, light and elegant little threads made, quite simply, of glass.

Fibre-optic cables, as these are known, carry their telephone signals which have been broken down into millions of fragments – digitized, rendered into the raw material with which computers like to treat – by reflecting them incredibly rapidly along their length. The fibres are thin, of near-perfect internal cleanliness, and have untold powers of internal reflection; so the signals, the minute bursts of light of fractionally differing frequencies for each of the calls they represent, hurtle along the lines with virtually none of the attenuation or distortion that was found in wire cables. The new cables are also highly secure – since they involve the transmission of light, it is all but impossible to tap into them without that light leaking away and being detected – so any customer wishing to be quite certain that no one is listening to his call across the sea is far better off transmitting it via a submerged cable than entrusting it to the open skies of the satellite system.

(I once made a call to London, in rather trying circumstances, from a remote island in the Southern Ocean. A gun was in my back, and I had been told by the soldier who held it to omit certain references or things would go rather badly for me. The consequent call was therefore a little more strained than was customary. When I was in England some months later, I received in the post an envelope from a ham radio-operator – a man I didn't know, who lived near Reading in Berkshire. It seemed he had a fairly impressive array of aerials in his back garden, and a powerful radio receiver. He had listened to my call with some amusement, he said; his envelope contained a tape recording of it – purely, he ventured, for my interest. This was a striking reminder of how insecure satellite communications – for that is how this call had clearly been routed – have come to be. Fibre-optic cables, we are assured by their makers and layers, have changed all that.)

The world's first deep-sea submarine fibre-optic cable was laid in 1985 between Tenerife and Gran Canaria, in the Atlantic; the first system that did not have to rely on cumbersome repeaters – bulky amplifiers which have to be inserted in the cable every 20 miles or so, like bottles in the neck of an ostrich – was called the Commando Fox Cable, and was laid for 80 miles in the Pacific between the island of Okinawa and a permanently moored offshore oil platform, also in 1986. And then in April 1989, things became serious, with the inauguration of the first trans-Pacific fibre-optic connection, the inelegantly titled HAW-4/TPC-3, which the publicists promptly titled "The Pacific Link".

Since so much of the business of the new Pacific involves money rather than politics, cultural exchanges or science, it was perhaps appropriate that the first calls between Japan and the United States along the Pacific Link were made by the chairmen of the two nations' principal stock exchanges. "This is not simply a technical leap forward," said one, ". . . we are witnessing the opening of a next-generation information infrastructure for the world." Indeed, replied the other – over a telephone call obligingly augmented by a video link so the participants could all witness the reactions of those around them, "the revolution of our time is an information revolution . . . we are at the threshold, in terms of financial markets, of speaking globally."

A pity, perhaps, that these two dullards could come up with nothing more inspirational! For the new cable did represent something quite extraordinary – not least a measure of man's conquest of an ocean barrier that, 500 years before the laying ships set out from port, had not even been crossed by man. The cable's statistics were impressive enough. It is 8,271 miles long, passing from Punta Arenas in Northern California to Makaha in Hawaii, then on to an undersea branching point in the deep waters south-east of Japan, with one leg passing on to Chikura, on the coast of Chiba prefecture, near Tokyo; and the other going to Tanguisson, on Guam. The section from Makaha to the branching unit is 3,332 miles long, and is far and away the longest fibre-optic cable ever laid in one operation.

The capacity of the Pacific Link is vast: 280,000,000 bits of digitized information can pass back and forth along it every second – meaning that 40,000 two-way telephone calls can be made simultaneously. A protocol agreed by Japanese and American phone companies in March 1989 means that the cable will support the so-called Integrated Services Digital Network – a new type of telephone service which, without venturing into its complexities, offers possibilities the like of which Alexander Graham Bell could never have imagined. "High fidelity conversations, for a start," a man from the Japanese company KDD once said to me. "You have high fidelity from your stereo – why be satisfied with calling your wife on the phone and have her sound like a chicken? With ISDN it should be possible for me to call someone in Florida and for him to sound exactly, and I mean *exactly*, as though he was standing next to me."

All the cable companies are now busily spinning their fibre-optic webs across the Pacific – Cable & Wireless touting for business on its so-called "digital highway" that will cross from Washington state to Tokyo, then onwards to Korea and Hong Kong; and A T & T offering its "intelligent network" of what it calls "lightguide services", which it evidently thinks is a fancier name than fibre-optic cable. A new trans-Pacific lightguide in the making, due to open in 1992, will carry 80,000 telephone calls simultaneously – more than a thousand times the number carried by the COMPAC, so recently decommissioned and so soon forgotten.

The satellites are not out of business, of course. Hughes and Ford are busy making them, Cape Canaveral, Kouro and Tanegashima are busily hoisting new drums into space, and there are plans to build a commercial spaceport at Cape York in northern Queensland, its backers hoping that the site close to the equator and the eternally summery weather will attract launchers by the score. The Chinese still hope to launch satellites for the West, their success with the launch of AsiaSat (performed in spite of political opposition after the Tiananmen incidents in June 1989) clearly boosting their hopes of doing so.

I was climbing the hills outside Vandenberg Air Force base in Southern California one weekday in the autumn of the same year when I fancied I heard a dull rumble, and a plume of smoke drifted from behind one of the distant hills. A commercial rocket venture, the first ever in which a number of private enterprises had come together to construct a private rocket, had failed spectacularly: the launcher had blown up on the pad. Satellites, it seemed then, were still vulnerable devices, their reliability never quite certain: their launch rockets blew up; if they managed to get up into space they found themselves in the wrong orbits, or just plain lost: their solar reflectors failed to deploy; they were eroded and abraded by cosmic dust, or hit by small asteroids and put out of action; and in any case the conversations conducted across them (which customers often disliked because of the quarter-second time delay that a badly balanced circuit could provoke) were insecure and potentially overheard by millions.

Whereas the old-fashioned way of transoceanic communication, the cable, was so elegant, so discreet, so pleasingly romantic, so very *right*. For that reason alone, and in salute to this progression from Fanning Island to fibre optics, I have come – dinosaur though I may be considered – to regard the undersea cable as more truly symbolic of the Ocean: it seems iconic both of the difficulties and the benefits of communicating over the vast distances imposed by so great a sea as the Pacific.

2

The Monster

Seattle would never have been much of a town had not a Mr William Boeing bought a boatyard on the shores of Lake Union in 1916, and started to make seaplanes. Some unkind people, however, have argued that Seattle is not much of a town even today (though they concede it is an exceptionally pleasant city surrounded by magnificent countryside, that it enjoys kindly weather, has relatively little crime and not too many slums, and is a good place to *live*), and that Mr Boeing's present giant of a company* might have been better run from elsewhere, somewhere less obviously *provincial*, like New York City or Chicago. They started saying this particularly vociferously in 1969 when the company, in the words of its then President, Mr Tex Boullioun, "came within a gnat's whisker of not making it" – of going bankrupt.

The reason for the company's appalling performance that year – blamed at the time on hayseed accountancy of a kind you never would have encountered (said these same critics) on Wall Street or Michigan Avenue – was quite simple when viewed with the benefit of hindsight: all blame fell on the costs of developing and building the most remarkable aircraft of its time, the one plane that has somehow

*The present Boeing Commercial Airline Company no longer has a Boeing on the board. William E. Boeing resigned after the government ordered the disintegration of his company, the United Aircraft and Transport Corporation, in 1934. He was, however, invited to the roll-out of the firm's first commercial jet, the 707, in May 1954. His wife Bertha christened the aircraft "the Boeing Jet Stratoliner and Stratotanker", a name which was not to last. A week after the ceremony the plane collapsed, its landing gear buckling under its enormous weight.

since come to serve as the unqualified symbol of the century. The Boeing 747. The jumbo jet.

The jumbo had its origins, as one might expect, with the only organization that could afford to think such grandiose thoughts: the American military. Specifically, the plane's roots can be traced back to a decision taken by the Pentagon in the early 1960s to talk to the country's three paramount aircraft makers, Boeing, Douglas and Lockheed, about building a mammoth new machine for the prime purpose of moving great numbers of men and armour at high speed over long distances. The new plane, said the Pentagon, should be at least twice the size of any existing jet – twice the size, for instance, of the Boeing 707 which, when rolled out a decade before, had seemed a veritable Leviathan.

The bid which the Pentagon invited had enormous implications: it required, for instance, the construction of engines – for a plane, as all designers will tell you endlessly, is only as good as its power plant – that delivered as much as 40,000 lbs of thrust. In the Sixties, this was a staggering figure, about three times the thrust then delivered by one of the engines on a 707. In the relatively unenlightened days of three decades ago, to build such monsters seemed well-nigh impossible: of the two American engine makers, only General Electric believed they were competent. Pratt & Whitney backed down.

The weeks and months during which the three makers imagined, planned and modelled the new aircraft were, to the engineers involved, gruelling indeed, and to the accountants even more so. And it was price that eventually won the day: the Pentagon awarded the contract to Lockheed, which underbid its competitors to a degree that made its triumph soon turn to ashes in its shareholders' mouths. The company went on to produce a transport plane that would be called the C-5A, powered by four GE engines, and still the supreme workhorse of the wartime skies.

So Boeing had lost what was at the time the most important aircraft contract of the jet age. It might have been chagrined. Instead the firm's manager contrived to allow the company's loss to evolve rapidly into a decision that was to change the face of commercial aviation, for more than a generation. Joseph Sutter, then the engineer in charge of all Boeing's commercial operations, had been alerted some weeks before that if the company lost the C-5A contract he would be placed in command of a totally new design team with the aim of producing a commercial equivalent of the giant new military transport. Sutter was on holiday when in August 1965, the Pentagon made its announcement about Lockheed's success: he was recalled, given charge of the 100 engineers who had been working on the failed military bid and ordered to get to work on designing the new machine. Thus did Mr Sutter become the ultimate creator of the 747 – the father, as some would have it, of the jumbo jet.

Wide-bodied jets have come to be so familiar a part of the everyday landscape that it is almost impossible to imagine their never having been invented. They have a solid, imperturbable look of inevitability about them. The evolutionary process from Wright through Blériot to Lindbergh and to the Sea of Tranquillity, or via the Dakota and the Stratofortress to the Stratocruiser, the Comet and the 707 seems to lead inexorably to the jumbo, the wide-bodies, the 747. Where next? is quite another question. Perhaps, *pace* the advocates of Concorde, supersonic planes are not to be with us for a while, and the plane of the coming decades is to be some kind of development – bigger, heavier, more brutally powered – of what we have now. There is the unspoken assumption that the 747 is somehow the now and future aircraft, a thought as beguiling as it is – to anyone with a hint of the visionary in his soul – repugnant.

Yet there was nothing inevitable about the 747. It would never have come about without the active support and cooperation of Pan American and its founder and then president, Juan Terry Trippe. It was Trippe who ordered the first twenty 707s in 1955, thus helping Boeing to inaugurate the jet age. This time, three days before Christmas 1965, he ordered twenty-five of Sutter's new monsters (and took options for eight more). This decision then represented the largest financial and technological gamble in the history of aviation. Without the order, Boeing could never have started the programme; as it is they committed some $2,000 million to building the aircraft – more than twice the total worth of the company itself. It was overextended to a terrifying extent – as was Pan Am – and one elderly Boeing executive now admits that thinking about the 747's early days "brings sweat to the palms of my hands".

The scale of the project was extraordinary. An entirely new factory had to be built in Everett, a then rather dismal lumber town on the mouth of the Snohomish River, thirty miles north of Seattle. The assembly building was to be the largest enclosed structure in the world – forty acres in extent, on a 783-acre site – and a special rail link (with specially enlarged box-cars for the huge assemblies they would be required to carry) was ordered to connect it to the main line to Seattle.

Two hundred different designs were advanced for the new plane, innumerable new variables being introduced into the equations: Pan Am, for example, wanted slightly wider seats than those on the 707 because, their ergonomists declared, the breadth of the American (and eventually the world) bottom was increasing. There was a plan to make the entire aircraft double-decked, as the Stratocruiser had been (passengers went downstairs for a stroll), but engineers vetoed this because of the potential difficulty in getting the passengers out quickly in the event of an emergency.

The diameter of the new fuselage was defined by way of a charming throwback to a slower form of transport, the ship (albeit the *container* ship, which mariners hardly regard as possessed of much charm). Pan Am, eager that their new plane could double up as an aerial freighter, decided that it should be able to carry, deep in its hold, at least two parallel rows of standard ships' containers – 40 feet long (or their half-size brothers), 8 feet wide and 8 high. Two of these placed side by side – a total width of rather more than 16 feet, with a minute gap between them – would fit in a circle almost exactly equal to nine of the newly-designed seats placed beside each other with two aisles separating them. The containers' width thus became the 747's fuselage diameter – meaning that anyone stuck in the middle of a five-wide block of economy seats at the back of a plane making its seemingly interminable trans-Pacific way from Tokyo to Los Angeles knows exactly whom to curse. A narrower plane might have meant a single aisle: a wider plane would have meant more room, and comfort, for everyone.

The familiar bulge at the rear of the cockpit had its origins with the needs of the cargo hauliers, too. The original idea was for cargo to be loaded through the aircraft's nose – meaning that the cockpit would be placed well above it. An elevated cockpit would require an aerodynamically efficient slope down to join the rest of the fuselage – a sloping surface containing a considerable amount of usable space. Sutter's design team planned to use this to contain the air-conditioning ducts, but Juan Trippe – as flamboyant as he was prescient – vetoed so prosaic a plan. He wanted the space used to make money – to have what Americans quaintly call a stateroom.

Boeing loathed the idea, but Trippe was the customer and was foot-ing most of the bills, so eventually, after much protestation, they caved in. So a strangely Victorian and decidedly non-aeronautical idea was born: a spiral staircase was constructed to link the existing passenger space with this new, oddly-shaped area above – leading to a space that would fill with two tons of extra weight which could include (depending on the airline) a baby grand piano, a bar or (as in one lunatic scheme) a small swimming-pool; and then, as the years went on, with fare-paying passengers.

The deadline for producing the first flying 747s was crippling: Pan Am and Boeing had agreed among themselves in December of 1965 that deliveries would begin in November 1969 – meaning that in less than four years a brand-new plane (and, more significantly still, a brand-new engine) would have to be developed, certified and made ready to fly. General Electric, who had won the contract for the C-5A, declined the invitation to build the power plant for the new craft, pleading it would take at least four years to develop. Rolls-Royce, who very much wanted to make the engine (and had a work-force of 70,000 already working on jet-engine projects of one kind or another) was turned down by Boeing, who thought (rightly as it turned out) that the much-vaunted Hyfil carbon-fibre turbine blades with which Rolls-Royce wanted to equip its new engines were no good. Sutter, who had a firm belief in titanium or other exotic alloys, called the Rolls-Royce invention "oatmeal blades".*

Pratt & Whitney, the remaining contender, agreed to build the engine – and to raise to an unheard of 5:1 the so-called "bypass ratio" of their engines, an engineering challenge which, if they could meet it, would raise the power of their engine to the 41,000 lbs of thrust which Sutter's design team figured was the minimum necessary to keep the new plane aloft.

---

*Sutter's scepticism was well-founded. Rolls-Royce succeeded in persuading Lockheed to buy Hyfil-bladed engines for its L1011 Tri-Stars, claiming that the use of fibre would strip 500 lbs from the weight of each engine. But one memorable afternoon in the summer of 1969, Rolls-Royce engineers performed a standard engine test to simulate bird-strike on an engine by firing a 4 lb chicken from a cannon directly into the fan assembly of a working engine. The fans should be able to "gulp" the bird with no ill-effects: but to everyone's astonishment, the Hyfil blades shattered. Thus began the long saga of bankruptcy and government bail-outs that was to engulf Rolls-Royce for the next decade – a saga essentially started with a 4 lb broiler fowl.

The development of jet bypass technology was essential to the construction of wide-bodied jets: had the concept been impracticable, none of today's monster planes could fly. Like the modern jet itself, the bypass was invented by Sir Frank Whittle, utilizing a principle which (he says) is as old as nature itself: "as old as the squid – if you push air back, you push yourself forward."

The basic jet involves what seems a combination of elegant simplicity and magic. Air drawn into the engine's nacelle is squeezed by a series of compressor blades until it is at very high pressure. Fuel is then injected into it, and ignited. The compressed air and fuel burn, very rapidly, and the hot gases expand enormously, rushing out of the exhaust of the engine housing – turning a turbine as they do so, which in turn rotates the compressor blades to compress still more air pouring in from the front. Air thus streams from the exhaust nozzle at a far higher speed than it is being taken in – with the result that the engine, and hence the aeroplane to which it is attached, moves forward.

A bypass engine takes this concept further by an order of magnitude. At the front of the nacelle is an enormous fan which, driven by the turbines that are turned by the exhaust gases, seems to chew its way into the air before it, seems almost to pull the engine forward. The air that its forty or blades bites into flows not into the engine as such, to be mixed with fuel and ignited in the doughnut-shaped combustion chambers, but is *bypassed* around these to be injected directly into the hot exhaust stream. It is then heated, rapidly, duly expands and is shot out of the rear of the engine – the bypass air producing as much as three-quarters of the engine's total thrust. (The fan itself also helps move the engine along by acting as an old-fashioned propellor.)

The consequences are fourfold. The fact that the engine is being pulled forward by a fan, and that the extra air being forced out of the exhaust is doing its own bit to push the engine forward, combine to give the engine far greater thrust than a non-bypass type. The engine is also a great deal quieter, since the larger volume of air moving through the wider-mouthed bypass engine flows less rapidly than it would if the engine were as small as its predecessors – less noise, and of kindlier rumble than the whining of older-generation engines. Fourthly, and crucially to the customers, the engine uses relatively less fuel since a high proportion of the air never mixes with it, but is merely heated by that which does.

In summary, a bypass engine is a high-thrust, low-noise, extremely economical type of engine – crucial to the success of wide-bodied jet airliners. In the late 1960s, and with only a forty-month deadline, it was an appallingly difficult project to design, build, certify and prove. That Pratt & Whitney dared to attempt it says something for the courage, or the foolhardiness, of the American manufacturers of the time.

Foolhardiness, indeed, appears to have been a dominant feature of the attitudes of many of those directly involved with the making of the 747 during the years between the signing by Pan Am of its Letter of Intent in December 1965, and the first commercial flight of a Pan Am 747 in January 1970. The blame is shared more or less equally by the three protagonists. Pan Am wanted a monster of ever-increasing size, appeal to the travelling public, and abilities. Boeing kept agreeing – helplessly but, as it appears from today's vantage point, mistakenly – to do whatever Pan Am demanded. And Pratt & Whitney tried gamely to keep up with the ever-expanding size and weight of the new plane by promising an engine that was beyond its abilities to build.

When the original contract was signed, it was agreed that the plane's take-off weight should be 655,000 lbs (at the time of the original handshake between the companies four months earlier, the idea was for a plane 50 tons lighter) and that it should carry 400 passengers for 5,900 miles at an altitude of 35,000 feet – well above the ceiling of the competing jets, so that purchasers could look down upon their rivals, as well as offer their passengers and crew calmer weather and their accountants the prospect of lower fuel consumption (which changes in inverse proportion to height above sea level). That was the plan; but during 1967 and 1968 the plane began to grow – a little longer here, a lot heavier everywhere* – and the targets for its performance began to drop. The weight increased to 680,000 lbs, then to 710,000; the range fell to 5,000 miles, the operating ceiling to 33,000 feet. And Pratt & Whitney were asked to rate their engine for more power still – as much as 43,500 lbs of thrust.

In short, the project was beginning to run out of control. There were real fears voiced in the Boeing boardroom that the much smaller

---

*Since the notorious "square-cube law" holds that if, while a plane is being designed, its designers allow it to grow, then its dimension increases by the square but its volume – and thus its weight – does so by the cube.

"jumbos" that Lockheed and McDonnell Douglas had now agreed to build, the L1011 and the DC-10, would eventually prove to be the planes actually justified by passenger demand and the realities of the airline industry, and that the Boeing 747 was set, like the Brabazon and the Spruce Goose, to be a white elephant of the sky.

Should Boeing delay the project, and think out its problems? Should Pratt & Whitney redesign the engines? Should Pan Am tone down the ferocity of its demands and ease the breakneck pace of its programme to acquire and introduce the new machines? To all these legitimate questions the answer was a resounding no, with the consequence that the jet ran into even greater problems. The plane's test engine started to change shape – to "ovalize", as alarmed mechanics put it. The company ran out of spare parts. It couldn't find enough trained engineers, so embarked upon a gigantic training programme and quite forgot, for a while, that it was in the business of building a new plane. In short, it was a mess.

However, at the end of September 1968 the first plane was rolled out of the new assembly building at Everett – a stunning demonstration to a fascinated world that the bold, quintessentially *American* plan had succeeded simultaneously on two fronts. The world's most remarkable plane had been built inside, and in tandem with the construction outside of the world's most remarkable assembly building – nearly 800 acres of aluminium-covered steel to build nearly 400 tons of titanium-finished aluminium, and to induce it to fly more people farther, and faster, than they had ever flown before. The sceptics – those who had *gulped* when they saw the first wooden mock-up of this oddly bug-eyed monster of a plane which looked as if no force known to man could lift it from the ground and keep it in the sky – were silenced. This new craft was a wonder, a massive and beautiful creature that would change the face of aviation – itself only six decades old, it was barely possible to realize – for ever.

But there were still dire problems. Pratt & Whitney could not make the right engines fast enough to keep pace with the assembly-line operation at Everett, which was beginning to churn out clones of Joe Sutter's plane at the rate of one every five days. Aircraft were emerging from the huge doors with wings, wheels and stabilizers – but with concrete blocks suspended from the engine mountings to prevent the planes from blowing over in a Pacific storm. One sightseer counted seventeen of the new planes standing out in the rain, blocks of cement dangling from under their wings as if they were destined for a Mafia funeral.

Then there was the matter of the engines that Boeing received from Pratt & Whitney, and tested: of the 87 that arrived in Everett, 60 were destroyed during the tests. The planes destined for service had terrific engine problems too; Pratt & Whitney had suggested they be run at higher temperatures to produce the desired thrust, but this caused both higher fuel consumption and increased costs, as well as hugely increased wear and tear to the engine parts themselves. Aircraft captains were having to shut down engines in mid-flight, to turn back or to limp on to their destination ports, late and anxious. And when the Pan American inaugural flight from New York to London started its take-off roll on 21 January 1970, an engine overheated and the plane had to abort its departure. The airline had anticipated this and had a spare plane, fully fuelled and laden with champagne and strawberries, waiting on the apron. But even *this* departure was delayed by a total of six hours: most of the problems, Boeing and Pan Am said lamely the next day, stemmed from an air traffic controllers' strike.

Everyone then began to talk litigation. Pan Am suffered enormous financial losses – the beginnings of a savage decline in fortunes which continues today, and which prompted the company to withdraw from trans-Pacific flying in the late 1980s. Boeing came to within the "gnat's whisker" of crashing. *Forbes* magazine talked of the firm as "dangerously" ailing", and prompted investors to look towards McDonnell Douglas as the star performer in the airline industry of the Seventies. But then a deal was eventually struck. Pan Am withheld $2 million of the $18500,000 cost of each plane until the aircraft performed as well as the original contract had specified: and Boeing managed to persuade Pratt & Whitney to assume all but half a million dollars of that penalty. The threat of a courtroom battle receded, and the three firms straightened their ties, slicked back their hair and got on with their various tasks.

And slowly, painfully so, the Boeing 747 stopped being the nightmare of the aviation world. The engines began to work properly. General Electric started to supply bypass engines of its own, and after the rescue of Rolls-Royce from Carey Street it, too, applied its phenomenal engine-making expertise to producing power plants for the 747. By the end of the 1970s the travelling public – after first rebelling at all the delays and cancellations that seemed to dog the plane – had fallen in love with it. There was a feeling abroad that anything so huge and so solid was sure to be safe – and even some of the celebrated accidents which have befallen the plane have done little to dampen popular enthusiasm. Within weeks of the first deliveries, airlines – especially state-run airlines, who liked the kudos of owning the biggest civil aircraft made and believed they derived great status from parking the gleaming machine at their capital city airport – were buying from Boeing in droves. The 747 started to make money – one of very few planes ever to manage to recover its development costs – and eventually, after four hundred or so had been sold, became one of the most celebrated "cash cows" within the Boeing company.

It is now more than two decades since the first 747 was rolled from the vast building in Everett. The building is now even more vast – still the biggest enclosed space on the planet, and as unimaginable in statistical terms as it is unbelievable at first sight. The figures make no real sense at all: according to the endless stream of press releases published by Boeing's public relations department, the structure contains 291 million cubic feet (mostly air: the height, which adds volume at a frightening rate for every additional foot, is needed to accommodate the tallest part of the tallest aircraft, which is, of course, the tail section of the 747 – 63 feet 5 inches above the ground. Boeing, presumably anticipating dramatic changes in the size of planes of the future, has made its building twice as high – 115 feet – as the current plane requires it to be). The railway that connects the building to Seattle (laid as part of the original 747 building plan of the mid-Sixties) is said to have the steepest gradient of any line in the country – steeper (going 6 feet upwards for every 100 feet along) than even the gradients in the Rocky Mountains. The earth that was moved to make way for the assembly building was half as much again as that shifted to build the Grand Coulee Dam (a statistic presented to impress residents of the Pacific north-west) and would be enough to build a dyke 10 feet high and 10 feet wide from (for East Coast residents) New York to Washington DC, or (for Britons) from London to Newcastle upon Tyne.

Quite a menagerie of jumbos has been housed within: the originals, the 747-100 series, now all but defunct and consigned to moulder with the less significant airlines; the 200s, the mainstays of today's middle-range fleets; the half-cargo, half-passenger Combis; the unnaturally foreshortened, ugly and unpopular 747-SPs, the "Edsel of the skies", which some airlines – SAA, China Airlines, Pan Am – use to ferry their loads across greater-than-usual distances;

and the two newer family members, the aircraft Singapore Airlines dubbed the Big Top 747-300, now discontinued, but which won immediate favour with the long-haul fliers; and the true Pacific aircraft, the 747-400, which will be described in greater detail later.

To see one of these craft being created – for the process seems more like creation than mere manufacture – is to marvel at the ingenuity of man. Inside the unbelievably vast cavern of steel girders and endless walls thousands of men swarm over and around what is very obviously a production line. Not a line that moves continuously, like that at Ford or General Motors, still it is recognizably a line, a kind of animated time-lapse photograph that displays the whole evolutionary progress of "The Plane". We see it from the moment of conception as a prodigious and glittering cigar of metal lying among a mess of naked ribs and wire sinews, to the moment when it is first clad with plates of shining aluminium, to the great birth-day when it emerges from the plant – another fully-fledged, fully-painted, engine-equipped, tyre-fitted version of the giant we see each day at every big airport in the world.

Every six days at the Everett plant – usually in the middle of the night, when there are fewer distractions – the Boeing production line moves. (A couple of years ago the line moved every twelve days. In 1990, with airlines frantic for new planes, and with an unprecedented Boeing machinists' strike in 1989 having severely complicated matters, the company doubled their work pace.) In this line there are seven positions, easily recognizable by innocents watching from above in the apartment-sized viewing platforms. At the back great wings are brought in from storage, made into matching pairs, and joined on to what is called a wing-stub box. Then a relatively small section of the fuselage – merely as small as the average house – is attached to the wings. In the third and fourth positions, to which the foetal craft is moved on an arrangement of hydraulic bags and rollers, the rest of the tubular body, the nose – along with the cockpit – and the tail are bolted and glued and riveted and otherwise conjoined. The undercarriage is added, so that the now-recognizable plane-to-be can be wheeled around – as indeed it is, to be parked in the remaining three positions on the slant, to allow more room in the assembly building. In positions five and six much of the interior work, the wiring and the hydraulics is completed, and at seven the engines are attached. Only then does the new 747 head out into the cool and drizzle for which Everett is famous.

I first saw the assembly building on such a day in a heavy, sheeting rainstorm, but I had no need to get wet dashing from car park to front door: the bus in which Boeing brought me from the airport simply drove directly into the heart of the building itself, through a doorway which, though prodigious by mere human standards, was a mere mousehole compared with the doorway beside it which allowed finished aircraft to move out (though never in: once constructed, they never return to where they were whelped). I was there to witness one of the more curious events of the airline world: the transfer of a jumbo jet from the ownership of builder to customer.

Every six days as the line inside the building has rolled forward – one new set of aluminium plates, ribs and rivets set down at Position 1, and one new aircraft rolled out from Position 7 – a customer (an airline) has to collect the new machine ordered two or three years before. A deposit has been paid. New timetables are being readied back home, presuming the delivery of the new craft. For Boeing and for the customer, timing is all: if Boeing doesn't sell its plane, then Everett Field fills up with billions of dollars' worth of unclaimed merchandise; if the customer doesn't get his machine, thousands of potential passengers will be stranded somewhere, hundreds of planned connections will be missed and an airline reputation, so crucial for business, will slip down a notch or two in the ratings.

So in the customers flock – each one to see his plane, check that all is working, pay over the money and fly it away. They come from almost everywhere – Tehcran, Dublin, Tokyo, Hong Kong, Chicago, Bangkok, Lisbon, Toronto – from the sixty-odd airlines that are sufficiently rich and important to drive jumbos around the world.

The customer crews, teams of directors and lawyers, accountants and engineers, pilots and navigators, plus a small group of stewardesses who reputedly fight like cats for the privilege of working a delivery flight, are put up in the best of the local hotels. They dine with their consuls, or with their company representatives. The lesser figures go sailing on Puget Sound, or wander the slopes of Mount Rainer, or eat soft-shell crabs on a pine-covered island. The senior people are taken out to Everett to see their new plane and make sure all is as expected – seats the right size, colour scheme perfect, lavatories in the right place; that the cockpit controls read accurately and the wheels are acceptably round (not always guaranteed, bearing in mind the 200 tons riding on top of them).

Then they fly it (Boeing already have, to make sure that the wings are the right way up and the engines blow the air out in the correct direction). If the pilots and engineers feel happy, then arrangements are started – lawyers briefed, accountants readied, bankers instructed and vaults opened – to do the deal. If they don't like what they feel – if the plane feels heavy or sluggish, or the engines make an odd noise – then they ask for changes and arrange to take it for a spin next day. And, if necessary the next day. And the next . . . .

(Boeing sometimes suspects that a few airlines organize several of these so-called "C-flights" in order to arrange time to get the money gathered together. One Middle East airline, whose plane was still parked at Everett Field on the day I was first there, had demanded something like seven C-flights, the pilots insisting, after receiving long-distance phone calls, that they had heard otherwise inaudible sounds from this engine, or that wheel, or suspected leaks from that gasket or this journal. Boeing sighs and does as it is bidden: better, its accountants say, to have an eventual sale, no matter how much time and energy is spent coasting around the skies above Washington State.)

But, finally, D – for Delivery – day. The night before, the customer has been given a banquet, the host often a burly Boeing figure with the title Vice President, Contracts, whose burliness is not unrelated to the fact that he has to attend a banquet almost every eight days. Though they are free to attend the party, the pilots are not allowed to drink, and in consequence are the only ones with clear heads when, shortly after breakfast next day, the Boeing bus arrives to take everyone from the hotel up north to Everett and the 747 Delivery Center. Here the final details are discussed: the route home, the weather, the fuel quantity, the passenger load for the journey; usually, if the destination is an appealing one, a few Boeing executives manage to get aboard to go shopping, but if the plane is off to Lagos or Riyadh, it goes all but empty. The plane I was travelling on was bound for Hong Kong.

In a small room off the main factory floor, pert waitresses serve canapés, hand round souvenir stickers and funny hats – this is the kind of party Americans do well, geared to keeping everyone happy while the final technical problems are sorted out. Over at the plane an engineer is working on the video system which has developed a flutter; someone has discovered that the fire-warning system is behaving erratically; a fuel bleed line has become blocked with metal shavings.

At last the shuttle buses arrive, and the forty who are off across the Pacific are taken out to clamber aboard the plane – gleaming in the early morning light. The pilot gives a thumbs-up; instrument lights glow green; the Boeing field's brilliant yellow fire-engines sidle away, and a small group of the men who helped build the plane stand to one side and watch, some with a small sorrow and some with evident pride, as another of their great masterpieces begins to edge away from the factory door and out on to the runway. A few moments later and the hundreds of tons of glittering new steel roar past them, and they wave and cheer as another "Boeing Big Top" lifts its nose, floats up into the air and heads off west, out to the coast.

At this point a Boeing captain is at the controls. He is there for one very simple reason: in law the plane belongs to Boeing, and its ownership will not change until one small detail has been definitively settled, to everyone's satisfaction.

The money.

There is not, quite frankly, a great deal to recommend the spot which is fixed on the globe at longitude 129° West of Greenwich and latitude 50° North of the Line. For the average man in the street, it is manifestly not a place at which to linger, either by accident or design. This unique (and, as it turns out, uniquely important) dot on the globe is in the middle of the sea – a foggy and stormy part of the north-east Pacific, some few score miles off the coast of Canada and 200 miles away from the frontier of the United States.

Two hundred miles *exactly*. This last figure is most important – the distance being the single aspect of the great mass of sea beneath 50°N latitude and 129°W longitude that gives it a very particular significance far beyond its ability to give pleasure or challenge to dolphin, albatross, or eel. For reasons that are a complex mixture of geographical accident, national politics and economic necessity, this point happened to have been chosen (during the years before I first visited Everett) as the site for the consummation of a particular type of business deal worth thousands of millions of American dollars every year.

The point at which these deals are fixed is not upon the face of the sea, but seven miles above it – precisely above these maritime coordinates. At this point sits a great, invisible sale-yard where Boeing sells – or sold, for the practice is now being changed to a duller, more businesslike and wholly unromantic means of transfer – many of its jumbo jets to the world. It was the spot in the sky where you handed over your cash and in return were given a triple set of keys to your brand-new plane.

There was a very sound economic reason why many new aeroplanes were sold this way – on the wing, as it were, rather than on the ground. The customer has so far paid about 30 per cent – a quarter down, with progress payments made during the years the craft has taken to assemble. Give or take the odd hundred thousand, there is around $89,675,000 left to pay. Boeing wants that money before it will part with the plane, but the customer wants to hand over only at the very last moment, interest rates on that kind of cash costing something in the region of thirty dollars a minute. And so the plane hurries out across the sea to the sales point, the navigator calling out the coordinates from his inertial navigation system screen.

"Steady on 50 North," he calls. "One twenty-eight, thirty, West." Then it is 129° West, then 129° 20' – precisely where he wants to be. He cries: "On coordinates. Two hundred miles out. Steady as we go!" And suddenly everyone gets very interested.

A complicated high-frequency radio circuit is opened: from the plane to the Boeing Company, from the plane to the customer's lawyers in Washington, to the customer's bankers in New York and, crucially, to the Boeing lawyers. A series of code numbers is read out – the customer's instructions to pay over the $89 million. The lawyers evidently agree, they instruct the bank accordingly and the bankers in New York, 3,000 miles back east, hand over the cheque (all transactions have to be done in mid-morning, Seattle time, before the Manhattan banks, three hours ahead, close shop for the day).

The Boeing lawyers call to verify the account details, that the money is there, the cheque won't bounce. The money is transferred. The lawyers issue a coded signal to Boeing, then Boeing sends up its final instruction: "Okay, Captain. We no longer own the plane. Hand over the controls, please. The deal is complete."

The Boeing captain then removes his silk gloves and steps out from the right-hand seat, out of the cockpit and into the cabin. The customer's pilot, who has been waiting anxiously for this moment, walks past him into his new cockpit, pushes back the seat and eases himself into it. The new leather squeaks. He takes hold of the controls, presses his feet against the elevator pedals and their unworn rubber pads, then utters some protocols down the microphone to the San Francisco Air Traffic Control and on to Hawaii Oceanic Control, about his intended route across the Pacific.

Finally he fiddles with some buttons, and the angle of the sun changes as the huge aircraft turns its nose off to the left.

The plane now belongs to the customer, and the directors back in the cabin open the first of their many bottles of Krug. They've spent nearly $90 million and, so far as one can see, they didn't feel a thing. Yet why was all this done over a crackling radio circuit, out at sea, out at longitude 129°W, latitude 50°N? Why not in an office, as one would imagine? Because, as one of the customer's directors explained with a grin, beyond the 200-mile limit no American tax – state, federal or municipal – can be levied on any commercial transactions. Washington State, in its wisdom, would have demanded 5 per cent sales tax on the purchase price of the plane if the deal had taken place inside the limit.

So the buyers, with Boeing's help, flew to a point just outside it, thereby conspiring to save themselves rather more than $4 million for a mere morning's work. More bottles of Krug are immediately opened as this happy realization begins to sink in, and many more will be opened as the plane rumbles smoothly across the limitless Pacific, towards its new home base and the beginning of its thousands of hours and uncountable route miles of life as a long-haul jet.

This delivery flight took place in May. It had been a cold and rainy morning in Everett when I left, and when I stepped on to the ramp at Kai Tak airport in Hong Kong thirteen hours or so later, it was humid and about 80°. Such observations are of less relevance or interest to a pilot than to his passengers: what counts to him is the weather along the route, up high. On this occasion the high-level weather had been mercifully placid and the captain had experienced no particular difficulty. Had the journey taken place in November, however, and had the plane been laden with 400 passengers, and not a mere 40 baggage-less wanderers like myself, the story would have been very different.

The westerly winds that blow at high altitudes in winter across the Pacific often do so with velocities of 200 knots or more – head winds that can slow the jumbo down to two-thirds of its normal cruising speed. A thirteen-hour trans-Pacific flight would thus turn into a fourteen- or fifteen-hour flight – far longer than the crew could work efficiently or, more importantly, than the 54,000-gallon fuel tanks could keep the plane aloft. The stark truth behind these figures is that while the 747-300, the Big Top jet aboard which I made that first flight, is an admirable plane for long-haul journeys, there is one part of the world it cannot guarantee to be able to cross without stopping – the Pacific Ocean. Only by dint of crossing at the narrowest point – Vancouver to Tokyo, say, or Seattle to Hong Kong – could the customers be offered a fair prospect of the plane getting over in one leap on most of the days it was scheduled to fly. Because the Pacific is so vast and the planes so relatively lacking in stamina, most of the other trans-Pacific routes are possible only at certain seasons of the year, or with only a limited number of passengers in the cabin. This was a harsh fact of life that airline planners and their paying passengers had to accept. If you wanted to cross from Los Angeles to Tokyo in December or February, you had a more difficult time of it than you would in May or July; flights operated with fewer seats available, or else there was a distinct possibility that the plane would be "diverted for reasons beyond our control", would "for operational reasons" have to make an additional unscheduled stop, or due to some other inexplicable but plausible cause be late arriving at its destination.

But then came the mid-1980s, and suddenly everyone wanted to cross the Pacific – and they wanted to cross it without stopping, whenever they wanted. They announced their loathing for airports like Anchorage, Honolulu and Nadi, where they were forced to halt their progress for refuelling and to wander, zombie-like, among the tat of the duty-free shops. They had booked their tickets for Tokyo, they said, so they wanted to go to Tokyo and to nowhere else. And come the mid-1980s the airlines started to listen to them.

This was the moment when the Pacific, in its conceptual sense, began to take off – the time when the Pacific economic boom had become a popularly established reality* and everyone – from Mr Reagan in his famous speech in Dublin to Mr Gorbachev in his equally famous address in Vladivostok – was urging the world to change its perspective view of itself. Aviation reflected the shift: this, as I have already noted, was also the time when most of the world's wide-bodied jets could fairly be said to have been aloft over the Pacific and not, as previously, over the Atlantic Ocean. (The date, some time in May 1984, is a matter of conjecture.) The only problem

*Though it was a decade earlier when the Pacific actually overtook the Atlantic in terms of the value of goods and services it produced, and traded.

was that most of these planes above the Pacific were forced to put down inside its boundaries, thus denying the passengers the benefits of uninterrupted progress Atlantic travellers had enjoyed ever since Shannon and Gander vanished from their travellers' lexicon. Something had to be done. A new aircraft needed to be built – in short, an aircraft for the Pacific.

Boeing was the obvious candidate to construct it, having so dominant a position among the builders of big aeroplanes. But Pan Am, which had provided the initial impetus for the 747 programme twenty years before, was by now a sadly arthritic airline and no longer a serious player in the Pacific theatre. (In 1985 it decided to withdraw totally from the Pacific and hand over all its routes to United Airlines.) In its place as the "seed customer" for the new plane was North-west Orient Airlines, based in the improbable and manifestly non-Pacific city of Minneapolis, Minnesota.

But being based among the wheat and the wild rice of the American heartland had long stimulated North-west's appetite for the far away. Spurred, no doubt, by lucrative contracts with the American military for transporting troops to and from the big bases in Korea, and by the holidaymaking needs of those in the Mid-West who wanted to escape from the cold to the coral reefs and beaches of the blue Pacific, the airline had long developed an intimate relationship with Asia. It flew in the north-west – to Seattle and Portland, Denver and Cheyenne; it flew in the Orient – to Seoul and Tokyo, Guam and Hong Kong. And crucially, as with most serious American carriers, it flew to New York City. By the mid-1980s the airline knew it wanted a plane that could fly non-stop between Kennedy and Narita airports, one of the most costly and prestigious routes, every day of the year.

When Mr Dean Thornton, President of Boeing Commercial Airplanes, sent a letter dated 28 February 1985 to a young man named Steven Rothmeier, recently appointed chairman of North-west, asking if he would like to be the launch customer for what Boeing was calling its "block change aircraft", North-west jumped at the chance. It could help design the aircraft, it could play a major role in determining its price, and it would receive huge publicity for being the first customer for a new generation of planes. Rothmeier, whose reputation for frugality is matched only by his keenness for secrecy, embarked on a bruising seven months of talks with Boeing about everything from the configuration of the cockpit to the costs of the

333

tyres. In September 1985 he placed an order for ten of the new planes, at a cost of $125 million each. Boeing began to build the new aircraft under the designation 747-400 – "the premier airliner", as Rothmeier was later to say, "for serving the trans-Pacific markets beyond the turn of the century . . ."

Outwardly the plane appears little different from the 747-300. Its fuselage is exactly the same size: 232 feet long, 63 feet from floor to top of tail, 32 feet from floor to top of the "bulge", while the bulge itself has the extra 18 feet sandwiched into it that distinguishes this generation of aircraft from the antediluvian jumbos, the -200s and the almost obsolete -100s. There is one very visible difference, however, in that the wings – themselves 6 feet longer than before – have apparently small (though actually man-sized) upwardly-angled tips, made of carbon fibre (the same Hyfil-like material that was very nearly the undoing of Rolls-Royce when the firm made fan-blades from it). The purpose of these "winglets", which give an oddly unfinished look to the plane, is to retain as much air as possible on top of the wing as it speeds across it in flight – it prevents the air from spilling off the end of the wing and scattering itself uselessly in the winds, and helps keep the machine in the air more efficiently.

There are two other significant and obvious changes. A new fuel tank bedded deep inside the tail assembly contains 3,300 extra gallons of aviation fuel (the normal payload is 53,985 gallons), and allows the plane to range 400 miles extra; and a new and totally electronic cockpit has everything that once was displayed on dials now shown on colour television screens. There is now no further use for a flight engineer, so the new 747-400 can be flown with just two officers in the front seats and no one else to keep watch on what they are doing.

The instrument panel – so simple, and so similar in appearance to a TV control room or the kind of background you glimpse behind a newsreader on one of the more unashamedly high-technology American networks – is known as "the glass cockpit", because it has so much. By contrast, an older cockpit looked more like the nerve centre of a water pumping station, with dials, levers and switches made of iron and bakelite. The existing cockpit has 42 dials immediately in front of the pilot's eyes, and uncountable dozens in the ceiling, beside his leg, behind his ears. The new glass cockpit has but six colour screens and six dials. Any information wanted by anyone on board – the temperature of the cabin around Row 58, the distance from the plane to the island of Guam or the number of gallons of fuel remaining in the port wing – can be flashed up on the screen in beguiling, cheerful full colour, and at the touch of a button.

Most of this can be dismissed as cosmetic; the extra fuel tank will provide a little more range, the more efficient wing surface will give a little more efficiency. What counts in the new aircraft, as in all its predecessors, is not so much the design of the airframe itself as that of the engine. And it has been in the technology of engine-making that the real recent breakthroughs have been made – breakthroughs which have enabled the gigantic distances of the Pacific to be spanned, as the world's economies have now dictated that they should.

However, the engine which has perhaps caused most interest among aviators is not an engine made on the Pacific, like the plane; nor is it made in the United States, though the engines constructed for the North-west Orient order were. The new engine, which was first placed on the 747-400s designated VR-HOO and VR-HOP and owned by Cathay Pacific Airways, of Hong Kong – perhaps the quintessentially Pacific airline – was made in Derby in England, in a plant just off the city ring road, by Rolls-Royce.

When the Cathay aircraft took off with four such engines bolted to her wings on 9 June 1989, the journey it completed twelve hours and fifty minutes later was the first trans-Pacific journey ever made by such machines. For Rolls-Royce, the flight was of enormous symbolic importance – and there was plenty of nail-biting as FAA inspectors demanded more and more signatures on more and more complicated paperwork before they would let such a combination of new plane and new engine make its debut in the skies.

As it happens the flight was completed without incident, the arrival in Hong Kong perfectly timed, the speed, range and fuel consumption exactly as predicted. Some of the forty-odd passengers aboard remarked on the apparent power of the engine – the plane seemed to tear itself away from earth in a vast hurry, someone said – and on the actual size of the engines, far larger than the Pratt & Whitneys and General Electrics mounted on other jumbos. But as is usually the fate of today's aircraft engines, most passengers barely even noticed their existence, taking them wholly for granted.

The parentage of the new engine lies with the egregious RB-211; the engine that, with its carbon-fibre blades and huge expectations, contributed to the near-collapse of Rolls-Royce eighteen years ago.

335

But the new technology which has enabled the engine to survive, then to be improved, advanced and upgraded to the point where it is now (as one aviation journal termed it) "the most exciting engine in the world", relates to twenty years of work on one crucial item, in particular, and the application in autumn 1988 of nearly half the total computing power of the British Isles to iron out a last-minute technical problem relating to its design.

This crucial item, the part of the modern RB-211 engine which has turned it into the key to tomorrow's Pacific travel, is the fan at the front – the only moving part of the engine visible to most passengers while they are being shepherded to the doorways. At first it appears no different from the fans at the front of any other engine – just the whirling spiral "eye", painted on and designed to help frighten birds away, and a number of blades, invariably seen turning slowly in the breeze – so perfectly balanced and frictionless in its bearings – while the plane waits to "spool up" for the take-off roll, or running down after a completed voyage.

A closer look into the mouth of the new Rolls-Royce engine – and the "Pacific" engine is formally known as the RB-211-524G – will show that there are rather fewer blades than in normal engines, and that each one is rather larger than usual. This simple difference is in fact the key difference – the fan-blades are nearly half as wide again as conventional fans and are known, in a throwback to language of an earlier era, as wide chord blades. (The word – signifying a line used to connect two points on a curve – was once, coincidentally, used in the charmingly pedantic language of another transport system, that of the Indian railways: "trains for Delhi to Calcutta," read the advertisements, "via the Grand Chord.")

The need for such fan-blades was obvious twenty years ago, when bypass engines were first brought into service. The usual, narrow blades of the fan were knitted together by struts known as snubbers – they had to be, otherwise vibration in the blades would have increased to the point where it destroyed the whole engine. But the snubbers complicated the air-flow through the blades, setting up strange vortices of air, tiny whirlpools that frustrated the engine's ability to compress it sufficiently to make the optimum jet-blast. To make blades so wide and strong as to allow the elimination of the snubbers was the engine-makers' dream. Rolls-Royce set its design team to work in 1969, when trans-Pacific non-stop flight was no more than a vague dream: it took until 1984 for the first such blades

336

to be placed in a working engine, and it was not until the summer of 1989 that the first engine with these blades made its Pacific debut.

Each blade is hollow – solid blades would have been prohibitively heavy. The design team, led by a figure who has become a living legend in the world of bypass jets, a tall and bespectacled enthusiast called Michael Howse, came up with a blade constructed from two sheets of pure titanium bonded to an inner shell made of pure titanium honeycomb – a manufacturers' nightmare, a thing of questionable strength that might deform in strange ways under extremes of temperature and pressure. Mathematical models of majestic complexity were built, hundreds of thousands of different sets of conditions were posited, slight modifications were made until, finally, the results suggested the blade would be strong and resistant and would thrust air smoothly down into the ever-hungry turbines.

Models were made, tests were applied. A gun was built that would fire defrosted 24-oz chickens at the blades in under a second – a simulation of a bird strike, a test which had been inaugurated with the original RB211 and had gone so badly wrong. But this time "the fan just ate the birds", as an article in *Flight International* reported drily. (Not so in a similar test performed by another engine maker in America, however: someone forgot to defrost the chickens, which promptly tore through the engine like bullets and destroyed it.) In another test an explosive device was rigged up that would tear off one of the blades while the engine was revolving at its maximum speed: the engine casing absorbed the energy of the resulting disaster (equivalent to a family car crashing into the engine at 30 mph) so well that parts of the rear of the engine were reusable afterwards. The front, though, was spectacularly wrecked.

In late 1988, just a few weeks away from delivery of the first four engines to the new Cathay aircraft then being built at Everett, what seemed a small crisis developed. Minute stresses noticed at the base of each of the turbine blades began to look, in mathematical terms, quite villainous: computer models predicted they might worsen and severely reduce the life of each engine (which cost about $7.5 million). So Michael Howse, *in loco parentis* to the new engine, ordered computer tests run to suggest improvements.

One of those tasks required the use of a supercomputer. Rolls-Royce needed to look at simulations, microsecond by microsecond,

337

of the precise conditions of the blades and the air in three dimensions, at a bewildering range of different temperatures and pressures. The firm has an arrangement with the Cray supercomputer at the Meteorological Office in Bracknell, Berkshire – a computer huge enough to deal with all the scores of thousands of minutely changing variables, changing in three dimensions, of a vast weather system.* When Bracknell is not busy, the firm can have access to the time on the machine. There was a period in September and October 1988 when Rolls-Royce were using the Bracknell Cray and every other piece of parallel processing equipment available – about half the total computing power in Britain was being wielded to solve the problem. It was solved – but how, and what was done to rectify it, is something the company is not willing to discuss.

The new Rolls-Royce engine now seems, after years of uncertainty, to have a definite cost advantage over both of its American competitors. The development of the wide-chord fan in Derby is said to be one of the most remarkable advances in aerodynamics engineering in years, and an increasing number of airlines are breaking the habits of years, and placing enormous faith in it. All the new British Airways jumbos are to be equipped with the engine, also those of Qantas, South African Airways and Air New Zealand. Cathay Pacific won the race to be the first to cross the Ocean with it in June 1989; then in August Qantas, with great flair, showed off the capabilities of the engines by flying their new -400 from London to Sydney non-stop – a distance of 11,156 miles which the plane managed in 20 hours 8 minutes. (It was one of the ugly, long-range Boeing 747-SPs that held the previous range record of 10,281 miles, when a South African Airways delivery flight in 1976 flew direct from Everett to Capetown.) But like the Qantas flight thirteen years later, the vast stride was accomplished because the plane had hardly

---

*Supercomputers are awesome Leviathans indeed, but not as mystical as their name suggests. They differ from so-called "mainframe" computers in their ability to conduct processing of information "in parallel", thus being able to deal with highly complex systems that undergo many changes simultaneously. It is erroneous to suppose that supercomputers will necessarily be of much value in discovering the Holy Grail of the technology, artificial intelligence. Only fundamental changes in computer architecture will enable machines to make rational decisions, and no existing or hypothetical supercomputer can do anything approaching that. But certainly the machine that is ultimately invented will be termed a "supercomputer", *post hoc, ergo propter hoc.*

any load – no passengers and no cargo. The realistic range figure offered for the 747-400 today – 7,370 miles – supposes the craft to be fully loaded with 412 passengers, with all their baggage and five pallets of cargo. Thus laden, the plane could make it from Sydney to Los Angeles without stopping, or from Hong Kong to Toronto, or Tokyo to New York – precisely the kinds of routes demanded by today's Pacific-minded business travellers. But these are routes only made possible by the development of engines with technology as innovative as that contained in the Rolls-Royce wide-chord fan.

Like the original jumbo of two decades before, the new plane was something of a victim of its own success. Orders flooded in – more than 200 had been ordered by 1989, and Boeing was being asked to make five of the aircraft each month – as well as the existing -300s and the less familiar varieties of freighters and combination freighter-passenger planes that other airlines demanded. There were problems with the Federal Aviation Administration, which was determined not to rush through the complicated process of certifying a new plane, despite Boeing's urgent need to get its aircraft flying on time. Other national certification bodies seemed to drag their feet, too: the Dutch Civil Aviation Authority held up the authorization of new jets for KLM, saying it wanted the hydraulic and electrical wires passing through the plane to be separated, for safety's sake, by a few more centimetres than the Everett designers had planned. And the crash of a Boeing jet in England in late 1988 led to fears – later proved to be groundless – that some Boeing products were not as rigorously checked for quality and safety as had once been the case. All these factors conspired to slow the production lines: the company had to hire hundreds of new engineers* to keep the planes emerging from the sliding doors and on to the apron at Paine Field at the proper rate. Even so, in late 1988 it had to announce "limited delivery dates" of the new aircraft, and airlines across the world which had already planned schedules around the new giant cursed under their breaths.

I flew home to Hong Kong on the first of the Cathay Pacific aircraft to be equipped with the new Rolls-Royce engines. Paddy

*The majority of the engineers came from the Lockheed C-5A production line, which was being shut down. There is a peculiar irony in that it was the award of the C-5A project to Lockheed in 1965 – and its loss by Boeing – that prompted Boeing to begin work on the 747 programme in the first place.

Anderson, a taciturn Ulsterman who brings most of the new planes home for the airline, had spent weeks on the new Rediffusion simulator at Kai Tak airport learning how to fly an aircraft with so unconventional a cockpit, so simple a set of controls. There was a real fear, one of his colleagues remarked, that life on the flight deck – already about as boring as any professional life could be – would now become anaesthetizingly so, and that the best-paid blue-collar job in the world would become as tedious as packing biscuits – yet with the most massive of responsibilities riding in the seats behind and sleeping in the cities below.

On this particular flight – delayed for two days by the zealousness of FAA officials – there was little time for anyone to be bored. Dozens of technicians swarmed in and out of the cockpit, monitoring the fuel flow (the plane consumed 9.3 tonnes of the stuff in climbing out of Paine Field to its cruising altitude of 35,000 feet), the aircraft trim, the engine temperatures, and the performance of the radios, radars and inertial navigation computers. There were experts in a wholly new art called HERF–damping – men who could install suppressors to prevent damage to the plane's electronics which might happen when it flew through the cone of high-energy radio waves produced by big short-wave transmitters, like those owned by the BBC or Voice of America. There was a specialist on how planes fared when they flew into thunderstorms, and how lightning strikes might affect the cockpit electronics. There were even two stewardesses modelling a new uniform, unhappy because it seemed to make everyone who looked at it go cross-eyed.

Two soberly-suited men rode across the Ocean purely to check on what they said were "spurious radio emanations" which had been detected coming from Taiwanese position beacons – signals that, considering the turmoil in China (this was but a few days after the events in Tiananmen Square) might well have had something to do with Taiwanese adventurism. The men would not say for whom they worked; there never was a hint of adventurism from Taiwan, and the signals were not detected again.

It was an otherwise unremarkable flight. VR-HOP reached her cruising altitude over Vancouver then headed north by east, along the Canadian and Alaskan coasts, following the Great Circle home. She passed overhead Port Hardy, at the northern tip of Vancouver Island; she passed over Kodiak (the seemingly Russian name is actually a Russian corruption of the Eskimo word for island); then left the American mainland for the first time in her career at Cape Newenham, above an American Air Force radar station that protects this remote outer perimeter of the United States.

She remained under Anchorage Oceanic Control as she sped westwards until, just over four hours out of Everett, she crossed the Greenwich anti-meridian, left west longitudes behind and began her long trek through the east longitudes. She passed over the Date Line, and Friday afternoon became Saturday afternoon; then over the mid-ocean reporting points of Nukks and Neeva, where she spotted two other eastbound jumbos below and beside her – for now she was on North Pacific Track Romeo 220, one of the most heavily used jetways on the planet – before being handed over by Anchorage ("Good day to you, Cathay, Anchorage out") to Tokyo ("Cathay Pacific Flight 2722, this is Tokyo Oceanic, how do you read me?").

After which it was downhill all the way – overhead Ninno, Nippi, Nytim, Nokka and Noho, landfall in Japan at a site known to airline pilots (but not to Japanese) as Inkfish, thence on to the town of Sendai (best known for its factory making wooden dolls), Niigata (rice), Nagoya (relics of the Tokugawa shoguns, as well as massive industry) and Kagoshima, where men and women pay small fortunes to be buried up to their necks in hot sand, or to loll in milky water made fragrant with floating oranges.

We passed over Naha, the capital of Okinawa, mentioning the fact of our passage to the ever-anxious American air traffic controllers below at the Kadena air base. We were handed on to the Mandarin-speaking controllers at Taipei Control, then passed swiftly over the Republic of China before reaching a waypoint called Magog – though not here the Satanic force at Armageddon, but the mythical Anglo-Saxon giant, a waypoint named to take account of our entering British colonial air space. We were now at the TOD – the "Top of the Drop", the moment when the captain spooled back the hard-working RB211-524Gs and our ever-lightening tube of aluminium and titanium began its slow descent into Hong Kong.

The familiar accents of the Cantonese controllers – "Welcome, Cathay 2722. Welcome home" – filled the earphones. It was now late evening, Saturday, and down below were the firefly lights of the fishing boats on their way home to Aberdeen. Some big container ships were churning towards Waglan Island light, the outer marker of the colony, the light at the end of the empire.

We overflew them all, spiralling lower and lower. Islands came into view – the Ninepins, Sung Kong, Po Toi (with its charming little Hakka cafés we would visit on junk trips), Lamma. Over Cheung Chau, the little dumb-bell-shaped island halfway between Lamma and Lantau, the biggest of all Hong Kong's many islands, we turned – a full 90° to the right, then 90° again – spotting the flashing light below Victoria Peak to our right, the only flashing coloured light in the territory.*

Then we were on track for Kai Tak, and the single runway that juts out bravely into the eastern harbour. A line of brilliant white strobe lights led us in over Stonecutter's Island, over Sham Shui Po and Mong Kok, where lives the highest concentration of mankind on earth. There was Kowloon Tong and there, right ahead, illuminated by blazing lights, the huge red-and-white checkerboard painted onto a hillside. Paddy Anderson waited until the checkers filled his wind-screen, then threw the plane to the right, a sudden 47° turn that, if poorly executed, leads us straight down on to the runway.

Huge skyscrapers and tenement blocks reared up to meet us. Canyons full of neon flared briefly below, one after another, as we passed low above the teeming streets of Kowloon. As always, I could see hundreds of television sets glinting their blue lights into hundreds of living rooms: I could see the same figures on each screen, a series of time-lapse photographs of some unknown drama being watched by people who were being watched from above by the cavalcade of aerial passers-by. The buildings flashed past nearer and nearer, faster and faster and faster until it was certain we were going to hit and then . . . suddenly the pillars of vertical concrete made way for a vast open space, and there below was a triple security fence, and just behind a huge advertisement for cigarettes painted on to a buttress, and dozens of silvery aircraft were parked on a brilliantly lit apron, and the lights of Hong Kong itself glittered on the distant skyline as we eased ourselves down and down until our wheels touched on Runway 13, Kai Tak, in the British Crown Colony, home at last.

It was 90 degrees outside, a laconic voice intoned, and the humidity was close to 100 per cent. Seattle, and Everett, and the pleasingly cool winds of Snohomish County, seemed suddenly a very long way away.

*The reason Hong Kong's abundance of neon manages to be both bright and dull is that none is permitted to flash or flicker, since to do so might confuse the pilots of planes arriving or leaving from the city-centre airport.

3

The Mac

Students of natural science who are offered an insight into the arcane mysteries of *cloning* – the art of mixing reproduction with mass-production, of marrying the techniques of the Kama Sutra and Henry Ford, so as to make immense numbers of genetically identical versions of the same living thing – are invariably given one example, a classic of its kind.

In many orchards around the world there exists a variety of apple tree known as the MacIntosh. It is a sturdy tree, the fruit is crisp and sweet, and is much liked by all who eat it. Yet it is not the happy consequence of a natural event, no gift from the Garden of Eden. It came about because a mutant tree was created by a long-forgotten horticulturist, and in a blatantly non-sexual manner. There was no fertilization of flowers, no need for bees or birds, nor winds or water, nor pistils or stamens; the horticulturist mated the plants by his own fiendish devices, and every MacIntosh apple tree that stands today is the result. Each one, moreover, is identical to the next; each looks and tastes just as every other. In short, each tree is a perfect genetic replication of its brother and sister tree, and of its parents, grandparents and the members of every generation before it, until its origin with the strange mutant production of that long-forgotten botanical genius. Each tree, in other words, is a clone.

This trivial morsel of information has more relevance than might be outwardly apparent to the world of personal computers. It also has some connection with the Pacific Ocean. And it has, though probably accidentally, a certain irony to it. But there is need for some background explanation.

343

The personal computing world, now firmly established in our midst, worships before the altars of two religions. The one, by far the larger, is dominated by the products of the International Business Machines Corporation, of Armonk, New York. IBM – Big Blue, as it is widely known – has been making personal computers since 1981, when it introduced a model known (somewhat unoriginally) as the PC. All IBM personal computers run on the basis of a set of internal instructions known by the initials MS-DOS, which stands for the maker, the MicroSoft Corporation (whose founder, Bill Gates, was to become the computer industry's first billionaire), and the software itself, the Disk Operating System.

As Mr Gates knows to his profit, MS-DOS has become the most successful small computer operating system of all time. It is not particularly easy to use: it makes a lot of demands on the user, who has to file away in his head all sorts of instructions and buzz-words in order to be able to make his computer work. But it had the distinct advantage of being the first operating system to be used for personal computers (nearly all those invented before IBM came along used it too) and, once it had been taken on board by IBM, to have become the virtual standard tool of the small computer industry. The original and the largest: were one to stick to the religious metaphor it would be the Catholic, the universal church, orthodox, ubiquitous and surviving both before and after the Great Schism.

Use of MS-DOS has since spread to a hundred and one other small computer makers. Compaq, Toshiba, Sharp, Grid, Leading Edge, Apricot, Tandy – all of these and nearly every other name, recognizable and unfamiliar, use MS-DOS. You switch on a Sharp portable in your hotel room, an IBM in your office or a Tandy 100 on your lap in the darkened hush of an aircraft, and after some clanking and whirring the same introductory message will come glowing on to your screen: the letter C, followed by the mathematical sign indicating greater than, >. The so-called "Command-line" or "C-prompt".

After you see that, where you next go with your computer – depending on the programs you have loaded into its memory – is up to you. If you want to remind yourself what you have, you type the letters "DIR" and a DIRectory of all your files scrolls up the screen. If you want to write a business letter, or some more pages of the book on which you are working, then you can type the letters "WS" and, if you have it, WordStar, one of the better-known word processing programs, suddenly becomes available to you. And so on.

The same prompt, the same command letters, the same use of keys on the keyboard to move the blinking cursor up and down the lines, or to the left or right – everything is similar for every kind of machine that uses the system. In shorthand one might well be tempted to call it the "IBM" system, although Mr Gates, whose company claims to be staunchly independent of the firms it supplies, would bridle at such a description. But so apparently derivative of the IBM system do all the machines that employ MS-DOS appear to be that they are lumped, generically, under the heading "IBM-compatible", or "PC-compatible". You decide you need a new computer, you telephone your supplier, and the first question is invariably: "You want IBM-compatible?"

These derivative machines are known also – and here is the first link with the world of fruit and orchards, as mentioned earlier – as IBM *clones*. They are genetically identical, perfect replicas of each other in those parts that matter. Though they may look a little different from the outside, and be offered at prices ranging across a wide spectrum, they are, in essence, the same.

Which sameness has its advantages. A Japanese portable machine that is "IBM-compatible" will contentedly allow itself to be linked to a real IBM deskbound model so that, for example, files can be transferred from one to the other. A Korean IBM-compatible computer can be connected to an American-made IBM-compatible printer, and it will gaily print such documents as it is commanded to do as though the two devices were made for one another. The IBM system, or to be more accurate the MS-DOS software, is in short popular, almost universally available, relatively inexpensive, efficient and fast.

It is also, to those who belong to what one might call the Protestant computer ethic, a system that is primitive, inelegant, cumbersome and tricky to learn. To make it work properly you need a lengthy and, to most people, quite incomprehensible manual by your side. (An example of the kind of instruction you need to know, picked at random from the MS-DOS manual, says: "Type:EDLIN USER JSM REPORT.MAY to create a file called REPORT.MAY in the USER \JSM subdirectory," which gives a fair flavour of the thing.) It is also wholly unsuitable for those millions of men and women whose first language relies – as do those of China and Taiwan, much of Japan and Korea and Singapore – on the use of ideographs rather than letters.

The second grand computing religion, the Protestant among operating systems, came about as a direct consequence of what can be called the Great Schism of 1983. It is a system whose inventors had sought a true reformation of the way that computers behave internally, and the way people can be taught to use them. Known quite simply as *the Apple Macintosh system*, it is radically different in every possible way from the MS-DOS approach to computing. In the view of enthusiasts whose eagerness for its grand simplicity and style verges on the evangelical – just as did the early acolytes of the Reformation – it offers a measure of access to the power of computing which is truly worldwide.

For the narrowly-defined purposes of this account the Apple Macintosh also appears to its apologists peculiarly suited to the unusual needs of those countries bordering the Pacific Ocean. Many nations use pictograms for their written language: nearly all these countries border the Pacific. For them, and for all those languages using unusual phonetic alphabets – including the Korean *hangul* script, and the Japanese *katakana* and *hiragana* – the Macintosh system is said by its boosters to be ideal. (The fact that Apple is a West Coast and thus a Pacific organization, while IBM in New York has its feet set firmly on the Atlantic shore, does not offer an entirely sustainable supporting argument. The MicroSoft Corporation, the author of MS-DOS, is itself based in California too.)

But the name Macintosh: did it spring from the fertile mind of Jeff Raskin, the Apple Computer programmer who was the first manager of the project, and who knew about the famous and well-liked variety of the fruit? Apple Computer in California says it has no idea. The name just "seemed kinda nice", its staff are wont to say over their arugula-and-balsamic-vinegar salads and their glasses of Simi Valley Chardonnay in the bars of Cupertino. But if the horticulturally-inclined programmer did so name it, then he christened it in suitably – though perhaps inadvertently – paradoxical style.

For while the *Macintosh apple* is a type example of a clone, the *Apple Macintosh* is utterly and completely the reverse. It is the one computer that cannot (despite the best efforts, it is reported, of gangs of Taiwanese fakers and forgers) *be* cloned. Its innards, the details of its uniquely complicated operating system, are held tight to the breasts of all but the most disloyal of Apple's employees.* The source code in which it is wrapped and written is protected from forbidden scrutiny by the most Byzantine arrays of security and secrecy. The IBM system is quite the opposite: it is widely available, well understood, inexpensive and saleable and can be cloned. Cheap and ubiquitous as they are, these IBM clones have come to be regarded, and indeed regard themselves, as the principal commercial enemies of Apple Macintosh and all for which it and its supporters stand. The Macintosh of the computer world stands alone, in stark contrast to its fruiting namesake, as the very opposite of what a clone is all about.

Steve Jobs – a curious, difficult, driven man, a combination of Howard Hughes and Walt Disney, part megalomaniac, part visionary, part populist – nurtured a passionate belief that the microchip was an invention that could trigger a true revolution in the personal lives of the world's entire population – with time and patience and creative thought, it could be taught to accomplish almost every task that man might set it. And so a computer must be built, he said, that people would truly love – a computer that could and would change the whole way people felt about computers, and would persuade them of his own unshakeable faith that computers could bring happiness and freedom to millions. The image of a cold, lifeless, inexpressibly stupid but awesomely powerful device doing little actual good for those who bought it, other than to offer a few days or weeks of the illusion of being at the leading edge of technology, learning and intellectual life – this image, Jobs decreed, must change. If it did not, then the computer would fade from public view, and the real benefits that ordinary people could enjoy from the proper application of computing power would be lost, perhaps for another generation or more. Indeed it was beginning to show: in the early 1980s there were signs that the computer craze was dying away, shops were closing down, firms were going out of business (Apple Computer itself was to run into monumental difficulties); the whole love affair with personal electronics had the look of a nine-day wonder.

*A problem developed in 1989 when some lines of the source code were leaked to a magazine by a disgruntled Apple worker. The company took a very dim view, and threatened all manner of sanctions. But in a very American way the stricter rules that were subsequently imposed on the employees were advertised rather flippantly. "I know a lot," proclaimed a button that workers were urged to wear pinned to their chests, "but I'm not telling."

Why (people were starting to ask) import such complicated, costly, mysterious and really rather intimidating arrays of silicon, solder, copper, ceramic and plastic into the *home*? Of course, though perhaps rather unfortunately, there was a real need for computers, progress being what it was; but they should be kept penned up, out of sight in air-conditioned, neon-lit rooms deep in the basement of vast corporate headquarters where, watched over by white-coated troglodytes and attended to by myopic and halitotic *idiots savants* they could perform the duties of booking us on aeroplanes, sending us our Social Security payments or analysing the complexities of the atom without our ever knowing exactly how or what they did. After all, you didn't generate your own electricity at home, or keep a milch-cow in the garden or a file of every copy of the *New York Times* in the basement. Other people did that for you; by the same token other people could keep the computers, and perform such miracles of arithmetic, Boolean algebra and algorithm creation as were essential to society's survival, out of sight and out of mind.

Mr Jobs and a few like-minded men and women living in California in the early Eighties decided that such thinking must be reversed. The computers which then existed – those made both by their own firm and by their competitors – were simply, they thought, not good enough, not so accessible and unintimidating as to prompt the kind of revolution in thinking that was wanted. In one of the many memorable phrases that one of their number was later to utter, they wanted the personal computer to offer "wings for the mind". So a new machine, something very different indeed, had to be created.

That machine, the Macintosh computer, was formally unveiled on 24 January 1984. Five years in the making, it was unlike almost anything that had gone before, except for its two intellectually distinguished but commercially disastrous antecedents, both of them now half forgotten. One of these was named the Apple LISA, the earlier one was named the Xerox Star. And it had many, many human creators. No one person would be so high-handed as to lay claim to having "invented" the Macintosh. But in the same way that Joe Sutter at Boeing will probably – and to his peers, fairly – come to be regarded by history as the father of the 747 jumbo jet, so one Alan Kay, graduate of the University of Utah, chamber musician and computer scientist of a high order, played the dominant role, the principal part of the *fons et origo* of the machine.

Alan Kay invented many things – not least the phrase "personal computer" itself – long before IBM launched their PC and so popularized the name in 1981. Indeed, back in 1968 Kay had designed such a computer. Called the Dynabook, it was small enough to tuck under the arm, had the ability to scan, recognize and read handwriting and could communicate with mainframe computers via radio links. The Dynabook was never built, but the idea sparked interest and Alan Kay at once came to be thought of as a visionary, a seer, the kind of figure who was breaking away from the traditional number-crunching massiveness with which the world's computers were then invested.

He also invented a language. A whole hierarchy of languages stands between ordinary human beings and the computers themselves, and it is the computer programmers and software engineers who are the interpreters of these strange tongues. At the lower, the computer end of the scale lies what is known as *machine language* – a series of ones and zeroes, the binary arithmetic chatter that signifies simply "on" and "off" to the electronic circuits of the microprocessors. This cannot be read by humans, other than those of cryptological bent who have plenty of time on their hands. Machine language passes into the microprocessor via a complicated piece of software known as a *compiler*, which translates it from a variety of low-level (but higher than machine-language) computer-speak known, generically, as *assembly languages*. This is a cumbersome set of instructions, and it uses a little English, but mostly it reads as gibberish to outsiders. The computer cannot understand it either, until the compiler churns it out as machine language. Further up the scale – closer to the humans – are middle-level tongues like *Pascal*, or the Bell Labs-designed *C*, and, higher still and thus even more easy to understand, *Cobol* and *Fortran*. (There is an innate *snobbisme* among programmers, those who write in *Pascal* cordially loathing those who can only manage *Cobol*, for example.) Further still up the hierarchy is the kind of high-level, object-oriented language like that written by Alan Kay; and at the very summit – but not so far invented properly – is *natural language processing*: sets of instructions for the computer which can be written, or spoken, in perfectly plain English. "Good morning – when I touch the red button, switch yourself off, will you?", which is an example of natural language processing, is still too complicated, in its subtler forms, to be implemented. The inventor who gets it right – as soon someone will – will have his parsnips amply buttered.

The language that Alan Kay invented was a bold enough departure from the conventional tongues of the time to form the undeniable base for a coming revolution. He called it Smalltalk, and it was both a high-level language – meaning that it was possible for relatively non-technical people to use it – and, importantly, though not a nature language, it was *object-oriented*. This meant that the user did not have to know or use a series of instructions based on code-like words: he used instead small pictures, icons, *objects*, to signify the instruction he was giving the computer. He wanted to open a file, so he moved his computer's cursor over an object on the screen that symbolized a file. He wanted to throw a document out of the computer – so he took a document and slid it across the screen until it reached a small picture of a dustbin and vanished inside it.

This was Alan Kay's stroke of genius. At a single stroke he removed computing from the bothersome, fussy, rather frightening world of codes, buzz-words and mathematical symbols, and made it instead amusing, friendly, welcoming and human. Ordinary men and women, he reasoned, could come to the screen on which were arranged these small recognizable pictures, and point to them, touch them, and the computer would then do something that related to these pictures. Power was literally at the fingertips of people who no longer had to be brave: as the Zen masters had it, the journey into the world of computing was to prove its own reward.

Alan Kay had another hero in the business, a technical genius called Douglas Englebart. Mr Englebart did not like the unfriendly way in which users of MS-DOS-based machines were told to move their cursor – the small blinking object on the screen indicating the letter or the line or the area of the screen to which you wanted to do something. On MS-DOS you pressed a key on the left of the keyboard and, simultaneously, you pressed another key on the right – one particular key to make the cursor go up a line, another to go down, a third to go left and so on. Cumbersome, inefficient and deeply boring.

Douglas Englebart then went out and invented something he called the mouse. In the words of the technical manuals of the day this was "a box the size of a cigarette packet used to move a cursor on a computer screen. The movement of the cursor matches the movement of the mouse. The mouse may also have one or two buttons . . ." It was, basically, a boxed-in, hand-held roller-ball, the direction of its rolling monitored constantly by a number of tiny electrical sensors which were connected (by something that looked very much like a tail – hence the *mouse*) to the computer, and to the cursor. Roll the ball to the left, the cursor slid across the screen to the left, exactly the same distance; roll the ball down, then up, then to the right – the cursor would do just the same. Provided you had a small piece of vacant territory, six inches by three, beside your keyboard, you could roll the mouse – and thus the cursor – anywhere you wanted, instantly.

The combination of Alan Kay's icons, his high-level Smalltalk language and Mr Englebart's mouse represented the seminal trinity of the new computing world. But there was one small problem. Alan Kay did not work for Apple Computer; he worked a few miles north of Cupertino, though still in Silicon Valley, at the Palo Alto Research Center of a serious rival corporation, Xerox. And there was a plan afoot to incorporate Smalltalk, the icons and the mouse in a brand-new Xerox computer to be called The Star.

At about the same time, down at Apple Computer a small team had already been assembled "to spec out what was going to be the personal computer of the 80s". No one knew of the plans afoot at Xerox PARC. John Couch, who had been hired from the Hewlett-Packard computer company, had collected some serious thinkers about him to work out what would be the natural successor to the Apple II. Steve Jobs was Apple's chairman: he told Couch that something had to be devised that "would allow me to replace everything that is currently in my office, but without changing the basic way that people did things". Couch reasoned that the major development required to accomplish such a task would be in the field of software: he therefore established a software development team and gave his project the name LISA – for no better reason than that all Apple software projects were given women's names (but this one was subsequently awarded an acronym, reverse-engineered to fit: it was said to stand for Local Integrated Software Architecture, as cumbersome as it was forgettable. Unkinder souls, notably *Time* magazine, said the name was that of a child of the mist, fathered by Mr Jobs; he maintained a dignified silence at the charge).

In the autumn of 1979 the LISA team heard, by way of a combination of technical papers and the bar-room gossip of Silicon Valley, that Xerox PARC was working on something interesting. A visit north was arranged in December 1979 – and computing history changed in a blink of an eye. Couch and his colleagues saw a demonstration of Smalltalk, they saw the icons and they saw Douglas Englebart's mouse. "We loved it," reported Bruce Daniels, one of Apple's LISA engineers. "What they were trying to put across was ease of use. It was almost a snap at that point. We all said: 'That's it. That's what we want to build.'" "None of what they were doing at Xerox was good enough," Mr Jobs recalled later. "But it was all in the right direction. We all said that it was basically what we wanted."

Apple history becomes a trifle hazy at this point; the legend dims. Within six months some crucial Xerox people, notably a young engineer named Lawrence Tesler, were persuaded, tempted or bullied into coming across to work for Apple. They came, and the mouse and something very like Smalltalk and the icons (though these latter were only incorporated into the LISA project at the last moment) came too. Were they purloined or borrowed, filched or plagiarized, handed over with a smile – or what? Apple says little other than to scoff at any suggestion – and there have been many – that the company was involved in even the slightest degree of chicanery. "Discussions were held," Apple says, "on the possibility of our acquiring certain technology from Xerox. Nothing came of these discussions." Xerox, who might have been expected to win some sympathy for having fallen victim in the affair, had there been one, took a full decade to take the case to court: a fight, of sorts, continues fitfully.

The Xerox Star computer work-station was duly built and was launched at a computer show in Houston in June 1981. "A lot of people from Apple went to the show," recalls Mr Tesler. "In a way it was like seeing Smalltalk the year before, in terms of inspiration." A journal of the day still reported nothing but friendliness between the two teams. "I think that Xerox see the fact that we're doing something like their product as giving them more credulity," Mr Tesler went on. "They won't be the only ones in the market with a mouse and icons and so on – so they've encouraged us." One is inclined to suspect there might be room for at least a small degree of scepticism.

In the middle of January 1983, Steven Jobs and his then six-year-old company (not that he was much older: 27), announced the birth of LISA. The computer had been four years in the making and had cost the company $50 million to build – a very considerable investment, even for a firm that had pioneered the personal computer (the Apple II was selling some four years before IBM came down from its high horse and decided to try to make computers for the man in the street) – and three quarters of a million of them had been sold. It was immediately obvious to all the reviewers that something quite new had suddenly appeared on the scene, and that computing was about to take a big step in a wholly new direction.

LISA, mouse-equipped, did indeed sport icons – lots of icons, some representing duties that the computer could perform on its own, others the different programs that might perform a stupendous range of tasks for the user. Open up one icon on which was the image of a printed page, and you would get a word processor; open another adorned with a small picture of an accounts book, the icon sitting near the first one on the monitor screen, and another quite different program – a means of doing accounts – would open in its place. Or maybe the first one would stay in place and the new one would overlay it for just those few moments that you wanted to perform the calculation: then you could click a button and it would vanish, leaving you alone with your word processor, as you were.

The screen was thus filled with objects that would guide you around what was called the "desk top" – an electronic mimic of what you might expect to find on an ideal desk. Here was a typewriter, there a calculator, a telephone was up at the top right, a calendar top left, a Rolodex with your partners' numbers near here, a sketchpad over there. And all worked, and much better and faster and more accurately than any of your own devices, even if you had them all: you could type a letter more cleanly, calculate your firm's payroll more rapidly, send a copy of your latest report to your advisers over the telephone line in microseconds, check the date of next Friday's lunch on the electronic calendar, find the telex number of the branch in Manchester from the electronic file and draw a three-dimensional sketch of your latest widget on the electronic pad before you. All this, easy to use, friendly and not requiring you to have more than a passing familiarity with the English language, was the result of 200 man-years of work, and the consequence of two million characters of computer code. It could be yours, the advertisements proclaimed, for $9,995.

LISA cost a lot of money. Probably that was the problem. IBM was mounting an aggressive advertising campaign for its new PC and, revolutionary a device though LISA clearly was, it was never allowed to succeed. It may well have taken the person of average intelligence a mere 21 seconds (Apple had run tests) to learn how to use her (and without need for a manual to be kept on hand all the time, as was essential in the MS-DOS world) – but $10,000 was a lot of money and Apple encountered considerable resistance. "Besides," said the computer press, "buyers could well be more receptive to MacIntosh, a LISA stepbrother to be announced later this year, and which will sell for half the price . . ."

MacIntosh (later to be written without the "embedded" capital letter which has become such an irritating feature of contemporary technobabble, as in QuickDraw, MacPaint and SuperCard) had its own origins about a year after Mr Couch started work on LISA. The idea, as drawn up in 1979 by an Apple II programmer named Jeff Raskin, was for a low-cost plug-in-and-go computer of great power and versatility – a $1,000 miracle machine. It would have all the power, resources and flexibility about to be built into LISA, but it would be cheap, or relatively so: the first "crankless computer", something that could be taken out of its box, plugged into the wall and used immediately. No hours or days spent sifting through manuals, no long and arduous learning curve, no curses that this option went unbought or that upgrade was unavailable. This would be like a Honda Civic or a Braun hairdryer: you'd unpack it and use it, and it would perform perfectly every time; so that, as Sony's Akio Morita said, even though it was just a few pounds of plastic and silicon and wire, you would eventually and inevitably grow to love it.

Mr Raskin's presence on the little team of engineers was soon to be eclipsed. Steven Jobs, whose inexperience and supposed eccentricities had prevented his admission to the LISA design team,* was able to persuade management to let him lead the Macintosh group. There was little enthusiasm in corporate headquarters: they were obsessed with LISA, with Apple III, and had given Mr Raskin's tiny team the smallest of budgets. Mr Jobs they thought could do little harm and would be well out of the way.

Literally. The Macintosh group, involved in designing what cynics were initially to call "Steve's folly", was consigned to a low-rent house behind a Texaco petrol station some way from the sleek structures more obviously within the corporate fold. The atmosphere within was rather like an American college fraternity house: noisy, cluttered and sophomoric, with rock music blasting from giant speakers, a host

---

*This even though he was Apple's founder and chairman: American companies can be tough places to work.

of self-consciously iconoclastic images – a pirate flag, since "it was more fun to be a pirate than join the Navy" – young men playing computer games, or table tennis, or a Bosendorfer piano "beer busts" held each Friday, and everyone encouraged to wear jeans and torn T-shirts and, if shoes at all, plimsolls.

Yet out of all this confusion came, slowly but surely, the Macintosh computer.

To design and manufacture a new machine that would be all that was embodied in the LISA, but in a cheaper, more compact and yet faster-running form, was considerably more difficult than it might at first appear. In those early days everything depended on memory: you needed a lot of memory for the computer to perform such a multiplicity of tasks with such elegance and ease as did LISA, but the chips that provided the memory were very expensive. In the Macintosh there would therefore have to be a great deal less memory – yet the machine must, the designers insisted, perform as LISA had. All the basic functions of what is known as the WIMP system – the Windows, Icons, Mouse and Pull-down menus – should work on Macintosh. So, the designers wondered – how to accomplish all this within the limitations imposed by cost – particularly the limitation of having only 128 kilobytes of random-access memory in the low-cost Macintosh, compared with the one thousand kilobytes that had been inserted onto the baseboard of every high-cost LISA?

Software and hardware were radically rewritten and redesigned, or written and designed from scratch, to build the first of the prototypes. The code for the better parts of the LISA software, in particular, was begged, borrowed and stolen from John Couch's group – notably an extraordinary refinement known as QuickDraw, invented by a cosmic wanderer, a neurochemist *manqué* named Bill Atkinson.

Put simply, QuickDraw allowed the appearance on the computer screen of any number of specific and defined regions – squares or circles or triangles or whatever you arbitrarily wanted to design. Often they were made to resemble something, to be icons that represented, say, a document, a file folder or an accounts book. If you were a programmer you would "put" your programs "inside" the appropriate icon; if you were an ordinary user, you could "put" your files, or things you had created, "into" the appropriate file. You hadn't actually put anything anywhere – but QuickDraw gave you the illusion that you had; and once the file or whatever was apparently safely "inside" its icon, then you could do various things to it. You could drag the document icon that held your latest piece of writing on top of another iconic representation of a file folder, and the document would, as if by magic, slip "inside" the file folder. There it might join a number of other documents already inside, and it would be arranged alphabetically, or by date, or however you wished. Then again, you could use your mouse to position your cursor on top of the document icon and click it twice, then lo! the actual document within the icon would open and you would see your words, or a picture you had drawn, or columns of tables, and you could do something with these words or lines or columns: add more words, insert a paragraph, draw a picture of a flower and shade its petals and leaves with different designs, or take the columns and multiply all the figures in them by 365, or seven, or whatever.

And then you could pull down a menu – a list of other things you might want to do – and by pointing your cursor to an instruction word on this menu and then clicking your mouse button you could tell the machine to, let us say, Save whatever work you had just done and then, having saved it, to pack it all away neatly back into its little document icon, whereupon you could slip this back into the image of the file folder and then close the computer down for the night.

On the other hand, you might use the pull-down menu to go on to tell the computer to Print the file that you had saved. In this case you would have the considerable luxury of knowing exactly how what you had written would look once it was printed because, as another demand of the Macintosh team, you would receive on the printer exactly what you saw on the screen. WYSIWYG, pronounced just as it appears, denotes that What You See Is What You Get, and it was a guiding principle of the Macintosh inventors.*

Finally, if you didn't like what you had done, you could slide the document icon down into the icon representing a rubbish bin, at the bottom right-hand side of the screen, whereupon the rubbish bin would suddenly fatten slightly, showing it had something inside it. A click on your mouse, and everything inside the bin would be thrown away. "Are you sure you want to throw this file away?" a message would ask you if the Macintosh detected something important – like a program – attached to the document; it was just trying to

---

*But WYSIMOLWYG, also pronounced as it suggests, was manifestly not a guiding force. Sceptics invented the term to indicate that What You See Is More Or Less What You Get.

make certain, to save you from yourself. But if you wanted to bid the document sayonara, a final click would make sure it was gone for ever.

These and a hundred other features, then, were to lie at the heart of what was to be called the new computer's User-Interface – the system that permits the user, the innocent and untutored human who has laid down cash for one of the machines, to come to make friends with it and let it show off the great power that such computers can wield. But to design all these features and sandwich them into just 128 kilobytes of memory was to take time and immense trouble. Initially, in fact, the task proved worse than impossible, no matter how elegant and tightly written the computer code that instructed the computer to perform as it had been designed to do. Mercifully – and at a critical stage – the Motorola Corporation came up with a brand-new and very powerful microprocessor, the hardware heart of a machine (in the same way that software is the soul of the machine). It was a chip called the 68000 and it was expensive – about $200, initially, for each tiny black beetle lookalike – but it permitted all the magic that Steven Jobs and his colleagues required to be performed, within the memory limitations they had set for themselves. They decided to abandon their earlier reliance on a tried and trusted microprocessor known as the Intel 6809, and instead to go ahead with the Motorola 68000 and gamble on its price coming down as the months went by.

They would also permanently engrave a number of Macintosh's unique features (including a tightly-written version of QuickDraw) into the read-only-memory. Into this 64 kilobyte-sized "archive", a small chip of vitally important memory that was inaccessible, unerasable and unchangeable, went what came to be called the toolbox – the elegantly constructed software routines which gave the Mac its unique look and feel.

But like LISA, Macintosh was more expensive than everyone had thought. The $1,000 miracle machine was not to be. With the 68000 microprocessor, the high-resolution monitor, the speaker and the serial port, the total cost would have to be $1,995. And the marketing chiefs at Apple, determined that this new product would have a send-off as remarkable as any in modern marketing history, wanted $500 to be added to the price. The money would pay the $1,600,000 bill that was required to make and screen a sixty-second television advertisement which even now, years after the event, remains one of the most enduring commercial images of all time.

It is known everywhere, still, as the "1984" advertisement. It won the Grand Prix at Cannes – it had been years since an American commercial had achieved such honours – and collected thirty-four other statuettes, plaques, medals and citations from around the world for its excellence. It scandalized some Apple shareholders and horrified some of the older guard of the advertising industry; but it was seen by 43 million American people, and not one of those who saw it ever forgot it.

There was one basic thought behind the advertising stratagem: the firm conviction that Macintosh was a remarkable computer, a machine which truly did have the potential to change the world. To match such a claim, therefore, an immensely strong and even shocking introductory commercial was needed to make the people who saw it change their minds. It was mid-1983 when Apple, which had by now scheduled a launch date for Macintosh for early 1984, approached its advertising agency, Chiat/Day of Los Angeles – agents also for Nike, Pizza Hut and Porsche. The company reminded them, if a reminder were necessary, of the Orwellian overtones of the year ahead: something, they ventured in a small voice, could surely be made of that?

And indeed it was. Big Brother, telescreens, zombies, doom-laden voice-overs, one young and beautiful woman – all of these images were arranged around a central story line that said, quite simply, *IBM is dominant and conservative and boring and a force for bad, and yet now, here and at long last, something is about to be revealed – and in fact will be revealed tomorrow – that is going to end this supposedly unchallengeable rule of Big Blue, once and for all.*

Ridley Scott, the British film director who had made such chilling visions of the future as *Bladerunner* and *Alien*, was hired to make the film. He in turn hired a number of British skinheads, about as unpalatable-looking specimens of humanity as could be found; other more normal-looking young men and women were paid to shave their hair and to be on call for one week of filming at Shepperton Studios in West London. A young, blonde female discus thrower was located, coached and hired. She would be the star. No lines had to be learned: none of the skinheads or extras would be seen speaking. There was to be no picture or image or even hint of the existence of any new kind of computer.

The film that resulted began with a thunderous roar of stamping feet. Hundreds of shaven-headed, grey and emaciated men, all in dark prison-blue overalls, all looking identical and glum, marched and shuffled in time through long glass tubeways and into a vast and cavernous hall, dimly lit, vaguely smoky, gloomy, dank and dire. Armed guards wearing samurai helmets and swinging black clubs stood by as the men were herded into rows, and silence fell as they waited for the screen at the front of the hall to come to life.

Each man stared ahead impassively as the lecture began. Big Brother, all-seeing, all-encompassing, brooking no argument or dissent, started to intone his instructions, his voice a bass monotone.

My friends – each of you is a single cell in the great body of the State. And today, that great body has purged itself of parasites. We have triumphed over the unprincipled dissemination of facts. The thugs and the wreckers have been cast out. And the poisonous weeds of disinformation have been consigned to the dustbin of history. Let each and every cell rejoice! For today we celebrate the first, glorious anniversary of the Information Purification Directive. We have created, for the first time in all history, a garden of pure ideology, where each worker may bloom secure from the pests of contradictory and confusing truths. Our Unification of Thought is a more powerful weapon than any fleet or army on earth. We are one people. With one will. One resolve. One cause. Our enemies shall talk themselves to death. And we will bury them with their own confusion.

It was, of course, nonsense, Newspeak – impressive, without content, rather frightening. Its final words were printed out on the screen, below the ranks of men listening, watching, their thoughts utterly controlled by the signs and the symbols about them.

Yet suddenly, from the back of the hall, came a slight commotion. In the distance, running up the central aisle, was the young woman – beautiful, fresh, in white running shirt and red shorts, and holding in her hands a sledgehammer. She ran, gracefully, purposefully, ever onwards. The film cut back to the ranks of grey-faced men . . . then back to the young blonde. Back to the shaven heads, the telescreen, the still-pontificating face . . . back to the girl, who had now arrived in the middle of the hall and had stopped, her face shining with exertion and with hope.

She began to whirl the hammer. Round and round went her arms and her lithe little body. Some of the men looked at her. Then suddenly, all her muscles taut, she released the hammer. It arced its way smoothly towards the screen and hit it, dead centre, exploding in a blinding shower of sparks. The voice stopped. Big Brother was no more. The screen was blank.

And then, up came the slogan. A voice-over, much more attractive and soothing, and the words on the screen itself: "On January 24th, Apple Computer will introduce Macintosh.

"1984 won't be like *1984*."

The commercial ran just once, during the third quarter of the American football SuperBowl played between the Washington Redskins and the Los Angeles Raiders. It lasted sixty seconds. Even the sports announcers were stunned: "Wow! What was that?" It became the most talked-about commercial for years, and the 43 million who saw it – and the even greater number who read about it, as the controversy – over its content, style and argument – was thrashed out in the public prints – realized they were playing bit parts in the very revolution for which Macintosh had been designed.

From that moment on it was time to get the computer sold, and into the hands of people who would carry forward the revolutionary thought that it embodied. The creative trials were over. The Macintosh did indeed sell, and over the coming months and years it became ever bigger and more powerful. More memory. Bigger screens. Full colour graphics. It was turned into a series of modules, so that you could buy bits of it and add other bits to it. A portable version was built. Strange and inventive software was created for it. A curiously evangelical crowd of supporters rallied to it – the most interesting, most energetic, most creative of America's (and the world's) computer community. Suddenly IBM and all that the elephantine organization stood for seemed out-of-date, out of step with the progress of modern thought. Macintosh had truly sparked a revolution.

In 1988, the National University of Singapore bought 450 Macintosh computers; and at about the same time another class of students at Stanford University in Northern California took delivery of a truck-load of the machines, to use during the coming academic year. Apple Japan had been firmly established and software engineers from Kagoshima to Sapporo were writing programs in *hiragana* and *katakana* and *kanji*. ChinaTalk and MacChina software was being engaged by programmers and less ambitious users in Taiwan, Kuala Lumpur and Manila and, to a lesser extent, in Peking and Shanghai too. (There is a version of the System software written in Taiwanese and another

in simplified Chinese, such as that now used in mainland China.)
Apple Australia reported record business. HangulTalk made it easy
to use the Mac in Korea. There was a new Thai operating system. To
my certain knowledge, there were Macintoshes to be found in offices
in Suva, Papeete, Santiago and Lima, as well as in Papua New Guinea,
Zamboanga, Hanapepe and Panama City.

Once I took a Macintosh to Ulan Bator, the capital of Mongolia,
and in an hotel room I showed it to a charming and, as it happens,
beautifully gamine young woman named Tsendsurene, or Serena.

I had first brought the computer into Russia by train from Poland,
and the customs officials at Brest-Litovsk seemed uninterested. But
three days later, as I returned to the Metropole Hotel in Moscow,
a worried-looking receptionist beckoned to me. Three men were
waiting for me, she said; it was most urgent. She took me upstairs,
drew back a curtain that concealed a door, and indeed there were three
men beyond, two of them in shabby brown suits of coarse tweed, the
third in a long plastic raincoat.

"We understand," they said as one, "that you have imported into
our country certain high-frequency equipment of an unspecified kind.
We wish to see it, and evaluate its possible dangers to the security of
the state."

Relieved that nothing more unpleasant was about to happen I went
upstairs – escorted – retrieved the Mac from its box, took it to the
men and explained what it did, and for what purpose I used it. They
grunted unsympathetically, then went into a huddle and emerged
to forbid me from using the device while within the borders of the
Soviet Union. I agreed; and they ensured my compliance with their
order by wrapping the machine in heavy string and sealing the knots
with red wax, sticks of which the raincoated man had in his pockets.
Finally they embellished the hardening red wax with an image of
what I assumed to be Feliks Edmundovich Dzerzhinsky – from
whose inspiration these men gained their employment – and left.

A month later I left the Buryat Autonomous Soviet Socialist
Republic via the frontier town of Naushki – where no Soviet
customs official was on hand to check that the seal had remained
unbroken – and entered the People's Republic of Mongolia, or Bügd
Nayramdakh Mongol Ard Uls. A week later still I was in the Hotel
Ulan Baatar, trying to keep warm while I idly jotted some notes of
my experiences on to the screen of the irrepressible (and seemingly
well insulated) Macintosh.

Serena knocked at the door, asking if she might arrange the following morning's visit to a neighbourhood lamasery. She then saw the screen, illuminated, covered with notes – about her, about Sukhi Bator (the great Mongolian hero), Genghis Khan and Josef Stalin (of whom there was a statue in town – one of the few still standing beyond Tiblisi, near where he was born).

She asked me to explain. I left the work I was doing by (as explained above) pulling down the menu, Saving, Quitting and placing the document safely in its file folder; then I showed her the start-up screen, littered with rows of small boxes, each containing some fascinating-looking icon, a clue to what would happen if the box were to be opened. I showed her how to move the mouse; I showed her how to click; and she opened the first of the boxes.

It was like Christmas morning. I retreated into the ante-room, and could hear from where she sat a series of gasps and squeals of delight, and then long periods of silence as, with rapt attention, she managed to get the machine to perform the various tasks she set it. She worked all afternoon and well into the evening, and it was dark and snow was falling before she stood up, stretched and rubbed her eyes.

Serena had little enough English. The Mongolian script is akin to Russian, and she said she thought in that script, and with a few Chinese characters thrown in for good measure. She had never used a computer before – had never seen one, except in magazines. But this one, she said proudly, she had learned how to use in less than thirty minutes. It was all so easy, and it made no difference that English was not her language. Everything on the computer screen was presented as images, as icons – unmistakable, no matter what the linguistic origins of the user.

It had been a demonstration, it seemed to me at that time, of just how powerful an icon the Mac had unwittingly become – how it was every bit as much a Pacific machine as that which flew across it seven miles up, or which linked its inhabitants' telephones and televisions from five miles below. Steve Jobs, Alan Kay and their colleagues, who had been labouring with such extraordinary passion on the American west coast ten years before, had created something whose symbolism, as a Pacific icon, was almost as great as its usefulness.

PLACES IN THE BASIN

There are scores of thousands of islands contained by what is now customarily called the Pacific Basin, thousands of villages, towns and cities, and more than fifty nation-states besides. On the surface, the vast differences between all these places and most of their peoples are much more apparent than any connections among them: making visits, say, to Santiago and Wellington, to Santa Barbara and Xiamen, or to Cooktown and Juneau, it is difficult to note any observable similarities – other than the fact that the same blue and imperturbable Ocean washes the beaches and groynes and the breakwaters and piers and harbour walls on the seaside of all these towns, and of many more. On one level, the Pacific seems to be their only common denominator.

Yet there is, perhaps, something more. It is relatively easy to demonstrate on another level the existence of a multiplicity of connections between this city and that, between this alien culture and another, between Pacific peoples of one kind and those thousands of miles away who appear to be quite different. The communications cable, Confucius, the computers, the cargoes, the monetary devices . . . all these icons and ideas tend to bind the disparate places and peoples of the region into one.

But still there is more. Deep, deep down, on a level only recognized by hints and murmurs, an inchoate, undefined sense of oneness, of coterminous identity is growing among some of the peoples and some of the places of the Pacific. It cannot be quantified, nor described; if it exists, it can only be felt. Over the past few years I have been fortunate enough to have travelled to many Pacific islands, to many Pacific villages, towns and cities, and to most of the Pacific nation-states, and I have here selected a few of them in an effort to capture this vague phenomenon – evanescent though it appears, chimera though it may well prove to be.

Hawaii's most northerly island, for one, seems to weave a most decidedly Pacific spell on those who visit; this island provides a fair starting point for a brief passage through and across the wide Pacific Sea. And yet, like the vague phenomenon of Pacific unity that seems to link it with other places and other times, it has a special fragility of its own: perhaps the wilderness I describe is fated to be a vanishing wilderness, and perhaps this and the other places I mention in the next few pages are special not merely because they link arms and voices with each other, but because they are all in some way or other at risk.

In Hawaii, the very wild is at risk. In the Australian Outback, the frontier of civilisation is disappearing fast. Deep in the jungles of Borneo an entire culture is dying because of the greed of man. The graceful ruins of a long-dead civilization are decaying for all to see on the curve of a river in Thailand. The particular magic of British Hong Kong seems now at risk in the countdown to the Chinese take-over in 1997. And the indescribable peace – after which the Pacific was named, and which once seemed so appropriately sited amidst the grace and beauty of the Fijian archipelago – is vanishing from there too, hostage to politics and religion, and the curses of modern times.

I

Kauai

Towards the back of the Pitt-Rivers Museum in Oxford, past the collection of shrunken heads from Borneo, across from the Transylvanian bagpipes and beside the British Columbian totem pole – in a glass case fitted with curtains which you must pull back in order to see the contents – is a Hawaiian ceremonial cape made of about twenty thousand of the tiny, bright yellow thigh-feathers of the o'o bird. Dating from the eighteenth century and said to be of incalculable value, it is certainly one of the most remarkably lovely things in any museum in England – its beauty enhanced by the knowledge that no birds had to die for it since Hawaiian tradition required that they be caught on sticky poles, relieved of their choicest plumage and then allowed to fly away.

The o'o bird – which is actually jet-black, save for its techni-coloured thighs – may not have suffered from King Kamehameha the Great's predatory court cape-makers, but it declined savagely at the hands of other nameless fates. It is mentioned in all today's ornithological literature (notably Pratt's *The Birds of the Tropical Pacific*) as being extinct – except, importantly, for one species that clings on in the most northerly island in the Hawaiian chain. (I am advised to discount "the event that amazed the birding world" – the discovery of a Bishop's o'o on Maui in 1981 – as an aberration.) No, the single species of this extraordinary bird which remains is *Moho braccatus*, the Kauaian o'o, and it lives, elusive but extant, in a dismally wet mountain-top slough called the Alakai Swamp on the island of Kauai.

The island of Kauai, which has many distinctions – one of the lesser being that it is the only Hawaiian island which cannot be seen

367

from any of the others – is a sanctuary for many survivors, avian and otherwise. Perhaps in part because of its physical isolation, for many years Kauai has been an island reliquary, a place where many of the people, the flora and fauna, the traditions – much of the *charm* – of the Old Pacific have come to rest and look like staying on. It was the first of the Sandwich Islands on which James Cook landed; the last of the Hawaiian islands to relinquish its regal independence and accept the suzerainty of King Kamehameha. In consequence it is an island with a certain sense of pride, and a place that is fighting hard not to be ruined.

But thousands of visitors stream in daily through Lihue airport, quite careless of all this. Jets arrive every thirty minutes, their passengers bound from the chill of the American continent (and, increasingly, from the big cities of Japan and the prosperous states of East Asia, just a date line away) for the beaches and resort hotels of the Kauaian shores. Watching this mass daily immigration – though it is far larger and more disagreeable in Waikiki, or the more celebrated parts of Maui – it is tempting to suppose that the old Hawaiian charm has already been submerged, even in Kauai, under the contemporary myth of the styrofoam *aloha* and all its horrid trappings.

"You had a leg reading yet?" asked the girl beside me on the plane, that brief parabolic excursion constituting the excuse for a flight between Honolulu and Lihue. Sue-Anne was from the South, from Mississippi, and this was her third vacation in Hawaii. She always came with her girlfriends Cindy and Tammy and they all thought the place was really neat, the beaches were neat, the food was neat, the guys were neat "and they have these really neat cliffs where these old fellows used to throw each other off and git fed to the sharks". The trio giggled horribly, then Sue-Anne repeated her curious, twanging query. "You had a leg reading yet?"

I knew a little of the geomantic reputation of Kauai and assumed that this was the connection. In fact, one of the people I was hoping to see was a woman from Pittsburgh who had settled in the old Kauaian sugar town of Hanapépé because she believed in the presence of "a vortex" nearby. On arrival she had changed her name from Ann Merritt to Roberleigh Hale because, she explained, "numerologically speaking, Ann Merritt sucks", and she was a woman deeply impressed by the strange "magick" of numbers. She was also very anxious about health – hers and that of those around her. So she bought herself a tiny hotel and now offers to her visitors a sombre regime of massages, strenuous bouts of colonic irrigation, meals purged of all free oils and dairy products, also phrenology, iris diagnosis, aromatherapy – and palm readings.

As with palm readings, so with leg readings – and thus I assumed (foolishly as it turned out) that Sue-Anne was a friend or at least a client of this celebrated Dr Hale of Hanapépé, purveyor of healthful vacations, astrological readings and interior irrigations. But before I could ask her the plane had shuddered to a halt on the Lihue runway and we were all rushing for the exit. I came across her later waiting for her bags; a pretty Hawaiian girl had just put a massive *lei* of frangipani around her neck and she was smiling broadly. "See here!" she cried, pointing at the rope of blossoms. "I got one again," she twanged. "I got a leg reading." So *that* was it. Her accent. She had never met Dr Hale, nor even heard of her, in her life.

The thousands of duly *lei*-greeted arrivals like Sue-Anne make only the most limited of forays into the island. Kauai is more or less circular, being the cone of an enormous volcano called Wai'ale"ale, and a narrow road runs along most of its circumference at sea-level. Wherever the road meets a beach, or more particularly (if the beach is on the windward side of the island, where the north-east trades bend the palms and stir up the surf) a stretch of sand protected by an offshore reef, some developer will have slapped down an hotel – and it is to scores of these dire establishments that the thousands all repair. The more affluent take trips by helicopter or Zodiac boat; the secretaries from Scranton, Pa., and the Chevrolet dealers from Cedar Rapids, Ia., – and Sue-Anne and her friends, no doubt – just bake in the sun, squeal at the colours of the tropical fish, take half-day excursions with "Cap'n Andy's Sailing Adventures", or frolic at endless and wholly artificial *luaus*, where the pig is put in an oven (rather than in a traditional *imu* pit) and its carcass is swabbed down with a ghastly Ohio-made synthetic called Likwid Smoke instead of being roasted above a fire of *kiawa* wood and hot chunks of basalt.

Tourists of whatever nationality sometimes have a special knack of ruining anywhere and anything that's perfectly good – and in Hawaii, it is often tempting to think that they've done so in spades.

But not quite . . . not on Kauai. A map will show that the island *péripherique* does not circle the island in its entirety. In the south it runs across the lower plains, where the old sugar barons – the Sinclairs, Robinsons, MacBrydes, and the heirs of the legendary

Gaylord P. Wilcox – tend to their cane-fields still. (But there is no refining these days, no delicious smell of boiling molasses and cane straw. Kauaian sugar is exported as a liquid in what look like oil-tankers, and goes thus unromantically to California.) In the west, the road wanders idly through sleepy, run-down, rather pleasant old mill towns, places like Hanapépé and Kekaha, and Waimea Town, where Captain Cook first came ashore and where there is a statue (a replica of the one that stands on the seafront back in Whitby). On the eastern side the road is much busier, taking the rental-car crowd from resorts to beaches, from sight ("Where Mitzi Gaynor washed that man right out of her hair") to sight ("Kilauea Lighthouse – the most northerly point in the Hawaiian Islands") to sight ("This fine home is owned by Billie Jean King, ladies and gentlemen, and this one by a group of young songsters named Crosby, Stills and Nash!").

But on the northern side there is no road at all. From the triple chain-link electrified fence around the Barking Sands Pacific missile range – where technicians track rockets rushing between Vandenberg Base and Kwajalein Island, and where others fire torpedoes into the sea and play complicated war-games with them – to a cluster of caves and Hawaiian holy sites and a tiny cove at Ha'ena State Park, there is a 15-mile arc of Kauaian coast around which not even the world's greatest highway engineer could ever imagine building a road.

The thick basalt layers have been lifted up and eroded into immense hanging valleys separated from each other by vast, almost sheer – but still green jungle-covered – walls thousands of feet high, with columns capped by elegant entablatures of iron-black lava.

The Na Pali coast, as these cliffs and valleys are known where they plunge suddenly into the raging ocean, is a wilderness of spectacular, almost frightening remoteness. It is well-nigh impossible to trek into it: the basalt is old and well eroded, and the rock faces which from a distance look so sturdy and knitted together by the lianas and ferns of the rain-forest are in fact quite rotten; given any applied pressure they will crumble like demarara sugar, robbing any walker of footholds and handholds and plunging him – like scores before him who have died and whose bodies have lain unrecovered for years – into the canyon below. There is a slippery, evil trail from Ha'ena State Park running west along the coast for 11 miles into the mystically-reputed Kalalau Valley; but in places this is only a few inches wide, and is no more than a thin stain of red mud on rocks that rise vertically on the landward side and on the other drop 1,000 feet, quite sheer, into the bottomless Pacific. It was from places along this trail that Sue-Anne's "old fellows' were once wont to "throw each other off and git fed to the sharks"; sacrifices were indeed made to appease Kanaloa, the God of the Sea and the Wind. The awesome cliffs and the potential for dizzying falls remain an ever-present warning to anyone who tries to pass along to Kalalau and its legendary Valley.

The state of Hawaii now forbids strangers to stay in the Valley for more than five days. This ordnance – which seems extraordinarily mean to anyone who makes it along the trail and reaches this deep green valley with its waterfalls, old taro plantations, orange groves and long white beach – was enacted because (as with so many of the world's most beautifully remote places) the Valley was once a magnet for those refugees from modernism who were known as hippies.

Back in the Sixties the secluded *cwms* of Na Pali became temporary grottoes for their alternative living. The valleys – Kalalau was the most celebrated, but Hankapi'ai, Honopu and Po'opo'oiki became briefly fashionable too – had mystic associations with long-vanished Hawaiian cultures, with men and women whose ghosts still drifted around their ruined *haeus* and tumbledown villages, and gave out the alluring siren-call of . . . Polynesia! So small hippy villages sprang up, little communities of white Americans in ragged clothes, with their grubby children and their dogs – and official Hawaii became briefly outraged and passed a law. Most of the hippies had gone within a year, but Kauai is a reliquary: some, like the o'o bird, cling on.

Na Pali is difficult to reach and equally difficult to police. And while the state still occasionally drops rangers and gangs of henchmen by helicopter, to check that no one outstays his welcome, the odd reclusive pair from the mainland can still be found eking out a living in the jungle. I found a couple in a corner of the beach one evening; they were quite naked, and had come down from their cave-home to bathe in the sea. They had lived wild for ten years and saw few outsiders, save for a grocer who bartered their marijuana plants for cigarettes and a few bottles of beer. They grew corn, oranges, guavas and taro (which they pounded into purple *poi* paste; the thicker it was the fewer fingers required to eat it, thus two-finger *poi* is a hippy favourite); they kept goats and pigs and chickens and insisted they were perfectly happy. The man – shaggy, deeply tanned and something of a sentimentalist – quoted a line from one Bernard Wheatley, a negro doctor who disappeared in Kalalau twenty years ago after having lived off the land for ten. "There is more here than just quietness. There is big peace. There is music in the wind and the surf. I like sundown best, and the moonlight on the ripples in the sand. I like to sit in my cave and watch Venus in the night sky." But this man didn't want to tell me his name, and once he had loped off back into the woods it was as though he had never been at all.

It is said to be impossible to climb up the head of Kalalau to the rim of the Valley, and to the huge forested wilderness of the Kokee State Park. However, the lip is reachable from the other side of the island: the 4,000 unclimbably vertical feet that separate the head of the Kalalau Valley from the Kokee lookout above can be bridged by walking back along the treacherous trail and then driving 70 miles around the metalled circumference of Kauai; then up the side of the immense Waimea Canyon (canyon connoisseurs say it is as deep and magnificent as the Grand Canyon of the Colorado, though the dark cindery rocks make it a lot less colourful) and along deep forest roads to Kokee Lodge and to the lookout itself.

It takes three hours if you have a decent car and the tourists are not bunched up looking at the Mitzi Gaynor site, in the parking lot of Charo's Restaurant or outside the Paradise Thrift Shop in Kapa'a where second-hand ("pre-worn") Hawaiian shirts are on sale at – being "collectors' items' – up to $150 a time. After these three hours of walking and driving you reach a point high up on the mountain rim where you can see down into Kalalau and watch eagles soaring half a mile below, almost halfway to where you stood at sea level in the heat, gazing up at this inaccessible ridge.

The rim is Kauai's most dramatic borderline. Below is the lushly dangerous valley-land where the human species goes – ancient Hawaiian, modern hippy, the legions of helicopter-borne travellers; above the rim is a wilderness inhabited only by Nature, a watery plain of foggy immensity, a place of primeval strangeness.

A walker can approach the Alakai Swamp, as it is known, along a footpath from the Kokee lookout. At first the path is well-travelled, and has the look of permanency, and you will meet an occasional hiker well wrapped against the increasing cool. But further along the path – the further inland – where the trail begins to thin and vanish into puddles of black mud, so blankets of thick grey fog snake down from the sky, eddies of the trade winds bringing down smothering slabs of wetness which make everything invisible and coat every branch and leaf with huge drops of fresh water. Thick coats of sphagnum moss cover the branches here. Ferns, some as tall as trees, others of cobweb-like delicacy, grow everywhere. Black feathered birds stand gloomily in the rain and mist, waiting for a brief glimpse of the sky and the chance to flutter on before the next shower.

The mud gets thicker, such paths as there are seem built on sliding rafts of decaying vegetation from which bubbles of gas rise ominously, like the belches of a sleeping god. People who slip off the pathways and into the swamp can be trapped for hours, held waist-deep in thick black mud. Some plants would drown if their roots went too deep into the quagmire, so natural selection has determined that the roots float beside them on the boggy surface and the plant, a stunted, blackened-looking thing, tries its best to tower above but looks sheepishly unable to do so.

The Alakai is a very odd place . . . . It is also the wettest in the world. A rain gauge at the summit of Mount Wai'ale'ale has recorded 50 feet of rain in some years, and an average of very nearly 500 inches annually. The damp, warm trade winds which sweep down from the landless ocean to the north-east of Kauai are caught in an immense funnel when they arrive at this most northerly island of the chain: the Anahola range in the north and the Haupu range in the east of Kauai direct them all on to Mount Wai'ale'ale, which in consequence is nearly always shrouded with cloud and drenched with rain. The rain falls almost as continuously on the 20 square miles of the Alakai – a tepid, wettening, rusting, mildewing rain that encourages everything to grow furiously and falls endlessly on the thick carpet of black mud and green foliage that it constantly creates. I came to love the rain of the Alakai: it made the place seem primeval, the mud like some comfortable proterozoic ooze. (A not wholly inappropriate metaphor, a state geologist later remarked: the volcanoes of Hawaii ranged along the suture-line that is the birthplace of the new Pacific – if the new Ocean is being created in Hawaii, he said, why not new life to go along with it?)

And it is in the Alakai that the Kauaian o'o is said to live. I went hunting for one; indeed, the glum-looking black birds which waited on dripping perches for the skies to clear could well have been o'os, but each time one flew off it did so when I was looking elsewhere and thus denied me the sight of its flashing ochre thighs. My guide,

373

however, said she had spent a year looking for one, but in vain: sea-eagles, yes, and a bewildering variety of frogs, insect-eating plants and honeycreepers. But not an o'o, nary a one. (A fanciful woman, wife of a teacher at Waimea School, apparently her present task – undertaken with the kind of studied seriousness found among Hawaiian eccentrics – was to compile an illustrated sex manual for centaurs, a job made difficult [she said] by her inability to draw *good hooves*. Centaurs, she assured me as we waited for the o'o's non-appearance, tended to favour the missionary position, somewhat different from the standard equine approach liked by regular horses. She liked Kauai for the same reason as Dr Hale, in that it was sited on a vortex of celestial power – she had been up at dawn, praying for the successful conclusion to the Harmonic Convergence of the Planets, due that particular day and visible (or whatever) from Kauai. "It is that sort of place," she said in a whisper. "We're into things like that on Kauai. Nowhere else in the States seems quite so tolerant.")

It seemed as good an epitaph as any for this most peculiar island. Down below me on the ring road were thousands of ordinary Americans, performing the unchanging Coppertone-and-Coors rituals of the perpetual summertime of this mid-Pacific American possession. Up here, on this wedge-shaped piece of swampy mountainside, and on the cliffs and in the valleys which drained the rains from it and took them back into the sea from which they had come . . . up here, all was so very, very different. "It is swampy and dangerous," wrote Isabella Bird when she visited Kauai a century ago and looked up to Wai'ale'ale and the misty acres of the Alakai. "It is very little explored, and little seems to be known of the area."

And it is much the same today. By-passed by the millions, loved by the few, a refuge for curious people, a homeland for strange plants and beasts and, it is said, the nesting-place and the resting-place for a tiny black bird; a bird that was once a symbol – known as far away as the University of Oxford – of the very essence of Hawaii, but which now, like so much of the essence of Hawaii itself, has almost vanished clear away.

2

Outback

In a formidably sober-looking report put out by the Security Pacific Bank at the beginning of the 1980s, and filled with high-minded predictions about what it was prescient enough to call The Pacific Century, one sentence stood out as most *unbankerly*: "The romantic legends of the Australian outback," the report concluded, "will shortly take over in the popular imagination from the traditional tales of the American West."

It all seemed just a little improbable. A bank – and what do banks know – was suggesting that Ned Kelly might become a more popular comic-book hero in America than Buffalo Bill? That schoolchildren might soon be learning about Burke and Wills instead of Lewis and Clarke? That the Bungle Bungles might take over as a fashionable destination in place of the Grand Canyon, Ayers Rock instead of Bryce and Zion? How far would it go? Would the dingo replace the coyote in popular disfavour? Would damper bread outstrip the Big Mac? Would the stetson be discarded in favour of the Akubra, and Oshkosh b'Gosh in favour of Drizabone? What other Antipodean heresies might the century bring?

And then along came Paul Hogan and *Crocodile Dundee*, and the predicted trend – or some of it, at least – duly got under way. Hollywood and the networks gave it all a push. Quantas hired a pretty girl to do some clever advertising, and for the balance of the decade the trans-Pacific jumbo jets were filled with eager American wanderers, off to see the delights of Down Under.

They went off to see the Opera House and the Harbour Bridge; the more intrepid of their number went to Alice Springs, the Barrier Reef and Ayers Rock; they learned to distinguish between a koala bear and a wombat, and a few played golf on a course in South Queensland that had more kangaroos than caddies.

But they would not – in any significant numbers, at least – go off to the Australian outback. Maybe the outback was simply too big, or too hot, or simply too wild. Maybe the land "at the back of Burke", as some say, all seemed a little terrifying. Maybe the Aboriginals who live there seemed a little strange, a little frightening. Whatever the reason, it seemed that in one way the Security Pacific Bank had been wrong: the lure of what locals call the Gaba – the Great Australian Bugger-All as mentioned earlier – simply failed to percolate the American psyche. But there are those who remain confident that, before very long, it will.

One such is the owner of a faraway cattle station known as Escott in North Queensland. Escott Station is a farm of a shade over 1,000 square miles, perched precariously on the southern lip of that huge munch of tropical sea known as the Gulf of Carpentaria. Imagine a square bounded by Washington and Baltimore, Gettysburg and Harper's Ferry, and you have the approximate size of Escott. Imagine, further, the sense of isolation enjoyed by the twelve men and women who live and make their being there – so far from city life and from people, so utterly ignorant of crowds, urban noise and pollution. And imagine their mixed feelings of relief and apprehension when, once in a while, the tiny station plane – of Nicholson River Airways, in honour of their temperamental local stream – rumbles down for a landing on the dusty strip, with those few aboard who have been persuaded to make the journey into this beautifully hostile corner of the world.

As I stepped down from the plane I was greeted by an emu called Burke. An emu – this one, anyway – is a bird about six feet tall, is mostly composed of neck, and by way of greeting makes a noise like a blocked drainpipe. But any chance of making a more detailed observation of it vanished in a maelstrom of dust as Digger, the family dog, rushed up and began chasing Burke along the airstrip. Then from behind the dust came Lyn Stolk, a plump lady from New Zealand who, with her husband Len, has been running the gigantic property since 1979. She led the three of us who had ventured this far into the outback through a picket fence – Digger unlatching the gate for us – out of the world of dust, and into an oasis of green.

The grass was thick and springy, cool and damp – dozens of lawn sprayers were tossing rainbows of fresh water in great fans and circles on every side. There were flowers – oleanders and hibiscus, bougainvillea and roses, and others of brilliant blues and yellows which I quite failed to recognize. A pair of enormous grey stork-like birds – brolgas, in the vernacular – appeared from the shade of a gum tree. More curious ornithology: a clutch of guinea-hens, three peacocks and a long black and white bird called a jabiru darted into sight. Wallabies, lazing in the shadows, turned their heads and loped off into the middle distance. Dozens of horses in the corral, their tails flicking aimlessly at the clouds of flies, looked towards our brief disturbance, but displayed not the slightest interest as the plane taxied along the strip and, with a brief roar of power, lifted off and back to the outside world.

Then all was quiet again, except for the increasing and gentle throb of the generator, and the occasional honking sound from Burke doing battle with Digger and a dingo bitch named Maggot who had been lately roused from her slumber. Lyn, who was arranging for bags to be carried to the neat little visitors' cottage nearby, left me beside the homestead building, where I cooled my toes in the pool and cooled my brain, as she put it, with a "stubby" of Fosters beer. After the heat and smell, the roaring and bucking of the plane which had taken three long hours to bring me here – a measure of just how far away from everywhere Escott Station really is – this peace and this cool seemed the ultimate idyll.

But the piercing clamour of a nearby dinner-bell brought me back to sudden reality: Escott Station, happy though Len and Lyn Stolk may be to accommodate visitors, is very much a working cattle farm, and those who venture there have to make way for the daily demands of outback labours.

Lunch is at noon, is prodigious – Queensland is four times bigger than Texas, and the steaks are built to match – and is eaten at great speed by a dozen stockmen who appear from all four corners of the station with dust on their boots and tucker on their minds. They seem taciturn. "G'day, mate" is about the extent of their conversation as they roar or canter in from the bush – four-wheel drives and work-horses left under the gum-tree shade – until, grimy and sweat-stained and replete, they lean back with a beer and a Winfield cigarette and tell you the story of the place.

"I imagine," said a sailor from the *Beagle*, when he stepped ashore south of the Gulf in 1836, "the time when this landscape will be dotted with white church spires." It reminded him so much of England –

rolling greenwoods, low hills, winding rivers – that he called the place Prince Albert Land and the flat, salty coastal flatlands The Plains of Promise.

Yet no church spires rise here today – there is only one town of any size, a place called Burketown, with 1,000 inhabitants – and the only inhabitants of the outback are station people like the Stolks of Escott, the people who run Punjaub Station 80 miles down the track, or those at Mount Oscar, at Almora or at Planet Downs.

Escott, which runs along both sides of the wide and tidal Nicholson, is in a way a memorial to the Britons who first settled here; the English-Scottish Australia Cattle Company bought the land and gave Escott, an acronym, its name. It is one of the larger properties, though some absentee landlords (including the prominent Texan, Bunker Hunt) have fair-sized spreads in the shires nearby. Len Stolk, who worked his way round Australia after arriving on a boat from Curaçao, was hired as a stockman at Escott in 1969: a decade later, when English-Scottish decided to pull out, he was offered the chance to buy the property at the knock-down price of $100,000.

The bank was doubtful, but eventually came up with a load which Len Stolk repaid in double-quick time. Escott, he now says with some deserved pride, is worth a cool $7 million, and is one of the more prosperous properties in northern Australia.

There are 8,000 head of cattle on the ranges; attendance to their needs, and mustering them for branding or shipping them off to the market at the railhead in Cloncurry 200 miles away is central to the functioning of the station. Visitors of a timorous nature can see the cattle that come close to the homestead – like Tomato, a beast as big as a Sherman tank who lumbers up the airstrip each day to demonstrate his insatiable demand for bottled beer and his appetite for anything on the farm that isn't bolted down: he was eating from a bag of cement one morning, his lips rimmed with white, and Lyn (aware of the disadvantages of concrete cud) was trying frantically to dissuade him from guzzling water to follow.

But those of a sturdier disposition – and few who brave the hardships of getting to Escott go there merely to sit around in armchairs – can watch the cattle being mustered. It is an unforgettable spectacle, not for the mild-natured or the fragile-boned and not (like most of rural Australia) for vegetarians.

We rose before dawn, when there was still a slight chill in the air. There was breakfast – steak, eggs, home-made sausage, fresh papaya, pineapple, coffee – before we clambered into stripped-down Toyota wagons for the hour-long ride to where cattle had been seen the day before.

One of the cars, battered beyond belief, had thick steel bars bolted to its sides and old car-tyres mounted fore-and-aft. There was no roof, but there was a thick steel roll bar from which hung dozens of strong leather straps with sturdy buckles. Two stockmen climbed on the back, two in front. Their mission: to catch each and every bull we saw and render them, as painlessly and rapidly as possible, into steers.

After a long and irksome hunt, by which time the temperature was well into the nineties, we spotted a herd lurking by a water-hole. There were fifty Brahman cows and two enormous bulls standing sentry, and the moment they saw us they took off in a grand stampede towards the trees. Hurtling behind them – gradually increasing our speed, the cars and the drivers totally oblivious to any obstacle – we smashed through bushes, over the man-sized anthills and through dry creeks as though we were on a four-lane highway, and everyone had to hang on for grim death to avoid being pitched onto the ground. If anyone did fall, we had been warned, the chase went on: no stopping for the foibles of mere humanity.

We split the herd, weaved and twisted around and isolated one of the bulls, then drove madly behind the great white animal urging it into open country, where we would have a chance to catch it and bring it down.

The speedometer juddered between 40 and 50 mph as we closed on the hapless bull. It turned. We turned behind it. It leapt a pool. We skirted it, lurching to one side and then the other, nearly spilling the crew, who gave a great war-whoop of laughter.

The distance between our front wheel and the bull's back legs was now twenty yards, now ten, now five, and then we were level and with a quick and brilliantly timed left snap of the wheel the driver hit the back end of the thundering beast and knocked its legs from beneath it. With a roar of enraged surprise and an unforgettable, expensive-sounding thud as two tons of furious bullmeat hit the deck, the felled animal was lost in a thick cloud of yellow dust.

Then, in a series of movements as brilliantly drilled as on a battle-field, the stockmen leapt from the wagon and held the bull's tail to immobilize it. Leather straps were whipped around its legs and buckles were snapped home, a tiny saw raced and the horns were cut

379

down by two inches. Then, with a small and wicked knife, with a flash and a flick and a couple of businesslike cuts, the bull became instant steer and lay puffing and snorting in the dirt.

"Watch out now – he'll be as mad as hell!" a stockman cried, before unclamping the buckles and jumping back up into the wagon. And the bull staggered to its feet, snorted, pawed the ground, charged the sides of the truck a couple of times – very nearly overturning it – before turning tail and racing off to join its chums. We saw him ten minutes later, running with the herd, untroubled by the fate which had befallen him, keen only to make sure nothing like it happened again. The newly shortened horns would act as his identification, the stockmen said, to ensure he was henceforward left in peace.

At the end of a day with the cattle, the horses or the crocodiles, as the sun slopes down below the gum-trees, the kangaroos emerge from the trees, the parrots and peacocks begin their evening rituals and dusty fist is clamped around an ice-cold can . . . time and urgency are allowed to wash away in the pleasant twilight, so the reality fades and the idyll of perfect outback peace surfaces again.

This, it seems, is the very heart and essence of Australia – the vast stillness and quietness of the bush, where one feels very well in the warm, dry air, and sleep is not far away, and when it comes is comfortable and deep. Security Pacific's prediction may yet turn out correct.

3

Teak Bandits

Up on the middle reaches of the Baram River, which flows like warm, slow treacle through the tropical rain forests of northern Sarawak, are a dozen or more logging camps – ugly agglomerations of Nissen huts, oil-tanks and warehouses, and old iron cranes which lift the 10-ton mahogany trunks down and on to the barges waiting to take them down to the sea and the waiting export ships.

But in recent years all of these camps, and a hundred more dotted around Sarawak, have fallen still. The bright orange LogMan "Special Power" bulldozers are parked, and leak oil on to the mud. The crane hoists swing idly in the breeze. Generators rust in the warm wetness and blankets of fungus stain the piles of rotting timber. Each camp is all but deserted, like a *Marie Celeste* beached deep in the jungles of Borneo.

There is a small Dayak village 100 miles upriver on the Baram, a place called Uma Bawang. Six hundred people live there, growing rice, bananas and pepper, and raising chickens. There is a tiny store that sells the Dayaks their current favourites from the "Great Outside": Wincarnis, ginseng extract, Arab Brand curry powder and beer. But these days there is not much demand for fishing tackle, the shopkeeper says: the Baram has been too dirty ever since the loggers came two years ago, and all the fishable fish have now gone. Those who make their living fishing or selling fishing tackle have in consequence no time for the loggers, nor has anyone else in Uma Bawang.

Yet they are close neighbours. A logging camp of the Marabong Lumber Company lies on the far bank, across the river from the village. Like the rest of the camps it is quite deserted, except for a watchman who shelters from the blazing sun and the afternoon drenches under a canopy of palm fronds. When I first visited, no one had worked in the camp since March, he said, and when asked why he pointed to a muddy welt of a track that led up the hill and into the darkness of the jungle itself. "Go look up there," he snarled. "You'll see why we have to stop."

The track bore the old scars of the tractors that until last spring ploughed into the forest, and dragged out the logs the lumberjacks had felled: the Philippine mahogany, the teak, the damar, the agatis tree, the Sarawak woods destined for the house-builders of Yokohama, the furniture makers and chopstick factories of Tokyo. But when I was there the track had no useful function, and it went nowhere . . . .

For there was a crude barrier built across it. A few stakes had been shoved into the mud and behind them was a shelter – a thatch-and-bamboo version of a Dayak longhouse – blocking all access between forest and camp. Beyond the barricade the forest is deep and gloomy, the tall trunks of the old hardwoods rising up to the thick canopy through which little light penetrates, but from which bird-song can faintly be heard.

A dozen Dayaks – specifically these are Kayans, one of the half-dozen agriculturist tribes to be found in Sarawak – stood beside the barrier. To an outsider they presented a remarkable appearance. The men had their hair cut in a strange monkish tonsure, and both men and women had their earlobes stretched down many inches with heavy brass weights. One man had the horns of a bearded pig wedged into holes in his upper ear, and they all sported tattoos of great complexity on their arms and legs. Some wore huge, oddly-shaped straw hats. A few carried long pangas, and one man had a shotgun. They looked menacing, and they are meant to.

"We are here to make sure no logging continues in our forest," says their leader, a young, well-educated, English-speaking Christian named Francis Maring. "You see what it has done. Our jungles, cut down. Our rivers, polluted. Our animals, dead. Our fish, gone. And these are *our* jungles, *our* rivers. They have been for many hundreds of years. Now these greedy people want them. These dirty politicians are giving our lands away. And now we are fighting back. The logging people will have to pass this blockade. We will stop them if they try."

So far, in this part of Sarawak, the loggers have not tried.

The Sarawak Police Commissioner arrived one day recently in a helicopter, and told Francis Maring and his Kayans they were breaking the law; but he did nothing, excusing himself by saying he had to leave in a hurry to visit other barricades put up by other tribes – the Kenyah, the Kelabit, the Murut and the fearsome (headhunters, by reputation) Iban – whose lands stretch along the coast from Kuching to Miri, and back through the jungle to the Indonesian frontier. Following his visit, the authorities had to come to the regretful conclusion that all logging has been brought to a halt in the Sarawak mountains – logging that brought $500 million into the provincial coffers last year alone, and which is considered Borneo's biggest industry by far.

The loss of revenue is now making the government – and by that one means the highly autonomous Sarawak government, and not the Malaysian government, which has no formal say in logging and land matters and preserved an embarrassed silence in the dispute – highly exasperated. It started off by taking action – dismantling barricades, arresting blockaders – against the one tribal group that is not only the most vulnerable but has perhaps the strongest reason to object to the loggers' avarice: the Dayak tribe known as the Punan, the people who started it all.

The Punan are the last remaining hunter-gatherer groups in Borneo, having no interest in settled community nor in agriculture. With blowpipes and curare-tipped darts, and lately with rifles too, they hunt for monkeys, tapirs, wild pigs and porcupines. They range, nomadically, from the Baram River eastwards and up into the hills to the south of Brunei. Romantics say the Punan have no interest in the trappings of the West; cynics say that whenever they happen to see a television – in a Kenyah's longhouse, say – they fall over themselves to watch *Dynasty*. The truth lies somewhere in between: like the Kalahari Bushmen, the Central African pygmies and the Andaman islanders, the Sarawak Punan are representatives of a vanishing way of living – a way of living for which the rest of the "civilized" world seems now to show scant respect.

Loggers have been ranging across the Punans' lands since the mid-Eighties, ever since the Sarawak government decided on a programme of massive exploitation of the huge natural resource that was sitting up in its central mountains. At first the bewildered Punan asked for money as compensation for what they saw as the theft of their land; they petitioned the Sarawak government in Kuching; they sent a delegation over to the federal government in Kuala Lumpur. But still the logging went on. And so in 1986 the Punan chiefs issued a public statement; its peculiar grammar and simplicity added to its eloquence:

> We see with sorrow the logging companies entering our country. In these areas where timber is extracted there is no more life for us nomadic people. Our natural resources like wild-fruit trees, sago-palms, wood-trees for blowpipe, dart-poison and other need will fall. Animals like wildboar, our daily food, and deer will flee. Rivers will be polluted and quickly overfished. In a likewise destroyed jungle it will be difficult to get the daily food, for us now as for our children and grandchildren later on. Also we already settled Punan tribes, although making shifting cultivation, always go hunting and working sago in the surroundings. Already now we have to complain about tractors destroying our cultivation, and planted fruit trees.
>
> So we now declare our wood reserved. We forbid any working by use of tractors in our areas. We don't sell the lands of our fathers.
>
> Please you, our Sarawak government and you Timber-Companies, respect our origin rights. All of us expect tractors leaving for ever. You have to look for other grounds than ours for extracting timber.

Six thumb-prints, of the tribal elders, were appended to the statement.

But it did little good. The tractors stayed put, the chain-saws continued to bring the mighty trees crashing down, the LogMan "Specials" hauled the timber away to the Baram. From the air, the logged areas of the Punan are now huge and the forests look quite ruined: vast scars straggle across what was once whole jungle, and the rivers run with ochre mud. On the ground it was a disaster: animals scared away, rivers useless, the air heavy with the stench of diesel, the jungles echoing to the harsh whine of the saws. The Punan took it all stoically for a few months and then, in the middle of 1987, they acted.

They threw up their barricades across logging roads; they built chains of boats across rivers; they mounted guard on the bulldozer bases; and they issued dark warnings about the accuracy of their blowpipes, and how silently fatal these could be to anyone foolish enough to work their land or destroy their trees. The other tribes quickly followed suit and the logging companies, fearful of a jungle war they would almost certainly lose, promptly stopped what they were doing. An industry that is vital to the local economy came quickly to a halt, and is still stuck fast today.

All manner of special interest groups have now joined the tribals' cause. (It is suspected, but not proven, that a young Swiss named Bruno Manser, who is living illegally with the Punan, has lent his intellectual support: certainly the Punan statements suggest a greater familiarity with the English language than might be expected deep in the heart of Borneo.)

Friends of the Earth ran an energetic office – mainly staffed by tribals – in the Baram river-town of Marudi. Survival International, the London-based group which works so tirelessly to protect the rights of the world's indigenes (and can surely now begin to hope for a Nobel Peace prize for its efforts), got on the case. Lawyers in Malaysia started class-action suits on behalf of arrested tribals, and planned to fight cases that would determine the precise rights to the land.

"Land – and who has the rights to it – is at the bottom of the case, as in so many disputes with indigenous peoples," said Marcus Colchester, a Survival official who was in Sarawak to investigate. "The tribals say, and we agree, that as they have lived on the land for thousands of years, it is theirs by right. It can't just be sold or given away. It's their land."

But as is so often the case, politics and commerce seem bent on dictating otherwise. Most of the wealth in Sarawak is made by the local Chinese – who own the majority of the logging companies. The logging concessions are in the gift of Sarawak's ministers, the majority of whom are now very rich men. Some of them, indeed, see no conflict of interest in owning concessions themselves – the Minister of Environment and Tourism, Mr James Wong, being one such. He owns the Limbang Trading Company, which controls a number of logging camps currently blockaded by the Punan, and he takes a robust view of the situation:

Logging roads go through the forest – but that makes it easier for the Punan to walk through the forest and search for game.

Yes, there will be a disruption in the water supply . . . but since the Punan are nomadic, they can move to another stream.

We must find out exactly what the Punans want. To stop logging completely is not possible. We don't know what to do with the nomadic Punans. We want them to settle down.

There was perhaps not much room for argument with a government minister who made profits from logging and who wanted nomadic peoples to "settle down". The stand-off between the tribals and their intellectual supporters on the one hand, and the Chinese businessmen and their political supporters on the other, continues even now.

Officials in the Sarawak chief minister's office hope for a compromise – one that urges the Punan to wake up to the realities of twentieth-century life, and urges the loggers to be more responsible in their management of the jungles. But the Punan are a proud people, and becoming prouder by the minute; and the businessmen, urged ever onward by the commercial demands of the Japanese – who have dozens of ships hungrily awaiting wood at the lumber terminal at Jalang Baram – are eager for more and more profit; as are the many politicians known to be in their pay.

Down in the jungle the tribal elders shake their heads, occasionally dismayed at the hot-headed actions of their youngsters, saddened by the destruction of their lands. "It would never have happened during Rajah Brooke's time," said a Kenyah headman who remembers the days when Charles Brooke ran Sarawak as a private fiefdom. "Now it is all greed, money, power. We would like a strong man from Kuala Lumpur to come and tell these local politicians to give us back our land. But there is no strong man left in Kuala Lumpur now. No one cares about us. We have our whole lives ruined, just so the Japanese can have a few million more houses."

4

Relics of Old Siam

Four hours up river from Bangkok on the Chao Phya River – or perhaps sixty minutes, if you decide to risk your life in one of those pencil-slim, water-borne Concordes currently favoured by Thailand's gondoliers – lies a most spectacular ruin, much visited but very little known. Ayuthaya was the capital of Siam for more than four centuries – from 1350, until 1767 when the Burmese sacked it and trampled everyone to pieces with their elephant cavalry. Now it is one of the great ruins of Asia, and as such it appears in all the tourist leaflets and is as obligatory a stop on a tour of Central Thailand as the Wat Arun or a live show in Patpong II.

But hardly anyone spends time in Ayuthaya. Each day, after luncheon, the great white boats from Bangkok slide up to the landing stages at Bang pa-In to disgorge their invading armies of package tourists, and at dusk the charabancs growl away with them in full retreat, leaving the old capital once more silent and deserted. Four hours appears to be the maximum permitted exposure to this most glorious display of Siamese history. To any but the most purblind visitor, it must seem that just as the tragic languor of the place begins to sink in, so a motor-horn barks and a guide bellows some instruction, and you are summoned away.

Yet it is entirely possible to stay a while in Ayuthaya – possible, inexpensive, delightful and, for anyone attempting to understand the complexities of Thai history, eminently desirable. But to do so you have to make a show of your independence – ignore the persuasive arguments of the Bangkok boatmen (though by all means take up their offers for lesser journeys, to the Grand Palace or the Floating Markets) and insist, though they will advise you otherwise, on a northbound bus, train or car. Travel up from Bangkok early one evening; the plains are dull, so there is no need to go by daylight. Take dinner at a café in the bustling little country town which is the sole living remnant of the old capital, and rise before the sun and *then* take a local boat. (A word of warning, drawn from the bitter experience of others: if you were incautious enough to allow the café-owner to flavour your curry with too much of that murderously hot green chilli known as *prick kee nu*, you will have risen long before dawn. So it is as well to demand, in a town that entertains so few *farangs* to dinner, that the chefs go easy on the peppers.)

I took my boat, a slender "long-tail" with its propeller set on a pivoted stem to help avoid the floating clumps of water-hyacinth, just before dawn. When King U-Tong established Ayuthaya in 1350 he chose a site at the confluence of three rivers – the Lop Bur, the Pasak and "Thailand's Mississippi", the Chao Phya – and then had a small canal constructed to turn his city into an easily defensible island. The island, lozenge-shaped, two miles by one, is itself incised by dozens of narrow *klangs*, or canals – meaning that a boat, and especially a narrow-boat, is an essential means of exploring the city.

I found mine moored behind my hotel, the steersman puffing contemplatively on a ragged cheroot. He agreed on 25 baht – a dollar – an hour, and once the deal had been struck and the cheroot tossed away, declared himself proud to be able to show me the city that sixteenth-century wanderers called the most beautiful in the East. "They said it was like your Venice," said my boatman, who was called Mr Sak. "Many canals. Much water. Many lovely buildings. But so many are knocked down by the Burmese. You have to imagine what it must have been like before the Burmese came."

Ayuthaya was a mere vassal state during the closing years of that most glorious and idyllic period in Thai history, the age of the kingdom of Sukhotai. The kings who ruled from Sukhotai are regarded even now with nostalgia and reverence – they were deeply religious, kindly, learned, accessible, paternal figures, men whose wisdom brought a golden era to Siamese history. But they were ultimately weak rulers, and down in Ayuthaya a new class of more martial figures began to assert themselves. By the mid-fourteenth century these men had seized power from the pious monarchs of the north. The kings of Ayuthaya, the so-called "Lords of Life", were quite different. They ruled as absolute monarchs, ambitious and nationalistic men who ran disciplined and ruthlessly organized courts: a strict ban on "amatory poems", amputation for anyone who kicked a palace door, a code of laws laying down that errant princes could be beaten to death by means of sandalwood clubs drummed against the napes of their royal necks.

The island-city built by the 33 Ayuthaya kings during their five dynasties and four centuries was appropriately regal in scale and style – a mix of architecture that managed to be both bombastic and reverential. There were huge palaces, wide moats, magnificently expensive temples, towering *prangs*, whole forests of brick *chedis*, endless rows of Buddhas and icons in gold and jadeite and marble. The Dutch, the French, the British and the Japanese were in Ayuthaya too. King Songham had permitted his cities to be used as entrepôts, and there was a bustling trade in silk, spices, hides, teak, tin and sugar. The traders built their embassies and houses and, in the case of the Dutch, a huge cathedral. Ayuthaya at its zenith had all the trappings of a major world capital, and was respected and admired by everyone who visited it.

But it was not to last. The Third Burmese Empire had designs on the Thai fiefdom in the south, and Ayuthaya came under attack – first by King Alaungpaya in 1760 (though he withdrew, having been injured by his own cannon-fire), and then again, and fatally, by Alaungpaya's son Hsinbyushin in 1767. The city was under siege for more than a year before the Ayuthayan guards gave up the struggle and the Burmese poured into the city on their squadrons of battle-elephants. Then, in an act of collective vandalism that is almost unmatched in Asia, they set this lovely old capital ablaze, ruined its palaces and forts, and melted every ounce of gold from every Buddha and icon in sight. By the end of the year the place was a total ruin, only the stumps of its temples and the foundations of its palaces remaining for the jungle grasses to reclaim.

But Thailand herself was to survive the assault. A young general, Phya Tak Sin, escaped the siege, set up a temporary headquarters on the Gulf of Siam and some months later travelled back to drive the Burmese occupation garrison out of the capital. The devastation he saw was too terrible: he spent barely a night among the ruins before leaving for the south, for the riverside town of Thonburi and the place they call "the village of wild olive groves" – Bangkok. But that is another story. While Bangkok was to grow and prosper, Ayuthaya was to moulder and decay in the steamy heat of the tropics, waiting for its rediscovery as a treasure-house of old Siam.

Old Mr Sak steered me slowly down the Pasak River, under the single road bridge that is Ayuthaya's only physical link with the outside world. Even at dawn the river was busy. Long trains of huge old rice-barges lumbered by. Fisherwomen cast nets, and sat smoking cheroots as they waited for them to fill. A boatload of young Buddhist monks, all in their deep red robes – one shoulder bare, as is the Thai custom – flashed past on the way to worship at a *wat* nearby. Their driver gunned his Evinrude to show off, and the monks stumbled over each other as the prow rose from the water. But they grinned and waved. Such a cheerful religion, Buddhism – so very little that is solemn.

We stopped at a temple, the Wat Phanan Cheong, which was built a few years before Ayuthaya herself and has long been popular with the local Chinese. The Buddha is almost unbelievably large – so tightly jammed inside the temple that it appears to be supporting the roof. Even at this hour the temple was full. Old ladies were lighting incense tapers, men were pasting tiny offerings of gold leaf on to the Buddha's feet and shins, schoolchildren were bowing low and reciting their morning mantras. Outside I paid 10 baht for a tiny caged bird, and set it free above the river to carry my wishes where they might be answered.

(After flying a few circles, the bird went straight back to its mistress, who re-caged it and sold it again ten minutes later. She did the same with terrapins and, said the ever-sceptical Mr Sak, made a small fortune doing so.)

Beside Phanan Cheong is a small Shinto shrine and a little cemetery – the remains of the Japanese community that once thrived here. But when in 1682 the shogun refused to recognize the usurper Prasattong as King of Thailand, the Japanese were murdered, or fled. To modern Japanese the tombs are holy relics, revered as war graves, and they are carefully tended by their Thai guardians.

A clockwise progress along the river – the way Mr Sak insisted on taking me each day – leaves the old city itself on the right bank. I would stop the boat every few yards and walk, or paddle up along a tiny klong to see the various ruins within. Some are magnificent; the Chandrakasem Palace has been turned into a most agreeable museum, and the Wat Raj Burana has been splendidly restored with huge *prangs*, superb gateways, rows of *chedis* standing on freshly mown lawns. The old royal palace, Wang Luang, was totally destroyed by the Burmese; but close by its foundations is

the marvellous line of the three identical *chedis* of the Wat Phra
Sri Sanphet, as dignified and harmonious an example of Buddhist
temple-building as you will see anywhere in Asia.

The huge Buddha at Phra Sri Sanphet is even more impressive than
that at Phanan Cheong, and the throngs of the faithful are greater,
their devotions louder. But this is where the foreign tourists tend to
start their wanderings (the boats from Bangkok arrive around 1 pm),
and it can become unbearably crowded. There are souvenir stalls, too
– an irruption of commerce that sits uneasily against the tranquillity
of other ruins nearby.

Pleasant hours can be spent wandering in the old city itself. One
can start at the island's western end, at the monument to the heroic
Queen Suriyothai. (In the great battle with the Burmese in 1549
the Queen, a great feminist, dressed in men's clothes and fought,
on her elephant, alongside her King. In one memorable cavalry
charge she saved her husband's life, but died in so doing. The
chedi that holds her ashes is one of Thailand's most sacred.) And
one can finish at the east, by the Phom Phet fortress, or the
attractive Wat Suwan Dararam, a place which is quite lovely at
dusk as the monks, framed by the magnificently restored columns and frescoes, chant their plain-song devotionals. And then,
being nearby, one can dine at a floating restaurant on the Pasak
River: there are two beside the Pridi Damrong Bridge, and the
road home.

However my own preference in Ayuthaya is for the unrestored, the
ruin *sensu stricto*, where some of the sadness of the saga of the capital
remains embedded in the stone. To see such a place one is forced
to look at the river's left bank, not the right. My own favourite
– somewhere that tells the essence of the Ayuthaya story, I like to
think – is beside the old Dutch cathedral of St Joseph (which still
stands, and from which you can hear Christian hymns on a Sunday
morning, sung in Thai.) Called the Wat Chai Wattanaram, it is a
place of silence and forlorn beauty on the bend of a river. There is
a mighty *prang*, covered with foliage, with small bushes growing
from its cornices and parapets. A single Buddha looks down from
a pedestal. Surrounding the *prang* are the subsidiary *chedis*, all more
or less intact but weathered like ancient stalagmites, the brown of
their stones rendered green by the plants clinging to every horizontal
surface. There are dozens of headless Buddhas, still sitting in con-
templative attitudes, still somehow radiating peace, still somehow

managing to look beatific and even forgiving to those ancient vandals to whom they fell victims.

Cattle wandered through the ruins and small black pigs rooted among the tussock grass. Flocks of brilliantly-coloured birds rose in alarm from the recesses of the old stones, like sudden rainbows and bursts of fire. Lizards lazed in the sun, prompting Mr Sak to wonder if there might be snakes in the deeper grass. He may well have been right. There was no one else in the grounds of the temple; boats no longer stopped here. The whole place had returned to the jungle, swamped in a green and feral wilderness beside the slow river.

It was like a lost city, somewhere which had slumbered for centuries, unvisited and undisturbed. Indeed, I thought, Wat Chai Wattanaram looked today as Ayuthaya itself must have looked before it was rediscovered and placed foursquare on all the tourist maps. It was perfectly quiet that morning but for the chatter of song-birds as I stood beside the river, gazing at the wrecked spires and domes and all those ranks of statues . . . despoiled, but still serene.

Two hundred years ago all of them – statues, temples, monuments, tombs – were intact. But then the Burmese elephant-squadrons made their final attacks, the fire-boats crossed the river, the soldiers from the North began their final rampage and the era of Ayuthaya was over. Elsewhere, where temples and palaces have been restored, the sights are impressive. But in this temple, above all others, the sense of deep and abiding tragedy – the real sense of Ayuthaya – remains. On this one spot beside the river stands a poignant reminder of the troubled history of the Thai people and their land. It is a discovery that the average day-visitor will never experience; but it is one well worth making, an essential way-station on any serious progress through the story of Siam.

5

Nervous Old Colony

Beside what the Cantonese still call "the Head Soldier's Flower Garden" and the rest of Hong Kong calls the zoo, a brand-new skyscraper opened for business in 1989, a stiletto of salmon-pink marble, the colony's own Trump Tower. The block, thirty storeys high (with flats still available for an average rent of $10,000 a month), is actually titled The Albany, a name that in such a faraway place as Hong Kong is heady with suggestions of luxury and nostalgia, of distant Mayfair and eternal discretion.

But no London traffic rumbles by outside. Those who live in this Albany are awakened each oriental morning by the cries of the red-cheeked gibbons, the tree-climbing kangaroos and the Palawan pheasants who live in the small botanical garden and zoo just below, which separates them from Government House a little way down the hill.

The building is owned by Swires, who if not the oldest are by general agreement the colony's most distinguished business house (and were long ago rewarded with P.O. Box 1, Hong Kong, to prove it), and it is crowned with two penthouses. One of them, the lower, is occupied by the British Trade Commissioner, the second most senior (after the Governor) of the British diplomats in the Territory. In the other, the grander of the two – and paying some undisclosed fraction of the market rental of $30,000 a month – lives a director of Swires, Miss Deng Lin-Yu.

Miss Deng (no relation to Deng Xiaoping, she insists with relief) was for many years better known in the colony by the Anglicised style of Lydia Dunn, until in 1988 when she was dubbed – on the urging of Mrs Thatcher, a great fan – Dame Commander of the

British Empire. Before the colonials had had a chance to come to grips with this name, Dame Lydia, she suddenly had another, for Mrs Thatcher saw in 1990 that the Queen appointed her a Baroness, no less. So she is at the time of writing formally known as Baroness Dunn of Hong Kong and Knightsbridge (where she has a flat). She is one of only two Hong Kong peers (the other is the Lord Kadoorie). By allowing herself to rise to such a pinnacle of this rather contrived segment of British aristocracy, Miss Dunn ended all suggestions that she might wish to be the first Chinese governor of the post-1997 Hong Kong (or Xianggang, as it will then be known).

It was when she first became Dame that Miss Dunn married a kindly-faced Welsh lawyer and former colonial Attorney-General named Michael Thomas. Since he was not to be ennobled there was some difficulty in knowing what to call the pair – Mr and Mrs Thomas, Dame and Mr Thomas, Lady Dunn and Mr Thomas, Lady and Mr Thomas, or Michael and Lydia, but whatever they care to be called they are without a scintilla of doubt the most celebrated couple in the colony. They are spoken of quite without irony as "royalty", with Lady Dunn variously cited as the colonial queen or princess, depending on the moment. Rare is the ball – and Hong Kong is a town with a *soi-disant* if somewhat threadbare social vibrancy, where in wintertime many balls are staged – that happens without them. Few are the pages of *Hong Kong Tatler* or its less stately rival, *The Peak*, that pass ungraced by their portraits.

And once their new quarters were open, and they turned out to be so splendid, so brilliantly and lustrously *tasteful*, so they served to display without shame what the couple themselves can be seen to represent: the apotheosis of Hong Kong life, a gorgeous symbol of the dream of every one of the six million Chinese who lives on these few square miles of Imperial turf.

A migrant businesswoman (formerly in the rag trade) from Shanghai, matched with an advocate from Wales . . . this unlikely (but in Hong Kong, all-too-common) combination has achieved undreamed-of social success in terms of money, standing, connections, influence and power. Big fish in small pool, some will say. *Some fish*, others would retort. And looking at the stupendous view from their immense drawing room – *some pool*.

"Hong Kong people are not a jealous people," Sir David Ford, the colonial secretary, remarked once – and when it comes to the attitude to wealth (though he was actually talking about something else, which we will come to in a moment), this is no doubt true. The ordinary Chinese who gazes enraptured from down among the gibbons and the Palawan pheasants, who sees the twinkling lights up in The Albany penthouse and wonders idly how the Baroness and her consort are living above, will have no truck with envy: quite simply, he wants what the Baroness has, he vows to acquire it and is quite certain that he *can* acquire it – either by work, by stealth, by chicanery or by cunning.

He feels none of the lip-curling resentment that such good fortune would engender in Britain: Lady Dunn, he knows only too well, came from China to Hong Kong and made good – and so can anyone else. This is the dictum by which the territory has lived for 150 years, and it applies across the board to all fortunate enough to live within.

It was of no consequence to the local Chinese that the happy couple were busy instructing the painters, the carpet-layers and the designers, and were hanging their original Chinnery and moving in the grand piano during the months when all Hong Kong – all China, indeed – was convulsed by the bloody events in Tiananmen Square. It was the anniversary of Bastille time too, and less kindly commentators in the local European press were whispering "*Qu'ils mangent de la brioche*" whenever the Baroness was mentioned, but no Chinese seemed perturbed. The way he looked at it was essentially that if he could order his Porsche, his mobile telephone or his strawberry dacquiri in the Harlequin Bar of the Mandarin Hotel the week after China had quietened down, then why shouldn't the fortunate Lady Dunn enjoy what her hard work and wealth had brought her, however unfortunate the timing?

But Sir David Ford was not, I have thought many times since, entirely right in his assessment of the Chinese and their allegedly limited capacity for envy. One of his better-known predecessors, Sir Jack Cater – there is a profusion of colonial knights in residence in Hong Kong at the end of its Imperial history, with the governor Sir David Wilson and the retired colonial secretary Sir David Akers-Jones at the social apex – immediately challenged him.

Ford had been defending the view that it was perfectly all right if London gave passports to and allowed in *some* Chinese – some of the very rich, and the very well connected – but then said to the remainder that it was all very regrettable, but limits were limits and there was simply no room for them in the Old Country. "Hong Kong people are not a jealous people," he said. It was at that point that Sir Jack Cater told him he was speaking nonsense:

> They may not be jealous about money. That's very true. But they are very jealous about passports, about their right to get out if they need to. If the people *down here* think that people *up there* are getting permission to live in Britain while they themselves are having to stay put and face the music, there'll be hell to pay. They won't stand for it.

Hence the dilemma that grips Hong Kong during her last few years as a colonial possession. The ordinary Chinese down at gibbon-level who gazes up at the Baroness's star-spangled penthouse may not mind that she can dine on Beluga, sleep between satin and keep constantly cool in perfumed air-conditioning while he eats fishballs, sleeps on a palliasse and only experiences summertime cool when he passes the doorway of the Sincere Company department store. But he minds a great deal that, when the chips are down and the Chinese Army is massing on the far side of the border fence, she can slip off to Kai Tak airport and fly out to Gatwick and be welcomed by the immigration officer with a smile and a stamp in her passport, while he – even if he could afford the fare – would not be permitted to get within 1,000 miles of Britain, despite the fact that for a century and a half it has been his ultimate mother country, a land to which he has paid unthinking fealty all his life. That, he thinks, is decidedly unfair.

Moreover, when he gets to thinking about it a little more, and discusses it with his co-workers, and perhaps has the odd glass or two of San Miguel, his mood may turn rather ugly. He may decide to try to somehow *get at* a person whom he perceives as being in a more fortunate position than himself, *passport-wise*.

Perhaps he may insult someone whom he knows has the precious document; the growing army of Cassandras here suggest he may even hurl a half-brick through a window, slash the tyres of a car or, heaven forfend, throw a punch . . . .

"Riots in the street may only be the half of it," commented Sir Jack, a man whose fondness for the colony is only exceeded by the decades he has lived here. "Those who have not may turn on those who have. And that very simple, very real possibility is beginning to make people here tremble a bit. Things could turn out very badly."

To make the outlook even more depressing, what if there is

unemployment – something quite unknown in Hong Kong for the last few years? What if the inevitable slowing of business with China leads to the shutting down of Hong Kong's factories? A closure of some of the dockyards? A sudden spattering of bankruptcies? What if, as Chairman of the Hong Kong Bank William Purves worried out loud in 1989, "the place doesn't start sparking again pretty soon?" Then the disgruntled thousands could become the incensed millions, and Britain would have an ungovernable nightmare on her hands. Not all the army in the land and there are only 8,000 British soldiers here, and no reinforcements within easy distance – could contain a Hong Kong on the loose.

So an icy cocktail of fear and apprehension has started to trickle down more than a few spines. At the turn of the decade the Chinese middle classes were struggling to get out while they could. More than a thousand of them – bank clerks, computer programmers, students in their last year of a law degree or a maths course – were pouring into the Canadian and the Australian consulates, seeking permissions and visas and places at schools in unlikely towns like Moose Jaw and Kalgoorlie. The American Consulate had a queue each morning that stretched for 300 yards. Even the Colombians, the Belizians and the Fijians had people knocking on their consulate doors, asking about residency, passports, visas and rights of abode. When Singapore announced in 1989 that it would allow in 25,000 people there was a riot outside the booth where they handed out application forms, and the police were called. The Chinese are *that* eager to leave.

But even among the more sedate, the very rich, the habituées of the Ladies' Recreation Club, the Hong Kong Club and the Helena May Institute, a new nervousness was abroad. Women with names like Dimity, Vanessa, Charlene and Amanda (but who preferred to keep their husbands' surnames out of print) were starting to say in increasing numbers and at an increasing volume something they had never even thought before – that they wanted to leave too, before the place came unstuck, became unpleasant, unbearable, even dangerous:

Of course I can go any time I like [said Vanessa, whose husband ran one of the colony's flashier hotels and who had lived here, in a splendidly gaudy mansion on The Peak, for the better part of three decades]. That's always been the case. But now, all of a sudden, Hong Kong's got an ugly feel about it. I can't rightly explain it. You could

397

always wear your jewels in public, never had to worry about safety or rudeness, the people were never insolent or anything like that. There was never any crime – not against us *gweilos*, at any rate. The Chinese may not have cared greatly for us – but they knew their place, that was the important thing.

But now you get the feeling that everything's different – that they actually now *don't* know their place, and that they don't like us very much any more. You see their looks in the shops – "*Oh, look at that bloody woman, she's all right, she's British, she's got a passport, she can go whenever she likes, we're stuck, and all thanks to the likes of her . . .*" – and you know it's going to get worse.

Frankly, my dear, I'm not so sure how much I will *trust the servants* in a year or so's time. The Filipinos are all right, of course. No argument with them . . . But the Chinese? Now all of a sudden I'm not so sure . . . . Will they turn on us? It's all our fault, they'll say. We sold them out, sold them down the river. Will they – I know it sounds faintly ludicrous, paranoid – will they one day creep in and stab us while we sleep?

That's why I've decided to go. It's been the very best of lives here, of course. A simply fabulous place. But I have this sense that it's coming apart at the seams. That old furrier in the Prince's Building, Mabel Woo Russell, she's closing down, you know. A sign of what's coming, perhaps. When the furriers start to pack up you know the old money's smelling something bad. Just what happened in Shanghai, of course. And if you can't trust your own staff . . . . Well, it's Australia for us. Couldn't stand the cold back home. But it's an awful shame. Bloody diplomats. Bloody Chinese. Mucking up what was a wonderful place. Wonderful place. Just look at that view – did you ever see such a thing?

So saying, she threw aside the damask curtains and there below, spread out across the warm night like a fabulous jewelled carpet, was all the wealth and vulgar abandon of Hong Kong – the world's most infamous borrowed place, with all that equally infamous borrowed time just about running out. And because of that simple chronological reality, behind the glitter, beneath the show – perhaps even in so sedate and confident a location as Lady Dunn's penthouse suite on top of The Albany too – a gnawing sense of fear has replaced the old Imperial style and swagger. It is a fear tinged with a certain sadness for poor old Hong Kong – a town that, thanks to the awful events of the Chinese summer of 1989, will never even seem to be the same again.

398

6

Return to the Native

The small advertisement buried in the personal columns of the *Sydney Morning Herald* in the Southern autumn of 1989 offered an unwitting insight into the tragedy of modern Fiji. "Shining Pearl," it began, "Trapped in a Stormy Sea."

Its author – one of those few who believe the Pacific not to be as pacific as its name – clearly had some talent as a copywriter. "Pretty, talented young Indian girl," she continued, "frustrated by evident lack of future in her troubled country, and seeking new life in Australia, hopes to correspond with and meet young man with a view to friendship and possible marriage. Write Box 1234, Suva."

Thus has life in modern Fiji become apparently intolerable for yet another wretched Miss Patel or Miss Chatterjee or Miss Singh – in this case an obviously educated and sensible young woman who, a year or so before, might reasonably have expected to live out her days in one of the 300 Western Pacific Islands – the Fiji group – which many Indians have long thought of as their own. Now she was wanting to leave: the emigration figures since 1989 have suggested that very considerable numbers of her friends and neighbours wanted to bale out too.

Marriage brokers in Sydney and Auckland are doing a roaring trade these days, bartering Gujerati and Punjabi brides by the boatload. Fiji Indians who have any connections – family, education, property, money – outside the islands are filling the outbound aircraft as fast as they can be carried away. One of the untidier legacies of the British Empire is being ruthlessly tidied up, as the Fiji Islands begin to return to the ownership of the Fijians themselves – a people who

399

have not been masters in their own house for the better part of this century.

The Indians are being made less than welcome by the government that was installed in Fiji in 1987 – after two instances of an uncharacteristically Pacific event, the *coup d'état* – by the Fijian Army. Colonels had been upset by the increasing power and influence of the Indians, descendants of sugar plantation workers who the British colonials had shipped in to work the canefields a century ago. When a government was elected that was openly sympathetic to the Indians – even wanting to share power with them – the nationalistic dam broke. The army took over the country, installed its own government, prodded it into action with a second display of sabre-rattling and then retired to the parade-ground to watch the demographics turn to their ethnic advantage. In early 1989 the new figures were published. Thanks to the emigration of so many Indians, they said, there was then an actual majority of ethnic Fijians in the islands. The statistics were probably not quite true – the last credible and disinterested count showed 330,000 Fijians and 347,000 Indians – and most neutral sources in the capital supposed the Indians still to have a slim majority. But the figures, though maybe no more than a triumphal piece of statistical sleight-of-hand, caused great celebration among the Fijian community, with much feasting and the spontaneous drinking of many gallons of *yaqona* – the local version of that slightly narcotic and very Pacific loving-cup, kava.

"Psst!" hissed an old man from a side door as I wandered through the Nuremberg-modernist corridors of the finance department in Suva on the day the figures were announced. I stopped. "Want some grog?" he asked. And he beckoned me into a room where ten middle-aged civil servants – all ethnic Fijians – had taken some time off from their paperwork to get mildly mellowed-out on *yaqona*. "Have some grog with us, man. Hear the news? We've got the numbers now, you know." And the men, all dressed in shirts, *sulu* skirts and sandals, passed round the half-coconut shell with its frothy grey contents. As I drank so they clapped, which I had also done when I took the little cup (once) and then again (twice) when I handed it back to the MC for passing on to the next drinker.

"*Bula!*" we all said. "*Vinaka!*" "Good health! Thank you!" "Yes," said the old man, hitching his *sulu* around the massive tree-trunks of his legs, "things will go much better for us all now we are getting those Indians where we want them."

A few days later, after leaving the tiny Fijian island of Wakaya, not more than a ten-minute flight from Suva, I was handed as a present a curious implement carved from wood. Though not one to look gift horses in the mouth, and despite being polite enough to utter proper gratitude, I have to confess that what I had been given looked neither obviously useful nor especially pretty. It had an intricately fashioned handle on one end and, on the other, four curved and menacing prongs, each six inches long.

"Know what it is?" asked the owner of the island, a Canadian businessman named David Gilmour. "A fork for eating human flesh. Exact replica of the one used to eat the Reverend Baker, to be perfectly honest. The last white missionary to be roasted and eaten, right here in the Fiji Islands."

Which event – the axing, roasting and eager scoffing down of the Wesleyan evangelist Dr Thomas Baker – took place in the summer of 1867, in a village in the west of the main Fijian island of Viti Levu; recent enough to provoke a slight shudder, yet distant enough to prompt relief, as well as to allow some derivative amusement. And serving, like the 1987 *coups d'état*, as another reminder of the vague undercurrent of violence which reverberates beneath nearly all discussions having to do with Fiji generally – and much of the Pacific generally, as it happens – as well as those to do with the tiny island of Wakaya in particular.

To place this apparently non-Pacific tendency in its proper context, it may be instructive to learn that Fijian men are the second biggest specimens of human being on earth (the Tongans, next door, are bigger still). Few are under six feet tall, and they like to sport vast moustaches and Afro haircuts. In spite of their national dress of calf-length *sulu* skirts and enormous leather sandals (the police wear particularly fetching white skirts with a Wild West fringe) they look much as you would imagine reformed cannibals to do – gentle giants, but with the gentility clearly a veneer beneath which lurk darker tendencies. Dormant volcanoes, to alter the metaphor to one more appropriate to Fiji since the islands, Wakaya included, are the relics of a vast volcanic plateau, a drowned mid-Pacific continent.

The first of these enormous Melanesians came to Fiji from some point to the north-west about 4,000 years ago and – perhaps behaving as their monstrous size suggests they should – have been going hammer and tongs at each other and at most outsiders ever since. Regard any chronology of modern times. "*1832: Coup d'état at Bau – Tanoa exiled.*" "*1837: Tanoa restored at Bau after bloody counter-coup . . .*" "*1843: Beginning of Bau-Rewa Wars.*" "*1844: Europeans expelled from Levuka . . .*" The Fijian landscape is littered with old forts and warlords' graveyards; and 8 ft spears and fearsome teak battle-axes are the central props of any *meke*, the Fijian dance extravaganza customarily performed for honoured guests.

On Wakaya, a 5 square mile scrap of lava and coral 20 miles to the east of Viti Levu, matters have been every bit as tumultuous down the years of its inhabited history. The island's *tui*, or hereditary leader, once found himself under impossible siege by forces loyal to the *tui Levuka* next door, and had all his villagers hurl themselves to their deaths from one of the 600-ft cliffs with which geology had blessed the place. Chieftain's Leap – Wakaya's answer to Masada, to Saipan or to the rock called Nakwa'am in South Korea – can these days be clambered up by anyone adventurous enough to get himself to Wakaya, and having a few daylight hours to spare.

Adventurous enough – and privileged enough too, for Wakaya Island is one of the very few morsels of the Fijian archipelago that is privately owned, and for which you need permission (or an invitation) to make a landing. It was first glimpsed by Captain Bligh of the *Bounty* during his enforced, post-mutiny cruise between Tahiti and Batavia in 1789. Three war-canoes sped out from what is now Homestead Bay; guessing that their intentions were not necessarily of the most friendly variety, Bligh turned tail and headed back out to sea again.

Fifty years later, a rather more courageous British naval officer named Captain Houghton landed on and staked a claim to Wakaya; crucially, he persuaded the then *tui* to hand it across in perpetuity for £200. The Fiji Land Commission has recognized the validity of the sale ever since; in spite of occasional grumbles from descendants of old Wakayans whom Brower and his friends booted off a century or so ago, the island remains privately held: unless one of the new breed of *coups d'état* turns out to be led by Marxists (these days a most improbable happenstance) it will stay private, and thus unique in this part of the South Pacific, for evermore.

David Gilmour, who owns it now, is a privileged man. He is Canadian and comes from fine Manitoba grain baron stock (father on the Winnipeg grain exchange). He went to the best Ontario schools and, using his skill and friendships, made millions out of unreconstructed entrepreneurship. He made particular friends with an exiled Magyar named Peter Munk, and went into venture after venture with him: gold mining, oil-well ownership, Danish design ("we bought workmen's mugs in Aalborg for ten cents each, covered them in white enamel and sold them in Greenwich Village for five dollars'), and hotels. In the late Sixties, Southern Pacific Hotels Ltd, a corporation with partners named Gilmour, Munk, Birchall and Khashoggi – Adnan, later indicted in New York and charged with all manner of villainy – started to buy up hotels in the blue waters of the Pacific, in a vast swathe from Alice Springs to Bora Bora.

In 1971, while he was surveying Southern Pacific's acquisitions in Fiji and preparing the ground for a new one – a wretchedly ill-timed (thanks to the oil embargo) development 20 miles from the Fijian capital, Suva – Gilmour flew by helicopter over Wakaya Island. It was the first of two closely linked moments that changed his life.

"It looked so wonderful, so perfect – tucked inside its fringing reef, quite unspoiled jungle, a tiny copra plantation, the manager's house, another couple of buildings, space for an airstrip . . ." Southern Pacific bought the island for $1 million, and announced plans to turn it into the ultimate South Seas resort. They spent $13 million more: they bulldozed roads, built a reservoir, put up a jetty, set up a landing strip – and then, basically, ran out of money.

Pacific Harbour, near-fatally hit by the energy crisis of the mid-Seventies, was – in spite of the construction of a costly golf course – soaking up funds. Another unfortunate venture, a piece of elaborate vanity inaugurated by Egypt's President Sadat which centred around the building of a resort in the shadow of the Pyramids, was suddenly cancelled for reasons of Cairene *realpolitik*. And the egregious Mr Khashoggi mysteriously started to appear more of a liability than an asset. The Wakayan visits of Nabila – either Nabila the daughter or *Nabila* the eponymous yacht – began to be less and less welcome.

It was about then that David Gilmour, who had a penny or two of his own and thus the ability to make choices, did what many middle-aged men in his enviable position perhaps should do: he took stock of himself. He took a long, hard look at the way his apparently phenomenally successful financial life was really going and wondered whether in purely human terms it *was* successful or whether the constant amassing of fortune meant that he was missing out on the sheer pleasures of living. Eventually, after long periods of introspection, he decided that in some ways his life was going awry, and he embarked on drastic and sudden measures. He had been tempted to change his life when he first saw Wakaya. Now, and at a stroke, he would.

So, digging deep into his pockets he bought out Messrs Munk's, Birchall's and Khashoggi's shares in Wakaya Island: he paid more than $3 million from his own pocket to become the sole owner of Wakaya Limited, of Air Wakaya, of Wakaya Shipping and, most recently, of the Wakaya Club. "I wanted to build my own home on a headland on Wakaya. I wanted to create something that was in perfect harmony with Fijian life. I wanted to show my respect for the people of the South Seas, and for the natural life and natural ways of this unspoiled part of the planet. And I wanted people to come and share it with me, people who would appreciate it as I did."

Had he intimated that such appreciation would carry with it the implicit condemnation of a way of life which had robbed him of a child, no one would have blamed him; but he has never said it . . . at least not in so many words.

For four years the thick Wakayan jungles hummed with the kind of mechanical activity they knew in the heady days just after Southern Pacific had bought the island. But under the new regime the plans were, mercifully, modified: where once the builders had planned to construct in marble and gilt, and in styles borrowed from Mussolini and Donald Trump, now Gilmour was building in teakwood and palm, in *tapa* bark and woven grass, in beach coral and seashells. His tiny hotel, tucked on to a beach at the northern end of the slender string of an island, was "really just a place where my friends, those I can't put up in my own home, can come and share the peace. I don't see it as terribly commercial, frankly. It will probably only break even. I just want people to come and savour the loveliness of this place, to have a chance at finding out what life really means, and at finding out who they really are."

I spent much of my time there strolling around the island's roads, gazing open-mouthed at the extraordinary clifftop views and being happily overwhelmed by flocks of wild deer (descended from those brought in by missionaries), scores of scurrying coal-black piglets, and a collection of wild grey horses too shy for me to attempt to ride. The birds, too, are unforgettable – Shining Parrots and Fan-tailed Cuckoos, Blue-crowned Lorikeets and Sacred Kingfishers, and black Peregrine Falcons that soar in the thermals and occasionally shoot off on the south-east trade winds at full speed, 100 miles an hour and more. There are said to be Birds of Paradise on Wakaya, too, though the *Field Guide* is silent on their presence, and I was never fortunate enough to spot one. I suspect they were mistaken for Silktails, puzzlingly difficult birds to classify, which are known to inhabit islands to the east of Viti Levu.

I clambered to the summit of Chieftain's Leap, and a few feet more to the summit of the highest hill, Korolevu; I went fishing for yellow-tail tuna and albacore; half a mile from shore I found a brilliant green brain coral so huge we called it Einstein, until we found one even larger the next day; I went reef walking, snorkelling and, had I had the courage, might even have gone scuba diving too. And there were books in each room – good old books, essays on Paul Gauguin and Robert Louis Stevenson, works by Herman Melville and Rupert Brooke – the cullings of a library of the best of all Pacific writers, those who knew as Melville did that this was "the mysterious divine Pacific", that Ocean which "zones the whole world's bulk about; makes all coasts one bay to it; seems the tide-bearing heart of the earth."

It was late one moonlit night, however, when I became quite certain why David Gilmour had decided to move and build a home in Wakaya, and to invite his friends down and persuade a few good people to buy small parcels of land and build their own homes around the cliffs.

The stars that southern autumn night were almost impossibly bright, and the distant thunder of the waves on the reef was soft and comforting. But every few moments the sound was drowned out by a rising chorus of Fijian voices, coming from a group of men sitting on *tapa* mats set out on the beachlawn, who were drinking *kava* and singing to each other and the night. They passed the *kava* cups around and drank deep of the milky, slightly stupefying grog; they chatted quietly under the starlight; they laughed; one would propose a song and then they would break into chorus after chorus, in perfect harmony, of some of the great Fijian folk songs – telling sagas of long ago and far away and always, of war and peace, of love and of triumph over disaster.

As a powerful businessman Gilmour may have made his life rich and triumphal, stitching together deals, selling Aalborg workmen's mugs for five dollars a time, drilling gold mines in Nevada, trading hotels in New Guinea like so many Monopoly properties, sipping

405

Krug aboard the *Nabila* and rubbing shoulders with Mr Sadat and constructing resorts in the shadow of the Pyramids and on the edge of the energy crisis. Yet since the mid-Eighties, and all that introspection, little of it seemed to count for very much.

Only now and here – in a battered old straw hat and a faded cotton shirt, as he sat on the *tapa* mat under the wide Pacific sky and we all listened to the cathedral swelling of the old Pacific songs – did he seem to have found a kind of peace which all his dealings and his power had never managed to bring him. He seemed a contented man at last, deep amid the calm and tropic murmurings of the South Seas.

Of course, to the young Indian woman who had placed her advertisement in the *Sydney Morning Herald*, the peace and calm we felt that night would seem alien indeed. For the past few years Fiji had meant a great deal otherwise to her, and to her kin. One can but observe and then regret such a fact, and apply a salve which says simply that if there truly is peace and contentment out there, on the greatest of all oceans, then it is not necessarily a contentment available to all – a truth that obtains in all the world, and not just this most immense portion of it.

CITIES ON THE RIM

I

Eastern Capital

The Chinese characters *Bei* and *jing* – hence Beijing – mean "Northern capital". Southern capital is *Nan-jing*, Western capital *Xi-jing*, and Eastern capital, *Dong-jing*. Dong-jing is what the Chinese call Tokyo – the easternmost capital city in the realms which have immediate relevance to the Middle Kingdom.

But in the realms of the new Pacific, Tokyo can no longer rightly be considered an eastern capital. It is out of the running in this particular context for the simple reason that it lies not at the eastern but at the western edge of the ocean. The city which sits foursquare on the eastern side – and which might thus more properly be termed the Pacific's *Dong-jing* – is that which has been much more obviously associated with things Western for all of its brief life – the City of the Angels, Los Angeles.

"The City of Dreadful Joy", Aldous Huxley called it. "A big, sprawling, incoherent, shapeless, slobbering civic idiot in the family of American communities," wrote Westbrook Pegler. A great hard-boiled city with no more personality than a paper cup, was the verdict of Raymond Chandler. Everyone at one time or another has apparently felt a need to attack Los Angeles – all the writers, the movie-makers, social scientists, journalists, politicians and armies of transients who either lived there or merely glimpsed her seemed to have gone on, inevitably and inexorably, to mount the most savage of broadsides against her for her vulgarity, her palpable lack of charity, her ugliness, tawdriness and gimcrack impermanence, her superficiality, her fads, her crime, her decadence and her smog. And *El Pueblo de la Reyna de Los Angeles de Porciúncula*, to give her the full title which the Spaniards who first settled there decided on – and a rather prettier title than perhaps she deserves – lay back in the sun, smiled wearily and took all this invective in her gigantic and confident stride.

Not even the most bilious of remarks seem to have upset her: not Philip Marlowe, for instance, who recalls pouring himself a stiff drink one evening and opening a window as he listened:

> . . . to the groundswell of the traffic on Laurel Canyon Boulevard and looked at the glare of the big angry city hanging over the shoulder of the hills through which the boulevard had been cut. Far off the banshee wail of police or fire sirens rose and fell, never for very long completely silent. Twenty-four hours a day somebody is running, somebody else is trying to catch him. Out there in the night of a thousand crimes people were dying . . . a city no worse than others, a city rich and vigorous and full of pride, a city lost and beaten and full of emptiness.

Mr Marlowe, whose global view was perhaps more jaundiced than most, could hardly be expected to talk in glowing terms of the town in which he stalked his prey. But even the gentlest and most congenially disposed of writers seem to take up a quillful of *aqua regia* when they try to recall Los Angeles. Gore Vidal, Joan Didion, H.L. Mencken . . . riffle through any book of quotations under "Los Angeles – see also Hollywood", and you will find page after unremitting page of the acidulous and the scathing.

Except that Oscar Wilde liked the place. Richard Henry Dana gasped with pleasure when his journey from Boston left him at the then small settlement in Southern California: "In the hands of an enterprising people, what a country this might be!" And earlier still the Spanish priest Father Juan Crespi, who was in at the birth of the stripling on 2 August 1769, remarked with some prescience that "this delightful place among the trees on the river has all the requisites for a large settlement."

Larger, by far, than the Blessed Crespi could possibly have imagined. The total population of the Los Angeles basin, the 500 or so square miles of gradually sloping smog that lie between the San Gabriel Mountains and the Pacific Ocean, is now getting on for 14 million. It will overtake New York to become America's largest city at the end of the century – the only city of the Western industrialized world still to be growing, and apparently with pride. Not unexpectedly, the Tokyo–Yokohama urban combination has been growing too. By 2010 Los Angeles will have 19 million people, and the total value of the region's output is currently growing each year by 3.5 per cent, compared with the 2.8 per cent of America as a whole.

From the welter with which it is just possible to describe and define this most gargantuan and ineffable of urban masses, one statistic seems to hang in the air whenever it is uttered: if all of the Southern California of which Los Angeles is clearly the capital – a freeway-stitched belt of wealth 200 miles long from Santa Barbara in the north to San Diego in the south – if all of this were to be counted as an independent nation it would rank as the eighth largest in the industrial world. If the group of seven industrialized nations, in other words, were to be expanded to a group of eight, then Southern California would take a place in the conference room beside Japan and Italy, Germany and the United Kingdom, as well as alongside the America she so cruelly diminished by her secession.

However, such statistics cannot define the city any more than a measure of volume can define a man. They cannot offer even a paltry attempt to define the sense of total wonder that all inbound fliers experience when suddenly, from out of the black void of the night-time Pacific, or from the occasionally firefly-speckled darkness of the Colorado or the Mojave deserts, leaps a carpet of sparkling jewels so vast, so wide, so magnificently colourful and pullulating and crawling with those endlessly intermingling cascades of freeway lights, that you might suppose you had left the planet and were about to land in another world, a place only recognized in dreams.

It was the first American city in which I lived, and the one in which I came first to realize my undying love-affair with America. I was seventeen and, in what came to seem a powerful double symbol – both of my own coming-of-age and of the absolute dominion of the car in this particular city – I learned to drive there. I was staying in a small frame house on Sycamore Street in Hollywood (with the splendidly unforgettable telephone number of Hollywood 3-3333), living with a pretty strawberry blonde with the improbable name of Janaire Skidmore, who owned a Corvette. She took me to Anaheim to see Disneyland a couple of days after I arrived in her town, having hitch-hiked down from San Francisco, and on the way back, despite my wholesale inexperience in matters automotive, gave orders that I should drive home. She was eighteen, and had to be obeyed.

We were on one of the approach roads leading to the Garden

Grove freeway, as I recall, and to return to the frame house on Sycamore Avenue we had to "go west until you get onto the San Diego, get up onto the Harbor freeway and then make a left on the Hollywood freeway – easy as pie", as Janaire insisted. The car had a leaking radiator hose, and steaming water would spray through holes in the bonnet and on to the windscreen. There was something wrong with the suspension. Janaire noticed my hesitation, and began to taunt me. I gunned the engine, slipped the gear-shift lever into "drive", turned on my indicator and set off up the ramp, and into everybody's nightmare.

It was rather like trying to board a moving express train. A river of steel and glass roared past on my left, five, six, eight lanes of it, all hurtling along quite careless of my presence at the outer edge. As I ventured towards the maelstrom, furious horns blared, the Doppler effect making it seem as though I were on the platform in *Brief Encounter*, deciding whether to end it all and hurl myself in the path of the Down Mail. In the end, and under the influence of Janaire's ceaseless and hortatory cries, I slipped in to a gap in the outer lane that had formed between a Peterbilt truck and a laggardly Volkswagen van, and then, safely in the stream myself, began to accelerate and change lane after lane after lane until I was safely tucked in beside the central crash barriers, protected from any cars that tried to enter as I had just done.

From that moment on, it all became a seamless passage of bliss. I was part of the stream, up on the wave, *doing the Los Angeles thing*. The city was racing, flashing past me on all sides, a tremendous gallimaufry of waving palm trees, rotating neon signs, tall office buildings and the glittering forecourts of a million petrol stations. Yet all my most immediate surroundings on the roadway – towering removal vans belonging to Bekins Storage or United Van Lines, pink and convertible Chevrolets with vanity plates saying "IMSEXY" or "ISCUMN" and with strawberry blondes aboard who indeed looked as though they well might be, bile-yellow Oldsmobile 225s driven by big black men in fedoras, stripped down, jacked-up, big-wheeled monster cars in midnight blue and black and billowing chrome and smoke in equal quantities, and posses of enormous Harley-Davidson FLH-1200 Electra-Glide police bikes, with reverse gear no less, driven by helmeted men in khaki shirts who sat so straight in the saddle you thought they had iron rods taped to their spines – all of this remained static, filling my fields of vision ahead, behind and to my right. I was part of a stream of steel, and the most extraordinary city in America was racing past me at 100 feet a second.

Back then there were – and still are now – seemingly endless rows of small and rather mean-looking houses visible from the Garden Grove and the San Diego freeways, as we zipped without mercy above communities, if any can be called such in so heartless a town, with undeservedly pretty names like Bellflower and Lakewood and Hawaiian Garden. Then we turned on to the Harbor freeway, heading north, and with the black slums of Watts and the memorably ugly towers of Simon Rodia* down to the right, we could see ahead the towers of the city herself. There were fewer now than then; downtown Los Angeles in the Sixties was grim and grimy, a few stumpy skyscrapers only, no architecture of any note, and drinkers of Ripple wine and white port more obvious on the streets than the bankers and stockbrokers who infest America's other downtowns. Today, though, there is a difference: there is more spring in the step of those who work in Los Angeles offices that lie between the Coliseum and Dodger Stadium, between Alameda Street and the Harbor freeway. The whole centre of the city has been, or is being, noisily transformed – not least because so many Japanese financiers have moved in and bought chunks of land and real estate for themselves, as we shall see shortly. After years of languishing with the Knoxvilles and the Detroits, Los Angeles proper can hold its head up high among the Houstons and Denvers, and even the Manhattans of this world.

But downtown is not – or was not – where the flame of the city was held, where resides the repute that made Los Angeles what it was, and to an extent still is. That came into view as we passed under the most complicated ganglion of freeways ever constructed – the so-called Merritt Four-Level Interchange – and squeezed ourselves westbound on to the iron river of the Hollywood freeway. We were passing signs for roads which have become more famous than the

---

*Rodia was an Italian immigrant who wanted to "do something big, and I did". His towers, a trinity of iron spirals decorated, like the temples of Siam, with fragments of faïence and seashells and the punts of wine bottles, stand only as a memorial to this remarkable man. He made them in his back garden – the tallest soars 99 feet – and once they were completed he gave his property to his neighbour and left, never to return. They are by most reasonable standards ugly, in the way that Antonio Gaudi's work in Barcelona can be thought of as ugly: but they are unforgettable, they tell an unforgettable story, and they have become a Los Angeles landmark.

destinations they were built to serve – Wilshire Boulevard, Beverly Boulevard, Hollywood and Vine. We were in the best-known town in the world. "Tell him you live in Hollywood," a salesman was quoted (in Collinson Owen's *The American Illusion*) as having said of a Frenchman, "and watch his eyes light up! All the world knows Hollywood. All the world wants to come to it. You can go to the naked savage living in darkest Africa, to the untutored Aborigine who bites raw meat with his sharpened teeth, so that the blood runs down his chin and you can say to him, 'I live in Hollywood,' and what will he say? He will reply, 'Yes, boss, I'se thinking of movin' there myself.'"

He would have to be one rich Aboriginal, these days. To rent one of the twenty-two cabanas around the pool at the pink stucco fairyland of the Beverly Hills Hotel (now owned by the Sultan of Brunei, a pleasing morsel of trans-Pacific symmetry) will cost him $75 a day, and then only if he happened to be a guest in the hotel, which will have set him back another two or three hundred. But the cabana will have a telephone – there are 52 telephone connections around the pool, since Hollywood legend required that one be paged (the loudspeakers are still there, and work) while sunning yourself at the pool, and to take the "Big Call" itself, before one officially existed as a Hollywood person. Our visitor from darkest Africa, or Australia (the quoted salesman having only a somewhat hazy sense of geography) would naturally require himself to exist once he had arrived, hence the necessity of the expense.

To buy more permanent accommodation would present a problem, too. Houses in Los Angeles are twice as costly as the average house elsewhere in America. In Hollywood, and in the plusher satellite towns of Bel Air, Beverly Hills and Brentwood, property is being subjected to the most grotesque of modern indignities, known by the suitably indecorous name of a "teardown". Time was when the old houses in Bel Air, with their high walls and Dobermans and snarling security guards and electronic gates, were surrounded by immense policies, with lawns and ha-has and croquet pitches and swimming pools and tennis courts: I once spent a weekend swooping low above them in a police helicopter to see if I could spot the celebrities of the moment, sunning themselves and looking for work in *Variety Daily* or the *Hollywood Reporter*. But such would be a futile pastime nowadays: the teardown phenomenon prompts speculators to buy up the comfortable old houses, 2,000 or 3,000 feet of amply monumental hedonism, and replace them with what are engagingly called "mansions" of 8,000 or 10,000 square feet, the better to attract the flashier type of buyer who is more easily parted from his money. One developer bought, for $1.7 million, a one-acre property in the flatlands below the Beverly Hills Hotel, and promptly ripped down the perfectly pleasant house – built in the Twenties – that stood on it. He spent another million building an immense and grotesque 8,000-square-foot palace on the site, and sold it for $4 million: his profit was a cool $1.3 million, and he ruined a small part of what in Hollywood terms was an old community, for ever.

The new buildings, like that just mentioned, are more than just ugly: being so big, they also swallow up almost all the pleasure-land that surrounded their well-spaced predecessors – perhaps only five or six feet will separate the bastions of mansion "A" from the flying buttresses of mansion "B". So no pools, no ha-has, and no chances for itinerant helicopter-riders to check on Joan Collins and her cellulite problem, or to see exactly how blue David Hockney's blue really was.

The dull roar of the perpetual affluence, the fatigue that is said to be induced by the relentless pursuit of pleasure, the tedium of everyday life in a parish of superlatives . . . all these are familiar by-products of the Hollywood publicity machine. And this does become apparent fairly readily.

I once stayed in a modestly legend-filled hotel on Sunset Boulevard, the Château Marmont.* As I walked through the door a concierge stepped from the shadows, asked for my name and then handed me a small envelope – a gift from a friend, he said. It turned out to contain a pair of keys, and a note. A Rolls-Royce Camargue, white with a black vinyl roof, would be waiting in the parking lot outside, it read. Yours for the next two weeks. Have a good time. (It was a quite unexpected thank-you from the Rolls-Royce motor company in England: I had recently driven one of their cars from London to

---

*Greta Garbo once lived there, as did Howard Hughes whose company, mentioned in an earlier chapter, still makes satellites near the Los Angeles airport. John Belushi killed himself there. Indeed it is entirely possible to spend a day seeing the houses where various celebrities died – at 12305 Fifth Helena Drive in Brentwood was discovered the body of Marilyn Monroe; at 7047 Franklin, Janis Joplin; Albert – Dr Cyclops – Dekker killed himself in a most unusual way, with syringes and a rope, and in the shower, at 1731 North Normandie; and Freddy Prinze went at 8825 Hollywood Boulevard.

Yalta, deep in Crimean Russia, and since nothing had fallen off and the car had not once failed to proceed, I had written kindly about the experience. Rolls-Royce professed themselves to be pleased, and for the next few months cars like the Camargue in Los Angeles turned up in parking lots in any hotel where I was booked to stay.)

But this was not a particularly pretty car, nor one eminently suited to the task at hand, which was to write an article about the gangs of East Los Angeles. My colleague, a tough photographer whose knowledge of gangland culture was profound, said it would be churlish to turn down the offer. Besides, he ventured, the gangs might like the machine.

Later that same day we were driving along Hollywood Boulevard and stopped at a red light. A bright red sports car pulled up beside us, and a tousle-haired blonde who had clearly been racing along a freeway, and was still chewing gum with the kind of nervous energy necessary for such adventure, looked over at us. "Jeezus!" she cried. "Is that a Rolls-Royce?" I looked over, past the photographer, and said that indeed it was. "Ugliest fucking car I ever saw," she returned. "Well," drawled the photographer in his best Finsbury Park accent, "you should know ugly, lady – just look in the mirror." I stood on the accelerator, and we left her in the dust. A nice Hollywood exchange, we agreed. The kind of exchange that makes one's day a little brighter.

But better was to come. We had arranged to meet a gang leader, a young Hispanic gentleman who had recently been released from Soledad prison after doing time for wounding a senior member of another gang, apparently rather grievously. Our friend was called Raul "Pinky" Estoban, he was 23 and, after asking a number of desperadoes in various bars, we found him lurking on the forecourt of an Exxon service station just near an exit ramp from the San Bernardino freeway. He was a small man, dressed in a rather torn white suit, and his visible skin seemed to have been covered with tattoos, all of which said the same thing: *Viva White Fences*. The White Fences gang was one of East Los Angeles' most venerable, and Pinky was proud to have been elected to run it. He showed us his tattoo collection: three on each arm, three on each shin (he rolled up his trousers), a small one on each ear-lobe, another across his stomach, one over his heart (and enclosed in a red caricature of same, suitably embellished with tattoo blood). He then rolled down his lower lip to show evidence of deeply painful tattooing there, and was about to unzip his fly when – since we were still standing in the Exxon station – I told him I thought we had seen enough to convince us of his unswerving loyalty to his clan. It was at this point that he spotted the car.

"You boys want pictures?" he said. "I no give pictures. Except maybe you let me drive the car?" He gestured towards the Rolls-Royce. My heart sank. The photographer nudged me: we needed the pictures, we had to do the trade. And so we let Pinky drive. He did so with enormous care and skill, first going to a friend's house and picking up a cigar, then to the house of another and more sinister man who lent him a machine gun. And that was how Pinky was content to spend the coming hour: driving a white Rolls-Royce along the Santa Ana freeway, puffing on a cigar and cradling a large machine gun under his arm (settling it on to his lap each time he managed, with unerring skill, to spot a Highway Patrol car or motorcycle in the rear-view mirror).

"This one great machine," he declared, as he slowed to take the last exit to East L.A. "One day I have one, perhaps, no?" I recounted the story of the morning's encounter with the blonde in the scarlet Stingray. "She say that?" he asked, in evident astonishment. "She truly say that?" His finger started stroking the trigger of the gun, in a most menacing way. "She say that while I drive, I blow her fucking head off." Another fine encounter, I remarked to the photographer, and we headed back into the smog-dusted sunset, back to the Château for the night.

We took dinner at Spago, one of the more fashionable Hollywood cafés of the day, run by an engaging fellow named Wolfgang Puck. (There is a copy of the place in Tokyo, of course.) The atmosphere was oddly vibrant, as though we were not just having dinner but were sitting down to a party to which Mr Puck had kindly invited us. The food was interesting and the company – which included a halfway up-and-coming actress named Pia Zadora – was, to a Hollywood ingenue, rather more so. But the *richesse* was only too apparent afterwards, for when I went outside to retrieve the car from one of the blond young men – all would-be actors, they always say – who are hired as automobile-fetchers by most Californian restaurants, and asked for "My car, please – it's a Rolls-Royce," with a smug air, he replied, "Oh yes, sir," and, with a look of quiet contempt, added, "I"ll need to know a little more information than *that*. We've got about twenty in the lot right now, and quite frankly, sir, I find they all look so alike." It was at that moment that I wished Pinky had been at my side, for sure.

There can be few other places in the world where such wealth is on permanent display, yet where such wretchedness is etched on so many faces too. The broken dreams for which the town is infamous are all too easily uncovered. I was down on Broadway one evening, looking around a miserable Mission for Women that had been established by a Westwood grand dâme, in the hope of saving a few old ladies before they disappeared through the fissures – tectonic and social – with which Southern California is so liberally scarred. I came across a woman from Tennessee who had come to the city six months before, on a Delta jet, with high hopes of becoming a bit player, maybe even a little more, in the television industry. So she had taken a hotel room in Burbank, and had gone to the agencies and waited for the calls . . . and had waited, and waited.

Then her money ran low and she moved out of Westwood into an hotel downtown, which was a great deal more seedy then (three years before) than now. She worked part-time as a telephonist, but had an argument with the manager and he threw her out. Within four months of flying in to Los Angeles International she was having to come to terms with the most awful reality of her life: that she would have to sleep out on the streets, in the centre of one of the richest cities in all history. She hadn't made it. She endeavoured to preserve some fragments of her dignity, washing herself and trying to darn the holes in her stockings, and keeping her cuffs tidy and hiding the brown stains. But eventually that became an impossible task too, and her spirits fell to the lowest of all possible points, and she began to take comfort in some cheap sweet wine she could get for a dollar and a half a pint, and drink from a brown paper sack. She found food in dumpsters at the back of the Pizza Hut, and cold and congealed and greasy though it was, it cost her nothing and reminded her of the riches all about her. And then the Mission took her in, and she sat out her afternoons in front of an old Zenith television, sitting on a shiny old armchair with cracked arms, next to a jabbering old woman in a print dress three sizes too short for her. The dream, such as she had enjoyed, was long gone; she could never afford to go back to Tennessee, where she had no friends in any case. She stared into the middle distance and nodded, and her eyes filled with tears. Los Angeles seemed then, as Philip Marlowe had said, a big angry city, a really hard place to live.

But these days millions want to live there, given the unending glory of the weather, the limitless possibilities for pleasure and reward and the apparently ceaseless booming of an economy which, since it is so very diverse – ranging from television films to the manufacture of jet planes, from banking to oil refining, from government to international trading – never seems to be seriously affected by a depression, a recession or a down-turn. Despite the image projected from Hollywood and the San Fernando Valley, this is not a one-product town: the film and television industries together directly employ only 75,000 people, and the total contribution the entertainment business makes to the economy is merely the employment of 7 per cent of the total labour force.

Finance – international, high-rolling corporate finance – is by contrast much more important. Los Angeles romped past San Francisco as the banking headquarters of the state in the late Seventies; by 1986, the value of its total banked deposits having doubled since 1980, it shot past Chicago to become the country's second banking centre after New York. Los Angeles now has $150 billion on deposit, New York $180 billion, and the gap between the two is narrowing. Some 180 out-of-state banks have offices in the city, and 130 of these are foreign – many Japanese. In the last five years the Japanese banks' share of the assets has risen from a tenth to a fifth, and Japanese investors now own more than a third of the central office buildings – in sharp contrast to the situation in San Francisco, where the Hong Kong Chinese have an enormous share of the local real estate market.

One immediate and human consequence of the new interest in banking is that the city centre, a dreary place just a decade ago, is now crammed with a gleaming array of skyscrapers, while the office workers who slave there enjoy restaurants, parks and museums in a city centre that, in the Sixties and Seventies, had almost ceased to exist. Flats are being built there, too, and there was a new magazine on the streets in the late 1980s promoting the value of centre-city living. And after years of having to fight freeway traffic,* there

---

*The new Century freeway, twenty years in the planning and $1.7 billion in the making, is due to open for traffic in 1993. Specialists predict it will be jammed solid with rush-hour traffic from the day it opens. Other plans – for making all existing freeways double-deck, and for removing crashed cars by helicopter snatch teams – are under serious consideration.

is a vague hint of hope for the millions of commuters: 4 miles of the city's first-ever underground railway, MetroRail, were being built at the end of the Eighties, and by the late 1990s – and after the expenditure of $4.5 billion – a full 20 miles of new subway should be open.

Critics have already condemned the scheme as being far too costly – it will be the most expensive in the world – and just not practicable for a city that, despite all I have just said about its newly gleaming downtown, really does not possess a core. There is no orderly and concentric arrangement of suburbs and city centre, as exists in London and Paris, San Francisco and Montreal: instead there are "nineteen suburbs in search of a metropolis", as H.L. Mencken wrote in 1925, and the patterns of population movement during the working day are Byzantine in the extreme – secretaries from Van Nuys heading off to work at the Arco headquarters downtown, cameramen from West Covina rushing to assignments in Century City, wealthy bankers in Newport Beach who work in offices in Westwood, waitresses in Whittier who serve lunch in Malibu. The web of wandering that produces the ever-mobile, always frantic, deadline-conscious Los Angeles is a product of history and topography – something that lends the city its strange charm, but makes for frightening inconvenience.

Yet however impossible the city can sometimes be, however polluted, traffic-choked, expensive and dangerous,* hundreds of thousands of men and women are still pouring in to live and work there. And most of them, it seems, are from Asia. No longer is Los Angeles what it was in Steinbeck's day, attracting the American legatees of the philosophy of "manifest destiny". Since 1981, when the city was officially 200 years old, white Angelanos have very nearly become a minority. Twenty-five per cent of the population is already Hispanic, 9 per cent is black (with precious few of those able to live today in Beverly Hills, even though the land where the community

---

*And not just crime. Brush fires detroyed 484 houses in Bel Air in 1961. Landslides topple others into the sea, or down canyon walls. Like so many on the Pacific's "ring of fire" the city is in the middle of an active earthquake zone, and since the 1989 tragedy in San Francisco, many residents are noting gloomily that it has been 140 years since anything over 7.0 on the Richter scale has hit. And the dog-breath heat of the Santa Ana winds causes everyone to become tense and uneasy; as Raymond Chandler wrote, the Santa Ana is when "meek little wives feel the edge of the carving knife and study their husbands' necks".

now stands was once owned by the grand-daughter of a black tailor), and 7 per cent is Asian.

It is this latter proportion that is set to rise most dramatically in the coming years – if not in numbers, then in the value of the community's combined effort. For although there will be 4 million more Hispanics in the city in 2010 (the percentage rising from 24 to 40) and the number of Asians will rise only from 7 to 9 or 10 per cent (increasing by an extra million souls) the output of a community that has proven itself to be of enormous energy and unstoppable entrepreneurial skill will undoubtedly be prodigious.

At the beginning of the decade the Orange County suburbs of Westminster and Garden Grove, for example, were a jumble of used-car lots and bean fields. The television automobile-evangelist Robert Schuller, whose vulgarly monstrous Crystal Cathedral was a Sunday-viewing landmark, preached from Garden Grove: it was known for little else. Today the area is known as "Little Saigon", sports tens of thousands of Vietnamese residents and an array of shops, markets and restaurants that serve as the focal point for the 120,000 who live in the region.

Monterey Park, five miles east of downtown, had a population in the mid-1980s that, like the rest of the San Gabriel Valley, was largely white or Hispanic: today it is more than 50 per cent Asian. A Taiwanese developer bought land there and decided to advertise it as the Chinese Beverly Hills: it has become the first suburban Chinatown, and attracts more new immigration from Hong Kong and Taiwan than anywhere else in the country.

The size and economic success of the city's sprawling "Koreatown" is legendary. The Koreans in Los Angeles are not street-corner vegetable sellers, as in Manhattan: here they have their own city, south of Wilshire Boulevard, and the pungent and unforgettable aroma of *kimchi* is as pervasive as it is in Seoul, or Pusan. Indeed, the scale of trans-Pacific migration is such that, although it is not quite possible to prove (given the numbers of illegal aliens who infest the region), it is said and widely believed that Los Angeles is the biggest Korean metropolitan area outside Korea itself, the second largest Chinese metropolitan area outside China, the second largest Japanese metropolitan area outside Japan, the largest Philippine ditto, and the largest Vietnamese as well. The fondness among Asians – though with the exception of the Japanese – for running small and highly flexible businesses has begun to show itself in the statistics: although only 17 of the Fortune 500 companies have their headquarters in Los Angeles, 95 per cent of the companies incorporated in the region have fewer than 50 employees. The employment of large numbers of new Hispanic and Asian immigrants, particularly illegal ones, in sweat-shops continues, however. One researcher was taken, blindfolded, to an immense warehouse where scores of immigrant workers were toiling in Dickensian conditions, producing motorcar wheels. The biggest surprise came when the researcher glanced at the labels on the wheels being packed for shipment: they read "Made in Brazil".

The city has become America's greatest gateway for immigrants from the new Pacific – as well as now being (by some measures) the busiest trading port in the country, far outstripping the Port of New York and New Jersey. The total value of oceanborne cargo passing into the ports of Los Angeles and Long Beach (where inbound container vessels are still dwarfed by the mighty Cunarder, the RMS *Queen Mary*, now settled in cement and used as an hotel) was $62 billion in 1986; Los Angeles International airport – LAX, as it is more universally known – currently adds a further $11 billion annually. The oceanborne total for Los Angeles is far ahead of New York; and while the New York total of air and sea trade is higher, it is growing more slowly and Los Angeles can be expected to catch up and overtake it, probably by 1995.

And as a player on the Pacific stage, it is crucial: as I have noted above, American trade with the countries grouped around the Pacific Ocean is now one third higher than with those of the Atlantic. Fully 60 per cent of that trade enters the United States through the two ports grouped around San Pedro Bay, and via the airport sandwiched between Century Boulevard, Imperial Highway, the San Diego freeway and the Pacific.

When I last arrived there, on a late evening flight from Detroit, having skimmed low over the twinkling lights of the desert, I placed my bags in the temporary care of a young woman whom I assumed, from her appearance, came from the Philippines. On the contrary, she said, she was from Samoa – Western Samoa, not the American island. Her parents still lived outside Apia and, once I told her I was from Britain, she remarked that she knew well where Robert Louis Stevenson was buried, and began to quote the epitaph he wrote for himself:

422

Under the wide and starry sky,
Dig the grave and let me lie.
Glad did I live and gladly die,
And I laid me down with a will.

Amid all the hubbub of the busiest and most modern and most insufferably crowded of the Pacific gateways – and yes, she said, she had arrived there a few weeks before, and had been offered a job by the officials who checked her in – we recited together as best we could:

This be the verse you grave for me:
Here he lies where he longed to be,
Home is the sailor, home from sea,
And the hunter home from the hill.

And all of a sudden the images of a quintessentially American Los Angeles seemed to fade from view and memory. Gone was the Hollywood sign from which a despondent Peg Entwhistle had leapt to her death* in the Thirties, after RKO refused to renew her contract. Gone was the view of surfer gridlock from the Malibu pier, and gone were the daiquiris and the arugula salad at Alice's Restaurant. "Gag me with a spoon" and "Barf me out" were lost from the lexicon. The Spruce Goose, the Universal Studios mock-up of the Red Sea that *really parts*, the Forest Lawn Cemetery, boysenberry jam, 1313 South Harbor Boulevard (a.k.a. Disneyland), the man who juggles with working chain-saws on the ocean-front walk at Venice, UCLA, the Polo Lounge, Bijan and all the other impossibly expensive shops on Rodeo Drive, the La Brea Tar Pits, the Comedy Store, the Brown Derby restaurant, the Capitol Records building, Frederick's lingerie shop, Graumann's Chinese Theatre with all its cement footprints, Griffith Park Observatory, Topanga Canyon, the 28 advertisements for cosmetic surgery, radial keratotomy, breast enlargement and smile enhancement that you find in the average copy of a Los Angeles magazine . . . all this faded into the background rumble of the airport.

With this young Samoan woman standing before me and quoting Robert Louis Stevenson, and telling me of her memories of Apia

*From the letter H.

423

and her dreams for her future, the city that lay just beyond the crawling cars outside the airport seemed suddenly to be a different, more substantial, more symbolic place: a city that was for the Pacific what New York had once been for the Atlantic: a great and majestic gateway and a great and dignified port, the natural eastern capital for the newest, busiest, richest and most populous quarter of the twenty-first-century world.

2

Metropolis West

Tokyo, capital of the Western Pacific, and probably one day capital of the world, is a city infatuated with thinking about the future – its future, Japan's future, the world's future – the future of everything. And a glance down Harumi–Dori Avenue on a glistening wet Friday evening can present a vision of urban life as futuristic as any imaginable. To anyone who has lived in the city that has been Japan's capital since 1868, the view is one of profound ordinariness: to a newcomer, it is as memorable a view of the coming nature of urban life as one is ever likely to encounter.

It was a Friday night, about 10 o'clock. I had just been with friends to a modish new restaurant called the Metropole: it was decorated in the style of a London club, with wood panels and rather decayed-looking marble columns made of heavy plastic. There was a small bust of Schiller, or perhaps it was Beethoven, or even Shakespeare, beside my table, and a crackling log fire, and a copy of *The Times* from the day before rolled up in that most quintessentially English of icons, the flat garden basket for rose-gathering made of wood strips, called a trug. The waiter, an androgynous functionary with hair that shone like obsidian and who wafted around like a faerie, dressed impeccably in the style of the Twenties, said that the paper was brought in daily straight from the London plane.

The restaurant, which was crowded with young Japanese, served Shanghainese food for no evident reason, given the decorative scheme: and so, from a table covered with Irish napery and Wedgwood and Royal Doulton china and glass, and with heavy cutlery from Asprey, we dined on entire steamed fishes patterned with onion-grass, on curious pork-filled dumplings, and vaguely

425

recognizable meats dressed with lotus-seed paste, and all washed down with (still more incongruously) a Momessin Fleurie at £100 a bottle. The bill for the four of us came to well over £400, and we all remarked afterwards that it had been (as indeed it should have been) tremendously good.

It was raining when we emerged, and I took a subway back to the hotel, not far from Hibiya Park and the outer ramparts of the Imperial Palace. In the park itself there was a pleasing, island-like tranquillity, though skyscrapers rose on every side: the moats and the massive stone walls of the palace rose abruptly to the north, and the shape of roofs which appeared to float above the parapets suggested the Japan of long ago – even though most of the structures are no more than thirty years old, the egregious "Flowers of Edo" having consumed their predecessors during the Second World War.*

I turned east, down Harumi-Dori Avenue, towards the Sumida River, on the estuary of which the original settlement of Edo had been built. Not far away was Nihonbashi – Japan Bridge – which spans a branch of the river. The five major post roads left from here in the days of the Tokugawa shoguns – the post roads that led into the *inaka*, the rather dismissive term the Japanese still use for anywhere in their country that is beyond the pale of the capital. Though an undistinguished iron structure built in 1911, the bridge is still the point from which all distances are measured, rather as Charing Cross is the cartographers' ground-zero in London.

But the images of Empire and shogunate were, it has to be said, mere fancies on my part. Harumi-Dori was very much a place of the twentieth or even the twenty-first century, and as I strolled along it – plunging ever out from the courtliness of old Tokyo, or such of it as remains – so I entered deeper and deeper inside the neon fantasia of Ginza, *the silver quarter*, where the old

---

*The phrase *Edo no hana* is an example of the gallows humour for which the Japanese are well known. It means, quite simply, fires. It was used to good effect in 1923, to describe the small – and from a distance probably rather pretty – blooms of flame that sprouted all across the city when, as a million women in paper houses were lighting their charcoal-fuelled *hibachis* for lunch, the Great Kanto Earthquake struck. 107,000 people died then; and again, when 139 American bombers struck Tokyo on one spring night in 1945, another 200,000 were consumed by fire. The particular fire that ruined the old Meiji palace was started by American incendiaries dropped on the night of 25 May 1945 – the Emperor and Empress safe in an underground bunker.

mint once had been – yet another reminder of her past; Tokyo's obsession with tomorrow is always coloured by a remembrance of yesterday.

Now everywhere, in the wild, throbbing and polychromatic confusion on all sides, was evidence of commerce. Here a mighty cylindrical glass and chrome tower, the San-ai Dream Centre, filled with scores of shops selling mini-skirts and tight sweaters and Wacoal computer-designed automatic memory bras to the teenaged girls with which Tokyo, more than any other city on earth, appears to be liberally supplied; there a night-club, with strips of pink-edged neon tracing a door from which legions of shouting and staggering men, all in dark blue suits and white shirts and with ties in a variety of states of askew, were emerging; here a tiny sushi bar, the crew-cut *itamae-san* slaving to slice and shape the slivers of blue-fin tuna, *awabi*, *torigai* and ark-shell, to ensure the rice below appears to have all its grains aligned, and to see that the *nori* in which the sushi-rolls will be wrapped is crisp and flexible, with the deep greenish colour and sheen of gold leaf; here, a little further along the street – halfway towards the vast Tsukiji fish market in which 190 tons of tuna are auctioned to the city's sushi bars each day – here is the Kabuki-za theatre where, if you've a mind to (and if you come before 9 pm), you may watch one of the lengthy "song, dance and skill" (the word's literal translation) dramas that remain so popular in modern Japan.

Here, then, is yet another illustration of the way old Japan intrudes amongst the glitter and clash of the modern city. Kabuki, a dramatic form five centuries old, is held in an atmosphere of theatrical informality that the West has not known since the days of the Globe or the music hall: the theatregoers eat their dinner in the stalls, walk about and in and out of the theatre, bellow at the actors and are in turn bellowed at by players who may suddenly weary of the plot and yearn for some inspiration from the audience. The television stations happily broadcast Kabuki, earning ratings that can sometimes – depending on the fame of the Kabuki star – compare favourably with those for baseball games or the late-evening diet of blurred pornography.

The structure of Kabuki is quite formal: there is, in a traditional programme, an historic play followed by a contemporary, domestic drama, and then a dance finale – the *jidaimono*, the *sewamono* and the *ogiri shosagoto* – all interleaved with dancing, and the whole affair lasting for as much as five hours. The historic plays, too, are hugely popular: none more so, perhaps, than the so-called *Chushingura*, or

Story of the Forty-Seven Ronin, which General MacArthur had banned during the Occupation. Indeed, one could say with some accuracy that the saga of *Chushingura*, especially once revived after MacArthur and his men had gone home, captured the imagination of the entire Japanese people and is powerfully representative of a crucially important aspect of Japanese morality. Despite our being buried among the neon cathedrals of Ginza, in a quarter of the city – of the world – that displays an extraordinary radiant energy and an almost erotic passion for the highest of technologies . . . despite all this, it will perhaps be useful to be reminded of the simple story of *Chushingura*, a saga whose effect on a people and a nation still has few equals.

A thick accretion of fiction clings now to the original tale – itself lengthy and complex, but from which can be distilled the elements which General MacArthur so feared and despised. All took place during the rule in Tokyo – or Edo, as it was then – of the shogun Tsunayoshi.* One *daimyo* named Asano claimed he had been insulted by another, the Lord Kira, and tried to kill him – in fact only wounding him. Tsunayoshi, recognizing the attack as a breach of feudal ethics, ordered Asano to commit *seppuku* – to slice open his own abdomen with two cuts, one vertical, one horizontal, and then eviscerate himself before dying. Despite protesting the apparent injustice – Kira had, after all, insulted him savagely – Asano did as he was bidden.

However, a number of his retainers decided to avenge their master's death – this being the aspect of the tale to which MacArthur took exception, since he felt it glorified the vengeance, the espousal of *Bushido*, that the Japanese might think of wreaking on the triumphant Americans. In the story the leaderless retainers (hence their name, *ronin*) wandered the length of the country, searching for Kira. They caught up with him one snowy night: the entire group stormed into his house in Edo and murdered him, cutting off his head and taking it to the grave where their master Asano lay. They then gave themselves up to the magistrates.

*His reign proved a fortunate time for the city's dogs. In a somewhat eccentric attempt to expiate his sin of failing to sire an heir, Tsunayoshi inaugurated a policy of extravagant solicitude for any dog, stray or domestic. Anyone found guilty of killing one might be executed. The shogun built kennels for strays, and dogs taken there were escorted in palanquins. His love for the beasts stemmed partly from his having been born in the Year of the Dog (according to the twelve-year animal cycle of Chinese mythology): he is known still as the Dog Shogun.

The case presented the shogunal government with a dilemma: the *ronin* had undoubtedly committed a breach of the peace, a murder; but at the same time there was widespread concern that during Tsunayoshi's reign the old ways of the *samurai* were being ignored, that a certain moral laxity was abroad. Moreover, the old Confucian codes insisted that the unjust death of a father or master must be avenged by the man's disciples or his sons. The feeling across seventeenth-century Edo was that the *ronin* should be pardoned, that theirs was an honourable crime, what in today's America would be termed justifiable homicide.

But the scholars of Edo ruled otherwise. Law and order, they said, had to be upheld in concert with the traditional standards. Only by committing suicide themselves could the *ronin* meet the apparently conflicting requirements of history and equity. By doing so they would in addition be meeting in the next world the master whose death they had avenged in this. And so, as ordered, the 46 (one had dropped out at an early stage in the story) committed hari-kiri. There was a massive outpouring of public grief: the men, it was said – and is still said today – exemplified the spirit of true warriors. Their tombs are still to be found in the temple of the Sengakuji, next to Lord Asano's grave, and such is the popular sentiment on the side of the *ronin* that many thousands of ordinary Japanese stand in line to visit their memorial, 300 years later.

It was from close to the theatre, perhaps a few yards back along Harumi-Dori, a little to the west of the junction with Showa-Dori, that I happened to glance back. It was quite late on the Friday night now; the rain had worsened and was hissing on to the streets, and the neon madness of Ginza reflected itself as great puddles and smears of carmine, chartreuse, aquamarine, jasmine, heliotrope and a million other colours besides. The buildings, immense disembodied pillars of light, rose from the low clouds that seemed to have settled from the storm. The streets were crowded, with cars and taxis and small buses, and thousands of men and women – mostly men, with lithe young women in short satin pants beckoning at them from some of the smaller neon-rimmed doorways – walking hurriedly through the fiery gloom.

Suddenly, from somewhere above and up a little way, came a hiss and a rumble and a thunderous roar. Above the roadway something blue and white and adorned with rows of brilliantly illuminated windows streaked across my field of vision. Whatever it was moved tremendously fast and I had the impression, what with the people and the neon, the cars, the rain and the flashing lights and movement of every speed and direction, that I was caught up in some immense and infernal machine: the sensation was not at all unpleasant – in fact, it was rather exciting – but there was a strange feeling of being quite out of control and that this city had simply become too complicated, too many-layered, multi-textured, polychromatic, babel-filled and crowded, and that the power of the individual had somehow become utterly subservient to the unstoppable demands of this urban firestorm.

It had been, of course, a bullet-train, the *shinkansen*. Tokyo Station* was but a few hundred yards up the track, and the specially-built *shinkansen* road (next to but separate from the ordinary, subsonic railway line) soared over Harumi-Dori just beyond the freeway bridge. The freeway leads south towards Yokohama and Kawasaki, north towards Niigata: it is choked with traffic for much of the day and so, as part of the drastic traffic management policies applied to the city, has its access roads closed for many hours daily. A common sight in the city centre is a queue of motorists several city blocks long, waiting before a freeway barrier: at a certain moment, either broadcast on the radio or familiar to those rash enough to drive in the city, the barrier lifts and the cars roar upward to join the ceaseless river of lorries and buses hurtling between the Sea of Japan and the Pacific, or points in between.

I looked at my watch; it was exactly a quarter past eleven. The bullet-train, invariably punctual to the second, would arrive at Tokyo *eko* in one minute. I had a timetable in my pocket. Only one train coming from the south arrived at 23.16 – the Hikari Number 30 *shinkansen* from Hakata, and the monster that had so startled me was undoubtedly it. It had completed the longest bullet-train journey it was possible to make: 1,180.9 kilometres from the terminus on the northern shore of the island of Kyushu, passing via Hiroshima and Kobe (though it had not stopped at Shin-Kobe station), Osaka and Nagoya. It had left Hakata at eleven minutes past five in the

---

*2,800 trains a day pass through Tokyo *eko*. There have also been two prime ministers assassinated there: the first, Takahashi Hara, was stabbed in 1921: a tiny chrysanthemum set into the marble of a stairway, and ignored by those who crowd across it, serves as memorial to the incident. Nine years later Yuko Hamaguchi was shot, but he was only wounded, dying many months later.

evening, and had borne its cargo of businessmen and women home to the capital in six hours and five minutes, at a mean speed of 194 kilometres an hour.

So splendid a symbol of modern Japan, one might suppose the *shinkansen* to be a wholly home-grown phenomenon, a consequence of the riches, technical expertise and astonishing propensity for hard work for which all Japan is known. But to the chagrin of many proud Japanese, the truth is somewhat different. The *shinkansen* lines were a World Bank project, and the freeways were, too. At the time they were being planned, and then built, Japan was the world's second largest recipient of foreign aid – India being the first. Today, now she has the structures in place to permit her people to travel so speedily and to arrive and depart with such enviable promptitude, the position is quite reversed: in 1989 Japan became the world's largest donor of foreign aid, overtaking the United States by hundreds of millions of dollars.*

Within half an hour, then, on my stroll from Hibiya subway station to the Kabuki-za theatre, so many layers of Tokyo were unveiled. The shogunate and the Emperor were there; the relentless search for pleasure, invariably erotic or narcissistic, was there too; the high-technology glitz of it all, the tradition, the quietude, the noise. Tokyo has this curiously pleasing anarchic quality about it, a circus-like performance of the eternally unexpected. What might be around the next corner? In Tokyo, you never quite know what is about to happen. It is a city on the edge, with all the benefits and trials such an existence offers and threatens.

As an example of the unexpected anarchy of modern Tokyo, I recall once being in the British Embassy, a singularly lovely old set of buildings, a laager of grey British houses set behind a wall off Uchibori-Dori Avenue, to the west of the Imperial Palace. I had been with an old friend (now a senior diplomat) and a Japanese politician, and we had been trying to work out how much to price a piece of land in Shinjuku – a part of western Tokyo that, because it is built on rock and thus likely to be relatively insulated from the travails of the coming second Kanto earthquake, sports a number of real, sub-American-style skyscrapers. It is a popular entertainment in Japanese

*Nearly half Japan's foreign development aid goes to countries in East Asia and the Pacific – particularly the Pacific islands. The slightly smaller sum of US assistance goes principally to the Middle East and Africa.

cafés to demonstrate the price of real-estate by pointing to a table, or the top of a sushi-bar counter, and guessing how much so small a tract of land would cost in, say, Marunouchi, Shimbashi or Chiyoda-ku. We settled for a book, a coffee-table book, *A Day in the Life of Japan*. The politician said 20,000 American dollars, my diplomat friend put it a little lower. The politician was probably right – and that was in 1988. By now its price, if not its value, might have doubled.

I came out of the embassy around tea-time. It was a crisp autumn afternoon, sunny and cold, with the acid smell of fallen maple leaves. The first of the winter Siberian winds was beginning to stream down from the hills, just as it did in Seoul and Peking at this time of year. The roofs of the Imperial Palace glittered in the sloping sun. Traffic on the avenue was lighter than usual: the evening rush-hour had yet to get under way.

"You fucking cunt!" The phrase came at me in a booming scream. It was a woman's voice, high-pitched, hysterical, and much amplified so that it thundered around the buildings. I glanced around, alarmed. The embassy guard, a tough-looking Mancunian, grinned out at me from his bullet-proof glass box and shrugged his shoulders apologetically as the stream of obscenities continued.

The voice came from a black panel truck parked outside the embassy, three huge horn loudspeakers mounted on the roof. Inside was a driver and beside him, a young Japanese woman in what looked like army fatigues. She was staring at me and speaking into a small microphone. "Stop looking at me, you filthy English pig. You make me sick!" And so she continued as I walked down the embassy steps and, with the outer perimeter guard assuring me no harm would come to me and urging me out on to the street, began my short stroll home.

I passed beside the van. The woman continued to shout and hurl all manner of abuse at me, then suddenly looked up and back at the embassy. "You, you four-eyed scumsucker!" she screeched, and since I was not wearing spectacles, I realized she was attempting, probably with some success, to gain the attention of someone else. Indeed a mild-looking *gaijin* – a clerkly figure from some bowel of the chancery – was emerging from the door, and it was now his turn to look alarmed, and to wonder how safe it was to leave the sanctuary of Earl Grey and yesterday's *Financial Times*. I looked up at the howling harpy, whereupon she returned my glance, gave me a thumbs-up and grinned. I fancied that she might have urged me to have a nice day, though this seemed rather disconsonant with her overall approach. We parted partners in some strange conspiracy, and I heard her healthily lambasting the hapless clerk until he, too, joined the roadway beyond the good lady's attentions.

Such protests are not uncommon in Japan. The law says that one citizen may shout and scream abuse at another provided one keeps moving, even if only very slightly – and indeed, and since I knew a little of the law, I was keen to see that the black panel truck was indeed inching its way, snail-like, along the avenue. As with a snail, it was tricky ever to see the van actually under way: but if I looked elsewhere, and then back again at the van a moment later, then its position was very definitely different. (The managing director of a Hong Kong airline, a mild Englishman of perfect manners, had met with such a protest while staying a few weeks earlier at the Hilton Hotel in Osaka: a travel agent, claiming he had been gypped in some previous dealing with the company, had hired a van of professional mobile protestors who spent the next day and night circling the Hilton screeching the most bloodcurdling insults at the man. He had to flee in the middle of the night and check in somewhere else, under an assumed name.)

There is infinitely more to the inherently complicated feeling of Tokyo than the presumption that one is living on the verge of anarchy. True, displays like this are disturbing at first; and the decadent excesses of the Tokyo consumer – gold-leaf sprinkled in the tea, room deodorizers set to detect the aroma of perspiration, mint-flavoured oxygen on sale for inhalation at a dollar a minute – can be as dismaying as they are amusing. But there is also a feeling that this is the city at its modern optimum – that if ever a city had captured the *zeitgeist*, had managed to be at a point in its psychological, architectural and infrastructural development that somehow exactly and indescribably matched the era, then that was Tokyo.

Brad Leithauser writes, half-admiringly, about the way Tokyo offers "that giddy, befuddling feeling that derives from a gleaming, unweathered architecture. Although the city's mapped outlines may still reflect – as the guidebooks tell us – the careful, concentric encampments by which both *shogun* and emperor protected themselves from insurrection, what strikes the stroller's eye is the unbroken newness of it all: block after high-tech block of buildings erected in the last few decades." But he also goes on to speak, rather less lyrically, about the potential problems, the "dislocation that comes from living in proximity to a future that threatens to engorge the past . . .", and wonders about the long-term psychiatric health of the Tokyo citizenry.

Other cities around the world seem to be somehow cocooned in another age, or in an expectation of one to come. New York had had its heyday half a century ago, Paris was *du fin de siècle*, and London's pinnacle of elegance and importance coincided with the Empire's climax. Seoul, on the other hand, is a city still a-building, in the hope of some future chance for glory, and Bangkok and Saõ Paulo have their eyes set well into the next decade too. San Francisco, though, is a city that seems to have something of the spirit of the times about her – a feeling, an energy, a vibrant power that Tokyo, above all, displays in abundance. Tokyo is a city obsessed about the future: but she is also very much a city of the present.

The company that manufactures the Memory Bra, Wacoal, plays an important role at the cutting edge of Tokyo's modern development. Its stores – in particular the Wacoal Kojimachi, all domed ceilings and a spaceship-shaped canopy – are architecturally fascinating. It also sponsors arts exhibitions and permanent displays, and owns a building on Aoyama-Dori called Spiral where the whole mélange of artistic energies of young Tokyo – and Tokyo is a very young city indeed, jammed solid with the "new human race", the *shinjinrui* – is on show, along with a steamy Thai-Japanese restaurant, a chic club where American rock bands perform and a bazaar that sells the minutely precise pieces of equipment – Bowie-knife-*cum*-radio-set-*cum*-paper-clip-dispenser-*cum*-electronic-pager – that the Japanese believe will bring an illusion of order and efficiency to their lives. Spiral is a place that plays benign host to all manner of creative madness from a community that appears to have become a reliquary for the *avant garde*, perhaps the only place left where the phrase can be used with a straight face. Arrays of video screens show experimental media productions. Soft female voices advertise coming attractions. Sound and light, pastel and bilious flickering and ever-changing, pulse around the gradually rising and falling walkways so that, as in Tokyo itself, there is a feeling of being trapped, stuck in molasses, in something that is delightfully insane and yet at the same time vaguely threatening.

But the architect of Spiral, Fumihiko Maki, is no youngster, and the building that he created is no hair salon in Knightsbridge or Wanchai, as likely to be pulled down and redeveloped tomorrow as it was to have been built yesterday. He is a former Harvard teacher, and is described as "part of the huge cadre of future-oriented thinkers now helping Tokyo's government overhaul and reconfigure the city for the next century . . ." Maki was quoted in 1988 as saying that he and his fellow Tokyoites were "experiencing an exciting moment that doesn't come often in the history of a city. Tokyo is ascendant, flourishing. We have the money, the opportunity and the tradition." He also pointed out what is as obvious about Tokyo as it is about Los Angeles – that it has no centre, no "downtown". "It is a chaotic labyrinth of small, interesting inner spaces, constructed from light, fragile materials and connected to each other by a complex network of grids, radials and spirals."

But the connection between all these "small, interesting inner spaces" is considerably more sophisticated than in Los Angeles, where only now is a subway about to be constructed, and one which will connect only a very few places to one another. In Tokyo such matters have long been well organized. To get from, say, Shibuya in the west, to Ueno in the northeast of Tokyo, or to Tokyo Disneyland in the east, is a matter of perfect simplicity. There are ten subway lines and eleven private railways operating in Tokyo, and each intersects with the other at least once, and in some cases many times, so that – with imagination and a skill that it can be most satisfying to develop – you can calculate the least expensive and the quickest way of getting from anywhere to anywhere. Moreover, you can do so secure in the knowledge that, while you may be squeezed half to death by the crowds, and may have more intimate sub-sexual contact with strangers than you might have bargained for (an aspect of Japan's sexual liberality that may dismay Westerners, though the degree is relatively harmless), you will get to your destination on time and in one piece, and have no truck with traffic jams or freeway killers or the Highway Patrol or wrecks that are common coin to the commuters on the far side of the Pacific.

Your only problem may come late at night, when the subways close down and the hordes of drunken *sararimen* from Ginza and the old red-light region of Shinjuku stagger home to where the faithful wives have been darning their *tabi* and affecting an insouciant disregard for their whereabouts. Drink and the Japanese male has never proven a wholly successful mixture, and carriage after subway carriage will be temporary home to a half-sleeping man who, if he tries to stand, will appear to do so on top of a set of greased ball-bearings, and will then almost certainly be sick into the bargain. Risk of being the victim of projectile vomiting is reason enough for most mortals to stay away from the last train of the Tokyo night.

"Ah!" a stranger to Tokyo might be exclaiming at this point. "That shows it!" The fact that you can be vomited over on a late-night train by a man who treats his wife like an animal and who gets drunk

435

because his life is so damnably tedious and structured and boring – that demonstrates that life for a Japanese is in fact dreadful, not at all the kind we in the West would wish to trade. Did not the distinguished European Commission head of external relations, Sir Roy Denman, say in 1979 that Japan was "a country of workaholics" and that they all lived in "what Westerners would regard as little more than rabbit-hutches"? And did not a sizeable number of Westerners feel smug at the knowledge that the Japanese standard of living – or way of life, at least – was so very poor, and did not an upwelling of *schadenfreude* replace for a moment the envy so many of us feel for the Japanese?

Sir Roy Denman, it turned out, was in the van of an inchoate Japan-is-dreadful movement, and following his remarks a perception coalesced around him to the effect that Japan in general, and Tokyo in particular, represented some kind of living hell: that Tokyo was the city on which Ridley Scott, the film director, modelled *Bladerunner*, with its appallingly prescient visions of tomorrow's urban nightmare. (A truer template for *Bladerunner* is to be found at the eastern end of Lockhart Road in Hong Kong's Wanchai, a combination of neon, filth and crime that is peopled with a cast of low-life characters drawn from the fleshpots of South China.) In fact, as is demonstrably clear to anyone who can afford to spend more than a weekend there, Tokyo is one of the most pleasant of all cities in which to live, and the Japanese seem to suffer no more from life in Tokyo than do Americans from life in New York or Los Angeles: probably, in fact, they suffer rather less. Sir Roy and his followers would do as well to spare their tears.

It is true that Japanese houses are small – particularly those in cities like Tokyo. But the figures show they are not that much smaller than anywhere outside Canada and the United States: sure, an American might well have a three-bedroomed house with an average floor area of 135 square metres, while a Japanese would have to cram the same number of beds into just 81 square metres. But is he that much worse off than the Frenchman, or the German? Apparently not: in Paris the average flat was only 5 square metres larger, and in Frankfurt and Munich, the average householder had only 15 square metres more. The Denman rabbit-hutches are more widespread a phenomenon, it seems.

It is also true that prices are terrifyingly high: a flat in Tokyo rents, on average, for $1,500 a month, while an equivalent apartment in New York would cost $500 less, and in Frankfurt a third of the Tokyo cost. And though the *sarariman* earns more, he can afford much less: a New Yorker has precisely twice the purchasing power of a Tokyoite, while a German living in Frankfurt has two and a quarter times as much. But other statisticians quibble about such figures: how do you create a "culturally neutral" basket of goods and services, such that one can properly compare what it really costs to live in Tokyo with how much one would spend in Chelsea or Manhattan? Quibbles aside, though – the sheer ability of the man from Marunouchi to enjoy himself as well as the man from Malibu is, in all probability, very limited indeed.

The Japanese office workers are given more holidays than their opposite numbers in America (though they invariably decline to take all of their entitlement), and they have no fewer than eighteen public holidays a year in addition. They can spend them overseas with far greater facility than can foreigners: the Japanese ability to afford almost anything abroad, a consequence of *endaka*, is legendary. Not that he would necessarily want to spend it in the big city, though: Tokyo has fewer public parks than New York – a tenth as much green space, in fact; but while walking across it the American is six times more likely than a Japanese to be murdered, 25 times more likely to be raped and 140 times more likely to be robbed. There is no inner-city problem to speak of in Tokyo (though you can see tramps disconsolately reading comic books on the benches in Tokyo station), and no racism – since there is essentially no race in Tokyo other than Japanese. The *burakumin* – the "special community people" who were once total outcasts, the *eta*, who tanned leather and once were the only meat-eaters, are still not treated well and their misery sometimes causes suicides. The Koreans, even though second- and third-generation immigrants, still have to be fingerprinted and carry special identity papers, and many jobs are denied them.* But their problem is as nothing compared with those still suffered by the American black or Hispanic, and the idea of urban ghettos and street violence of the kind seen in Harlem and the Bronx is total anathema to the 19 million who live in relative harmony in the great sprawl of Tokyo.

The generally serene life of the Japanese – family stability, job security counting for more than one might think – and his good

*Though soon this may all end; in May 1990 the new Japanese Emperor, Akihito, formally apologized to the Korean president and his people for the "wrongs" committed over the preceding years – most notably, of course, the invasion and colonization of the country between 1910 and 1945. But implicit in the apology, which some Koreans said was still not enough, was better treatment for those ethnic Koreans who still lived in Japan.

diet – fish and rice and beer and saké – leads him to expect four years more life than his American or German counterpart, and when he does die he will be only a sixth as likely to succumb to a heart attack as his British opposite number (though three times as likely to die of stomach cancer). And even though in 1988 the average Tokyo businessman – 53 per cent of whom own their own homes – spends 85 minutes a day commuting, he was spending 100 minutes a day in 1975 – so conditions in the city are getting better, and life is becoming ever more convenient and enjoyable. Rabbit-hutches? Workaholics? Maybe so, compared with Westchester County and Santa Monica – but if the other side of the coin includes a secure job, a happy family, a crime-free city and a content old age, is the trade perhaps not worthwhile?

These two great cities, the Eastern Capital of Los Angeles and the City of Tokyo that teeters on the edge of the Western Pacific, are ineluctably entwined as the twin capitals of the Ocean, the two ends of the axis upon which tomorrow's world spins. They have their similarities. Their populations are of a similar magnitude. Both are port-cities, and their peoples involved in an astonishing diversity of industries and activities. They are both modern, recently reconstructed cities that seem preternaturally prone to disasters – fires and earthquakes in the West, just earthquakes in the East. Both cities have developed during their short modern histories and in what urban scientists regard as a curiously non-classical way, with many different centres of population, and little by way of a clearly defined downtown to which all mankind is attracted each morning and from which he is expelled each nightfall. Transport is a key element in both *metroplexes*, to use the modish descriptive: the car dominates in Los Angeles, the train in Tokyo – and in both pollution is a plague. Yet there is a certain chic about living in either place and surviving all that the urban turmoil can hurl at one: those who live beyond the confines of either city are regarded by those within as hayseeds, as rude provincials – a phenomenon truer in Japan, perhaps, than in America.

Most crucially of all, both places are cities of the world. Tokyo and Los Angeles are no longer to be thought of as merely properties of the nations on whose coasts they happen to stand. They have a role to play in the global scheme that transcends the minor inconveniences of national boundaries. Los Angeles gives the world many things: to pick two of its products, almost at random, it provides the world with the great bulk of its entertainment, and its factories provide the satellite machinery which is hurled into space and allows us each to talk to one another; Tokyo, on the other hand, provides us with televisions, radios, personal stereos and cameras and, perhaps rather more importantly, with cars. Its bankers lubricate the world's financial enginework and, as the country becomes increasingly a creditor nation, so it will exert a greater and greater degree of influence over the way the world, and its citizens, live and work and have their being.

Between them the cities permit us the wherewithal to do, and to talk and to be entertained and to have fun. They do not by any means enjoy a monopoly in granting us these rights, but they do play a crucial and a growing role in doing so.

This global role which has been gifted to Los Angeles and Tokyo has come to be reflected in the character of the cities themselves, and in a curiously contrasting way. For the progress of the one city from its previous merely national to its present-day truly transnational standing, turns out to be the precise antithesis of that of the other.

The writer George Woodcock reported on an aspect of this in Tokyo thirty years ago. He noticed the way that the Japanese who inhabited the capital – and in those immediately post-Olympic days it was a rather dowdy town, only just starting to show signs of its coming greatness – he noticed how they were displaying all the attributes of a cannibalized culture, something the haughtily nationalistic Japanese would have been loath to admit. For example, he wrote: their style and manner of writing came largely from China; their political constitution came from the British; both the beer that they drank and the halls in which they drank it were of obvious German heritage; the uniforms of the university students were, and remain, pure Hapsburg Austria; and the attractive little middy blouses worn by the schoolgirls were Victorian, and English. There were tiny cake-shops all over town: clearly *patisseries*, and French; there were an immense number of coffee-shops: these were Italian; the fashions in art and dress – all were pure American. The Tokyo middle classes loved then, as they love today, the works of Manet and Monet and Picasso: a visit to the art sales departments of any branch of the Sogo, Matsuzakaya or Mitsukoshi department stores will demonstrate their reverence for this sometimes affordable

439

luxury; while their corporations, underlining the public preference for Western art, will buy Van Gogh rather than one of the bird-and-twig pictures that are customarily favoured (or so it is supposed) by most Eastern people.

"At first we were bewildered at the very incongruity," George Woodcock wrote, "of this mixture of the strange and the familiar, and then amazed at the zest for having the best of both worlds, which seems to be the most outstanding characteristic of the modern Japanese."

And all this assimilation of the best foreign culture could be accomplished, the Japanese had found, without the need for any significant assimilation of the people who had invented that culture in the first place. Sure, there were expatriates in Tokyo all right – American stockbrokers, teachers of English, and Frenchmen who had come to study the niceties of Japanese fashion in the style of Kenzo and Issey Miyake. But was there a *quartier* in Shinjuku? A ghetto at the back of Tokyo station? A bustee or a Jewtown, or anywhere described as Apache territory, to be found between Kashima and Yokohama?

Most assuredly there was not. All the products, styles, fashions, pretension, sounds and foods of the world were in Tokyo, but none of the people who had made them. To all intents and purposes, Tokyo was Japanese only: it had managed to absorb the essence of the world without for a moment diluting its own self, its ineffable sense of the Japanese identity.

The very opposite is true of Los Angeles. Here, thanks to the continuing American experiment in forging human alloy from the disparate elements of the races, men and women of every nation, ethnic type and religious persuasion on earth are to be found living in every kind of circumstance in those 1,000-odd square miles between the San Gabriel Mountains and the sea. There may be no Hispanics in Tokyo: there are millions upon millions of them in Los Angeles. There are no communities of East European Jews in Tokyo: the synagogues are filled on Saturday everywhere from Beverly Hills to the Harbor freeway. No blacks are in evidence around Tokyo Bay, except on the far side of the gates of America's Yakusaka naval base: millions live in Watts and its neighbouring slums, and there are many middle-class blacks in every quarter of the town. There are in addition Koreans, Haitians, New Zealanders, South Vietnamese, Japanese – sizeable numbers of Japanese, in fact, huddling together for comfort and security – Papuans, Solomon Islanders. The little girl from Western Samoa whom I found at the airport: none like her, or of any of the other groups, are to be found in Tokyo, nor ever will be. Everything – their food, their music, their style of life – everything that they are is in Tokyo: but they are not. They are in Los Angeles.

And Los Angeles takes them all in, thanks them for coming, and then relentlessly and shamelesssly strips away and persuades them each to forget all the culture and separate identity they each brought with them. It may take a generation or two before a Korean from south of Wilshire Boulevard thinks of himself as an American, and takes to coleslaw more readily than *kimchi*. It may be even longer before all the elements of Pidgin are purged from a Port Moresby man who now works at the docks in Long Beach. The traces of longing for a decent Pavlova may linger in the mind of that man from Christchurch who now drives to work in his Camaro along the San Diego freeway.

But even if slowly, the great forcing machine that is America will assuredly render all of these men and women down into the grist of these United States, and make them equal partners in all the richness and the might and the bland homogeneity that on the surface is the most visible aspect of the American way.

Los Angeles thus, like all of America, takes in the world and her people and makes them all-American. Tokyo, on the other hand, has restricted herself to taking in the world, yet has herself remained purely Japanese. She is still possessed of her old identity; Los Angeles is proudly making do with her new one. Equal and opposite, the new poles of the world, the cities are playing their new-found roles as the urban point and counterpoint of the coming century.

THE WAVE

There is a shiny black building in Roppongi, perhaps the most modish of Tokyo's villages, in which one may buy almost anything that appeals to man's sense of hearing. Seven storeys tall and decked out in black and grey metallic tiles and in a lambent green neon, the store is curved and patterned to resemble a cross between an immense Wurlitzer juke-box and a stacking system for the high-fidelity enthusiast. There are other passing resemblances, too: a similarity, for instance, to the old Capitol Records building on the far side of the Ocean, in Hollywood; some architectural propinquity to parts of the engineworks from the Starship *Enterprise*, or even to parts of a film much admired in Japan, *Alien*.

The store is called "The Wave", and its basic business is the selling of records to members of the *shinjinrui*, the "new human race", with which Japanese society currently abounds.

But The Wave is more than a store. It reminded me, the first time I stepped from its lift, of an Eastern version, an ultra-modern version of the old Pitt Rivers Museum in Oxford, where the founders had organized their collections typologically – all mirrors together, all knives, all bagpipes, all guns – rather than by their age, or the country of origin. Here was everything, in short, that made a sound – from wind chimes and bone-pipes and nose-flutes, in a long evolutionary chain that passed via trumpets and alp-horns, balalaikas and zithers, Jew's harps, kazoos, glockenspiels, dulcimers and bombardons to CD players, digital audio tapes, Walkmans and Moog synthesizers.

Although it might prove something of a trial to pick up a fine Cremona at The Wave, and though disappointed visitors have

445

reported that the stock of Bosendorfers and Steinways is not what it once was, in all other ways the spectrum of sound-production is represented in its entirety. Every vinyl record, every polycarbonate compact disc, every tape – cassette, eight-track, reel-to-reel, metal, ceramic and digital – known to have been recorded is discoverable, somewhere, within the seven floors of The Wave. As, curiously, is also a gallimaufry of strange and wonderful, largely Californian-published books and journals – on low fashion, sexual eccentricity, bizarre photography, violent fantasy. An American who wandered in one afternoon recently found himself in the midst of a Wave exhibition called Bondage Week. There were young blonde models in black leather restraints, treatises on knots and magazines on leather, and sado-masochistic films played silently on scores of TV monitors. It was an indication, he later remarked, that the dark side of Japanese life was rarely far from the surface. Others might observe that the store was displaying the quintessence of Japanese society, an amalgam of the old obsessions and the new technologies, and all set against a backdrop of sound waves, rhythms, harmonies and all the instruments that ever made or played them.

To me, The Wave represented rather more than a simple exposition of the bizarreries of Japan. Rather, it seemed to offer a new kind of cultural mélange, a combination of the technical and artistic best – or worst, depending on your taste – that came from both sides of the Pacific and which, in a manner having much to do with the ascendancy of the region, has brought the two coasts together in a cultural lockstep.

I mentioned at the outset of this venture that what prompted my consideration of the Pacific as a real entity, rather than a figment of a writer's imagination or an item on some geopolitician's wish-list, was the new certainty that the inhabitants of the nations grouped by geographical accident around the Ocean's coasts had started to look inwards, at themselves, rather than much caring any longer for the view of those beyond, or behind. They were concerned less with looking over their shoulders, with watching nervously how their antics were being received by some bossy mother-nation beyond their Ocean's shores. They looked instead across the huge blue expanse of water, and they communed with each other – Shanghai with Santiago, Sydney with Hong Kong, Jakarta with Lima and, in this particular case, Roppongi with Hollywood – and by doing so perhaps they achieved a kind of Pacific identity.

This identity is perhaps ineffable and inchoate. It may prove to be

446

both ephemeral and evanescent. But I doubt it. The shape of the thing, the identity of Pacific Man, all is becoming slowly clearer, looming up through the fog. The trans-Pacific links – even such as are so trivially but undeniably colourfully exhibited at The Wave store – between the science that brought forth digital audio-tape and the expressive energy that gave us Monterey music, the links between the efficient processes which render Toshiba sound chips affordable and the intellectual freedoms which allow the graphic artists of Cupertino to draw things the like of which they have barely imagined, the links between the sudden fascinations of affluent Tokyo (leather-fetishism today, leather handbags tomorrow) and the high priests of personal liberalism across in the American West – such links as are being forged in the post-colonial, post-socialist, end-of-history, high-technology, environmentally-conscious new era look like enduring.

If this thesis is believed, they – or others that replace and subvert them – will quite probably form the basis of the social, intellectual, economic and human alliances of the future. If they achieve this, then they will form the underpinnings of the world's new political structure, the world in which the Pacific will be in consequence the focus of human energy and existence.

It was not always so. The Pacific – by which not so long ago one meant the South Seas – was once the place for exotic oblivion, for adventure, contemplation and escape. As recently as 1913, a widely accepted image of the Pacific and its shores held that:

> Warm perfumes like a breath from vine and tree
> Drift down the darkness. Plangent, hidden from eyes,
> Somewhere an *eukaleli* thrills and cries
> And stabs with pain the night's brown savagery;
> And dark scents whisper; and dim waves creep to me,
> Gleam like a woman's hair, stretch out, and rise;
> And new stars burn into the ancient skies,
> Over the murmurous soft Hawaiian sea.

Rupert Brooke, much more widely known for writings that reflected the savagery of the European War, "The Soldier" and "Grantchester", had been to the Pacific, and it had left an indelible impression upon him. He sailed first to Hawaii in the summer of 1913, and there wrote the sonnet starting as above. Finding Honolulu "a dreadfully American place", he swiftly moved on to Samoa, and to Fiji. His declaration, written after he had been to see where Stevenson was buried on a hilltop above Apia, rings now as clearly as it must have done eight decades ago:

> It's all true about the South Seas. I get a little tired of it at moments, because I am just too old for Romance. But there it is; there it wonderfully is; heaven on earth, the ideal life, little work, dancing and singing and eating; naked people of incredible loveliness, perfect manners, and immense kindliness, a divine tropic climate, and intoxicating beauty of scenery.
>
> . . . if ever you miss me, suddenly, one day, from lecture room B in King's, or from the Moulin d'Or at lunch, you'll know that I've got sick for the full moon on these little thatched roofs, and the palms against the morning, and the Samoan boys and girls diving thirty feet into a green sea or a deep mountain pool under a waterfall – and that I've gone back.

Brooke was smitten, as a dozen famous passers-by before him; Paul Gauguin, for instance:

"I have escaped everything that is artificial and conventional," he wrote from Tahiti, in *Noa Noa*. "Here I enter into Truth, become one with nature. After the disease of civilization, life in this new world is a return to health."

Gauguin had a fair taste of the Pacific to begin with. His father was French, but his mother was half Peruvian Creole, and his early days were spent in that rather threadbare capital city, Lima. Perhaps it was something about those early sunsets – not that Lima's dismal, misty climate would provide many: young Paul must have been taken down to the coast at Miraflores – that prompted his later love for natural beauty, for romance and primitivism. He was fascinated by pre-Colombian Peruvian pottery, without a doubt, and admitted deriving visual inspiration from those early Pacific designs. Whatever, he returned to the Ocean when he was 43 and stayed for almost all the rest of his life, immersed in the world of the "natural".

His sojourn proved both an idyll and a revelation. Gauguin was one of the first truly perceptive Europeans to realize the coming agony of the old Pacific – to realize that here was Paradise, and that it was being desecrated by the growing interest and avarice of the white man. He had come, he wrote, to paint "these nymphs. I want to perpetuate them, with their golden skins, their searching animal odour, their tropical savours." Instead, what he found was the evidence of coming ruin. The white man, with his greed, his diseases, his penchant for order and control, for legal codes and assimilation, and for power, was stealing away the very things which had drawn him to the Pacific in the first place.

Gauguin was deeply disappointed, and used both paintbrush and pen to inveigh bitterly against what he saw as the racist venality of the French colonial administration – against the venality of all the European conquerors and exploiters of the Pacific.

What he witnessed had much to do with that old saw – first told by Jomo Kenyatta and repeated by Archbishop Tutu before the American Congress – about the seductive force that can be brought to bear when God and Empire conspire. "When the missionaries came," Kenyatta said, "we had the land and they had the Bible. 'Let us pray,' said the missionaries. We closed our eyes. When we opened them again, they had the land and we had the Bible."

The consequence, at least in the islands of the Pacific Ocean, was to reduce huge numbers of the population to a state of idle catatonia, a life apparently wearying and pointless:

> The natives, having nothing, nothing at all to do, think of one thing only – drinking. Many things that are strange and picturesque existed here once, but there are no traces of them left today; everything has vanished. Day by day the race vanishes, decimated by the European diseases. There is so much prostitution that it does not exist . . . one only knows a thing by its contrary, and its contrary does not exist.

But he painted, and his paintings remain the most vivid contemporary image of the Pacific. His stature has become eponymous: what Kafka is to bureaucracy, Paul Gauguin is to the Ocean and its people. I recall once sitting in a bar in Nuku'alofa, the capital of Tonga. The barmaid, wearing a brightly flowered lava-lava and white blouse, and with a hibiscus tucked behind her ear, was tall and olive-skinned, a cascade of thick black hair falling to her waist. She was inexpressibly handsome, with wide dark eyes and deeply sensual full lips. Her breasts swelled darkly beneath the cotton, and her hips swayed to some unheard rhythm as she walked to the table. "Look at

449

her," breathed my companion, who had flown in from London only that morning. "Pure bloody Gauguin! Exactly what one expects! Just what I was dreaming of!"*

And this girl did not smile. She had on her face an expression that mixed arrogance and contempt, indifference and sadness, contemplation and reverie. Maybe, to crude *palangis* that we were, this expression was her main attraction. The girls in Paul Gauguin's pictures do not smile either; they stare vacantly into space, lost and sorrowful, dreaming of what once they were. "*D'où venons-nous? Que sommes-nous? Où allons-nous?*", Gauguin's most famous work, was finished shortly before he tried to commit suicide. *Nevermore*, my own favourite, shows a woman just like the girl in Tonga, quite naked, lying on a bed, her body surrounded by a scattering of blooms from the Pacific's most famous and most fragrant flower, the gardenia known as *tiare tahiti*.† A dark couple whisper in the background. The walls of the young woman's room are covered with blooms and birds, all tropical shapes and symbols, and by the single, crudely drawn word, "Nevermore".

But it is the girl's expression which haunts: as Alan Moorehead writes, "she is waiting for nothing, hoping for nothing." Indeed, he says, all Gauguin's women appear "supine, defeated, despairing and beautiful . . . they gaze in a reverie into the lost past. They have no hope at all. They see nothing but the broken stones of their *marae*, their lost idols, the great legendary war-canoes with their tattooed warriors in their elaborate robes, the forgotten dances and rituals of the *arioi*."

Before Gauguin, Herman Melville had been angered by the desecration of the Pacific's traditional life and culture. He was perhaps the first writer of true genius who decided to wander the Pacific. That he did so in 1841, having sailed from New Bedford on the whaler *Acushnet*, serves to remind one both how lately was the Pacific penetrated – it had only been "discovered" by Balboa in 1513, and first

---

*William Manchester, in *American Caesar*, found the Western image of Pacific femininity deeply influenced and corrupted by the Hollywood scriptwriters. Instead of lithe young women in fitting sarongs who dived for pearls and seduced missionaries, "in reality the proportions of women there were closer to those of duffel bags." While I accept there are many obese ladies, wearing the all-enveloping Mother Hubbard smocks forced upon them by Western missionaries, this young lady in Nuku'alofa was pure Gauguin.
†The title also of Rupert Brooke's finest South Sea poem.

crossed by Magellan in 1522 – and how recently had the desecration begun. Melville's two great Pacific books, *Typee* and *Omoo*, present a sustained attack on the debasement of the island culture, particularly by the missionaries: "The voluptuous Indian, with every desire supplied, whom Providence has bountifully provided with all the sources of pure and natural enjoyment, and from whom are removed many of the ills and pains of life – what has he to desire from the hands of civilization?"

But the most perceptive of the Pacific's recent chroniclers, even when one thinks of Maugham, Conrad and Dana and the poet Robinson Jeffers, whose epigraph appears at the beginning of this book – more acute and shrewd and more omniscient than all these is the work of that great Edinburgh lighthouse-builder's son turned Samoan chief, Robert Louis Stevenson. He first came to the Ocean in 1888, and stayed there until he died six years later.

"The Pacific," Stevenson wrote, "is a strange place. The nineteenth century exists there only in spots: all around is a no-man's land of the ages, a stirabout of epochs and races, barbarisms and civilizations, virtues and crimes."

He travelled far and wide around this vast, deep sea. Aboard the yacht *Casco* in which he arrived from San Francisco, or the schooner *Equator*, or the cargo-ship *Janet Nichol* which took Robert and Fanny on an eastbound voyage from Sydney, he visited dozens of the "hot and healthy islands" of the Pacific tropics. He went to the Marquesas, the Tuamotus and to the Society Islands, where Tahiti lies; he visited Australia and New Zealand, Hawaii, New Caledonia, the Marshalls, the Cooks. He stopped in Niue, Kiribati, Tuvalu, Tokelau, American Samoa and what is now called Western Samoa. He came to be known on Samoa as *Tusitala*, the story-teller.

He was saddened by what he saw as the engulfment of the island-ers' lives by "our shabby civilization". He wrote lyrically about the islands, he took up causes with great passion, and penned furious letters to *The Times*, 9,000 miles away in London, whenever he wanted prompt attention paid to his steady cavalcade of concerns. But his most prescient interest was alerted when a typhoon hit Apia, the Samoan capital, on the night of 16–17 March, 1889.

Like the "fateful five minutes" at the Battle of Midway half a century later, these few hours of climatic turmoil in mid-Pacific on St Patrick's Day Eve were purely by chance to bring about a mighty change in the face of world politics. The telling of this change, and of Stevenson's reporting on it, marks a re-connection between what might have seemed a byway in this narrative and the major realities of today's Pacific – a re-establishment of the link between the languorous island-states of the inner Ocean, and the tough and powerful nation-states strung along its thousands of miles of margin.

In the late 1880s the three great powers of the day – Germany, the United States and Britain – were all jockeying for influence in the Samoan Islands. None of the three wanted the group badly enough to annex it; but equally each had traders – dealing mainly in copra and palm oil – who wished their respective countries to exercise more control over the turbulent, eternally warring Polynesian population. In 1887 the Germans had had enough of this foolishness, deposed the Samoan king and installed a puppet ruler of their own. The Samoans rebelled at a German move not actually sanctioned by the Berlin government, and by early 1889 warships from all three nations had gathered in the shelter of Apia Harbour. There were seven capital vessels anchored there when the typhoon struck and, so eager was each nation to demonstrate its power over the islands, that none would budge despite the ferocity of the storm.

In the end four of the vessels were sunk, and 200 sailors were drowned. Two other ships were beached and damaged. The German warship *Eber* went down; the USS *Trenton* and *Vandalia* were finished; the *Nipsic* was refloated and limped away with *Vandalia*'s funnel; the German vessel *Adler* was reef-bound and stayed put, rusting imperturbably until the 1950s and now buried under the Apia cricket pitch. Only the Royal Navy displayed the style of seamanship that was necessary: HMS *Calliope* managed to battle her way clear of the anchorage and put to sea.

The outcome of this tragedy – "a marking epoch in world history", Stevenson called it – was twofold. First, it triggered a series of diplomatic conferences that eventually confirmed the division of the Samoan islands into two: a Western group, placed initially under German control and then, following the Great War, under a League of Nations mandate administered by New Zealand; and an Eastern group – the islands of Tutuila, Aunu'u, Ta'u, Olesega, Ofu and Rose – which little by little and treaty by treaty were handed over to the United States, which controls them to this day. (Western Samoa is now independent.)

The second outcome of the storm was a more direct consequence of the humiliation felt by the American admirals at the loss of their three vessels. Ever since the Civil War the US Navy had been allowed to run down; but under the presidencies of Benjamin Harrison and, later, of William McKinley and his ebullient Vice-President, Teddy Roosevelt, matters were reversed. The old watchword of "manifest destiny" was heard again – the phrase coined in the 1840s to justify the annexation of Texas, the occupation of Oregon and the war with Mexico. Now it was being employed once more to justify America's expansion into the Pacific, and excuses were hurriedly seized upon by its advocates – Republicans to a man – to stimulate action.

In 1889 the excuse was the loss of the three vessels in Apia harbour: the reward was the granting to the United States of what (a decade later) would be full control over Eastern Samoa. Four years after the Apia storm the Americans overthrew Queen Lili'uokalani of Hawaii, and began the process that was to lead to the islands' incorporation into the United States.* Five years later still, with cries of "Remember the *Maine*" ringing in the doughboys' ears, the United States took Guam and the Philippines. What happened in Apia harbour in March 1889 signalled the beginnings of the American Empire – the empire which was still battling gamely, but in vain, when Vietnam fell in 1975. Even today some Americans like to think of the Pacific as American territorial waters – "the American lake" is how it is frequently put – and the commanders inhabiting the bunkers in Hawaii from which they administer their forces there, do so with the certainty of both might and right.

Five years after the typhoon, Robert Louis Stevenson – still in his beloved Samoa – died very suddenly aged just 44. He was buried at the top of a hill, with almost all the honours accorded to a Samoan chief. It is a place of pilgrimage, a long way from anywhere, visited by thousands who have come to regard the man as one of the best storytellers in any language, and whose writings have a special resonance no matter how long ago or far away they were written. Jack London came here. A list of writers from Jorge Luis Borges to Virginia Woolf, via Graham Greene and Conan Doyle, would have

---

*Though one island, Niihau, voted against statehood, and remains implacably opposed to American interference. It is a privately-held island, just off the coast of Kauai, where the 500-odd inhabitants speak Hawaiian, and frequently indicate their disdain and dislike for the American style of life on offer on the neighbouring islands. No one may visit Niihau without permission of the owners.

come if they could. But the Pacific is wide and Apia is far, so they admire Stevenson in their writings and let him rest alone.

Though not entirely alone. Fanny's ashes were brought to the mountain-top when she died twenty years later, and the pair lie under the epitaph that Stevenson wrote for himself, and which the young woman in Los Angeles airport had proved such an adept at quoting:

> Under the wide and starry sky,
> Dig the grave and let me lie.
> Glad did I live and gladly die,
> And I laid me down with a will.

I started this account of the new Pacific in Tonga, just a few miles west of Samoa. A few miles but, thanks to the existence of Professor Dowd's International Date Line snaking between the islands, one entire day ahead. Dusk in Apia on a Monday is dusk in Nuku'alofa on a Tuesday; and so the reverse of the sentence with which I began this book is true: that while the first dawn in the Pacific is the first dawn in the world, so the last moments of any day's dusk in the Pacific are the last moments of that day's dusk on the planet. An obvious corollary, yet worth repeating for whatever symbolism it holds.

And I believe, in a way, that it does hold some. For the process which began with the discovery of all those "hot and healthy islands" in the middle of this giant Ocean, which progressed through the gifts of weapons and war and disease, the indelible imprints of colonialism and still more war, through the terrors of the atom-bomb testing in Bikini and Christmas Island, and which still continues beneath the French "possession" of Mururoa . . . the process has ended the marvel that once was the Pacific life, the life in which Gauguin once sought purity and nature and true Romance. Now, so much of what remains is a grotesque pastiche of Pacific romance, preserved in a taro basket for the benefit of tourists from Tokyo, Los Angeles and Sydney. The dawn of the New Pacific has coincided with the drawing down of blinds upon the Pacific way of life.

And yet, not quite. I write these closing words in my study in Hong Kong, having just put down the telephone after a conversation that somehow seems typical of the New Pacific, and of its pleasing links with the constancy of the old.

It is easy to forget the old. My study window overlooks the bustle

454

and throng of a colony that is fast changing its identity as it hurtles towards its reunion with China. The window rattles with the endless reverberation of a city that seems never to be finished with making itself. There is a park opposite, and if I narrow my eyes I can see flamingoes and monkeys, a Palawan pheasant. But the park is overshadowed with new apartment blocks a-building, all swathed in fragile-looking bamboo scaffolding. There is the constant flash and sparkle of welders' torches, and cranes' arms swing back and forth lifting cement and ironwork into place. This penultimate bastion of British Imperial might in the East – Pitcairn still shows no sign of wishing to emerge from beneath the Imperial blanket – is readying herself to go out with at least the trappings, if not necessarily the actuality, of consequence.

The telephone call came from Hawaii – from the Big Island, where a friend was staying for a week on his way between Hong Kong and San Francisco. I had sent him a fax message, telling him that what with my wife lying on a beach somewhere in southern Thailand and with him sunning himself in Hawaii while I was freezing to death on an improbably cold weekend in Hong Kong – "cold northerly winds emanating from a high pressure ridge in Mongolia' was how the Royal Observatory described it – I was frankly envious. He had called to tell me not to be. It was, he said, sheeting down with rain, and he was gazing down from his window at the palm trees leaning into a full gale and white horses ruffling the surface of Kealakekua Bay.

"But it's still Hawaii,' he went on. "There's something magical about it. Something timeless, despite all that the modern world has done to the place. There is a certain spirit of the Pacific, and it hasn't quite gone yet. I can't explain. But perhaps you know what I mean."

Kealakekua Bay was where the islanders killed Captain Cook in 1779 – a tragic error, a replay of the killing of Magellan in the Philippines 250 years before. But no sinister memory attaches to the place now. It is quite lovely, and the Pacific that stretches away to the sunset can look peaceful and immense – and does so, on more clement days than this.

Then, having replaced the phone in its cradle, a small idea came to me, an idea which lodges behind my reason for writing about the islands, and of their romance and beauty, at the close of a book which has largely been concerned with the weightier matters of the nations lying around the Ocean's edge.

What ties the Pacific together? What unites it, makes something so vast and disparate enjoy at least the beginnings of a sense of unity? I have tried to answer the question on a number of occasions, by suggesting that the nations ranged around the Ocean edge look to each other now for support, for profit and advance – that they look inward, not outward, and that a certain unity is born of that new perspective.

What this telephone call had made me realize in addition is the consequence of the fact that passages made between the peripheries of the region can (and now often do) compel or persuade the wanderer to halt for a while within the Pacific itself. A traveller from Hong Kong to San Francisco may well sojourn briefly in Hawaii. One wandering between Tokyo and Los Angeles can (and often does) stop awhile in Guam. A businessman proceeding from Sydney to Vancouver may profitably arrest his progress on the islands of Fiji; and perhaps one going from Auckland to Santiago might stop on Easter Island, or even on Juan Fernandez, of which Daniel Defoe had heard when he wrote the saga of Robinson Crusoe.

Slowly the idea of Polynesia, and that of Micronesia and Melanesia too (though it is Polynesia which most accurately reflects what one might call the Pacific spirit) is becoming familiar in the huge community that lies beyond. It is becoming familiar and, dare one say it, becoming a subject of some pride as well. The spirit of the Ocean, a feeling that somehow never attached to the other oceans of the world, is imperceptibly giving a patina to those whose homes are in Seattle or Brisbane, Kagoshima or Valparaiso. Perhaps the ancient Polynesian seaways which once united the Ocean's shores are once again, though unseen and half-forgotten, bringing them and all who live upon them closer together.

The economics of the New Pacific are undeniable; as are the military realities, and the sheer power of so many of the nations of the region. But up and away from such concerns, and on a more cosmic level – how fine and pleasingly symmetric it would be to bring the old Pacific navigators finally into a picture from which they have so long been excluded, and to ponder on the notion that, as with their endless journeys all those scores of years ago, so this Ocean which has given the world everything from silks to silicon may still be linked together by the stars.

MAPS

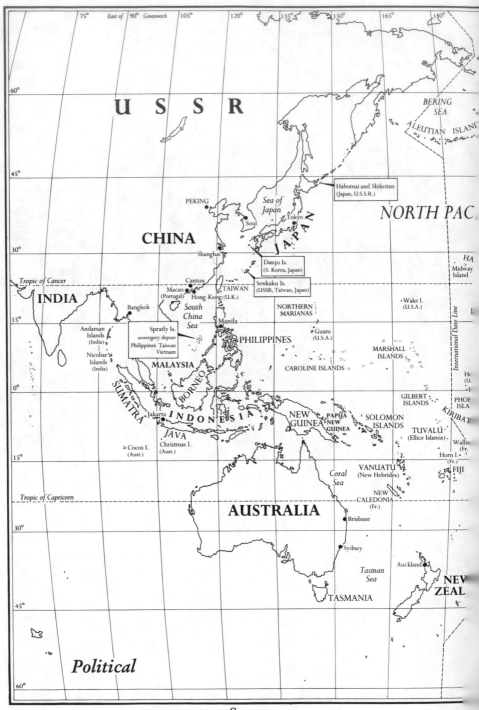

Political

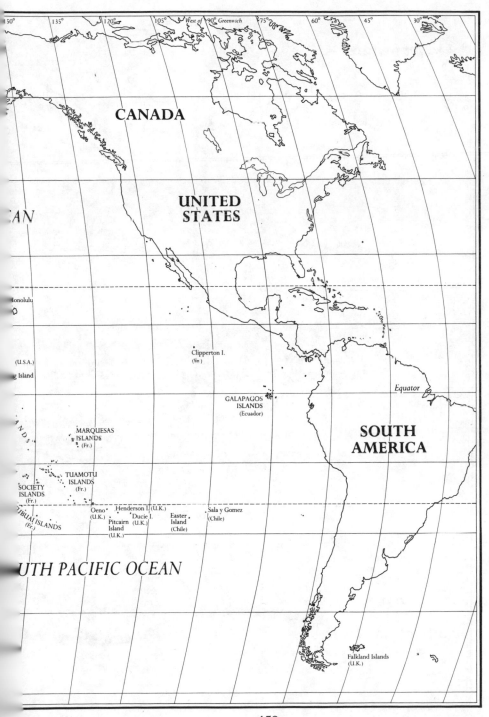

CANADA

UNITED
STATES

CAN

Honolulu

(U.S.A.)

g Island

Clipperton I.
(Fr.)

GALAPAGOS
ISLANDS
(Ecuador)

West of 90° Greenwich

Equator

SOUTH
AMERICA

NDS

MARQUESAS
y ISLANDS
(Fr.)

TUAMOTU
ISLANDS
(Fr.)

SOCIETY
ISLANDS
(Fr.)

Oeno
(U.K.)

Pitcairn
Island
(U.K.)

Henderson I. (U.K.)

Ducie I.
(U.K.)

Easter
Island
(Chile)

Sala y Gomez
(Chile)

TIBUAI ISLANDS
(Fr.)

UTH PACIFIC OCEAN

Falkland Islands
(U.K.)

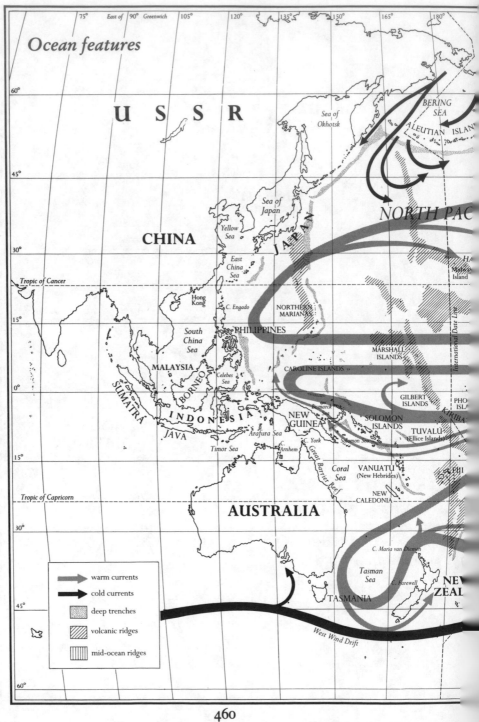

Ocean features

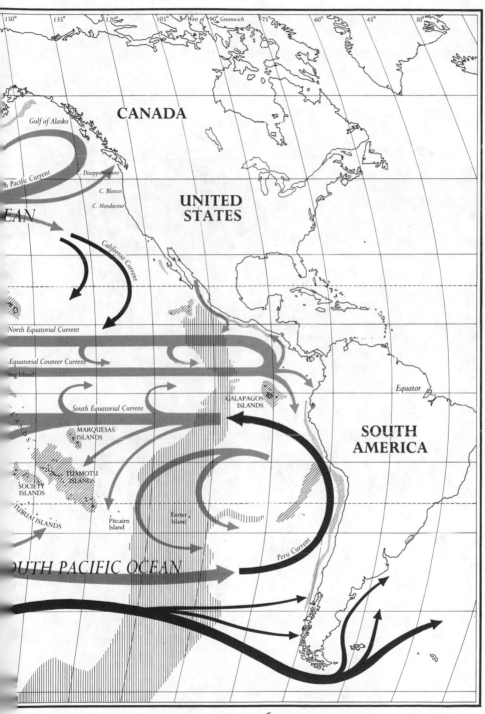

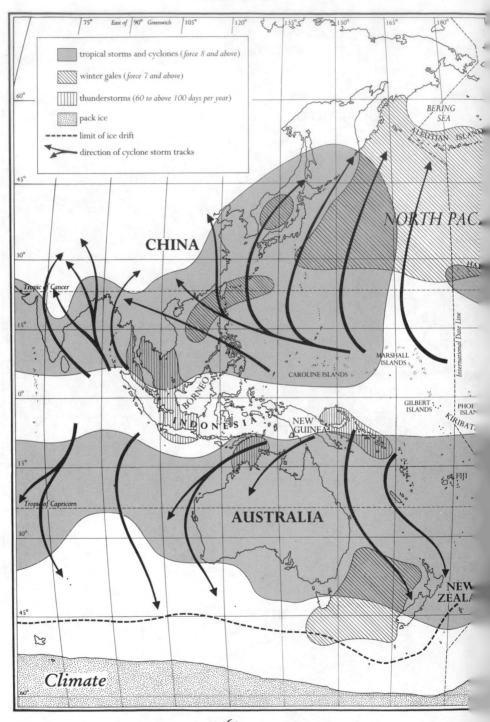

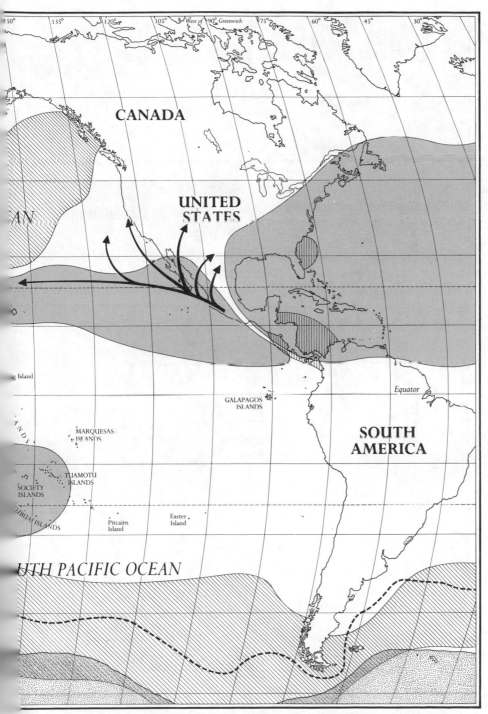

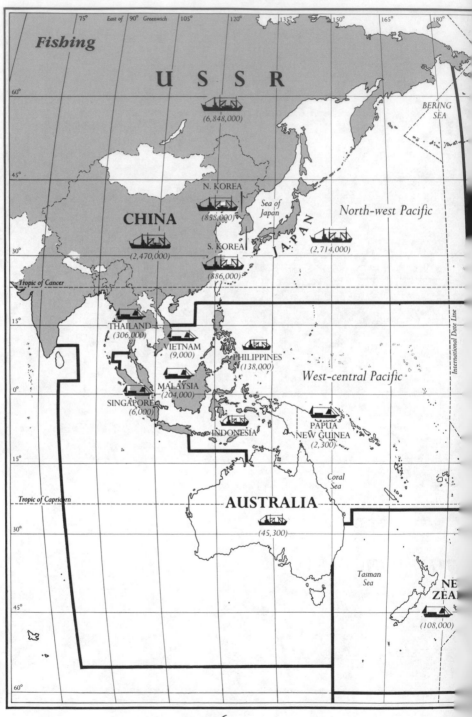

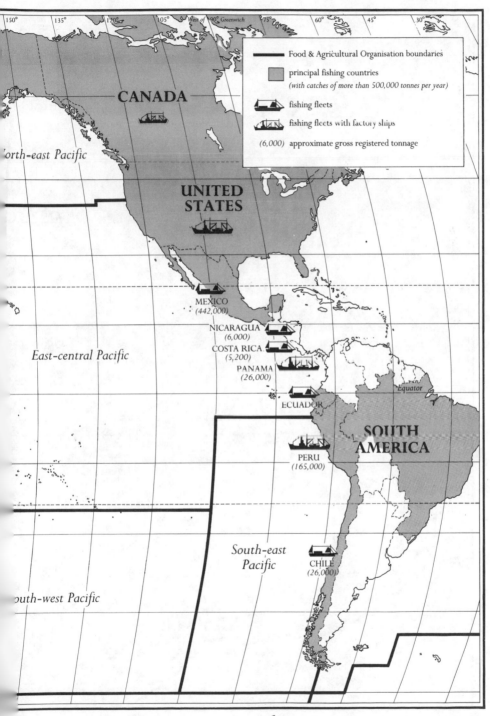

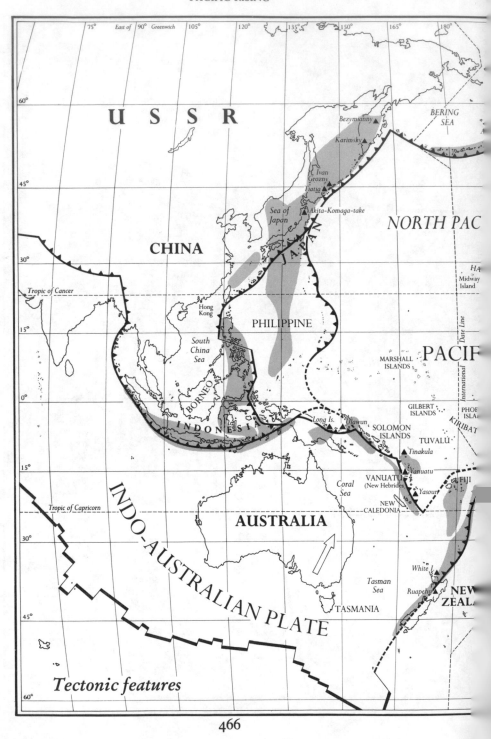

Tectonic features

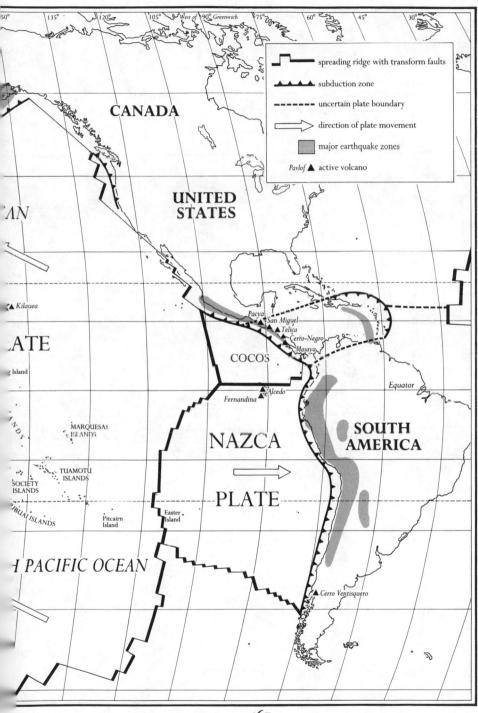

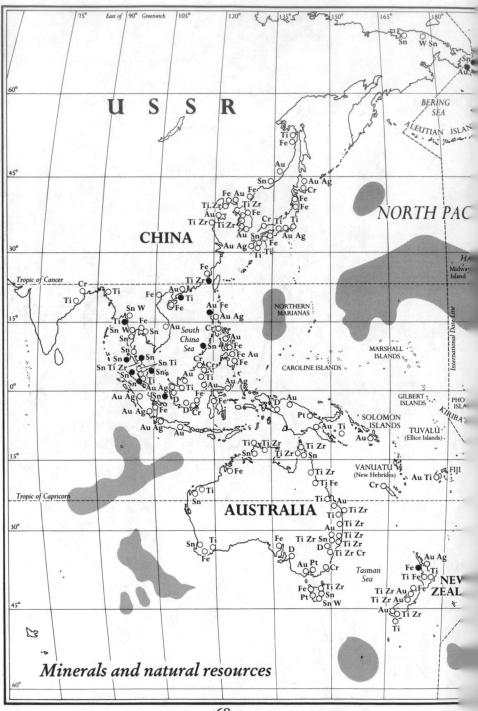

Minerals and natural resources

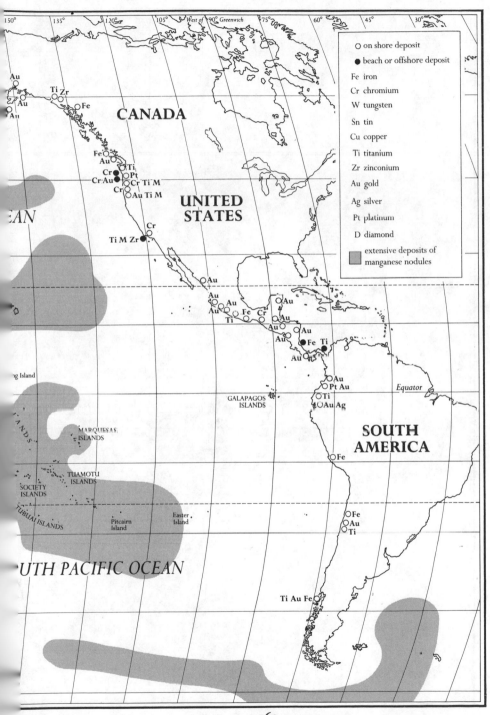

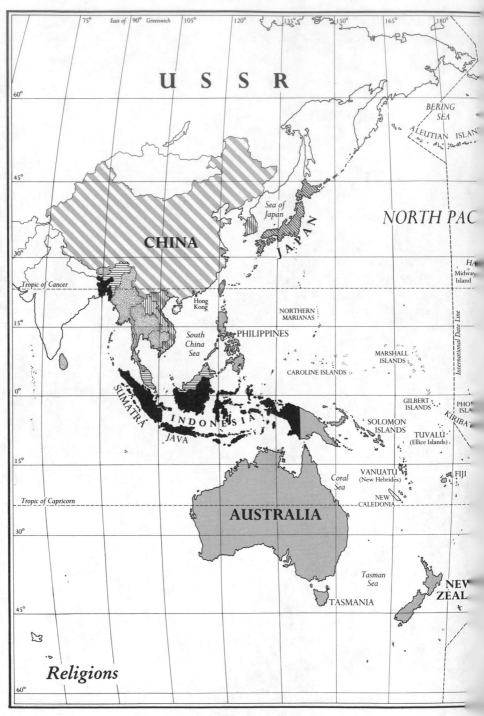

Religions

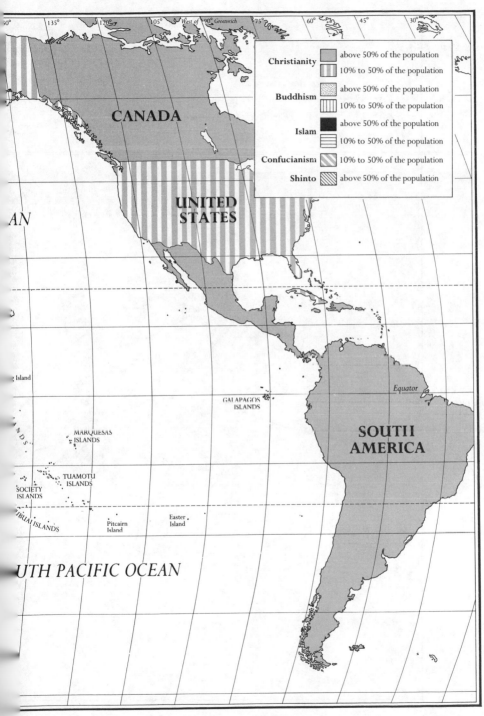

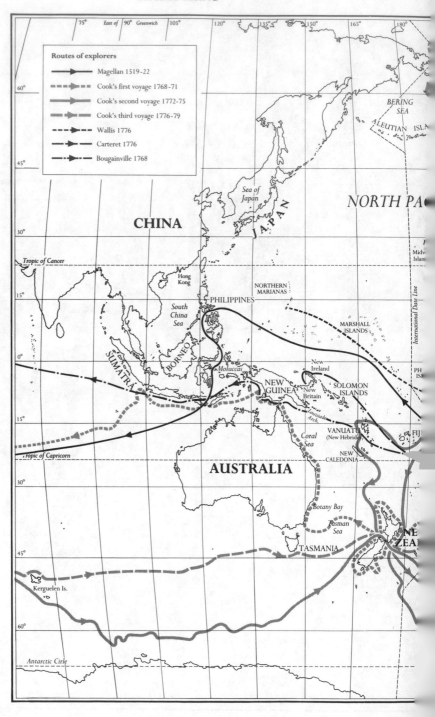

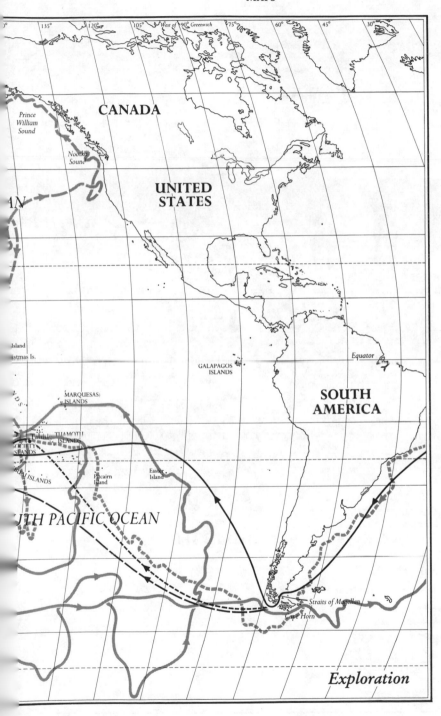

Exploration

Defence

Major potential combatants

- total army strength
- total major surface combatants (ships)
- total other capital ships
- total submarines
- total air force aircraft
- nuclear weapons

(figures are 1989, unless otherwise stated)

USSR
1,500,000 men
49
216
327
11,320

Chita

930,000 men
2
854
23

Sakhalin Island
Sovetskaya Gavan
Vladivostok
Petropavlovsk
Habomai and Shikotan

N. Korea
Wonsan
56
5170
92

Seoul
S. Korea
Takeshima (Liancourt) Rocks
Misawa
JAPAN
63
309
14
156,000 men

Yoko Suka
Sasibo
Danjo-gunto rocks

CHINA
2,300,000 men

TAIWAN
36
400 (1988)

Senkaku Is
Okinawa
28
3
442
550,000 men

VIETNAM
270,000 men
2
Paracel Is
Cam Ranh Bay
Spratly Is

2
330
Guam

PHILIPPINES
68,000 men

MARSHALL ISLANDS

CAROLINE ISLANDS

INDONESIA
215,000 men
15
72
105

SUMATRA
JAVA

NEW GUINEA
Torres Strait

SOLOMON ISLANDS

GILBERT ISLANDS
KIRIBATI

TUVALU (Ellice Islands)

Timor Sea

Coral Sea

VANUATU (New Hebrides)
NEW CALEDONIA
FIJI

AUSTRALIA
31,000 men
12
6
300

Tasman Sea

TASMANIA

NEW ZEALAND

BERING SEA
ALEUTIAN ISLAND

NORTH PAC

Midway Island

International Date Line

Tropic of Cancer
Tropic of Capricorn

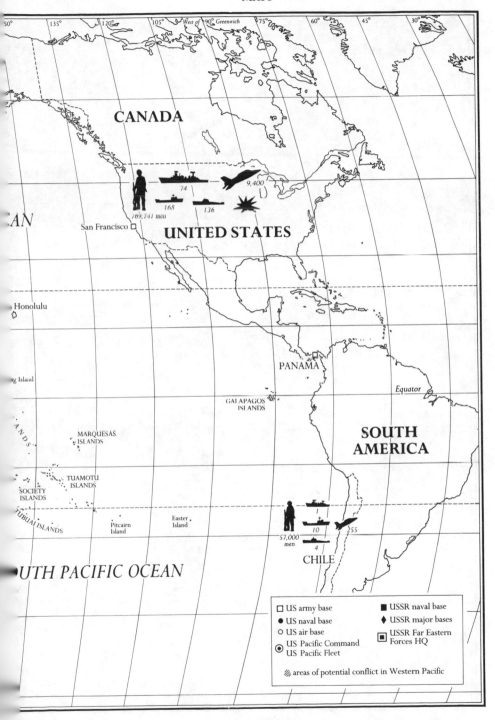

Overseas Chinese

USSR
8,797 (1978)

BERING SEA

ALEUTIAN ISLAN

CHINA
93% of 1080m (1987)

NORTH KOREA
10,000 (1983)

SOUTH KOREA
30,000
(1983)

JAPAN
79,122 (1982)

NORTH PAC

Tropic of Cancer

LAOS
10,000
(1983)

THAILAND
4.5m (1978)

Hong Kong
98% of 5⋅6m

TAIWAN
98⋅4% of 19⋅7m (1987)

Bangkok

CAMBODIA
50,000 (1983)

VIETNAM
700,000
(1983)

Manila

PHILIPPINES
1m (1983)

NORTHERN MARIANAS

Midway Island

International Date Line

MALAYSIA
31⋅8% of 17⋅36m
(1980)

Singapore
2,038,000
(1989)

CAROLINE ISLANDS

MARSHALL ISLANDS

INDONESIA
6m (1983)

PAPUA NEW GUINEA
5,000 (1971)

SOLOMON ISLANDS
5,000 (1979)

NAURU
1,400 (1979)

GILBERT ISLANDS

KIRIBAT

TUVALU
(Ellice Islands)

PHOE ISLA

SAMO
10,000 (198

AUSTRALIA
172,483 (1986)

Coral Sea

VANUATU
(New Hebrides)

NEW CALEDONIA

FIJI
7,000

Tropic of Capricorn

Sydney

Tasman Sea

TASMANIA

NEW ZEAL
16,000 (19

4.5m (1978)   number of overseas Chinese

● cities with appreciable Chinatowns

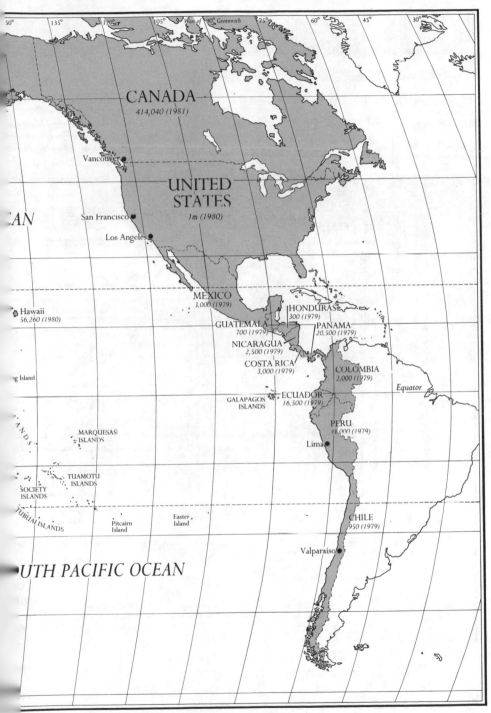

CANADA
414,040 (1981)

Vancouver

UNITED
STATES
1m (1980)

San Francisco

Los Angeles

Hawaii
56,260 (1980)

MEXICO
3,000 (1979)

HONDURAS
300 (1979)

GUATEMALA
700 (1979)

PANAMA
20,500 (1979)

NICARAGUA
2,500 (1979)

COSTA RICA
3,000 (1979)

COLOMBIA
2,000 (1979)

GALAPAGOS
ISLANDS

ECUADOR
16,500 (1979)

Equator

PERU
18,000 (1979)

MARQUESAS
ISLANDS

Lima

Island

TUAMOTU
ISLANDS

SOCIETY
ISLANDS

TUBUAI ISLANDS

Pitcairn
Island

Easter
Island

CHILE
950 (1979)

Valparaiso

SOUTH PACIFIC OCEAN

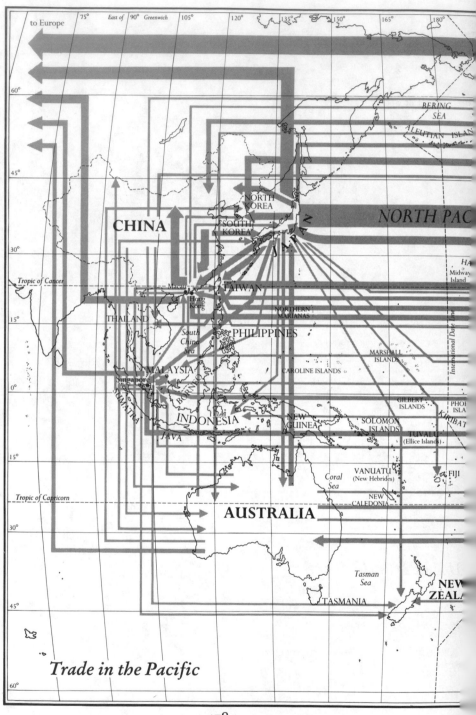

Trade in the Pacific

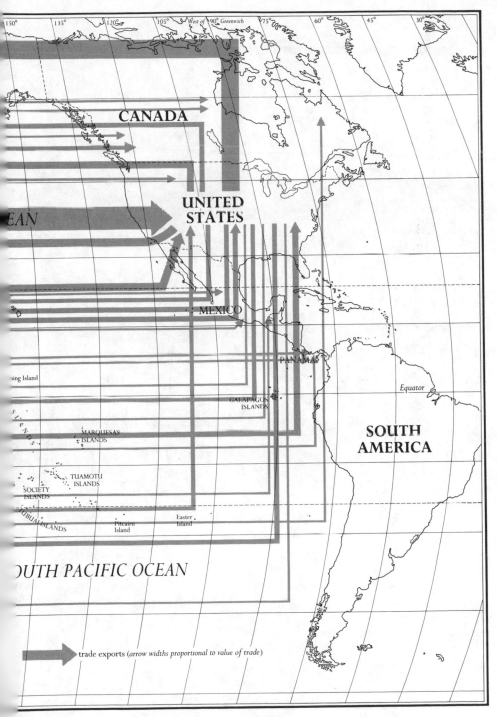

trade exports *(arrow widths proportional to value of trade)*

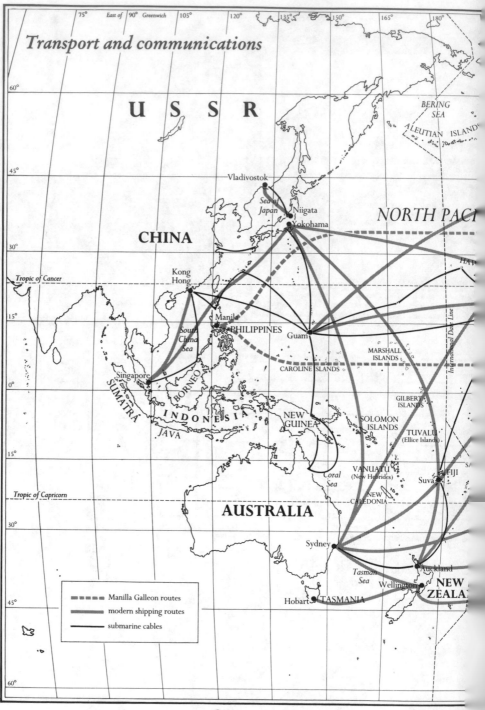

Transport and communications

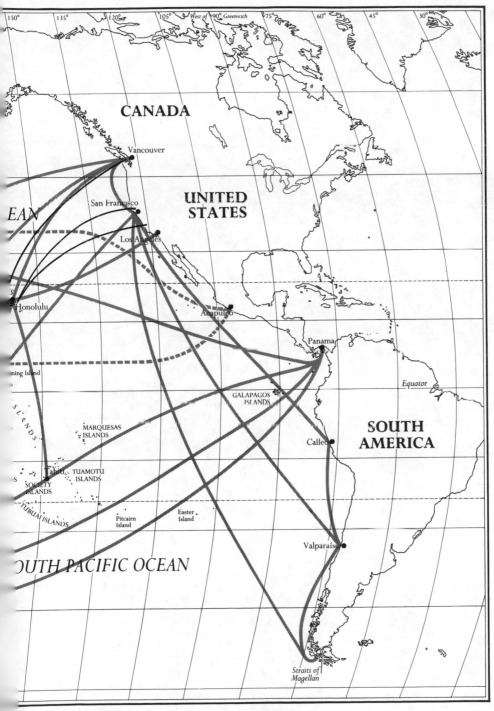

FURTHER READING

It is perhaps something of a surprise to find that there is no single book about the Pacific which even attempts to have the kind of magisterial authority that Fernand Braudel gave to his mighty study of the Mediterranean, published in 1949. Maybe the Pacific is too vast an entity to have tempted the historians. Maybe it has not, until today, been regarded as an entity worthy of consideration as a whole. Some such reason must be adduced for the poverty of literature: works like Felix Riesenberg's *The Pacific* (London 1947) and John Gunther's somewhat partisan *Inside Asia* (London 1939) were all that existed to satisfy the curiosity of the generalist.

It was not until the mid 1980s that Professor Osker Spate filled the void by embarking on his three-volume work, *The Pacific Since Magellan* (Sydney, 1988). Standing at the high-water mark of published knowledge about the Ocean, this massive and some-times daunting work of scholarship could profitably be consulted in conjunction with another four-volume work, the discovery of which came to me as a consummate joy: the Royal Navy Intelli-gence Division's utterly comprehensive *Handbook of the Pacific Islands* (London, 1943) contains every available fact about every known and unknown island, islet, skerry and rock within the confines of the sea, and while some details may have changed in the half-century since its publication the broad brushstrokes remain as fresh and vivid today as they must have seemed during the dark days of war. *A History of the Pacific*, written by Glen Barclay (London 1978), is competent and reasonably concise. Michael Macintyre's splendidly illustrated *The New Pacific* (London, 1985), which was related to the massive BBC television series he produced in the same year, has become a standard.

Other works that have lately become available, and which lay claim to relating the saga of the Pacific, are invariably more concerned simply with the Asian quadrant of it. Thus Eric Downton's *Pacific Challenge* (Toronto, 1986), David Aikman's *Pacific Rim* (Boston, 1986), and *The Pacific Century* by Staffan Burenstam Linder (Stanford, 1986) are all, in my view, offered under misnomers: each is readable – Eric Downton's particularly so – but none can lay claim to being a real Pacific book. *The Four Little Dragons*, by Brian Kelly and Martin London (New York, 1989), *The Third Century* by Joel Kotkin and Yoriko Kishimoto (New York, 1988) and Dick Wilson's skilfully prescient *Asia Awakes* (London, 1970) make no such pretence and are thus perhaps more successful.

Robert Elegant's *Pacific Destiny* (New York, 1990) is a skilful reworking of John Gunther's book of half a century before but, once again, concerns itself with less than its title implies.

The most comprehensive and wholly Pacific book to concern itself with modern development is *Rethinking the Pacific* by the celebrated scholar Gerald Segal (Oxford, 1990). Its thesis runs precisely counter to mine – the Pacific, Dr Segal declares, has not now nor ever can have a truly common purpose, nor a common destiny. But disagreement aside, it is a formidably good book and should be required reading.

James Fenton's pleasingly eccentric style of reporting is evident in *All the Wrong Places* (New York, 1988), and Ian Buruma's *God's Dust* (London, 1989) presents an absorbing study of a part of the region: both should be devoured by anyone eager to learn about contemporary politics and society in what it is now becoming fashionable to call the North-West – that band of countries stretching from Rangoon to Vladivostok, and which lies in the upper left-hand side of a Pacific map.

I made much use of the well-known Lonely Planet *Survival Guides*, and the *Insight Guides*, as well as the New Moon Publications *Handbooks* to the various countries. The *South American Handbook*, published every year in Bristol, is unrivalled for its coverage of the Latin Pacific. The *All-Asia Guide* published annually in Hong Kong by the Far Eastern Economic Review contains invaluable data too.

These, then, comprise what one might call the general Pacific books. But I also consulted, and in many cases enjoyed, a number of other more specialized works, and these are listed below in the approximate order of my own book's somewhat erratic progress around the Ocean.

The best book on the Date Line is Derek Howse's *Greenwich*

Time and the Discovery of Longitude (London, 1980). I employed to advantage both Sir Harry Luke's *Islands of the South Pacific* (London, 1962) and *Tonga*, by James Siers (Wellington, 1987) when trying to learn about the Friendly Isles. *On Fiji Islands* by Ronald Wright (New York, 1986) stands as perhaps the most delightful of all modern South Seas books. Alan Moorehead's classic though contentious *The Fatal Impact* (London, 1966) tells much of the destructive impact of colonialism – all too evident on islands like Fiji and Tahiti. *The South Pacific Handbook* (Chico, California, 1989) told me how to find what and where. *The Polynesians*, by Peter Bellwood (London, 1987) was crammed with technical information. *The Forgotten Islands of the South Seas* by Bengt Danielsson (London, 1957) is an evocative account, while Rupert Brooke's collected poems and letters from the South Seas (London, 1931) were even more perfect for those idle moments by the moonlit taffrail.

Jan Morris has written a characteristically luxuriant account of old and new and future *Hong Kong – Xianggang* (London, 1988). C.P. Fitzgerald's *China: A Short Cultural History* (London, 1935) is an extraordinary primer on the Pacific community's largest member. *To Get Rich is Glorious*, a distillation of Orville Schnell's brilliant articles about China written for the *New Yorker* (New York, 1984) may seem a little dated in view of recent events in Peking but still has enormous value.

Vasco Núñez de Balboa has surprisingly few biographers: Kathleen Romoli's *Balboa: Discoverer of the Pacific* (New York, 1953) has a title that may irritate some anti-colonialists, but is the best work by far. Ian Cameron's story of the building of the Panama Canal, *The Impossible Dream* (London, 1972) is a superb coda to Balboa's historic foray into Darién. Cameron has done great justice also to *Magellan* (London, 1974), and the second volume (the Southern Voyages) of Samuel Eliot Morison's *The European Discovery of America* (New York, 1974) relates (with the finest of maps and photographs) a host of other absorbing details from the extraordinary tale of Magellan and his crew. *The Portuguese Seaborne Empire* by C.R. Boxer (London, 1969) adds a further dimension to the tale. *A Short History of the Philippines* by Teodoro Agoncillo (New York, 1969) tells of the end of the great captain-general, but this time as seen through the eyes of those who more understandably favoured the great chieftain who struck him down, Lapu Lapu. Stanley Karnow writes splendidly about America's Philippine colony in *In Our Image* (New York, 1989).

Lynne Withey has also retold the story of Captain Cook's *Voyages of Discovery* (London, 1987).

For an account of the rocky underpinnings of the Pacific I turned to *The Geophysics of the Pacific Basin and Margin* (Washington, 1976): I can hardly confess to having enjoyed it, but it had its uses.

I have long enjoyed Linda Christmas's *The Ribbon and the Ragged Square* (London, 1986), a sympathetically executed portrait of Australia. *Poor Nation of the Pacific*, edited by Jocelynne Scutt (Sydney, 1985) added a different perspective of the Australian landscape. The ore-carrier that takes the readers from Australia to Japan passed through an area of islands that is well described in the impressively academic but nonetheless very readable *The Japanese Colonial Empire 1895–1945* (Princeton, 1984). Japan herself has many chroniclers: I relied on the late Richard Storry's *A History of Modern Japan* (London, 1960), *The Sun at Noon* by Dick Wilson (London, 1986), *Hirohito* by Leonard Mosley (New Jersey, 1966), and the enchanting account written by the then young (but now Emperor) Akihito's tutor, Elizabeth Gray Vining, *Windows for the Crown Prince* (London, 1952). The colected *Writings from Japan* of Lafcadio Hearn (London, 1984), Oliver Statler's *Japanese Pilgrimage* and *Japanese Inn* (both London, 1983) are timeless.

For the great saga of the Japanese economic revival, David Halberstam's astonishing account of the Nissan Motor Company in *The Reckoning* (New York, 1986) is without equal. But I also enjoyed *Yen!* by Daniel Burstein (New York, 1988), and Akio Morita's account of the building of his Sony empire in *Made in Japan* (London, 1987).

Passing through the Aleutian Islands makes one inevitably think of the Pacific War, and I read with interest John Costello's work of the same title (London, 1981) and Edwin Hoyt's *Japan's War* (London, 1986). Other military details come from the excellent annals of the *Pacific Defence Reporter*, and from Douglas Stuart's *Security Within the Pacific Rim* (Aldershot, 1987). John Keegan's account of the history-making crucial five minutes in the Battle of Midway in his masterly *The Second World War* (London, 1989) was of enormous value.

Seattle, Past to Present, by Roger Sale (Seattle, 1976) was most useful – especially dealing with the anti-Chinese riots in the late nineteenth century – and the fascinating subject of the overseas Chinese is exhaustively covered by the writer Pan Ling (who also writes as Lynn Pan) in *Sons of the Yellow Emperor* (London, 1990).

I relied shamelessly on her fact-studded, superbly written book, and to a lesser extent on Garth Alexander's *The Invisible China* (New York, 1973) and Wang Gungwu's *A Short History of the Nanyang Chinese* (Singapore, 1959). In *The Big Four* by Oscar Lewis (San Francisco, 1938) there is a vivid account of the Chinese workers on the American trans-continental railroad, the first link between the Atlantic and Pacific coasts: but Lewis relates too, as his primary purpose, the story of Stanford and Crocker, Hopkins and Huntington, giants and visionaries in the story of America's Pacific development. *The Outer Coast* by Richard Batman (San Diego, 1985) relates some of the extraordinary maritime derring-do off the California cliffs.

The other Pacific icons are detailed at greater length too. John Newhouse, another New Yorker writer, talks of the development of the jumbo jet in *The Sporty Game* (New York, 1982); and John Sculley presents his account of the making of the Apple Macintosh in *Odyssey* (New York, 1987). Hugh Barty-King's *Girdle Round the Earth* (London 1979) – a surprisingly well-written company history of Cable and Wireless – had many details about the mid-ocean cable-stations. And *The Religions of China* by Max Weber (New York, 1951) offers the most complete, if not the most readable, account of Confucius.

There are some classics: Arthur Grimble's *A Pattern of Islands* (London, 1952) is essential reading, even if Grimble is now judged rather more harshly than before. Though recently exposed as something of a fraud, *Coming of Age in Samoa* (London, 1928) placed Margaret Mead in the forefront of world anthropologists, and her study is still an excellent read. Lucas Bridges in *The Uttermost Part of the Earth* (London, 1951) talks eloquently of Pacific Chile and Tierra del Fuego. And Isabella Bird's *Six Months in the Sandwich Islands* (London, 1890) still reads as delightfully as ever. *The Moon and Sixpence*, by Somerset Maugham, is based on the life of Paul Gauguin. And should the wholly fictional Pacific be preferred, there is plenty of Conrad, and Melville, Jack London and Richard Henry Dana.

But of all the South Pacific books Robert Louis Stevenson's *In the South Seas* (London, 1900) remains my abiding favourite. Nicholas Rankin's biography of RLS, published in 1987, is an admirable companion; and were I to take one book with me the next time I set out for the palm trees, the warm blue waters and the coral strands, it would be Rankin's *Dead Man's Chest*, as perfect an account of a true Pacific Man as has been written to this day.

Index